D0164004

FIFTH EDITION

Drugs, Society, and Criminal Justice

CHARLES F. LEVINTHAL
Hofstra University

LORI BRUSMAN LOVINS
University of Houston—Downtown

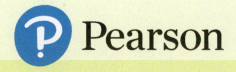

Vice President, Portfolio Management: Andrew Gilfillan
Portfolio Manager: Gary Bauer
Editorial Assistant: Lynda Cramer
Vice President, Product Marketing: Brad Parkins
Product Marketing Manager: Heather Taylor
Product Marketing Assistant: Liz Bennett
Director, Digital Studio and Content Production: Brian Hyland
Managing Producer: Jennifer Sargunar
Content Producer: Rinki Kaur
Manager, Rights Management: Johanna Burke

Manufacturing Buyer: Deidra Headlee
Creative Digital Lead: Mary Siener
Full-Service Management and Composition: Integra Software Services Pvt. Ltd.
Full-Service Project Manager: Vigneswaran Balachandran
Cover Design:
Cover Photos:
Printer/Binder: LSC Communications, Inc.
Text Font: ElectraLTStd-Regular
Cover Printer: LSC Communications, Inc.

Copyright © 2020, 2016, 2012 by Pearson Education, Inc. 221 River Street, Hoboken, NJ 07030. All Rights Reserved. Manufactured in the United States of America. This publication is protected by copyright, and permission should be obtained from the publisher prior to any prohibited reproduction, storage in a retrieval system, or transmission in any form or by any means, electronic, mechanical, photocopying, recording, or otherwise. For information regarding permissions, request forms, and the appropriate contacts within the Pearson Education Global Rights and Permissions department, please visit www.pearsoned.com/permissions/.

Acknowledgments of third-party content appear on the appropriate page within the text. PEARSON and ALWAYS LEARNING are exclusive trademarks owned by Pearson Education, Inc. or its affiliates in the U.S. and/or other countries.

Unless otherwise indicated herein, any third-party trademarks, logos, or icons that may appear in this work are the property of their respective owners, and any references to third party trademarks, logos, icons, or other trade dress are for demonstrative or descriptive purposes only. Such references are not intended to imply any sponsorship, endorsement, authorization, or promotion of Pearson's products by the owners of such marks, or any relationship between the owner and Pearson Education, Inc., authors, licensees, or distributors.

Library of Congress Cataloging-in-Publication Data

Names: Levinthal, Charles F., 1945- author. | Lovins, Lori Brusman, author.
Title: Drugs, society, and criminal justice / Charles F. Levinthal, Hofstra University, Lori Brusman Lovins.
Description: Fifth edition. | Boston : Pearson, [2020]
Identifiers: LCCN 2018041679| ISBN 9780135180037 | ISBN 0135180031
Subjects: LCSH: Drug abuse. | Drugs of abuse. | Drug abuse and crime. | Drug abuse–Prevention.
Classification: LCC HV5801 .L493 2020 | DDC 362.290973–dc23 LC record available at https://lccn.loc.gov/2018041679

10 2022

ISBN 10: 0-13-518003-1
ISBN 13: 978-0-13-518003-7

BRIEF CONTENTS

CONTENTS

CHAPTER 16

Deterrence through Drug Testing   366

In this fifth edition of Drugs, Society, and Criminal Justice, I am pleased to welcome a coauthor, Dr. Lori Brusman Lovins of the Department of Criminal Justice at the University of Houston—Downtown. My collaboration with Dr. Brusman Lovins has had a transformative impact on the pedagogy, focus, and state-of-the-art coverage in this edition. Continuing in the spirit and execution that have been hallmarks of previous editions, the fifth edition provides students in the criminal justice field of study with a thorough and comprehensive introduction to the major facts and issues concerning criminal justice and drug-taking behavior. Its core mission remains to provide an understanding of (1) the multiple challenges that drug abuse brings to our society, (2) the drug-control policies we have enacted to meet those challenges, (3) the range of international and domestic law enforcement efforts that provide the implementation of our present-day drug-control strategy, and (4) the systems of criminal justice that have been established to deal with the prosecution and adjudication of drug-law offenders.

What's New in the Fifth Edition?

- **Through the contribution of Dr. Brusman Lovins**, there is now a dedicated section of the book (Part Two) that examines the full spectrum of topics in criminal justice that bear upon drug abuse in our society—ranging from drug–crime relationships to drug-law penalties and enforcement to adjudication and correctional procedures for drug-law offenders.

- **An overall reorganization of chapters** in Drugs, Society, and Criminal Justice, Fifth Edition, provides a greater focus on the connection between drug-taking behavior and the criminal justice system. In the new edition, Part One (Chapters 1–3) serves as the foundation for issues of criminal justice through an understanding of drug problems in America and in the rest of the world as well as an understanding of the history of drug-control policy in America. Part Two (Chapters 4–7) is devoted to addressing major issues with regard to drugs, crime, and criminal justice. Part Three (Chapters 8–13) deals with fundamental and theoretical issues of drug-taking behavior in general and with respect to specific drugs of abuse. Part Four (Chapters 14–16) focuses on substance-abuse prevention and treatment, tobacco regulation, and drug testing.

- **Updated coverage of drugs and drug abuse in this edition** has been guided by the recognition of the devastating social and personal impact of an ongoing drug abuse crisis in America today. Chapter 9 (Opioids) focuses on the specific concerns related to opioid abuse and opioid overdose deaths, while other chapters focus on other major drugs of abuse such as cocaine and methamphetamine (Chapter 10) and hallucinogens and depressants (Chapter 12). Drug-taking behavior relating to other drugs with significant abuse potential—namely alcohol and nicotine in tobacco products—will be examined as well. Despite the fact that they are historically legal commodities and their recreational use by adults do not bear directly on the criminal justice system, there are significant ramifications for the public safety and public health of our nation. Alcohol misuse and abuse and tobacco use will be covered in Chapters 13 and 15, respectively. Finally, the social, political, and health-related issues surrounding the use of marijuana in America today will be given a special treatment in Chapter 11, with particular attention given to concerns that are being hotly debated and are continually in flux.

- **New and expanded coverage in Chapter 2 of this edition** deals with the significant issues of drug-related crime and law enforcement that relates to an increasingly sophisticated system of global illicit drug trafficking. Up-to-date coverage includes the unending challenges brought by the influx of illicit drugs across the U.S.–Mexico border, the destabilizing impact of narcoterrorist organizations in Afghanistan and Colombia, and transnational narcoterrorist organizations operating across international borders. Global illicit drug trafficking remains a constantly "moving target," and in this edition the latest law enforcement issues and developments are addressed.

- **An expanded number of** Drug Enforcement . . . in Focus **features in this edition** emphasize the important role that domestic and international law enforcement agencies play in the implementation of drug-control policies. New examples include: Efforts to Move Marijuana from a Schedule I to a Schedule II Controlled Substance (Chapter 3), Diversion Programs for Low-level, First-time Offenders (Chapter 7), and A New Technology in Drug Testing (Chapter 16). Addressing a broader perspective on drug use and abuse in America, an expanded number of **Drugs ... in Focus features** provide insights on selective topics. New examples include: Opioid Crisis Intervention Courts: A Response to the Opioid Epidemic (Chapter 9), Cannabis Skin Care Products without the High (Chapter 11), and Does Uber Save Lives? (Chapter 13).

- **A new series of updated** Numbers Talk **features**, positioned near the beginning of each chapter, provide the opportunity for often surprising "numerical" insights into aspects of current patterns of drug-taking behavior. They serve to draw the reader into the chapter and help to set the stage for classroom discussion.

- Several pedagogical features from the previous edition have been updated in the fifth edition. **Portrait features**, one in each chapter, enable us to put a "human face" on the discussion of drugs, society, and criminal justice, reminding us that we are dealing with issues that affect real people in all walks of life, now and in the past. **Quick Concept Checks**, embedded in the chapters, provide opportunities to test oneself on basic concepts in the text. **Review Questions** and the **Critical Thinking: What Would You Do?** features at the end of each chapter provide the means for summarizing one's knowledge about facts in the chapter and re-examining the information in the text through an application to a real-world situation. **Running Glossaries** and **Pronunciation Guides** are helpful to see the definition of terms in the immediate context of the material and to have difficult-to-pronounce terms spelled out phonetically. On a personal and professional level, **Help Line features** provide important facts that can be used to recognize specific signs of drug misuse or abuse, effective ways to respond in drug-related emergency situations, and guidance concerning circumstances that may present some degree of personal harm.

Instructor Supplements

Instructor's *Manual with Test Bank*. Includes content outlines for classroom discussion, teaching suggestions, and answers to selected end-of-chapter questions from the text. This also contains a Word document version of the test bank.

***TestGen*.** This computerized test generation system gives you maximum flexibility in creating and administering tests on paper, electronically, or online. It provides state-of-the-art features for viewing and editing test bank questions, dragging a selected question into a test you are creating, and printing sleek, formatted tests in a variety of layouts. Select test items from test banks included with TestGen for quick test creation, or write your own questions from scratch. TestGen's random generator provides the option to display different text or calculated number values each time questions are used.

***PowerPoint Presentations*.** Our presentations are clear and straightforward. Photos, illustrations, charts, and tables from the book are included in the presentations when applicable.

To access supplementary materials online, instructors need to request an instructor access code. Go to **www.pearsonhighered.com/irc**, where you can register for an instructor access code. Within 48 hours after registering, you will receive a confirming e-mail, including an instructor access code. Once you have received your code, go to the site and log on for full instructions on downloading the materials you wish to use.

Alternate Versions

E-Books. This text is also available in multiple eBook formats. These are an exciting new choice for students looking to save money. As an alternative to purchasing the printed textbook students can purchase an electronic version of the same content. With an eTextbook, students can search the text, make notes online, print out reading assignments that incorporate lecture notes, and bookmark important passages for later review. For more information, visit your favorite online eBook reseller or visit **www.mypearsonstore.com**.

Acknowledgments

Dr. Brusman Lovins and I acknowledge with great appreciation the professionalism of the editorial and production team at Pearson Education: Editor Gary Bauer and Content Producer Rinki Kaur. It has been a pleasure to work with them all. We would also like to thank the reviewers for their valuable inputs in this edition: Albert Kopak, Western Carolina University; Beth Wiersma, University of Nebraska - Kearney; John Hazy, Youngstown State University; Kilby Raptopoulos, University of Arkansas - Little Rock; Sue Mahan, University of Central Florida.

From Dr. Brusman Lovins: "I would like to thank my academic mentor, Dr. Edward Latessa, at the University of Cincinnati. Dr. Latessa not only connected me to this project, but exposed me to a much wider world of corrections. He has been a continuous source of support and guidance. I want to express my appreciation to Dr. Levinthal (Chuck), who warmly welcomed me to join him in writing this edition and showed much patience, respect, and helpful guidance as we worked together. Finally, unending thanks are extended to my husband, Brian, and our three boys, Sam, Henry, and Walter, who endured a few sacrifices during this book writing journey but did not waiver on their love and encouragement."

From Dr. Levinthal: "My family has been a continuing source of strength, patience, and encouragement. I will always be particularly grateful to my wife, Beth, and our wonderful sons, David and Brian, for their love, understanding, and support."

An Invitation to Readers

Your reactions to *Drugs, Society, and Criminal Justice*, Fifth Edition will always be welcome. Please send any comments or questions to the following e-mail address: charles.f.levinthal@hofstra.edu. Thank you.

The Challenge of Drugs in Our Society

chapter 1

Understanding the Drug Problem in America

After you have completed this chapter, you should have an understanding of the following:

- The impact of drug-taking behavior on society and society on drug-taking behavior
- Definitions and distinctions regarding drugs and drug use
- The problem of drug toxicity
- Drug-related hospital emergencies and drug-related deaths
- Prevalence rates for drug use in the United States
- Illicit drug accessibility through Internet Web sites known as the "Dark Web"

For Juvenile Court Judge Marilyn Moores, of Marion County, Indiana, the social impact of the opioid crisis in America can be seen on a daily basis—in the sad faces of children literally being left behind. In her community, the demands on child welfare services have reached a breaking point.

> We're seeing many younger children than we had seen before... lots and lots of opioid-addicted babies following their releases from NICUs (neonatal intensive care units) where they went through withdrawal from the opioid addiction they suffered in utero. We see kids—little itty-bitty kids—that are found in car seats in the backs of cars where parents have overdosed in the front seat. And because of the age of the children, we can't safely leave them with addicted parents ... We have kids who are sleeping in the Department of Child Services office because there are no homes for them that can be quickly found.[1]

There is no question that we live in a world where drugs are all around us. We have become accustomed to hearing about all the drug-related arrests and thousands of drug-law offenders being incarcerated in prisons and jails, the unending interception and confiscation of illicit drugs at our borders, and most importantly, the devastating effects of drug abuse among our families and friends in our neighborhoods and communities.

We have dealt with these issues for quite a while, but in recent years we have faced a new reality that is unique in its impact on our society and on our personal lives—the present-day epidemic of opioid abuse in America. Approximately 72,000 lives were lost in 2017 from a drug overdose, about 14 percent more than had been lost in 2016 and twice as many as had been lost in 2007.

Approximately 49,000 of the total drug overdose deaths in 2017 involved an opioid drug (either heroin, prescription opioid or synthetic opioid). On average, 134 Americans died of an opioid overdose on a given day during that year. Since the beginning of the twenty-first century, opioid abuse has claimed close to 500,000 American lives. No age group, geographic region, racial or ethnic group, or socioeconomic category of Americans has escaped this national calamity.

Across the nation, public-safety first responders have been overwhelmed each day with multiple opioid overdose emergency calls; medical examiners (calling themselves "last responders") have found themselves contending with finding room in morgues that are beyond capacity. Social service agencies have had to keep up with the demands of children needing to be placed in foster care due to opioid abuse conditions at home. Drug-related car crashes have become so commonplace in some communities that rescue crews immediately administer the opioid antidote, naloxone (Narcan), to any unresponsive driver they find, on the presumption that an opioid overdose was the cause. The criminal justice system is strained with greatly increased numbers of opioid abusers among the population of drug-law offenders. Meanwhile, large quantities of heroin and synthetic opioids continue to be smuggled across our borders and from overseas, with only a small fraction being confiscated by federal officials (see Chapter 2).

It is clear that the opioid crisis poses a clear and present danger to the public health and public safety of our entire nation. But even though opioid abuse has dominated the headlines, it should be recognized that present-day drug abuse takes many forms. For example, more than 14,000 lives were lost in 2017 to cocaine abuse, and 10,000 lives were lost to methamphetamine (meth) abuse (see Chapter 10). As we have seen in the past (Chapter 3), specific forms of drug abuse fall out of and into favor over time. Contending with the problems of drug abuse in America has been as difficult as aiming at a moving target that can switch direction at a moment's notice. Meanwhile, through the years problems of chronic alcohol abuse have never gone away (see Chapter 13).[2]

We pay a heavy price, amounting to expenditures of hundreds of billions of dollars, for the treatment of drug abusers and individuals with drug-related diseases, as well as a criminal justice system that is expected to implement drug-control policies at federal, state, and local levels. Beyond these expenditures, however, we are aware all too well of the costs of drug abuse that cannot be calculated in monetary terms: the consequences of drug-related crime, the deterioration of communities where drug-related crimes occur, and, in a larger sense, the decline in our collective sense of social order, the diminishment of personal dignity and self-worth, and finally the devastation in personal relationships among our families and individuals around us.

An accused drug-law violator is led away by an agent of the Drug Enforcement Administration (DEA) on an otherwise quiet, residential street in Billings, Montana.

Numbers Talk. . .

134	In any given day in 2017, the average number of Americans who died from an overdose of opioids (heroin, prescription opioid or synthetic opioid).
72,000	Estimated number of drug overdose deaths in the United States in 2017.
40,000	Estimated number of motor vehicle fatalities in 2017.

Sources: National Institute on Drug Abuse (2018, August). Overdose death rates. Rockville, MD: National Institute on Drug Abuse. National Safety Council (2018). 2017 estimates show vehicle fatalities topped 40,000 for second straight year. Accessed from: https://nsc.org/road-safety/safety-topics/fatality-estimates.

The purpose of this book is to explore a wide range of issues associated with **psychoactive drugs**, that is, those specific drugs that influence the functioning of the brain and hence our behavior and experience. A particular focus will be on psychoactive drugs that are dealt with through the criminal justice system in the United States. The principal drugs of this type include opioids, cocaine and methamphetamine, hallucinogens and depressants, and marijuana. Since their impact on societal well-being is enormous, there will be also chapters on alcohol and tobacco.

Given the problems we face with respect to drug abuse, we can ask the following questions: What are we doing about it? Specifically, what is the role of the criminal justice system in the United States in dealing with drug abuse today? How effective have our public policies and the criminal justice system been in meeting the challenges of drugs in our society?

Understanding Drugs and Society

There are essentially two ways of looking at the relationship between drugs and society.

First, we can examine the impact of our society on drug-taking behavior. There are a series of sociological risk factors, comprising elements of our present-day culture that increase the likelihood of certain undesirable forms of drug-taking behavior. Drug use is, at least in part, a consequence of how we feel about ourselves in relation to our family, to our friends and acquaintances, to our life experiences, and to the community in which we live. Risk factors a͙ cal and psychological in nature. As we will see ͙ all three risk factors (biological, psychological, and ͙ cal) are often acting in combination. It is for that reason we consider a **biopsychosocial model** as a way of understanding the range of motivating circumstances for drug-taking behavior (Figure 1.1).

Second, we can consider the relationship in reverse. We can examine the impact of certain forms of drug-taking behavior on society, specifically the consequences of drug-related crime and other forms of antisocial behavior. As a nation, we have established over the years drug-control policies at federal, state, and local levels (Chapter 3) as a response to the negative impact of drug-taking behaviors. The implementation of federal drug-control policies has been the responsibility of specific agencies within the U.S. Department of Justice, such as the Drug Enforcement Administration (see Chapter 2), with its focus on the control of international and domestic drug trafficking and the enforcement of federal drug laws. Federal courts and correctional facilities for federal drug-law offenders are administered under the U.S Attorney's Office

psychoactive drugs: Drugs that affect feelings, thoughts, perceptions, and behavior.

biopsychosocial model: The idea that drug-taking behavior can best be accounted for through the consideration of a combination of biological, psychological, and sociological risk factors in an individual's life.

FIGURE 1.1

Understanding the interplay of drug-taking behavior and society through the biopsychosocial model. Note: The criminal justice system is an implementation of drug control policies established at state and federal levels. Components of the criminal justice system include law enforcement agencies, criminal courts, and correctional systems.

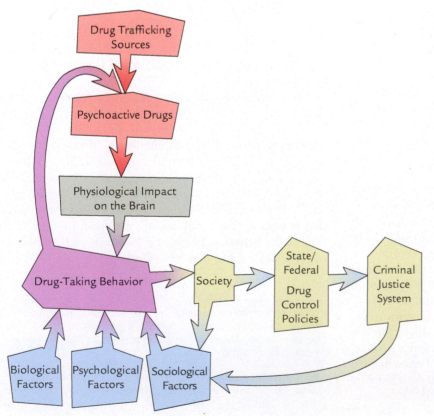

...ns (Chapter 7). State courts and cor-... administered under equivalent agen-...idual U.S. state.

...s that it is possible that the implementa-... policies designed to reduce drug abuse ... sociological risk factors, in that they tend ... kelihood of further drug-taking behavior (see Cha...... In other words, it is possible that, in some instances, the criminal justice system itself sets up a behavioral "feedback loop" that can increase rather than reduce the incidence of drug-taking behavior.

Definitions and Distinctions

Whichever way we look at the relationship between drugs and society, the fact remains that drugs and society have a profound impact on our daily lives—all the more reason to be clear on the meaning of the terms we use. The next sections cover the principal definitions and distinctions that will form the basis for understanding drugs and society. We begin with a basic definition that helps us to distinguish between drugs and nondrugs.

What Is a Drug?

It seems as if it should be relatively easy to define what we mean by the word **drug**. Minimally, there should be a set of criteria that can be used to distinguish a "drug" from a "nondrug." Unfortunately, it is more challenging than we would expect it to be.

The standard approach is to characterize a drug as *a chemical substance that, when taken into the body, alters the structure or functioning of the body in some way*. In doing so, we are accounting for examples such as medications used for the treatment of physical and mental disorders, as well as alcohol, nicotine, and the typical street drugs. Unfortunately, this broad definition also could refer to ordinary food and water. Because it does not make much sense for nutrients to be considered drugs, we need to refine our definition, adding the phrase, *excluding those nutrients considered to be related to normal functioning.*[3]

Even with this qualification, however, we may still be on slippery ground. It is true that we can now effectively eliminate the cheese in your next pizza from consideration as a drug, but what about some exotic ingredient in the sauce? Sugar is safely excluded, even though it has significant energizing and therefore behavioral effects on us, but what about the cayenne pepper that burns your tongue? Where do we draw the line between a drug and a nondrug in this case?

There are two major lessons that we learn from the seemingly simple task of arriving at a definition. First, there is probably no perfect definition that would distinguish a "drug" from a "nondrug" without leaving a number of cases that fall within some kind of gray area. The best we can do is to set up a definition, as we have, that handles most of the substances we are likely to encounter.

The second lesson is more subtle. We often draw a distinction between drugs and nondrugs not in terms of physical characteristics but rather in terms of whether the substance in question *was intended to be used primarily as a way of inducing a bodily or psychological* change. By this reasoning, if the pizza maker intended to put that spice in the pizza to make it taste better, the spice would not be considered a drug; it would simply be another ingredient in the recipe. If the pizza maker intended the spice to intoxicate you, raise your blood pressure, or quicken your heart rate, then it could possibly be considered a drug (see Drugs ... in Focus on page 5 for a guide to drug names). In other words, a designation of a chemical substance as a drug cannot be made without considering *how it might be used.*

Ultimately, the problem is that we are trying to reach a consensus on a definition that fits our intuitive sense of what constitutes a drug. We may find it difficult to define pornography, for example, but (as has been said in the halls of the U.S. Supreme Court) we know it when we see it. So it may be with drugs. Whether we realize it or not, when we discuss the topic of drugs, we are operating within a context of social and cultural values, a group of shared attitudes about what kind of behavior (that is, what kind of drug-taking behavior) is acceptable and what kind is not. These values and attitudes have manifested themselves over the years in social legislation and a criminal justice system that is designed for the purpose of regulating the use of specific drugs and specific forms of drug-taking behavior (see Chapter 3).

Instrumental Drug Use versus Recreational Drug Use

What could be the intent or motivation of the drug user with respect to this kind of behavior? Based upon the intent of the individual, drug use can be categorized as either instrumental or recreational.[4]

By **instrumental use**, we mean that a person is taking a drug with a specific socially approved goal in mind. The user may want to stay awake longer, fall asleep more quickly, or recover from an illness or its aftereffects. If you are a medical professional on call over a long period of time, taking a drug with the goal of staying alert is considered acceptable by most people as long as the drug does not interfere with one's duties. Recovery from an illness and achieving some reduction in pain are goals that are unquestioned. In these cases, drug-taking behavior occurs *as a means toward an end that has been defined by our society as legitimate.*

---

drug: A chemical substance that, when taken into the body, alters the structure or functioning of the body in some way, excluding those nutrients considered to be related to normal functioning.

instrumental use: Referring to the motivation of a drug user who takes a drug for a specific purpose other than getting "high."

The instrumental use of drugs can involve prescription and nonprescription (over-the-counter, abbreviated OTC) drugs that are obtained and taken for a particular medical purpose. Examples include an antidepressant prescribed for depression, a remedy for a cold, an anticonvulsant drug to control epileptic seizures, or insulin to maintain the health of a person with diabetes.

In contrast, **recreational use** means that a person is taking the drug not as a means toward a socially approved goal but for the purposes of acquiring the effects of the drug itself. The motivation, generally speaking, is to experience a pleasurable feeling or achieve a positive state of mind. *Whatever happens as a consequence of recreational drug-taking behavior is viewed not as a means to an end but as an end onto itself.* Smoking tobacco is a form of recreational drug-taking behavior as is involvement with street drugs, in that the goal in both cases is to alter one's mood or state of consciousness.

This seems simple enough, but there will be instances in which the distinction is less than clear. Drinking an alcoholic beverage, for example, is considered as recreational drug-taking behavior under most circumstances, but when moderate amounts are recommended by a physician for a specified therapeutic or preventative purpose (see Chapter 13), alcohol drinking might be considered instrumental in nature. You can see that whether drug use is judged to be recreational

recreational use: Referring to the motivation of a drug user who takes a drug only to get "high" or achieve some pleasurable effect.

Drugs . . . in Focus

Understanding Drug Names

The names we give to a particular drug can range from a tongue-twisting generic or pharmaceutical term to a catchy commercial word used for marketing purposes to often-colorful street slang. It is important to keep straight the different circumstances in which a drug name is used. We will focus on four major categories: brand names, generic names, natural-product names, and street names.

Brand names
Once a pharmaceutical manufacturer receives governmental approval for marketing a newly developed drug, it is given exclusive rights, referred to as a *drug patent*, to a specific brand name identifying the drug that is being sold. The brand name is a registered trademark that cannot be used by any other manufacturer for the life of the patent. As examples, while under patent, the drug Januvia, developed for the treatment of Type 2 diabetes mellitus, was marketed under that brand name by AstraZeneca Pharmaceuticals, and the cholesterol-lowering drug Crestor was marketed under that brand name by Merck & Co., Inc. A drug patent is granted for a fixed period of 20 years, beginning from the first year of an arduous multi-stage FDA approval process.

Generic names
Every pharmaceutical drug has a generic name as well. Doctors and other designated health-care professionals will often write prescriptions for a particular drug using its generic name (if the patent has expired) rather than its brand name since it is considerably less expensive. Once a drug patent has expired, a drug formerly available under its brand name becomes available under its generic name, sometimes alongside its brand name equivalent. For example, the nonprescription analgesic drug Tylenol is marketed by McNeil Consumer Healthcare in North America and its "sibling" Panadol is marketed by GlaxoKlineSmith in the United

Kingdom and other countries outside North America under their original brand names. Since the patents have long since expired, they are also marketed as generic drugs under their generic names acetaminophen and paracetamol (para-acetylaminophenol), respectively. Illicit drugs are referred to by federal and state authorities by their generic names, unless they are botanical products (see later). Examples are cocaine hydrochloride, heroin, dextroamphetamine, methamphetamine, lysergic acid diethylamide (LSD), and phencyclidine.

Natural-product names
In some cases, drug names refer to (1) plants from which the drugs originate (for example, marijuana, opium, coca, and amanita mushrooms), (2) chemical entities isolated directly from plants (for example, morphine and codeine from opium poppies, cocaine hydrochloride from the coca plant, THC from marijuana, psilocybin from psilocybe mushrooms, and mescaline from peyote cactus), or (3) chemical entities derived directly or indirectly from plants through a specific chemical process (for example, alcohol created as a result of the fermentation of grains, free-base cocaine and crack cocaine created from a chemical modification of cocaine hydrochloride).

Street names
Street names refer to slang terms generated by a subculture of drug users for a particular illicit drug or combination of illicit drugs. Any listing of street names is bound to be incomplete, as the slang names are always changing. Nonetheless, some street names have been around for a long time. Examples are "speed" for methamphetamine, "smack" for white heroin, "black tar" for Mexican heroin, "speedball" for a combination of heroin and cocaine, "grass," "weed," or "pot" for marijuana, and "coke" for cocaine. More extensive listings of street names for major drugs can be found on pages 182, 202, and 210.

or instrumental is determined in no small part by the circumstances under which the behavior takes place. As we will see, social attitudes toward forms of drug-taking behavior have had a significant impact on the establishment of drug-control policies and drug-control laws.

Illicit (Illegal) versus Licit (Legal) Drugs

Psychoactive drugs that traditionally receive the greatest amount of attention are the ones officially defined in the United States as **illicit (illegal) drugs**. By definition, criminal penalties are imposed on their possession, manufacture, or sale, according to federal and state-level statutes. The best-known examples of illicit drugs are heroin, cocaine, and (except in some U.S. states) marijuana, as well as "club drugs" such as methamphetamine (meth), Ecstasy, LSD, PCP, ketamine, and GHB. Other equally important psychoactive substances, however, are **licit (legal) drugs**, such as alcohol, nicotine in tobacco products, caffeine, and certain prescription medicines used to treat a wide range of mental disorders. In the cases of alcohol and nicotine in tobacco products, legal access carries a minimum-age requirement. In the case of prescription medicines, legal access is limited to approval by specific health-care professionals. In the case of caffeine, there are no restrictions at all to its legal access.

The designation of a particular drug as being either illicit (illegal) or licit (legal) depends upon the society within which legality is defined. In short, the legal status of a particular form of drug-taking behavior is established on the basis of historical, cultural, and sometimes religious decisions rather than on the physical properties of the drug itself. Tobacco, for example, has deeply rooted associations in American history, dating to precolonial days. Although tobacco use is objectionable to many individuals and harmful to the health of the smoker and others, tobacco remains a legal commodity, though presently under federal regulations.

Except for a period between 1920 and 1933, known as the Prohibition Era, alcohol has been a drug that holds legal status in the United States within the bounds of the law, despite the fact that alcohol consumption can be harmful to individuals who become inebriated, potentially harmful to others who may be impacted by the drinker's drunken behavior, and harmful to one's health when consumed on a chronic basis. Elsewhere in the world, the legality of a drug or class of drugs is determined on the basis of the religious attitudes of a particular society. A prominent example is the illegality of alcohol use in nations whose laws incorporate the teachings of the Islamic religion.

In the United States, the legal or illegal status of marijuana is complicated by two important factors. The first factor is the specific region within the United States having the jurisdiction authority over marijuana use. On a federal level, marijuana use is officially designated as an illegal act (see Chapter 3), while in several U.S. states it is not. The issues surrounding the present-day jurisdictional conflict between the federal government and U.S. states with respect to marijuana use will be examined in Chapter 11.

The second factor considers whether marijuana has been used for either instrumental or recreational purposes. The instrumental use of marijuana for the treatment of specific medical conditions is legal in certain U.S. states, while in some U.S. states recreational use of marijuana is legal as well (see Chapter 11). In some U.S. states, the recreational use of marijuana remains an illegal form of drug-taking behavior but has been "decriminalized" under the law, in that penalties for infractions involve a monetary fine rather than criminal prosecution.

Misuse, Abuse, and Dependence

Distinctions need to be made between three terms that reflect the *long-time* consequences of drug-taking behavior. These consequences fall into three categories: drug misuse, drug abuse, and drug dependence.

Drug misuse typically applies to cases in which a drug is used with an instrumental goal in mind but in an inappropriate manner. For example, drug doses may be increased beyond the level recommended for its use in the mistaken idea that if a little is good, more is even better. Or doses may be decreased from the level recommended for its use with the intention of saving money by making the drug supply last longer. Prescription drugs may be continued longer than they were intended to be used or combined with some other drug. In the case of alcoholic misuse, the social or celebratory occasions of alcohol drinking may develop into a state of intoxication that can lead to inappropriate behaviors that are harmful to the drinker or to others.

Drug misuse of prescription or nonprescription drugs can be dangerous and potentially lethal, particularly when alcohol is combined with medications that depress the nervous system. Drugs that have this particular feature include antihistamines, antianxiety medications, and sleeping medications. Even if alcohol is not involved, however, drug combinations still represent serious health risks, particularly for the elderly, who often take a large number of separate medications. This population is especially vulnerable to the hazards of drug misuse.

In contrast, **drug abuse** is typically applied to cases in which a licit or illicit drug is used in ways that produce some form of physical, mental, or social impairment. The primary motivation for individuals involved in drug abuse is recreational. Drugs with abuse potential include not only the common street drugs but also legally available psychoactive substances, such as caffeine and nicotine (stimulants), alcohol, sedatives, and inhaled solvents (depressants), and a number

illicit drugs: Drugs whose manufacture, sale, or possession is illegal.

licit drugs: Drugs whose manufacture, sale, or possession is legal.

drug misuse: Drug-taking behavior in which a drug is used inappropriately.

of prescription or OTC medications designated for medical purposes but used by some individuals exclusively on a recreational basis. In Chapter 9, we will examine significant concerns about the abuse of prescription pain medications, such as Vicodin, Percocet, and OxyContin.

The term **drug dependence** is typically applied to conditions that extend beyond the consequences of drug abuse. There are more intense experiences on the part of the individual, such as feelings of intense craving for the drug and preoccupation in obtaining it as well as tendencies to increase the amount of the drug (referred to as drug tolerance) and display withdrawal symptoms when the drug use has stopped.

While it is important in many instances to make distinctions among misuse, abuse, and dependence as problematic aspects of drug-taking behavior, there are occasions when no value judgment is made or implied as to the motivation of the individual involved or the consequences that may result. In those occasions, we will simply refer to drug-taking behavior as *drug use*.

Drugs versus Substances

Because the general public often fails to recognize alcohol and nicotine as drugs (see Chapters 13 and 15), despite the significant problems associated with their use, health-care professionals have felt the need to substitute the word "substance" instead of "drug" in terminology when referring to drug-related diagnosis and treatment. Consequently, problems of drug-taking behavior are referred to as consequences of substance misuse, substance abuse, or substance dependence, respectively.

In guidelines for the diagnosis and treatment of problems related to substance use, the American Psychiatric Association and associated health professional organizations draw upon specific behavioral criteria. The degree of impaired control that an individual has over his or her substance use is assessed by occasions in which a substance is taken in large amounts or over a longer period of time than the individual originally intended or by evidence of persistent desire to cut down or regulate a pattern of substance use. In the most current guidelines adopted in 2013, referred to as the *Diagnostic and Statistical Manual of Mental Disorders, Fifth Edition (DSM-5)*, behavioral criteria that had formerly been used to designate conditions of substance abuse and substance dependence as separate entities in earlier versions of the guidelines are now combined (with some modification) into a single condition, referred to as *substance use disorder*. Under the general diagnosis of substance use disorder, problems associated with drug use are now considered along

a continuum, ranging from relatively mild to severe (see a more complete discussion of the DSM-5 on pages 145–146).

On the Matter of "Addiction"

It is common in everyday conversations about excessive forms of drug-taking behavior that we use the term "addiction" or the phrase "drug addict." In broad terms, use of this term or phrase refers to an individual's dependence on a particular form of drug use and the presence of serious personal and social problems that are directly associated with that dependency. For the general public, the connotation of the word "addiction" is that an individual has abused a particular drug to such an extent that he or she no longer has the capability of stopping, that there is now some significant impairment in self-control. In that sense, addiction is a disorder of a normal process necessary for our survival. Every day, we find behavioral ways to satisfy bodily needs for food and water, for example, but the behavior typically ends once those needs have been satisfied. Addiction can be viewed as a useful shorthand way of saying that an important feedback loop of behavior has been disrupted.

Nonetheless, as convenient as it is to refer to the condition of drug dependence as an addiction, we need to be careful in doing so. We want to avoid perpetuating certain long-held negative social beliefs and prejudices toward people who suffer from this condition. Labeling an individual with a drug addiction as "a drug addict" can have a stigmatizing effect that impedes efforts on his or her part to seek out substance dependence treatment. While it is acknowledged that addiction is a serious *recurring* condition and that successfully treated individuals need to view themselves as being "in recovery" rather than "recovered," it is not helpful to adopt an implied expectation of inevitability (as implied in the expression "Once an addict, always an addict"). Unfortunately, only one out of ten individuals in the United States in need of treatment for a problem with illicit drug or alcohol use actually receives treatment in a specialty facility (see Chapter 14). Clearly, any progress toward reducing the social consequences of drug-related problems through treatment will depend on individuals avoiding a sense of shame, or a sense of denial that these problems exist in the first place.

While the behavioral aspects of drug misuse, drug abuse, or drug dependence are important to identify, it is equally important to emphasize the increasing opportunities for physical harm to occur. There will always be potential risks to one's physical well-being. As we all know, significant consequences can be life-threatening or life-ending. The next section will examine a major area of concern with respect to drug-taking behavior—the problem of drug toxicity.

The Problem of Drug Toxicity

When we say that a drug is toxic, we are referring to the fact that it is, to some degree, dangerous or in some way interfering with a person's normal functioning. Technically, any substance, no matter how benign, has the potential for

drug abuse: Drug-taking behavior resulting in some form of physical, mental, or social impairment.

drug dependence: Drug-taking behavior that involves not only some form of physical, mental, or social impairment in an individual's life but also more intense experiences such as feelings of drug craving, drug tolerance, and/or withdrawal when drug use has stopped.

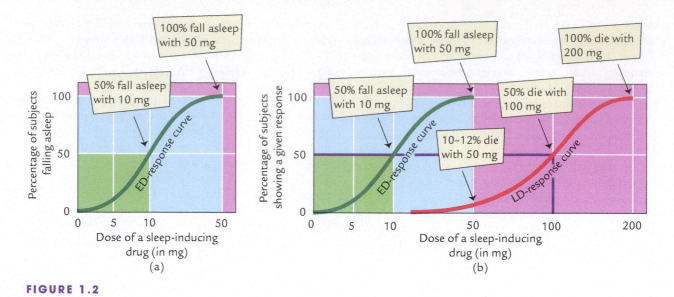

FIGURE 1.2

(a) An effective dose (ED)-response curve, and (b) an ED-response curve (left) alongside a lethal dose (LD)-response curve (right).

toxicity if the **dose**—the amount of the substance taken—is high enough. The question of a drug's safety, or its relative safety, when compared to other drugs, centers on the possibility that it can be toxic *at relatively low doses*. We certainly do not want people to harm themselves accidentally when taking the drug in the course of their daily lives. When there is a possibility that the *short-term* effects of a particular drug might trigger a toxic response, then the drug is identified as having some level of **acute toxicity**.

To understand the concept of toxicity in more detail, we need to examine an S-shaped graph called the **dose-response curve** (Figure 1.2a). Let us assume we have the results of data collected from laboratory tests of a hypothetical sleep-inducing drug. Increases in the dose level of the drug will produce the desired sleep-inducing effect in an increasingly large percentage of a test population of mice. As illustrated in Figure 1.2a, a dose of 10 mg will cause 50 percent of the population to fall asleep. With a dose of 50 mg, 100 percent will have done so. Some variability always exists in an individual reaction to any drug; some mice may be internally resistant to the drug's effect, while others may be quite susceptible. We cannot predict *which specific animal* might fall asleep with 10 mg of the drug, only that the probability of a given animal doing so is 50 percent.

We define the **effective dose (ED)** of a drug having a specific effect on a test population in terms of probabilities, from 0 to 100 percent. For example, the ED50 of a drug refers to the effective dose for 50 percent of the population; ED99 refers to the effective dose for 99 percent of the population. In this example, the ED numbers refer to the drug's effect of *producing sleep* on a specific proportion of the population being exposed to the drug. The same drug may be producing other effects (muscular relaxation, for instance) at lower doses; these drug effects would have their own separate dose-response curves. Remember that we are looking at

the properties of a specific drug *effect* here, not at the overall properties of the drug itself.

Now we can look at Figure 1.2b, where the effective dose-response curve is represented next to another S-shaped dose-response curve, also gathered from laboratory testing, only in this case the "response" is death. It makes sense that the second curve is shifted to the right because the **lethal dose (LD)** would generally require a higher dosage of a drug than the dosage necessary to produce a nonlethal effect.

Emphasis should be placed on the word "generally," because the lethal dose-response curve may overlap with the effective dose-response curve (as it does in this example). In the example shown, although a 100-mg dose needs to be taken to kill 50 percent of the test population, a dose of as little as 50 mg (or less) is lethal for at least a few of them. The LD50

toxicity (tox-IS-ih-tee): The physical or psychological harm that a drug might present to the user.

dose: The quantity of drug that is taken into the body, typically measured in terms of milligrams (mg) or micrograms (μg).

acute toxicity: The physical or psychological harm a drug might present to the user immediately or soon after the drug is ingested into the body.

dose-response curve: An S-shaped graph showing the increasing probability of a certain drug effect as the dose level rises.

effective dose (ED): The minimal dose of a particular drug necessary to produce the intended drug effect in a given percentage of the population.

lethal dose (LD): The minimal dose of a particular drug capable of producing death in a given percentage of the population.

of a drug refers to the lethal dose for 50 percent of the population; LD1 refers to a relatively lower dose that is lethal for only 1 percent of the population.

In order to arrive at an idea of a drug's overall toxicity, we need to combine the effective and lethal doses of a drug in a ratio. The ratio of LD50/ED50 is called the **therapeutic index**. For example, if the LD50 for a drug is 450 mg, and the ED50 is 50 mg, then the therapeutic index is 9. In other words, you would have to take nine times the dose that would be effective for half of the population in order to incur a 50 percent chance of death in that population.

It can be argued that a 50 percent probability of dying represents an unacceptably high risk even for a drug that has

> **therapeutic index:** A measure of a drug's relative safety for use, computed as the ratio of the lethal dose for 50 percent of the population to the effective dose for 50 percent of the population.

Drugs . . . in Focus

Acute Toxicity in the News: Drug-Related Deaths

The following is a listing of prominent celebrities in the entertainment world who have died since 1970 either as a direct consequence or as an indirect consequence of drug misuse or abuse.

Name	Year of Death	Age	Reasons Given for Death
Janis Joplin, singer	1970	27	Overdose of heroin and alcohol
Jimi Hendrix, singer and guitarist	1970	27	Overdose of sleeping pills
Elvis Presley, singer and actor	1977	42	Cardiac arrhythmia suspected to be due to an interaction of antihistamine, codeine, and Demerol (a painkiller), as well as Valium and several other tranquilizers
John Belushi, comedian and actor	1982	33	Overdose of heroin combined with cocaine
River Phoenix, actor	1993	23	Cardiac-respiratory arrest from accidental combination of heroin and cocaine
Jonathan Melvoin, keyboardist for the Smashing Pumpkins rock band	1996	34	Overdose of heroin
Chris Farley, comedian and actor	1998	33	Overdose of heroin and cocaine
Bobby Hatfield, singer, the Righteous Brothers	2003	63	Heart failure following overdose of cocaine
Mitch Hedberg, comedian	2005	37	Heart failure due to "multiple-drug toxicity," including heroin and cocaine
Heath Ledger, actor	2008	28	Acute intoxication from combined use of six prescription medicines for pain, anxiety, insomnia, and nasal congestion
Michael Jackson, songwriter and entertainer	2009	50	Cardiac arrest due to an intramuscular administration of propofol (brand name: Diprivan), possibly interacting with a number of antianxiety medications
Greg Giraldo, comedian	2010	44	Overdose of prescription medication and alcohol
Amy Winehouse, singer	2011	27	Accidental alcohol poisoning, resulting from a lethal blood–alcohol concentration of 0.42 percent
Whitney Houston, singer and actress	2012	48	Accidental drowning, with chronic cocaine use and heart disease as contributing factors
Cory Monteith, television actor "Glee"	2013	31	Overdose of heroin and alcohol
Philip Seymour Hoffman, actor	2014	46	Overdose of heroin
Prince, songwriter, singer, actor and director	2016	57	Overdose of fentanyl
Tom Petty, songwriter and singer	2017	66	Overdose from a combination of fentanyl, fentanyl analogs, oxycodone, and other drugs

Note: Celebrities whose drug-related deaths have been attributed to the toxicity of nicotine, tars, or carbon monoxide in tobacco products are not included in this listing.

Source: Various media reports.

genuine benefits. To be more conservative in the direction of safety, the ratio of LD1/ED99 is often calculated. Here we are calculating the ratio between the dose that produces death in 1 percent of the population and the dose that would be effective in 99 percent. Naturally, this second ratio, called the **margin of safety**, should be as high as possible for a drug to be considered relatively safe to use. As before, the higher the ratio, the greater the difference between effectiveness and lethality. In other words, the wider the margin of safety, the safer (less toxic) the drug in question. Clearly, the margin of safety for the hypothetical drug examined in Figure 1.2 would present serious toxicity issues. Bear in mind, however, that any index of drug toxicity assumes that the drug is being consumed by itself, without any other substances being consumed at the same time. If something else is administered along with the drug in question (whether it is another drug or some food product), then the margin of safety can potentially change. The important issue of drug interactions, particularly drug interactions with alcohol, will be taken up in Chapter 8.

The U.S. Food and Drug Administration (FDA) requires that therapeutic index and the margin of safety are calculated by recognized pharmaceutical companies during the development of new drugs. Obviously, the goal is for these ratios to be as large as possible, considering that an individual might unintentionally take a higher-than-recommended dose of the drug. We do not want the consumer to be in danger if this happens. But what about the toxicity estimates in the consumption of illicit drugs? The unfortunate reality of street drugs is that the buyer has no way of knowing what he or she has bought until the drug has been used, and then it is frequently too late. It is an extreme case of *caveat emptor* ("Let the buyer beware").

Few if any illicit drug sellers make any pretense for being ethical businesspeople; their only objectives are to make money and avoid prosecution by the law. Frequently, the drugs they sell are diluted with either inert or highly dangerous ingredients. Adulterated heroin, for example, may contain a high proportion of milk sugar as inactive filler and a dash of quinine to simulate the bitter taste of real heroin, when the actual amount of heroin that is being sold is far less than the "standard" street dosage. At the other extreme, the content of heroin may be unexpectedly high and lead to a lethal overdose, or the adulterated product may contain animal tranquilizers, arsenic, strychnine, insecticides, or other highly toxic substances. Cocaine, LSD, marijuana, and all the other illicit drugs that are available to the drug abuser, as well as look-alike drugs that are unauthorized copies of popular prescription medications, present hidden and unpredictable risks of toxicity. Even if drugs are procured from a friend or from someone you know, these risks remain. Neither of you is likely to know the exact ingredients. The potential for acute toxicity is always present.[5]

Given the uncertainty that exists about the contents of many abused drugs, what measure or index can we use to evaluate the effects of acute toxicity on individuals in our society? A natural tendency is to look first to the news headlines; think of all the well-known public figures who have died as a direct consequence of drug misuse or abuse (Drugs ... in Focus).

It is possible that such examples have been misleading. In the past, it could have been argued that celebrities were not representatives of the drug-using population in general and that the drugs prevalent among celebrities, because of their expense, were not representative of the drugs most frequently encountered by the rest of society. However, in light of the current nationwide drug epidemic, recent reports of drug-related deaths among celebrities appear to be more of a mirror of present-day society than an anomaly. To gain more definitive understanding about drug toxicity in the general population, we must turn to emergency departments of hospitals where drug-related cases are treated as well as medical examiners where drug-related deaths are recorded.

Drug-Related Hospital Emergencies

The extent of hospital emergencies associated with a major drug of abuse, as reflected in the number of **drug-related emergency-department (ED) visits**, varies considerably from drug to drug and from year to year. ED-visit statistics for a given year can only be a "snapshot" of problems in drug-taking behavior at that point in time. The dominance relationship among specific drugs of abuse with respect to hospital emergencies will be in constant flux. Beginning in the 1980s, for example, cocaine and crack cocaine abuse was the dominant drug-related problem, particularly among urban communities of major cities (Chapter 10). In the late 1990s and early 2000s, the focus was on methamphetamine abuse, particularly as experienced in nonurban regions of the United States (Chapter 10).

Obviously, heroin and other opioids have become the primary focus of concern in recent years. Figure 1.3 shows the number of ED visits in 2015 involving an overdose of heroin and other opioids, cocaine, or methamphetamine. Heroin and other opioids accounted for about 84 percent of these ED visits, with cocaine and methamphetamine accounting for about 6 percent and 10 percent, respectively. While heroin accounted for a majority of all opioid-drug ED visits that year, about one-third involved opioid drugs other than heroin, primarily opioid medications such as oxycodone and hydrocodone.

In the past, tracking the extent of a particular medical condition requiring an ED visit on a national level was an arduous, labor-intensive task, since information had to be

margin of safety: The ratio of a lethal dose for 1 percent of the population to the effective dose for 99 percent of the population.

drug-related emergency-department (ED) visit: An occasion on which a person visited an ED for a purpose that was related to recent drug use.

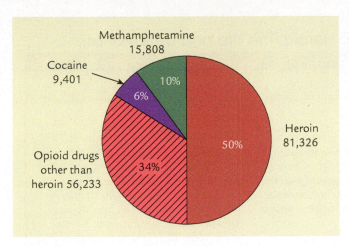

FIGURE 1.3

Estimated numbers in the United States of drug-poisoning-related emergency department (ED) visits in 2015, involving heroin, opioids other than heroin, cocaine, or methamphetamine.

Source: Centers for Disease Control and Prevention. (2018, August 31). *Annual Surveillance Report of Drug-Related Risks and Outcomes — United States, 2018.* Atlanta, GA: Centers for Disease Control and Prevention, Table 3B. Accessed from: https://www.cdc.gov/drugoverdose/pdf/pubs/2018 cdc-drug-surveillance-report.pdf.

extracted from billing data. As a result, there would be a considerable time delay before it was possible to determine the extent of any large-scale public health emergency such as the current opioid abuse epidemic. The 2015 data described above comes from this former record-keeping process. Fortunately, patient data can now be collected electronically in near real-time and viewed within 24–48 hours of an ED visit. As a result, there is an opportunity to track opioid overdose emergencies or any condition requiring an ED visit in a timely fashion. Using electronic data records, the Centers for Disease Control and Prevention reported in 2018 that opioid overdose ED visits had increased 30 percent from the third quarter (July–September) of 2016 to the third quarter of 2017. Of the four regions of the United States in the analysis,

the Midwest showed the greatest increase (60%) over this period of time. Information regarding opioid overdose deaths will be reviewed in the next section.[6]

It should be pointed out that among hospital emergency records in any given year, the overwhelming proportion of **drug-related ED visits** continues to be associated with *excessive alcohol consumption*, either as a direct consequence of alcohol consumption or automobile accident injuries that have resulted from alcohol consumption. The number of ED visits in such cases far outstrip the number of ED visits resulting from any form of illicit drug-taking behavior. The range of toxicity issues related to alcohol use and misuse will be reviewed in Chapter 13.

Drug-Related Deaths

According to the Centers for Disease Control and Prevention, drug overdose is presently the leading cause of accidental death in the United States and the leading cause of death among Americans under the age of 50, with about two-thirds of overdose deaths reported in 2017 being due to either a prescription opioid or illicit opioid drug (see Chapter 9). Figure 1.4 shows the changing pattern in drug overdose cases from 1999 to 2017. While the number of cocaine overdose cases exceeded the number of overdose cases involving opioids in 1999, opioids have subsequently become dominant. The dramatic rise in heroin overdose deaths began around 2010 and deaths due to synthetic opioids around 2013.

Clearly, the most significant factor in the escalating numbers of opioid overdose deaths has been the sharp increase in the abuse of the synthetic opioid, fentanyl, as well as fentanyl analogs (chemical variations of fentanyl) that have been combined with heroin sold to opioid abusers. One extremely potent fentanyl analog, called *carfentanil*, has been estimated to be as much as 5,000 times more potent than heroin itself. Carfentanil is used as a tranquilizer for elephants and other large animals, but it has never been intended to be consumed by humans.[7]

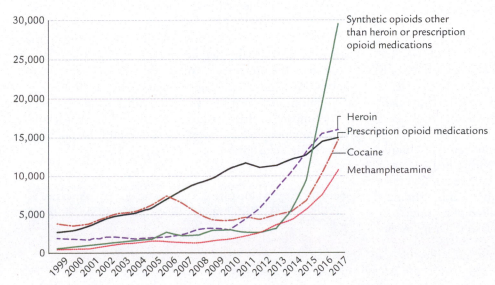

FIGURE 1.4

Drugs involved in U.S. overdose deaths, 1999–2017.

Source: National Institute on Drug Abuse (revised September 2017). Overdose death rates. Accessed (March 12, 2018) https://www.drugabuse.gove/relate-topics/trends-statistical/overdose-death-rates.

Erik lived in a suburban Long Island, New York community, and heroin killed him in 2008 at the age of 19. His mother, Linda D., never imagined what she was up against. "You worry," she has said, "about them smoking pot. You worry about them driving recklessly. You worry about them not using their seat belt. You worry about that phone call in the middle of the night. You don't worry about heroin. Because it didn't exist in my mindset."

In the last few years, the reality of heroin in the suburbs and small towns of America, previously considered to be immune from its deadly reach, has hit home with a sudden and unexpected vengeance. As a director of a local drug-counseling center has expressed it, "They're starting younger, they're starting with more substances, they have better access, everything is cheaper, and they have more money." You would call a perfect storm. Heroin arrests have doubled; rehabilitation-facility admissions of those 21 and under for prescription pain reliever dependence have tripled or quadrupled in many cases.

In the case of Erik, it began after an emergency appendectomy with a prescription for Vicodin. Erik gradually entered into a shadowy world of drug-taking behavior. Finding new supplies of Vicodin, then shifting to OxyContin, was easy. "It sounded grimy and sleazy," a teenager would say in reference to her own dependence on prescription pain relievers, "but at the time it was just what I did. Everyone knows someone who can get them for you."

At some point in early 2008, according to Linda, "The oxys dried up." Erik turned from pills to heroin. "It started at a party," she has said, "Someone said to him, 'Oh, try this.'" By May, Linda and her husband realized Erik was using heroin. In the weeks that followed, they tried to convince him to get help. The family's insurance covered Erik's first trip to a rehabilitation facility in update New York, but when Erik left after three days, they told the family that he had used up their insurance company's "once in a lifetime" rehabilitation coverage. They tried to convince public hospitals to admit Erik, but he was denied. In the meantime, Erik's parents were finding injection needles around the house and discarded rubber tubing. They desperately tried to cobble together funds to pay for rehabilitation, but they didn't succeed in time. Erik died in July.

If Erik had rejected his parents' efforts to get him help, they would have faced considerable legal obstacles. In New York State, no one, even a minor, is required to get treatment for substance abuse. Parents can petition a county probation department to have a drug-abusing child designated as a Person in Need of Supervision (PINS), but a court order has to be issued by a judge for a PINS child to be admitted for treatment. Even then, the child may leave at any time regardless of medical advice to stay.

Sources: Alter, S. (2009, November 12). Push for heroin help. *Newsday*, p. A5. Archibold, R. C. (2009, May 31). In heartland death, traces of heroin's spread. *The New York Times*, pp. 1, 24. Lefkowitz, M. (2009, June 14). Heartbreak of addiction hits home. *Newsday*, pp. A4–A6. Muhuri, P. K.; Gfroerer, J. C.; and Davies, C. (2013, August). Associations of nonmedical pain reliever use and initiation of heroin use in the United States. *CBHSQ Data Review*. Rockville, MD: Substance Abuse and Mental Health Services Administration. Deutsch, K. (2013). Thriving online marketplace. *Newsday*, p. A3.

Detailed information regarding recent developments in opioid abuse is discussed in Chapter 9.

Understanding Chronic Drug Toxicity: How Many Drug Users?

The statistics regarding hospital emergencies and overdose deaths are staggering and disturbing, but we are speaking only of the occasions resulting from *acute* drug toxicity. In order to evaluate the impact of **chronic toxicity** as well, it is important to examine the numbers of individuals who are drug users over an extended period of time.

We would not be so concerned about acute or chronic toxicity levels of psychoactive drugs if we lived in a society in which very few or any individuals were engaged in that form of behavior. If a drug were so toxic (in other words, extremely poisonous), no one except individuals attempting suicide or exposed to that drug by accident would take it. Drug toxicity in that case would affect relatively few people. Unfortunately, surveys of prevalence rates with regard to major psychoactive drugs indicate substantial numbers of drug users and therefore substantial potential for the incidence of drug toxicity.

Prevalence rates will be examined here in two ways. First, the degree of recent exposure to specific drugs will be assessed by the prevalence rate of drug use during the past year. Second, the degree of current drug use will be assessed by the prevalence rate of drug use during the past month. In general, prevalence rates can be thought of as a "multiplier" that allows us to gain a rough estimate of the impact of drug toxicity on our society as a whole. How many people have been or are presently engaging in drug-taking behavior?

chronic toxicity: The physical or psychological harm a drug might cause in the course of drug use over an extended period of use.

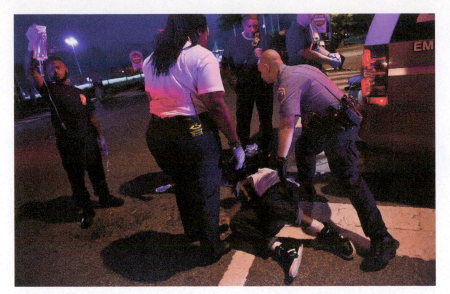

Dealing with drug-related emergencies is a continual challenge for emergency medical service (EMS) crews.

Credit: Radius Images/Alamy Stock Photo

Prevalence Rates of Drug Use in the United States

Naturally, there are problems in obtaining a full picture of drug-taking behavior in America today. Since we cannot conduct large-scale random drug testing, the only alternative is simply to ask people about their drug-taking behavior through self-reports. We encourage honesty and arrange the data-collection procedure so as to convince the respondents that their answers are strictly confidential, but the fact remains that any questionnaire is inherently imperfect because there is no way to verify the truthfulness of what people say about themselves. Nevertheless, questionnaires are all we have, and the statistics on drug use are based on such survey measures. Comprehensive reports of the prevalence rates of many forms of drug use among Americans across the life span, referred to as the National Survey on Drug Use and Health (NSDUH), are issued on an annual basis by the U.S. Department of Health and Human Services. Reports on prevalence rates specifically among secondary school students, as early as eighth-graders, college students, and young adults, are issued on an annual basis through the Monitoring the Future (MTF) program at the University of Michigan.

We begin with NSDUH statistics related to current levels of illicit drug use in the U.S. population at large, and more detailed statistics for specific age groups within that population. Current drug use is defined as any drug use within the previous month. Five major drugs will be highlighted: heroin, cocaine, methamphetamine, hallucinogens, and marijuana. It should be noted that marijuana is included among illicit drugs surveyed in the NSDUH data, owing to the official stance of the U.S. federal government with respect to marijuana.

Illicit Drug Use among Individuals Aged 12 and Older

Figure 1.5 shows that between 28 and 29 million Americans, 12 years or older were current illicit drug users in 2016. This number accounts for about one in ten individuals in this population.[8]

Figure 1.6 shows the prevalence of current illicit drug users in age groups 12–17, 18–25, and 26 years or older in 2016. It is clear that the greatest number of current drug users were between 18 and 25 years of age.[9]

Specific prevalence rates in 2016 with regard to five major drugs among Americans, 12 years or older, as well as among individuals in three age groups are shown in Table 1.1. It is apparent that marijuana users account for about 84 percent of the total number of illicit drug users in the United States (as defined by the U.S. federal government). Among Americans aged 12 or older, cocaine use in 2016 outnumbered heroin use by about four to one. Since the number of heroin overdose deaths in 2016 was greater

Quick Concept Check **1.1**

Understanding Margins of Safety

Check your understanding of the concept, margin of safety, by answering the following questions.

The following seven drugs have been studied in large populations of laboratory animals and the LD1 and ED99 dosages for each drug have been established.

	LD1	ED99
DRUG A	100 mg	50 mg
DRUG B	40 mg	2 mg
DRUG C	500 mg	10 mg
DRUG D	35 mg	5 mg
DRUG E	140 mg	20 mg
DRUG F	150 mg	1 mg
DRUG G	150 mg	10 mg

Rank order Drugs A through G in terms of their margins of safety, from the greatest margin of safety (safest) to the smallest margin of safety (least safe). Determine which drugs might be "tied" in their margins of safety.

Answer: The correct rank order is Drug F (safest), Drug C, Drug B, Drug G, Drugs D and E (tied), and Drug A (least safe).

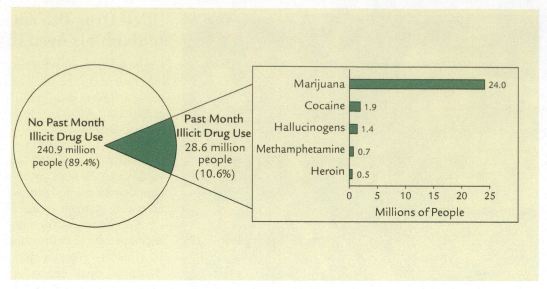

FIGURE 1.5

Numbers of current illicit drug users among individuals aged 12 or older in 2016.

Source: Center for Behavioral Health Statistics and Quality, Substance Abuse and Mental Health Services Administration (2017, September). *Key Substance Use and Mental Health Disorders in the United States. Results from the 2016 National Survey on Drug Use and Health.* Rockville, MD: Center for Behavioral Health Statistics and Quality, Substance Abuse and Mental Health Services Administration, Figure 15.

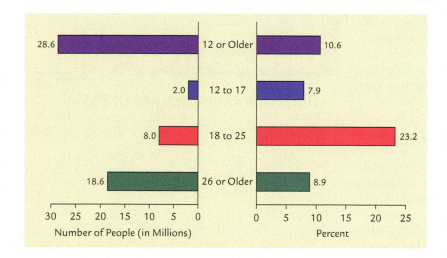

FIGURE 1.6

Percentages of current illicit drug users among individuals aged 12 or older and age group in 2016.

Source: Center for Behavioral Health Statistics and Quality, Substance Abuse and Mental Health Services Administration (2017, September). *Key Substance Use and Mental Health Disorders in the United States. Results from the 2016 National Survey on Drug Use and Health.* Rockville, MD: Center for Behavioral Health Statistics and Quality, Substance Abuse and Mental Health Services Administration, Figure 16.

than cocaine overdose deaths in 2016, a relative judgment of heroin toxicity relative to cocaine toxicity can be made. Since heroin overdose deaths in 2016 outnumbered cocaine overdose deaths among far fewer individuals, we can conclude that heroin use carries a substantially higher level of drug toxicity than does cocaine use. In other words, in relative terms, heroin is by far the more dangerous drug.[10]

Illicit Drug Use in Special Populations

Since 1975, the Monitoring the Future (MTF) project at the University of Michigan has provided detailed information about drug use among subpopulations in the United States that include three levels of secondary school students (eighth, tenth, and twelfth graders) and college students. The advantage of surveying secondary school students from year to year is that we are able to examine trends in adolescent drug-taking behavior over time and compare the prevalence rates for one drug relative to another over the years. We can assume that the degree of overreporting and underreporting stays relatively constant over the years and does not affect interpretation of the general trends. Additionally, it is possible to predict future changes in prevalence rates among high school seniors based upon present changes in prevalence rates among eighth and tenth graders, since these students will progress to higher grades in succeeding years (based on the "cohort effect" in survey research).

TABLE 1.1

Current illicit drug users and prevalence rates in 2016 among Americans, 12–17, 18–25, and 26 or older.

DRUG	AGE			
	12 or older	12-17	18-25	26 or older
Heroin	475,000	3,000	88,000	383,000
	0.2%	<0.1%	0.3%	0.2%
Cocaine (including crack cocaine)	1,900,000	28,000	532,000	1,300,000
	0.7%	0.1%	1.6%	0.6%
Hallucinogens (including LSD)	1,400,000	114,000	668,000	608,000
	0.5%	0.5%	1.9%	0.3%
Methamphetamine	667,000	9,000	65,000	594,000
	0.2%	<0.1%	0.2%	0.3%
Marijuana	24,000,000	1,600,000	7,200,000	15,200,000
	8.9%	6.5%	20.8%	7.2%

Source: Center for Behavioral Health Statistics and Quality (2017, September). *National Survey on Drug Use and Health. Illicit drug use in the past month.* Rockville, MD: Center for Behavioral Health Statistics and Quality, Substance Abuse and Mental Health Services Administration.

To examine various degrees of drug use, MTF questions are phrased in four basic ways:

1. Whether an individual has ever used a certain drug in his or her *lifetime*. The percentage of those saying "yes" is referred to as the lifetime prevalence rate.
2. Whether an individual has used a certain drug *over the past year*. The percentage of those saying "yes" is referred to as the annual prevalence rate.
3. Whether an individual has used a certain drug *within the past 30 days*. The percentage of those saying "yes" is referred to as the past-month prevalence rate and is equivalent to the designation of "current drug use" in the NSDUH surveys.
4. Whether an individual has used a certain drug *on a daily basis during the previous 30 days*. The percentage of those saying "yes" is referred to as the daily prevalence rate.

These questions distinguish three important degrees of involvement with a given drug. The first question focuses on the extent of experimentation, referring to individuals who may have taken a drug only once or twice in their lives but have stayed away from it ever since. The second and third questions focus on the extent of current but moderate drug use. The fourth question focuses on the extent of heavy drug use.

Illicit Drug Use among Secondary School Students

A graph of year-to-year changes in annual prevalence rates for illicit drugs among U.S. high school seniors since the inception of the Monitoring the Future program in 1975 (Figure 1.7) resembles something of a roller-coaster ride. In 1975, the statistics were looking quite scary. By the end of the 1970s, prevalence rates for illicit drug use had reached historically high levels. In 1979, about one-half of high school seniors reported smoking marijuana or using an illicit drug of some kind in the past year. At that time and continuing into the mid-1980s, 12 percent (one in eight seniors) reported using cocaine or crack cocaine in the past year. Fortunately, annual prevalence rates for illicit drug use among high school seniors showed a steep decline through the 1980s, ending at a historically low level (27%) around 1992. In other words, illicit drug use had dropped by about 50 percent. But at that point, a dramatic reversal occurred. Prevalence rates took a sharp upward turn during the decade of the 1990s. The bottom line is that, in terms of illicit drug use in this demographic group, the situation in 2017 remains somewhere between the worst of times (in 1979) and the best of times (in 1992).

There is optimism that prevalence rates among seniors might decline from present levels in the near future. The reason is that the annual prevalence rate for illicit drug use among eighth graders in 2017 declined from the previous two years (from 15 percent to 12–13 percent). Since it is likely (though not certain) that the present drug-taking inclinations of eighth graders will continue over their succeeding high school years, we might be seeing a decline in illicit drug use among seniors reporting in 2021.[11]

Illicit Drug Use among College Students

According to the MTF survey, college students reported in 2017 a higher annual prevalence rate (42%) in the use of illicit drugs in general, relative to high school seniors. As is the case with other surveys, illicit drug use was clearly dominated by marijuana smoking. Table 1.2 shows the lifetime, annual, and 30-day prevalence rates among college students with respect to five major types of drugs: the use of heroin, cocaine, hallucinogens, methamphetamine, and marijuana.[12]

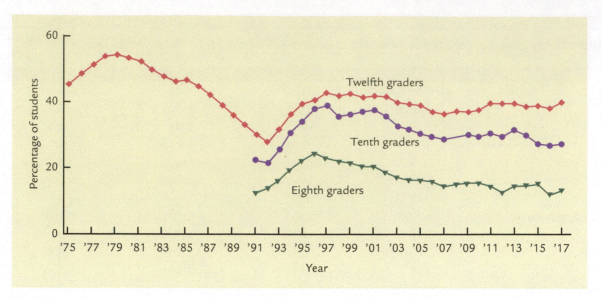

FIGURE 1.7

Trends in annual prevalence of illicit drug use among eighth, tenth, and twelfth graders.

Note: Updated statistical information from the University of Michigan survey is available at the end of December of each year through the Web site: http://www.monitoringthefuture.org.

Source: Based on data from Miech, R. A.; Johnston, L. D.; O'Malley, P. M.; Bachman, J. G.; Schulenberg, J. E.; and Patrick, M. E. (2018). *Monitoring the future: National survey results on drug use. 1975-2017, Vol. I: Secondary school students.* Ann Arbor, MI: Institute for Social Research, The University of Michigan, Table 4-1b.

TABLE 1.2

Prevalence rates (in percentages) for six illicit drugs among college students, aged 19–22, in 2017.

	EVER IN LIFETIME	IN PAST 12 MONTHS	IN PAST 30 DAYS
Heroin	0.1	<0.1	<0.1
Cocaine	6.5	5.0	1.3
Hallucinogens	7.2	4.0	1.2
Methamphetamine	0.6	0.4	<0.1
Marijuana	50.5	38.3	21.2

Note: For more current information, consult the Web site for the Monitoring the Future study: http://www.monitoringthefuture.org.

Sources: Based on data from Schulenberg, J. E.; Johnston, L. D.; O'Malley, P. M.; Bachman, J. G.; Miech, R. A.; and Patrick, M. E. (2018). *Monitoring the future: National survey results on drug use, 1975–2017, Vol. II: College students and adults aged 19–55.* Ann Arbor, MI: Institute for Social Research, The University of Michigan, Tables 2-1, 2-2, and 2-3.

Quick Concept Check 1.2

Understanding Prevalence Rates of Drug Use in the United States

Check your understanding of prevalence rates of drug use in the United States by marking the following statements as true or false.

1. The MTF survey conducted by the University of Michigan represents drug use information from all 17- to 18-year-old individuals in the United States.
2. The trend in illicit drug use from the early 1980s to the present has been a steady decline.
3. Prevalence rate for marijuana use among college students is less than the prevalence rate among high school seniors.
4. From the cohort data in the MTF survey, it is possible to predict that the prevalence rate for illicit drug use among high school seniors in 2021 will be substantially higher than the prevalence rate reported in 2017.
5. Lifetime prevalence rates are indications of the most extreme involvement with illicit drugs.

Answers: 1. false   2. false   3. false   4. false   5. false

The Problem of Drug Accessibility through the Internet

One of the current drug-related problems in America today, and one of the major challenges for law enforcement agencies, is the easy accessibility to illicit drugs through Internet Web sites, where drug transactions can be made with considerably greater anonymity and ease than had ever been possible. According to law enforcement officials, Internet transactions on these sites are accessed through special browsers with purchases made with virtual, difficult-to-trace currencies such as bitcoins, and delivered through the ordinary mail. The shadowy world of Internet trade is referred to as the "Dark Web."

In 2013, authorities took down the most notorious online marketplace for drugs, known as the Silk Road (see Drug Enforcement . . . in Focus), but recently a great number of other Web sites have taken its place. One of the leading markets of this kind reportedly comprises as many as 23,000 listings for opioids and more than 4,000 for fentanyl alone, along with a wide range of pills, powders, and nasal sprays. The distribution of the powerful opioid, fentanyl, has been particularly suited for Dark Web transactions since a quantity of fentanyl sufficient to get nearly 50,000 people high can fit into a standard first-class envelope.

Presently, tens of thousands of consumers are estimated to have access to these sites. While arrests are continually

Drug Enforcement . . . in Focus

Dealing with High-Tech Drug Dealing: Policing the "Dark Web"

In October 2013, the FBI in conjunction with the Drug Enforcement Administration succeeded in shutting down an online Internet marketplace called Silk Road. From February 2011 to October 2013, Silk Road was available as a Web site for Internet customers to buy a range of illicit drugs (among other items such as weapons) in an anonymous and untraceable transaction. Silk Road users could access the Web site using encrypted software that hid their personal computer IP addresses. As a result, they could not be identified. Money transactions were accomplished via Bitcoins, a digital form of currency that could be purchased online with real money. Buyers were instructed to have shipments delivered to post office boxes or locations other than their home. When deliveries were completed, Bitcoins were transferred from buyer to seller through a secure escrow account on the site. At the time it was shut down, Silk Road was estimated to have 900,000 active users and annual sales worth $30 million. The FBI had identified Silk Road as the most sophisticated and extensive criminal marketplace on the Internet.

From a criminal justice perspective, here was an example of the difficulty in keeping up with present-day technologies that, while originally developed for legitimate applications, could be exploited for carrying out illegal transactions. Department of Justice and Postal Service authorities struggled to track down the server location of Silk Road and prosecution proceeded slowly, until the owner, 29-year-old Ross William Ulbricht, made a simple mistake. According to court records, the U.S. Customs

and Border Protection agency had intercepted at the Canadian border a package of allegedly forged identification documents containing Ulbricht's photograph. More than 100 undercover purchases through Silk Road had been made by authorities, as they built a criminal case.

After the original Silk Road was closed down, however, Web sites similar to Silk Road, collectively referred to as the Dark Web, took its place. Marketplace sites such as Agora, White Rabbit Anonymous, Silk Road 2.0, Outlaw Market, and Evolution made use of increasingly sophisticated encryption technology to allude law enforcement agencies in their effort to identify the customers involved. In 2014, the number of illegal drug listings on 10 of the largest online drug markets had risen to more than 40,000, twice the number in the previous year.

In late 2014, an international raid jointly conducted by cybercrime units of Europol and federal law enforcement agencies in the United States succeeded in closing down Silk Road 2.0 and as many as 400 other Web sites, as well as arresting the man behind the operations of Silk Road 2.0 and some associated individuals in Europe.

Sources: Deutsch, K. (2013, October 3). Drug mart shut. *Newsday*, p. A3. Deutsch, K. (2013, September 23). High-tech drug dealers: Sources say Feds are probing. *Newsday*, p. A3. Segal, L. (2013, November 6). How the silk road was reborn. *CNN Money*. Accessed from: http://money.cnn.com/2013/11/06/technology. Wakefield, J. (2014, November 7). Huge raid to shut down 400-plus dark net sites. *BBC News Technology*. Accessed from: http://www.bbc.com/news/technology-29950946.

being made, the technological tools that have made the Dark Web possible in the first place are so widely available that it is unlikely that Internet accessibility of illicit drugs will be completely curtailed anytime soon. Often, sites are taken down for only a matter of days before they reappear under a new name or format. As a former federal prosecutor has put it, "It's only going to increase, and increase the types of communities and markets that might not have had as easy access before."[13]

A screen shot of the now-defunct Web site "Silk Road 2.0," showing various items available for sale.

Source: U.S. Department of Justice, Washington, D.C.

Summary

Understanding Drugs and Society

- Psychoactive drugs are those drugs that affect our feelings, perceptions, and behavior.

- An understanding of drugs and society requires an examination of the impact of our society on drug-taking behaviors as well as an examination of the impact of drug-taking behaviors on society. In the first case, it is important to consider the biological, psychological, and social risk factors that increase the likelihood of drug-taking behavior. In the second case, it is important to consider the consequences of drug-related crime and other forms of antisocial behavior. Agencies within the Department of Justice focus on reducing the negative impact of drug-taking behavior.

Definitions and Distinctions

- Drug use is considered either instrumental or recreational, depending on the intent of the user. Designation of drugs as illicit (illegal) or licit (legal) is dependent upon the society in which drug use occurs.

- Drug misuse refers to cases in which a prescription or nonprescription drug is used inappropriately. Drug abuse refers to cases in which a licit (legal) or illicit (illegal) drug is used in ways that produce some form of impairment. Drug dependence refers to cases in which the individual has intense experiences in connection with drug use, such as feelings of drug craving, drug tolerance, and/or feelings of withdrawal when drug use has stopped.

The Problem of Drug Toxicity

- A drug's harmful effects are referred to as its toxicity. Acute toxicity refers to the physical or psychological harm a drug might present to the user immediately or soon after the drug is ingested, as measured by a drug's therapeutic index or margin of safety. The therapeutic index is computed as the ratio of the lethal dose for 50 percent of the population to the effective dose for 50 percent of the population. The margin of safety is computed as the ratio of a lethal dose for 1 percent of the population to the effective dose for 99 percent of the population.

- Chronic toxicity refers to harmful effects when drug use extends over a period of time. Assessments of the chronic toxicity of a particular drug include statistics on drug-related health consequences as well as socioeconomic costs. The impact of chronic toxicity for a particular drug on society needs to be evaluated in terms of the prevalence rate of use.

Drug-related Hospital Emergencies and Drug-related Deaths

- Acute toxicity associated with a major drug of abuse is reflected in the number of drug-related emergency-department (ED) visits and drug-related deaths. The statistics vary considerably from drug to drug and from year to year, making the nature of drug toxicity something of a "moving target." From 2015 statistics, heroin and other opioids have become the dominant source of drug toxicity, accounting for more than eight out of ten (84%) hospital emergencies.

- Lethal cases of drug overdose represent the leading cause of accidental death in the United States today and the leading cause of death among Americans under 50. The recent rise in drug overdose deaths in the United States has been dominated by opioid overdose deaths, specifically through the increased availability of illicit synthetic opioids such as fentanyl and fentanyl analogs.

Prevalence Rates of Drug Use in the United States

- Information concerning illicit drug use among the general population is reported in the annual National Survey of Drug Use and Health by the Department of Health and Human Services. Information concerning illicit drug use among subpopulations such as secondary school students and college students is gained through annual reports by the Monitoring the Future (MTF) program at the University of Michigan.

- Between 28 and 29 million Americans, 12 years or older, were current illicit drug users in 2016, as indicated by reports of drug use within the past month. Marijuana users (defined by the U.S. federal government as an illicit drug) accounted for about 84 percent of the total number of illicit drug users in the United States. Among Americans, 12 years or older, cocaine use in 2016 outnumbered heroin use by more than four to one.

- From 2000 to 2017, prevalence rates of illicit drug use among secondary school students have been fairly stable at a level of about 38–40 percent. College students reported in 2017 a higher annual prevalence rate (42 percent) in the use of illicit drugs in general, relative to high school seniors. As is the case with other surveys, illicit drug use in 2017 was clearly dominated by marijuana smoking.

The Problem of Drug Accessibility through the Internet

- One of the current drug-related problems in America today, and one of the major challenges for law enforcement agencies, is the easy accessibility to illicit drugs through Internet Web sites. Drug Web sites are accessed through special browsers, transactions are made with virtual, difficult-to-trace currencies such as bitcoins, and illicit drugs are delivered through the ordinary mail. The shadowy world of Internet trade is referred to as the "Dark Web."

- A prominent example has been the online Internet marketplace Web site, Silk Road, offering Internet customs a range of illicit drugs (among other items such as weapons) for purchase through anonymous and untraceable transactions. Silk Road was closed down by cybercrime units of Europol and federal law enforcement agencies in the United States in 2014.

Key Terms

acute toxicity, p. 8	drug, p. 4	effective dose (ED), p. 8	margin of safety, p. 10
biopsychosocial model, p. 3	drug abuse, p. 6	illicit drugs, p. 6	psychoactive drugs, p. 3
chronic toxicity, p. 12	drug dependence, p. 7	instrumental use, p. 4	recreational use, p. 5
dose, p. 8	drug misuse, p. 6	lethal dose (LD), p. 8	therapeutic index, p. 9
dose-response curve, p. 8	drug-related ED visit, p. 10	licit drugs, p. 6	toxicity, p. 8

Review Questions

1. Distinguish between brand names, generic names, and street names given of present-day drugs.
2. Distinguish between (a) instrumental and recreational drug use, (b) illicit (illegal) and licit (legal) drugs, (c) misuse, abuse, and dependence, and (d) drug use and substance use
3. Define the following: ED, LD, ED99, LD1, ED50, and LD50. Explain how these terms are used in the computation of a therapeutic index and a margin of safety for purposes of evaluating a particular drug's level of toxicity.
4. Summarize the 2015 estimates of hospital emergencies with respect to heroin, cocaine, hallucinogens, methamphetamine, and marijuana.
5. Summarize the current estimates of drug overdose deaths. In what way could you say that heroin is by far more dangerous than cocaine?
6. Summarize the general trends in the pattern of illicit drug use among high school seniors in the United States from 1975 to 2017.
7. Summarize the general relationship between drug use among college students, relative to that of high school seniors.
8. Why has it been particularly difficult for law enforcement to close down the Dark Web?

Critical Thinking: What Would You Do?

Suppose that you were a state legislator considering new regulatory laws with respect to psychoactive drugs. What would be your argument in favor of making a distinction between "hard drugs," such as heroin, cocaine, and methamphetamine, and "soft drugs," such as marijuana and hallucinogens? On what basis would you make such a distinction? What would be the counterarguments to this proposal? What considerations would be made with respect to federal regulations currently in place?

Endnotes

1. Adapted from Scott, S. (2017, December 17). The foster care system is flooded with children of the opioid epidemic. Interview with Juvenile Court Judge Marilyn Moores, Marion County, Indiana. *NPR Now*, WNYC Radio. Quotation of Judge Moores.in https://www.npr.org/2017/12/23/573021632/the-foster-care-system-is-flooded-with-children-of-the-opioid-epidemic.

2. Eckholm, E. (2009, May 28). Governments' drug-abuse costs hit $468 billion, study says. *The New York Times*, p. A15. National Institute on Drug Abuse (2007). *The economic costs of drug abuse in the United States, 1992–2002*. Washington, D.C.: Office of National Drug Control Policy.

3. Jacobs, M. R.; and Fehr, K. O'B. (1987). *Drugs and drug abuse: A reference text.* Toronto: Addiction Research Foundation, pp. 3–5.

4. Goode, E. (2012). *Drugs in American society* (8th ed.). New York: McGraw-Hill Higher Education, pp. 11–15.

5. Treaster, J. B.; and Holloway, L. (1994, September 4). Potent new blend of heroin ends eight very different lives. *The New York Times*, pp. 1, 37.

6. Centers for Disease Control and Prevention (2018, March 6). Vital Signs: Trends in emergency department visits for suspected opioid overdoses—United States, July 2016–September 2017. *Morbidity and Mortality Weekly Reports. Early release/Volume 67*. Atlanta, GA: Centers for Disease Control and Prevention. Centers for Disease Control and Prevention (2017, August 31). *Annual Surveillance Report of Drug-Related Risks and Outcomes—United States, 2017.* Surveillance Special Report 1. Atlanta, GA: Centers for Disease Control and Prevention. Accessed from: http://www.cdc.gov/drugoverdose/pdf/pubs/2017-cdc-drug-surveillance-report.pdf

7. Centers for Disease Control and Prevention, *Annual Surveillance Report of Drug-Related Risks and Outcomes—United States, 2017.* Katz, J. (2017, September 3). New count of 2016 drug deaths shows accelerated rate. *The New York Times*, p. 14. McLaughlin, K. (2017, March 23). Underground labs in China are devising potent new opiates faster than authorities can respond. *Science News*, American Association for the Advancement of Science, Washington, D.C. National Institute on Drug Abuse (revised September 2017). Overdose death rates. Accessed from: https://www.drugabuse.gov/related-topics/trends-statistics/overdose-death-rates.

8. Center for Behavioral Health Statistics and Quality (2017, September). Illicit drug use in the past month. *Key Substance Use and Mental Health Disorders in the United States. Results from the 2016 National Survey on Drug Use and Health.* Rockville, MD: Substance Abuse and Mental Health Services Administration.

9. Center for Behavioral Health Statistics and Quality, Figure 16.

10. Center for Behavioral Health Statistics and Quality, Illicit drug use in the past month

11. Miech, R. A.; Johnston, L. D.; O'Malley, P. M.; Bachman, J. G.; Schulenberg, J. E.; and Patrick, M. E. (2018). *Monitoring the future: National survey results on drug use 1975–2017, Vol. I: Secondary school students.* Ann Arbor, MI: Institute for Social Research, The University of Michigan, p. 108.

12. Schulenberg, J. E., Johnston, L. D.; O'Malley, P. M.; Bachman, J. G., Miech, R. A.; and Patrick, M. E. (2018). *Monitoring the Future: National survey results on drug use, 1975–2017, Vol. II: College students and adults ages 19–55.* Ann Arbor, MI: Institute for Social Research, The University of Michigan, Tables 2-1, 2-2, and 2-3.

13. Popper, Nathaniel (2017, June 11). Drug trade rises in dark corners of the Internet. *The New York Times*, pp. 1, 19. Popper, Nathaniel (2017, July 7). Online bazaar for drugs goes dark, startling users. *The New York Times*, p. B4.

chapter 2

Understanding the Drug Problem in Global Perspective

The darting eyes of the driver, his tight grip on the steering wheel as he began to cross the U.S.–Mexico border: sufficient telltale signs for the Customs and Border Protection officer on duty at the busy DeConcini Port of Entry in Nogales, Arizona, to be suspicious of someone with something to hide. Sure enough, the car carried a Mexican citizen with a border-crossing card, his wife, and two small children—and a load of illicit drugs. Four pounds of methamphetamine were found in the passenger's backrest and seven pounds of heroin between the engine and the dashboard. It was a relatively small seizure operation but repeated often during the day. In 2016, more than 300 pounds of heroin had been seized at the Nogales border point alone.

It has gotten so bad, according to the agents who spoke to me, smuggling operations so brazen that shipments would some-times have visible markings identifying their cartel of origin. Earlier that morning, the letters "LEY" were spotted in black lettering on some heroin bricks that had been intercepted at the border the previous day. "Probably Sinaloa guys sending it through Chino Leya," said an agent in charge. He later explained that Chino

Leya was one of the drug distribution organizations in the Sinaloa Cartel, which controls the routes that run through Arizona, with destinations in Cleveland, New York, and New Jersey. Evidently, the drug traffickers didn't want their shipment to get lost in transit.

It was a typical day in the life of the Customs and Border Protection agents, small victories on a day-to-day basis, despite the acknowledgment that all their efforts accounted for only a very small percentage of drugs that would make it through the border without detection.[1]

Illicit drugs are a global problem and a global business. They are a global problem in that illicit drugs impact upon hundreds of millions of individuals in nations around the world, just as they impact upon Americans. In fact, some countries face problems that are more far-reaching, as we will see. It is clear that problems of acute and chronic toxicity arising from illicit drug abuse are the same no matter where in the world illicit drugs are found. Hospital emergencies, drug-related deaths, and conditions of substance abuse in general are facts of life everywhere. Illicit drugs are also a global business, in that illicit drugs are the products of an international commercial enterprise, referred to as the **global illicit drug trade**. Every day, this shadowy business manages to deliver sufficient supplies of illicit drugs to customers in practically every region of the world. Its operations rest upon an enormous and ever-changing drug-trafficking network that is sustained on brutality, opportunism, greed, and, in some countries, a continuing pattern of political corruption.

Estimates of the total worth of the global illicit drug trade range from $28 billion to $280 billion or upwards of $400

global illicit drug trade: An international business encompassing the cultivation, manufacture, distribution, and sale of illicit drugs in practically all regions of the world.

billion. Of that total, a minimum of $64 billion is estimated to be generated through U.S. drug sales alone.[2] Understandably, it is difficult to come up with exact figures, but it is safe to say that the global illicit drug trade has always been and will continue to be a financial success.

Given its success, however, outlets are needed for spending all that money. Drug trafficking is inherently a cash-intensive business, and hundreds of thousands to millions of dollars of cash proceeds must be somehow moved from point A to point B, placed into a formal banking system, or disguised as legitimate business earnings. In other words, illicit drug proceeds must be "laundered" in order to be realized as profits by drug-trafficking organizations, hence the term "money laundering." Historically, the term is derived from an early practice of American gangsters who owned chains of laundromats as a way of channeling their illegal profits through a legal business. Today, with such huge amounts of money involved, money laundering tactics need to be much more sophisticated. A number of methods are currently employed, including bulk cash smuggling, trade transactions in which proceeds are used to purchase consumer goods that are later resold individually for cash, and manipulations of formal banking procedures. International law enforcement authorities are continually challenged to circumvent these tactics (see Chapter 4).

Ultimately, financial success for the global illicit drug trade rests upon a steady demand for their products. In this respect, participants in the global illicit drug trade are no different from leaders of legitimate businesses. So long as demand stays high, suppliers will have the upper hand. Where are the customers for this enormous business enterprise? How many people worldwide are currently illicit drug users? How does the United States compare to other nations in this respect? And, most importantly, what is the extent of health-related problems in the world that result from the toxicity of illicit drugs?

Two international surveys provide information about prevalence rates of illicit drug use and associated health-related consequences of drug-taking behavior on a global basis. The first survey is the World Drug Report (WDP), compiled and published annually by the United Nations Office on Drugs and Crime (UNODC), an agency that coordinates

Numbers Talk. . .

60,000	The number of killings and disappearances of Mexico citizens over a six-year period as result of drug-related violence. Some estimates have been higher, up to 70,000 killings.
98	Percentage of drug-related murders and disappearances in Mexico that are never followed up or possible perpetrators hunted down. In some regions of Mexico, the percentage is 100 percent.
300,000	The estimated death toll in Colombia during the 10-year period (1948–1958) referred to as *La Violencia*.

Sources: AnimalPolitico (2013, July 17). Retrieved from http://www.animalpolitico.com/2013/07/98-de-los-homicidios-de-2012-en-la-impunidad/#axzz2ZJH5vQG5. (accessed in translation, September 1, 2013). Miroff, N. (2012, December 2). A new General in Mexico's drug war. *Newsday*, pp. A32–A33. Richani, N. (2002). *Systems of violence: The political economy of war and peace in Colombia.* Albany, NY: State University of New York Press, pp. 23–28. Second statistic, information courtesy of InsightCrime.org.

information from 98 countries on a variety of illicit drug-related issues.[3] The second survey is the European School Survey Project on Alcohol and Other Drugs (ESPAD), a survey of prevalence rates for illicit drug, alcohol, and tobacco use among adolescents 15–16 years old in 36 European nations. Since nearly all European nations prohibit the sale of alcohol and tobacco to minors in a similar way to that of the United States (see Chapters 13 and 15), prevalence rates in the ESPAD survey can be considered to reflect the prevalence of underage drinking and underage smoking as violations of regulations regarding alcohol and tobacco use, respectively.[4] ESPAD statistics can be compared to the 10th-grade student data in the Monitoring the Future study (Chapter 1). Together, the two surveys allow us a glimpse into the global picture of drug-taking behavior.

The Global Problem of Illicit Drug Toxicity

According to the UNODC, an estimated quarter of a billion people, approximately 5 percent of the global population aged 15–64, used drugs at least once in 2015. While the extent of drug toxicity experienced by so many people in the world can be difficult to fathom, a statistic has been devised that captures it in a single number. The **disability-adjusted life years (DALYs) statistic** refers to the years of "healthy life" lost as a result of premature death and disability caused by drug use, essentially an indicator of drug toxicity. In 2015, an estimated 28 million years of "healthy life" were lost worldwide due to drug use.[5]

The DALYs statistic provides a look at overall drug toxicity levels on a worldwide basis, but prevalence rates and drug toxicity vary considerably among nations and across drug types. One nation might have a high prevalence rate for Drug X and a low prevalence rate for Drug Y, while another nation might have a low prevalence rate for Drug X and a high prevalence rate for Drug Y. The consequences of drug toxicity for different drugs may vary from nation to nation as well. Fortunately, the World Drug Report breaks down the prevalence rates and toxicity levels for individual illicit drugs among individual nations.

Worldwide, approximately 190,100 drug-related deaths were reported in 2015. Table 2.1 shows the disproportionate share of the United States in this total, accounting for more than one in four cases (27 percent) in the world, despite representing only 5 percent of the world's population. Other nations such as the Russian Federation, the United Kingdom, and Canada experienced large numbers of drug-related deaths as well. In terms of the impact of drug-related cases themselves, you can look to the rate per million individuals who were affected in each country. Some countries reported fewer cases in 2015, but their impact nonetheless was significant. In Iceland, for example, 45 drug-related deaths were reported, but, due to a relatively small population, the impact on individuals in Iceland was nearly as great as the impact in the

TABLE 2.1

Drug-related deaths in 10 countries in 2015.

COUNTRY	NUMBER OF INCIDENCES	RATE PER MILLION IN POPULATION
Australia	1,808	116.2
Canada	2,394	104.5
El Salvador	568	160.1
Iceland	45	221.2
Kenya	1,387	56.1
Russian Federation	8,189	81.1
Sweden	765	124.5
United Kingdom	2,949	66.7
United States	**52,404**	**245.8**
Venezuela	197	55.3

Note: Marijuana is listed as an illicit drug due to its status in most countries as well as the federal government of the United States.
Source: United Nations Office on Drugs and Crime (2017). World Drug Report 2017. Vienna: United Nations Office on Drugs and Crime. Statistical tables.

United States. Overall, opioids accounted for almost 12 million of the 28 million DALYs reported worldwide in 2015.[6]

The annual prevalence rates of four illicit drugs (heroin, cocaine, methamphetamine, and marijuana) in eight countries in 2015 are shown in Table 2.2. The prevalence rate for heroin in the United States (0.59 percent) was somewhat higher than the worldwide prevalence rate, though lower than that of the Russian Federation (1.44 percent), Jamaica (0.70 percent), and Nigeria (0.70 percent). Prevalence rates for cocaine in the United States and the United Kingdom were about seven times higher than rates reported worldwide. The United States reported about four times the worldwide prevalence rate in the use of methamphetamine and marijuana.

Clearly, marijuana is far and away the most frequently used drug among the four drugs listed in Table 2.2, with a worldwide prevalence rate of approximately 4 percent. Worldwide, there were approximately 183 million marijuana users, compared to 18 million heroin users, 37 million methamphetamine users, and 17 million cocaine users in 2015.[7]

European Prevalence Rates for Illicit Drugs, Alcohol, and Tobacco

While the World Drug Report provides information about worldwide illicit drug use in a population ranging from 15 to 64 years old, the focus of the ESPAD survey is on drug use among adolescents. The ESPAD statistics regarding lifetime prevalence rates for a wide range of drugs are

Disability-adjusted life years (DALYs) statistic: An index of the number of years of "healthy life" that would be lost as a result of premature death and disability caused by drug use.

TABLE 2.2

Annual prevalence rates (percentages) for drug use with respect to four illicit drugs in 2015.

COUNTRY	HEROIN	COCAINE	METHAMPHETAMINE	MARIJUANA
Bermuda	0.15	1.30	0.10	10.90
France	0.52	1.10	0.30	11.10
Israel	0.53	1.07	1.01	8.88
Jamaica	0.70	0.98	0.81	7.21
Nigeria	0.70	0.70	1.40	14.30
Russian Federation	1.44	0.23	0.39	3.49
United Kingdom	0.73	2.20	0.10	6.50
United States	**0.59**	**2.30**	**2.90**	**16.50**
Worldwide	**0.37**	**0.35**	**0.77**	**3.8**

Source: United Nations Office on Drugs and Crime (2017). *World Drug Report 2017.* Vienna: United Nations Office on Drugs and Crime. Statistical tables.

based on a sample of approximately 100,000 European students aged 15–16 years old, closely matched in methodology to the 10th-grade sample of American students as reported in the Monitoring the Future survey (Chapter 1). The average lifetime prevalence rates for illicit drugs, heroin, cocaine, methamphetamine, marijuana, alcoholic beverages, and tobacco (cigarettes) are shown in Table 2.3, alongside comparable data for American 10th graders.

The bottom line is that American adolescents are less likely than their European counterparts to use cigarettes and alcohol, but more likely to use illicit drugs. The United States ranks lowest in the proportion of students using tobacco or alcohol, compared to students in 36 European countries. With respect to other forms of drug use, however, the United States ranks near the top of the list. Among European nations, levels of marijuana use in the Czech Republic (37 percent) and France (32 percent) are comparable to that of the United States.[8]

The Global Problem of New Psychoactive Substances (NPS)

A major concern among drug-control authorities around the world is the emergence of several hundred new drug formulations. While these formulations are related chemically to known illicit drugs, in many cases their behavioral effects are significantly greater. These new psychoactive substances are created in clandestine laboratories, principally in China, by making minor alterations in the molecular structure of known psychoactive compounds. The proliferation of these new drugs (sometimes referred to as "designer drugs") has greatly complicated drug-control efforts.

Of particular concern are NPS that are analogs of extremely potent opioid, fentanyl (see later in the chapter); others are identified by simply letters and a number. Examples of NPS of this type are AH-7921, U-47000, AH-21, and MT-45

TABLE 2.3

Lifetime prevalence rates for four illicit drugs (heroin, cocaine, methamphetamine, and marijuana), alcohol, and tobacco among users 15–16 years old in the United States, Europe, and two European countries.

DRUG/DRUG ACTIVITY	UNITED STATES (%)	EUROPE (%)	CZECH REPUBLIC (%)	FRANCE (%)
Illicit drugs	35	18	37	32
Heroin	1	1	1	2
Cocaine	3	2	1	4
Methamphetamine	1	2	1	1
Marijuana	31	16	37	32
Any alcoholic beverage	47	80	96	50
Tobacco (cigarettes)	20	46	66	63

Note: More recent statistics for users 15–16 years old in the United States are available (see Figure 1.7), but 2015 prevalence rates are entered here for comparable analyses to European counterparts.

Source: Based on data from The European Monitoring Centre for Drugs and Drug Addiction (2017). *The 2015 ESPAD report: Substance use among students in 36 European countries.* Stockholm: The European Monitoring Centre for Drugs and Drug Addiction, Tables 5, 6, 7a, and 7b.

Quick Concept Check 2.1

Understanding Prevalence Rates in America and Worldwide

Check your understanding of the annual prevalence rates in the U.S. adult population relative to the average worldwide by circling "Higher" or "Lower," as appropriate.

1. Heroin	Higher	Lower
2. Cocaine	Higher	Lower
3. Methamphetamine	Higher	Lower
4. Marijuana	Higher	Lower

Check your understanding of the lifetime prevalence rates among 10th graders in the U.S. population relative to the average among European youths of comparable age by circling "Higher" or "Lower," as appropriate.

5. Illicit drugs in general	Higher	Lower
6. Marijuana	Higher	Lower
7. Any alcoholic beverages	Higher	Lower
8. Tobacco (cigarettes)	Higher	Lower

Answers: 1. Higher   2. Higher   3. Higher   4. Higher
5. Higher   6. Higher   7. Lower   8. Lower

(see Chapter 9). It is as if a well-understood set of viruses that have been tracked over the years were now mutating into new forms. Between 2009 and 2016, 106 countries and territories reported to the UNODC that as many as 739 different NPS compounds had been introduced as new illicit drugs.

One NPS category, based on variations in the molecular structure of a group of compounds found in marijuana plants called *cannabinoids* (see Chapter 11), illustrates the challenges faced by drug-control officials. Soon after the synthetic cannabinoid JWH-018 (known as Spice or K2) appeared on the scene in 2010 as a new recreational drug, several countries placed it on their own prohibited-drug lists. It was not long, however, before another compound with similar psychoactive properties, referred to as JWH-073, took its place. At that point, JWH-073 was added to the prohibited-drugs list, only to be followed by further variations. Making matters worse, regulatory agencies in some countries have been relatively slow in their response to the emergence of NPS, allowing a foothold to be established among drug users before they can be officially banned.[9]

The Global Illicit Drug Trade and Criminal Justice

It is clear that prevalence rates for illicit drugs around the world constitute a substantial "demand" for the global illicit drug trade that continues to provide a "supply."

Obviously, the "suppliers" are highly motivated to get their product to the customer, and they do so with great success, despite the concerted efforts of international drug-control authorities to thwart their operations. How does the global illicit drug trade do it? Where are the drug-trafficking routes that deliver illicit drugs to drug users? What is the extent of "collateral damage" brought on by the global illicit drug trade?

It would be an ideal situation if international drug-control authorities were able to identify, at any precise moment, all of the illicit drug-trafficking routes in the world and all of the means by which drugs are distributed. But unfortunately, two principal factors are working against them in this respect.

The first factor is the extraordinary agility on the part of the global illicit drug trade in adapting to changing law enforcement circumstances. Typically, drug-trafficking operations are highly mobile; operations can often be moved within hours, making it relatively easy to shift illicit drug activity to another location. One country might be dominant with respect to drug trafficking one year, while a neighboring country might be dominant the next year. The reality is that drug-trafficking patterns are in a constant state of flux, with drug-control agencies playing "catch up" time after time. In effect, updated maps of drug-trafficking routes cannot ever be completely accurate because the "ink never dries" fast enough before routes change again.

The second factor is the limitation in the ways that are available to law enforcement for keeping track of drug-trafficking activities. The principal method is to examine, on an ongoing basis, confiscated shipments of illicit drugs in drug-seizure operations and raids on illicit drug laboratories and distribution sites. While yielding information about drug trafficking, this approach is far from perfect. Confiscated drugs are by no means a random sample of the drugs involved in a specific drug-trafficking system. Drug seizures and laboratory raids may correlate with the *extent* of drug trafficking in a particular region, but the *quantity* of confiscated drugs may be related more to the intensity of drug-control campaigns in that region or else the ease by which drugs are intercepted by drug-control authorities. In other words, we cannot know the extent to which the magnitude of a drug seizure is related to law enforcement agents being clever or drug traffickers being stupid!

While we recognize that illicit drug-trafficking patterns can change, it is nonetheless useful to draw upon the information we have at our disposal in order to gain an understanding of the global forces at work. The focus here will be on the best-known international trafficking routes, past and present, in five categories: heroin, cocaine, marijuana, methamphetamine, and finally three other illicit drugs (LSD, PCP, and ketamine). In the past, a particular drug has had its own unique trafficking pattern. In recent years, however, there has been a growing trend toward "multitasking" on the part of the global illicit drug trade, with distribution systems designed to deliver multiple categories of illicit drugs through the same pipeline. As we will see, this is particularly the case with respect to present-day drug trafficking in Mexico.

The Trafficking of Heroin and Other Opioids

Opioids are a diverse group of drugs, some of them (such as heroin) being derived from morphine, the active ingredient in raw opium (see Chapter 9), and others (such as fentanyl) having similar "opiate-like" properties but synthesized entirely in the laboratory. The abuse of heroin and fentanyl or in combination represents the dominant opioid problems today (Chapter 1). We will take up the trafficking patterns of heroin and fentanyl separately, since they have distinct origins, histories, and routes of distribution.

Heroin, Turkey, and the "French Connection"

From the 1930s to the 1960s, heroin trafficking into the United States centered on a close association of American and Corsican Mafia organizations with clandestine heroin-producing laboratories in Marseille, France. Although most of the raw opium itself was produced and transported from Southeast Asia, Turkish farmers grew opium poppies as well. The main markets for these local farmers were the pharmaceutical companies that manufactured morphine and other opium-based medications for legitimate purposes, but part of their crop would be left to the side and later diverted to morphine laboratories operated by criminal groups in the area. Morphine would then be shipped to Corsican-controlled heroin laboratories in Marseilles. From Marseilles, the heroin would be transported to New York, where American Mafia groups controlled its distribution in major U.S. cities. The pattern of heroin trafficking during this period of time became known as the "French Connection."

By the late 1960s and 1970s, a series of successful "French Connection" prosecution cases, conducted by a coordinated team of international law enforcement agencies, had led to the demise of this heroin-trafficking system. The supply of opium to Marseilles was cutoff when production in Turkey was curtailed, beginning with the 1968 opium crop. Major traffickers were either captured and imprisoned by French and American authorities or killed by fellow criminals within their own organizations. Heroin trafficking shifted from France and Turkey to more direct sources in Southeast Asia and Southwest Asia.[10]

FIGURE 2.1

The nations of the Golden Triangle.
Source: Public Radio International, Minneapolis, MN.

The Golden Triangle in Southeast Asia

In the 1960s and 1970s, the dominant source of heroin for the U.S. market was the so-called **Golden Triangle** of Southeast Asia, an area comprising the countries of Thailand, Burma (Myanmar), and Laos (Figure 2.1). Heroin from the Golden Triangle was usually sold as a white or off-white powder, and, considering its place of origin, was called **China White** on the street. Southeast Asian heroin was smuggled into the United States primarily via containerized maritime cargo from such locations as Taiwan and Hong Kong and often was concealed among legitimate commodities. The cargo shipments traveled to major ports of entry along the West Coast of the United States and western Canada, where they were transported eastward to cities such as Chicago and Detroit. Since the 1980s, however, the role of the Golden Triangle region as a source of heroin in the United States has greatly diminished as heroin trafficking to American users has shifted to sources in the Western Hemisphere. Today, direct Southeast Asian heroin markets are primarily in Asia and Australia.[11]

The Golden Crescent in Southwest Asia

Currently, the single largest source of heroin for *worldwide* consumption is the so-called **Golden Crescent** of Southwest Asia, an area comprising the countries of Pakistan, Afghanistan, Iran, and regions of the former Soviet Union such as Tajikistan and Kyrgyzstan. Within the Golden Crescent, the dominant player is clearly Afghanistan and, in particular, the southwest Afghan provinces of Farah, Hilmand, and Kandahar, next to the border with Iran and Pakistan. In years when crop yields are high, Afghanistan alone has the capacity to supply approximately 90 percent of the world's heroin; in years of relatively low crop yields, the percentage dips to about 75 percent, with other regions in

---

Golden Triangle: A once-dominant opium-producing region of Southeast Asia comprised the nations of Thailand, Burma (Myanmar), and Laos.

China White: A street name for heroin from the Golden Triangle nations of Southeast Asia.

Golden Crescent: A major opium-producing region of Southwest Asia, comprising Pakistan, Afghanistan, Turkey, Iran, and former regions of the Soviet Union.

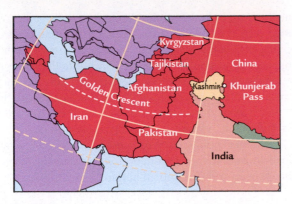

FIGURE 2.2

The nations of the Golden Crescent.
Source: Global Times.

Myanmar and Laos (part of the Golden Triangle) making up the extra quantities needed for the global marketplace.

Special units of the Drug Enforcement Administration, called Foreign-Deployed Advisory Support Teams (FAST), have been trained by U.S. Special Forces in Afghanistan since 2005 to blunt the impact of the country's heroin trade by destroying opium processing laboratories and targeting heroin traffickers. Raids by U.S. and Afghan counter-narcotics units, such as an October 2016 seizure of more than 20 tons of heroin (the "largest known seizure of heroin in Afghanistan, if not the world" according to officials), reduced the flow of heroin trafficking money to the Taliban for their use in meeting operational expenses. Nonetheless, even raids of this magnitude have not been sufficient to stem the tide of heroin trafficking in the region. Interestingly, the reason given by opium farmers themselves for growing opium poppies remains essentially economic; less than 1 percent of

the Afghan farmers claim that their decisions are dictated by the encouragement of the Taliban or other anti-government groups. A typical Afghan farmer makes 10 times more money from growing opium poppies than another other crop.[12]

Relatively little of the heroin from Afghanistan or other countries in the Golden Crescent region (Figure 2.2), however, is destined for the U.S. market. Nonetheless, owing to its importance with respect to heroin trafficking for the rest of the world, it is important to examine the ways in which heroin trafficking from this region is accomplished.

In recent years, three major trafficking systems for Golden Crescent heroin have been identified by international drug-control agencies: (1) a northern route, (2) a Balkan route, and (3) a southern route through East, West, and Central Africa. The northern route extends through Tajikistan, Kyrgyzstan, Uzbekistan, and Turkmenistan to Kazakhstan (formerly part of the Soviet Union) and the Russian Federation itself. The Balkan route is the principal trafficking corridor for Afghan heroin to sizable markets in the Russian Federation and Western Europe, extending through Iran (via Pakistan), Turkey, Greece, and Bulgaria. Judging from data gained through heroin seizures, a relatively minor but growing southern trafficking route extends from the East African nations of Benin and Tasmania to Nigeria with destinations in Western Europe. In the case of the southern route, Golden Triangle nations have traditionally supplied the bulk of the raw opium for processing, but in recent years the demands from Western Europe have increased to such an extent that "the African connection" now brings significant quantities of heroin from Afghanistan as well (see Figure 2.3 on page 28).[13]

Heroin Trafficking in Mexico and Colombia

At the present time, despite its dominant role in the worldwide heroin trade, the heroin-trafficking operations in Golden Crescent nations have little or no impact on heroin consumption in the United States. Instead, the dominant players in heroin trafficking to markets in the United States in the twenty-first century are the Western Hemisphere nations of Mexico and Colombia.

For many years, Mexican heroin was crudely processed with many impurities, resulting in a much-disparaged powder version (called brown heroin) that was, at the time, considered inferior to the more refined China White heroin coming out of Southeast Asia. The Mexican variety is typically black or brown in color and has a sticky consistency, hence its name **Black Tar** or "Tootsie Roll" on the street. Despite its darker color, Mexican heroin processing methods have "improved" so as to achieve considerably higher levels of purity. At the same time, street prices have dropped dramatically, so that Mexican heroin is both relatively strong and relatively cheap.

Nasrullan Khan, Kandahar's deputy counter-narcotics officer, inspects a cache of opium and heroin seized in a recent raid.

Credit: Steve Chao, Al Jazeera.

> **Black Tar:** A form of heroin, generally brownish in color, originating in Mexico.

Although Mexico cultivates only 2–7 percent of the world's opium, Mexico's opium production is significant because virtually all the Mexican opium is converted into heroin and destined for the United States. Most of the opium in Mexico is grown by small, independent farmers known as *campesinos* in rural areas of Sinaloa, Chihuahua, Durango, and Guerrero. Typically, individual traffickers or trafficking organizations pay a prearranged price for the opium crop, the equipment used in harvesting, and food for the farmer's family. A middleman or broker then collects the opium and transports it to a clandestine laboratory for processing into heroin. Mexican heroin is smuggled into the United States primarily overland across the U.S.–Mexico border via private and commercial vehicles. Smaller quantities of Mexican heroin often are carried across the border by illegal aliens or migrant workers who hide the drugs in backpacks, in the soles of their shoes, or on their bodies.[14]

By global standards, Colombia produces relatively little heroin (less than 5 percent of the world's total estimated production). However, most of the heroin produced in Colombia is destined for the United States. At one time, heroin was transported from Colombia directly to the United States by couriers traveling on commercial flights from one of the Colombian airports to international airports in Miami, Atlanta, or New York. Couriers (known as "drug mules") often swallowed small pellets of heroin that had been placed in condoms or balloons, or wrapped in latex from surgical gloves. They also concealed heroin in body cavities, taped it to their bodies, or concealed it in their clothing or shoes. Larger quantities of heroin into the United States were smuggled by transporting the drug in suitcases containing heroin sewn into the seams of clothing. Alternatively, Colombian heroin traffickers recruited Mexican couriers to transport South American heroin into the United States through rural areas of Mexico then across the Mexico–U.S. border via private or commercial vehicles crossing at border checkpoints. As already noted, Mexico has since developed its own heroin production and trafficking system for both Mexican and Colombian heroin.[15]

Heroin Trafficking Today

At the present time, the global heroin trafficking network is a complex system with the Golden Triangle nations, Golden Crescent nations, and Mexico being the dominant suppliers for various destinations around the world. Heroin trafficking, originating in the Golden Crescent region and destinations in Western, Central and Southeastern Europe, and the Russian Federation, follows a variety of routes, including a circuitous "Southern route" that extends through and around Africa. The Golden Triangle distributes heroin through more localized routes into Central Asia and Australia. Finally, heroin from sources in Mexico and Colombia enters Mexico, then is transported into the United States, primarily through its southwest border (Figure 2.3).[16]

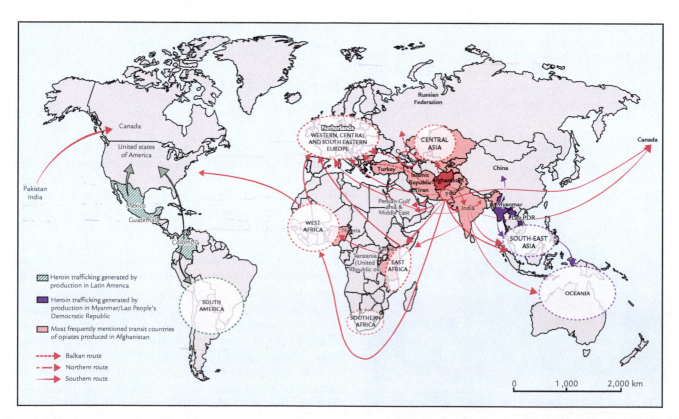

FIGURE 2.3

The complex heroin trafficking network, supplying the world.

Source: United Nations Office on Drugs and Crime (2017). *World Drug Report 2017.* Vienna: United Nations Office on Drugs and Crime. PowerPoint Slide 10.

The Trafficking of Fentanyl and Fentanyl Analogs

Fentanyl has been widely applied in clinical settings as a licit synthetic opioid drug, owing to its extremely strong analgesic and anesthetic properties (see Chapter 9). In its licit form, fentanyl has been diverted, on a small scale, by drug traffickers from the legitimate market to illicit use or sale. On a much larger scale, illicit fentanyl or precursors for manufacturing fentanyl is presently created in clandestine laboratories in China, then shipped directly to the United States via the U.S. Postal Service and other express mail services or shipped to Canada and Mexico for later transport across the northern and southwest borders. Wherever the final destination for fentanyl or fentanyl precursors, a variety of hotel rooms or private homes, known as "fentanyl mills," are typically employed for mixing fentanyl with heroin or pressing fentanyl into counterfeit pills that are intended to pass as legitimate prescription pain medications (Figure 2.4).

As noted earlier, illicit fentanyl is responsible for enormous increase in opioid-related overdose deaths in recent years. Adding to the dangers involved, a synthetic fentanyl analog called carfentanil, with a potency that is 100 times that of fentanyl and used on a legitimate basis only as a tranquilizing agent for elephants and other larger mammals, has recently entered the illicit drug market. According to reports of the Drug Enforcement Administration, mail-order shipments of carfentanil have been seized having markings that indicate Chinese points of origin. Destinations for these shipments have included Ohio and several other U.S. states on the East Coast from Rhode Island to Florida.

Until recently, adequate technology for the interdiction of opioids from overseas on a large scale has not been available. However, in 2018, the International Narcotics Trafficking Emergency Response by Detecting Incoming Contraband with Technology (INTERDICT) Act became law, authorizing the installation of thousands of newly developed portable drug-screening devices at major international

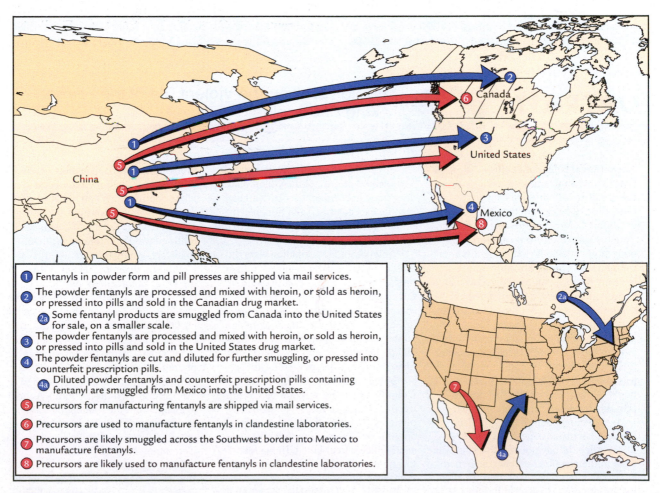

FIGURE 2.4

Trafficking routes for illicit fentanyl and fentanyl precursors.

Source: Drug Enforcement Administration (2017). *2016 National Drug Threat Assessment Summary.* Washington, D.C.: Drug Enforcement Administration, U.S. Department of Justice, Figure 83.

airports and international mail delivery centers that will be sensitive enough to detect fentanyl, fentanyl analogs, and other synthetic opioids. The law also authorizes the support of hundreds of scientists to analyze the data collected from these devices and determine the origin of the shipments and their intended recipients.[17]

The Trafficking of Cocaine

Cocaine is derived from the leaves of the coca shrub, grown in the high-altitude rain forests and fields that run along the slopes of the Andes in South America (see Chapter 10), commonly referred to as the Andean Region. Due to the volatility of the global illicit drug market, the country with the "distinction" of being the number-one coca producer in the world varies from year to year. At one time, virtually all the world's coca was cultivated in Bolivia and Peru, but frequent crop

---

cartel: An organization centered on the manufacture, distribution, and/or sale of illicit drugs.

Medellin and Cali drug cartels: Two major Colombian drug cartels that controlled much of the illicit drug distribution in South America from the mid-1970s to the mid-1990s.

---

eradication campaigns resulted in a decline in coca production in these countries. In recent years, Colombia has become dominant in coca cultivation and the manufacture of cocaine. Cocaine is routed west into Europe through Colombian drug-trafficking organizations, while cocaine destined for the United States is routed through Mexico for further distribution across the Southwest border or else by air or sea (see Drug Enforcement ... in Focus in Chapter 10).

Until the early 1970s, Cuban organized crime groups controlled the importation of cocaine from Colombia into the United States, but, by the mid-1970s, control of the cocaine industry had shifted from Cubans to Colombians themselves. For the next two decades, its production and distribution would be under the control of well-organized Colombian-led criminal organizations (referred to as **cartels).** The most powerful organizations of this type were the **Medellin and Cali drug cartels** (named after cities in Colombia that were their home bases).

Prior to the advent of drug cartels in Colombia, cocaine smuggling had been on a small scale and quite primitive by today's standards. As the demand for cocaine in the United States exceeded supplies, however, more sophisticated trafficking methods were developed. The infamous Medellin Cartel led by Pablo Escobar (see Portrait) employed fleets of small airplanes loaded with cocaine in remote Colombian airfields. The huge profits gained from Medellin operations were invested in

---

PORTRAIT

Pablo Escobar: The Violent Life of the Former "King of Cocaine"

The criminal career of Pablo Escobar began in earnest at the age of 26 with his first drug bust. We can be certain that he had been in trouble before, but this was his first drug bust, an arrest for possession of 39 pounds of cocaine. What made this arrest unusual was that the arresting officer was later mysteriously murdered and as many as nine judges were so intimidated by death threats that they refused to hear the case. In the succeeding years, Escobar joined two other criminal entrepreneurs to form the Medellin Cartel, named after their home town. The cartel they created was to set the standard for its organizational discipline as well as the vicious brutality by which the cartel operated.

In a fleeting attempt to legitimize himself, Escobar at one point ran for political office. It may not be surprising that he won the election and became a member of the Colombian Congress. In effect, his intention was to gain immunity by being part of the government. His political career did not last very long, however, and soon Escobar returned to a more lucrative renegade status in Colombia.

In 1984, the Medellin Cartel controlled 80 percent of the Colombian drug trade in cocaine. Escobar's annual income exceeded $2.75 billion, placing him on the *Forbes* magazine listing of the wealthiest people in the world.

Violence and assassination were the tools of his trade. Police officers, judges, public officials, and journalists were his targets. Public bombings and drive-by shootings were commonplace. Three presidential candidates, the Colombian attorney general, more than 200 judges, 100 police officers, and dozens of journalists were murdered, their deaths attributed to Escobar and his cartel. A Colombian jetliner was bombed, resulting in 107 deaths. In 1990, Escobar offered a "bounty" of $4,000 (a huge amount by Colombian standards) for each police officer killed. In the following month, 42 police officers were murdered.

In 1991, the Colombian government offered immunity from prosecution and the use of extravagant facilities of a mountainside ranch if Escobar would turn himself in. He accepted this arrangement,

though his criminal activities were merely directed from the ranch itself and the violence continued. When the government decided to move him from the ranch, Escobar was tipped off and escaped. What followed was the most famous manhunt in history, lasting for over a year. The Central Intelligence Agency (CIA) and the Drug Enforcement Administration (DEA) joined Colombian police in the chase. In 1993, a brief telephone call to his family was intercepted by authorities and telephone lines were severed, isolating Escobar (before the advent of cell phones) from communicating with the outside. A relatively small 17-men swat team surrounded his last stand. As he tried to escape from the rooftop, he was killed by a barrage of bullets. So ended the ignominious career of Pablo Escobar—the Colombian King of Cocaine.

Sources: Brooke, J. (1990, June 7). In the capital of cocaine, savagery is the habit. *The New York Times*, p. 4. Watson, R.; and Katel, P. (1993, December 13). Death on the spot: The end of a drug king. *Newsweek*, pp. 18–23.

increasingly sophisticated cocaine labs, better airplanes, and even a private island in the Bahamas where their planes could refuel. In the meantime, the Medellin Cartel became known as the prototype for the modern-day drug cartel with an organization that can be characterized as an onion-like layering of power and responsibility. Kingpins at the center directed operations, and groups of self-contained cells were managed by a small number of cartel managers. Each cell specialized in a different aspect of the drug business, such as production, distribution, smuggling, or money laundering. If police arrested members of one cell, a second or third cell would step up operations to fill the vacuum. Members of each of cells rarely were connected directly with any of the leaders of the cartel.

During his ascendency to power, Pablo Escobar and the other leaders of the Medellin Cartel set out to crush any opposition from law enforcement or the Colombian government by a campaign of terror and brutality. They were considered responsible for the murder of hundreds of government officials, police, prosecutors, judges, journalists, and innocent bystanders. Their flamboyant lifestyle, combined with their total disregard for human life, became their trademark.

In contrast, the Cali Cartel was more subdued in their operations, relying instead on political corruption over violence, conducting their business in a discreet and business-like manner, and reinvesting much of their profits from the illicit drug trade into legitimate businesses. The Cali Cartel relied heavily on political bribery for protection. At one point, the former president of Colombia, Ernesto Samper, and hundreds of Colombian congressmen and senators were accused of accepting campaign financing from the cartel. The Medellin Cartel relied on small airplanes and speedboats, whereas the Cali Cartel smuggled most of its shipments in large cargo ships, hiding the drugs in all types of legitimate cargo, from cement blocks to bars of chocolate. During the 1980s, the two cartels shared the cocaine-trafficking market into the United States, with the Medellin Cartel controlling the market in south Florida and the Cali Cartel controlling the market in cocaine in New York. The Cali Cartel later expanded into cocaine markets in Europe and Asia and through alliances with other organized crime groups such as the Japanese Yakuza.

By the mid-1990s, both cartels had met their downfall. Escobar himself was killed as he tried to escape in a final confrontation with Colombian police in 1993. The Cali Cartel outlasted the Medellin Cartel for a few years, but its leaders were eventually tracked down and arrested as well. The vacuum created by the demise of the Medellin and Cali Cartels led to a decentralization of cocaine trafficking in the region. Production and trafficking operations were taken over by smaller independent Bolivian, Peruvian, and Mexican organizations (called "cartelitos").

Present-day trafficking of Colombian cocaine is routed through Honduras, then on to Mexico, where the drugs are smuggled across the border into the United States in hidden

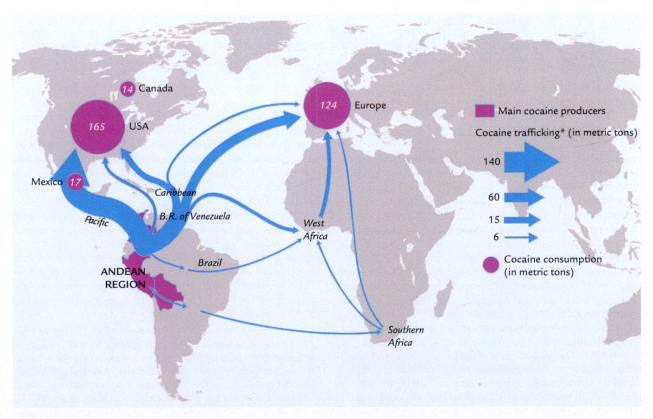

FIGURE 2.5

Patterns of cocaine trafficking from origins in the Andean Region of South America.

Source: United Nations Office on Drugs and Crime (2010). *World Drug Report 2010.* Vienna: United Nations Office of Drugs and Crime, Map 6, p.70.

compartments inside passenger vehicles or combined with legitimate cargo in commercial trucks. Other transborder routes have not been devised as well. In 2015, an underground drug tunnel was discovered that ran from Mexicali, Mexico, to the All-American Canal on the U.S. side of the border near Calexico, California. Thirty-one kilograms of cocaine were seized by U.S. federal agents. In October 2015, the Columbian government ended over 15 years of aerial eradication of coca because of concerns that the herbicide, glyphosate, used in killing coca plants, caused health problems among the community. The DEA assessment has been that, as a result of this action, coca production in Colombia has risen substantially and will continue to rise in the foreseeable future (Figure 2.5).[18]

The Trafficking of Marijuana

Mexico is currently the major foreign source for marijuana smuggled into the United States. Most of the marijuana trafficking, whether grown in Mexico or transported through Mexico from other locations such as Colombia, takes place at the U.S.–Mexico border.

A Mexican federal agent crawls through a hidden U.S.–Mexico border tunnel previously used to transport drugs from Mexico to the United States. See Drug Enforcement . . . in Focus for an update on DEA operations on the U.S.–Mexico border.

Credit: Sandy Huffaker/Getty Images News/Getty Images

Drug Enforcement . . . in Focus

Massive Drug Tunnels Underneath the Border

From 2008 to 2013, more than 75 cross-border drug-trafficking tunnels were detected and shut down (most of them in California and Arizona), reflecting a trend in getting illicit drugs into the United States from Mexico. An image comes to mind of tunnels barely wide enough for one man to crawl through (see the above-mentioned photo), and many of the tunnels have been indeed small. But some of them have been substantially bigger. In 2013, a massive and sophisticated tunnel was uncovered by the San Diego Tunnel Task Force, comprising agents with ICE, DEA, and Customs and Border Protection. Stretching the length of five football fields (about one-third of a mile) at a depth of about 35 feet, it was equipped with lighting, ventilation, and an electric rail system.

The tunnel connected a warehouse in Tijuana, Mexico, with a warehouse in the Otay Mesa industrial park south of downtown San Diego, just north of the Mexico border. It was estimated that it had taken years and tens of millions of dollars to build the tunnel, and it was just completed and ready for operation when federal agents descended (literally) and closed it down. More than eight tons of marijuana and several hundred pounds of cocaine were seized.

As it often happens in interdiction cases, careful surveillance and a few lucky breaks made the difference. Earlier in the week, a box truck was pulled over by police in a nearby town for traffic violations and three tons of marijuana was found concealed inside. Another five tons of marijuana was found in another box truck attempting to leave the Otay Mesa warehouse that turned out to be the "U.S. entrance" to the tunnel. The cocaine was also found in a van that authorities had earlier observed leaving the same warehouse site. While the tunnel uncovered in 2013 was immense, it was only the eighth large-scale drug tunnel that had been discovered in the San Diego area since 2006.

Despite the success of the operation, drug-control authorities expect that more tunnels will be built. Whether or not all of them will be detected is another matter. The tunnel uncovered in 2013 was the eighth large-scale drug tunnel discovered in the San Diego area since 2006.

Sources: Drug Enforcement Administration (2017). *2016 National Drug Threat Assessment Summary.* Washington, D.C.: Drug Enforcement Administration, U.S. Department of Justice. Feds shut down massive new cross-border drug tunnel south of San Diego. News Release, Drug Enforcement Administration, U.S. Department of Justice, Washington, D.C., October 31, 2013. Massive new cross-border drug tunnel shut down south of San Diego. News Release, Immigration and Customs Enforcement, U.S. Department of Homeland Security, Washington, D.C., October 31, 2013.

As a result of increased detection and monitoring of air traffic at the border, most of the marijuana that enters the United States from Mexico is smuggled by land. Drug-trafficking organizations operating from Mexico employ a wide variety of methods for smuggling marijuana when crossing the border, such as concealing the drug in false vehicle compartments located in doors, fuel tanks, seats, or tires. Marijuana often is hidden in tractor-trailer trucks among shipments of legitimate agriculture products, such as fruits and vegetables. Smaller quantities of marijuana can be smuggled across the border by horse, raft, and backpack. Once the marijuana is smuggled successfully across the border, traffickers consolidate the shipments at "safe houses" in southern U.S. cities. For large quantities of marijuana, transport through cross-border underground tunnels from Mexico to sites in California and Arizona has been a frequent option (see Drug Enforcement ... in Focus). From 1990 to 2016, 225 tunnels were seized by federal drug-control authorities.[19]

The Trafficking of Methamphetamine

During the early 1990s, methamphetamine reemerged as a popular recreational drug in the United States after an earlier period of popularity in the 1960s and 1970s. Methamphetamine has a similar chemical structure to that of amphetamine, but it has a more pronounced effect on the central nervous system (see Chapter 10). It is a white, odorless, and bitter-tasting crystalline powder and is commonly referred to as "speed," "meth," and "crank." The primary precursor chemicals for the manufacture of methamphetamine, ephedrine, and pseudoephedrine are obtained by purchasing inexpensive over-the-counter cough-and-cold medications. Throughout the 1970s and 1980s, the production and trafficking of methamphetamine were controlled by motorcycle gangs such as Hell's Angels and other groups. It has been estimated that between 1979 and 1981, money obtained from selling methamphetamine accounted for 91 percent of the Hell's Angels finances. Today, methamphetamine is still often referred to as "crank" because motorcyclists would hide the drug in the crankshafts of their motorcycles.

In the mid-1990s, drug-trafficking organizations based in Mexico and California began to take control of the production and distribution of methamphetamine, setting up large-scale "superlabs" that were capable of producing as much as 10 pounds of methamphetamine in a 24-hour period. The entry of these organizations into the methamphetamine trade resulted in a significant increase in the supply of high-purity, low-cost methamphetamine.

At the same time, supplies of methamphetamine appeared as produced by smaller independent "mom and pop" laboratories, obtaining the ingredients necessary for manufacture from retail and convenience stores. The rural regions of southern and midwestern U.S. states were particularly suited for small-time methamphetamine (meth) cookers with operations in trailers or mobile homes located in secluded heavily forested

areas. Cooks would typically dispose of highly toxic wastes from the production process by dumping the material into a nearby lake, pond, or stream. The proliferation of laboratories was fueled by the expansion of Internet sites providing access to methamphetamine "recipes." At the time, these methamphetamine laboratories were described as "chemical time bombs" because of the frequent explosions and fires that were triggered by the highly flammable and toxic chemicals needed for methamphetamine production (see Chapter 10).

Since 2005, methamphetamine trafficking has shifted from the domestic meth labs to foreign sources. The federal Combat Methamphetamine Epidemic Act, passed in 2005, drastically reduced the availability of large quantities of pseudoephedrine, a necessary precursor chemical for meth production. As a result, domestic production of meth has decreased substantially, replaced by production in Mexican laboratories. In order to circumvent the scarcity of pseudoephedrine, Mexican traffickers have utilized an alternative precursor, Phenyl-2-Proponone (P2P). According to recent analyses by the Drug Enforcement Administration, 78 percent of meth samples seized by drug-control authorities show that P2P was the precursor used in the production process. Meth is then smuggled across the southwest border in liquid or powder form. Once across the border, clandestine laboratories in the United States convert meth into a crystalline form, referred to as *crystal meth* (see Chapter 10).[20]

The Trafficking of LSD, PCP, and Ketamine

Lysergic acid diethylamide (LSD) is a clear or white, odorless crystalline material that is soluble in water (see Chapter 12). The drug is usually dissolved in a solvent for application onto paper, commonly referred to as blotter paper or blotter acid. Blotter acid consists of sheets of paper soaked or sprayed with LSD and decorated with a variety of colorful designs and symbols. A sheet of paper LSD blotter may contain hundreds of small, perforated, and one-quarter-inch squares, with each square representing one individual dose. LSD may also be found in tablet form (microdots), in thin squares of gelatin ("window panes"), or in a dissolved liquid form that can be stored in an eyedrop container or glass vial. Eyedroppers allow users to disperse hundreds of doses of LSD at large parties or concerts by administering the drug on the tongue.

LSD is commonly produced from lysergic acid, which, in turn, is chemically derived from the ergot fungus. Since ergot is not readily available in the United States and is regulated under the Chemical Diversion and Trafficking Act, most of the production of LSD is believed to come from sources located abroad, such as Europe and Mexico. Since the 1960s, nearly all the LSD that is produced in the United States has originated from a small number of laboratories operating in northern California.

Typically, LSD trafficking is accomplished in two ways. The primary method of transportation is by mail, using overnight delivery services. LSD is frequently concealed in greeting cards, plastic film containers, or articles of clothing that are mailed to a post office box established by the recipient. The post office box is usually listed under a fictitious name or business, and no return address is typically provided on the package or envelope. Rock concerts also have been a traditional means of distributing LSD. Throughout the 1970s and 1980s, traffickers used concerts of the rock band The Grateful Dead as a network to distribute and sell both large and small quantities of LSD.

Phencyclidine (PCP), a synthetic drug first used in medical anesthesia but now classified as an illicit hallucinogen (see Chapter 12), is produced in clandestine laboratories either in Mexico or in the United States and distributed under a variety of street names, such as angel dust, rocket fuel, killer weed, embalming fluid, ozone, or Sherman (because the drug supposedly "hits you like a Sherman tank").

Ketamine is known by the street names Special K or simply K (not to be confused with the synthetic cannabinoid that is called K2 or Spice). Ketamine is a drug that is chemically similar to PCP but produces fewer symptoms of confusion, irrationality, and violence. Since it is currently available as a legitimate medication as an injectable, short-acting anesthetic for animals and humans, ketamine is frequently sold on the street after being stolen from either hospital or veterinary facilities, or else smuggled into the United States from Mexico. In clinical use, ketamine is found in liquid form for injection, but ketamine sellers prefer to market the drug in a powdered or crystallized form. In this way, ketamine powder can be snorted, smoked (sprinkled on tobacco or marijuana), or ingested by being dropped into a drink, with an effect similar to that of PCP.[21]

Drug Trafficking as a Moving Target

The emphasis in examining drug-trafficking patterns has been on nations that have historically participated in the global illicit drug trade. In recent years, however, drug-trafficking organizations have emerged involving nations that had not been part of the traditional illicit drug cultivation and trafficking business. In some cases, an expansion of global drug trafficking has been off-shoots of well-established trafficking organizations. Mexican drug traffickers, for example, have managed to establish strongholds in other Central American countries such as Guatemala and Honduras. Colombian traffickers now have major operations in nearby Venezuela; trafficking routes extend as far as West Africa. Dominican traffickers are particularly active on the East Coast of the United States in the distribution of cocaine and heroin, in cooperation with Mexican and Colombian organizations. Asian drug traffickers are active on the East Coast and West Coast of the United States in the distribution of marijuana and MDMA (Ecstasy), the latter of which is typically imported from China, Belgium, and the Netherlands to Canada or produced in Canada then smuggled into the United States (see Chapter 11).[22]

Drug Trafficking/Violence: The Mexican Connection

During the 1980s and early 1990s, the United States began to exert immense pressure on drug-trafficking organizations operating in the Caribbean and south Florida. As a response, traffickers in Colombia formed alliances with Mexican trafficking groups for the purpose of transporting cocaine across the southwest border of the United States. With the disruption of the Medellin and Cali drug cartels in Colombia, Mexican cartels groups such as the Amado Carrillo-Fuentes Organization (ACFO) and the Arellano-Felix Organization (AFO) began to consolidate their power and dominated drug trafficking along the Mexico–U.S. border and in many American cities. By the late 1990s and early 2000s, after the loss of their leaders who were either imprisoned or killed during capture, the power and influence of these particular organizations declined significantly, only to be replaced by other trafficking groups that are seemingly intent on outdoing each other in brutality and callous disregard for human life.

Today, it is difficult to fully appreciate the scope of Mexico's involvement in illicit drug trafficking and the impact of Mexican drug trafficking on American illicit drug users (Figure 2.6). Drug-control authorities have confirmed that Mexico is responsible for the major portion of illicit drugs smuggled into the United States. In addition, prescription opioid medications such as OxyContin (see Chapter 9) as well as other prescription drugs are manufactured in clandestine Mexican laboratories. At the same time, Mexico continues to be a major transit location for illicit drugs destined to the United States from South America. According to the U.S. Department of Justice, Mexican drug cartels have gained drug-trafficking operations in more than 1,000 U.S. cities and towns, smuggling multiton quantities of illicit drugs and unauthorized prescription drugs across the U.S.–Mexico border.

The statistics of drug-related violence in Mexico are staggering. There have been more than 164,000 civilian casualties in Mexico from 2007 to 2014 that have been related to drug-trafficking activities. This number can be compared to approximately 21,000 civilian casualties in Afghanistan and approximately 81,000 civilian casualties in Iraq during the same period. Many homicides in Mexico have been reported simply as "disappearances."

The horrific effects on daily life in the countryside are difficult for most Americans to grasp. The brutality associated with the continual battles for control over illicit drug trafficking among Mexican drug cartels is an ever-present reality. Over the years, thousands of Mexicans have suddenly never been seen by their families again, most likely never to be found. One cabinet member in the Mexican government has described his nation as a society in which killing someone can be viewed as normal or natural. It is not surprising that in a 2013 survey, more than 72 percent of the Mexican population reported feeling insecure in their own country, and more than half reported that insecurity was the main concern in their lives.[23]

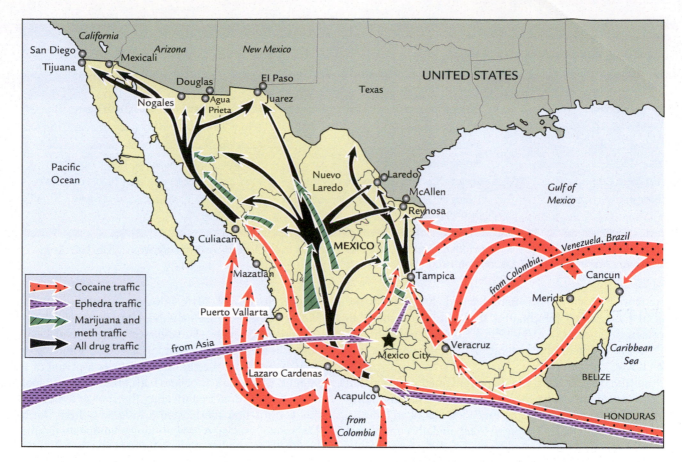

FIGURE 2.6

Drug-trafficking routes in Mexico. Ephedra refers to a plant-based stimulant, once marketed as a dietary supplement but since banned in the United States in 2004.

Source: Google Image. http://www.geo-mexico.com/wp-content/uploads/2011/01/Drug_routes_2010_800.jpg

The Continuing Drug Cartel War in Mexico

Over more than 20 years, criminal prosecutions of drug cartel leaders have been cited as indicators of major victories by law enforcement agencies in the long-standing war against drug trafficking in Mexico, but it is difficult to be optimistic that significant improvements will be made in that regard in the near future. All too often, power struggles among drug cartels and within each of them are ignited when a cartel leader is removed. The result is an increased level of violence rather than a period of calm as rival cartels sense a vacuum in the structure of the illicit drug trade and an opportunity to become the new dominant power. Individuals within each cartel will begin to outdo each other in brutality as they fight for the vacant top spot in the organization or dominance among rival cartels. The current roster of Mexican drug cartels, listed in Table 2.4, will be constantly changing, as will the dominance relationships among them. The shifting dominance relationships can be seen clearly through the history of the Sinaloa Cartel and its leader as given in the following section.

The Rise and Downfall of El Chapo

Few drug cartel leaders in recent years have been followed as extensively by the media as the notorious leader of the Sinaloa Cartel, Joaquin Guzmán, best known by his nickname, El Chapo. As it has been widely reported, the final capture of El Chapo and his extradition to the United States for prosecution in 2016 ended a yearlong manhunt and a frustrating series of twists and turns that created deep concerns among American drug-control authorities over the competence of Mexican authorities in handling drug trafficking in their country.

In 1989, the war over dominance in Mexican drug trafficking between the (now defunct) Arellano-Felix Cartel and the then-emerging Sinaloa Cartel had escalated into bloody confrontations as gunmen of each cartel battled to kill the leader of the other. In 1993, Cardinal and Archbishop of Guadalajara Juan Ocampo died in the cross-fire of one of these battles, leading to a massive public outcry and a nationwide manhunt for the perpetrators of the killing. Under a false passport, El Chapo fled to Guatemala where he had paid a Guatemalan military official $1.2 million as a bribe

TABLE 2.4

Major drug cartels in Mexico in 2017.

NAME	PRINCIPAL BASE OF OPERATIONS IN MEXICO	DRUG-TRAFFICKING PRODUCTS
Sinaloa Cartel	State of Sinaloa	Heroin, cocaine, marijuana, and meth
Jalisco New Generation Cartel	State of Jalisco	Primarily meth, also heroin, cocaine, and marijuana
Juarez Cartel	State of Chihuahua	Marijuana, cocaine, recently heroin and meth
Gulf Cartel	State of Tamaulipas	Marijuana, cocaine, less so heroin and meth
Los Zetas Cartel	Eastern, Central, and Southern Mexico	Marijuana, cocaine, recently heroin and meth
Beltran-Leyva Cartel	States of Guerrero, Morelos, Nayarit, and Sinaloa	Heroin, cocaine, marijuana, and meth

Source: Drug Enforcement Administration (2017, October). 2017 National Drug Threat Assessment Summary. Washington, D.C.: Drug Enforcement Administration, U.S. Department of Justice.

to remain in hiding. His attempt failed, however, as the official soon passed information about his whereabouts to Mexican authorities, and in 1995 El Chapo was returned to Mexico, arrested, and sentenced to imprisonment in a federal Mexican prison.

For the next six years, El Chapo remained in prison, but his existence there was hardly a harsh one. During his imprisonment, El Chapo's lifestyle far exceeded that of an ordinary incarcerated inmate. He managed to retain daily control over expanding Sinaloa Cartel operations. Associates brought him suitcases of cash to bribe prison officials. Prison guards themselves became his personal servants; regular visits from his mistress were overlooked by prison authorities. Not surprisingly, the extent of collusion between El Chapo and prison staff, not to mention $2.5 million of his personal funds, would set the stage for a relatively easy prison escape in 2001.

From 2001 to 2014, under the ruthless leadership of El Chapo, the Sinaloa Cartel battled and eventually won over rival cartels for dominance in drug trafficking in Mexico. Meanwhile, the elusiveness of El Chapo from authorities, even in the face of national manhunts for his capture, soon made him a near-legendary figure in Mexican folklore. Stories abounded, for example, of his habit of strolling into local restaurants, his bodyguards confiscating the patrons' cellphones, eating a meal, and then leaving after paying for everyone's tab, all without detection by authorities. According to law enforcement intelligence reports, Sinaloa gunmen carried surface-to-air missiles to bring down government aircraft on the occasions in which it was necessary to protect El Chapo from being captured. During this period, El Chapo himself was ranked as the 10th richest man in Mexico with a net worth amounting to an excess of $1 billion.

In 2014, Mexican authorities finally succeeded in recapturing El Chapo, and now he was sentenced to a maximum-security prison, supposedly the most secure facility in all of Mexico. In July of 2015, however, it was evident that the facility was far from secure enough to prevent El Chapo from escaping once more. Surveillance cameras had been positioned in his prison cell, but coverage had somehow missed a small section in the shower area. Over a period of several months, El Chapo's associates had constructed a 30-foot-deep underground tunnel connecting the shower area to an outside construction site located a mile away from the prison. The tunnel was large enough to accommodate lighting and air ducts for ventilation. A motorcycle was found in the tunnel and officials presume that this may have been the means for El Chapo's escape. In the several months while this elaborate tunnel or its connection to the prison was being built, no reports of unusual construction noise had been made by prison officials.

At this point, El Chapo was at large once again, but not for long. In October 2015, he was captured while hiding in the Sierra Madre mountains, and now extradited to the United States under bilateral international drug-trafficking agreements. In January of 2017, El Chapo pleaded not guilty to a 17-count indictment in U.S. District Court in New York for money laundering and drug trafficking, as well as numerous kidnappings and murders that he had allegedly directed in Chicago, Miami, New York, and other U.S. cities while in Mexico. In November 2018, the trial of El Chapo finally began. His charges included trafficking $14 billion in illicit drugs and running a criminal enterprise that the government has called "the world's largest and most prolific drug trafficking operation."[24]

Drugs and Narcoterrorism

The term **narcoterrorism** has been used in a number of ways when referring to the intermingling of political activity with illicit drug trafficking. In the case of Afghanistan, narcoterrorism has been applied to the violence waged by Afghan insurgent groups such as the Taliban, using profits from heroin trafficking as a means for funding their political activities. In the case of Colombia, narcoterrorism has referred to the

narcoterrorism: A term referring to anti-government political groups in which their operations have combined political insurgency and illicit drug trafficking.

Quick Concept Check 2.2

Understanding International Drug Trafficking

Check your understanding of global drug trafficking by matching the organization name or term (on the left) with the appropriate identification (on the right). *Note:* Some of the answers may not at all be used.

1. The French Connection
2. The Golden Crescent
3. Black Tar
4. Medellin Cartel
5. Sinaloa Cartel
6. Hell's Angels
7. FARC
8. China White
9. Drug mules
10. The Golden Triangle

a. A present-day drug cartel in Mexico
b. Human couriers carrying drugs either in their bodies or on their person
c. A major anti-government organization in Colombia
d. A name for Mexican heroin
e. Southeast Asian nations, including Laos and Vietnam
f. Southwest Asian nations, including Afghanistan
g. The chemical name for PCP
h. A major drug cartel in Colombia, led by Pablo Escobar
i. A name for Asian heroin in the 1960s and 1970s
j. An early trafficking organization of methamphetamine
k. Animals used to transport illicit drugs across the Rio Grande River from Mexico to the United States
l. A trafficking route of heroin in Europe, discontinued in the late 1960s and 1970s.

Answers: 1.l 2.f 3.d 4.h 5.a 6.j 7.c 8.i
9. b 10. e

---

violence stemming from a long-standing political struggle between the Colombian government and powerful cocaine-traficking organizations within Colombia. As we will see, there exists an extensive network of "transnational" narcoterrorism as well, operating throughout the world with no regard to international borders.

Narcoterrorism in Afghanistan and Colombia

In Afghanistan, the blurriness between drug trafficking and political insurgency has been particularly significant, given the recent history of American military engagement in that country. Profits from Afghan heroin, for example, allegedly helped to finance Taliban terrorist activities within Afghanistan during the 1990s, although that Al Qaeda forces benefited directly from the heroin trade has been largely refuted. The U.S. 9/11 Commission Report on the September 11, 2001, attacks concluded in 2004 that the drug trade was a source of income for the Taliban, but it did not serve the same purpose for Al Qaeda. Specifically, there is no reliable evidence that Osama bin Laden was personally involved in drug trafficking or that he made his money through drug trafficking.[25]

Interestingly, in 2001, the Taliban announced a comprehensive ban on the cultivation of the opium poppy, purportedly for religious reasons. As a result, opium production plummeted from 3,676 metric tons the previous year to 74 metric tons by the end of 2001. U.S. officials believe that the ban was most likely an attempt by the Taliban to raise the price of opium, which had declined significantly following a particularly abundant crop season in 2000. After the fall of the Taliban in 2002, Afghan growers resumed opium cultivation, and production increased to 2,865 metric tons in 2003. Although the Afghanistan government has officially banned the cultivation of opium poppies, decades of war and political unrest have left the criminal justice system in disarray, and it has been difficult for the ban to be enforced. From the standpoint of U.S. strategic interests in Afghanistan, there has been a troublesome conflict between efforts to reduce the cultivation of opium in the rugged, mountainous areas of Afghanistan, on the one hand, and efforts to encourage regional Afghan warlords in these regions to divest themselves from a profitable opium-trade involvement in order to support the central government and oppose the Taliban, on the other.[26]

With respect to Colombia, U.S. foreign policy was originally focused strictly on supporting anti-drug programs in that country. During the Clinton presidency in the 1990s, economic aid to Colombia rose to a previously unprecedented level of $88 million, but this money was tightly restricted to police and counterdrug efforts and not intended to support Colombia's war against insurgent groups. The focus was to reduce the influence of major drug cartels that were dominant in Colombia at the time. In 2002, George W. Bush changed the U.S. strategy by granting the Colombian government the funding to combat terrorism as well as drug trafficking, two struggles that in the view of the Bush administration had become one. Under the Bush administration, Colombia was awarded $650 million, an eightfold increase, in U.S. aid, to begin a unified campaign against drug trafficking and the activities of groups designated as terrorist organizations.[27]

For more than a half-century, rebel insurgency in the form of leftist guerrilla organizations opposed to the established Colombian government has dominated the political landscape. It is estimated that from 1948 to 1958, more than 300,000 people were killed during a civil war within Colombia, a horrific period that has since been referred to as *La Violencia* (the Violence).[28] Combined with a history of unstable central governments and a long-standing culture of violence, illicit drug trafficking in Colombia was bound to exacerbate an already volatile political situation. It was evitable that political insurgency would become intertwined with illicit drugs.

From its founding in 1960, the public agenda of the Revolutionary Armed Forces of Colombia (known as FARC by its initials in Spanish) was to represent the people of rural Colombia against repression under the central government, exploitation of natural resources by multinational corporations, and political influence by other nations, specifically the United States. In reality, it became the agent of widespread kidnappings, murders, and social intimidation. In recent years, several world governments, including the United States, European Union, and Canada, joined in officially classifying FARC as a terrorist organization.[29]

At its peak, FARC claimed approximately 18,000 members, though a substantial number of them were identified as minors forced to join and fight along with the adults. The organization became concentrated primarily in the southeast region of Colombia, in an area of more than 42,000 square kilometers (16,200 square miles), the approximate size of Kentucky.

In the late 1990s, several cocaine producers elsewhere in Colombia shifted their crops to FARC-controlled territory, and experimentation with coca plants resulted in a stronger coca leaf with a higher cocaine yield. FARC essentially created a coca-based economy within its sphere of influence. Due to a scarcity of paper currency in the area, farm workers were paid in coca paste (see Chapter 10). They sold their excess "wages" to cocaine traffickers, who in turn refined the coca paste into cocaine for shipping to the United States. Meanwhile, FARC collected taxes on the trade, charged the traffickers for protection from authorities, and collected a fee for the use of remote runways for planes to take the cocaine away. There was even an "export tax" on all cocaine shipped from FARC-controlled territory. At one time, FARC was considered to be the richest insurgent organization in history.[30]

Yet, despite the riches that FARC accumulated from cocaine trafficking, its political power began to wane. Major FARC leaders were arrested on charges of cocaine importation conspiracy and extradited to the United States. A ceasefire and talks of a negotiated peace settlement between FARC and the Colombian government began in 2011, but it was unclear whether a political agreement would ever be achieved. As a testament to the fact that terrorist activity was not at an end, 19 Colombian soldiers were killed in 2013 in a FARC ambush near the Venezuelan border. Nonetheless, a disarmament agreement between FARC and the Colombian government was finally achieved in 2016. The terms included relinquishing 8,000 guns and 1.2 million pieces of ammunition to the United Nations in return for amnesty for rank-and-file guerrilla fighters. Guerrilla commanders who were accused of war crimes, however, would be subject to prosecution in a military tribunal.

To conclude, Colombians have paid a very heavy price for decades of political conflict and illicit drug trafficking in their country. An independent commission reported in 2013 that, since 1958 (the year that *La Violencia* supposedly ended), there have been more than 250,000 conflict-related deaths, more than 27,000 forced disappearances, and between 5 and 8 million people forced from their homes. On the one hand, Colombia looks to a more stable political future. In 2018, Rodrigo London, former FARC rebel commander, announced his candidacy for president, under the newly formed political party Common Alternative Revolutionary Force (conveniently retaining the Spanish acronym, FARC). It remains unclear whether the Colombian people will be forgiven with their votes. On the other hand, the dismantlement of FARC as a military force will lead to a disengagement from control over coca-producing provinces where they have been dominant for decades. If this occurs, it is possible that there will be a new round of violence in these regions as local organizations wrestle among themselves to fill in the void.[31]

Transnational Narcoterrorism

A significant development in narcoterrorism has been the emergence and continuing influence of individuals and groups, operating across international borders, without specific allegiances to individual nations. They are financed by powerful private donors (called shadow facilitators), and their criminal operations include arms trafficking, money laundering (see Chapter 4), kidnap-for-ransom, extortion, and racketeering, as well as drug trafficking. According to the Counter-Narcoterrorism Operations Center of the DEA, an Algeria-based Muslim jihadist group called Al Qaeda in the Lands of the Islamic Maghreb (AQIM), designated by the U.S. Department of State as a foreign terrorist organization, has been active for several years in West African nations such as Kenya, Tanzania, Ghana, Guinea-Bissau, and Nigeria, with a primary focus on trafficking Colombian cocaine through West Africa to destinations in Europe. Some of the AQIM profits have financed the Hezbollah in the Middle East, who in turn has received support from the government of Iran. The DEA has identified Hezbollah as having a significant role in cocaine trafficking and drug-related money laundering between South America, West Africa, Europe, and the Middle East.

Besides concerns about illicit drug trafficking, there is the extremely worrisome prospect of terrorist organizations acquiring access to highly toxic substances, such as chemical weapons, for use as weapons of mass destruction (Drugs … in Focus).[32]

Drugs . . . in Focus

Sarin and Chemical Warfare: Neurotoxicity on the Battlefield

The compound sarin is considered one of the most toxic and rapidly acting of known chemical warfare agents. It can be easily and quickly evaporated from a liquid to a gaseous state and released into the environment. People can be exposed to sarin by breathing sarin gas, consuming food or water that has been contaminated with sarin, or touching surfaces containing sarin residue. It is essentially a toxic psychoactive drug in a form that can be readily used as a weapon of mass destruction. Victims exposed to sarin have difficulty in breathing, lose control of bodily functions, and at a later stage develop violent twitching and jerking of the body. Ultimately, exposure to sarin can lead to death by asphyxiation as victims become comatose and suffocate in a series of convulsive spasms.

Sarin is classified as a nerve agent, since it affects a critical function of the central nervous system, specifically the control of muscle contraction and relaxation. Normally, brief muscle contractions are controlled by the release of the neurotransmitter, acetylcholine, which causes a stimulation of muscle fibers. Shortly afterward, the enzyme acetylcholinesterase causes a breakdown of the acetylcholine molecule, resulting in a period of relaxation. Relaxation of muscle fibers is critical because the muscle must "rest" before contracting again. Sarin works by inhibiting the action of acetylcholinesterase. As a result, acetylcholine is continually released, and without an "off-switch," muscle fibers are constantly stimulated. The twitching and jerking of the body are consequences of the continual contraction of muscles. Eventually, diaphragm muscles cannot function to allow air into the lungs, and the victim no longer can breathe.

An international agreement, the United Nations Chemical Weapons Convention, was established in 1997. The treaty stipulates that the development, production, stockpiling, and use of all forms of chemical weapons, including sarin and a variation called VX, are prohibited. Sarin gas has been used during the Iran–Iraq War in the late 1980s and in a terrorist attack on a subway station in Tokyo in 1995. In April of 2017, the poison was used in a deadly chemical bomb attack in the town of Khan Sheikhoun in a rebel-held part of northern Syria, according to the Turkish Health Ministry who observed the aftermath of the attack and conducted autopsies on three of its victims. The Syrian Observatory for Human Rights, a UK-based monitoring group, put the death toll from the attack at 86, including 33 children and 18 women. In addition, hundreds were sickened in what has been considered one of the worst atrocities so far in the six-year-old Syrian war. The Syrian government has denied responsibility for the attacks.

Sources: Centers for Disease Control and Prevention (2013, May). *Facts about Sarin.* Atlanta, GA: Centers for Disease Control and Prevention. Gussow, L. (2005). Nerve agents: Three mechanisms, three antidotes. *Emergency Medicine News, 27,* 12. Kingsley, P.; and Barnard, A. (2017, April 6). Banned nerve agent sarin used in Syria chemical attack, Turkey says. *The New York Times online.* https://www.nyti.ms/2oEKfDs.

Summary

The Global Illicit Drug Trade

- The global illicit drug trade encompasses the cultivation, manufacture, distribution, and sale of illicit drugs in practically all regions of the world.

- Estimates of the total worth of the global illicit drug trade range from $28 billion to $280 billion or upwards of $400 billion. Of that total, a minimum of $64 billion is estimated to be generated through U.S. drug sales alone.

The Global Problem of Drug Toxicity

- An estimated quarter of a billion people, approximately 5 percent of the global population aged 15–64, used drugs at least once in 2015. An estimated 28 million years of "healthy life" were lost worldwide due to drug use. Approximately 190,100 drug-related deaths were reported worldwide.

- Relative to the rest of the world, prevalence rates in the United States were somewhat higher for heroin, seven times higher for cocaine, and four times higher for methamphetamine and marijuana.

- Worldwide, there were approximately 183 million marijuana users, compared to 18 million heroin users, 37 million methamphetamine users, and 17 million cocaine users in 2015.

Trafficking of Heroin and other Opioids

- Heroin trafficking, originating in the Golden Crescent region and destinations in Western, Central and Southeastern Europe, and the Russian Federation, follows a variety of routes, including a circuitous "Southern route" that extends through and around Africa. The Golden Triangle distributes heroin through more localized routes into Central Asia and Australia. Heroin from sources in Mexico and Colombia enters Mexico, then is transported into the United States.

- Fentanyl and fentanyl precursors are created in clandestine laboratories in China, then shipped directly to the United States via the U.S. Postal Services and other mail services or shipped to Canada and Mexico for later transport.

Trafficking of Cocaine

- Most of the world's coca cultivation and cocaine production takes place in the Andean countries of South America. Currently, the primary cocaine producing nation is Colombia.
- The Medellin and Cali cartels in the 1970s, 1980s, and 1990s were the dominant cocaine-trafficking organizations, infiltrating political life at all levels throughout Colombia and were responsible for the murder of hundreds of government officials and innocent bystanders during the height of their power.
- Present-day trafficking of Colombian cocaine is routed through Mexico, crossing the border into the United States in hidden compartments inside passenger vehicles or combined with legitimate cargo in commercial trucks.

Trafficking of Marijuana, Methamphetamine, LSD, PCP, and Ketamine

- Mexico is currently the major foreign source for marijuana smuggled into the United States. Most of the marijuana trafficking, whether grown in Mexico or transported through Mexico from other locations such as Colombia, takes place at the U.S.–Mexico border.
- Methamphetamine had been manufactured by domestic clandestine laboratories from ingredients that can be acquired through retail outlets. Federal restrictions on the availability of these ingredients have shifted production to facilities in Mexico where it is later smuggled into the United States.
- LSD, Phencyclidine (PCP), and ketamine are produced in clandestine laboratories either in the United States or in Mexico with later transport across the U.S.–Mexico border.

Drug Trafficking and Social Violence in Mexico

- Mexico is responsible for the major portion of illicit drugs smuggled into the United States. In addition, prescription opioid medications such as OxyContin as well as other prescription drugs are manufactured in clandestine Mexican laboratories. Mexico continues to be a major transit location for illicit drugs destined to the United States from South America.
- Mexican drug cartels have gained drug-trafficking operations in more than 1,000 U.S. cities and towns, smuggling multiton quantities of illicit drugs and unauthorized prescription drugs across the U.S.–Mexico border.
- There have been more than 164,000 civilian casualties in Mexico from 2007 to 2014 that have been related to drug-trafficking activities.
- Mexican drug cartel organizations have dominated illicit drug production and trafficking in the country for decades. Arrests and prosecutions of major drug cartel leaders, most prominently the leader of the Sinaloa Cartel Joaquin Guzmán ("El Chapo") in 2015, have been a major effort of international drug-control agencies. However, drug-trafficking operations in Mexico continue largely unabated.

Narcoterrorism

- Narcoterrorism refers to the practice of combining illicit drug trafficking in the financing of anti-government insurgency groups around the world. Examples of groups of this type are the Taliban in Afghanistan and the Revolutionary Armed Forces of Colombia (known as FARC, by its initials in Spanish) in Colombia. In Afghanistan, international drug-control activities have been intertwined with ongoing counterinsurgency efforts.
- Transnational narcoterrorism refers to illicit drug-trafficking revenue being used by insurgency groups to finance transnational terrorist activities, such as arms trafficking, money laundering, kidnap-for-ransom and extortion, and racketeering.

Key Terms

BC Bud, p. xx
Black Tar, p. 27
cartel, p. 30

China White, p. 26
disability-adjusted life years
   (DALYs) statistic, p. 23

global illicit drug trade, p. 22
Golden Crescent, p. 26
Golden Triangle, p. 26

Medellin and Cali drug cartels,
   p. 30
narcoterrorism, p. 36

Review Questions

1. How do American adults compare to adults around the world with respect to the annual prevalence rates for illicit drugs in general, heroin, cocaine, methamphetamine, and marijuana? How do American adolescents compare to their European counterparts?
2. Describe the patterns of heroin trafficking for most of the world and for the United States specifically. Describe the present-day Mexican involvement in the trafficking of a range of illicit drugs.
3. Why would drug-trafficking cartels be particularly dominant in the northern regions of Mexico?
4. Discuss the use of the term narcoterrorism as it has been applied to drug-control initiatives in Afghanistan and Colombia. How are these nations different from each other in terms of narcoterrorism?

Critical Thinking: What Would You Do?

You are a federal DEA official who has recently been informed that a major drug lord in Honduras, presently the leader of the dominant cocaine-trafficking organization in that country, has agreed to provide significant information concerning drug-related corruption activities of top Honduran political figures as well prominent banking families in the country, in exchange for leniency in the prosecution by authorities of crimes committed while in power, his placement in the witness protection program, and passage of relatives to the United States who would be subject to reprisals. His cooperation would be a crucial step in reducing what has been called "state-supported drug trafficking" in Honduras. Presently, Honduras is the gateway for massive amounts of cocaine headed for the United States through Mexico, and it has been impossible to make inroads in stemming the tide of Colombian cocaine into U.S. cities. However, this individual has admitted to having "caused" 78 deaths in Honduras during a 10-year period, including the murders of a lawyer, two journalists, an antidrug government official, and several innocent bystanders.

Do you recommend that the U.S. government enter into this agreement?

Endnotes

1. Adapted from Santos, F. (2017, January 8). Outwitting the mules. An excerpt from the article, An opioid tide from coast to coast. *The New York Times*, pp. 10–11. Paraphrased quotation on p. 11.

2. Drug Enforcement Administration (2017). *The Drug Threat Assessment 2016 Summary*. Washington, D.C.: Drug Enforcement Administration, U.S. Department of Justice. Thoumi, F. E. (2005, Winter). The Numbers Game: Let's all guess the size of the illegal drug industry! *Journal of Drug Issues*, 35, 185–200. United Nations Office on Drugs and Crime (2013). *Drug trafficking: Introduction*. Vienna: United Nations Office on Drugs and Crime. Zagaris, B.; and Elders, S. (2001, May). Drugs trafficking and money laundering. *Foreign Policy in Focus*, p. 1.

3. United Nations Office on Drugs and Crime (2017). *World Drug Report 2017*. Vienna: United Nations Office on Drugs and Crime.

4. European Monitoring Centre for Drugs and Drug Addiction (2017). *The ESPAD Report 2015*. Lisbon: European Monitoring Centre for Drugs and Drug Addiction.

5. United Nations Office on Drugs and Crime (2017). *World Drug Report 2017*. Vienna: United Nations Office on Drugs and Crime. Key findings.

6. United Nations Office on Drugs and Crime (2017). *World Drug Report 2017*. Vienna: United Nations Office on Drugs and Crime. Key findings and statistical tables.

7. United Nations Office on Drugs and Crime (2017). *World Drug Report 2017*. Vienna: United Nations Office on Drugs and Crime. Statistical tables. United Nations Office on Drugs and Crime (2017). *Fact sheet on statistics and trends in illicit drugs*. Vienna: United Nations Office on Drugs and Crime.

8. The European Monitoring Centre for Drugs and Drug Addiction (2017). *The 2015 ESPAD report: Substance use among students in 36 European countries*. Stockholm: The European Monitoring Centre for Drugs and Drug Addiction, Tables 5, 6, 7a, and 7b.

9. United Nations Office on Drugs and Crime (2017). *World Drug Report 2017*. Vienna: United Nations Office on Drugs and Crime. Booklet 4.

10. McCoy, A. W. (2003). *The politics of heroin: CIA complicity in the global drug trade*. Revised edition. Chicago, IL: Chicago Review Press, pp. 46–77.

11. Drug Enforcement Administration (2017). *2016 National Drug Threat Assessment Summary*. Washington, D.C.: Drug Enforcement Administration, U.S. Department of Justice.

12. Chao, S.; and Victor, P. J. (2015, May 7). "They'll never stop us": The drug runners fueling Afghanistan's epidemic. *Al Jazeera.com*. Fuller, T. (2015, January 3). Myanmar returns to what sells: heroin. *The New York Times*, pp. A6, A9. Meek, J. G. (2016, December 15). DEA: Heroin haul largest ever in Afghanistan, "if not the world." *ABC.com*. Retrieved from https://abcnews.go.com/International/dea-heroin-haul-largest-afghanistan-world/story?id=44216333

13. United Nations Office on Drugs and Crime (2013). *World Drug Report 2013*. Vienna: United Nations Office on Drugs and Crime.

14. Drug Enforcement Administration (2017). *2016 National Drug Threat Assessment Summary*. Washington, D.C.: Drug Enforcement Administration, U.S. Department of Justice.

15. Ibid.

16. United Nations Office on Drugs and Crime (2017). *World Drug Report 2017*. Vienna: United Nations Office on Drugs and Crime. Booklet 2.

17. Drug Enforcement Administration. Press Release (2016, September 22). DEA issues carfentanil warning to police and public. Washington, D.C.: Drug Enforcement Administration, U.S. Department of Justice. Schumer: Stop drug at JFK (2018, January 8). *Newsday*, p. A26.

18. Drug Enforcement Administration (2017). *2016 National Drug Threat Assessment Summary*. Washington, D.C.: Drug Enforcement Administration, U.S. Department of Justice. Goldstein, J.; and Weiser, B. (2017, October 7). A murderous drug lord partners with the U.S. *The New York Times*, pp. A1, A6–A7.

19. Drug Enforcement Administration (2017). *2016 National Drug Threat Assessment Summary*. Washington, D.C.: Drug Enforcement Administration, U.S. Department of Justice.

20. Ibid.

21. Drug Enforcement Administration (2017). *Drugs of Abuse: A DEA Resource Guide, 2017 edition*. Washington, D.C.: Drug Enforcement Administration, U.S. Department of Justice.

22. Ibid.

23. Archibold, R. (2013, June 23). Mexico pursuing vanished victims of its drug wars. *The New York Times*, p. A6. Associated Press (July 24, 2013). Mexico's drug war boils over again in Michoacan as gang gunmen stage attacks on federal police. Results of the National Survey on Victimization and Perception of Public Safety 2013, National Institute of Statistics and Geography, Aquacalientes, Mexico. Public Broadcasting System (2015, July 27). Frontline Newsletter: "Mexico's Drug War." Washington, D.C.: Public Broadcasting System.

24. Ahmed, A.; and Archibold, R. C. (2015, July 13). Drug kingpin escapes prison through tunnel. *The New York Times*, pp. A1, A3. Feuer, A. (2018, January 13). Prosecutors with stack of evidence on El Chapo. *The New York Times*, p. A17. Feuer, A. (2018, October 10). Who might testify against El Chapo? Among others, some ex-confederates. *The New York Times*, p. A17. Keefe, P. R. (2014, May 5). The hunt for El Chapo. *New Yorker Magazine*, pp. 38–49. Machias, A.; and Tasch, B. (2015, July 30). This astounding mistake led to "El Chapo" Gusmán's prison escape. *Business Insider Online*.Riley, J. (2018, November 13). Trial begins for "El Chapo." *Newsday*, pp. A2–A3.

25. National Commission on Terrorist Attacks upon the United States (2004). *The 9/11 Commission Report*. New York: W. W. Norton, Chapter 5, Section 4.

26. Filkins, D. (2010, June 22). U.S. money-financing Afghan warlords for convoy protection, report says. *The New York Times*, p. A4. Risen, J. (2010, September 12). Propping up a drug lord, then arresting him. *The New York Times*, pp. A1, A18. Shah, T.; and Rubin, A. J. (2012, April 12). In poppy war, Taliban aim to protect a cash crop. *The New York Times*, pp. A4, A7.

27. Isaacson, A. (2003). Washington's new war in Colombia: The war on drugs meets the war on terror. *NACLA Report on the Americas, 36*, 5–11.

28. Palacios, M. (2007). *Between legitimacy and violence: A history of Colombia, 1875–2002*. Durham, NC: Duke University Press. Richani, N. (2002). *Systems of violence: The political economy of war and peace in Colombia*. Albany, NY: State University of New York Press, pp. 23–28.

29. Livingstone, G. (2004). *Inside Colombia: Drugs, democracy, and war*. New Brunswick, NJ: Rutgers University Press, p. 180. Shanty, F. G.; and Moshra, P. P. (2007). *Organized crime: From trafficking to terrorism*. Santa Barbara, CA: ABC-CLIO, p. 323.

30. Guillermoprieto, A. (2002, May). Waiting for war. *New Yorker*, pp. 48–55.

31. Associated Press (2018, January 28). Ex-Guerilla launches historic presidential bid in Colombia. *The New York Times*. https://www.nytimes.com/aponline/2018/01/28/world/americas/ap-lt-colombia-farc-elections.html. Brodzinsky, S. (2013, July 29). FARC peace talks stoke hope—and unrest in Colombia. *Christian Science Monitor, Weekly Digital Edition* (accessed August 29, 2013). Colombia-FARC peace talks eye political participation in hope of integrating rebel army into government. *Huffington Post*. Accessed from: http://www.huffingtonpost.com/2013/08/10/colombia-farc-political-participation_n_3737572.html.

32. Counter-Narcoterrorism Operations Center (2013, November). *Combating transnational organized crime*. Washington, D.C.: Drug Enforcement Administration, U.S. Department of Justice.

chapter **3**

Drug-Control Policy in America

Miguel proudly calls himself a fourth-generation Mexican American. Today, he works for a major accounting firm in Los Angeles, and he and his family live in the suburbs. I asked Miguel if he would tell me some of the family stories about marijuana and the old days.

"It's funny," he said, "Marijuana has really gone mainstream. It's all around you. Even my boss smokes marijuana!"

"But it wasn't funny back in my great-grandfather's day. Damn, the prejudice was out there. White people didn't like us, even though we were picking their fruits and vegetables twelve, fourteen hours a day. Sure we had marijuana then; our families brought it with us when we came across from Mexico. It was how we relaxed, probably the only way we could."

Miguel grew more serious. "But whites didn't see it that way. The stories you would hear about us ... they would say that marijuana made us violent and angry. They would spread outlandish stories that marijuana made us fearless and super-strong, that we were ready to attack a police officer, even if a gun was drawn on us. They would claim that it took two or three policemen just to hold us down. Can you believe that?"[1]

The use of psychoactive drugs has been a part of human life in almost every culture and in every age of recorded history. Drugs have been used in the context of religious rituals, health care, celebration, and recreation. An understanding of the history of drug regulation forms the basis for an understanding of present-day drug policy and the problems associated with it.

Over the course of our nation's history, attitudes toward certain drugs and certain forms of drug-taking behavior have fluctuated between enthusiastic acceptance and passionate rejection. Heroin, marijuana, cocaine, and numerous other drugs all have had periods of approval and periods of disapproval. In the late 1800s, for example, cocaine was widely accepted as a stimulant drug (see Chapter 10). This was followed by a rejection in the early 1900s and a brief reemergence of approval in the early 1980s, followed by another period of rejection beginning in the mid-1980s and extending to the present day.[2]

American drug-control policy also has had its own historical swings, with policies themselves not always being founded on rational decision-making and empirical data. Decisions to outlaw some drugs while legalizing others have been all-too-often based on fear, hysteria, politics, ethnic prejudice, and racism.[3] As we will see, public disapproval of a particular drug has been instigated by attitudes toward a specific minority group associated with the drug, rather than genuine concerns about the effects of the drug itself. The negative associations of opium with Chinese immigrants working on the American railroads in the nineteenth century, cocaine with African Americans, alcohol (specifically beer) with Germans, and marijuana with Mexican immigrants in the twentieth century have been unfortunately a part of the history of drugs in America.[4] It is important to examine the history of drug use and drug-control policy in the United States, as well as the ideology that drives such policy in order to arrive at the best strategies for dealing with the present-day problems of drug abuse.

Drug Regulation in the Nineteenth Century: Laisse-Faire

The use of drugs in America has been widespread for both medical and recreational purposes. Morphine was identified as the active ingredient in opium, a drug that had been in use for at least 3,000 years and had become the physician's most reliable prescription to control the pain of disease and injury by the end of the nineteenth century. Morphine quickly became a common treatment for pain during the Civil War, a time during which a surgeon's skill was often measured by how quickly he could saw off a wounded patient's limb. Unfortunately, in subsequent years, morphine dependence among Civil War veterans would be so widespread that it was called the "soldier's disease." Doctors also recommended morphine injections for women to treat the pain associated with "female troubles," and by the late 1890s, morphine dependence among women made up almost half of all cases of drug dependence in the United States (see Chapter 9).[5]

Cocaine, having been extracted from South American coca leaves, was also a drug in widespread use and taken quite casually in a variety of forms. The original formula for Coca-Cola (as the name suggests) contained coca until 1903, as did Dr. Agnew's Catarrh Powder, a popular remedy for chest colds. In the mid-1880s, Parke, Davis, and Company (merged with Pfizer, Inc. in 2002) was selling cocaine and its botanical source, coca, in more than a dozen forms, including coca-leaf cigarettes and cigars, cocaine inhalants, a coca cordial, and an injectable cocaine solution.[6] A Viennese physician named Sigmund Freud, who was later to gain a greater reputation for his psychoanalytical theories than for his ideas about psychoactive drugs, called cocaine a "magical drug." Freud would later reverse his position when a friend and colleague became dependent on cocaine (see Chapter 10).[7] In the latter part of the nineteenth century in the United States, cocaine was a popular ingredient in over-the-counter medications. These products were totally unregulated, and customers included children as well as adults.

During the nineteenth century, America's public attitude toward drug use was one of **laissez-faire**, roughly translated from the French as "allow [people] to do as they please," which means that there was little regulation or control of drugs. In fact, the United States was the only major Western nation that allowed the unlimited distribution, sale, and promotion of psychoactive drugs during this period. The result was a nation of medicinal and recreational drug users that has been described as a "dope fiend's paradise."[8]

> **laissez-faire (LAY-say FAIR) (Fr.):** The philosophy of exerting as little governmental control and regulation as possible.

Numbers Talk. . .

.38	Caliber bullets in revolvers adopted by many southern police departments in the early 1900s, believing that cocaine would make African Americans unaffected by .32 caliber bullets.
11	Estimated percentage of American troops in Vietnam in 1971, who were regular users of heroin.
1 in 5	Number of inmates incarcerated in the United States for a drug offense.

Sources: Musto, D. F. (1989, Summer). America's first cocaine epidemic. *The Wilson Quarterly*, pp. 59–64. McCoy, A. W. (1972). *The politics of heroin in Southeast Asia.* New York: Harper & Row, pp. 220–221. Wagner, P.; and Sawyer, W. (2018, March). Mass Incarceration: The Whole Pie 2018. Prison Policy Initiative. Retrieved from https://www.prisonpolicy.org/reports/pie2018.html.

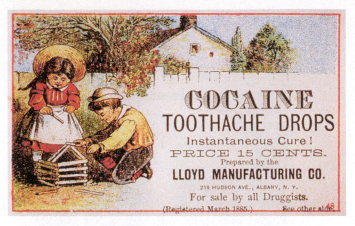

In the latter part of the nineteenth century in the United States, cocaine was a popular ingredient in over-the-counter medications for children as well as adults. These products were totally unregulated for safety or effectiveness.

Two major factors explain why there were no major drug-control policies during this period. First, unlike many European nations, the United States did not have any agencies regulating the medical field, and because doctors and pharmacists were unlicensed, it was not difficult to call oneself a doctor and distribute drugs. The American Medical Association (AMA) was established in 1847, but only a fraction of practicing health professionals were members during the 1800s. Doctors of this era had no choice but to rely upon untested and potentially toxic chemicals to treat both physical and psychological disorders. A second factor was the issue of states' rights. During the nineteenth century, the prevailing political philosophy, especially in southern states, was a belief in the strict separation of state and federal powers. Therefore, the regulation of drugs was left to the states, most of which had few, if any, drug laws. For the federal government to pass laws limiting the use of any drug would have been viewed as a serious challenge to the concept of states' rights.[9]

Drug Regulation in the Early Twentieth Century: The Beginning of Controls

By 1900, the promise of medical advances in the area of drugs was beginning to be matched by concerns about the health risks that some of these drugs could produce. Two important factors behind the movement toward drug regulation in the beginning of the twentieth century were (1) the continuing problems associated with patent medicines and (2) the association of drug use with certain minority groups.

Pure Food and Drug Act of 1906

Between the late 1800s and early 1900s, hundreds of **patent medicines** were sold that included such ingredients as alcohol, opium, morphine, cocaine, and marijuana. The term "patent medicine" for products of this kind can be misleading. Generally, one thinks of a patented product as being officially registered with the federal government, providing the producers with the exclusive right to sell that product. However, around the turn of the twentieth century, patent medicines were not registered with the federal government or any regulatory agency, and their formulas were usually kept secret. Manufacturers were not required to list the ingredients on the bottle label or the package in which they were sold. Patent medicines were advertised for mail-order purchase in newspapers and magazines or available through traveling medicine shows.

As the popularity of patent medicines grew, cases of accidental poisoning from ingredients in these medicines became widespread. In 1905, a series of scathing articles appeared in the widely read *Collier's Weekly* magazine that documented the dangers of unregulated patent medicines. These articles were followed the next year by Upton Sinclair's novel *The Jungle*, depicting in gruesome detail the unsanitary conditions of the meat packing industry in Chicago. Responding to public outcry for regulatory reform, President Theodore Roosevelt proposed a federal law that would regulate misbranded and adulterated foods, drinks, and drugs. The **Pure Food and Drug Act of 1906** became the first drug regulatory law in American history, establishing the requirement that all packaged foods and drugs list the ingredients on the label of the product.[10]

The new law did not prevent potentially harmful drugs from being sold, but it did require manufacturers to identify specific drugs that were contained in these patent medicines. Thus, cocaine, alcohol, heroin, and morphine could still be in patent preparations as long as they were listed as ingredients.[11] It was not until President Franklin D. Roosevelt signed into law the Federal Food, Drug, and Cosmetic Act of 1938 that drugs and cosmetic products not only were required to be accurately identified but manufacturers were required to demonstrate through research studies that their products were safe (when used as directed) prior to being marketed. The law also established the U.S. Food and Drug Administration (FDA) as the federal enforcement agency in charge of insuring the safety of commercial drugs. The Kefauver-Harris Amendment of 1962 extended the power of the FDA further by requiring evidence that commercial drugs were clinically effective as well as safe.

patent medicine: A drug or combination of drugs sold through peddlers, shops, or mail-order advertisements.

Pure Food and Drug Act of 1906: Federal legislation requiring all packaged foods and drugs to list the ingredients on the label of the product.

Quick Concept Check 3.1

Understanding the History of Drugs and Drug-Taking Behavior

Test your understanding of the early history (prior to 1914) of drugs and drug-taking behavior by matching the statement on the left with one of the associated drugs, names, or terms on the right.

1. Dependence on this drug among Civil War veterans was so common that it was called the "soldier's disease."
2. This drug was associated with Chinese immigrants working on American railroads during the 1800s.
3. This drug was used in Dr. Agnew's Catarrh Powder, a popular remedy for chest colds.
4. A drug or combination of drugs sold through peddlers, shops, or mail-order advertisements.
5. This major figure of the twentieth century gained an early reputation for promoting cocaine as a "magical drug."
6. The novel, *The Jungle*, by this American author, was influential in gaining public support for the Pure Food and Drug Act of 1906.

a. opium
b. cocaine
c. Upton Sinclair
d. patent medicines
e. morphine
f. Sigmund Freud
g. marijuana

Answers: 1. e. 2. a. 3. b. 4. d. 5. f. 6. c.

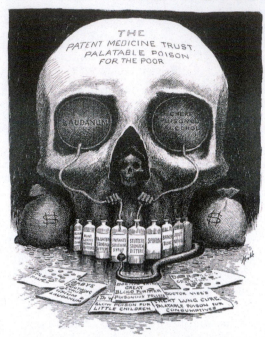

In a June 1905 issue of the widely read Collier's Weekly magazine, the cover (entitled "Death's Laboratory") dramatically depicted the dangers of patent medicines. A scathing exposé of the patent medicine industry, written by Samuel Hopkins Adams, appeared in the magazine four months later.

Harrison Act of 1914

Whereas the Pure Food and Drug Act of 1906 focused on drug safety, by the second decade of the twentieth century, calls for expanded drug regulation were unfortunately spurred in large part by a growing prejudice against minority groups in America believed to be involved in certain forms of drug use. As we will see, this social phenomenon impacted upon the eventual prohibition of opium and heroin, cocaine, and marijuana, as well as the temporary prohibition of alcohol.

The movement toward federal drug-control legislation, in general, was met with resistance from southern politicians, who believed that such actions were yet another intrusion of the federal government into state affairs. It has been suggested that, in order to overcome this resistance from southerners during this time, a propaganda campaign was launched that associated African Americans with cocaine. Southern newspapers began publishing "reports" of the cocaine-induced raping of white women and demonstrations of superhuman strength.[12] One of the more bizarre myths was that cocaine made African Americans unaffected against .32 caliber bullets, a claim that

is said to have caused many southern police departments to switch from .32 caliber to .38 caliber revolvers. The propaganda campaign was successful; southerners became more afraid of African Americans and cocaine than of an increase in federal power and eventually offered their support for federal drug regulation.[13]

Another example of how racism became interwoven with drug policy was the identification of Chinese workers with the smoking of opium. After the Civil War, the United States had imported thousands of Chinese workers to help build the rapidly expanding railroads. The Chinese brought with them the habit of smoking opium, which many Americans believed led to prostitution, gambling, and overall moral decline. When the major railroad systems were completed, Chinese workers began to settle into western cities such as San Francisco. Working for low wages, the Chinese, some Americans feared, were taking jobs from whites and provided "big bosses" of business with the opportunity to use cheap Chinese labor as a means of preventing the organizing of unions. Hostility and violence against the Chinese became commonplace. The first antidrug legislation in the United States was an ordinance enacted in 1875 by the City of San Francisco prohibiting the operation of opium dens (establishments where smoking of opium took place). Other states followed San Francisco's lead by prohibiting opium smoking, and in 1887, Congress prohibited the possession of smokable opium.[14]

The origins of the landmark **Harrison Act of 1914** can be traced back to an issue of foreign trade and international diplomacy. While many Americans detested the Chinese and their habit of smoking opium, at the same time, the U.S. government wanted to open up commercial trade with China. China refused to purchase American goods, however, as a protest against the poor treatment of Chinese people in the United States. To establish some degree of goodwill with China and to improve its foreign trade position, the United States initiated a number of international conferences to address the issue of control measures over the worldwide production and distribution of narcotics, especially opium. Recognizing the enormous population of opium abusers within their own country, Chinese leaders were eager to participate in such conferences.

At an international conference held in The Hague in 1912, the United States was accused of maintaining a double standard in the negotiations. According to the Chinese delegation, the U.S. government was attempting to establish international agreements to regulate the drug trade while at the same time having no domestic policy over drug production and distribution within its own borders. Having recognized China's criticism in this regard, Congress set out to establish its own regulatory drug-control policy. The Harrison Act, named after its sponsor, Representative Francis Burton Harrison of New York, was enacted in 1914. The full name of the legislation was the Harrison Narcotics Tax Act.[15]

The Harrison Act was designed to regulate drug abuse through government taxation and became the basis for narcotics regulation in the United States for more than a half century. The act required anyone importing, manufacturing, selling, or dispensing cocaine or opiate drugs to register with the Treasury Department, pay a special tax, and keep records of all transactions. Because the act was a revenue measure, enforcement was made the responsibility of the Department of the Treasury and the commissioner of the Internal Revenue Service.

Because it was specifically stated in the language of the Harrison Act, cocaine became included alongside opiates as target drugs for law-enforcement control, resulting in its being referred to as a narcotic as well. Although application of the term "narcotic" to cocaine was clearly incorrect ("narcotic" literally means "stupor-inducing," and cocaine is anything but that), the association unfortunately stuck for many years. Later, several restricted drugs, including marijuana

Harrison Act of 1914: Federal legislation regulating through government taxation the importing, manufacturing, selling, or dispensing of cocaine or opiate drugs. The law effectively changed the status of cocaine and opiates from licit to illicit substances in the United States.

and the hallucinogen peyote, also were officially classified as narcotics without regard to their pharmacological characteristics. Today, many people still think of any illegal drug as a narcotic, and for many years, the bureau at the Treasury Department charged with drug enforcement responsibilities was the Bureau of Narcotics, and its agents were known on the street as "narks."

Technically, the Harrison Act did not make opiates or cocaine illegal. Physicians, dentists, and veterinarians could prescribe these drugs "in the course of their professional practice only." What this phrase meant was left to a good deal of interpretation. The Treasury Department viewed the maintenance of patients on these drugs, particularly opiates, as beyond medical intentions, and the Supreme Court upheld this interpretation in 1919. As a result, thousands of physicians in the United States found themselves in violation of federal law.

Eventually, physicians stopped issuing prescriptions for drugs now covered under the Harrison Act. A new class of criminal was created as a consequence, driving individuals to seek drugs through the black market. In what would become a continuing and unfortunate theme in the history of drug enforcement legislation, the Harrison Act failed to reduce drug-taking behavior. Instead, it created a new lucrative market for organized crime that continues to the present day.

Marijuana and the Marijuana Tax Act of 1937

As with opium and cocaine, significant public concerns about marijuana did not surface until the drug became linked to a minority group—namely, migrant Mexican workers. During the 1920s, Mexican laborers immigrated to the United States to perform jobs that white workers refused to do, such as picking cotton, fruit, and vegetables on large farms in the Southwest. Some of the Mexican workers smoked marijuana as a drug of entertainment and relaxation. When the Depression struck the United States, many white workers would take just about any job they could get, and public opinion supported sending the Mexican workers home. Many white laborers in the Southwest began to band together and form organizations such as the "Key Men of America" and the "American Coalition," whose goal was to "Keep America American." Leaders of these organizations believed that marijuana and the problems with Mexican immigration were closely connected, and many southwestern police chiefs agreed. Newspaper stories began to circulate telling of how marijuana made users become sexually excited and violently insane (see Chapter 11).[16]

The first commissioner of the newly formed Federal Bureau of Narcotics (FBN), Harry J. Anslinger, saw the marijuana issue as a way to gain national attention and extend the power of FBN. Congressional committees heard testimony from Anslinger, relying on unsubstantiated tales of murder, insanity, and sexual promiscuity that were brought on by marijuana use. According to the FBN, marijuana was a "killer weed." Movies produced and released in the 1930s, such as *Reefer Madness* (now a cult classic) and *Marihuana: Weed with Roots in Hell*, supported Anslinger's propaganda campaign by depicting innocent young people committing terrible acts under the influence of marijuana. The result was the **Marijuana Tax Act of 1937**, which did not outlaw marijuana but required that a tax be collected on its manufacture and sale. Each time marijuana was sold, the seller had to pay a tax of as much as $100 per ounce for a transfer tax stamp. Failure to possess such a stamp was a federal offense, and not surprisingly, tax stamps were rarely issued. The 1937 law effectively made marijuana illegal, but the drug was not officially prohibited until the enactment of the Controlled Substances Act of 1970.

Alcohol Regulation in America: The Prohibition Era

In the late 1700s, prominent physicians, writers, and scientists began to consider the adverse effects of alcohol consumption and tried to formulate some kind of social reform to mitigate them. The goal at that time, however, was to reduce the consumption of distilled spirits (liquor) only. It was a *temperate* attitude toward drinking (hence the phrase **temperance movement**) rather than an insistence on the total prohibition of alcohol in all its forms.

In nineteenth-century America, political and religious groups, particularly in primarily nonurban U.S. states, saw excessive alcohol consumption in social and moral terms. In their view, drunkenness led to poverty, a disorderly society, and civil disobedience. In short, it was unpatriotic at best and subversive at worst. When we hear the phrase "demon rum," we have to recognize that many Americans during the nineteenth century took the phrase quite literally. Liquor was demonized as a direct source of evil in the world.

The temperance point of view toward liquor consumption spread like wildfire. In 1831, the American Temperance Society reported that nearly 2 million Americans had renounced strong liquor (having "taken the pledge") and that more than 800 local temperance societies had been established. With characteristic succinctness, Abraham Lincoln observed, in an 1842 address before a national temperance organization, that prior to the temperance era, the harm done by alcohol was considered to be a result of the "abuse of a very good thing," whereas his contemporaries now viewed the harm as coming "from the use of a bad thing."[17] By the 1850s, 12 U.S. states (more than one-third of the nation at the time) and two Canadian provinces had introduced legislation forbidding the sale of "alcoholic" (distilled) drink.

Whether or not they were justified in doing so, temperance groups took credit for a drastic change that was

Even though this 1874 engraving shows a temperance crusader in full battle regalia, relatively few temperance activists resorted to physical violence.

occurring in the levels of alcohol consumption in the United States. From 1830 to 1850, consumption of all types of alcohol plummeted from an annual per capita level of roughly 7 gallons to roughly 2 gallons, approximately today's consumption level. It is quite possible that this decline encouraged the temperance movement to formulate its ultimate goal: a prohibition of all forms of alcohol consumption.

In 1880, the Woman's Christian Temperance Union (WCTU) was formed, with its goal being a total prohibition of alcohol. The WCTU's primary target was a highly visible fixture of late-nineteenth-century masculine American life: the saloon. These establishments were vilified as the source of all the troubles alcohol could bring. Saloons were seen as a significant threat to American women in general:

> *Bars appeared to invite family catastrophe. They introduced children to drunkenness and vice and drove husbands to alcoholism; they also caused squandering of wages, wife beating, and child abuse; and, with the patron's inhibitions lowered through drink, the saloon led many men into the arms of prostitutes (and not incidentally, contributed to the alarming spread of syphilis).*[18]

The American experience in World War I proved the turning point in the path toward national prohibition. During the war, anti-immigrant sentiment had begun to flourish, especially against German Americans, who were prominent in the beer

Marijuana Tax Act of 1937: Federal legislation regulating through government taxation the manufacture and sale of marijuana. The law effectively changed the status of marijuana from a licit to an illicit substance in the United States.

temperance movement: The social movement in the United States, beginning in the nineteenth century, that advocated the renunciation of liquor consumption.

Soldier's disease code for addiction to morphine

industry. A campaign was launched to convince Americans that the production of beer was part of a German plot to undermine America's willpower and deplete the cereal grains that were needed to make food for the soldiers in Europe. Prohibitionists were dominantly rural white Protestants, generally antagonistic toward Irish and Italian immigrants, who were gaining political power in metropolitan areas such as Chicago and New York. To many who were behind the movement, prohibition represented a cultural battle between America's Protestant rural towns and America's "sinful," immigrant-filled cities.[19]

The era in American history commonly known as **Prohibition** began in December 1917, when Congress passed a resolution "prohibiting the manufacture, sale, transportation, or importation of intoxicating liquors," the simple wording that would form the basis for the Eighteenth Amendment to the U.S. Constitution. It should be noted that it did not forbid purchase or use of alcohol, only in its production and distribution. The Volstead Act of 1919, authored by Representative Andrew Volstead of Minnesota, provided for the mechanism for federal enforcement by creating a Prohibition Bureau under control of the Treasury Department. By the end of the year, the necessary 36 states had ratified the amendment, and Prohibition officially took effect in January 1920.

Prohibition failed to produce an alcohol-free society and spurred numerous social problems. Many citizens, especially in the large cities, had little regard for the new law and continued to consume alcohol in nightclubs and bars known as **speakeasies** or "blind pigs." Alcohol itself became dangerous to consume because dangerous adulterants such as kerosene could be found in the cheaper "brands" of liquor, producing paralysis, blindness, and even death.

Because of Prohibition, the decade known as the "Roaring Twenties" became one of the most lawless periods in American history. Criminal organizations controlled the manufacture and distribution of "boot-leg" alcohol, smuggling huge quantities of liquor into the country. Court systems

Prohibition: A period between 1920 and 1933 in the United States when alcohol manufacture and sale was illegal.

Volstead Act of 1919: Federal legislation establishing the enforcement of the Eighteenth Amendment (Prohibition) of the U.S. Constitution.

speakeasies: Business establishments that sold liquor illegally during the Prohibition era.

PORTRAIT

Eliot Ness and the Untouchables

Shortly after graduating from the University of Chicago with a degree in business administration and political science, Eliot Ness accepted an appointment as an agent with the U.S. Treasury Department's Prohibition Bureau during a time when bootlegging was rampant throughout the nation. The Chicago branch of the Prohibition Bureau had a particular reputation for corruption, and it was difficult to find an honest law enforcement agent working in the city. Widely regarded as a model of reliability and honesty, Ness was given the job of assembling and leading a team to go after the liquor operations of famous gangster Al Capone. Capone was one of the most powerful bootleggers in the country with a multimillion-dollar operation of distilleries, breweries, and speakeasies in the Chicago area.

Ness was given the personnel records of the entire Prohibition Bureau, from which he carefully selected a special team to serve under his direction. One of Ness's first operations was to shut down 18 of Capone's operations in Chicago in one night. The raids were all scheduled to occur simultaneously so that they could make a clean sweep before the news got out to Capone. Given the poor reputation of the average prohibition agent, Ness's men made sure that no one in the raiding parties had the opportunity to make a telephone call before the raid. With a sawed-off shotgun in his arms, Ness and his men charged through the front door, yelling, "Everybody keep his place! This is a federal raid!" The operation was a success. Eighteen stills were shut down, and 52 people were arrested. Over the coming months, Ness and his team closed down numerous illegal stills and breweries worth an estimated $1 million (about $15 million in today's dollars).

Capone, feeling the pinch of Ness's operations, believed that every man had his price and made several attempts to bribe Ness and his men, but he had no success. In one instance, a man threw an envelope filled with cash into a car driven by one of Ness's men. Ness's agents caught up with the car and threw the money back into the gangster's car! Ness later called a press conference to talk about Capone's failed bribery attempt. The intent was to show Capone's organization that there were still law enforcement agents who could not be bought. The press conference was carried by newspapers around the country, one of which coined the term "The Untouchables."

Ness's war with Capone came to an end in 1931 when Al Capone was convicted of tax evasion. Capone, with his extravagant lifestyle, had not filed an income tax return for several years, and even though his lawyers continually warned him of his vulnerability to the Internal Revenue Service, Capone always felt that he was above the law.

Some of his critics at the time argued that Ness simply craved the spotlight and used his crusade against Capone to gain attention to himself. Ness responded to this issue by explaining why he took the job: "Unquestionably, it was going to be highly dangerous. Yet I felt it was quite natural to jump at the task. After all, if you don't like action and excitement, you don't go into police work. And what the hell, I figured, nobody lives forever!"

Many years later, Ness and his unit's exploits became popularized through a TV series, The Untouchables (1959–1963), and the 1987 film costarring Kevin Costner and Sean Connery.

Sources: Heimel, P. W. (1997). *Eliot Ness: The real story.* Coudersport, PA: Knox Books. Kobler, J. (1971). *The life and world of Al Capone.* New York: G. P. Putnam's Sons.

handling the prosecution of violators of the Volstead Act were stretched beyond their limits. By the time Prohibition ended, nearly 800 gangsters in the city of Chicago alone had been killed in bootleg-related battles. In the countryside, operators of illegal stills (called "moonshiners" because they worked largely at night by the light of the moon) continued their production of homemade liquor, despite the efforts of an occasional half-hearted raid by U.S. Treasury agents (locally known as "revenooers").

Unfortunately, federal agents in the Prohibition Bureau soon developed a reputation as being inept and corrupt. The bureau itself became viewed essentially as a training ground for bootleggers because agents frequently left law enforcement to embark upon their own criminal enterprises. One of the Prohibition Bureau's heroes, Eliot Ness, became famous for organizing a team of agents known as "The Untouchables," so-named because of their reputation for honesty and refusal to take bribes. In 1931, Eliot Ness and his Untouchables were able to arrest, prosecute, and eventually convict one of the most notorious crime figures of the time, Al Capone (see Portrait).[20]

The early years of Prohibition, however, did show positive effects in the area of public health. Alcohol-related deaths, cirrhosis of the liver, mental disorders, and alcohol-related crime declined in 1920 and 1921, but in a few years, the figures began to creep up again, and the level of criminal activity associated with illegal drinking was clearly intolerable.[21]

By the end of the decade, it was obvious for the vast majority of Americans that the "noble experiment" (as it was called at the time), despite its lofty aims, was not working. The significant social problems brought on by Prohibition were beginning to put pressure on political leaders to reconsider the concept of alcohol prohibition. In addition, there was an increasing need to restore the federal revenue dollars from taxes on alcohol, in order to help finance Depression-era programs. Before Prohibition, taxes on alcohol had been one of the primary sources of revenue for the federal government.

In 1933, President Franklin D. Roosevelt, having campaigned on a platform to repeal the Volstead Act, signed the necessary legislation that became the Twenty-first Amendment; ratification was swift. Alcohol was restored as a legal commodity, and regulatory control over alcohol was returned to the individual states. Prohibition as a national policy was over.[22] State prohibition laws were gradually repealed. In 1966, Mississippi, the last "dry" state, became "wet" as alcohol regulation returned once more to local authorities.

Drug Regulation in the Late Twentieth Century: A "War on Drugs"

While the post–World War II social scene showed clear acceptance for alcohol and tobacco use, the general perspective on drugs such as heroin, marijuana, and cocaine was quite the opposite—drugs were bad and illegal, and "no one you knew" had anything to do with them. Illicit drugs were seen as the province of criminals, the urban poor, and nonwhites.[23]

During this period, a whole class of drugs and drug-taking behavior was outside the mainstream of American life. Furthermore, an atmosphere of fear and suspicion surrounded people who took such drugs. Commissioner Anslinger, who took on the evils of marijuana, accused the People's Republic of China in the 1950s of selling opium and heroin to finance the expansion of communism. Drug abuse now became un-American, and Congress became convinced that penalties for illicit drug use were too lenient. Federal legislation in 1951 and 1956 increased the penalties of previously enacted marijuana and narcotics laws, lumping together marijuana and opiates under uniform penalties. A minimum sentence of two-year imprisonment was mandated for first-time offenders and up to 10-year imprisonment for repeat offenders; the sale of heroin to individuals under the age of 18 was made a capital offense. The basis of these laws was the belief that strict drug laws and an increase in drug-law enforcement would curb future drug demand.

During the 1960s, the basic premises of American life—the beliefs that working hard and living a good life would bring happiness and that society was stable and calm—were being undermined by the reality of the Vietnam war abroad and social unrest at home. The large adolescent and college-aged cohort born after World War II, often referred to as the "baby boomers" or "hippie" generation, was challenging many accepted cultural norms and the established hierarchy. Many young people were searching for new answers to old problems, and their search led to experimentation with drugs that their parents had been taught to fear. The principal symbol of this era of defiance against the established order, or indeed against anyone over 30 years of age, was marijuana. No longer would marijuana be something foreign to Middle America. Marijuana, as well as new drugs such as LSD and other hallucinogens, became associated with the sons and daughters of white middle-class families. Illicit drug use, once a problem associated with minority populations, inner cities and the poor, was now a concern for all Americans.

Along with the turbulence of the period came a disturbing increase in heroin abuse across the country. In the early 1970s, reports surfaced estimating that up to 15 percent of the American troops returning home from Vietnam had been heroin abusers. As detailed in Chapter 2, organized crime groups in Europe established the "French Connection," in which opium grown in Turkey was converted into heroin in southern French port cities, smuggled into America, and then sold on the streets of major cities. A new form of crudely processed heroin from Mexico, known as "Black Tar," was beginning to be sold throughout western United States. Heroin abuse increased in many inner cities, and heroin abuse was later connected to a rise in the crime rate, specifically a growing number of robberies and burglaries committed by heroin abusers to get money to buy drugs (see Chapter 4).[24]

The Controlled Substances Act of 1970

For President Richard Nixon, elected in 1968 on a platform of law and order, illicit drug use became a major political issue. He declared a "total war on drugs," ordering his senior staff to make the reduction of drug abuse one of its top priorities. In 1970, the Nixon administration persuaded Congress to pass the **Comprehensive Drug Abuse Prevention and Control Act**, popularly known as the "Controlled Substances Act" and abbreviated as the CSA. The act was passed to consolidate the large number of diverse and overlapping drug laws as well as the duplication of efforts by several different federal agencies. The act also established five schedules for the classification of drugs, based upon their approved medical uses, potential for abuse, and potential for producing dependence. Because of the 1970 Controlled Substances Act, the control of drugs was placed under federal jurisdiction regardless of state regulations, which made it one of the most important drug-control legislative acts in the nation's history.

The 1970 act also shifted the administration of federal drug enforcement from the Treasury Department to the Department of Justice, creating the **Drug Enforcement Administration (DEA)**. The DEA was given the control of all drug enforcement responsibilities, except those related to ports of entry and borders, which were given to the U.S. Customs Service (now renamed as the U.S. Customs and Border Protection). DEA agents were to conduct drug investigation, collect intelligence about general trends in drug trafficking and drug production, and coordinate efforts among federal, state, and local law enforcement agencies. The DEA's mission today remains both domestic and foreign. Agents are stationed in foreign countries, and although they do not possess arrest powers, they act as liaisons with foreign law enforcement agencies. Both the DEA and the Federal Bureau of Investigation (FBI) share responsibility for enforcement of the Controlled Substances Act of 1970, and the director of the DEA reports to the director of the FBI, who in 1982 was given responsibility for supervising all drug-law enforcement efforts and policies (Drug Enforcement ... in Focus).

President Nixon also believed that reducing the supply of drugs from overseas sources could curb drug abuse in the United States. In the 1970s, the federal government estimated that 80 percent of the heroin reaching the United States was produced from opium poppies grown in Turkey. In an attempt to reduce the amount of heroin coming into the United States, the Nixon administration threatened to cut off aid to Turkey if that country did not put an end to the export of opium. Nixon also promised Turkey millions of dollars in aid to make up for the subsequent losses resulting from reduced poppy cultivation. Initially, this action did lead to a shortage of heroin on American streets in 1973. The decline in heroin availability, however, did not last long. In 1974, Mexico became a primary source of opium production, and in response, the U.S. government began to finance opium poppy eradication programs in Mexico (see Chapter 2).[25]

A "demand-reduction" response of the Nixon administration to drug abuse, particularly with regard to the increase in heroin dependence, was to finance a number of treatment programs for drug-dependent individuals. These treatment programs ranged from inpatient detoxification and therapeutic communities to newly created methadone outpatient programs. Methadone is a long-acting opiate that is taken orally in order to prevent heroin withdrawal symptoms for up to 24 hours (see Chapter 9). Methadone maintenance programs were designed to wean heroin abusers off heroin by allowing them to have a better chance at employment and ending the need to commit crimes to maintain their abuse. After an initial report of the drug's success in 1966, methadone's popularity quickly spread. Methadone maintenance programs represented the first time that the federal government made a commitment to drug-abuse treatment in the community.

By 1972, some of the Nixon administration's antidrug programs appeared to be working. There was a national network of methadone treatment centers and evidence of successful eradication efforts. Turkey had agreed to stop growing opium, and Mexico was cooperating with U.S. law enforcement. The price of heroin was up, the purity level was down, and there was a decrease in the number of drug overdose cases. When President Gerald Ford took office in 1974, however, the nation's attention was diverted from drug abuse to other issues, such as unemployment, inflation, and an energy crisis. Illicit drug use was no longer a dominating issue. Ford's policy toward illicit drug use was based on the attitude that drug abuse was here to stay, and that the emphasis of government actions should be on containing rather than eliminating the problem. The administration also believed that some drugs were more dangerous than others were and that antidrug policies should be directed at controlling the supply and demand of those drugs that posed the greatest threat to society.

President Jimmy Carter, elected in 1976, was more tolerant toward drug use than President Ford and even favored decriminalization of the possession of small amounts of marijuana. President Carter stated, "Penalties against possession of a drug should not be more damaging to an individual than the use of the drug itself, and where they are, they should be changed. Nowhere is this clearer than in the laws against the possession of marijuana in private for personal use."[26] By 1978, 11 states followed Carter's lead and decriminalized small amounts of marijuana. California and Oregon made possession of one ounce or less of marijuana a citable misdemeanor with a maximum penalty of $1,000, and there were

Comprehensive Drug Abuse Prevention and Control Act of 1970 (Controlled Substances Act): Federal legislation establishing five categories (schedules) of controlled substances based on their approved medical uses, potential for abuse, and potential for producing dependence. The law also shifted the jurisdiction for drug-law enforcement from the Treasury Department to the Department of Justice. It is often referred to as the CSA.

Drug Enforcement Administration (DEA): The principal federal agency under the U.S. Department of Justice, responsible for enforcing laws and regulations related to controlled substances being illicitly trafficked in the United States.

Drug Enforcement . . . in Focus

The Drug Enforcement Administration Today

The Drug Enforcement Administration was established in 1973 under President Nixon to create a single federal agency for the enforcement of federal drug laws and consolidate drug-control responsibilities previously held by the Bureau of Narcotics and Dangerous Drugs (formerly the Federal Bureau of Narcotics under Harry J. Anslinger), the Office of Drug Abuse Law Enforcement, and other federal agencies. The DEA became the lead agency for domestic enforcement of the Controlled Substances Act of 1970 in conjunction with the FBI and Immigration and Customs Enforcement (ICE), as well as sole responsibility for U.S. drug investigations in foreign countries. These responsibilities remain the mission of the DEA today. As of 2018, the DEA employs more than 10,000 men and women, including more than 4,600 Special Agents (see badge in photo). In addition, more than 1,600 DEA employees are specialists in three programs:

- The DEA Intelligence Program is responsible for tactical intelligence information that facilitates the arrests, seizures, and interdiction of violators of the Controlled Substances Act and strategic intelligence information focusing on patterns of drug trafficking around the world. More than 750 Intelligence Specialists are employed in the El Paso Intelligence Center (EPIC) in Texas.
- The DEA Diversion Control Program is responsible for the investigation and support for the prosecution of cases in which controlled substances such as OxyContin and other opioid pain medications (see Chapter 9) that are manufactured for legitimate medical use but diverted through illegal distribution channels. Nearly 600 diversion investigators are employed in seven regional offices in the United States.

- The National Forensic Laboratory Information System (NFLIS) is a nationwide system of nearly 300 federal, state, and local forensic laboratories that analyze the contents of drugs seized by the DEA and report to the DEA Diversion Control office as to patterns of illicit drug availability. More than 300 forensic chemists employed by the DEA are involved in this program.

The annual budget of the DEA is $2.1 billion for FY 2018. The agency is officially under the U.S. Department of Justice in Washington, D.C.

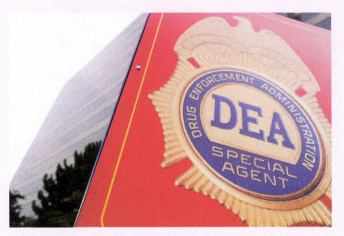

The DEA Special Agent badge marks the entrance to the DEA headquarters in Arlington, Virginia.

Source: The Drug Enforcement Administration, U.S. Department of Justice, Washington, D.C. Assessed from https://www.dea.gov/.

---

no increased penalties for repeat offenders.[27] Relaxed attitudes toward drugs reached a peak in 1979, a year when an estimated 51 percent of high school seniors reported having smoked marijuana, and 28 percent reported using an illicit drug other than marijuana over the past 12 months, the latter being about twice the level reported in 2017 (see Chapter 1).[28]

Drug Regulation 1980–2000: Renewed Efforts at Drug Control

With the decade of the 1980s came significant changes in the mood of the country in the form of a social and political reaction to earlier decades. If the media symbol formerly had been the "hippie," now it was the "yuppie," a young, upwardly mobile professional. The political climate became more conservative in all age groups. With regard to drugs,

the concern about heroin dependence was being overshadowed by a new fixation: cocaine. At first, cocaine took on an aura of glamor and (because it was so expensive) became a symbol of material success. The media spotlight shone on a steady stream of celebrities in entertainment and sports who used cocaine. Not long after, however, the harsh realities of cocaine dependence were recognized. The very same celebrities, who had accepted cocaine into their lives, were now experiencing the consequences; many of them were in rehabilitation programs, and some had died from cocaine overdoses. To make matters worse, in 1985, a new form of cocaine that was smokable and cheap, "crack," succeeded in extending the problems of cocaine dependence to the inner cities of the United States, to segments of American society that did not have the financial resources to afford cocaine itself. In the glare of intense media attention, crack dependence soon took on all the aspects of a national nightmare.

In the 1970s, there had been generally a lack of public interest and even some tolerance of drug use. As mentioned earlier, in several U.S. states there was even a trend toward deregulation. In the 1980s, however, the lack of public interest in drug use began to shift as grassroots groups began to demand that something be done about "America's drug problem." During the presidency of Ronald Reagan, drug abuse became a major political and social issue. President Reagan declared an all-out war on drugs, and First Lady Nancy Reagan launched her "Just Say No" campaign, which focused mostly on white middle-class children, who had not yet tried drugs. Reagan's war on drugs focused on a policy of controlling the supply of drugs by increasing the budgets of drug enforcement agencies and providing foreign aid to such countries as Colombia, Peru, Bolivia, and Mexico to encourage anti-drug programs. Demand was to be reduced by enacting laws that imposed some of the harshest penalties ever for drug-law violators.

With popular sentiment once again turned against drugs, Congress rewrote virtually all of the nation's drug laws in record time. In 1984, Congress passed the **Comprehensive Crime Control Act**, which increased the penalties for violations of the Controlled Substances Act and expanded asset-forfeiture law, allowing both local and federal drug enforcement agencies to keep most of the money made from the sale of seized assets (see Chapter 6). Two years later, Congress passed the **Anti-Drug Abuse Act of 1986**, which placed mandatory minimum sentences for federal drug convictions, eliminating a judge's discretion in pronouncing a sentence. Different mandatory minimum sentences were to be given for possession of powder and crack cocaine, again demonstrating the linkage between racism and U.S. drug control policy. The new law imposed a prison sentence of 5 to 40 years for possession of 500 grams of powder cocaine or 5 grams of crack cocaine. This mandatory sentence could not be suspended, nor could the offender be paroled or placed on probation. The Anti-Drug Abuse Act of 1986 also created a "kingpin" statute under which the heads of drug-trafficking organizations could receive mandatory life imprisonment if convicted of operating a continuing criminal enterprise.

One of the most important drug laws passed in the 1980s was the **Anti-Drug Abuse Act of 1988**. This legislation created a cabinet-level position of Director of National Drug Control Policy, later to be referred to in the media as the "Drug Czar," whose job was to coordinate federal activities with respect to both drug supply and demand reduction. The first director was former Education Secretary William J. Bennett, who believed that individual users of drugs should accept moral responsibility for their behavior. Bennett believed that drug laws should be strict so that drug users would understand that involvement in the illegal drug trade has clear consequences. The law created harsher penalties for the possession of drugs; penalties for selling drugs to minors were enhanced; and the act reinstated the death penalty for anyone convicted as a "drug kingpin" or anyone convicted of a drug-related killing. The act also addressed alcohol use, especially the problem of drunk driving, by providing federal money to states that instituted tough penalties for drunk drivers. Lastly, the act addressed the issues of drug use in schools and in the workplace by requiring educational institutions and businesses to establish a system to ensure that students and workers remained drug free. This provision later established the basis for drug testing in schools and in the workplace (see Chapter 16).

The wave of antidrug legislation in the 1980s (see Drugs ... in Focus) profoundly changed America's criminal justice system. Law enforcement budgets increased, as more officers had to be hired to enforce drug laws. The number of drug violators increased to the highest level ever, and courts became backlogged with drug case after drug case. The number of inmates in U.S. prisons and jails rose nearly 100 percent from 1985 to 1996, and the budget for prisons increased by more than 160 percent.[29] Prison building became one of the biggest public works projects in America; hundreds of new prisons sprang up across the country. Fortunately, by the end of the 1990s, the extent of crack abuse had greatly diminished, crime rates had begun to fall, and rates of illicit drug use began to decline. It is still being debated, however, whether these changes were due to the "get tough" policy on drugs, and whether the mass incarceration of mainly minority Americans was justified.

"Just say no" was a popular slogan coined by First Lady Nancy Reagan during the "war on drugs" era in the early 1980s.

Credit: Doug Mills/AP images

Comprehensive Crime Control Act of 1984: Federal legislation increasing penalties for drug possession and trafficking under the Controlled Substances Act and expanded laws regarding asset forfeiture of major drug traffickers.

Anti-Drug Abuse Act of 1986: Federal legislation establishing mandatory minimum sentences for federal drug convictions and creating special penalties for major leaders of drug trafficking organizations.

Anti-Drug Abuse Act of 1988: Federal legislation creating a cabinet-level "Drug Czar" position to coordinate all federal drug-control activities.

Drugs . . . in Focus

A History of American Drug-Control Legislation

1794   A federal tax on whiskey leads to the Whiskey rebellion in western Pennsylvania (see Chapter 13).

1868   The Pharmacy Act of 1868 requires registration of those individuals dispensing drugs.

1875   The Anti-Opium Smoking Act is passed in San Francisco.

1906   The Pure Food and Drug Act requires all packaged foods and drugs to list the ingredients on the label of the product.

1914   The Harrison Act is designed to regulate opiate and cocaine abuse through government taxation.

1919   Congress passes the Eighteenth Amendment, which outlaws the manufacture and sale of alcohol.

1933   Congress passes the Twenty-first Amendment, which repeals the Eighteenth Amendment.

1937   The Marijuana Tax Act places a tax on the manufacture and sale of marijuana.

1938   The Food, Drug, and Cosmetic Act requires all drugs and cosmetics are tested for safety (when used as directed) prior to being marketed. The U.S. Food and Drug Administration (FDA) is established to insure the safety of commercial drugs.

1962   The Kefauver-Harris Amendment extends the power of the FDA to ensure the effectiveness as well as safety of commercial drugs.

1970   Comprehensive Drug Abuse Prevention and Control Act, popularly known as the Controlled Substances Act, establishes five schedules for the classification of drugs based upon their approved medical uses, potential for abuse, and potential for producing dependence.

1984   The Comprehensive Crime Control Act enhances the penalties for violations of the Controlled Substances Act and expands asset-forfeiture law, allowing both local and federal drug enforcement agencies to keep the majority of the money made from the sale of seized assets.

1986   The Anti-Drug Abuse Act of 1986 establishes mandatory sentences for federal drug convictions, eliminating a judge's discretion in pronouncing a sentence.

1988   The Anti-Drug Abuse Act of 1988 increases penalties for drug offenses involving children and creates a cabinet-level position of Director of National Drug Control Policy, often referred to in the media as "Drug Czar."

1996   Arizona Proposition 200 and California Proposition 215 are passed, which legalize the use of marijuana for medicinal purposes within these two states (see Chapter 11).

1996   The Comprehensive Methamphetamine Control Act increases the penalties for trafficking and manufacture of methamphetamine and its precursor chemicals.

2000   GHB (gamma-hydroxybutyrate) is added to the list of Schedule I controlled substances.

2003   The Illicit Drug Anti-Proliferation Act, aimed at the promoters of "raves," holds persons accountable for knowingly renting, leasing, or maintaining any place where drugs are distributed or manufactured.

2004   The Anabolic Steroid Control Act of 2004 adds several new steroids and steroid precursors to the list of controlled substances.

2004   The U.S. Food and Drug Administration (FDA) issues regulations prohibiting the sale of dietary supplements containing ephedrine.

2005   The Combat Methamphetamine Epidemic Act establishes nationwide sales restrictions on precursor chemicals and law enforcement initiatives for the seizure of domestic methamphetamine laboratories.

2008   The Ryan Haight Online Pharmacy Consumer Protection Act increases regulations on both doctors and pharmacies related to online controlled substance prescriptions.

2009   The Tobacco Control Act gives the FDA authority to regulate the sale and manufacture of tobacco products (see Chapter 15).

2010   The Safe and Secure Drug Disposal Act allows users of the controlled prescription medication to dispose of them safely by delivering them to authorized entities.

2012   The Synthetic Drug Abuse Prevention Act adds 26 chemicals to Schedule I controlled substances and extends authority of the DEA over the introduction of new synthetic drug formulations.

2012   Recreational marijuana use is legalized in Colorado and Washington.

2014   Recreational marijuana use is legalized in Alaska and Oregon, as well as in the District of Columbia.

2016   Recreational marijuana use is legalized in California, Massachusetts, Nevada, and Maine.

2018   Recreational marijuana use is legalized in ten U.S. states and the District of Columbia, with additional states considering moves toward legalization.

The 1990s can be characterized as a period of relatively little political interest in drug-abuse issues. During his first term in office from 1992 to 1996, President Bill Clinton reduced the staff of the Office of National Drug Control Policy by 83 percent, a move that he ascribed to keeping his campaign promise to reduce the White House staff by 25 percent. As the 1996 election approached and a rise in marijuana use among youth became publicized, Clinton was subject to criticism that he had neglected America's drug problem. In response, Clinton declared his own war on drugs and appointed a retired four-star military general, Barry McCaffrey, to be his "Drug Czar." Clinton urged Congress to appropriate a $100 million increase in the budget for drug interdiction and increased foreign aid to stop the supply of drugs at their source. In addition, he signed the **Comprehensive Methamphetamine Control Act** into law in 1996. Designed to curb the use of methamphetamine, this act increased funding for identifying and dismantling small clandestine "meth labs" that were appearing across the country and increased restrictions on the sale of precursor chemicals used in the manufacture of methamphetamine (see Chapter 10).

Drug Regulation in the Twenty-First Century: The Impact of 9/11

After the events of September 11, 2001, when four planes were hijacked by the terrorist group al-Qaeda, two of which were flown into the World Trade Center in New York, one which struck the Pentagon in Washington, and the last of which crashed in a field in Pennsylvania, killing in total nearly 3,000 people, the war on terrorism became a dominating concern. As discussed in Chapter 2, President George W. Bush combined programs aimed at drug-abuse control with programs aimed at enhancing national security. In effect, the war on drugs became intertwined with the war against terrorism in one all-encompassing policy. Foreign aid to Colombia was increased enormously, not only to fight drug trafficking but also to support Colombia's domestic war against insurgent groups within the country.[30]

At the same time, economic and political aspects of U.S. foreign policy have complicated efforts to control global drug trafficking, as discussed in Chapter 2. Diplomatic relations with Mexico, for example, have been strained by the fact that Mexico continues to be not only a major trafficking route for cocaine from South America and heroin from Mexico itself but also a source of marijuana cultivation and a manufacturing source of methamphetamine and illegal medications. Efforts to reduce the cultivation of opium in the rugged, mountainous areas of Afghanistan have been intertwined with efforts to control the political influence of regional warlords, whether they have terrorist associations or not. The interconnected and sometimes opposing goals of America's drug-control policy and global foreign policy continue to be a major challenge in the effort to regulate drug-taking behavior both in the United States and around the world.[31]

Quick Concept Check 3.2

Understanding the History of U.S. Drug-Control Legislation

Test your understanding of American drug-control legislation by matching the statement on the left with the associated drug on the right.

Note: An answer may be used more than once.

1. It has been suggested that, in order to get federal drug legislation passed in 1914, a propaganda campaign was launched that associated African Americans with this drug.
2. The opposition to this drug was intertwined with a negative reaction toward German, Italian, and Irish immigrants.
3. Legislation that made this drug an illegal substance in 1937 was linked to drug-taking behavior among Mexican migrant workers.
4. The Nixon Administration initiated programs in the late 1960s that promoted this opioid as a therapeutic strategy for treating heroin.
5. During Jimmy Carter's presidency in the late 1970s, several U.S. states voted to decriminalize this drug.
6. Federal legislation passed in 1996 funds law enforcement efforts to close down small clandestine laboratories that were manufacturing this drug.
7. In 2012, drug compounds used to develop this drug were added to the CSA as a Schedule I controlled substance.

a. marijuana
b. methamphetamine
c. synthetic marijuana
d. morphine
e. alcohol
f. heroin
g. methadone
h. cocaine

Answers: 1. h. 2. e. 3. a. 4. g. 5. a. 6. b. 7. c

The connection between the war on drugs and the war on terrorism has been evident at the domestic level as well. The **USA PATRIOT Act of 2001**, enacted as a response to the

Comprehensive Methamphetamine Control Act of 1996: Federal legislation increasing penalties for methamphetamine trafficking and setting limits on the purchase of precursor materials for methamphetamine production.

USA PATRIOT Act of 2001: Federal legislation authorizing federal agents to carry on telephone and electronic surveillance in drug-control operations, increased money laundering enforcement, and expanded operations at the U.S. border.

September 11 attacks, increased the ability for federal authorities to tap telephones and wireless devices, monitor Internet communications, and tighten the enforcement of money laundering activities, as well as protect U.S. borders. These powers were directed toward not only possible acts of terrorism but also other criminal acts such as drug trafficking. The **USA PATRIOT Improvement and Reauthorization Act of 2005** (often referred to as "PATRIOT II") extended the original legislation, relaxing certain provisions that had been criticized as being restrictive of individual civil liberties, tightening other provisions regarding law enforcement powers, and closing some loopholes in the 2001 act with regard to terrorist financing.

Significantly, PATRIOT II contained a subsection called the **Combat Methamphetamine Epidemic Act** that restricted access to over-the-counter cold medications that could be used to manufacture methamphetamine (see Chapter 10). Limits on the amounts purchased were established, and consumers were required to provide photo identification and sign in a store log at the time of purchase. In addition, funding was authorized for the federal Meth Hot Spots program, intended to support state and local law enforcement agencies in the investigation and prosecution of individuals committing methamphetamine offenses.

Within this timeframe, there was also increased concern over the availability of synthetic drugs. While MDMA (ecstasy) had first gained popularity earlier in the 1980s, the "raves" of the 1990s, where such drugs were often used, became the target of drug legislation. The **Illicit Drug Anti-Proliferation Act of 2003** amended the CSA to offer stiff sanctions to those who established venues where such drugs were made, distributed, or consumed. This act demonstrated a shift from targeting the users of these drugs to the establishments that help facilitate the drug's use. The act also provided the DEA with funding for education on the dangers of club drugs.

During the early twenty-first century, attention was also drawn to the issue of prescription drug abuse. The **Ryan Haight Online Pharmacy Consumer Protection Act of 2008** was named after an 18-year-old who died after overdosing on prescription painkillers he obtained on the Internet

from a doctor he had never met. This legislation was designed to help regulate the distribution of controlled substances via the Internet. Specifically, the statute amended the CSA by requiring a face-to-face medical evaluation prior to issuing an online prescription, as well as registration and reporting requirements for pharmacies. Soon after the Ryan Haight Act, additional legislation was passed, aimed also at preventing the problem of prescription drug abuse, particularly among adolescents who consumed unused prescription medications in the home. In 2010, the **Safe and Secure Drug Disposal Act** allowed users of controlled prescription medication to dispose of them by delivering them to designated entities authorized to take them. The DEA is seeking to expand this Act by offering mail-in options, "take-back day" events and collection box locations for safe and convenient disposal of dangerous medications.[32]

In 2012, in an effort to combat the growing problem of synthetic marijuana issue, President Obama signed the Food and Drug Administration Safety and Innovation Act, which includes the **Synthetic Drug Abuse Prevention Act** provision. This act adds cannabimimetic agents to Schedule 1 of the CSA. Examples of these drugs include "Spice," "K2," "Blaze," and "Red X Dawn," which prior to this legislation were legally available in shops and on the internet (see Chapter 11).[33] While these designer drugs are chemically different from cannabis, they offer similar effects as natural cannabis, and users often opt for these drugs to escape drug detection, despite their unpredictable and often dangerous effects.

While the government was legislating against the use of synthetic marijuana, the perception of natural marijuana as a relatively benign drug was growing. A 2017 national poll found that most Americans supported the legalization of marijuana—61 percent in favor and 33 percent against.[34] As of late 2018, ten U.S. states and the District of Columbia have legalized the possession, sale, or use of marijuana for recreational purposes; 33 states and the District of Columbia have approved the use of marijuana for medical purposes.[35] Given this trend in the public acceptance and in several states, legalization of marijuana has had a significant impact on the criminal justice system. Data from 2011 suggests that California alone paid more than $60 million to incarcerate marijuana offenders, who spent an average of 13 months in confinement. Moreover, California was imprisoning African

USA PATRIOT Improvement and Reauthorization Act of 2005: Federal legislation modifying the USA Patriot Act of 2001, to satisfy certain civil liberty concerns and close certain loopholes in the previous law.

Combat Methamphetamine Epidemic Act of 2005: A portion of the USA PATRIOT Improvement and Reauthorization Act of 2005, setting limits on the sale of over-the-counter medications typically used as precursor materials for methamphetamine production and increasing support for law enforcement agencies involved in methamphetamine control operations.

Illicit Drug Anti-Proliferation Act of 2003: Legislation aimed at the promotion of "raves" amended the CSA to include increased penalties for establishments that were considered to be contributing to the production, distribution or consumption of drugs.

Ryan Haight Online Pharmacy Consumer Protection Act of 2008: An amendment to the CSA, which increases regulations on both doctors and pharmacies, related to online controlled substance prescriptions.

Safe and Secure Drug Disposal Act of 2010: An amendment to the CSA that allows users of controlled prescription medication to dispose of them by delivering them to authorized entities.

Synthetic Drug Abuse Prevention Act of 2012: Legislation adding cannabimimetic agents (synthetic marijuana) to the listing of controlled substances in the CSA.

Americans at 10 times the rate of other races for marijuana offenses.[36] Hence, the legalization of marijuana has had major ramifications for the California criminal justice system, and more importantly, for minority communities in California and other states (see Chapter 11).

Drug-Control Policy Today: Public Health and Public Safety

In general, societal problems associated with drug use and abuse can be broken down into two broad and somewhat overlapping areas of concern: public health and public safety.

Addressing public health concerns requires the efforts of psychiatrists, psychologists, drug-abuse counselors, and other health professionals, who focus on the effects of the use and abuse of a substance (or multiple substances) on one's physical health and psychological well-being. The decision to treat an individual with a drug problem is based on behavioral criteria. For example, an individual might have persistent intentions or make persistent efforts to cut down on drug-taking behavior or fail on a recurring basis to meet major responsibilities at work, school, or home. While the treatment for these difficulties may be specifically tied to the type of drug that is involved, the diagnosis is based solely on the adverse behavioral consequences of drug use, not on the nature of the drug itself. Whether the drug is judged as legal or illegal is not an issue. The strategy of health professions in addressing the public health concerns of drug-taking behavior, through the application of the current fifth edition of the *Diagnostic and Statistical Manual* (DSM-5), will be examined in Chapter 8.

Addressing the public safety concerns, however, rests upon the efforts of governmental officials and professionals in the field of criminal justice. In this latter case, five specific categories of drugs (referred to as Schedules I through V) have been established under the Controlled Substances Act of 1970, based upon accepted medical benefits and their potential for abuse. These categories represent the official stance of the U.S. government with regard to the degree to which public access to a specific drug should be allowed. Under this system, the guiding principle for viewing drug-taking behavior from a criminal-justice perspective is that drugs with the fewest medical benefits and the greatest potential for abuse (Schedule I controlled substances) should be the drugs with the most stringently restricted availability to the public, as established by law. In addition, the possession and trafficking of these drugs should carry the most severe criminal penalties. The set of decisions as to which drugs are listed in a particular category is directly tied to the prevailing national drug-control policy at the time. As we will see in Chapter 11, conflicts have arisen between the U.S. federal government that has established marijuana as a Schedule I controlled substance and individual U.S. states that have legalized recreational marijuana use.

It is clear that public health and public safety concerns frequently overlap when addressing the overall problems of drug use and abuse. In order to achieve the most productive solutions to the drug problem in our society, health professionals and criminal-justice professionals coordinate their efforts as much as possible. A good example of this collaboration has been the creation of specialized drug courts for nonviolent drug-law offenders (Chapter 7).

Federal Drug-Control Policy: Five Schedules of Controlled Substances

From the perspective of the U.S. federal government and criminal-justice professionals under federal jurisdiction, the legality of various forms of drug-taking behavior is defined along the five-category system created more than 40 years ago under the Controlled Substances Act. Each category or schedule defines a particular chemical substance in terms of its potential for medical use and its potential for abuse. The guiding principle is that those substances having the lowest potential for medical use and the highest potential for abuse (Schedule I controlled substances) should be the substances whose availability to the public is most stringently restricted. In addition, the possession and trafficking of Schedule I controlled substances (with the exception of marijuana) carry the harshest criminal penalties. Schedule II controlled substances are prescribed medications that are the most tightly regulated; no prescriptions for Schedule I controlled substances are permitted. Table 3.1 lists the major drugs under Schedules I through V. The specific criminal penalties for possession and trafficking of controlled substances will be outlined in Chapter 5.

Attitudes Driving America's Drug Policy

When drug regulations are discussed, it is important to consider the ideological stance that drives the policy. It is the ideology, or belief about the problem, that forms the basis of drug-control strategies. For example, if you believe that drug use is inherently immoral, you might consider a strategy that removes those drug users from society, or else punishes users for having committed an immoral act. If, on the other hand, you believe that the people who use drugs are troubled individuals who abuse substances because of the circumstances in their lives, your strategy is likely to look much different. You might advocate for treatment and alternative programs other than jail or prison. Recall that the WTCU believed that drinking was immoral, as were the establishments that provided the alcohol (saloons). Hence, their strategy was to fight for the prohibition of alcohol, which they won (for a time). Recall that President Carter believed that the nation was doing more harm than good to individuals being incarcerated on low-level marijuana convictions. This led to his advocacy for marijuana decriminalization. These are both very different perspectives or beliefs about substance use, each leading to different responses for dealing with drug problems.

One way to conceptualize attitudes toward crime is through the dichotomy of conservative versus liberal perspectives.[37] The conservative perspective focuses on deterrence strategies, such as tough laws that dissuade criminal behavior

TABLE 3.1

Summary of controlled substances schedules under the Controlled Substances Act.

SCHEDULE I:

Criteria: high potential for abuse; no accepted medical use

Restrictions: research use only; drugs must be stored in secure vaults

Examples: heroin, LSD, marijuana, MDMA (Ecstasy), mescaline, methqualone, methcathinone (khat), peyote, psilocybin

SCHEDULE II:

Criteria: high potential for abuse; some accepted medical use, though use may lead to severe physical or psychological dependence

Restrictions: no prescription renewals permitted; in cases of medical use, drugs must be stored in secure vaults

Examples: amphetamines (Dexedrine, Adderall), cocaine, coca leaves, codeine, hydrocodone (Vicodin)*, methadone, methamphetamine, methylphenidate (Ritalin), morphine, oxycodone (Percocet, OxyContin), phencyclidine (PCP)

SCHEDULE III:

Criteria: high potential for abuse; accepted medical use, though use may lead to low or moderate physical or psychological dependence

Restrictions: up to five prescription renewals permitted within six months

Examples: anabolic steroids and other testosterone-based compounds, ketamine

SCHEDULE IV:

Criteria: low potential for abuse; accepted medical use

Restrictions: up to five prescription renewals are permitted within six months.

Examples: antianxiety medications, antidepressant medications, choral hydrate, phenobarbital, temazepam (Restoril) triazolam (Halcion)

SCHEDULE V:

Criteria: minimal potential for abuse; widespread medical use

Restrictions: minimal controls for selling and dispensing

Examples: cough-control medications containing small amounts of codeine and diarrhea-control medications containing small amounts of opium or morphine

*As of 2014, hydrocodone (Vicodin) is now reclassified as a Schedule II controlled substance. Prior to 2014, it was classified under Schedule III. The reclassification was a result of concerns over widespread overprescriptions of hydrocodone and diversion of the drug to nonmedical recreational use.

Note: A full listing of drugs categorized as controlled substances in Schedules I through V can be found in publications of the Drug Enforcement Administration, http://www.justice.gov/dea.

Source: Based on data supplied by the Drug Enforcement Administration, U.S. Department of Justice, Washington, D.C.

in general as well as laws that are aimed at incarcerating those who violate specific drug laws. The liberal alternative is to invest in rehabilitating drug offenders, offering drug treatment services in lieu of long prison sentences. A liberal ideology focuses on diverting first-time drug offenders from punitive criminal justice responses via the use of drug courts and other alternatives to incarceration. Regarding law enforcement, conservatives call for increased police presence, drug interdiction and intense street-level law enforcement, while liberals call for improved police–community relationships to help communities work with law enforcement on drug problems. With regard to prevention efforts, conservatives might use drug testing to deter individuals from drug use, whereas liberals might be more inclined toward drug education to help prevent drug use.

Unfortunately, ideology rather than evidence about policy effectiveness often drives policy.[38] This is true for both liberal and conservative strategies. For example, the Drug Abuse Resistance Education (DARE) program has been around since the 1980s, despite limited evidence of the model's support in preventing children from using drugs (see Chapter 14). Similarly, there is only limited evidence that long prison sentences succeed in deterring individuals from engaging in future crime.[39] Despite knowing this, we continue to see policies focused on long terms of incarceration, such as proposals by President Trump to fight to the opioid epidemic by advocating for increased criminal penalties, including mandatory minimum sentences, for drug dealers and traffickers.[40]

Drug-Control Policies: From Conservative to Liberal?

Attempts to regulate drugs in America have taken place through much of the twentieth century, including a war against the ills of marijuana in the mid-1900s and an earlier 23-year-long criminalization of the use of alcohol. It should be recalled, however, that it was President Nixon who initiated the "war on drugs" by supporting conservative policies aimed at harsh responses to drug law violations, while supporting at the same time drug treatment programs and harm-reduction remedies, such as methadone maintenance, which can be seen as a more liberal strategy toward drug abuse. Later, President Reagan renewed President Nixon's "war on drugs" but with a more consistently conservative stance on drugs and crime, such as initiating mandatory minimum sentences to target drug offenders. A significant consequence of this policy have been a sharp increase in lengthy prison sentences for a range of nonviolent drug offenders.

America is still facing the consequences of four decades of conservative drug control policy. One of the more apparent consequences is the great expansion of the prison population between the 1970s and 2010. This is largely attributable to policies directed specifically toward drug offenders, which will be discussed in more detail in Chapter 5.

Drug Enforcement . . . in Focus

Efforts to Move Marijuana from a Schedule I to Schedule II Controlled Substance Category

The Drug Enforcement Administration classifies marijuana in the most restrictive of the five-category drug regulatory system, reserved for drugs deemed as having the greatest potential for abuse and as having no medicinal value. So why does marijuana have a Schedule I rating, and why is this important?

When the Controlled Substances Act was established in 1970, unsure where marijuana should fall, President Nixon formed a commission to study the drug and advise the DEA as to where it should be placed. The commission found that marijuana appeared to be a less serious threat to public health than other Schedule 1 drugs and recommended that the drug remain a controlled substance, but that citizens could be allowed to possess small amounts of marijuana for personal use. Yet, given the social and political climate during the beginning years of the "war on drugs," marijuana ultimately remained on the highest classification tier.

The fight to reclassify marijuana to a lower drug class has been waged practically from the year the classification system was designed. The National Organization for the Reform of Marijuana Laws (NORML) was the first group to file a petition to the DEA for the reclassification of marijuana. After a 22-year battle, the petition was rejected. In 2002, the Coalition to Reschedule Cannabis filed a similar petition, which was once again declined by the DEA. Since that time, the Federal Drug Enforcement Administration has conducted its own analyses of marijuana, only to conclude that it should remain a Schedule I controlled substance. The primary reason for the denial of petitions and recommendations against reclassification is the lack of sufficient high-quality medical research to recognize the drug as having medicinal value (see Chapter 11).

Why does this classification matter? By definition, Schedule I substances incur the harshest legal penalties for distribution and possession. In light of marijuana being classified as a Schedule I controlled substance, many jurisdictions around the country have taken steps to decriminalize the possession of small amounts of marijuana, recognizing the enormous burden that prosecuting this particular crime places on the present-day criminal justice system and communities.

In a recent attempt to reclassify marijuana, a lawsuit was filed against Attorney General Jeff Sessions and the DEA in a U.S. District Court claiming that the current scheduling of marijuana violates due process, as it lacks a rational basis. The hope was that reclassification would pave the way to national legalization of marijuana. The federal judge denied the reclassification request, again leaving marijuana as a Schedule I controlled substance. Congressional proposals are currently addressing the issue of rescheduling marijuana within the CSA.

Sources: Nordrum, A. (February 2015). Why is Marijuana a Schedule I Drug? *International Business Times.* http://www.ibtimes.com/why-marijuana-schedule-i-drug-1821426; Madappa, A. (February 2018). Marijuana to Stay a Schedule I Drug, Federal Judge Denies Reclassification. *International Business Times: Inforwars,* https://www.infowars.com/marijuana-to-stay-a-schedule-i-drug-federal-judge-denies-reclassification/.

The rate of incarceration in 1972 rose from 161 U.S. residents per 100,000 to 707 U.S. residents per 100,000 in 2012, by far the highest in the world.[41] Moreover, the rate of incarceration was much higher for minority and low-income populations. After a long period of "tough on crime" legislation aimed at drug offenders in particular, there are signs now of a shift toward a more liberal crime control agenda.

While the trend of marijuana legalization and decriminalization is a reversal of the earlier stance by FBN commissioner Harry Anslinger in the 1930s and 1940s who deemed marijuana as a "killer weed" (see Chapter 11), cannabis, from which marijuana is derived, remains classified as a Schedule I controlled substance by the U.S. federal government. Changing marijuana from a Schedule I to a Schedule II drug would have major ramifications, among them being the fact that doctors are permitted to write prescriptions for Schedule II but not Schedule I drugs. While some changes in the American landscape have occurred that suggest a more liberal viewpoint toward drug-taking behavior, there is still resistance among some government officials against making further departures from conservative drug-control policies. Chapters 4–7 in Part Two will explore in more detail the interrelationships among drug-taking behaviors, violence, and crime and the criminal justice system. The drug–crime relationship will be explored, as well as the range of criminal penalties for drug violations and the significant long-term consequences of these penalties on American society. Issues regarding the most effective strategies to be employed by law enforcement and corrections in combating drug crime and managing drug offenders will also be addressed. Overall, these chapters will ask a basic question: What is the most effective role of the criminal justice system in dealing with the challenges of drug abuse in America?

Summary

Drug Regulation in the Nineteenth Century: Laissez-Faire

- Medical advances in the mid-1800s allowed isolation of the active ingredients within many psychoactive substances. For example, morphine was identified as the major active ingredient in opium.
- During the nineteenth century, there was little regulation or control of drugs, and the U.S. government imposed no limitations on their distribution, sale, and promotion. The result was a century of widespread and uncontrolled medicinal and recreational drug use.

Drug Regulation in the Early Twentieth Century: Controls Begin

- The effects of drug dependence began to become a social concern. The two most important factors that fueled the movement toward drug regulation in the beginning of the twentieth century were (1) the abuse of patent medicines and (2) the association of drug use with socially marginalized minority groups.
- The Pure Food and Drug Act of 1906 was the first regulatory law on drugs in American history, requiring all packaged foods and drugs to list the ingredients on the label of the product.
- The Harrison Narcotics Tax Act (generally referred to as simply the Harrison Act) of 1914 was the first of several legislative efforts to impose criminal penalties on the use of opiates and cocaine.
- The Marijuana Tax Act of 1937 required that a tax stamp be issued to anyone selling marijuana. Tax stamps, however, were rarely issued, making marijuana essentially illegal. The drug was prohibited in this way until the Controlled Substances Act of 1970.
- Passage of the Eighteenth Amendment resulted in the national prohibition of alcohol in the United States from 1920 to 1933.

Drug Regulation in the Late Twentieth Century: A "War on Drugs"

- During the 1940s and 1950s, the use of illicit drugs such as heroin, cocaine, and marijuana was outside the mainstream of American life.
- Legislation during the 1950s imposed increasingly severe penalties for drug violations.
- In the 1960s and 1970s, the use of marijuana and hallucinogenic drugs among young people of all races and classes spread across the nation, along with an increase in problems related to heroin.
- President Richard Nixon declared a "total war on drugs," directing the reduction in drug abuse as one of America's

top priorities. Two aspects of this initiative were the international pressure on specific foreign nations to reduce the source of illicit drugs entering the United States and the establishment of drug-abuse treatment programs.

- The Controlled Substances Act of 1970 established a federal drug-control system based upon a classification of drugs into five Schedules of Controlled Substances, designated as Schedule I through V. Under this act, a drug has been "scheduled" based on its approved medical use, potential for abuse, and potential for producing dependence.
- By the end of the 1970s, drug-control policy in the United States shifted to a position of relative tolerance with regard to drug-taking behavior. In some U.S. states, the possession of small amounts of marijuana was decriminalized.
- A decline in heroin abuse in the 1980s was matched by an increase in cocaine abuse and the emergence of crack as a cheap, smokable form of cocaine.
- During the 1980s, a wave of federal drug legislation, including the Comprehensive Crime Control Act of 1984 and Anti-Drug Abuse Act of 1986 increased the penalties for the possession and trafficking of illicit drugs. As a result, the number of drug violators rose to record levels, and courts became backlogged with drug cases. The number of inmates in U.S. prisons and jails rose nearly 100 percent from 1985 to 1996.
- The 1990s can be characterized by a general lack of political interest in drug abuse, as the rate of incarceration of drug offenders continued to climb.

Drug Regulation in the Twenty-first Century: The Impact of 9/11

- After the events of September 11, 2001, the war on drugs became intertwined with the war on international and domestic terrorism.
- The USA PATRIOT Act of 2001 was enacted as a response to the September 11 attacks, increasing the ability for federal authorities to monitor communications related to possible terrorist activities, tighten money-laundering enforcement, and increase the protection of U.S. borders. These powers were directed toward other criminal acts, including drug trafficking.
- The reauthorization of the PATRIOT Act legislation, known as PATRIOT II, included a program to restrict access to over-the-counter cold medications that could be used in the manufacture of methamphetamine.
- Other regulations put into place include legislation targeting "raves," distribution of controlled substances by pharmacies and doctors online, measures aimed at safe prescription medication disposal (particularly opioids), and regulation of the compounds used to make synthetic marijuana.

Drug-Control Policy Today: Public Health and Public Safety

- The problems associated with drugs and alcohol can be broken down into the overlapping categories of public health concerns (treatment needs of drug abusers) and public safety concerns (a criminal justice response to drug abuse).

- The five-category classification of controlled substances established by the Controlled Substances Act (CSA) remains the official stance of the federal government with regard to the legal use of drugs. Substances in the first category, designated as having the lowest potential for medical use and the highest potential for abuse (Schedule I controlled substances) are those substances with the most restricted access to the public and the harshest criminal penalties for their possession or trafficking. Schedule II through V controlled substances have progressively greater potential for medical use, lower potential for abuse, and greater opportunities for access to the public.

- Ideology about drugs, rather than data on effective practices, often drives policy decisions. Liberal and conservative ideologies offer different strategies for dealing with drug crimes. A liberal ideology focuses on treatment and diversion from incarceration, while a conservative ideology focuses on a tough stance on drug law violations.

- There is some evidence of a shift from the more conservative legislation that has driven tough penalties for drug crimes since the 1970s to a more liberal response, as evidenced by the trend toward marijuana decriminalization and legalization.

Key Terms

Anti-Drug Abuse Act of 1986, p. 53

Anti-Drug Abuse Act of 1988, p. 53

Combat Methamphetamine Epidemic Act of 2005, p. 56,

Comprehensive Crime Control Act of 1984, p. 53

Comprehensive Drug Abuse Prevention and Control

Act of 1970 (Controlled Substances Act), p. 51

Comprehensive Methamphetamine Control Act of 1996, p. 55

Drug Enforcement Administration (DEA), p. 51

Harrison Act of 1914, p. 47

Illicit Drug Anti-Proliferation Act of 2003, p. 56

laissez-faire, p. 44

Marijuana Tax Act of 1937, p. 48

patent medicine, p. 45

Prohibition, p. 49

Pure Food and Drug Act of 1906, p. 45

Ryan Haight Online Pharmacy Consumer Protection Act of 2008, p. 56

Safe and Secure Drug Disposal Act of 2010, p. 56

speakeasies, p. 49

Synthetic Drug Abuse Prevention Act of 2012, p. 56

temperance movement, p. 48

Volstead Act of 1919, p. 49

USA PATRIOT Act of 2001, p. 55

USA PATRIOT Improvement and Reauthorization Act of 2005, p. 56

Review Questions

1. Describe the public attitude and the official stance of the federal government with respect to the use of opiate drugs prior to and subsequent to passage of the Harrison Act of 1914.

2. Discuss the positions for and against having a national prohibition of alcohol in the United States. Provide some reasons why a policy of national prohibition failed.

3. Discuss the developments in drug-control policies related to the "war on drugs" subsequent to the events of September 11, 2001.

4. Describe the criteria for listing a particular drug in the five-category system of scheduled controlled substances under the Controlled Substances Act of 1970, and provide two examples of drugs that are listed in each of the five categories.

5. Discuss the importance of ideology in driving the strategies used to combat the drug problem in America.

Critical Thinking: What Would You Do?

Given what we know about the impact of alcohol prohibition in the 1920s, what advantages and disadvantages might there be for a national legalization of marijuana? How might this impact on the way that marijuana is classified on the existing schedules of controlled substances, according to the Controlled Substances Act of 1970?

Endnotes

1. Fictionalized reflections of a modern-day Mexican-American, based on historical accounts of anti-Mexican prejudices in the first part of the twentieth century.

2. Musto, D. F. (1999). *The American disease: Origins of narcotics control* (3rd ed.). New York: Oxford University Press, pp. 1–28.

3. Goode, E. (2005), *Drugs in American Society* (6th ed.). New York: McGraw-Hill, pp. 86–115.

4. Ashley, R. (1975). *Cocaine: Its history, uses, and effects.* New York: St. Martin's Press, pp. 66–71. McGirr, L. *The war on alcohol: Prohibition and the rise of the American state.* New York: Norton, pp. 31–37. Musto, *The American dream*, p. 6.

5. Sneader, W. (1985). *Drug discovery: The evolution of modern medicines.* New York: Wiley, pp. 15–47. Stearns, P. N. (1998). Dope fiends and degenerates: The gendering of addiction in the early twentieth century. *Journal of Social History, 31*, pp. 809–814.

6. Bugliosi, V. (1991). *Drugs in America: The case for victory.* New York: Knightsbridge Publishers, p. 215.

7. Freud, S. (1884). Über Coca (On Coca). *Centralblatt für die gesammte Therapie, 2*, pp. 289–314. Translation by S. Pollak (1884, December). *St. Louis Medical and Surgical Journal, 47*, pp. 502–505.

8. Brecher, E. M. (1972). *Licit and illicit drugs.* Boston: Little, Brown, p. 3.

9. Musto, *The American disease*, pp. 1–28.

10. Filler, L. (1976). *The muckrakers.* Stanford, CA: Stanford University Press, p. 153. Young, J. H. (1961). *The toadstool millionaires: A social history of patent medicines in America before regulation.* Princeton, NJ: Princeton University Press.

11. Goldberg, J.; and Latimer, D. (2014). *Flowers in the blood: The story of opium.* New York: Skyhorse Publishing.

12. Helmer, J. (1975). *Drugs and minority oppression.* New York: Seabury Press.

13. Cloyd, J. W. (1982). *Drugs and information control: The role of men and manipulation in the control of drug trafficking.* Westport, CT: Greenwood.

14. Musto, *The American disease.* Goldberg and Latimer, *Flowers in the blood.*

15. Goldberg and Latimer, *Flowers in the blood.*

16. Musto, *The American disease.*

17. Lincoln, A. (1842/1989). Address to the Washingtonian temperance society of Springfield, Illinois. *Speeches and writings, 1832–1858.* New York: Library of America, p. 84.

18. Quotation in Lender, M. E. and Martin, J. K. (1982). *Drinking in America: A history.* New York: Free Press, p. 107. Okrent, D. (2010). *Last call: The rise and fall of Prohibition.* New York: Scribner.

19. Cashman, S. D. (1981). *Prohibition.* New York: Free Press. Coffey, T. M. (1975). *The long thirst: Prohibition in America, 1920–1933.* New York: Norton, pp. 196–198. Gusfield, J. R. (1963). *The symbolic crusade: Status politics and the American temperance movement.* Urbana, IL: University of Illinois Press. Sinclair, A. (1962). *The era of excess: A social history of the prohibition movement.* Boston: Little, Brown.

20. Woodiwiss, M. (1988). *Crime, crusaders and corruption: Prohibition in the United States, 1900–1987.* Totowa, NJ: Barnes and Noble.

21. Blocker, J. S. (2006). Did Prohibition really work? Alcohol prohibition as a public health innovation. *American Journal of Public Health, 96*, 233–243. Lerner, M. A. (2007). *Dry Manhattan.* Cambridge, MA: Harvard University Press.

22. Musto, D. F. (1996, April). Alcohol in American history. *Scientific American*, pp. 78–83. Sournia, J. C. (1990). *A history of alcoholism.* Cambridge, MA: Basil Blackwell, p. 122.

23. Sinclair, *The era of excess.*

24. Helmer, *Drugs and minority oppression.* Schlosser, E. (2003). *Reefer madness: Sex, drugs, and cheap labor in the American black market.* Boston: Houghton Mifflin, p. 245.

25. Brecher, *Licit and illicit drugs*, p. 188. Musto, *The American disease.*

26. Marshall, E. (1971). Cold turkey: heroin. The source supply. *New Republic, 165*, pp. 23–25.

27. Carter, J. E., Jr. (1979). President's message to the Congress on drug abuse. *Federal Strategy for Drug Abuse and Drug Traffic Prevention*, pp. 66–67.

28. Himmelstein, J. L. (1983). *The strange career of marijuana: Politics and ideology of drug control in America.* Westport, CT: Greenwood.

29. Miech, R. A.; Johnston, L. D.; O'Malley, P. M.; Bachman, J. G.; Schulenberg, J. E.; and Patrick, M. E. (2018). *Monitoring the future: National survey results on drug use, 1975–2017, Vol. I: Secondary school students.* Ann Arbor, MI: Institute for Social Research, The University of Michigan, Table 4.2.

30. Bureau of Justice Statistics (1998). *U.S. Department of Justice sourcebook of criminal justice statistics.* Washington, D.C.: Bureau of Justice Statistics.

31. Isaacson, A. (2003). Washington's new war in Colombia: The war on drugs meets the war on terror. *NACLA Report on the Americas, 36*, pp. 5–11.

32. Lacey, M. (2008, December 5). Hospitals now a theater in Mexico's drug war. *The New York Times*, pp. A1, A18. Shanker, T. (2008, December 23). Obstacle in bid to curb Afghan trade in narcotics. *The New York Times*, p. A6.

33. Drug Enforcement Administration, History, 2009–2013, U.S. Department of Justice, Washington, D.C.

34. Ibid.

35. Quinnipiac University National Poll. Release Details. August 3, 2017. Accessed from: https://poll.qu.edu/search-releases/search-results release-detail?ReleaseID=24777.

36. ProCon.org (2018, November 13). 33 legal medical marijuana states and DC. Assessed from: https://medicalmarijuana.procon.org/view.resource.php?resourceID=000881.

37. Males, M. (2011, November). *Misdemeanor marijuana arrests are skyrocketing and other California marijuana enforcement disparities.* San Francisco, CA: *Center on Juvenile and Criminal Justice.*

38. Walker, S. (2015). Sense and Nonsense about Crime, Drugs and Communities (8th ed.). Stamford, CT: Cengage Learning.

39. Cullen, F. and Jonson, C. (2012). *Correctional Theory: Context and Consequences.* Thousand Oaks, CA: Sage Publications.

40. National Institute of Justice (2016, May). Five Things about Deterrence. NCJ 247350. Washington, D.C.: U.S. Department of Justice.

41. Allen (2018, February). *Trump Says He Will Focus on Opioid Law Enforcement, Not Treatment.* Shots: Health News from NPR. Accessed from: https://www.npr.org/sections/health-shots/2018/02/07/584059938/trump-says-he-will-focus-on-opioid-law-enforcement-not-treatment.

42. National Research Council (2014). *The growth of incarceration in the United States: Exploring the Causes and Consequences.* Washington, D.C.: The National Academies Press. Accessed from: https://doi.org/10.17226/18613.

PART TWO
Drugs, Crime, and Criminal Justice

chapter 4

Drugs and Crime

In 2017, 78-year-old physician Shepherd Odom pleaded guilty in Montgomery Alabama to charges of drug distribution and conspiracy to commit money laundering. The charges stemmed out of an ongoing investigation of a "pill mill" operating out of his clinic. Although Dr. Odom had sold his interest in the business to his partner, Dr. Gilberto Sanchez (age 55)—who also pleaded guilty to drug distribution, health-care fraud, and money laundering—he had remained involved in the business's affairs.

According to court records, Dr. Odom wrote multiple prescriptions for fentanyl patches to patients without any medical justification. As with other "pill mills," most of the controlled substances unlawfully dispensed were opioids. In conjunction with his partner, Dr. Odom also engaged in money laundering from the illegal drug distribution in the practice, through transfers of proceeds by Dr. Sanchez into Dr. Odom's personal checking account. In June 2018, Dr. Odom received a sentence of five years' probation and fined $750,000. On consideration of Dr. Odom's age, his sentence was considerably lighter than a potential 20 years in prison.

The collaboration of the Drug Enforcement Administration (DEA), Internal Revenue Service (IRS), Department of Health and Human Services (DHHS), Montgomery County Sheriff's office, Alabama Board of Medical Examiners, Montgomery Police Department, and

After you have completed this chapter, you should have an understanding of the following:

- The distinctions among drug-defined crime, drug-related crime, and drug-using lifestyle
- The drug–crime connection in juveniles
- The drug–crime connection in adult offenders
- Psychopharmacological circumstances in drug-related crime
- Economically compulsive circumstances in drug-related crime
- Systemic circumstances in drug-related crime
- Social structures in illicit drug trafficking
- Gangs and drug-related crime
- Money laundering and drug-related crime

Opelika Police Department in the successful prosecution of Dr. Odom underscores the importance of coordination among criminal justice and public health agencies in criminal cases of this kind.[1]

For law enforcement officers and other criminal justice professionals who contend with drugs and crime on a daily basis, the drug–crime connection is all too real and an inarguable fact of contemporary society. For the general public, the news headlines about "drive-by shootings" and "neighborhoods under siege" reinforce the common assumption that drugs and crime are inextricably bound together.

Criminal justice researchers also do not dispute the existence of a drug–crime connection. Drug abuse is a clear risk factor for criminal behavior. Hence, those who engage in regular drug abuse are more likely to become justice involved, and with continued use, are more likely to be repeat offenders.[2] Many paths link illegal drug use and crime. Illegal drug use in and of itself can lead to arrest. Drug users also tend to spend time with other drug users, which puts them at increased risk for a range of criminal behaviors. Users often sell drugs or engage in other criminal behavior, such as theft, to feed their addiction. Manufacturers and dealers are often motivated by money rather than addiction, but also tend to engage in a range of criminal behavior, such as assault and extortion. This chapter will explore the various paths between drug use and crime, as well as the nature of this relationship. Does drug use lead to crime or does crime lead to drug use? Is there an alternative explanation for the undeniable link between drug use and crime?

> **drug-defined crime:** A violation of laws that prohibit the possession, use, distribution, and manufacture of illegal drugs.

Defining the Terms

In order to understand the complexities of the drug–crime connection, it is important to differentiate three general categories of the drug–crime relationship: (1) drug-defined crimes, (2) drug-related crimes, and (3) drug-using lifestyle.

Drug-defined Crimes

Drug-defined crimes are offenses in violation of laws prohibiting the possession, distribution, or manufacture of specific drugs or specific quantities of drugs. The drugs in question have been identified as controlled substances under the federal Controlled Substances Act (see Chapter 3) or state law. The possession of cocaine or heroin, the manufacture of LSD or other hallucinogens, and the sale of methamphetamine are all examples of drug-defined offenses, though the severity of the offenses and the penalties imposed vary widely (see Chapter 5). Naturally, offenses involving Schedule I controlled substances, which are regarded as having the greatest potential for abuse and with no accepted medical use, carry the most severe penalties.

For the most part, drug-control laws are uniform across jurisdictions in the United States, allowing us to speak of a drug-defined crime in the same way no matter where we are in the country. But in a few instances, federal authorities and state authorities may have different positions on whether a certain form of drug-taking behavior is a drug-defined crime. The nonmedical use of marijuana, for example, qualifies as a drug-defined crime on a federal level and in all U.S. states other than those that have legalized marijuana possession. One U.S. state may classify a particular drug under a different schedule of controlled substances than another U.S. state. The issues surrounding medical marijuana and nonmedical use of marijuana will be examined in Chapter 11.

The impact of drug-defined crimes on the criminal justice system and on society at large is immense. Consider these statistics:

Numbers Talk. . .

1,664	Number of armed pharmacy robberies in the United States in 2015 and 2016. Top-ranked states for armed robberies were California, Indiana, and Ohio.
36	Percentage of high school youth in the United States who in 2017 reported ever using marijuana.
20	Percentage of youths in grades 9–12 in the United States who reported in 2017 being either offered, sold, or given an illicit drug by someone on school property.

Sources: Information courtesy of the Office of Diversion Control, Drug Enforcement Administration, U.S. Department of Justice, Washington, D.C. Kann, L.; McManus, T.; Harris, W.; Shanklin, S.; et al. (2018, June 15). Youth Risk Behavior Surveillance—United States, 2017. *Morbidity and Mortality Weekly Report.* Atlanta, GA: Centers for Disease Control and Prevention, U.S. Department of Health and Human Services.

- In 2016, of the approximately 10.7 million arrests in the United States, the highest number (nearly 1.6 million) was made for a drug-defined criminal offense.[3]

- Roughly 84 percent of drug-defined criminal offenses in 2015 were for *possession* of a controlled substance; approximately 39 percent involved marijuana (a drop of 10 percentage points since 2013); 20 percent involved heroin, cocaine, or their derivatives; 5 percent involved synthetic or manufactured drugs; and 20 percent involved other controlled substances.[4]

- Nearly half (92,000) of all federal prisoners were serving time for a drug-defined offense. Among female prisoners, 59 percent were serving time for a drug offense.[5]

Drug-related Crimes

In contrast to drug-defined crimes, **drug-related crimes** are offenses that do not involve a violation of a drug law *per se*, but rather involve a violation of a law of some other type. The criminal act is, in some way, associated with illicit drug-taking behavior.

In 1985, Paul J. Goldstein published a seminal article on a conceptual framework for understanding the connection between drugs and violent behavior, presenting a model that has become a widely adopted conceptual tool for researches in this field. In his Tripartite Model, there are three basic categories under which drug-related violence may occur (Figure 4.1).

- In the first category, an act of drug-related violence is committed as a result of the perpetrator being under the influence of the drug itself at the time of an aggressive act. Symptoms of intoxication are an obvious cause for such behavior in most cases, but it is possible that withdrawal symptoms could be the instigating factor in drug-related violence, as long as the withdrawal symptoms have a direct influence on the behavior at the time. The assumption is that the drug intoxication (or withdrawal from it) reduces the customary inhibition we have over our actions and, as a result, we become aggressive and violent. These circumstances are collectively referred to as **psychopharmacological violence**.

- In the second category, an act of drug-related violence is committed because of the perpetrator's need to gain money for a future purchase of drugs. Robbery (particularly armed robbery), unlike other forms of theft, is classified as a violent offense, since it involves taking property from a person by force or threat of force. Robbery for the purpose of supporting a drug habit would therefore fall under this category, which includes pharmacy robberies, to be discussed later in the chapter (see Portrait). These circumstances are collectively referred to as **economically compulsive violence**.

- In the third category, an act of drug-related violence is committed based on participation in the business of drug trafficking (see Chapter 2) or in a subculture with involvement in an ongoing pattern of drug-taking behavior. Associated activities in this category of drug-related crimes include violent acts exhibited by a dealer toward a user or another dealer for stealing drugs or money, or gang violence that is related to drug-dealing activities. These circumstances are collectively referred to as **systemic violence** (Figure 4.1).[6]

> **economically compulsive violence:** A drug-related crime in which violence is committed in order to obtain money to buy drugs.
>
> **systemic violence:** A drug-related crime in which aggressive acts occur as part of a pattern of violent behavior when existing in an organization that is involved in illicit drug trafficking and distribution.

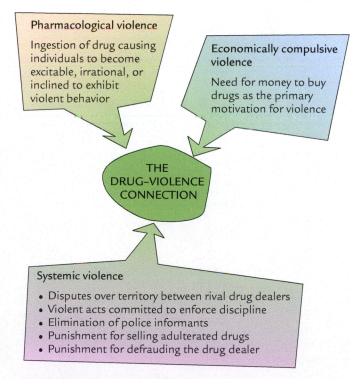

FIGURE 4.1

The Goldstein Tripartite Model of drugs and violence, showing the importance of distinguishing three major types of drug-related violence.

Source: Based on the model presented in Goldstein, P. (1985). The drug-violence nexus: A tripartite framework. *Journal of Drug Issues,* 15(4): 493–506.

> **drug-related crimes:** An offense in which a drug contributes to the commission of a crime, either by virtue of the drug's psychopharmacological effects, the economic need to secure the drug, or drug trafficking.
>
> **psychopharmacological violence:** A drug-related crime in which a violent act is committed while the perpetrator is under the influence of a particular psychoactive substance, with the implication that the drug itself caused the drug-related violence to occur by altering one's mental state.

In many cases, drug-related crimes are violent in nature, but there are also instances of drug-related criminal activities that do not involve violence. Goldstein's Tripartite Model could be applied to these nonviolent criminal behaviors as well (see Figure 4.2). For example, being under the influence of a substance impairs judgment and might contribute to poor decision-making. Poor decision-making might accompany a range of impulsive, yet nonviolent, criminal behaviors, such as joy riding, vandalizing of property, or driving under the influence. These instances would fall under the category of *pharmacological crime*. The embezzlement of funds in a company in order to support the expenses of chronic cocaine abuse would seldom involve violent behavior, yet such instances would fall under the category of *economically compulsive crime*. Chronic drug users will often steal money and property from family members to support a drug habit or break into unoccupied dwellings (breaking and entering), circumstances that would not be a violent offense, yet would fall under the category of economically compulsive crime. Likewise, money laundering of funds acquired through drug-trafficking transactions would not necessarily

involve violent behavior, but it would qualify as a *systemic crime*. Systemic crimes also include prostitution activities, which are often committed to support a drug habit. In some cases, the categories described here may not be mutually exclusive. Imagine that a drug user's withdrawal symptoms were so severe and money was so scarce that the drug user stole money or drugs from another drug dealer to support his or her drug habit. All three categories of drug-related criminal activity would apply under these circumstances.

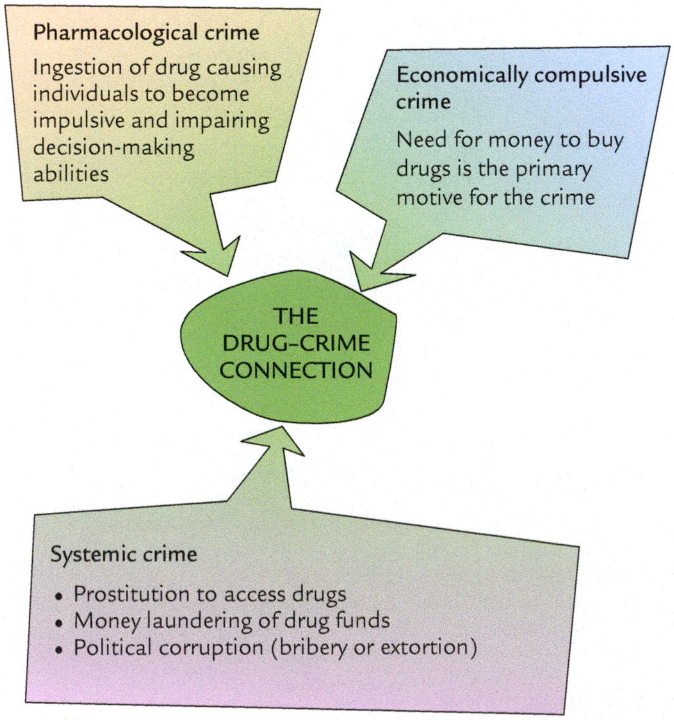

While the Goldstein model is not perfect, its significance lies in the fact that it has enabled criminal justice professionals and drug-control policy-makers to make a clear distinction between drug-related crimes caused directly by drug use (psychopharmacological) and drug-related crimes driven by money (economically compulsive and systemic). Unfortunately, it is impossible to arrive at an overall proportion of drug-related crimes in each category, since there are so many variables to consider, such as the abused drug in question, the historical period being examined, and the society in which these crimes are committed. Nonetheless, there is no question that the share of violence in economically compulsive and systemic categories far exceeds that of psychopharmacological violence. In other words, drug-related crime and violence can be viewed more as a matter of drug marketing and drug buying than as a matter of drug use *per se*.[7]

The images of violence associated with drug-related crimes that are psychopharmacological or economically compulsive in nature (sexual assaults while under the influence of a drug, armed robberies carried out in order to gain drug money) are the images that most often come to mind. However, it can be argued that violence associated under systemic circumstances have the potential for being the most intense and socially far-reaching. The social violence associated with gangsters involved in liquor trafficking during the Prohibition era in the 1920s and the violent urban lifestyle of individuals in drug trafficking at the height of the crack cocaine epidemic in the late 1980s (Chapters 3 and 10) are two examples from the past. Of course, a prime example is the culture of violence associated with the present-day global illicit drug trade. As we saw in Chapter 2, systemic violence has been carried out in order to settle territorial disputes among rival international drug-trafficking groups. At a local level, systemic violence has been carried out to impose punishments for defrauding a drug dealer or being a police informant, to intimidate public officials, or simply to assert the authority of the leader of the group over its members. Later in the chapter, we will examine the culture of violence in certain types of gangs and the forms of drug-related crime that occur in the context of a deviant subculture.

Drug-using Lifestyle

Drug-using lifestyle is the third category often used to describe the drug–crime relationship. This category focuses more on the intersection of drugs and crime based on a more general deviant lifestyle. Drug abusers often fail to participate in conventional activities, such as legal work and recreation.

Pharmacological crime
Ingestion of drug causing individuals to become impulsive and impairing decision-making abilities

Economically compulsive crime
Need for money to buy drugs is the primary motive for the crime

THE DRUG–CRIME CONNECTION

Systemic crime
- Prostitution to access drugs
- Money laundering of drug funds
- Political corruption (bribery or extortion)

FIGURE 4.2

The Goldstein Tripartite Model of drugs and violence, as applied to nonviolent criminal behaviors.

Source: Based on the model presented in Goldstein, P. (1985). The drug-violence nexus: A tripartite framework. *Journal of Drug Issues, 15*(4): 493–506.

In addition, due to their drug-using lifestyle, they tend to be exposed to a myriad of risk factors for criminal behavior. Hence, drug-using lifestyle looks beyond the drug use itself and effects from that use, as well as ancillary criminal behaviors drug users and dealers engage in to access drugs. This category examines how the drug-involved lifestyle leads to a pattern of criminal justice involvement.

Risk factors for criminal behavior are well established in the literature. Specifically, risk factors have been identified that predict the likelihood of repeat offending. Top among these risk factors are criminal history, criminal attitudes, criminal associates, and antisocial personality features. Other important risk factors are substance abuse, lack of prosocial leisure activities, lack of education/employment, and lack of family attachment and support. The more risk factors that are present, the more likely a person is to engage in a future law violation.[8]

When you think of an individual living a drug-using lifestyle, consider exposure to these risk factors. Individuals who use on a regular basis tend to use with others, or at minimum regularly interface with drug dealers to access their supply (*criminal associates*). Spending time with criminal peers provides the opportunity for individuals to sharpen their own skills at illegal behaviors, like drug use and theft. Criminal peers also reinforce a type of thinking that is used to justify continued drug use or criminal behavior. For example, drug users may tell themselves, "My use isn't hurting anyone," or "My kids aren't affected—I never use in front of them," or "Their insurance will cover the cost of the stuff I stole" (*criminal thinking*). These individuals also spend much of their time using drugs or engaging in activities that enable them to access drugs, which leads to *unemployment* and a *lack of prosocial leisure activities*. Likewise, the focus for individuals with a drug-using lifestyle is on the short-term goals of doing what must be done to obtain and use drugs. Little focus is given to long-term goals like *educational achievements*. Finally, law-abiding family and friends often cutoff those with a drug-using lifestyle, as they have been burned too many times. Hence, the lifestyle of a drug user is often what leads to the revolving jail door. Even when individuals are motivated to stop using drugs, when they expose themselves to risk factors (old friends, old ways of thinking, or lack of productive activities like work or school), reoffending is easily predictable.

Lack of conventional activities and connections is another important factor that connects the drug-using lifestyle to crime. Consider a juvenile who has gotten into trouble for drug use. This youth might be moved from his or her neighborhood school to an alternative school, where he or she now spends every day with others also in trouble for delinquent behavior. If this youth did have friends that stayed out of trouble, responsible parents might disallow their child from hanging out with a friend that's been

arrested. This youth might have trouble getting a job or finishing school due to his delinquent history. Hence, both the exposure to criminal elements and lack of exposure to conventional elements creates risk for future offending behaviors. Both of these circumstances tend to be present for individuals with a drug-using lifestyle. Interventions to assist those with this lifestyle will be discussed in Chapter 7. The next section will explore how a person might fall into a drug-using lifestyle.

Perspectives on Drug Use and Crime

Historically, the process by which there is a connection between drug use and crime has been explored through three major perspectives.

- The first perspective is called the *enslavement model*, also referred to as the "medical model." It asserts that individuals become forced into a life of crime and drug abuse either because of social situations such as poverty or from a personal condition such as a physical disorder. In other words, criminal activity and drug use or abuse exist together, arising from a common adverse set of circumstances in one's life.

- The *predisposition model*, also referred to as the "criminal model," asserts that drug abusers are far from law-abiding citizens in the first place and that they have already been involved in criminal activity prior to initial drug use. A predisposition toward criminal activity is increased by the fact that criminals exist in social subcultures in which drug use is readily accepted and encouraged.

- The *intensification model*, essentially a combination of the previous perspectives, asserts that drug use tends to perpetuate a life of crime. In essence, according to this perspective, criminal careers have already begun in the life of the individual, but the degree of criminality is intensified by one's involvement with drug use. The intensification model is able to account for two basic conclusions in the drug–crime research literature: (1) criminal careers typically begin prior to drug use and (2) criminal activity declines substantially during times of drug abstinence.[9]

Collecting the Statistics on Drugs and Crime

In order to arrive at evidence-based conclusions about the relationship between drugs and crime, it is important to analyze the best available statistical data on this question. We will examine two sources of information: (1) information about adolescent drug use and juvenile delinquency and (2) information about adult drug use and criminal offenses.

drug-using lifestyle: Drug use and criminal behavior as part of a deviant way of life, characterized by lack of conventional activity and exposure to criminal risk factors.

Drugs and Delinquency

On odd-numbered years, the Centers for Disease Control and Prevention, an agency of the U.S. Department of Health and Human Services, conducts a nationwide survey of nearly 15,000 students in grades 9 through 12 through the Youth Risk Behavior Surveillance (YRBS) program. Behaviors assessed in the YRBS include alcohol, tobacco, and illicit drug use and sexual risk behaviors associated with unintended pregnancy or sexually transmitted diseases, as well as delinquent behaviors such as carrying a weapon or being in a physical fight.[10] Table 4.1 shows the prevalence rates of drug use and delinquent behaviors in 2009, 2011, 2013, 2015, and 2017.

Drawing upon responses in the YRBS survey, researchers found a strong relationship between drug use and delinquency. Twice as many students who reported consuming five or more drinks in a row within a few hours on at least one day (the criterion for binge drinking, see Chapter 13), using marijuana one or more times, or even using cocaine one or more times also reported carrying a weapon or engaging in a fight on at least one day in the past year, when compared to students who consumed fewer than five drinks, did not use marijuana, or did not use cocaine. While there have been changes in prevalence rates and delinquent behaviors among adolescents sampled in the YRBS program in succeeding years (see Table 4.1), it is not unreasonable to assume that the relationship between drug use and delinquent behaviors has remained basically the same.[11]

Drugs and Adult Crime

A federal data collection program called the Arrestee Drug Abuse Monitoring (ADAM II) survey provides information about drug use among men who have been arrested for any criminal offense. Under this program, all males arrested in five selected U.S cities are required to report prior use of 10 illicit drugs and submit to urinalysis tests (see Chapter 16) within 48 hours of their arrest. Figure 4.3 shows the percentage testing positive for four major illicit drugs (marijuana, cocaine, heroin, and methamphetamine), multiple drugs, and any of the 10 drugs being investigated.

ADAM II statistics indicate that drug use among an arrestee population is much higher than in the general U.S. population (see Chapter 1). In 2013, the last report conducted, at least two-thirds of the arrestees tested positive for at least one illicit drug, with the percentage varying from 63 percent in Atlanta, Georgia to 83 percent in Chicago and Sacramento, California. From 12 percent to 50 percent of arrestees (depending upon the city where an arrest was made) tested positive for more than one drug. The most common substances identified during testing were, in descending order, marijuana, cocaine, heroin, and methamphetamine. Distinct regional differences were noted, with methamphetamine use being identified with arrestees primarily in the western regions of the United States.[12]

Another survey examines drug use among criminal offenders at a later stage in the criminal justice process. In this study, prison inmates are interviewed to check the pattern of illegal drug use prior to their incarceration. In 2002, one-half of them reported symptoms of a substance use disorder involving an illicit drug at a previous time and two-thirds had received drug treatment of some sort. The prevalence rate of severe substance use disorder (see Chapter 8) was especially high for property crimes, with the prevalence rate as high as 74 percent for those serving time for burglary.[13]

A more direct examination of the connection between drug use and adult crime, however, can be made through information provided by the *victim* of a criminal act. The 2008

TABLE 4.1

Prevalence rates for alcohol use, marijuana use, cocaine use, illegal prescription drug use, and selected risk behaviors among students in the youth risk behavior surveillance (YRBS) surveys in 2009, 2011, 2013, 2015, and 2017

	2009 (%)	2011 (%)	2013 (%)	2015 (%)	2017 (%)
Had five or more drinks of alcohol in a row (within a couple of hours) on at least one day in the past 30 days	24	22	21	18	14
Used marijuana one or more times in the past 30 days	21	23	23	22	20
Ever used any form of cocaine one or more times	6	7	6	5	5
Ever took prescription drugs without a doctor's prescription	20	21	18	17	14
Engaged in a fight one or more times in the past 12 months	32	33	25	23	24
Carried a weapon on at least one day in the past 12 months	18	17	18	16	16

Sources: Kann, L.; McManus, T.; Harris, W.; Shanklin, S.; et al. (2018, June 15). Youth Risk Behavior Surveillance—United States, 2017. *Morbidity and Mortality Weekly Report*. Atlanta, GA: Centers for Disease Control and Prevention.

Percentage Testing Positive for Any of Ten Drugs		Percentage Testing Positive				
0 20 40 60 80 100	Marijuana	Cocaine	Heroin	Methamphetamine	Multiple Drugs
Atlanta, GA — 63	34	33	6	<1	12
Chicago, IL — 83	52	24	14	<1	20
Denver, CO — 74	48	20	8	16	27
New York, NY — 73	44	32	8	0	23
Sacramento, CA — 83	60	7	18	51	50

FIGURE 4.3

Urinalysis results for illicit drug use among male adult arrestees in five U.S. cities in 2013.

Source: Based on data from the Office of National Drug Control Policy (2014, January). *ADAM II:2013 Annual report. Arrestee Drug Abuse Monitoring Program II.* Washington, D.C.: Office of National Drug Control Policy, Executive Office of the President, Tables 3.3–3.8.

National Crime Victimization Survey (NCVS) has addressed the extent to which the victim of a violent crime believed that the perpetrator was under the influence of alcohol or other drugs. As shown in Figure 4.4, nearly half of the victims (47 percent) were unable to say whether the perpetrator was under the influence of alcohol or drugs, but for those who had an opinion, approximately one-half of these victims felt that the perpetrator was either under the influence of alcohol, or drugs, or a combination of alcohol and drugs. In 14 percent of the cases, the perpetrator was identified as being specifically under the influence of alcohol, but in about three out of ten cases, the victim reported that the perpetrator was not under the influence of alcohol or drugs at the time of the crime. Surveys of victims of rape or sexual assault have indicated a similar pattern regarding the victim's perception of the perpetrator at the time of the crime (see Chapter 12).[14]

Surveys bearing on the *chronological sequence* of drug-taking behavior and adult crime, however, do not permit us to see the drug–crime connection as a clear *directional* cause-and-effect process. Several studies of drug users in Miami, conducted during the 1970s and 1990s, found that the only drug use that preceded the first crime they committed was the use of alcohol and marijuana. Use of more expensive drugs, such as heroin and cocaine, usually did not begin until two to four years after their first crime. A survey of inmates in Michigan, California, and Texas prisons found that only 20 percent of those who used drugs reported that their drug use began prior to their first crime, and more than 52 percent reported that they began using drugs and committing crimes at about the same time. The National Youth Survey Family Study, conducted by the University of Colorado, found that the initial involvement in criminal activity often *preceded* drug use. In a 10-year survey of more than 1,700 youths aged 11–17 years old, the first criminal offense preceded their first alcohol use in 63 percent of cases, and their first criminal offense preceded their first marijuana use in 93 percent of cases.[15]

Women, Drugs, and Crime

Males make up approximately 85 percent of the criminal justice population. It is therefore not surprising that aside from prostitution, females have lower arrest rates for all crime

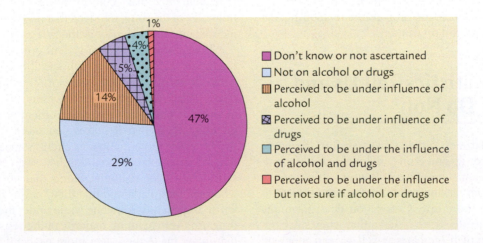

FIGURE 4.4

Perceptions of victims of a violent crime with regard to alcohol and/or drug use by the perpetrator at the time of the crime.

Source: Based on data from the Bureau of Justice Statistics (2011, May). *Criminal victimization in the United States, 2008. Statistical tables.* Washington, D.C.: Bureau of Justice Statistics, U.S. Department of Justice, Table 32.

categories. While males make up a sizably larger portion of the U.S. corrections population, the crimes leading to arrest and incarceration do vary by gender. Generally, females are less likely to commit violent crimes than males. In 2015, the majority of male offenders in state prisons were incarcerated for a violent offense (54 percent) versus 35 percent for women. Women were more likely than men to be incarcerated for a property offense (28 percent versus 18 percent) and for a drug offense (25 percent versus 15 percent).[16] Hence, while men are more likely to be arrested and incarcerated than women (leading to far more males in prison for a drug offense than females), when the type of crimes that lead to incarceration are examined, women are much more likely to be incarcerated for nonviolent drug and property offenses than males.

These data are consistent with the pathways theory of crime, which argues that a woman's path to the criminal justice system is quite different from the male pathway; justice involved girls and women often experience trauma and victimization, which leads to drug and alcohol abuse and eventual criminal justice involvement.[17] The economic marginalization of women in society also makes it more difficult for women to meet bail as well as court fines and fees. Mandatory minimum sentences have also lead to higher growth rates in incarceration for women, as first time, non-violent female drug offenders who would have typically gotten community supervision were serving lengthy mandatory sentences for drug offenses.[18]

The rate of drug problems among women also appears higher for those incarcerated. In a special government report examining drug problems among prisoners, more females in prison (47 percent) and jail (60 percent) were reported using drugs in the month before their current offense than males in prison (38 percent) and jail (54 percent). Drug dependence and abuse was also higher among female versus male state prisoners (69 percent versus 57 percent) and sentenced jail inmates (72 percent versus 62 percent).[19] These data, along with the high rates of reported childhood and adult victimization among females, also lend support to the pathways theory of crime for women. Hence, the drug–crime relationship appears particularly impactful on women.

What the Statistics Tell Us and What They Do Not

Undoubtedly, the statistics in the surveys confirm the opening supposition that drugs and crime are linked together, but, as persuasive as they may be, most of them establish only a *correlation* between drugs and crime, not a causal relationship between drugs and crime. Correlation does not imply causation. In other words, if we observe that when drug use increases, criminal activity increases as well, we can conclude that the two behaviors are correlated. Yet we cannot say *necessarily* that there are no directional cause-and-effect relationships going on. If there is a cause-and-effect relationship between *a third variable* and drug use and, at the same time,

a cause-and-effect relationship between that variable and criminal activity, then it is likely that there will be a correlation between drug use and criminal activity as a result.

As an example, consider the relationship between substance use and delinquency discussed earlier. It may be that a youth begins to get into trouble with the law due to a pattern of substance abuse. However, it could also be that a youth who engages in skipping school, theft, or fights also begins to use alcohol and drugs as part of a continuum of "rebellious" behavior. It might also be that a youth is associating with a peer group that engages in problem behaviors, so that spending time with negative peers leads to a range of delinquent acts, including substance abuse. This is quite different than concluding that it was the substance use itself that caused the youth to engage in delinquent behavior.

Despite the limitations, statistical information about drug-related crime allows us some insight into the nature of drugs and crime. In particular, we can examine the important features of three specific forms of drug-related crime.

Regarding Psychopharmacological Crime

The ADAM II surveys have the potential for gaining an insight into a causal relationship (in this case, a psychopharmacological relationship) between drug use and crime, but even here, the presence of a drug in the bloodstream of an arrestee after an interval up to 48 hours following the arrest does not necessarily indicate that the arrestee was under the influence of the drug *at the time of the crime*. The main criticism of pharmacological explanations from the standpoint of ADAM II data rests on the fact that traces of a drug (referred to as metabolites) can be detected in a standard urinalysis drug test for a period of time after the user no longer feels intoxicated by the drug. This length of time can range from a matter of days to two months in the case of marijuana (see Table 13.3). Therefore, testing positive for a drug only indicates that the individual *might* have committed the crime while under the influence of the drug, if indeed that drug has the potential for inciting criminal behavior in the first place.

If we are speaking of a violent crime, it is important to recognize the degree to which specific drugs might be capable of inciting violent behavior. In some instances, the physiological nature of the drug itself makes the possibility of violence quite unlikely. A prominent effect of marijuana, for example, is that it makes you more lethargic than active, in effect quite mellow in circumstances in which there may be some interpersonal conflict. A study of 559 males in Philadelphia, for example, found that 96 percent of those who used marijuana said that they "never" or "almost never" felt an urge to hurt someone while under the influence of the drug. An overwhelming majority of the respondents said that marijuana made them feel more peaceful and passive than before its use.[20] Yet, the Philadelphia study did find that individuals who used marijuana were significantly more likely than nonusers to have committed multiple criminal offenses. The results of this study show that marijuana use on its own may not have caused crime *per se*, but may have been part of a lifestyle of people who commit crime. The relationship may be due to the fact that the same types of people who are most likely to commit crime—young males of lower socio-economic status—are also the same types of people who are most likely to use drugs (Drugs ... in Focus).[21]

Increased attention has turned to the use of synthetic cannabinoids or synthetic marijuana (e.g., "Spice" or "K2"). This drug has been on the rise, likely due to its availability on the Internet and its ability to escape detection with most drug tests. Unlike traditional marijuana, intoxication with synthetic cannabinoids has been associated with symptoms such as paranoia, auditory/visual hallucinations, agitation, and suicidal ideation. The term "Spiceophrenia" has been coined to exemplify the more extreme side effects from this class of drugs, some of which could be associated with violence. A similar case can be made from the instances of violent behavior among phencyclidine (PCP) abusers (see Chapter 12). [22]

In terms of its psychopharmacological effect, heroin produces a passive state of mind (hence the expression, "being on the nod"), thus reducing the inclination toward violent behavior. In fact, as rates of heroin abuse rise, the incidence of crimes against individuals (as opposed to crimes against property) declines.[23]

In contrast, psychoactive stimulants such as methamphetamine and cocaine or the hallucinogen PCP (known as "angel dust") produce an on-edge frame of mind and a social paranoia that can potentially lead to violent behavior (see Chapters 10 and 11). In the case of crack cocaine, crack smokers have the reputation of being irritable, paranoid, and inclined to lash out at another person at the slightest provocation. Yet, even in these cases, we need to be careful in interpreting statistical data linking violence with the abuse of these drugs. For example, in a study conducted at an Atlanta medical center, more than half of all patients being treated for acute cocaine intoxication were reported to be aggressive, agitated, and paranoid just prior to and at the time of hospital admission. It is impossible to determine whether these patients were mentally unstable prior to their taking cocaine. People who have long-standing psychological disorders may be overrepresented in any population of cocaine abusers.[24]

Of all the psychoactive drugs that we could consider in the context of psychopharmacological violence, the one with the widely reported links to violent behavior toward individuals is *alcohol*. Of course, millions of people drink alcohol and never become violent, but the chances that violence will occur are increased when people are drinking. In such cases, the violence is clearly pharmacological because the effects of being drunk from the ingestion of alcohol are apparent almost immediately. There is a very short lag time between alcohol consumption and behavioral consequences, and there is little doubt that a causal relationship is operating.

In the area of violence against women alone, 30 percent of women worldwide who have been in a relationship report that they have experienced some form of physical or sexual violence by their partner. Risk factors for both intimate partner and sexual violence include harmful use of alcohol.[25] Males

involved in violent spousal abuse commonly report having been drinking or having been drunk during the times that abuse has occurred. Use of alcohol decreases inhibitions as well as rational thought and decision-making skills. Other risk factors for intimate partner violence include poor communication between partners and marital discord and dissatisfaction. Regular, problematic use of alcohol contributes to these relationship problems as well. Alcohol abuse poses as a risk factor for both perpetrators of violence as well as victims, suggesting individuals are also more likely to be victimized physically or sexually when intoxicated. Moreover, violent crime outside the home is strongly related to alcohol intoxication. The more violent the crime, the greater is the probability that the perpetrator of the crime was drunk while committing it.

On the one hand, from the statistical evidence, it is clear that more crime and violence is alcohol related than is related to all forms of illicit drugs combined. Perhaps, this is because so many people consume alcohol so often in their lives. In other words, it may be that the preeminence of alcohol in psychopharmacological crime is simply because the hours of alcohol intoxication exceed the hours of intoxication from the entire range of all illicit drugs. However, alcohol is also the champion in terms of violent acts *per hour of intoxication*, far ahead of marijuana, which is the most prevalent of illicit drugs. Therefore, it is not the overall availability of alcohol in our society nor the number of people involved in alcohol consumption that is of issue here.

On the other hand, for any psychoactive substance that we may consume—licit or illicit, dependence or nondependence producing, alcoholic or nonalcoholic—the majority of occasions of chemical intoxication in our lives do not motivate us to commit a crime. As discussed earlier, victimization surveys have shown that, from the victim's perspective, alcohol intoxication on the part of the offender accounts for only 14 percent of instances in which a violent crime has occurred. On the other side of the coin, 76 percent of these instances do not involve alcohol intoxication (or at least the victim is not aware of the offender being drunk).[26]

Whether or not alcohol or other drugs have a direct bearing on the committing of a criminal offense, their psychopharmacological effects may be sought after and experienced in conjunction with criminal activity. Drugs may be used before a criminal offense to bolster courage in the planning of criminal activity or afterward to celebrate success. Prostitutes may turn to alcohol and drugs as a method of coping with the stresses of their way of life. In these cases, psychopharmacological factors in drug-taking behavior are intertwined with a criminal lifestyle rather than a critical element in the instigation of a specific crime.

Regarding Economically Compulsive Crime

The evidence bearing on economically compulsive crime in the late 1980s and 1990s is overwhelming and from today's perspective quite frightening. A 1990 study of 611 adolescent (principally crack cocaine) users in Miami, Florida, for

Drugs . . . in Focus

From HeroinGen and CrackGen to BluntGen: The Rise and Fall of Drugs and Violence

From a sociological point of view, the impact of drug use on violent crime over the last 40 years or so can be examined in terms of the dominant drug of abuse at a particular time. Sociologists Bruce D. Johnson, Andrew Golub, and Eloise Dunlap have divided the drug scene in inner-city New York City into three distinct eras, each defined by a specific drug subculture and set of shared social norms. Each subculture has been guided by a set of expected behaviors that have dictated what subculture participants must do, what they must refrain from doing, and what the consequences are for noncompliance. An agreed-upon set of norms defining their conduct allows participants to function as if on "automatic pilot."

The HeroinGen

According to their analysis, the period 1960–1973 was the era of heroin injection and a subculture of heroin-abusing participants (the heroin-injection generation, or HeroinGen for short). In the peak year of 1968, the HeroinGen members were between 15 and 25 years old. Quite often, they had grown up in a subculture of alcohol abuse, with their parents being heavy alcohol consumers. In mid-adolescence, HeroinGen members were turned on to marijuana, but by 1964–1965, heroin had hit the New York streets in a major way. The promise was that heroin would give them a better high than marijuana or alcohol, and a process of introduction into heroin use began. A dominant feature of the subculture was the act of robbery. Handguns were rarely carried or used; instead, knives and blunt instruments were the weapons of choice.

The CrackGen

Crack cocaine became available around 1984 in New York City and other metropolitan communities. Subculture members, born between 1955 and 1969, came of age during the height of the cocaine/crack era (1985–1989). For these individuals, called the Crack Generation or CrackGen, conduct norms were quite different from those of the HeroinGen. Crack use was carried out in intensive binges. Hyperactivity, rapid cycling between euphoria and dysphoria, and paranoia dominated their behavior.

Sales of crack became so profitable that the entire illicit drug industry revolved around it. Vicious competition between crack dealers ensued. The key factor was "keeping the money and product straight." At this point, handguns became commonplace. There were 218 recorded drug-related homicides in New York in 1988 alone, as well as other forms of systemic violence.

The BluntGen

By the 1990s, remaining members of the CrackGen were in their thirties and increasingly isolated as they continued their compulsive drug-taking behavior. In their place were members of the Marijuana/Blunt subculture (BluntGen, for short). Born in the 1970s, the BluntGen smoked marijuana as a cigar. They would combine funds in a peer group to buy marijuana, occasionally committing a crime to get money for their purchases. They saw no need for handguns.

Evidence shows that members of the BluntGen viewed the ravages of the lives of HeroinGen and CrackGen members as a reason to limit their pursuit of drug-taking behavior to the use of marijuana and alcohol. The subculture of assault and disregard for human life had been transformed into a subculture of "stay safe, stay alive." Rates of violence and nondrug-related criminality, relative to that of an earlier era, declined sharply.

Conduct norms of the BluntGen have affected alcohol abuse in a positive way, and there are indications that patterns of drug-taking behavior may have changed. From studies in California and other U.S. states that have legalized medical marijuana in recent years, marijuana has become a substitute for alcohol for young people, reducing the problems typically associated with alcohol. Technically, marijuana in these states is legal only for medical use, but it is nonetheless widely available. Information about a possible decline in alcohol abuse in U.S. states, where marijuana is legal for either medical or nonmedical use, is not yet available.

Note: Since 2006, the drug subculture in America has changed dramatically. It is likely that there is a new "OpioidGen" era that is quite different from the HeroinGen era of years past.

Sources: Johnson, B. D.; Golub, A.; and Dunlap, E. (2006). The rise and decline of hard drugs, drug markets, and violence in inner-city New York. In A. Blumstein and J. Wallman (Eds.), *The crime drop in America*. New York: Cambridge University Press, pp. 164–206. Quotations on pages 173, 178, 180, and 186. Nagourney, A.; and Lyman, R. (2013, October 27). Few problems with cannabis for California. *The New York Times*, p. A1, A19.

example, showed that 59 percent participated in 6,669 robberies over a 12-month period, averaging 31 robberies per individual. While most of these robberies were carried out to obtain drugs, they were not always break-ins and holdups. Sometimes the crime involved the theft of drugs from drug dealers or other users.[27] Nonetheless, a large proportion of the crimes committed to obtain drug money involved violent acts directed against individuals within the community. Particular targets included storekeepers, children, and the elderly. In a later study, reported in 1998, interviews with 699 crack cocaine users in Miami regarding the number of crimes and arrests during the previous 90 days revealed that more than

1,700,000 offenses had been committed, roughly 28 per person each day! However, offenses included procuring drugs, drug sales, prostitution, and gambling—all activities that could occur multiple times in a 24-hour period. Nonetheless, there were nearly 5,000 offenses involving robberies and assaults. Roughly seven crimes of this sort were committed per person over the 90-day period. Yet, fewer than 1 percent of the offenses resulted in arrest.[28]

While the prevalence rate for drug-related crime is lower than it was during the 1990s and the percentage of arrests per drug-related offense is considerably higher, the incidence of economically compulsive crime is still high. According to a 2004 study of state prison inmates, about 4 in 10 of all property-crime offenders admitted that they committed their current offense in order to get money to buy drugs or to obtain drugs. Moreover, inmates incarcerated for a property offense were more likely to be diagnosed with a substance disorder than any other crime type.[29]

If economically compulsive crimes are indeed driven by money, to what extent are they related to "market conditions" (that is, the price of the drug at the time)? The dynamic features of economically compulsive crimes are important elements in public policy decisions about drug use. For example, if we artificially reduced the price of heroin (by providing a greater amount of heroin on the street), could we reduce economically compulsive crimes among heroin users?

In the early 1970s, when heroin abuse was particularly problematic, it was found that elevations in heroin prices (caused by reducing its availability) coincided with a higher level of property crime; when heroin prices were low, the crime level decreased. The implication was that heroin abusers committed property crimes in order to maintain a stable consumption of heroin. Therefore, the deliberate elevation of heroin prices tended to increase the incidence of property crime among heroin users. But price increases for heroin had

PORTRAIT

David Laffer: Pharmacy Robber and Killer of Four

Arguably the most famous bank robber in American history, Willie Sutton, was once asked by a reporter in an interview why, over a 40-year criminal career, he robbed banks. "Because that's where the money is," he explained. It has become a famous quote, and probably the most well-known quote by a lifelong criminal.

For a time, it was not the banks that were being robbed but the local pharmacies. Why pharmacies? To update Willie Sutton's explanation: "Because that's where the drugs were." To be more specific: "That's where the OxyContin was." During the years when cheap heroin had not yet been seen as an alternative to high-price OxyContin, opioid abusers with limited financial means turned to a criminal route. Pharmacy robberies became commonplace in practically every region in America, in states as disparate as Oklahoma, Ohio, California, and Oregon. The Drug Enforcement Administration (DEA) reported more than 800 drug-related pharmacy robberies in 2016, which was a slight decrease (5 percent) since 2015, but in several states, such as Indiana and California, the rate of pharmacy robberies had more than doubled since 2009.

In 2011, hundreds of armed robberies were reported across the country, but in one incident on Long Island, New York, the situation had gotten deadly. David Laffer (depicted here) killed four people in a robbery of a suburban pharmacy. Court records

revealed that he had acquired nearly 12,000 opioid pain medication pills in the four years leading to the robbery. Laffer was later convicted and sentenced to life imprisonment without parole.

From a street sale alone, the 80 mg dosage of OxyContin became a prime target for theft. A single pill at this dosage cost $80 on the street, so a heist of even a few bottles could add up to real money. Meanwhile, pharmacists had to contend with some difficult choices: Suspend all sales of OxyContin, depriving the many patients with genuine pain-control issues? Institute security measures such as those instituted by banks? Hire guards around the clock to protect themselves?

Some pharmacies (particularly those that were independently owned) upgraded their surveillance cameras, installed bulletproof glass-enclosed counters, and installed buzzers at the door for customers. Time-release locks on the safes used to store narcotics were put in place to reduce the number of burglaries. In one countermove, a pharmacist in Maine took to attaching a tracking device on specific bottles of OxyContin, reserved for a potential pharmacy robber, which successfully led to the location of the perpetrator. Some pharmacists greatly restricted their stock supplies of Oxycodone or OxyContin products and have no regrets in telling this to their customers.

Several U.S. states increased the minimum jail time for second-degree robbery,

when a pharmacist was threatened but no weapon was shown (a typical scenario in pharmacy robberies), from three months to three years. In the words of a county prosecutor in Washington State, this change was needed because word would travel fast on the street about what easy target pharmacies were and how much profit could be made from robberies.

While the incidences of armed robbery in a pharmacy received most of the media attention, a five-year analysis report of pharmacy experiences nationwide issued in 2015 by the Pharmacists Mutual Insurance Company concluded that break-ins were far more common, representing about 72 percent of pharmacy theft cases, followed by employee theft. A national pharmacy crime database, called RxPatrol, was established to monitor pharmacy theft, in cooperation with the DEA.

Sources: Brown, J. (2011, June 23). The oxycodone curse. Newsday, p. A8. Goodnough, A. (2011, February 7). Pharmacies under siege from robbers seeking drugs. The New York Times, p. A14. Peddie, S.; Van Sant, W.; and Lewis, R. (2012, January 8). The fear in the pharmacies. Newsday, p. A3, A4. Pharmacists Mutual Companies (2015). Pharmacy Crime: A review of Pharmacists Mutual Experience, Algona, IA. Information courtesy of the Drug Enforcement Administration, U.S. Department of Justice, Washington, D.C.

Credit: Suffolk County Police Department

no impact on the incidence of other forms of criminal behavior among heroin users nor did they reduce the number of heroin users themselves.[30]

Does the heroin price–property crime relationship, as noted in the 1970s, hold for other historical periods or other drugs of abuse? In the case of methamphetamine abuse during the 1990s, the picture appears to have been somewhat different. The passage of federal legislation beginning in 1996 greatly restricted public access to ingredients used in the manufacture of methamphetamine (see Chapter 10) and resulted in dramatically higher methamphetamine prices. Higher prices led to a general *reduction* in methamphetamine-related property crimes as well as a decline in methamphetamine use, particularly among light users. Since methamphetamine abuse was a relatively new phenomenon at the time, the preponderance of methamphetamine users were in a "light user" category. Evidently, fewer property crimes were committed because there were fewer light methamphetamine users to commit them. Heavy methamphetamine users showed less of a change in their drug usage or criminal behavior.[31]

The way in which property crime rates respond to higher drug prices, therefore, may depend on *the character of the drug user population.* Property crimes may be more likely to be reduced as drug prices increase when the population in question is comprised of significant numbers of newly initiated drug users. For these individuals, the level of drug usage would be relatively low, and they would be the ones who were inclined to give up the drug (perhaps switching to other forms of drug use) when the methamphetamine costs rise. The population of heroin users in the 1970s comprised fewer individuals of this type. Long-standing heroin users, less inclined to relinquish their drug of choice, would engage in greater levels of property crime as costs rise.

While the literature of drug-related economically compulsive crime has traditionally focused on heroin and cocaine use, it is important to point out that, in recent years, a more current example of economically compulsive crime has emerged in the form of pharmacy robberies carried out for the purpose of securing prescription pain medications, predominantly OxyContin. This chapter's Portrait depicts a particularly deadly incident of this type, occurring in 2011.[32] While in recent years, the availability of the less costly opioid, heroin, has increased, pharmacy robberies across the United States have only decreased slightly (actually increasing in some states). Perhaps this decreasing trend in pharmacy robberies will continue as heroin becomes increasingly easy to access, or robberies will continue to support those users who decide to avoid the overdose dangers of heroin, or decide that most costly pills are preferable to injections of street heroin.

Regarding Systemic Crime

The vast majority of drug-related crime in the United States stems from essentially three expensive illicit drugs: heroin, cocaine/crack cocaine, and methamphetamine. It has been estimated that these drugs represent 80 percent of all revenues in the black market of illicit drugs. It is no surprise that a combination of the costliness of compulsive drug-taking behavior and the limited incomes (at least from legitimate sources) of drug users would lead to drug-related crime.[33] Added to this situation is the dynamic pattern of supply and demand that gives, as we know, the upper hand to the drug supplier over the drug customer (Chapter 2). All of these factors provide the necessary ingredients for a thriving system of systemic crime.

In the world of systemic crime, it is difficult to separate criminality from drug use, in that the business of drug distribution *is built upon* drug use and the subculture of drug dealers is *defined by* criminality. A substantial number of drug users may become involved in drug distribution as their drug-using careers progress and hence become part of a criminal subculture that uses violence to maintain control over its operations. In general, there may not be a direct relationship between drug use and crime but rather an indirect relationship that has been called by the U.S. Department of Justice, hence the term **interactional circumstances**.

The prominence of systemic violence associated with crack cocaine abuse during the 1980s was particularly striking in the lives of young urban males. For those living in socioeconomic circumstances that offered few opportunities for future advancement, the enticement of acquiring great wealth, beyond anything that could be attained through legitimate means, was a strong factor in their participation in drug distribution operations. It was common for successful drug dealers to keep large stores of illicit drugs to show off their wealth and success; they were, in effect, role models in their society. Individuals recruited into crack cocaine distribution would become more likely to be involved in drug use, despite the warning that, as a drug seller, they should not be "their own best customer." Drug use would be an intrinsic part of an overall criminal lifestyle within a deviant subculture, in line with the subcultural recruitment and socialization theory of drug-taking behavior (Chapter 8).

As the involvement of a youth in crack distribution increased, it was more likely that the person would become involved in violent crime. The enormous value of the drug itself relative to its quantity (the contents of a plastic sandwich bag often being worth thousands of dollars) was a major factor in increasing the intensity of interpersonal relationships. Transactions were conducted under great uncertainty, as the other party could be a law enforcement informant.

In addition, the subculture was characterized by the most violent drug users being the people most highly regarded by young people. Many adolescents living in communities dominated by the crack cocaine market felt the need to prove that they could be brutal in order to avoid being harassed by their peers. It can be argued that the pressure to be an accepted member of such a community was more responsible for a drug abuser's committing frequent violent acts than the effects of the drugs themselves or the need for money to buy drugs.

interactional circumstances: The idea that there may not be a direct relationship between drug use and crime but rather an indirect relationship.

It is impossible to know how much of the violence among drug dealers during this era, or any period since then, can be attributed to the nature of illicit drug distribution operations or the inclination of individuals prior to their involvement. Particularly in the 1980s, violent drug dealers tended to live and carry out their operations in poor, inner-city neighborhoods, where violence was a common occurrence, independent of the illicit drug business. In other words, violent behavior might have been a "job description" in drug dealing markets. In a perverse example of natural selection, dealers who were dead or arrested and imprisoned over time made way for dealers who were better able to employ violence, intimidation, and manipulation by corruption for the purposes of maintaining their status and livelihood. The prominence of guns, particularly handguns, in this subculture tended to increase the lethality of the violence, and this element of the subculture continues today.[34]

Not surprisingly, when street sales of crack cocaine declined in the 1990s, there was an accompanying decline in homicide rates and violent crime in areas where crack sales had been dominant. When community policing procedures succeeded in breaking up drug gangs and large street-level drug markets, the result was a change in the pattern of drug buying and selling.[35] As drug distribution operations moved indoors from the streets, territoriality battles were unnecessary. A drug business could hire fewer numbers of people, relying more on trusted friends than easily replaceable (and potentially unpredictable) workers. As a result, there was less conflict among people in a particular drug-selling operation. There were fewer robberies by drug users since drug sales could be limited to known "customers."[36]

Fundamental Questions about Drugs and Crime

Although the literature on the nature of the relationship between drugs and crime is complex, we can still arrive at a few tentative conclusions, based upon research, about the process by which drugs and crime are bound together. It comes down to answering three fundamental questions. References to pages in the chapter that bear upon these conclusions are included.

Does Drug Use Cause Crime?

- Of all psychoactive drugs, licit or illicit, the drug with the highest potential for causing aggressive and violent behavior is alcohol. The circumstances tend to be psychopharmacological. From the perspective of victims, however, the prominence of alcohol as a drug intoxicant in the execution of a criminal act is moderate at best. See page 71.
- Most of the criminal offenses that are associated with illicit drugs are related to either cocaine (or crack cocaine), heroin, or methamphetamine. The circumstances tend to

be economically compulsive, but the incidence varies by the specific drug involved, the drug user population, and the environment under which drug use is occurring. See pages 71–74.
- Marijuana use has only a minor direct effect on drug-related crime, other than it represents a drug-defined crime in jurisdictions defining it as such. See page 64.

Does Crime Cause Drug Use?

- Persons who are predisposed to commit crimes also use drugs. Therefore, it is likely that an individual involved in criminality will be in a position to become involved in drugs. See pages 66–67.
- Despite the frequently observed developmental pattern of "crime first" and "drug use second," however, it is uncertain whether there is a causal relationship in this regard. See page 70.

Do Drug Use and Crime Share Common Causes?

- A strong case can be made for drug-related crime to be caused by a third factor or set of factors. In other words, social risk factors lead to deviant behavior, and deviant behavior includes both drug abuse and criminal behavior. See pages 66–67.
- Frequently, for example, individuals with a greater chance of abusing drugs have a number of socioeconomic disadvantages, such as a low level of education, a broken family, little or no social supervision, and low social status, which also produce a greater chance of criminal behavior.[37] See pages 65–67.
- While the effects of marijuana may not directly motivate a user to commit crime, both marijuana use and crime may be common characteristics of an overall deviant lifestyle.[38] In short, the type of person who is a heavy drug user also could be the type of person who is likely to have short-term goals supported by illegal activities and is more likely to be exposed to situations and persons that encourage criminal behavior.[39] See pages 74–75.

Social Structures in Illicit Drug Trafficking

In Chapter 2, the aggregate impact of the global illicit drug trade was examined in detail. In this section, we will address the inner workings of an individual drug-trafficking operation.

As with other businesses, the operational design of an illicit drug business can be divided into various "stages" of production and distribution that include (1) cultivation and manufacturing, (2) importation, (3) wholesale distribution, and (4) retail distribution. For drugs such as cocaine and heroin, peasant farmers living in remote locations in the world carry out the actual cultivation and initial processing. Growers then sell the drugs to importers or drug traffickers who smuggle large quantities into the United States and other worldwide markets. Once inside the United States, the drugs are sold to wholesalers who later sell smaller quantities to lower-level retail sellers or street dealers, often in adulterated forms.

In general, drug dealers at the retail ("street") level follow two types of drug distribution models: (1) the freelance model and (2) the business model.[40] As we will see, the first model can evolve into the second, as the character of drug dealing matures from an informal style of interaction to a more formal one.

Independent individuals working together without a previously established relationship characterize the **freelance model** of retail drug distribution. These dealers and buyers are not part of any large-scale drug organization. It is a "cash only" business, in that the buyer must pay for the drugs at the time of purchase. Both wholesalers and retailers usually do not "front" the drugs, and the price of a drug is negotiated at the time of the buy. Dealers may have many different buyers, some of whom they never see again after a given transaction is completed. If transactions occur successfully, dealers and buyers may negotiate similar arrangements on a more regular basis, but there is no expectation that they will cooperate in the future.

The freelance model typically is associated with the street sale of marijuana and hallucinogens such as LSD and MDMA (Ecstasy). Marijuana sellers are more likely to operate independently than as part of an organized operation, and marijuana often is sold through acquaintance or referral networks. LSD and MDMA are sold principally at concerts, nightclubs, and raves, where sellers and buyers do not know each other, providing a level of anonymity combined with a sense of being part of a common subculture.

In the early years of crack cocaine abuse, from 1984 to 1987, the freelance model dominated as the means by which crack was sold and distributed. The principal drug dealer was a "juggler" who would buy a supply of 10–20 vials of crack and sell them at a standard retail price, approximately twice the initial cost. When the supply was sold, the juggler would "re-up" by obtaining a new supply that would then be sold. Through several cycles, a freelance seller could make up to 50 deals a day. Since most of these freelancers used their product themselves, however, the quantity of sales did not produce substantial incomes. Less than 10 percent of dealers during this period had lengthy drug-dealing careers.[41]

In contrast, the **business model** of street dealing characterizes a structure organized as a "business" in a hierarchical fashion with numerous individuals occupying a range of roles. At the center of the business model is the crew boss who receives a supply of drugs from the wholesaler. Drugs are "fronted" at each level of the organization. The wholesaler fronts the drugs to the crew boss, who then divides the drugs and fronts them to street dealers, often called "runners." Runners most often are young (aged 14–23) males recruited from inner-city neighborhoods. Each crew boss may have as many as 20 runners working under his direction. Runners are assigned to work at a particular street location, sell only at a given price, and then hand over all of the money to the crew boss. As the drugs are sold, the money flows up the chain, from runners, to crew boss, and back to the wholesaler. Prices are agreed upon before the drugs are fronted. At the end of the day, each runner is paid in money or drugs for his or her work. To avoid rip-offs and robberies, each crew is guarded by an armed lieutenant who supervises several street sellers.

Quick Concept Check 4.1

Understanding the Drug–Crime Connection

Check your understanding of the drug–crime connection by matching one of the three aspects of this relationship (on the right) with the following drug situations (on the left).

Note: Some of the answers may be used more than once.

1. A teenager suddenly behaves in a violent manner toward a classmate and pulls out a knife after ingesting a drug.
2. A drug dealer kills a subordinate for stealing money gained from a street deal.
3. A woman engages in prostitution in order to gain money to buy drugs.
4. A man robs a store in order to get money for heroin.
5. One drug dealer is killed for encroaching on another drug dealer's territory.
6. A man who is intoxicated with alcohol rapes a woman.

a. Psychopharmacological crime
b. Economically compulsive crime
c. Systemic crime

Answers: 1. a 2. c 3. b 4. b 5. c 6. a

---

freelance model: A model of retail drug distribution in which dealers and buyers transact their business with relative anonymity, outside of the structure of a large-scale drug organization.

business model: A model of retail drug distribution in which drug transactions are conducted within a hierarchically structured organization.

Crack cocaine (crack, for short) dealing organizations, located in urban neighborhoods, best exemplify the business model of street dealing. In contrast to the freelance dealer, business model dealers and crew bosses who managed to limit their personal use of crack would soon make more than $1,000 per day. Competition among crack dealers would necessitate "protectors," whose worth was often measured by their violent inclinations and ability to instill fear in others. Thus, the subculture of crack abuse would become enmeshed in an environment of systemic violence.[42]

Gangs and Drug-Related Crime

The association between drug-trafficking activity, gang membership, and violent crime is well documented. Gang members who sell drugs are significantly more violent than gang members who do not sell drugs and are more violent than drug sellers who do not belong to gangs. In a study conducted among gang members in Rochester, New York, for example, 30 percent of youth who participated in gangs committed more than two-thirds of property and violent offenses throughout adolescence and 86 percent of all serious crimes.[43]

In order to understand the details of this association, however, we need to distinguish between two fundamentally different types of gang organizations: (1) outlaw motorcycle gangs primarily in western U.S. states, notably the Hell's Angels, the Outlaws, the Bandidos, and the Pagans and (2) street gangs in urban communities, such as the Crips and the Bloods in Los Angeles. Since the late 1980s, law enforcement authorities as well as researchers have recognized both organizations as having become the "new faces of organized crime" in America.[44] The question is the relationship between the criminal activity in general and drug-related crime in particular. The two types of gang organizations have their unique history and present-day involvement in drug-related crime.

Outlaw Motorcycle Gangs

Motorcycle clubs can be divided into either conventional or deviant categories. By far, the greatest proportion of clubs are of the conventional type, comprised of men and women who

A motorcycle gang out in force.

Credit: Uncleroo/Shutterstock

join together based on a common interest in motorcycles, riding together for pleasure and companionship, behaving in accordance with the norms of society. A very small percentage of clubs are of the deviant type, comprised of individuals who engage in unconventional, often criminal, behavior. In essence, these "clubs" function as outlaw gangs and their behavior is characteristic of a deviant subculture (see Chapter 8). In contrast to the popular image of mythic figures rebelling against the norms of society or misunderstood social misfits, members of outlaw motorcycle gangs (OMGs) typically have a history of violent behavior and criminal records that include offenses such as drug trafficking, racketeering, brawling, weapons possession, and homicide. Dating back to 1970s and 1980s, outlaw motorcycle gangs have been principal dealers and traffickers of methamphetamine, and their association with this drug continues today. As mentioned in Chapter 2, the name, crank, for methamphetamine originated from the practice of concealing the drug in the crankshaft of motorcycles. Their association with methamphetamine continues today, but the trafficking of methamphetamine has since been taken over by Mexican drug-trafficking organizations and outlaw motorcycle gangs play an increasingly minor role.[45]

One may believe that outlaw motorcycle gangs are a thing of the past. However, the 2015 National Gang Report found that OMGs have established new chapters and have increased membership by recruiting from more conventional biker clubs, such as sports bike clubs.[46] The 2015 shoot-out at a Twin Peaks restaurant in Waco, Texas, between the Bandidos and Cossacks serves as a grim reminder that OMGs are alive and well. The Cossacks were dubbed by the Texas Department of Public Safety as an emerging motorcycle gang, while the Bandidos have been deemed a highly organized criminal enterprise, involved in crimes such as racketeering, drug trafficking, murder, and extortion. The deadly shoot-out, where 9 were killed and 20 injured, allegedly stemmed from the Cossacks wearing a Texas bottom rocker patch on the back of the members' vest, which was not approved by the more powerful Bandidos.[47] The 2015 National Gang report suggests that the larger OMGs often require monthly payment for patches, which is used to help finance their criminal activities. This event exemplifies threats that OMGs continue to pose.

Street Gangs

The association between street gangs and drug selling became particularly striking in the 1980s during the height of crack cocaine abuse in inner-city neighborhoods. In contrast to outlaw motorcycle gangs, the largest proportion of street gangs involved in drug sales during this time comprised of individuals between 15 and 16 years of age. The prevalence of gang members aged 18 years or older increased when drug sales reached higher levels. White and Hispanic/Latino gang members tended to be more prevalent in neighborhoods where drug involvement was relatively low, and African American gang members tended to be more prevalent in neighborhoods where drug involvement was high. The extreme levels of systemic violence during this period were attributed in large part to the drug distribution activities of street gang members and their leaders.[48]

On the other hand, gang members during this period were not dealing drugs in an organized and structured way, and in an analysis of drug dealing in San Francisco, the types of drugs and style of dealing varied across the demographic characteristics. African American gangs sold crack cocaine near housing projects and small corner stores; Latino gang sold crack cocaine, marijuana, and heroin along major roads, often blending in with shoppers and passengers waiting for public buses. Asian gangs stayed out of public places, restricting drug sales, primarily powder cocaine, to private transactions by phone or pager.[49]

In 1995, the National Youth Gang Center was established as a federal center for statistically tracking and monitoring gang activity. In light of National Youth Gang Surveys conducted annually since then and other studies, a general picture of American street gangs over a period from 1996 to 2009 has emerged that relates to the issue of drug-related crime in this subculture.

First, tracking studies show that gang problems in the United States declined substantially between 1996 and 2001 but increased steadily between 2001 and 2009. A more recent 2015 survey of law enforcement showed 49 percent of jurisdictions reporting increased street gang membership in the prior two years, while 43 percent indicated membership stayed the same, and just 8 percent reported reductions[50]. While large cities consistently have the highest prevalence rate for gang activity (86 percent of law enforcement agencies reporting gang problems), there has been significant gang activity in suburban counties (52 percent reporting gang problems) and smaller cities (33 percent reporting gang problems).[51]

Second, there continues to be a high prevalence rate for violent crime among gang members and drug traffickers. In a 2014 study of gangs in two locations of Arizona, the majority of gang members reported engaging in violent acts, with 80 percent reporting that they had jumped or attacked people and 51 percent reported killing a person. Drug trafficking consisted primarily of sales of marijuana (80 percent), crack cocaine (51 percent), and powder cocaine (48 percent). Drug sales were highly correlated with violent offenses.[52] According to the 2015 National Gang Report, the most prevalent crimes committed by street gangs were street-level and large-scale drug trafficking, assaults, threats, and intimidation and robbery. Neighborhood-based gangs posed the most significant threat.

Third, street gangs in western and southwestern U.S. states have strong working relationships with Mexico-based and Central America-based drug-trafficking cartels. Gangs had traditionally been the primary organized retail or mid-level distributors of drugs, but now are purchasing drugs directly from the cartels, eliminating the mid-level wholesale dealer.[53]

Prison Gangs

While prisons should theoretically be a place to escape a gang lifestyle, gang activity is rampant in prison environments. Prison gangs are defined by the National Gang Intelligence Center as a self-perpetuating criminal organization that originates in the prison system, and operates both inside and outside the prison walls. While prison gangs are often perceived as a "prison" problem, these gangs affect communities nationwide. The threat of prison gangs is clear inside the prison walls, where withdraw from the gang can easily lead to death. However, prison gangs often order crimes from street gangs and serve as brokers for drug and related crimes between street gangs and Mexican Transnational Criminal Organizations.[54]

Most prison gangs formed in the early to mid-1960s; they typically form along racial and ethnic lines. Examples of prison gangs include the Aryan Brotherhood, Black Guerilla Family, and the Mexican Mafia. Each of these prison gangs were formed in California prisons.

Prison gangs range from tightly to loosely structured organizations. They are responsible for much of the drug and weapon smuggling inside the prison, with drugs being the primary contraband controlled by the gangs. Often, corrupt staffs assist prison gang members with smuggling contraband, which also includes cell phones, allowing members to communicate

Quick Concept Check 4.2

Understanding Gangs and Social Structures in Illicit Drug Trafficking

Check your understanding of gangs and other social structures in illicit drug trafficking by matching each drug situation given on the left with a term or name on the right.

Note: Some of the answers may be used more than once or not at all.

1. The drug dealers and buyers are not part of any large-scale drug organization.	a. Freelance model
2. Hell's Angels, the Outlaws, the Bandidos, and the Pagans are examples.	b. Business model
3. Urban groups in western and southwestern U.S. states work closely with Mexico-based or Central American-based drug cartels.	c. Outlaw motorcycle gangs
4. Street drug dealing is organized in a hierarchical structure of drug distribution.	d. Motorcycle clubs
5. The model of crack cocaine dealing was dominant in the early years of crack cocaine abuse, 1984–1987.	e. Street gangs
6. The Crips and the Bloods are examples.	f. Prison gangs
7. Often formed along racial and ethnic lines.	

Answers: 1. a   2. c   3. e   4. b   5. a   6. e   7. f

to other gang members in and outside of prison. The goals of prison gangs are similar to that of other gang organizations—increase power, territory, and money. According to the 2015 National Gang Report, nearly 70 percent of corrections respondents reported an increase in prison gang membership in the previous two years.[55] Hence, prison gangs have become an increasing threat, contributing to the U.S. drug market.

Money Laundering in Drug-Related Crime

Because practically all transactions in the illicit drug business are conducted in cash, a conspicuously large number of small bills can render drug traffickers vulnerable to law enforcement interdiction. Drug traffickers cannot simply deposit their profits into a local bank. The Bank Secrecy Act of 1970 requires that financial institutions in the United States report cash transactions of $10,000 or more to the Internal Revenue Service (IRS), and these institutions must identify the depositors and the sources of the money. Drug traffickers, therefore, must rely on a variety of money laundering methods to convert bulk amounts of drug profits into legitimate revenue. **Money laundering** refers to the process where illegal sources of income are disguised to make them appear legitimate. Money laundering conceals the illegal sources of money and gives the money a legitimate history.

One of the simplest methods of money laundering is called "smurfing," by which a number of persons, or "smurfs," deposit random amounts of less than $10,000 into variously named accounts at many different banks. Using 20 smurfs, for example, each depositing $9,000 in cash, a trafficker could launder as much as $180,000 in less than an hour and circumvent the regulations of the Bank Secrecy Act. After the money is deposited, it can be withdrawn by the trafficker to purchase money orders in U.S. funds, which are sent out of the country to purchase more drugs or for safekeeping. It can be a quite successful technique, except for the fact that traffickers have to give each of their smurfs a cut of their profits. Therefore, smurfing is not the most profitable method of money laundering.

A second technique of money laundering is for traffickers to ship the money abroad and deposit it in banks located in countries that have few, if any, money laundering regulations. Commonly called "offshore banks," unregulated banks in the Caribbean nations that were formerly British colonies, such as the Cayman Islands, have become favorite laundering havens. With the seventh largest deposit base in the world, the Cayman Islands have more than 550 banks, only 17 of which have a physical presence, operating without any requirement to report transactions. Typically, these offshore banking havens have very strict policies with regard to nondisclosure, effectively shielding foreign investors from investigations and prosecutions from their home countries.[56]

One of the oldest methods of money laundering is for drug traffickers to operate a cash-based retail service business such as laundromats, car washes, vending-machine routes, video rentals, or bars and restaurants, mixing the illegal and legal cash and reporting the total as the earnings of the cover business. In fact, the term "money laundering" is said to originate from Mafia ownership of laundromats in the United States during Prohibition. Bootleggers needed to show a legitimate source for their monies, and laundromats were chosen because they were cash transaction businesses. Later, in the 1970s, the Mafia used pizza parlors to launder money made from the sale of heroin. Acquiring a legitimate business to launder money serves to provide drug traffickers with a reportable income for tax purposes.

Profits in the global illicit drug trade have grown to such immense levels that ordinary businesses have become inadequate in handling the funds for money laundering purposes. Money laundering has included bribing employees of financial institutions, acquiring financial institutions themselves, as well as conducting large business loans and real estate transactions. The globalization of financial markets through the growth of international trade and the expansion of international corporations have provided a range of opportunities for the conversion of illegal proceeds into what appear to be legitimate funds.[57]

The combination of globalization and Internet technology has raised concerns about money laundering to new levels of complexity. In recent years, Internet providers, known as digital currency exchange (DCE) services, allow individuals to exchange legal tender (U.S. dollars, for example) into a form of electronic currency or exchange one form of electronic currency for another. The DCE transactions are made through Web sites rather than any physical location, and the process is independent of traditional banking or money transfer systems. Since the DCE is made anonymously, it has been a convenient vehicle for money laundering of funds acquired through the illicit drug trade or other illegal enterprises (Drug Enforcement … in Focus).

Until the Money Laundering Control Act of 1986 officially criminalized money laundering, the practice was not technically illegal. Federal drug-control authorities had to prosecute drug dealers on the basis of activities outside of money laundering. Since then, however, a series of legislative actions have strengthened the regulatory controls over this practice. Considering the globalization of illicit drugs, money laundering controls have been instituted around the world, and the U.S. Department of State has responsibility over issues related to international money laundering, through the Bureau for International Narcotics and Law Enforcement Affairs. Each year, an International Narcotics Control Strategy Report on Money Laundering and Financial Crimes is issued, listing regulatory controls in more than 200 nations and jurisdictions. It is important to note that the financial success of a modern-day drug-trafficking organization is based not only on its ability to produce, distribute, and sell drugs but also on its ability to launder the money made from the illicit drug business.[58]

> **money laundering:** The process where illegal sources of income are concealed or disguised to make the sources appear legitimate.

Drug Enforcement . . . in Focus

The New Money Laundering: Digital Currency Exchanges

In May of 2013, Liberty Reserve, one of the world's largest DCE companies, and seven principal employees of the company were indicted for conducting an international money laundering operation. The investigation and takedown involved law enforcement action in 17 countries. Liberty Reserve was alleged to have had more than 1 million users worldwide (more than 200,000 in the United States alone) who had conducted since its founding in 2006 approximately 55 million anonymous transactions, worth more than $6 billion.

According to indictment records, Liberty Reserve allowed users to open accounts without validation of their identities. The Liberty Reserve Web site offered a "shopping cart interface" that "merchant" Web sites could use to accept currency transfers as a form of payment. The "merchants" included illicit drug trade organizations as well as traffickers of stolen credit cards, and personal activities proceeded without registration with the U.S. Department of Treasury. As Preet Bharara, Manhattan District Attorney, said at the time of the indictment:

"... the only liberty that Liberty Reserve gave many of its users was the freedom to commit crimes ... and it became a popular hub for fraudsters, hackers, and traffickers. The global enforcement action ... is an important step toward reining in the 'Wild West' of illicit Internet banking."

Whether or not the indictment of Liberty Reserve will lead to prosecutions of other digital currency firms remains to be seen. One prominent digital currency in circulation, Bitcoins, operates with greater transparency, but there are Web sites (some of them suspiciously with names like Bitlaundry and Bitcoinlaundery!) that evidently use Bitcoins in their transactions. Needless to say, they will be subject to intense scrutiny, as law enforcement authorities continue to grapple with this new form of financial crime.

Sources: Manhattan U.S. Attorney announces charges against Liberty Reserve, one of the world's largest digital currency companies, and seven of its principals and employees for allegedly running a $6 billion money-laundering scheme. Press release of Manhattan District Attorney's Office, New York, U.S. Department of Justice, May 28, 2013. Quotation of Preet Bharara, U.S. District Attorney. Perlroth, Nicole (2013, May 29). Unlike Liberty Reserve, Bitcoin is not anonymous—yet. *The New York Times, Bits.* http://bits.blogs.nytimes/com.

Summary

Understanding Drug Use and Crime

- Empirical studies on the relationship between alcohol and drug use and the commission of crime are unanimous in their findings: Crime and drug use are strongly correlated. Individuals who drink alcohol and/or use drugs are significantly more likely to commit crimes than are individuals who neither drink nor use illegal drugs. Jail and prison inmates in the United States have much higher rates of drug use relative to the general population. Drug and property offenses are also the most common offense types for female offenders, whose substance use appears to be a significant contributor to their criminal justice involvement.

- Drug-defined crimes are specific law violations related to possession, use distribution, and manufacture of illegal substances. Drug-related crimes are law violations that are not specific to drugs but are associated with drug-taking behavior. Finally, a drug-using lifestyle involves criminal behavior that occurs as part of a more general deviant way of life associated with ascertaining and using drugs.

- Psychopharmacological crime refers to the possible effects of a drug on an offender committing a crime, that is, the drug in question is assumed to cause violent or criminal behavior while the drug is actually present in the individual's system. Alcohol is regarded as the psychoactive drug with the greatest potential for psychopharmacological violence or crime.

- Economically compulsive crime refers to circumstances in which drug use may lead users to commit crimes to obtain money to buy drugs or to support some form of drug-taking behavior. Several studies have shown that economically compulsive crime is a major component of the link between drugs and crime. Whether drug prices coincide with increases or decreases in crimes of this type appears to depend upon the historical period examined and the specific drug of abuse.

- Systemic crime refers to drug use and crime being intertwined in the lifestyle of a deviant subculture or an organization involved in illicit drug trafficking and distribution.

The Social Structure of the Illicit Drug Dealing

- The illicit drug business can be divided into the following "stages" of production and distribution: (1) cultivation and manufacturing, (2) importation, (3) wholesale distribution, and (4) retail distribution. In this sense, the illicit drug business is no different from that of a foreign or domestic commodity on the legitimate market.

- At the retail level, drug dealers follow either the freelance model in which dealers and buyers transact their business with relative anonymity or the business model in which drug transactions are conducted within a hierarchically structured organization.

Gangs and Drug-Related Crime

- The association between drug-trafficking activity, gang membership, and violent crime is well documented. Gang members who sell drugs are significantly more violent than gang members who do not sell drugs and are more violent than drug sellers who do not belong to gangs.
- Three fundamentally different types of gang organizations are involved in drug trafficking and distribution: (1) outlaw motorcycle gangs primarily in western U.S. states, (2) street gangs in urban communities, such as the Crips and the Bloods in Los Angeles, and (3) prison gangs, located in nearly all, large penal institutions. Since the late 1980s, law enforcement authorities as well as researchers have recognized these organizations as having become the "new faces of organized crime" in America.

Money Laundering in Drug-Related Crime

- To escape the attention of law enforcement agencies, the enormous amount of income gained from "cash only" drug distribution and sales must be converted into legitimate revenue in a process called money laundering.
- One method of money laundering, called "smurfing," is to enlist a number of individuals to deposit random amounts of less than $10,000 into accounts at many different banks. A second method is to ship the money abroad and deposit it into banks located in countries with few, if any, banking regulations. A third method is to operate cash-based retail service businesses that serve as "fronts" for illegal drug distribution activities. A fourth method is to employ digital currency exchange services on the Internet, where transactions can be carried out anonymously.

Key Terms

business model, p. 76
drug-defined crime, p. 64
drug-related crime, p. 65
drug-using lifestyle, p. 66

economically compulsive violence, p. 65
freelance model, p. 76

interactional circumstances, p. 74
money laundering, p. 79

psychopharmacological violence, p. 65
systemic violence, p. 65

Review Questions

1. Describe the difference between drug-law crime, drug-related crime, and drug-using lifestyle.
2. Describe the following three types of drug-related violence, as established in the Goldstein model: psychopharmacological violence, economically compulsive violence, and systemic violence. Give one example of a criminal act in each of these categories.
3. Why do the characteristics of the user population matter when explaining the relationship between the price of illicit drugs and illicit drug use?
4. For each of the three explanations for the drug–crime connection, describe the findings of one research study that support that explanation.

5. Distinguish between the features of the freelance model and business model of retail drug distribution.
6. Distinguish between outlaw motorcycle gangs, street gangs, and prison gangs with respect to their history and present-day involvement with drug trafficking.
7. Describe the operations of DCEs in terms of their money laundering of funds from illegal criminal activity, including drug trafficking.

Critical Thinking: What Would You Do?

Suppose you were in a position to reduce the prevalence of heroin abuse in your community by manipulating the price of heroin, either making it more or less available or artificially increasing or decreasing its street value. Would you decide to make heroin cheaper or more expensive? Describe your policy decision. How do you justify your decision? Discuss what ramifications you believe your policy might have not only on future heroin use but also on future use of other illicit drugs.

1. Adapted from a posting by the United States Drug Enforcement Administration, New Orleans Division News, published December 11, 2017. https://www.dea.gov/divisions/no/2017/no121117.shtml.

2. Bonta, J.; and Andrews, D. (2017). *The Psychology of Criminal Conduct* (6th ed.). New York, NY: Routledge.

3. Federal Bureau of Investigation: Uniform Crime Report. *Crime in the United States 2015*. Washington, D.C.: U.S. Department of Justice, Table 18.

4. Federal Bureau of Investigation: Uniform Crime Report. *Crime in the United States 2015*. Washington, D.C.: U.S. Department of Justice. Arrests for Drug Abuse Violations Table.

5. Carson, E. A. (2016, December). Prisoners in 2015. *Bureau of Justice Statistics Bulletin*. Washington, D.C.: U.S. Department of Justice.

6. Goldstein, P. J. (1985, Fall). The drugs/violence nexus: A tripartite conceptual framework. *Journal of Drug Issues*, 493–506.

7. Caulkins, J. P.; and Kleiman, M. (2011). Drugs and crime. In M. Tonry (Ed.), *Crime and criminal justice*. New York: Oxford University Press.

8. Bonta and Andrews, *The Psychology of Criminal Conduct*.

9. Goode, E. (2015). *Drugs in American Society* (9th ed.). New York, NY: McGraw-Hill Education.

10. Centers for Disease Control and Prevention (2013). *Youth risk behavior surveillance system: 2011 National overview*. Atlanta, GA: Centers for Disease Control and Prevention, U.S. Department of Health and Human Services.

11. Eaton, D. K.; Kann, L.; Kinchen, S.; Shanklin, S.; Ross, J.; Hawkins, J.; et al. (2008, June 6). Youth risk behavior surveillance—United States, 2007. *Morbidity and Mortality Weekly Report*. Atlanta, GA: Centers for Disease Control and Prevention, U.S. Department of Health and Human Services. Eaton, D. K. et al. (2010, June 4). Youth risk behavior surveillance—United States, 2009. *Morbidity and Mortality Weekly Report*. Atlanta, GA: Centers for Disease Control and Prevention, U.S. Department of Health and Human Services. Eaton, D. K. et al. (2012, June 8). Youth risk behavior surveillance—United States, 2011. *Morbidity and Mortality Weekly Report*. Atlanta, GA: Centers for Disease Control and Prevention, U.S. Department of Health and Human Services. Kann, L.; McManus, T.; Harris, W.; Shanklin, S.; et al. (2016). Youth Risk Behavior Surveillance—United States, 2015. *Morbidity and Mortality Weekly Report*. Atlanta, GA: Centers for Disease Control and Prevention, U.S. Department of Health and Human Services.

12. Office of National Drug Control Policy (2014, January). ADAM II: 2013 Annual report. *Arrestee Drug Abuse Monitoring Program II*. Washington, D.C.: Office of National Drug Control Policy, Executive Office of the President, Tables 3.3–3.8.

13. Karberg, J. C.; and Doris, J. J. (2005). *Substance abuse, dependence, and treatment of jail inmates*. Washington, D.C.: Bureau of Justice Statistics, U.S. Department of Justice.

14. Morgan, R.; and Kena, G. (2017). *Criminal Victimization, 2016*. Bureau of Justice Statistics. Washington, D.C.: U.S. Department of Justice, Table 32.

15. Elliot, D. S.; Huizinga, D.; and Menard, S. (1989). *Multiple problem youth: Delinquency, substance use and mental health problems*. New York: Springer-Verlag. Inciardi, J. A. (1979). Heroin use and street crime. *Crime and Delinquency*, 25, 335–346. Inciardi, J. A.; and Pottieger, A. E. (1994). Crack-cocaine and street crime. *Journal of Drug Issues*, 24, 273–292. Inciardi, J. A.; Horowitz, R.; and Pottieger, A. E. (1993). *Street kids, street drugs, street crime*. Belmont, CA: Wadsworth.

16. Carson, A.; and Anderson, E. (December, 2016). *Prisoners in 2015*. Washington, D.C.: U.S. Department of Justice, Bureau of Justice Statistics.

17. Daly, K. (1994). *Gender, crime and punishment*. New Haven, CT: Yale University Press.

18. Bloom, B.; B. Owen; and S. Covington. (2003). *Gender responsive strategies: Research, practice, and guiding principles for women offenders*. Washington, D.C.: U.S. Department of Justice, National Institute of Corrections.

19. Bronson, J.; Stroop, J.; Zimmer, S.; and Berzofsky, M. (June 2017). *Drug Use, Dependence, and Abuse Among State Prisoners and Jail Inmates, 2007–2009*. NCJ 250546. Washington, D.C.: Bureau of Justice Statistics, U.S. Department of Justice.

20. Goode, E. (1972). Excerpts from marijuana use and crime. In *National Commission of Marijuana and Drug Abuse, Marijuana: A signal of misunderstanding*, Appendix, Vol. 1. Washington, D.C.: U.S. Government Printing Office, pp. 447–453.

21. Goode, E. (2005). *Drugs in American society* (6th ed.). New York: McGraw-Hill, pp. 329–350.

22. Petersen, R. C.; and Stillman, R. C. (1978). Phencyclidine: An overview. In R. C. Petersen; and R. C. Stillman (Eds.), *Phencyclidine (PCP) abuse: An appraisal* (NIDA Research Monograph 21). Rockville, MD: National Institute on Drug Abuse, pp. 1–17. Papanti, D.; Orsolini, L.; Francesconi, G.; and Schifano, F. (2014). "Noids" in a nutshell: everything you (don't) want to know about synthetic cannabimimetics. *Advances in Dual Diagnosis*, 7(3), 137–148, https://doi.org/10.1108/ADD-02-2014-0006

23. De La Rosa, M.; Lambert, E.Y.; and Gropper, B. (Eds.), (1990). Introduction: Exploring the substance abuse-violence connection. In *Drugs and violence: Causes, correlates, and consequences* (NIDA Research Monograph 103). Rockville, MD: National Institute on Drug Abuse, pp. 1–7.

24. Roth, J.A. (1994, February). *Psychoactive substances and violence: Research brief*. Washington, D.C.: National Institute of Justice. Tyner, E. A.; and Fremouw, W. J. (2008). The relation of methamphetamine use and violence: A critical review. *Aggression and Violent Behavior*, 13, 285–297.

25. World Health Organization (November, 2017). *Violence Against Women: Intimate partner violence and sexual violence against women, fact sheet*. Geneva, Switzerland. Retrieved from http://www.who.int/mediacentre/factsheets/fs239/en/

26. Boyum, D. A.; Caulkins, J. P.; and Kleiman, M. A. (2011). Drugs, crime, and public policy. In J. Q.; Wilson; and J. Petervilia (Eds.), *Crime and public policy*. New York: Oxford University Press, pp. 368–410. Bureau of Justice Statistics, *Criminal victimization*, Table 32. Bushman, B. J. (1993, October). Human aggression while under the influence of alcohol and other drugs: An integrative research review. *Current Directions in Psychological Science*, 2, 148–152. Caulkins and Kleiman, Drugs and Crime. Collins, J. J.; and Messerschmidt, P. M. (1993). Epidemiology of alcohol-related violence.

Alcohol Health and Research World, 17, 93–100. Foran, H. M.; and O'Leary, K. D. (2008). Alcohol and intimate partner violence: A meta-analytic review. *Clinical Psychology Review, 28,* 1222–1234. Goode, *Drugs in American society,* pp. 343–346. Kuhns, J. B.; and Clodfelter, T. A. (2009). Illicit drug-related psychopharmacological violence: The current understanding within a causal context. *Aggression and Violent Behavior, 14,* 69–78.

27. Inciardi, J. A. (1990). The crack–violence connection within a population of hard-core adolescent offenders. In M. De La Rosa; E. Y. Lambert; and B. Gropper (Eds.), *Drugs and violence: Causes, correlates, and consequences* (NIDA Research Monograph 103). Rockville, MD: National Institute on Drug Abuse, pp. 92–111.

28. Inciardi, J. A.; and Pottieger, A. E. (1998). Drug use and street crime in Miami: An (almost) twenty-year retrospective. *Substance Use and Misuse, 33,* 1839–1870.

29. Bronson, J.; Stroop, J.: Zimmer, S.; and Berzofsky, M. (2017, June). *Drug Use, Dependence, and Abuse Among State Prisoners and Jail Inmates, 2007–2009.* NCJ 250546. Washington, D.C.: Bureau of Justice Statistics, U.S. Department of Justice.

30. Silverman, L. P.; and Spruill, N. L. (1977). Urban crime and the price of heroin. *Journal of Urban Economics, 4,* 80–103.

31. Rafert, G. (2007, October 23). Illicit drug policy in the United States: Will increased drug prices reduce use and drug-related crime? Presentation at the Crime and Population Dynamics 2007 Summer Workshop, Berkeley, C. A.; Rhodes, W.; Johnston, P.; Han, S.; McMullen, Q.; and Hozik, L. (2002, January). *Illicit drugs: Price elasticity of demand and supply.* Washington, D.C.: The National Institute of Justice, U.S. Department of Justice.

32. Information courtesy of the Drug Enforcement Administration, U.S. Department of Justice, Washington, D.C.

33. Caulkins and Kleiman, Drugs and crime.

34. Boyum, Caulkins, and Kleiman, Drugs, crime, and public policy.

35. Blumstein, A.; and Rosenfeld, R. (1998, October). Assessing the recent ups and downs in U.S. homicide rates. *National Institute of Justice Journal, 237,* 9–11. Curtis, R. (1998, October). The improbable transformation of inner-city neighborhoods: Crime, violence, drugs, and youths in the 1990s. *National Institute of Justice Journal,* 16–17. Reuter, P. (2009). Systemic violence in drug markets. *Crime, Law, and Social Change, 52,* 275–284.

36. Harris, J. (1991). *Drugged America.* New York: Four Winds Press, p. 117.

37. Ibid., p. 112.

38. Bureau of Justice Statistics (1992). *Drugs, crime, and the justice system: A national report from the Bureau of justice statistics.* Washington, D.C.: U.S. Department of Justice.

39. White, J. (1991). *Drug dependence.* Englewood Cliffs, NJ: Prentice Hall, p. 200.

40. Alder, P. (1985). *Wheeling and dealing.* New York: Colombia University Press. Hamid, A. (1990). The political economy of crack-related violence. *Contemporary Drug Problems, 17*(1), 31–78. Johnson, B. D.; Hamid, A.; and Sanabria, H. (1992). Emerging models of crack distribution. In T. Mieczkowski (Ed.), *Drugs, crime and social policy: Research, issues, and concerns.* Boston: Allyn and Bacon. Preble, E.; and Casey, J. (1969). Taking care of business: The heroin user's life on the streets. *International Journal of Addictions, 4,* 1–24.

41. Johnson, B. D.; Golub, A.; and Dunlap, E. (2006). The rise and decline of hard drugs, drug markets, and violence in inner-city New York. In A. Blumstein and J. Wallman (Eds.), *The crime drop in America.* New York: Cambridge University Press, pp. 164–206. Office of National Drug Control Policy (2004, January). *Pulse check: Trends in drug abuse, drug markets and chronic users in 25 of America's largest cities.* Washington, D.C.: Office of National Drug Control Policy.

42. Johnson; G.; and Dunlap (2006). The rise and decline of hard drugs, pp. 164–206. Office of National Drug Control Policy (2002, April). *Pulse check: Trends in drug abuse.* Office of National Drug Control Policy (2004, January). *Pulse check.* Vannostrand, L. M.; and Tewksbury, R. (1999). The motives and mechanics of operating an illegal drug enterprise. *Deviant Behavior, 20,* 57–83.

43. Maxson, C. (2011). Street gangs. In J. Q. Wilson; and J. Petersilla (Eds.), *Crime and public policy.* New York: Oxford University Press, pp. 158–182.

44. Barker, T.; and Human, K. M. (2009). Crimes of the Big Four motorcycle gangs. *Journal of Criminal Justice, 37,* 174–179. Bellair, P. E.; and McNulty, T. L. (2009). Gang membership, drug selling, and violence in neighborhood context. *Justice Quarterly, 26,* 644–669. Howell, J. C.; and Decker, S. H. (1999, January). The youth gangs, drugs, and violence connection. *OJJDP Juvenile Justice Bulletin.* Washington, D.C.: Office of Juvenile Justice and Delinquency Prevention, U.S. Department of Justice. McDermott, E. J. (2006, Winter). Motorcycle gangs: The new face of organized crime. *Journal of Gang Research, 13,* 27–36.

45. McDermott, Motorcycle gangs.

46. National Gang Intelligence Center (2015). *2015 National Gang Report.* U.S. Department of Justice, Washington, D.C.

47. A "War" on Wheels: The Biker Shootout at Waco, and What Came Next. (2016, April 7). *National Public Radio,* Retrieved from https://www.npr.org/2016/04/05/473085140/a-war-on-wheels-the-biker-shootout-at-waco-and-what-came-next.

48. Bellair and McNulty, Gang membership drug selling, and violence in neighborhood context. Howell, J. C.; and Gleason, D. K. (1999, December). Youth gang drug trafficking. *OJJDP Juvenile Justice Bulletin.* Washington, D.C.: Office of Juvenile Justice and Delinquency Prevention, U.S. Department of Justice. Decker, S.; Katz, C. M.; and Webb, V. J. (2008). Understanding the black box of gang organization: Implications for involvement in violent crime, drug sales, and violent victimization. *Crime and Delinquency, 54,* 153–172.

49. Joe-Laidler, K.; and Hunt, G. P. (2012). Moving beyond the gang-drug-violence connection. *Drug: Education, Prevention and Policy, 19,* 442–452.

50. National Gang Intelligence Center, *2015 National Gang Report.*

51. Howell, J. C.; Egley, A.; Tita, G. E.; and Griffiths, E. (2014). Gang problem prevalence trends in the U.S. In C. L. Maxson; A. Egley; J. Miller; and M. W. Klein (Eds.), *The modern gang reader (4th ed.).* New York: Oxford University Press, pp. 55–60.

52. Decker, S. H.; Katz, C. M.; and Webb, V. J. (2014). Understanding the black box of gang organization: Implications for involvement in violent crime, drug sales, and violent victimization. In C. L. Maxson; A. Egley; J. Miller; and M. W. Klein (Eds.), *The modern gang reader (4th ed.).* New York: Oxford University Press, pp. 166–178.

53. National Gang Intelligence Center (2011). *2011 National Gang Threat Assessment: Emerging Trends*. Tallahassee, FL: National Gang Intelligence Center.

54. National Gang Intelligence Center, *2015 National Gang Report*.

55. Ibid.

56. Mark, C. (1995, September). Where the world's crooks go to do their dirty laundry. *Christian Science Monitor*, 1.

57. Motivans, M. (2003, July). *Money laundering offenders, 1994–2001*. Washington, D.C.: U.S. Department of Justice. Office of National Drug Control Policy (2002, January). *ONCP fact sheet: International money laundering and asset forfeiture*. Washington, D.C.: Office of National Drug Control Policy. Wankel, H. D. (1996, February 28). *DEA congressional testimony: Money laundering by drug trafficking organizations*. Washington, D.C.: U.S. Department of Justice.

58. Bureau for International Narcotics and Law Enforcement Affairs (2013, March). *International Narcotics Control Strategy Report. Vol. II: Money laundering and financial crimes*. Washington, D.C.: U.S. Department of State.

Drug-Law Penalties

A federal judge walked back to his chambers in a particularly depressed mood. That afternoon, he had carried out yet another mandatory minimum sentencing. While many of his colleagues feel otherwise, he feels that the policy is just plain wrong—that it has forced him to put thousands of people in prison, sometimes for the rest of their lives, for crimes that he doesn't believe warranted such harsh punishment. Mandatory minimum sentencing has tied his hands.

He is required to treat the low-level addict involved in drug distribution to feed his addiction and the for-profit drug dealer as comparable cases to adjudicate, so that both of them end up receiving the same sentence. He does not agree with the recent statements of U.S. Attorney General Sessions that mandatory minimum sentences lead to consistent and fair decisions. As a judge, he emphasizes that he has a duty to uphold the law, even when he doesn't agree with it. So, the mandatory minimum sentences will continue to be applied to many people who need help with an addiction more than long periods of confinement—people who appear before his judicial bench on a regular basis.[1]

After you have completed this chapter, you should have an understanding of the following:

- The principal phases of judicial events in the criminal justice system

- How drug-law violators are represented in the U.S. criminal justice system

- Federal and state penalties for drug trafficking and simple possession

- How drug-law penalties from the 1970s to present time have impacted the criminal justice system

- Sentencing policies and their impact on mass incarceration

Each year, more than 10 million individuals in the United States are arrested on criminal charges by state or local law enforcement agencies. Of this group, more than 1.6 million arrests are made for drug-related offenses. Overall, approximately 298,000 drug-law offenders are incarcerated in U.S. prisons, about one in five prisoners of the total prison population.[2] Based on the sheer number of drug-law violators, procedures established for addressing these crimes and the individuals who commit them have a significant impact on the criminal justice system as a whole. This chapter focuses on the process of criminal justice following the arrest of drug-law violators, specifically the penalties and sentencing that are currently imposed in these cases. To begin, what are the phases of the criminal justice system for arrestees in general?

The Phases of Criminal Justice

For adult offenders, an extended sequence of judicial events begins following their arrest (Figure 5.1). These events consist of four phases: (1) prosecution and pretrial services; (2) adjudication in an arraignment and trial, and pending conviction of the criminal charges; (3) sentencing and sanctions; and (4) imposition of a fine, probation, and/or incarceration in a correctional facility. At multiple points in each phase, judicial mechanisms are in place to protect innocent individuals from being unjustly prosecuted. In such circumstances, individuals who have been accused of a crime may exit the system entirely (i.e., they will be set free). The basic features of each phase are as follows:

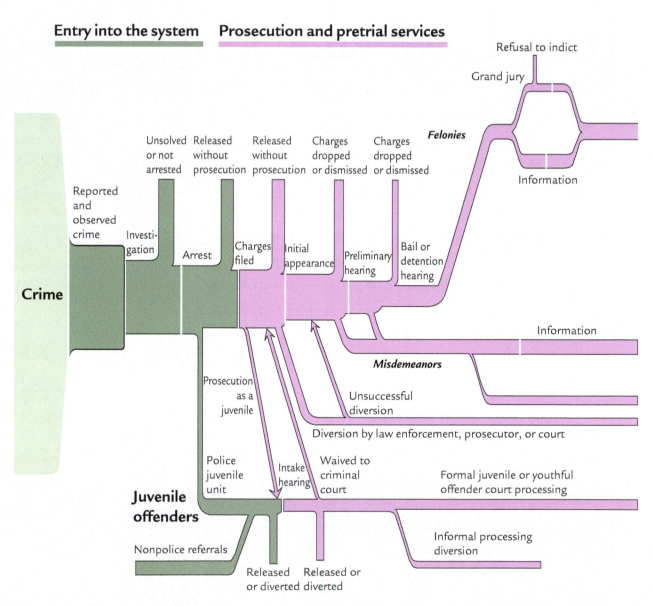

FIGURE 5.1

A flowchart of the phases of judicial events in the criminal justice system, as described on pages 86–88.

Note: Procedures vary among jurisdictions. The weights of the lines are not intended to reflect the relative size of caseloads in each phase.

Source: Bureau of Justice Statistics. *Criminal justice system flowchart.* Accessed (May 12, 2018) from: *http://www.bjs.gov/content/largechart.cfm.*

- During the **prosecution and pretrial services** phase, law enforcement officers involved in the arrest present information about the case to the prosecutor, who decides if formal charges are to be filed. If charged with a crime, the suspect must appear before a judge without unnecessary delay, and if counsel has not yet represented him or her, a state-appointed defense attorney is provided. The judge sets the conditions of pretrial release and bail if circumstances warrant them, and determines in a pretrial hearing whether there is probable cause to believe that the accused has committed a specific crime within the jurisdiction of the court. If the judge so rules, the case proceeds to trial.

- During the **adjudication** phase, a formal indictment is filed in the trial court, leading to arraignment. At arraignment, the accused is informed of the charge or charges, advised as to the rights of a criminal defendant, and required to enter a plea of guilty or not guilty. A trial proceeding takes place, leading to acquittal or conviction by a judge or jury.

prosecution and pretrial services: The first phase of the criminal justice system in which an individual is formally charged of a crime, receives defense counsel, and (after a ruling by a judge) proceeds to trial.

adjudication: The second phase of the criminal justice system in which an individual is formally indicted and arraigned. A plea of guilty or not guilty is entered, and a trial proceeding takes place.

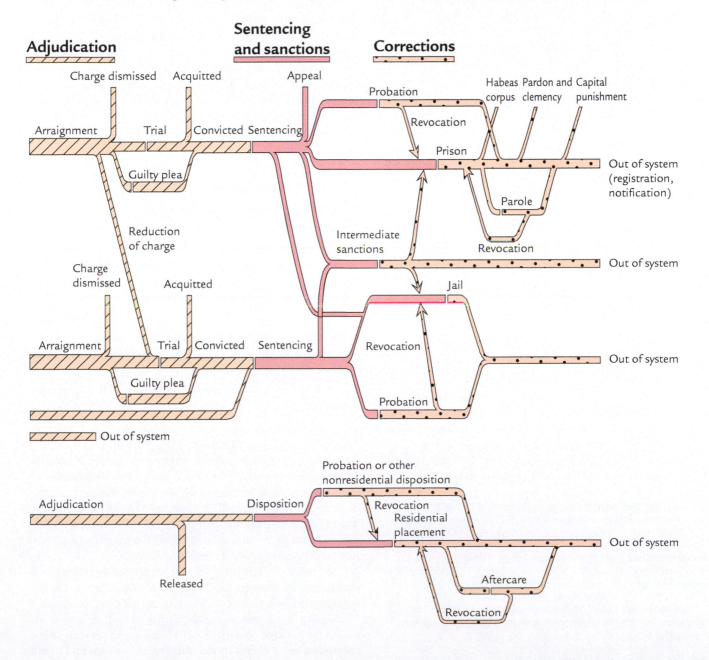

Numbers Talk. . .

5	The percentage of the adult population globally who used drugs at least once in 2015.
17	The percentage of individuals with drug-use disorders who are provided with treatment each year.
33	The percentage of prisoners who have used an illicit substance while incarcerated.

Source: United Nations Office on Drugs and Crime (2018). *World Drug Report 2017.* Vienna: United Nations Office on Drugs and Crime.

- During the **sentencing and sanctions** phase, assuming a conviction judgment has been reached, a sentence is imposed by the judge or (in capital cases) the jury. Possible sentences include one or more of the following: death penalty, a specific term to be spent confined in a prison, jail, or other correctional facility, probation, fines, or a requirement that the offender pay compensation (referred to as *restitution*) to the victim or victims.

- In cases in which a fine is imposed, arrangement must be made for the fine to be paid. Individuals convicted of a crime can be offered **probation**, or community supervision, in lieu of prison or an extended jail term. Community supervision is typically considered for lower-level offenses and/or for defendants without a significant criminal history. In cases in which a sentence involves **incarceration**, the offender "serves time" generally in a local jail (if the sentence is less than one year) or a state prison (if the sentence is more than a year). If sentenced under federal charges, incarceration is carried out in a federal correctional facility. Later, if eligible for **parole**, a prisoner receives a conditional release prior to serving the full prison term. In that case, the individual is required to be supervised by a parole officer in the community for the balance of the unexpired sentence. Violation of parole conditions can be the basis for revocation, or returning to prison.[3]

It should be noted that juvenile offenders (defined as individuals either 16, 17, or 18 years old or younger, depending on the U.S. state having jurisdiction) can be prosecuted and tried as adults under certain circumstances. However, in the vast majority of cases, juvenile offenders enter into an alternative juvenile justice system (see Figure 5.1) that has distinct differences from adult criminal proceedings. First of all,

sentencing and sanctions: The third phase of the criminal justice system in which a defendant, if convicted, receives a sentence and/or sanctions judgment by a judge or jury.

incarceration: The fourth phase of the criminal justice system in which a convicted defendant, if sentenced to imprisonment, enters a correctional facility.

probation: A sentence to a community supervision term, whereby individuals are monitored according to conditions set by the judge.

parole: A conditional release from prison prior to serving the full term of one's sentence.

referrals can be made not only by law enforcement officers but also by school officials, social service agencies, neighbors, or parents who have determined that specific behaviors of the juvenile require intervention by a formal judicial process. Second, juvenile justice decisions often divert the case out of a judicial system to alternatives such as counseling or educational programs, or youth may be placed on community supervision. In some cases, however, courts may order juveniles removed from their homes to foster homes, treatment facilities, or facilities with secure confinement. Following release from a treatment facility, there is often a period of aftercare.

Drug-Law Violators in the Criminal Justice System

In the United States, more than 1.6 million arrests were made in 2017 for a drug-law violation of some kind. To put it in perspective, compare this statistic to the average number of arrests made for other categories of crime:

- 519,000—Major violent crime (murder, manslaughter, forcible rape, robbery, or aggravated assault)

- 1,241,000—Major property crime (burglary, larceny-theft, or motor vehicle theft)

- 1,358,000—Driving under the influence (DUI) or drunkenness[4]

There are more than *three* times as many drug-law arrests compared to all types of major violent crimes, and slightly more than for major property crimes or crimes related to alcohol consumption. Figure 5.2 shows the distribution of drug-law arrests according to either the sale/manufacturing or possession of a controlled substance. Heroin and cocaine were the top sale/manufacturing arrests (36 percent), while possession of marijuana accounted for the majority of all possession arrests (43 percent) in 2017.[5]

When you consider the percentage of state and federal prison inmates in the United States who are presently incarcerated because of a drug-law conviction, the impact of drug-law enforcement on the criminal justice system becomes particularly striking. In 2016, about 47 percent of the approximately 189,000 inmates in federal prisons and about 15 percent of nearly 1.3 million inmates in state prisons were serving sentences for a drug-related offense. Overall,

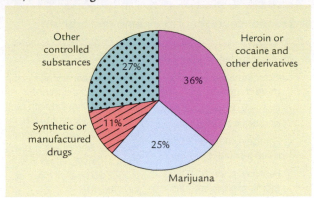

Sale/Manufacturing

Other controlled substances 27%

Heroin or cocaine and other derivatives 36%

Synthetic or manufactured drugs 11%

Marijuana 25%

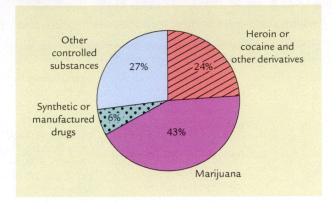

Possession

Other controlled substances 27%

Heroin or cocaine and other derivatives 24%

Synthetic or manufactured drugs 6%

Marijuana 43%

FIGURE 5.2

Drug-law arrests in 2017 according to the type of violation and the controlled substance involved.

Note: Arrests for sale/manufacturing accounted for 15 percent and arrests for possession accounted for 85 percent of all drug-law arrests in 2017.

Source: Federal Bureau of Investigation (2017, November). *Crime in the United States 2017.* Washington, D.C.: Federal Bureau of Investigation, U.S. Department of Justice, as posted by Drug War Facts, *https://www.drugwarfacts.org/chapter/crime_arrests#arrests=&overlay=table/annual-drug-arrests.*

there were approximately 286,000 drug-law offenders in U.S. prisons, about one in five prisoners of the total prison population.[6]

The preponderance of drug-law offenders in America's prison system has long been a subject of great concern and the impetus, as we will see, for reforms in the ways that drug-law violators are dealt with in the criminal justice system. What are the penalties that have been imposed on these individuals? The current status of criminal penalties for drug-law offenses, at the federal and state level, will be the topic of the next section.

Criminal Penalties for Drug-Law Offenses

Criminal drug-law offenses and their respective penalties fall into two broad categories. In the first category, referred to as **drug trafficking**, the offense is defined as the unauthorized manufacture, distribution by sale or gift, or possession with intent to distribute any controlled substance. In the second category, referred to as **simple possession**, the offense is defined as having a controlled substance on one's person or under one's control without intention to engage in sale or distribution. Cases of simple possession require that the amount of drugs seized is small enough to suggest it is for the purpose of personal use only, and that there were no large amounts of cash, baggies, or other items that would indicate the intention to sell or distribute.

Laws related to controlled substances exist on both the state and federal level. Hence, while most drug arrests are made at the local level, anyone arrested for a drug crime can be charged with a federal offense. This is most likely when the crime is made by a federal officer, the offender crosses state lines, or the arrest is made on federal land, like a national park. Prison sentences are often longer for federal crimes due to federal mandatory minimum sentence laws and because the federal Bureau

of Prisons has no parole option. The next section will examine federal penalties for drug crimes in more detail.

Federal Penalties for Drug Trafficking

The current federal law with regard to drug trafficking is a result of statutes originating in the Controlled Substances Act of 1970 and subsequently revised in 1986, 1988, and 2010. As mentioned in Chapter 3, penalties for drug trafficking are most severe for Schedule I and II controlled substances (Table 5.1). Federal penalties for drug trafficking in marijuana, while officially a Schedule I controlled substance, are treated separately (Table 5.2). As a result of the Anti-Drug Abuse Acts of

drug trafficking: The unauthorized manufacture of any controlled substance, its distribution by sale or gift, or possession of such a substance with intent to distribute it.

simple possession: Having on one's person any illicit or nonprescribed controlled substance for one's own use.

A simple street drug transaction constitutes the most basic form of drug trafficking.

Credit: Luka Lajst/E+/Getty Images

TABLE 5.1

Federal trafficking penalties for Schedules I, II, III, IV, and V controlled substances (except marijuana and hashish)

SCHEDULE	SUBSTANCE/QUANTITY	PENALTY	SUBSTANCE/QUANTITY	PENALTY
II	Cocaine 500–4,999 grams mixture	**First Offense:** Not less than 5 years and not more than 40 years. If death or serious bodily injury, not less than 20 years or more than life. Fine of not more than $5 million if an individual, $25 million if not an individual.	Cocaine 5 kilograms or more mixture	**First Offense:** Not less than 10 years and not more than life. If death or serious bodily injury, not less than 20 years or more than life. Fine of not more than $10 million if an individual, $50 million if not an individual.
II	Crack cocaine 28–279 grams mixture		Cocaine Base 280 grams or more mixture	
IV	Fentanyl 40–399 grams mixture		Fentanyl 400 grams or more mixture	
I	Fentanyl analog 10–99 grams mixture		Fentanyl analog 100 grams or more mixture	
I	Heroin 100–999 grams mixture	**Second Offense:** Not less than 10 years and not more than life. If death or serious bodily injury, life imprisonment. Fine of not more than $8 million if an individual, $50 million if not an individual.	Heroin 1 kilogram or more mixture	**Second Offense:** Not less than 20 years, and not more than life. If death or serious bodily injury, life imprisonment. Fine of not more than $20 million if an individual, $75 million if not an individual.
I	LSD 1–9 grams mixture		LSD 10 grams or more mixture	
II	Methamphetamine 5–49 grams pure or 50–499 grams mixture		Methamphetamine 50 grams or more pure or 500 grams or more mixture	**Two or More Prior Offenses:** Life imprisonment. Fine of not more than $20 million if an individual, $75 million if not an individual.
II	PCP 10–99 grams pure or 100–999 grams mixture		PCP 100 grams or more pure or 1 kilogram or more mixture	

SUBSTANCE/QUANTITY	PENALTY
Any amount of other Schedule I and II substances	**First Offense:** Not more than 20 years. If death or serious bodily injury, not less than 20 years or more than life. Fine $1 million if an individual, $5 million if not an individual.
Any drug product containing *gamma*-hydroxybutyric acid	**Second Offense:** Not more than 30 years. If death or serious bodily injury, life imprisonment. Fine $2 million if an individual, $10 million if not an individual.
Flunitrazepam (Schedule IV) 1 gram	
Any amount of other Schedule III drugs	**First Offense:** Not more than 10 years. If death or serious bodily injury, not more than 15 years. Fine not more than $500,000 if an individual, $2.5 million if not an individual.
	Second Offense: Not more than 20 years. If death or serious injury, not more than 30 years. Fine not more than $1 million if an individual, $5 million if not an individual.
Any amount of all other Schedule IV drugs (other than one gram or more of flunitrazepam)	**First Offense:** Not more than 5 years. Fine not more than $250,000 if an individual, $1 million if not an individual.
	Second Offense: Not more than 10 years. Fine not more than $500,000 if an individual, $2 million if other than an individual.
Any amount of all Schedule V drugs	**First Offense:** Not more than 1 year. Fine not more than $100,000 if an individual, $250,000 if not an individual.
	Second Offense: Not more than 4 years. Fine not more than $200,000 if an individual, $500,000 if not an individual.

Source: Drug Enforcement Administration, U.S. Department of Justice, Washington, D.C.

1986 and 1988, a number of special circumstances are considered in decisions to increase the penalty that is imposed:

- Penalties are doubled for first-offense trafficking of Schedule I or II controlled substances if death or bodily injury results from the use of such substances.

- Penalties for the sale of drugs by a person over 21 years of age to someone under the age of 18 are increased to up to double those imposed for sale to an adult.

- Penalties for the sale of drugs within 1,000 feet of an elementary or secondary school are increased to up to double those imposed when the sale is made elsewhere.

- Fines for companies or business associations are generally 2.5 times greater than for individuals. In either case, penalties include the forfeiture of cars, boats, or planes that have been used in the illegal conveyance of controlled substances.[7]

TABLE 5.2

Federal trafficking penalties for marijuana, hashish, and hashish oil Schedule I controlled substances

Marijuana 1,000 kilograms or more marijuana mixture or 1,000 or more marijuana plants	**First Offense:** Not less than 10 years or more than life. If death or serious bodily injury, not less than 20 years, or more than life. Fine not more than $10 million if an individual, $50 million if other than an individual. **Second Offense:** Not less than 20 years or more than life. If death or serious bodily injury, life imprisonment Fine not more than $20 million if an individual, $75 million if other than an individual.
Marijuana 100–999 kilograms marijuana mixture or 100–999 marijuana plants	**First Offense:** Not less than 5 years or more than 40 years. If death or serious bodily injury, not less than 20 years or more than life. Fine not more than $5 million if an individual, $25 million if other than an individual. **Second Offense:** Not less than 10 years or more than life. If death or serious bodily injury, life imprisonment. Fine not more than $8 million if an individual, $50 million if other than an individual.
Marijuana 50–99 kilograms marijuana mixture, 50–99 marijuana plants Hashish more than 10 kilograms Hashish oil more than 1 kilogram	**First Offense:** Not more than 20 years. If death or serious bodily injury, not less than 20 years or more than life. Fine $1 million if an individual, $5 million if other than an individual. **Second Offense:** Not more than 30 years. If death or serious bodily injury, life imprisonment. Fine $2 million if an individual, $10 million if other than an individual.
Marijuana less than 50 kilograms marijuana (but does not include 50 or more marijuana plants regardless of weight) 1–49 marijuana plants Hashish 10 kilograms or less Hashish oil 1 kilogram or less	**First Offense:** Not more than 5 years. Fine not more than $250,000, $1 million if other than an individual. **Second Offense:** Not more than 10 years. Fine $500,000 if an individual, $2 million if other than individual.

Source: Drug Enforcement Administration, U.S. Department of Justice, Washington, DC.

Federal Penalties for Simple Possession of Controlled Substances

Federal penalties for simple possession of a controlled substance in *any* of the five schedules are much simpler. First-time offenders for simple possession face a maximum of one-year imprisonment and a fine of between $1,000 and $5,000. Second-time offenders face a maximum of two years and a fine of up to $10,000.[8]

Felonies, Misdemeanors, and State Drug Laws

Since all federal penalties for drug trafficking, whatever the circumstances or the category of controlled substance, carry a minimum of one-year incarceration and fine (see Tables 5.1 and 5.2), the offenses are, by definition, considered **felonies**. Offenses that carry a penalty of up to one-year incarceration and fine or a fine alone are considered, by definition, **misdemeanors**.

Federal penalties set the standard for the punishment of drug-law offenses in the United States, but most drug-related offenses are prosecuted at the state level rather than the federal level, and state regulations for drug trafficking and simple possession can vary greatly. In the case of simple possession of a controlled substance, penalties depend on the drug involved and the statutes of the particular U.S. state where the violation has occurred. An offense might be a misdemeanor in one state and a **felony** in another. Detailed information regarding penalties for simple possession is available through state-specific Web sites. Obviously, from the standpoint of a drug-law offender, the degree of variation in drug-law statutes from state to state can have an enormous impact on his or her life.

Drug Paraphernalia

Certain other aspects of drug-taking behavior, such as the day-to-day regulation of alcohol sales and distribution, are regulated primarily by state and local municipalities, unless interstate commerce is involved. U.S. states and local municipalities have also taken on regulatory authority with regard to **drug paraphernalia**, products whose predominant use is to administer, prepare, package, or store illicit drugs. Nearly all U.S. states have statutes making it unlawful to sell these items to minors, unless they are accompanied by a parent or legal guardian. In addition, the importation, exportation, and advertising of drug paraphernalia are prohibited.[9]

felony: A criminal offense for which a sentence carries a minimum of one-year incarceration and a fine.

misdemeanor: A criminal offense for which a sentence carries an incarceration of up to one year and a fine or a fine alone.

drug paraphernalia: Products that are considered to be used to administer, prepare, package, or store illicit drugs.

Rethinking Drug-Law Penalties: 1970s–Present

Prevailing attitudes toward crime and punishment in the 1970s and 1980s, particularly with respect to drug-law violations, was quite different than they are today. Public outcry over dramatic increases in drug use and criminal behavior associated with it during this time resulted in a criminal justice system that emphasized deterrence, incarceration, and general retribution toward drug-law offenders. Official statements of the Office of National Drug Control Policy, such as the following issued in 1989, summarized the punitive stance:

> To prevent people from using drugs, drug enforcement activities must make it increasingly difficult to engage in any drug activity with impunity ... we need a national drug law enforcement strategy that casts a wide net and seeks to ensure that all drug users—whatever its scale—face the risk of criminal sanctions.[10]

Quick Concept Check 5.1

Understanding the Criminal Justice System

Check your understanding of the fundamental aspects of the criminal justice system by matching the terms/events on the left with the identifications/definitions on the right.

1. Misdemeanor penalty
2. Felony penalty
3. Federal penalty for simple possession (first offense)
4. Judges determine whether there is probable cause that a crime has been committed
5. Drug paraphernalia
6. Parole
7. Arraignment
8. Probation

a. Part of the adjudication phase
b. Part of the prosecution and pretrial services phase
c. Conditional release from imprisonment prior to serving the full term of the sentence
d. Imprisonment for a minimum of one year and a fine
e. Maximum of one-year imprisonment and a $1,000–5,000 fine
f. Up to one-year imprisonment and a fine or a fine alone
g. Regulated primarily by state and local municipalities
h. Community supervision as an alternative to incarceration

Answers: 1. f 2. d 3. e 4. b 5. g 6. c 7. a 8. h

In light of the social mood, at that time, toward drug-taking behavior in general and the criminal activity associated with crack cocaine abuse in particular (see Chapter 3), new laws were enacted that required the imposition of severe criminal penalties for drug-law offenses. The result was a policy that established mandatory minimum sentences.

The Issue of Mandatory Minimum Sentencing

In 1973, the so-called Rockefeller Drug Laws, named for former New York Governor Nelson A. Rockefeller, were enacted. Under this legislation, among other provisions, a mandatory minimum sentence of 15 years to life imprisonment was established as the penalty for simple possession of more than four ounces (112 grams) of heroin, cocaine, or any other "narcotic" drug. This criminal penalty at the time was equivalent to the penalty for second-degree murder.

For many years, the Rockefeller Drug Laws represented the harsh and inflexible policies toward drug-law violations that were being enacted across the nation. While the penalties for marijuana possession in New York State were relaxed in 1979, the overall effect of the 1973 legislation on the criminal justice system, particularly with respect to nonviolent violators, was devastating. Drug offenders as a percentage of the prison population in New York tripled from 1973 to 1994. Similar statutes stipulating **mandatory minimum sentencing** for drug offenders produced similar effects in other U.S. states as well. Arguably, no other legislative policy had contributed more to the increase in the number of drug offenders in U.S. prisons than the policy of mandatory minimum sentencing.[11]

Essentially, mandatory minimum sentencing required a judge to impose a fixed minimal term in prison for individuals convicted of certain crimes, regardless of the individual's role in the crime or other mitigating circumstances. Guidelines for sentences were based on the type of drug, the weight of the drug, and the number of prior convictions; offenders were required to serve their entire sentence (or in some states a minimum of 85 percent) without parole. Under federal law, for example, anyone convicted of selling 500 grams of powder cocaine received a minimum prison sentence of five years. A judge could issue a sentence shorter than the mandatory minimum only if the defendant provided "substantial assistance" or cooperation in the prosecution of another offender. This meant that if the defendant implicated someone else in a crime (rightly or wrongly), he or she could possibly escape a mandatory sentence. Even then, however, the prosecutor, not the judge, had the power to decide whether this "assistance" was valuable enough to warrant a reduction in sentence.

Proponents of mandatory sentencing believed that the policy was an effective deterrent to drug use and drug trafficking because it enhanced awareness of the consequences of breaking

> **mandatory minimum sentencing:** A policy that requires a judge to impose a fixed minimal term in prison for individuals convicted of certain crimes, regardless of the individual's role in the crime or other mitigating circumstances.

the law and kept drug offenders off the streets. Supporters of tough sentences for drug crimes claimed that the "drug epidemic" had a devastating effect on many communities, and the law was needed to protect these vulnerable communities by keeping drug offenders in prison. It was argued that mandatory sentences made the task of judges easier by allowing each offender to be sentenced equally under the law. Judges no longer had to weigh conflicting evidence in the course of deciding how much time a convicted offender would spend in jail or prison. In addition, mandatory sentences aided prosecutors and law enforcement authorities because the prospect of sentences tended to persuade lower-level drug dealers to testify against upper-level ones (Drug Enforcement ... in Focus).

Critics of mandatory minimum sentencing maintained that these inflexible penalty sentences filled American prisons with minor players, such as drug abusers, rather than major drug traffickers. They argued that as federal and state governments continued to spend billions of dollars on the operation of existing prisons and the construction of new ones, they neglected other social needs, such as drug-abuse prevention, education, and treatment. It is not uncommon for some U.S. states to have faster-growing prison budgets than drug-abuse treatment and education budgets, a particularly disturbing trend given the potential for effective drug-abuse treatment programs to be available. The practice of making false accusations against innocent parties by defendants in a desperate effort to reduce their sentence times became rampant.[12]

Since 1992, however, sentencing reforms have caught hold with the American public and, more specifically, state legislators. State laws regarding mandatory sentencing have been modified or rescinded, largely through the lobbying of such organizations as the Families Against Mandatory Minimums (FAMM), the U.S. Sentencing Commission, the American Psychological Association, the National Association of Criminal Defense Lawyers, and

Drug Enforcement . . . in Focus

Penalties for Crack versus Penalties for Cocaine: Correcting an Injustice

Under the 1986 Anti-Drug Abuse Act, the penalties for possession of crack (the smokable form of cocaine) were much more severe than those for possession of cocaine itself (the powder form). A mandatory minimum prison sentence of five years was imposed upon conviction of possessing more than 500 grams of powder forms of cocaine, whereas the possession of as little as 5 grams of crack could result in the same penalty. This became known as the "100-to-1 rule," referring to the threshold in the drug quantity for an equivalent prison sentence. In addition, in 1988, the federal penalty for possession of more than 5 grams of cocaine powder was set at a minimum of one-year imprisonment; the penalty for possessing an equivalent amount of crack was set at a minimum of five years.

This disparity, according to critics of this policy, had resulted in far more African Americans in prison for five years or more than white drug offenders. Why? Statistics showed that whites were more likely to snort or inject cocaine, whereas African Americans were more likely to smoke cocaine in its cheaper crack form. The differential effects of drug-law enforcement for the two forms of cocaine were reflected in a drug-offense inmate population that became divided along racial lines. On the one hand, 90 percent of crack cocaine convictions involved African Americans; on the other, nearly two-thirds of powder cocaine abusers in the United States were white. Moreover, it was more common for offenses relating to the possession of powder cocaine to be prosecuted under state regulations, under which mandatory minimum sentences frequently did not apply.

In 2007, the U.S. Sentencing Commission, the agency that establishes guidelines for federal prison sentences, unanimously voted to lighten punishments retroactively for some crimes related to crack cocaine possession. As a result, the stark disparity that had existed for more than 20 years in penalties for powder cocaine and crack cocaine was narrowed, and more than 19,000 prisoners became eligible for early release. As many as 17,000 others incarcerated for a crack-related offense, however, could not benefit from the change. These prisoners had been given the absolute minimum term in the first place or were arrested with huge amounts of crack cocaine.

In 2010, the Fair Sentencing Act was signed into law, officially narrowing the gap between penalties involving crack cocaine and powder cocaine. Under the new regulations, the amount of crack cocaine subject to the five-year minimum sentence was increased from five to 28 grams. The former "100-to-1 rule" (500 versus 5) was changed to the "18-to-1 rule" (500 versus 28). In addition, the Sentencing Commission was directed to review and amend its guidelines to increase penalties for persons convicted of using violence while trafficking in illicit drugs. Table 5.1 reflects the current penalties for the two forms of cocaine. While some continue to fight to eliminate the crack/power cocaine disparity altogether, there have been no legislative changes in this policy since 2010.

Sources: Hatsukami, D. K.; and Fischman, M. W. (1996). Crack cocaine and cocaine hydrochloride: Are the differences myth or reality? *Journal of the American Medical Association, 276,* 1580–1588. Stout, D. (2007, December 12). Retroactively, panel reduces drug sentences. *The New York Times,* pp. A1, A31. Weinreb, A. (2010, August 4). *Obama signs fair sentencing act into law.* http://news.suite101.com. Wren, C. S. (1997, July 22). Reno and top drug official urge smaller gap in cocaine sentences. *The New York Times,* pp. A1, A12.

the American Bar Association. At one time, in Michigan, possession with intent to deliver more than 650 grams of heroin or cocaine carried a mandatory life sentence with no chance of parole. This law now has been changed to 20 years to life, with the possibility of parole after 15 years. In Mississippi, sentencing laws that had required drug offenders, even those convicted of simple possession of a controlled substance, to serve 85 percent of their sentence, no matter the circumstances of their incarceration, now have reduced the maximum sentence to less than 25 percent. As of 2009, judges in New York who had previously been permitted no discretion in sentencing now have leeway in deciding whether a drug offender should be sent to a substance abuse treatment center instead of prison. Changes in New York State law have permitted thousands of inmates convicted of nonviolent drug offenses to apply for reduced sentences or to have sentences set aside.

The Justice Reinvestment Initiative is a public–private partnership aimed to improve public safety and cost savings for taxpayers by limiting use of prison to serious and repeat offenders, and investing in alternatives to incarceration. This initiative contributed to many state sentencing reforms. In 2011, Kentucky distinguished between serious drug trafficking and drug peddling, assigning less harsh sentences to those who sell small drug amounts for personal use, and

North Carolina required first-time drug offenders convicted of possession to be placed in diversion programs. During this same timeframe, Ohio and South Carolina eliminated the disparity between crack and powder cocaine offenses. In 2015, Alabama created a new felony category for the lowest level drug offenses, requiring community corrections programs as a sentence rather than prison. In 2016, Alaska reduced drug possession cases from a felony to misdemeanor, and Maryland removed penalty enhancements for repeat low-level drug offenders and increased access to residential treatment services.[13] These are just a few examples of the state-level sentencing reform efforts related to drug offenses that are aimed at reducing lengthy periods of confinement.

At the federal level, a major U.S. Supreme Court decision in 2007 ruled that federal district judges had broad discretion to impose what would be, in their judgment, reasonable sentences in criminal proceedings, even if federal guidelines were more stringent (Portrait).[14] The Fair Sentencing Act of 2010 was bipartisan legislation passed by Congress aimed at repealing mandatory minimum sentences related to federal crack sentencing laws (discussed in more detail under "Drug Enforcement … in Focus"). Following suit, in 2014, the U.S. Sentencing Commission voted unanimously to reduce the penalties for drug trafficking for an array of drug types by two "offense levels," leading to less mandatory time

PORTRAIT

Former State Senator John R. Dunne—Drug Warrior/ Drug-War Reformer

In 1973, John R. Dunne, Republican state senator of New York, was leading the charge for legislation that became known as the Rockefeller Drug Laws. It was a time of public panic. New York and other states around the country were contending with dramatic increases in illicit drug use (specifically heroin) and suffering its criminal and social consequences. Harsh mandatory minimum sentencing seemed to be the answer.

A quarter-century later, it was clear that the laws had done more harm than good. By 2001, Dunne himself was fully convinced that reform was more than overdue. The laws, according to Dunne, did nothing to reduce the drug trade, instead "the only thing they've done is to fill the prisons." Case in point: Daniel Boyd (not his real name), 46-year-old father of four with no criminal record, serving time in maximum security for 15 years to life after signing for a FedEx package delivered to his uncle's house that turned out to contain cocaine. Records would show that while most

drug users and drug traffickers were white, 94 percent of New York's inmates convicted of drug-law offenses were either African American or Latino.

Even after resigning his state senate seat in 1989, Dunne acted on his conscience and became the leading advocate for drug-law reform in New York. He appeared in emotional television commercials alongside an African American grandmother from upstate New York whose family had been destroyed by the policy of mandatory minimum sentencing. The appeals that Dunne had made and the connections to former colleagues in the State Senate were powerful, but the move to reform was frustratingly slow. It was difficult to dislodge conservative legislators from their tough-on-drugs stance. Some legislators saw the reforms as jeopardizing local economies that were dependent upon the operation of state prisons and the people who worked there. In 2002, reform legislation was stalled.

It was not until 2009, under former New York State Governor David A.

Patterson, that legislators reached an agreement. Mandatory prison sentences were eliminated for most drug offenses. Judges were given more leeway in sentencing decisions, drug courts and other alternatives to incarceration were expanded, drug-law penalties were reduced, and, importantly, about 1,500 people incarcerated at the time under the old drug laws were allowed retroactive resentencing. John R. Dunne and fellow reformers had finally succeeded in writing a new chapter in the history of drug legislation in the state.

Sources: New York's Rockefeller Drug Laws: Explaining the reforms of 2009. www.drugpolicy.org. Perlman, E. (2000, April). Public safety and justice: Terms of imprisonment. *www.governing. com.* Goldberg, M. (2002, August 5). Reforming Rockefeller drug laws. *www. alternet.org.* Peters, J. W. (2009, March 26). Albany reaches deal to repeal '70s drug laws. *The New York Times.* www.nytimes. com. The John R. Dunne Fund of the New York Bar Foundation. *www.tnybf.org.*

Quick Concept Check 5.2

Understanding Mandatory Minimum Sentences

Check your understanding of the impact of mandatory minimum sentencing on drug offenders by marking the following as true or false.

1. The Rockefeller Drug Laws in New York are an early example of legislation that enforces mandatory minimum sentences.

2. Mandatory minimum sentences increase a judge's discretion in sentencing drug offenders.

3. Mandatory minimum sentences have vastly contributed to the increase in the number of drug offenders in U.S. prisons.

4. The Justice Reinvestment Initiative has worked to maintain mandatory minimum sentencing.

5. The Fair Sentencing Act of 2010 has equalized punishment for powder and crack cocaine.

Answers:
1. true 2. false 3. true 4. false 5. false

Sentencing Policies and Mass Incarceration

Sentencing policies during the height of the War on Drugs were part of a larger movement in the United States to get tough on crime, with drug-related crime viewed as a central component to be contained. Crime growth in the 1980s was associated with a desire for specific policies of intensified punishment for drug offenses. Besides mandatory minimum sentencing, other policies included (1) "three strikes and you're out" sentencing in which life sentences were imposed on those convicted of more than two violent or serious felonies and (2) "truth in sentencing" laws in which parole was either restricted or abolished, requiring convicted individuals to serve their full sentences.

These policies had a substantial impact on the growth of incarceration between 1980 and 2010. Longer sentence lengths drove up the rate of incarceration, many because of mandatory minimum sentences. "Truth-in-sentencing" reforms, popular during the 1990s, were aimed at the restriction or abolition of parole so that individuals served their full sentences. Similarly, "three strikes" laws resulted in life sentences to those convicted of more than two violent or serious felonies. These laws affected sentence length, which also drove the rate of incarceration.[16] More people were going to prison and staying in prison longer.

By 2015, there were over 2 million people incarcerated in jails and prisons, approximately one quarter for drug offenses.[17] The United States incarcerates more people for drug offenses than any other country, and the rise of incarceration appeared largely attributable to drug offenses.[18] In 1980, the rate of incarceration in a state facility was approximately 15 per 100,000. By 2010, this rate increased nearly 10 times, to 143 per 100,000.[19] Hence, the increase in the incarceration rates in the United States over a four-decade timeframe appears largely attributable to "get tough" policies, particularly those aimed at drug offenders.

Since the rise in incarceration began, it had a disproportionate effect on African Americans and Latinos. The critical question is whether the differences in imprisonment are due to differences in criminality (e.g., African Americans and Latinos committing crime at a higher rate than whites), or differences in case processing (e.g., African Americans and Latinos being more likely to be arrested, prosecuted, and incarcerated than whites). The reality is that the disparities in incarceration rates between races appear to be a result of both differences in offense rates and case processing. While it is difficult to untangle the causes of high rates of incarceration among minorities, it is clear that an increased racial disparity in imprisonment rates, relative to arrests, particularly since the 1980s, is linked to the severe sentencing laws enacted in the 1980s and 1990s; this is particularly clear for drug offenders.[20] African Americans, for example, are arrested for drug offenses at a higher rate than whites. This is related to police emphasis on street-level dealers, with drug laws being enforced with vigor in low-income, minority communities. Minorities are also more likely to be

being sentenced. This amendment was made retroactive, resulting in over 30,000 federal cases being granted a motion for sentence reduction.[15] Despite this shift, in 2017, Attorney General Jeff Sessions (serving under President Trump) charged federal prosecutors to apply strict enforcement of the law to drug offenders, utilizing the mandatory minimum guidelines. This was a significant shift from the position of President Barak Obama and Eric Holder, previous Attorney General in the Obama administration.

Incarceration.

Credit: Tatagatta/Shutterstock.

sentenced to prison, and as discussed, longer sentences have been imposed for offenses related to crack cocaine that disproportionally impact African Americans.[21]

Gender has been explicitly intertwined with race and social class in the impact of policies of the War on Drugs. Incarceration rates have increased more rapidly for females than males since the early 1970s.[22] In the 1980s, the term "crack baby" emerged (see Chapter 10), and women began to be prosecuted with lengthy sentences for exposing their unborn child to crack cocaine. While the goal was to protect the unborn fetuses, a crackdown on drug-addicted minority women also led them to avoid prenatal care and drug treatment, due to fear of reprisal. In 2010, more than half of women sentenced to prison committed either a property or drug-related crime, compared to just 35 percent of men.[23] This suggests that women are more likely than men to be in prison for a nonviolent crime. Approximately seven in ten women under correctional sanction have children under the age of 18.[24] Hence, the impact of female incarceration rates for nonviolent offenses extends not only to the women themselves but to their children and communities as well.

A New Direction

The year 2010 marked the first time the United States saw a downward trend in rates of imprisonment since 1972.[25] Early in the twenty-first century, as noted earlier, several U.S. states began to reform their mandatory minimum sentencing laws, particularly with an aim to decrease the sentence length for drug or other low-level, nonviolent offenders.[26] Greater attention was also given toward rehabilitative efforts. Examples include

- expanded use of "good time" sentence adjustments (reductions in incarceration) for participation in prison-based rehabilitation and education programs;

- diversion efforts for first- and second-time drug, and other nonviolent offenders;

- putting more effort and resources toward reentry services that help incarcerated individuals' transition back to the community; and

- expanded use of drug courts and other alternatives to incarceration for higher risk and need offenders.

Like prisons and jails, the population of individuals on community supervision (primarily probation) has also seen a slight, but steady decrease since 2010.[27] Not only are lower-level offenders being diverted from jails and prisons but also from lengthy community supervision terms. For example, since 2012, Alabama and Hawaii have shortened probation terms. Likewise, Georgia passed bipartisan legislation in 2017 that limits time served for technical violations (i.e., violations of the conditions of supervision), allows judges to decrease probation time for good behavior, and requires supervision services for offenders to use evidence-based practices (practices that are backed by research). Similarly, Minnesota, Oklahoma, and Louisiana proposed or had pending bills in 2017 that would reduce probation and/or parole terms.[28] The longer an individual is on community supervision, the more likely that person is to violate the terms of supervision and end up in jail or prison. Hence, this movement toward more manageable community supervision terms will contribute to continuing the downward trend of incarceration in the United States. Chapter 7 will address in more detail correctional interventions, such as specialty courts and treatment strategies aimed at helping drug and other offenders make long-term behavioral changes that keep them from reoffending. This is another important strategy for addressing those that violate the law related to drug and alcohol issues.

Summary

The Phases of Criminal Justice and Drug-Law Violators in the Criminal Justice System

- The criminal justice system in the United States consists of four phases of judicial events: prosecution and pretrial services, adjudication, sentencing and sanctions, and corrections. At each phase, defendants may exit the system if no further action is required.

- More than 1.6 million arrests are made each year for a drug-law violation of some kind.

- According to 2016 statistics, about 50 percent of federal prisoners and about 16 percent of state prisoners are being incarcerated solely for a drug-law violation.

Criminal Penalties for Drug-Law Offenses

- Federal guidelines for drug-law violation penalties make the distinction between drug trafficking and simple possession of controlled substances. In addition, separate

guidelines are made for drug trafficking of marijuana and controlled substances other than marijuana.

- Federal drug trafficking penalties are most severe for controlled substances in Schedule I and Schedule II categories.

- For all schedules, the federal penalty for a first-time simple possession offense is a maximum of one-year imprisonment and a fine of between $1,000 and $5,000.

- State penalties for drug trafficking and simple possession can vary greatly from federal penalties.

- U.S. states and local municipalities have regulatory authority for the sale and distribution of drug paraphernalia that is associated with illicit drug use.

Rethinking Drug-Law Penalties: 1970s–Present

- Mandatory minimum sentencing has required a judge to impose a fixed minimal length of imprisonment for individuals convicted of certain crimes, regardless of a person's role in the crime or other mitigating factors. Strict mandatory minimum sentencing laws in New York have been referred to as the Rockefeller Drug Laws, enacted in 1973.

- In recent years, there has been a significant shift toward providing judges with a greater degree of discretion in their sentencing of drug offenders. Penalties with respect to powder cocaine and crack cocaine were revised because of the Fair Sentencing Act of 2010, to reduce a disparity that had been considered unjust.

Sentencing Policies and Mass Incarceration

- Between the early 1970s and late 2000s, mandatory minimum sentences and other "get tough" strategies contributed to a substantial rise in the rate of incarceration in America, which disproportionally affected minorities and women.
- The incarceration rate in the United States declined in 2010, the first time it had done so since 1972.
- Use of lengthy community supervision terms is also undergoing reexamination, with a greater focus on rehabilitation and effective reentry for nonviolent, drug-abusing offenders.

Key Terms

adjudication, p. 86
drug paraphernalia, p. 91
drug trafficking, p. 89
felony, p. 91

incarceration, p. 86
mandatory minimum
   sentencing, p. 92
misdemeanor, p. 91

parole, p. 87
probation, p. 86
prosecution and pretrial
   services, p. 86

sentencing and sanctions,
   p. 86
simple possession, p. 89

Review Questions

1. Describe the judicial events in the four phases of the American criminal justice system.
2. Describe the special circumstances that require an imposition of increased federal penalties for drug trafficking. Discuss the arguments that these special circumstances should have stricter penalties.
3. Briefly describe the historical events that created the mandatory minimum sentences for drug-law offenders.

4. How did mandatory minimums and other get-tough strategies contribute to mass incarceration?
5. Discuss the ways that the "War on Drugs" impacted minorities and women.
6. How might more recent reforms that have contributed to the decline in the incarceration impact drug offenders?

Critical Thinking: What Would You Do?

This chapter reviewed important criminal justice policies that worked to remove drug users and dealers from the street, but also vastly increased the number of nonviolent drug offenders undergoing long prison sentences. If your goal was to continue the current trend of decreasing the number of people in prison, what changes would you put in place to address those who violate drug laws? Would you change some of the current drug polices? If yes, how?

Endnotes

1. Adapted from an interview by Rachael Martin of Judge Mark Bennett of Iowa, appearing on Morning Edition of National Public Radio on June 1, 2017. https://www.npr.org/2017/06/01/531004316/a-federal-judge-says-mandatory-minimum-sentences-often-dont-fit-the-crime
2. Federal Bureau of Investigation. *Crime in the United States 2016*, Table 18.
3. Bureau of Justice Statistics. *Criminal justice system flowchart*. Accessed (May 12, 2018) from: http://www.bjs.gov/content/largechart.cfm.
4. Federal Bureau of Investigation. *Crime in the United States 2016*.
5. Federal Bureau of Investigation (2017, November). *Crime in the United States 2017*. Washington, D.C.: Federal Bureau of Investigation, U.S. Department of Justice, as posted by Drug War Facts, https://www.drugwarfacts.org/chapter/crime_arrests#arrests
6. Carson, E. A. (2018, January). Prisoners in 2016. *Bureau of justice statistics bulletin*. Washington, D.C.: Bureau of Justice Statistics, U.S. Department of Justice, Tables 12 and 13.

7. Drug Enforcement Administration, U.S. Department of Justice, Washington, D.C. *Statutes of the* Controlled Substances Act of 1970, *as amended and revised in 1986 and 1988.*

8. Drug Enforcement Administration. Yeh, B. T. (2012, December 13). *CRS Report to Congress: Drug offenses: Maximum fines and terms of imprisonment for violation of the Federal Controlled Substances Act and related laws.* Washington, D.C.: Congressional Research Services, United States Congress.

9. Healey, K. (1988). *State and local experience with drug paraphernalia laws.* Washington D.C.: U.S. Government Printing Office, pp. 69–73.

10. Office of National Drug Control Policy (1989). *National Drug Control Strategy.* Washington, D.C.: Office of National Drug Control Policy, Executive Office of the President, p. 18.

11. Gray, M. (2009, April 2). New York's Rockefeller drug laws. *Time Magazine Online,* http://content.time.com/time/nation/article/0,8599,1888864,00.html.

12. Donohue, J. J., III; and Siegelman, P. (1998). Allocating resources among prisons and social programs in the battle against crime. *Journal of Legal Studies, 27,* 30–43. Horowitz, H.; Sung, H-E.; and Foster, S. E. (2006, January–February). The role of substance abuse in U.S. juvenile justice systems and populations. *Corrections Compendium, 31*(1), 1–4, 24–26.

13. Public Safety Performance Project (2017, January 22). *Justice Reinvestment Initiative Brings Sentencing Reforms in 23 States. The Pew Charitable Trusts,* http://www.pewtrusts.org/en/research-and-analysis/issue-briefs/2016/01/states-modify-sentencing-laws-through-justice-reinvestment.

14. Associated Press (2009, December 20). Prison population to have first drop since 1972. Greenhouse, L. (2007, December 11). Justices restore judges' control over sentencing. *The New York Times,* pp. A1, A28. Peters, J. W. (2009, March 11). Legislation to overhaul Rockefeller drug laws advances swiftly. *The New York Times,* p. 20. Stout, D. (2007, December 12). Retroactively, panel reduces drug sentences. *The New York Times,* pp. A1, A31.

15. U.S. Sentencing Commission (October, 2017). *U.S. Sentencing Commission 2014 Drug Guidelines Amendment Retroactivity Data Report.* Washington, D.C.: U.S. Department of Justice.

16. National Academy of Sciences (2014). *The growth of incarceration in the United States: Exploring causes and consequences.* Washington, D.C.: The National Academies Press, p. 54.

17. Kaeble, D.; and Glaze, L. (2016). *Correctional Populations in the United States, 2015.* NCJ 250374. Washington, D.C.: U.S. Department of Justices, Bureau of Justice Statistics.

18. Justice Policy Institute (2008, January). *Substance Abuse Treatment and Public Safety.* Washington, D.C.: Justice Policy Institute, p. 1. http://www.justicepolicy.org

19. National Academy of Sciences (2014). p. 47.

20. Ibid., p. 95.

21. Ibid., p. 98.

22. Ibid., p. 64.

23. Guerino, P.; Harrison, P. M.; and Sabol, W. J. (2011). *Prisoners in 2010.* NCJ 236096. Washington, D.C.: U.S. Department of Justice, Bureau of Justice Statistics.

24. Greenfeld, L. A.; and Snell, T. L. (1999). *Women Offenders.* NCJ 175688. Washington, D.C.: U.S. Department of Justice, Bureau of Justice Statistics, Special Report.

25. Guerino, Harrison, and Sabol, *Prisoners in 2010.*

26. Greene, J. A. (2003). *Smart on crime: Positive trends in state-level sentencing and corrections policy.* Washington, D.C.: Families Against Mandatory Minimums.

27. Kaeble, D. (2018, April). *Probation and parole in the United States, 2016.* NCJ 251148. Washington, D.C.: U.S. Department of Justices, Bureau of Justice Statistics.

28. Stateline (2017, April 26). Doing less time: Some states cut back on probation. *The Pew Charitable Trusts,* http://www.pewtrusts.org/en/research-and-analysis/blogs/stateline/2017/04/26/doing-less-time-some-states-cut-back-on-probation.

chapter **6**

Drugs and Law Enforcement

After you have completed this chapter, you should have an understanding of the following:

- Efforts to control the production and/or cultivation of illicit drugs

- The role of law enforcement in illicit drug interdiction

- Street-level drug enforcement operations and procedures

- Asset forfeiture and the federal RICO statute

"I was on the upper level of a municipal garage looking down over a housing development playground in a less desirable part of the city," Sgt. Ramos said to me with a smile as he told me his favorite story. "Not surprisingly, there weren't any children in the playground. The only people there were five or six young males just standing around, doing a whole lot of nothing. To the experienced eye, it was obvious that a 'crew' had taken over the playground, doing a brisk business in broad daylight. Evidently, they had no fear of the residents of the development, and no one knew that police were around."

"It was easy to get those guys. The 'buy-walk' operation was completed in a matter of minutes (though it had been planned well in advance). Meanwhile, it was a hot summer day, and many of the windows in the 15-story building were open. Mothers and grandmothers sunned themselves by these open windows."

"As we led those guys off, we all heard a sound usually reserved for a baseball game. All those mothers and grandmothers were giving us a loud round of applause, heckling and cat-calling the men now in cuffs. They were showing their appreciation for us giving back the playground that had been built for their children and grandchildren. This gave us more satisfaction and pride in our job than any grand jury could have."[1]

The criminal justice system in the United States is responsible for protecting the public from individuals and groups that are deemed harmful to social order in our communities. In the context of drug-taking behavior, the criminal justice system is designed to respond to the social problems of drug abuse by fulfilling a threefold mission: (1) the enforcement of drug-defined and drug-related laws, (2) the adjudication through a court system of individuals who have violated these laws, and (3) the implementation of penalties for those convicted of drug-defined and drug-related offenses through a correctional system.

This chapter will focus on the operations of criminal justice professionals, both domestic and international, who are responsible for the *enforcement* of drug laws. The specific law enforcement objectives include crop eradication, the control of refining agents and solvents used in the processing of plant-based material into illicit drugs, the control of precursor chemicals used in the manufacture of illegal drugs, the interdiction of illicit drugs at our borders, the arrest of criminal offenders in violation of drug laws, and the use of asset forfeiture and other means to reduce the financial gains of those involved in illicit drug trafficking. Chapter 7 will focus on the correctional systems that deal with drug-law offenders after they are apprehended and arrested by law enforcement officers.

The 2017 federal drug-control budget is $31.1 billion, a growth of 1.7 percent from 2016. This includes $1.1 billion in new funding specifically for battling the opioid/heroin epidemic. Just over half of the budget was allocated to prevention and treatment (51 percent), while the remaining funding (49 percent) was apportioned for domestic law enforcement, drug interdiction, and international control programs (Figure 6.1). Together, these latter efforts represent the "supply reduction" side of the drug-control equation, with the "demand reduction" portion represented by drug treatment and prevention. Figure 6.1 shows the increased emphasis placed on demand reduction efforts since 2015, while supply reduction efforts have changed minimally. "Demand reduction" strategies that form the basis for substance abuse treatment and prevention programs will be reviewed in Chapter 14.

In general, "supply reduction" attempts to strike at the sources, availability and access to illicit drugs—going after the cultivation of plants that produce drugs, illegal producers and smugglers of drugs, and subsequent trafficking of these drugs. Drug-law enforcement programs are divided into three major areas: (1) source control, (2) drug interdiction, and (3) street-level enforcement.

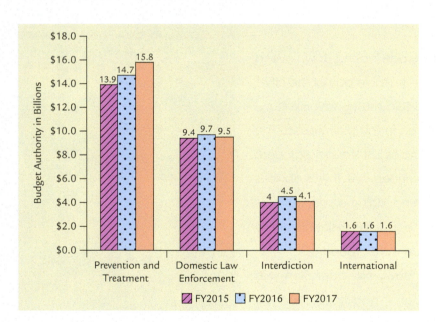

FIGURE 6.1

Allocations of the U.S. federal drug-control budget by function from fiscal year (FY) 2015 to 2017.

Source: Based on Figure 1. Drug Resources by Function from the Office of National Drug Control Policy (2016, December). *National Drug Control Strategy: FY 2017 Budget and Performance Summary.* Washington, D.C.: Office of National Drug Control Policy, p. 10.

Numbers Talk. . .

$30 billion	Value of assets and drugs seized from drug-trafficking organizations by the Drug Enforcement Administration between 2005 and 2016
28,881	Number of domestic drug-law violation arrests made by the Drug Enforcement Administration in 2016
98.5	Percentage decrease in use of stop-and-frisk in New York City from 2011 to 2017

Source: Drug Enforcement Administration, U.S. Department of Justice, Washington, D.C.; New York Civil Liberties Union (2018, April 2). Stop-and-Frisk Data. Accessed from: https://www.nyclu.org/en/stop-and-frisk-data

Source Control

Source control programs are aimed at limiting the cultivation and production of illicit drugs. There are four approaches in source control: (1) crop eradication, (2) control of refining agents for the processing of plant-based illicit drugs and precursor chemicals for the manufacture of illicit drugs, and (3) the U.S. certification process. In most cases, source control involves operations in foreign countries (such as the eradication of opium poppy fields in Afghanistan), but there are instances in which source control involves domestic locations as well. The dismantling of methamphetamine laboratories in a rural county of Missouri would be an example of source control within our own country.[2]

Crop Eradication

Crop eradication is the strategy of reducing the availability of illicit drugs through the destruction of opium poppies, coca plants, and marijuana plants in their countries of origin, or the elimination of the means by which they are cultivated. Crops are eradicated by manual or mechanical removal of the plants themselves or by fumigation with herbicides (chemicals that kill plants) that are either sprayed or dropped from the air as pellets that melt into the soil when it rains. Eradication programs are driven by the premise that decreasing marijuana cultivation and opium and coca cultivation for the production of heroin and cocaine, respectively, makes these drugs more expensive and less available to drug users. Chapter 4 dealt with the question of whether a reduced availability of illicit drugs results in a significant decrease in drug use or drug-related crime.

There is a continuing controversy over the benefits of crop eradication as a component of U.S. drug policy. On the one hand, proponents have argued that crop control is cost-effective in reducing the supply of illicit drugs because the drugs (specifically heroin and cocaine) cannot enter the illicit drug market if the plants by which they are derived (opium poppies and coca) have not been cultivated and harvested.

Coca plants are destroyed in a crop eradication program in Colombia. These efforts have been financed, in large part, by the U.S. Department of State through the Andean Counterdrug Initiative.

Ideally, there would be no further need for drug interdiction or domestic law enforcement. Another argument in favor of crop eradication is that it is easier to locate and destroy opium poppies and coca than it is to confront the supplies of illicit drugs later on, either in transit through drug-trafficking routes or at the street level where they are sold.

On the other hand, opponents have argued that it is highly questionable whether crop eradication can ever be successful in reducing the supply of illicit drugs. The available evidence has shown that, on a global level, there has rarely been more than a 10 percent decrease in the *worldwide* cultivation of any one type of illicit crop in any given year, despite massive crop eradication efforts. Even when there is a reduction in the cultivation of a particular crop, such as opium poppies or coca, in one part of the world, there is typically an increase in the cultivation in a neighboring country or another part of the world. This phenomenon is often likened to a continuing game of "whack-a-mole."

In addition, opponents argue that crop eradication is not cost-effective in terms of work-hours that are required to do the job. Manual removal of coca plants, for example, involves more than 20 work-hours of effort in order to get rid of one hectare (about 2.5 acres) of coca. Aerial fumigation is obviously more cost-effective, but it is not permitted in some countries, and where it is permitted, there are adverse environmental effects. Herbicides have produced irreversible contamination of local water supplies, and the relocation of planting fields to previously uncultivated land has resulted in extensive deforestation and a reduction in valuable rain forest resources.[3]

While the debate continues, there has been no argument that in many impoverished regions of the world, crop eradication programs have had serious economic and political consequences. For many poor farmers, the cultivation of opium poppies or coca represents their only source of significant income. Even when governments have promoted alternative crops such as corn, banana trees, and rubber, as has been done in Peru, Afghanistan, and other nations, farmers have resisted because these alternatives are far less profitable for them and their families.[4] It has been acknowledged by some U.S. officials that opium poppy eradication programs in Afghanistan may have encouraged many poor Afghan farmers to align themselves with insurgents and other groups in opposition to the central Afghan government.[5]

Chemical Controls

There are two opportunities to exert chemical control over the availability of illicit drugs. The first is the monitoring and control over refining agents and solvents that are

source control: Law enforcement actions that reduce or eliminate the cultivation and production of illicit drugs in foreign countries.

crop eradication: Programs in which opium poppies, coca plants, and marijuana plants are destroyed in their countries of origin, prior to transport overseas.

required for the processing of plant-based materials such as coca and opium poppies into cocaine and heroin. For example, *acetic anhydride* is an essential chemical for converting opium into heroin (see Chapter 9), and control over this chemical has been central to efforts to reduce heroin production in Afghanistan. Similarly, *potassium permanganate* is an essential oxidizing agent for converting coca into cocaine (see Chapter 10).

The DEA maintains programs to regularly monitor and track large shipments of acetic anhydride and potassium permanganate entering the United States and provides assistance to other countries in their internal monitoring and control. But many nations lack the capacity to determine whether the import or export of chemicals is related to illicit drug production or else they fail to meet goals for reducing the availability of these chemicals because of internal political pressures. The problem has been complicated by the fact that acetic anhydride and potassium permanganate are often transshipped through third-party countries to disguise their purpose or destination. A further complication is the fact that there are legitimate environmental benefits in the use of acetic anhydride and potassium permanganate, such as in the disinfecting of waste water. Therefore, it is difficult to monitor supplies of these chemicals within foreign countries, since it cannot be determined whether they are being used for legitimate domestic purposes or illegitimate purposes in the production of illicit drugs.[6]

The second opportunity for chemical control is the monitoring and control of **precursor chemicals** and other substances used in the manufacture of illicit drugs. For example, ephedrine and pseudoephedrine (a common ingredient in cough-and-cold remedies) are essential for the manufacture of methamphetamine (see Chapter 10). As a result of the Combat Methamphetamine Epidemic Act of 2005, substantial limitations in the availability of pseudoephedrine have been imposed in the United States, but serious problems remain with the continuing export levels of ephedrine and pseudoephedrine elsewhere in the world. Table 6.1 lists the top five exporting countries of ephedrine and pseudoephedrine, compared to the United States.[7]

U.S. Certification

The United States attempts to control the production of illicit drugs in foreign countries through a diplomatic program, referred to as **certification**. Enacted by Congress in

precursor chemicals: Substances required for the production of illicit drugs. Examples are acetic anhydride and pseudo-ephedrine for the production of methamphetamine.

certification: The process by which the United States has the option of withholding foreign aid to a country if that country is judged to be noncompliant with U.S. counterdrug efforts, by virtue of its participation in major illicit drug production and/or trafficking.

drug majors: Countries identified as being major producers or major transit countries for illegal substances.

TABLE 6.1

Top five exporting countries and the United States—Ephedrine and Pseudoephedrine, 2013–2015

EPHEDRINE	APPROXIMATE QUANTITIES IN KILOGRAMS		
	2013	2014	2015
India	59,000	85,000	57,000
Germany	92,000	40,000	19,000
United Kingdom	1,000	4,000	9,000
Singapore	31,000	10,000	9,000
Denmark	3,000	2,000	2,000
Top five total	186,000	141,000	97,000
United States	265	2	9

PSEUDOEPHEDRINE	APPROXIMATE QUANTITIES IN KILOGRAMS		
	2013	2014	2015
India	440,000	356,000	355,000
Germany	389,000	314,000	314,000
Taiwan	52,000	312,000	221,000
China	91,000	66,000	68,000
Switzerland	92,000	35,000	43,000
Top five total	1,063,000	1,082,000	1,001,000
United States	7,000	2,000	1,000

Note: One kilogram equals 2.2 pounds.

Source: Based on data from Bureau for International Narcotics and Law Enforcement Affairs (2017, March). *International Narcotics Control Strategy Report, Vol. I: Chemical controls.* Washington, D.C.: U.S. Department of State.

1986, certification is a process in which the U.S. government evaluates the cooperation of foreign countries in counterdrug efforts. Each year, the president is required to compile a list of countries that have been determined to be major illicit producing and/or drug transit countries (referred to as "**drug majors**"). Countries on this list are then divided into two categories: (1) those that are fully compliant with U.S. counterdrug efforts ("certified") and (2) those not compliant with U.S. efforts ("decertified"). If a country is decertified, U.S. law requires that all foreign aid be withheld until the president determines whether the country should be certified. In addition, U.S. representatives to multinational banks such as the World Bank and the International Monetary Fund are required to vote against any loans or grants to a decertified country.

Obviously, decertification can have significant adverse consequences for the economy as well as the political stability of a nation, but it is rare that decertification is fully implemented. Under the law, the president has the option of waiving the removal of foreign aid from a decertified nation if it is determined that continued assistance is vital to U.S. national interests. In 2017, the following 22 nations were identified as "drug majors": Afghanistan, The Bahamas,

Belize, Bolivia, Burma, Colombia, Costa Rica, Dominican Republic, Ecuador, El Salvador, Guatemala, Haiti, Honduras, India, Jamaica, Laos, Mexico, Nicaragua, Pakistan, Panama, Peru, and Venezuela. Of these, two countries received official decertification: Bolivia and Venezuela. However, it was determined not to suspend aid to Venezuela because such action would jeopardize vital U.S. interests.[8] Opponents of U.S. certification have argued that decertification serves merely as an international "score card" with little or no impact on the worldwide illicit drug supply or the global illicit drug trade. Nonetheless, the U.S. certification has been useful to exert pressure on certain nations to be more aggressive in their drug-control policies.[9]

Drug Interdiction

Denying drug traffickers the use of air, land, and maritime routes into the United States in order to prevent illicit drugs from being smuggled across our borders is a strategy known as **drug interdiction**. It is a reasonable goal in law enforcement, but consider the following difficulties: The entirety of our international border with Mexico and Canada extends nearly 7,000 miles. Each day, according to the U.S. Customs and Border Protection (CBP) agency, more than 1 million passengers and pedestrians are processed via air, sea, or land travel. More than 282,000 individuals enter the United States in privately owned vehicles, and over 80,000 truck, rail, or sea containers must be processed. In 2017, nearly 8,000 pounds of drugs were seized by CBP.[10]

An additional challenge comes from drug traffickers themselves, who come up with increasingly bizarre ways to circumvent standard interdiction controls; customs officials must leave (literally) no stone unturned. A shipment of boa constrictors from Colombia, for example, was once confiscated with their intestines stuffed with condoms full of cocaine.[11] In 1994, federal agents at JFK International Airport in New York noticed an emaciated and ailing sheepdog on a flight from Bogota, Colombia. X-rays and surgery revealed that 5 pounds of cocaine in 10 rubber balloons had been surgically implanted in the dog's abdomen. New York Police Department detectives later arrested a 22-year-old man from New Jersey when he came to claim the animal. The dog fortunately survived the surgery to remove the condoms and was taken to the Canine Enforcement Training Center in Virginia, where its handlers named it, appropriately enough, "Cokie."[12]

With tightened security after September 11, 2001, the use of air cargo as a method of smuggling drugs into the United States led to an extreme alternative. Drug traffickers resorted to using women from Colombia and other Andean nations as well as other regions of the Caribbean as drug "mules." The women would swallow as many as 50 condoms filled with cocaine or heroin and then board a flight on a commercial airline. They were given a topical anesthetic to deaden the throat before ingesting the condoms and then

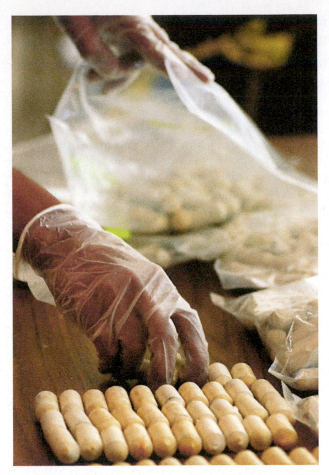

A police officer collects heroin capsules after displaying them during a news conference in Panama in 2004. A police operation uncovered some 15 kilograms of heroin, one of the largest confiscations in Panama, from a group of five Colombians.

told to use laxatives to help them "retrieve" the condoms after reaching their destination. Unfortunately, these condoms would sometimes break and leak into the stomach, causing a drug overdose and death. Most of these "mules" were women who were desperate for money and entered the business willingly, but there were an increasing number of women who were forced into the drug trade. The traffickers were known to kidnap a woman's children or other family members and threaten to kill the hostages unless the woman successfully smuggled drugs into the United States.[13]

In recent years, changes in airport security have caused traffickers to scale back their smuggling of drugs through airports entirely and instead direct their drug shipments over land routes. Most of this smuggling occurs at the U.S.–Mexico border, where drug traffickers use various strategies ranging from concealed compartments in cars, minivans, and commercial trucks to clandestine underground tunnels (see Chapter 2).[14]

drug interdiction: Efforts to prevent illicit drugs from being transported across the U.S. border.

Federal Agencies Involved in Drug Interdiction

The primary federal agencies involved in drug interdiction include the DEA, the U.S. Immigration and Customs Enforcement (ICE) agency, the U.S. Customs and Border Protection (CBP) agency, the U.S. Coast Guard, and the U.S. military. Of these agencies, only the DEA has drug-law enforcement as its sole responsibility. Employing more than 4,000 officers with the authority to make arrests and carry firearms, the DEA investigates major drug-law violators, enforces regulations governing the manufacture and dispensing of controlled substances, and performs various other functions to prevent and control drug trafficking. DEA agents also work overseas, where they engage in undercover operations in foreign countries, work in cooperation with foreign governments to apprehend major drug traffickers, help to train foreign law enforcement officials, and collect intelligence about general trends in drug trafficking, drug production (illicit farming operations and laboratories), and criminal organizations operating in the illicit drug trade.

As a result of the creation of the U.S. Department of Homeland Security in 2003, two major federal agencies were formed: U.S. Customs and Border Protection and U.S. Immigration and Customs Enforcement. CBP agents are responsible for patrolling all land and coastal borders as well as ports of entry into the United States, detecting and arresting immigrants attempting to cross U.S. borders illegally, and controlling any form of contraband (including illicit drugs) from entering the country. Nearly 20,000 CBP officers screen incoming travelers, conveyances, and cargo at more than 300 ports of entry across the United States, often working with drug detection dogs. Special agents within the CBP are responsible for conducting investigations of drug-trafficking and money laundering activities. The Marine Branch of the CBP is responsible for interdicting drugs in nearshore waters by stopping and searching incoming vessels that behave suspiciously, especially small boats with large engines commonly referred to as "go-fast boats." The Air Branch is responsible for interdicting suspicious aircraft, such as small low-flying aircraft operating at night. Once a suspicious aircraft has been detected, it is normally tracked and forced down by high-speed chase planes and then searched. CBP inspectors are not hampered by constitutional protections that typically limit the power of other law enforcement agencies; they can search a person, vehicle, or container at ports of entry or near to a U.S. shoreline without probable cause.

ICE agents are responsible for enforcing immigration laws not only at U.S. borders but in all 50 U.S. states. ICE has the authority to cooperate with state and local law enforcement agencies in the identification, processing, and deportation of illegal immigrants and to assist in investigations of human trafficking, drug trafficking, and money laundering. Like CBP agents, ICE agents do not need probable cause or warrants for operations at port of entry, only a degree of suspicion that there is an occurrence of wrongdoing. The primary responsibility of ICE is to prevent illegal entry into the United States, but ICE agents often work closely with DEA and CBP agents (see Drugs . . . in Focus) when cross-border individuals are involved in drug trafficking.[15]

The U.S. Coast Guard is the lead federal agency for maritime drug interdiction and shares responsibility for air interdiction with the Air Branch of the CBP. The Coast Guard is a key player in combating the flow of illegal drugs to the United States by denying smugglers the use of maritime routes in the "transit zone," a 6-million-square-mile area including the Caribbean, the Gulf of Mexico, and the Eastern Pacific. Coast Guard ships can stop and board any maritime vessel operating within a 12-mile radius of U.S. shoreline. Like CBP and ICE inspectors, Coast Guard personnel do not have to establish probable cause before boarding and searching a vessel at sea.[16]

In recent years, Coast Guard agents have had to contend with drug traffickers using semi-submersible submarine-like boats as a means for transport. These semi-subs are either self-propelled vessels or towed by other vessels, and they are capable of carrying up to 12 metric tons of cargo. As a response to the Coast Guard's tactic of using snipers in helicopters to shoot out engines on drug traffickers' speedboats, these new

Members of the U.S. Coast Guard law enforcement team gather in Miami around more than 5,000 pounds of cocaine seized from a Honduran fishing boat off the coast of Colombia. The drugs were discovered hidden in compartments within the fuel tank, and eight Colombians were arrested. The 110-foot boat was later towed to Miami and confiscated.

vessels are especially designed with engines beneath water level. In 2008, a major Coast Guard interdiction operation succeeded in the capture of one of these semi-subs off the coast of Guatemala and seized approximately 7 metric tons of Colombian cocaine (see photo on page 104).[17]

The U.S. military supports the drug interdiction efforts of federal and state drug enforcement agencies by providing air and ground observation and reconnaissance, environmental assessments, intelligence analysts and linguists, and transportation and engineering support. Military training teams also teach civilian law enforcement officers such skills as combat lifesaving, surveillance techniques, and advanced and tactical military operations that can be used in counterdrug operations. Military personnel can support counterdrug efforts, but they cannot search or arrest drug traffickers. Law enforcement agencies and the military both benefit from this relationship. Police are able to use military resources, and service members are able to practice their military skills in real-world situations.

The U.S. military is also active in drug interdiction by working with military units in foreign countries and international law enforcement agencies. Intelligence, strategic planning, and training are provided for antidrug operations in several Latin American countries, such as Colombia, Mexico, Peru, and Bolivia. A key element of the military's antidrug program in Latin America is its Tactical Analysis Teams (TATs), made up of a small number of U.S. Special Forces and military intelligence personnel. These teams gather intelligence and plan operations that are carried out by host nations and DEA agents.[18]

Military Operations and Domestic Law Enforcement

Technically speaking, the Posse Comitatus Act of 1878 forbids the military to be used as a law enforcement agency within the borders of the United States. The law was designed originally to bar federal troops from policing southern states after the Civil War and to protect Americans against abuses by their own military by dictating that federal troops could not enter private land or dwellings and could not detain or search civilians. In 1988, however, Congress expanded the National Guard's role in drug interdiction and allowed the guard to be actively involved in drug-law enforcement. In 2010, President Obama ordered up to 1,200 additional National Guard troops to be stationed in the Southwest, joining a few hundred Guard members previously assigned to help local law enforcement officials in reducing drug smuggling along the U.S.–Mexico border.

How did the National Guard operation manage to circumvent the Posse Comitatus Act? The key to National Guard involvement in drug operations is the word "federal" in the language of Posse Comitatus Act. Since 1912, the National Guard has had a two-tier mission to serve both the state and federal governments. Guard units involved in antidrug operations typically work for the state government under the supervision of a state governor. Therefore, while the soldiers' salary and other benefits are paid by the federal government, it has been argued that they are not bound by the Posse Comitatus Act. Since the U.S. Coast Guard is a

Quick Concept Check 6.1

Understanding Law Enforcement Agencies in Drug Control

Check your understanding of drug-law enforcement agencies involved in domestic and international drug control by matching the activity/responsibilities on the left with the agency, organization, or individual on the right.

Note: Some of the answers may be used more than once.

1. Monitoring and tracking large shipments of acetic anhydride and potassium permanganate into the country
2. Drawing up a list of nations that do not comply with U.S. counterdrug efforts
3. Enforcing laws regarding noncitizen individuals at U.S. borders and in all 50 U.S. states
4. Stopping and boarding-suspicious maritime vessels within a 12-mile radius of U.S. shoreline
5. Possible engagement to supplement security and law enforcement policing along the U.S.–Mexico border
6. Drug-law enforcement as its sole responsibility
7. Operating in antidrug programs in Latin America through Tactical Analysis Teams (TATs)
8. Patrolling all land and coastal borders as well as ports of entry into the United States

a. The president
b. Drug Enforcement Administration (DEA)
c. U.S. Customs and Border Protection (CBP)
d. U.S. Immigration and Customs Enforcement (ICE)
e. U.S. Coast Guard
f. National Guard
g. U.S. Special Forces

Answers: 1. b 2. a 3. d 4. e 5. f 6. b 7. g 8. c

military unit within the Department of Homeland Security, it has been authorized to operate outside the restrictions of the Posse Comitatus Act as well.

According to legal experts, the National Defense Authorization Act of 2011 essentially repealed the Posse Comitatus Act, leaving open the opportunity for all branches of the U.S. military to be involved in law enforcement, when authorized by the president. This development greatly concerned libertarians who viewed the Posse Comitatus Act as a long-standing protection against the development of a militarized police state. Others have argued, however, that for several years the issue had been a moot point, since state and local police forces have gained the weapons and tactical equipment that allow them to operate in a militarized fashion.[19]

Profiling and Drug-Law Enforcement

Over the years, drug-law enforcement agents have often developed "drug courier profiles" to help in the identification of potential drug traffickers. In *United States v. Sokolow* (1989), the U.S. Supreme Court ruled that drug courier profiles at airports could be used as a legitimate law enforcement tool, the Fourth Amendment to the U.S. Constitution notwithstanding. In this case, Andrew Sokolow, a young African American male dressed in a black jumpsuit with gold jewelry, purchased two airline tickets in Miami with $1,200 in cash. Sokolow flew from Honolulu to Miami, planning to return to Hawaii 48 hours later. He also was traveling under a false name, did not check any luggage, and appeared very nervous. Drug agents stopped him at the Honolulu airport and used a drug-sniffing dog, which led them to 1,063 grams of cocaine in his carry-on luggage. Chief Justice William H. Rehnquist stated, "While a trip from Honolulu to Miami, standing alone, is not a cause for any sort of suspicion, here there was more: Surely few residents of Honolulu travel from that city for 20 hours to spend 48 hours in Miami during the month of July." In a seven-to-two decision, the Court ruled that the drug courier profile could provide a "reasonable basis" for officials to suspect that a person is transporting drugs.

The most significant criticism of drug courier profiling is that some law enforcement authorities or individual law enforcement officers have created their own profiles based solely on race, ethnicity, or national origin rather than on the behavior of an individual, a practice that has become known as **racial profiling**. In the late 1990s, racial profiling became a major topic of controversy. National and local media reports often proclaimed that racial profiling was a significant social problem, and national surveys confirmed that most Americans agreed. In a 2014 Reason-Rupe Poll, 70 percent of respondents disapproved of the practice of racial profiling. When responses were broken down by race and age, 65 percent of whites and 80 percent of nonwhites disapproved this practice, while 77 percent of those aged under 34 and 66 percent of those over 55 disapproved.[20]

One of the most common complaints about racial profiling was the claim that police were stopping vehicles simply because the race of the driver did not appear to "match" the type of automobile he or she was driving. In a widely publicized case, Dr. Elmo Randolph, a 42-year-old African American dentist, was stopped more than 50 times spanning eight years while driving a BMW car to his office near Newark. New Jersey state troopers, believing that Dr. Randolph was "driving the wrong car," would pull Dr. Randolph over, check his license, and ask him if he had any drugs or weapons in his car. Randolph claims that he did not drive at excessive speeds and that he had never been issued a ticket.[21]

racial profiling: A practice of arresting or detaining an individual for possible drug violations, based on race, ethnicity, or national origin rather than on the individual's behavior.

A study was conducted by the New Jersey State Police in 1999 on the question of race and ethnicity of persons stopped by state troopers. It was found that New Jersey state troopers had indeed engaged in racial profiling along the New Jersey Turnpike. Although individuals of color comprised 13.5 percent of the New Jersey Turnpike population, they represented 41 percent of those stopped on the turnpike and 77 percent of those searched.[22] The study's findings led to a federal monitor being appointed from 2001 to 2009 to oversee efforts by New Jersey to address racial profiling in the state. Subsequent studies have identified racial profiling by police in other U.S. states as well.

In 2003, under a Department of Justice directive, racial and ethnic profiling was officially banned at all federal agencies with law enforcement powers, the only exception being investigations involving terrorism and national security. In 2006, the International Association of Chiefs of Police issued an extensive training guide for state and local authorities to implement a commitment to bias-free policing (Drug Enforcement ... in Focus).[23] Despite this, in a recent large-scale study on over 60 million patrol stops from 20 U.S. states between 2011 and 2015, it was found that African American drivers were more likely to be stopped than either white or Latino drivers, and that both African American and Latino drivers were more likely to be searched. Further analysis showed that African American and Latino drivers were searched on the basis of less evidence than white drivers.[24]

Street-Level Drug-Law Enforcement

As the third area of drug-law enforcement, street-level operations are the responsibility of federal agencies, state agencies, or local sheriffs' and police departments. Increasingly, these different agencies are joining forces and working together to form multijurisdictional drug task forces. Most of these task forces are coalitions of five or more local and state agencies that work closely with federal law enforcement agencies. Multijurisdictional task forces allow agencies at different levels of government to share funds, personnel, and intelligence and allow drug agents to track drug traffickers across many different jurisdictions. At the local level, a majority of local police departments and more than 70 percent of sheriffs' offices serving 25,000 or more residents have officers assigned to a multiagency drug task force.

Three major strategies for disrupting street-level drug markets can be employed.

- The first strategy involves the police policy only. One specific police-only approach is "hot-spots policing," where operations such as crackdowns and raids, as well as undercover operations and intensive patrolling are conducted within a geographically small, drug-ridden area.

- The second strategy goes beyond the police to the community-at-large. The advantage of community-wide approaches is that they can be focused less on a particular geographic area, and more on all levels of the community through the use of community-improvement partnerships. Examples include knock-and-talks (discussed later), foot and bike patrols, and arrest diversion.

■ The third strategy involves geographically focused approaches that include multiple communities and constituencies such as nonpolice entities. Studies on street-level drug law enforcement strategies have underscored the importance of community involvement in accomplishing a reduction in street-level drug trafficking.[25]

In the next sections, specific law enforcement operations conducted to disrupt street-level drug markets (undercover and non-undercover) will be examined.

Undercover Operations in Drug Enforcement

For street-level enforcement of drug laws, police departments employ a variety of undercover and non-undercover operations. Undercover operations include (1) the reverse sting, (2) the controlled buy, (3) the buy-bust, and (4) the buy-walk.

■ The **reverse sting** is a drug-law enforcement operation in which undercover agents pose as drug dealers and sell a controlled substance or imitation version of a controlled substance to buyers. Community policing programs have made reverse stings popular because such operations can be used as a method of "cleaning up" a neighborhood. The reverse sting operation also makes money for law enforcement because asset forfeiture laws allow agencies to keep at least part of the proceeds made in these operations. The logistical planning of a reverse sting operation is described in Drug Enforcement ... in Focus on page 108.

■ In the **controlled buy** operation, an undercover informant buys the drug under the supervision of the police. The informant may be a paid informant or a person who has

reverse sting: A law enforcement operation in which an undercover agent posing as a drug dealer sells a controlled substance, or an imitation of it, to a buyer and subsequently arrests the purchaser.

controlled buy: A law enforcement operation in which an undercover informant buys an illicit drug under the supervision of the police.

Drug Enforcement . . . in Focus

Updating Police Behavior during Traffic and Street Stops

In 2011, almost 63 million U.S. residents, aged 16 or older (one-fourth of the population), had one or more contacts with police, either in traffic or on the street, during the past 12 months. One-half of these contacts were involuntary or police initiated. A survey conducted by the Bureau of Justice Statistics in the U.S. Department of Justice came to the following conclusions with regard to racial or ethnic disparities in the conduct of the police or the frequency of an individual being stopped.

Traffic Stops

• A greater percentage of African American drivers (7 percent) and Latino drivers (6 percent) were ticketed in a traffic stop than white drivers (5 percent). A greater percentage of African American drivers (2 percent) were stopped and allowed to proceed with no enforcement action than white (1 percent) or Latino drivers (1 percent).

• There was no statistical difference in the percentage of white drivers (50 percent) and African American drivers (55 percent) who were stopped and given a ticket, although Latino drivers (60 percent) were more likely to be ticketed than white drivers.

• About 84 percent of white drivers believed that there was a legitimate reason for a traffic stop, compared to 67 percent of African American drivers and 74 percent of Latino drivers.

• A greater percentage of white drivers (89 percent) in a traffic stop believed the police acted properly than did African American drivers (83 percent). There was no statistical difference in this regard between white drivers and Latino drivers (87 percent).

• It was more likely that the police acted properly if the race or ethnicity of the police officer matched that of the driver (83 percent) than if the race or ethnicity did not match (74 percent).

Street Stops

• About 62 percent of individuals stopped on the street by police were white, 12 percent were African American, and 15 percent were Latino. The demographic profile of the population in this age range is 69 percent white, 11 percent African American, and 13 percent Latino.

• A greater percentage of those stopped on the street by police and believed the police acted properly were white (77 percent) than were African American (38 percent) or Latino (63 percent).

• Among individuals stopped on the street because the police suspected them of something, 62 percent believed that the reason for the stop was legitimate. No demographic breakdown on this statistic was available on this question.

Source: Bureau of Justice Statistics (2013, September). *Special Report: Police behavior during traffic and street stops, 2011.* Washington, D.C.: Bureau of Justice Statistics, U.S. Department of Justice.

been convinced by agents to "roll over" on other traffickers because they themselves have been charged with the possession or trafficking of an illicit drug. In the latter case, criminal charges against the informant may be either reduced or dropped for their participation in the operation. After agents have gained confidence in the informant, the informant is allowed to set up a controlled buy. Before the informant enters the dwelling in which the buy is to take place, he or she is usually searched to insure that there are no drugs on his or her person before conducting the buy. After the buy has been made, the informant is again searched and asked to turn over the drugs bought in the transaction. To protect the identity of the informant, arrests are usually not made at the time of the buy. Warrants are obtained and later executed within 10 days.

- In a **buy-bust** operation, an undercover agent makes a buy, and immediately thereafter, the seller is arrested for the drug sale. During a buy-bust, an undercover agent sets up a drug deal for a specified time and location. A cover team monitors the transaction via surveillance equipment, which is either hidden on the agent or in the room. After a "bust signal" is given by the undercover agent, a cover team rapidly moves in to make the arrest. Generally, the undercover agent is also "arrested" to protect his or her identity.

buy-bust: A law enforcement operation in which an undercover agent makes a buy, and immediately thereafter, the seller is arrested for the drug sale.

Drug Enforcement . . . in Focus

The Anatomy of a Reverse Sting Operation

A reverse sting is a complex undercover operation, typically requiring 20 or more police officers in order for the operation to be executed safely and efficiently. Typically, seven police vehicles are involved. The following diagram shows an example of the overall logistical arrangement:

- Vehicle 1 (an inconspicuous panel van without rear or side windows, for example) accommodates the officers making the arrest. Three officers employ weapons during the arrest; two others search and handcuff the arrestee or arrestees.

- Vehicles 2 and 3 (unmarked cars, for example) accommodate two officers. Vehicles should park on each side of Vehicle 1 if needed to block the suspect's vehicle at the time of takedown.

- Vehicle 4 is used for surveillance.

- Vehicles 5 and 6 are marked police cars each with two uniformed police officers inside. These vehicles are in the perimeter of the takedown area and are available to provide coverage in case the suspect or suspects flee the area.

- A prisoner transportation van is nearby to make sure the arrestee or arrestees are taken to the police station for booking.

Source: Lyman, M. D. (2007). *Practical drug enforcement* (3rd ed.). Boca Raton, FL: CRC Press, pp. 248–253. Drawing on page 250.

ANATOMY OF A STING OPERATION

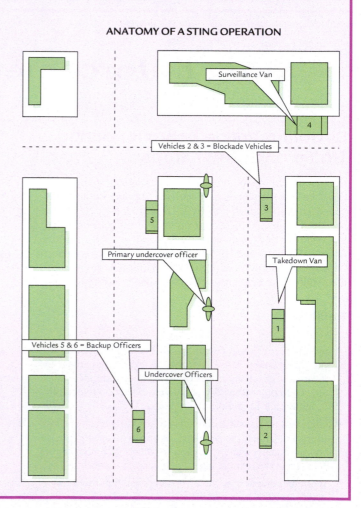

Police officers arrest drug offenders in a drug bust in Tampa, Florida.

- In a **buy-walk** operation, an undercover agent buys drugs but does not arrest the dealer at the time of the deal. The drug deal is used to obtain a warrant for the dealer that is served at a later time. The advantage of this operation is that it protects the identity of the undercover agent while at the same time ensuring his or her immediate safety during the time of the operation. Buy-walk operations are often used when a drug deal takes place at the residence of a drug dealer and officer safety is a concern.

Undercover Operations and the Issue of Entrapment

In order for an arrest of an individual for a drug-law violation (i.e., small-scale drug trafficking) to lead to a conviction, the case has to be presented that the police agent acting undercover had not induced the arrestee to commit a crime that was not contemplated beforehand. Otherwise, a defendant can claim that he or she has been a victim of **entrapment**.

The concept of an entrapment defense was first established in a Prohibition Era decision of the U.S. Supreme Court, *Sorrells v. United States* (1932). In this case, a federal agent in North Carolina had been informed that a local factory worker named Sorrells was a "rum-runner" in violation of the Volstead Act prohibiting the sale of liquor (see Chapter 3). According to court testimony, the agent posing as a tourist visited Sorrell's home and began a lengthy conversation, reminiscing about stories of their time in World War I. After being asked three times whether he could get some liquor and claiming that he "did not fool with whiskey," Sorrells left his home and returned with a half-gallon, which he sold the agent for $5. Sorrells was immediately arrested, but later he appealed his case. The court ruled that the investigation was a "gross abuse of authority" and that "the agent had lured the defendant, otherwise innocent, to [committing the crime] by repeated and persistent solicitation." In a unanimous decision, the Court reversed Sorrells' conviction.[26]

In a later case, *Sherman v. United States* (1958), an informant and a man named Sherman met in a hospital where they were being treated for substance abuse. According to

court testimony, in the course of their hospital stay when it was apparent that they were having a hard time, the informant asked Sherman where he could get some drugs. The informant acted as though he was suffering from withdrawal and continually pressed Sherman to do something about it. Finally, Sherman was persuaded to get drugs from his supplier and gave them to the informant. The prosecution in Sherman's trial argued that a conviction was justified because Sherman's past drug use predisposed him to commit the crime. The Court ruled that a prior history of criminality was not sufficient to establish a predisposition, and Sherman was cleared of charges.[27]

In *Jacobson v. United States* (1992), the U.S. Supreme Court ruled on a reverse-sting operation specifically related to a child pornography investigation but applicable to drug cases as well. In their decision, the government was guilty of repeatedly inducing Jacobson to order pornographic material. The Court ruled that ". . .in their zeal to enforce the law. . .government agents may not originate a criminal design, implant in an innocent person's mind the disposition to commit a criminal act so that the government may prosecute."[28]

Under present-day guidelines, police agents engaging in a form of undercover operation must show clearly that coercive or persuasive tactics were not used. It must also be demonstrated that the idea of committing the crime came from the defendant rather than the police agent (Portrait).[29]

Non-Undercover Police Operations

Undercover operations are not the only way to combat drug crimes, just a few examples of non-undercover operations include (1) the knock and talk, (2) the raid, and (3) the crackdown. Also important are some of the more recent diversion strategies being used by law enforcement, including drug diversion programs.

- The **knock and talk** is an operation that is used when officials receive information that an individual is dealing drugs but do not have probable cause to seek a search warrant. In

buy-walk: A law enforcement operation in which an undercover agent buys drugs but does not arrest the dealer at the time of the deal. The drug deal is used to obtain a warrant for the dealer that is served at a later time.

entrapment: Actions by undercover police agents that are intended to induce an individual to commit a crime that was not contemplated beforehand. In order to argue against the charge of entrapment, it must be demonstrated that the idea of committing the crime came from the defendant rather than the police agent.

knock and talk: A law enforcement operation in which agents ask for permission to search a residence for illicit drugs after asking the suspect whether anyone in the residence has been engaged in drug production or dealing.

Former Commissioner William J. Bratton—The Face of American Policing

In 2016, Commissioner William J. Bratton stepped down as the New York City police commissioner, after a 45-year career in public service. He began his career in Boston in 1970, where he eventually became police commissioner in 1992. He first served as commissioner of the New York Police Department from 1994 to 1996. He then served as the Chief of the Los Angeles Police Department from 2002 to 2009, returning to his position as New York police commissioner for a second time in 2014, where he resumed leadership of a 35,000-member department, the largest in the nation. While police commissioner between 1994 and 1996, he had been widely credited for reducing crime in New York City, instituting a computerized crime-tracking system to monitor criminal activity and the police response to it, and cracking down on corruption in local precincts. Bratton, under the leadership of Mayor Giuliani, put more police officers on patrol in high-crime areas of the city and held police commanders accountable for crime in their precincts. The focus was on what has been called the "broken windows" theory of policing, emphasizing smaller but highly visible crimes of disorder. For example, a person would be stopped for an open container of alcohol, with the intent on finding probable cause to frisk for drugs or guns. As a result, the number of police stops as well as arrests increased substantially. In the end, New York City witnessed a significant reduction in crime, enough to land Bratton on the cover of Time Magazine, with the cover title "Finally We're Winning the War Against Crime. Here's Why."

When Bratton took the position as police chief in Los Angeles, the LAPD had been plagued with police scandals and racial tension. Maintaining his "law and order" stance, the numbers of stops and arrests increased and a greater control over police conduct was achieved. By the time he left in 2009, the situation had improved. Tensions within the department and between the community and police were greatly reduced.

During his second stint as New York police commissioner in 2014, crime was at an all-time low, and attention turned from strict law enforcement to issues involving racial tension between police and the community. The news conference announcing his reappointment in December 2013, Bratton made it clear that there was a need to "bring police and community back together." "What we want to create is an environment where stop-and-frisk as we knew it ends." The newly elected New York City mayor, Bill de Blasio, who had campaigned against the abuses of stop-and-frisk policing, quickly added that Bratton meant "the overuse of stop-and-frisk, the unconstitutional use of stop-and-frisk, the targeting of young men of color regardless of whether they'd done anything wrong. That's going to end." Indeed it did. The rate of stop-and-frisk actions by the police plummeted in New York City (see later section of the chapter).

A focus on community policing with the support of the community behind those who are responsible for protecting them was Bratton's goal during his second term. As he put it, "In this city, I want every New Yorker to talk about 'their police …,' 'my police.'" Some have argued that Bratton never relinquished his aggressive policing approach that had resulted in vast increases in criminal justice involvement for minorities. Others have championed Bratton as taking on crime, corruption, and community relationship problems in some of America's biggest police departments.

Sources: Baker, A and Goodman, D. (2016, July 25). Bratton, Who Shaped and Era in Policing, Tries to Navigate a racial Divide. *New York Times.* Accessed from: https://www.nytimes.com/2016/07/26/nyregion/william-bratton-new-york-city-police-commissioner.html. Quotations of William J. Bratton and Bill de Blasio from the appointment news conference, New York City, December 5, 2013.

---

this case, agents arrive at a suspect's residence, knock on the door, identify themselves as police officers, and ask permission to enter the residence. Once inside, agents ask the suspect if anyone in the residence is producing or dealing drugs. After the suspect responds to the allegations, agents ask for permission to search the residence for illicit drugs.

The element of surprise obviously is an important factor in the success of the knock and talk. If there has been no prior warning, suspects do not expect law enforcement officers to knock on their door and confront them with an allegation. To "confuse" suspects, agents often make misleading allegations. To find evidence against a marijuana dealer, agents may state that they believe the suspect is producing methamphetamine at his residence. Knowing that such charges are ridiculous, even though they are dealing in marijuana, suspects usually allow a **consent search**. Agents state that approximately 75–85 percent of drug dealers waive their constitutional right to privacy and consent to a search. When later asked why they consent to such a search, dealers often state, "I thought I would have been in worse trouble if I didn't let you search" or "I didn't know I had the right to refuse." Once evidence of illicit drug trafficking is found, agents typically make an arrest or return with a **search warrant**.[30]

- The **raid** is an unexpected visit by police that uses the element of surprise to arrest drug offenders. This operation tends to target drug use and low-level drug dealing at

> **consent search:** A procedure in which law enforcement agents ask and receive permission from a suspect to inspect a residence or vehicle for illicit drugs.
>
> **search warrant:** A court-ordered document providing law enforcement agents the right to search a residence or vehicle for illicit drugs.
>
> **raid:** A law enforcement search and seizure operation in which a team of law enforcement officials uses the element of surprise on a residence or business to make drug arrests.

both private residences and commercial establishments (like clubs). Targets for raids are often identified via multiple citizen complaints or calls for service related to criminal or disruptive behavior around a specific dwelling. Multiple officers or agents participate in the raid in order to make multiple arrests, and the outcome is often publicized so as to deter other drug offenders. Unlike the knock and talk, a raid is a search and seizure operation requiring a search warrant.

The limited evaluations that have been conducted on the effectiveness of raids on suspected drug-using establishments show short-term effects on drug crimes and related criminal behavior, but these effects dissipate, particularly in high crime areas.[31]

- The **crackdown** is an operation where law enforcement abruptly escalates activity and presence in drug hot-spot areas. Police operations during a crackdown often involve a number of uniformed officers and undercover agents. They are highly visible to increase the actual and/or perceived threat of arrest. Crackdowns tend to target both drug use and dealing of harder drugs like crack cocaine and heroin, as well as drug-related offenses such as property or violent crimes. This operation uses a deterrent approach with the goal of disrupting the street-level drug market activities.

Studies conducted on the effectiveness of crackdowns at decreasing criminal activity show, like raids, that there is a short-term impact on drug and related criminal behavior. However, displacement of the criminal behavior, where the crime simply moves to another location or stops temporarily, and then resumes once the crackdown is over, is often an issue. Despite this possibility, positive long-term results can still be realized if a specific crackdown is followed up with "seeding programs" to help prevent the drug market from resuming.[32] The term "seeding programs" comes from a community-based U.S. Department of Justice (DOJ) **"Weed and Seed"** initiative, which was a multiagency approach whereby law enforcement would "weed" out drug, violent and gang activity in high crime areas, and community organizations would infuse the community with prevention, treatment and human service programs ("seeds").

- The **drug diversion program** is an intervention by law enforcement targeting low-level drug offenders, typically marijuana users. In this intervention, law enforcement issues warnings rather than arrests for low-level drug crimes, in order to divert minor drug offenders away from the criminal justice system. Some of these programs have mandatory education components, where offenders participate in brief interventions. This strategy aims to both decrease pressure on the criminal justice system (e.g. jail overpopulation), as well as prevent low-level drug offenders from dealing with the long-term impact of a criminal record. Most diversion programs for offenders occur at the pretrial stage of the criminal justice system. What is unique about law enforcement diversion initiatives is they occur even earlier in the criminal justice process, preventing arrests and bookings for criminal behavior.

In 2011, Seattle Washington began piloting a program called Law Enforcement Assisted Diversion (LEAD), which targets low-level drug and prostitution crimes in a pre-booking diversion program. This initiative involves multiagency collaboration, so that individuals that would otherwise be arrested are diverted from jail and prosecution to community-based treatment and social services agencies. Services include mental health and substance abuse treatment, health care,

---

Quick Concept Check 6.2

Understanding Drug-Law Enforcement Operations

Check your understanding of drug-law enforcement operations by matching the descriptions on the left with the types of operations on the right.

1. An undercover informant makes a drug buy under the supervision of the police.
2. A law enforcement officer finds marijuana on a suspect and makes a social service referral rather than arresting him.
3. An undercover agent buys a controlled substance from a drug dealer, and immediately makes an arrest.
4. A cadre of law enforcement officers increases police activity in a high crime area.
5. A police officer, posing as a drug abuser, buys illicit drugs from a suspected drug dealer. The dealer is later arrested for drug trafficking.
6. Agents use "drug courier profiles" and identify at an airport an individual bringing cocaine into the United States.
7. Colombian drug-control officials spray herbicides on fields of coca.
8. Using the element of surprise, agents ask permission to enter and then search a suspected drug dealer's home without a search warrant.
9. DEA agents rush a nightclub where they have had multiple reports of drug use and sales.

a. the knock and talk
b. the undercover buy
c. the controlled buy
d. the buy-bust
e. interdiction
f. crop eradication
g. raid
h. crackdown
i. drug diversion program

Answers: 1. c   2. i   3. d   4. h   5. b   6. e   7. f   8. a   9. g

housing, and job training. Evaluation of the LEAD program suggests that diverted individuals were significantly less likely to be rearrested during the evaluation period, compared to those exposed to the conventional law enforcement response.[33] These findings are consistent with similar programs in Australia and the United Kingdom that show a positive impact of drug diversion on public safety. Diversion programs have also been useful in dealing with low-level drug and alcohol offenders and are currently being adopted throughout the United States.

The Legacy of "Stop-and-Frisk" in Marijuana Arrests

In 2011, the United States District Court for the Southern District of New York ruled in a class action lawsuit on behalf of the minority citizens of New York City that the widespread practice of suspicion-less stops and frisks of African Americans and Latino suspects by the New York Police Department (NYPD) violated the Fourth Amendment rights of the suspects. The NYPD program had been a practice by which a police officer who reasonably suspected that a person who has committed, is committing, or about to commit a felony or misdemeanor may stop and question that person. In 2011, 684,000 people were stopped under these circumstances, with the vast majority being African Americans and Latinos, signifying a problem with racial profiling. In 2013, the United States Court of Appeals upheld the ruling, and since then, "stop-and-frisk" operations declined significantly in New York City, to just over 10,000 in 2017.[34]

crackdown: A law enforcement operation whereby officers abruptly increase visible police activity in a high drug-crime area in order to disrupt the street-level drug market activities.

weed and seed: A strategy aimed at the targeted reduction of violent, drug, and gang-related crime, involving law enforcement crackdowns on crime in that area (weeding), and community organizations restoring the neighborhood by infusing social service interventions for residents (seeding).

drug diversion program: A law enforcement strategy that involves diverting low level drug offenders (typically marijuana users) from arrest with a warning; some include a social service or educational component.

asset forfeiture: A process used in drug-law enforcement in which cash, automobiles, homes, and other property are seized if these items have been acquired or used as a result of criminal activity.

Racketeer Influenced and Corrupt Organization (RICO) statute: A section of the Organized Crime Control Act of 1970, pertaining to the prevention of criminal infiltration of legitimate businesses. The statute became the basis for the prosecution of money laundering activities of criminal organizations.

In 2018, an investigation by the *New York Times* revealed that current arrestees for petty marijuana possession offenses in New York City were disproportionately African American or Latino. The report showed that the police arrested African Americans on low-level marijuana charges at eight times the rate of whites over a period of three years, with Latinos arrested at five times the rate of whites. An editorial in the *New York Times* argued that the findings reflected the extent to which marijuana use has remained a punishable offense for African American and Latino New Yorkers, while informally legalized for white, middle-class citizens of the city. The adverse social and personal effects on individuals involved in these arrests (who are typically dismissed later in court on condition that the individual stays out of trouble for a year) can be significant. Future denials for jobs, housing, and college financial aid are possible consequences of a low-level marijuana arrest. Recently, appeals to the U.S. Department of Justice have been made to examine this issue.[35]

Asset Forfeiture and the RICO Statute

Asset forfeiture refers to the seizure by the government of cash, cars, homes, and other property that the government claims are the result of criminal activity, based on a concept of law that can be traced to biblical and pre-Judeo-Christian times. Early English law, for example, recognized a kind of forfeiture, known as "deodand," which required forfeiture of the instrument of a person's death. The instrument causing death was considered "guilty property," either by being capable of doing further harm in general or used specifically on the perpetrator in retribution by the deceased's family. During the Civil War, the Confiscation Act of 1862 authorized forfeiture procedures against southern rebels and their sympathizers who possessed property in the North. The seized property could then be used for supporting the Union cause in waging the war.

Modern-day authorization for this strategy in law enforcement was created as part of the Organized Crime Control Act of 1970. A section of this legislation, known as the **Racketeer Influenced and Corrupt Organization (RICO) statute** (or simply, RICO), pertained to the prevention of criminal infiltration of legitimate businesses. It was a response to the practice of criminal organizations to funnel profits gained from criminal activity, whether drug related or not, into financial dealings of an unrelated commercial enterprise. For decades, the RICO statute has formed the basis for the prosecution of cases in which criminal organizations have made efforts to circumvent detection by law enforcement.

The 1970 Controlled Substances Act provided, in part, for the forfeiture of property used in connection with controlled substances. In 1978, the law was expanded to allow federal authorities to include all profits from drug trafficking and all assets purchased with drug profits as items subject to forfeiture. The scope of the statute was further amended in 1984 with the Comprehensive Crime Control Act to include all property that was used, or intended to be used, in a drug offense, from simple possession to mass distribution. Many states have passed legislation authorizing their own asset forfeiture procedures when dealing with the violation of state drug laws. Forfeiture is particularly useful in drug-law enforcement because it reduces the financial incentive to reap the often-enormous profits that are involved in drug trafficking and disrupts a drug-trafficking organization by seizing any vehicles, boats, planes, or property used to transport or produce illicit drugs. As shown in Table 6.2, the DEA made 15,613 domestic seizures of nondrug property and cash, valued at approximately $722 million in 2013, as a result of drug investigations. Between 2007 and 2016, the DEA and other federal agencies conducted nearly 100,000 cash seizures, resulting in nearly 5.4 billion dollars seized.[36] Currently, the management and care of more than $1.7 billion worth of property seized through the federal asset forfeiture program is the responsibility of the U.S. Marshals Service.[37]

There are two types of forfeitures: criminal (*in personam*) forfeitures and civil (*in rem*) forfeitures. The distinction between criminal and civil forfeitures is based upon whether the penalty pertains to a person or a thing. Criminal forfeitures are primarily against a specific person and result after a conviction for a crime to which the forfeited property is related. This can occur upon showing during the course of sentencing or plea bargaining that the property is contraband (illegally obtained through the profit of a crime). Such criminal forfeitures are subject to all the constitutional and statutory procedural safeguards available under criminal law, and both the forfeiture case and the criminal case are tried together. Forfeiture must be included in the indictment of the defendant, which means that the grand jury must find a basis for the forfeiture as well as punishment for the criminal offense itself.

Civil forfeitures, on the other hand, are *in rem* actions based upon the unlawful use of property, irrespective of its owner's culpability. Traditionally, civil forfeiture has operated on the premise that the property itself is the guilty party, and the fact that the forfeiture of the property affects an individual's property rights is not considered. With civil forfeiture, the defendant does not need to be convicted or even charged with a crime because it is contended that the property "itself" is guilty. The property owner's guilt or innocence is therefore irrelevant, and civil forfeiture proceedings can be pursued independently or in lieu of a criminal trial. Profits from both criminal and civil asset forfeiture seizures fund victim compensation and law enforcement efforts.

Of these two types of asset forfeiture, it is civil asset forfeiture that has been under the most scrutiny, particularly by civil libertarians concerned with the rights of due process. Nonetheless, in recent years, civil asset forfeiture has been the weapon of choice in combating illicit drug trafficking and distribution in America. Critics of this practice argue that forfeiture laws distort law enforcement priorities and lead to widespread abuse of power, since money or property can be seized from individuals without an arrest or even the pursuit of criminal charges. Law enforcement officials, on the other hand, argue that civil forfeiture allows them to combat drug crime by attacking the economic viability of drug trafficking organization, all the while raising money for future law enforcement operations. By allowing agencies to rely on asset forfeiture as a source of revenue, critics claim, the law enforcement priorities have shifted from crime control activities to "funding raids."

Local, state, and federal agencies have found it advantageous to pool their separate personnel and resources into a multiagency drug task force that are frequently able to finance themselves, at least in part, through asset forfeiture. The **Equitable Sharing** program permits state and local authorities to share seizures with the federal government, so that regulations under federal rather than state forfeiture laws can be applied. In states with stronger anti-forfeiture laws, this program allows state and local law enforcement to circumvent the more restrictive state laws. The anti-forfeiture laws are designed to protect civil liberties, and often restrict how profits from forfeiture are disbursed. Under the Equitable Sharing program, up to 80 percent of the proceeds from the seizures are returned to local law enforcement agencies, which is higher than many states allow. In 2015, then Attorney General Eric Holder suspended portions of the Equitable Sharing program, but within a year this suspension was lifted.[38] A 2011 study found that agencies in jurisdictions with more restrictive asset forfeiture laws received

---

TABLE 6.2

Major DEA asset seizures in 2013

TYPE OF SEIZED ASSET	NUMBER OF SEIZURES	APPROXIMATE SEIZED ASSET VALUE
Cash	9,133	$410,970,000
Firearms	605	$19,000
Real property	291	$33,853,000
Vehicles	3,813	$52,192,000
Vessels	45	$1,794,000
Aircraft	26	$2,525,000
Financial accounts	978	$213,853,000
Jewelry/precious items	256	$4,065,000
Total	15,613	$722,126,000

Note: Total assets seized in 2011 and 2012 were valued at $770,786,000 and $833,737,000, respectively.

Source: Information courtesy of the Drug Enforcement Administration, U.S. Department of Justice, 2014.

Equitable Sharing: A federal program that allows state and local law enforcement to seize property under federal rather than state laws, by sharing the seized assets with federal authorities.

more proceeds from Equitable Sharing, supporting the notion that these jurisdictions use this program to bypass their own state laws.[39]

While it is claimed that forfeiture promotes the accomplishment of law enforcement goals, it turns out that 80 percent of seizures are unaccompanied by any criminal prosecution.[40] This may stem from the fact that, for many law enforcement agencies, civil forfeiture creates a temptation to depart from legitimate law enforcement goals in order to maximize funding. Some police departments now prefer to arrest drug buyers rather than drug sellers by employing a "reverse sting," the chief attraction being the confiscation of a buyer's cash rather than a seller's drugs.

Supporters of asset forfeiture claim that the lack of criminal prosecutions in such a large number of forfeiture cases is attributed to the need for police and prosecuting attorneys to offer a substantial bargaining chip in plea-bargaining negotiations. Defendants may be given the choice of not fighting the civil forfeiture procedure in exchange for avoiding criminal prosecution. This type of arrangement would benefit both the prosecutor and the prosecuted. The government would be able to "punish" defendants in legally weak cases that involve inadmissible or insufficient evidence, and the defendant would escape the monetary and social costs of a criminal conviction. Advocates of forfeiture also argue that forfeiture is an effective tool because it deters criminal activity, saves taxpayers' money by allowing law enforcement to self-fund many of their operations, and increases police officer morale.[41]

A series of U.S. Supreme Court decisions in the 1990s have established the constitutionality of asset forfeiture actions, while setting certain limits on its use. In *United States v. 92 Buena Vista Avenue* (1993), the Court ruled that the government was prohibited from seizing assets that were gained through a drug transaction if those assets were later obtained by a new and innocent owner. On the other hand, in *Bennis v. Michigan* (1996), it was decided that property (in this case, a car) could be seized if it was used in the commission of a crime, even though it might have been owned by an individual not involved in the crime. The Court also ruled in *United States v. Ursery* (1996) that forfeiture statutes did not violate the double jeopardy clause of the U.S. Constitution.[42]

In 2000, the **Civil Asset Forfeiture Reform Act** was enacted to meet objections that in some cases asset forfeiture proceedings placed too great a burden on individuals who eventually were found innocent. At the time, it was reported that 80 percent of individuals who had their property seized by federal authorities as a result of a drug-law violation arrest were never formally charged with a crime. Yet, in some cases, the seized property had been destroyed so it could not be recovered. The law now requires a stricter burden-of-proof standard with regard to the involvement of the property in the crime before it is seized. If found innocent, defendants have five years to make a claim on the seized property after it has been confiscated by the government.[43]

Civil Asset Forfeiture Reform Act: A law enacted in 2000 to ensure that individuals involved in asset forfeiture proceedings were not jeopardized if they were eventually found innocent.

Summary

- More than $31 billion is spent annually on the federal drug-control budget. About half (51 percent) is allocated toward treatment and prevention, while the other half goes to drug-law enforcement. This represents a recent shift toward a greater focus on "demand reduction" as a strategy in drug-control policy. In the past, budget allocations had been weighted to a greater degree toward a strategy of "supply reduction."

- There are three general areas of present-day drug-law enforcement: (1) source control, (2) drug interdiction, and (3) street-level enforcement.

Source Control

- Source control involves actions focusing on reducing the cultivation and production of illicit drugs. The four approaches to source control are crop eradication, control of agents used in the processing of illicit drugs, control of precursor chemicals for illicit drug manufacture, and the U.S. certification program.

- Crop eradication programs involve the destruction of opium poppies, coca plants, and marijuana plants in their countries of origin. Crops are eradicated both manually and with herbicides. Critics point out that these programs have been responsible for causing environmental damage and disrupting the local economy of many rural regions of the world.

- Agents of the U.S. Drug Enforcement Administration (DEA) regularly monitor and track large shipments of precursor chemicals to prevent them from reaching the producers of illicit drugs, as well as specific refining agents used to convert coca to cocaine and opium to heroin.

- "Certification" is a procedure by which the U.S. government evaluates the cooperation of foreign countries in counterdrug efforts.

Interdiction

- Interdiction programs are designed to prevent illicit drugs from being smuggled across the U.S. border by denying drug traffickers the use of air, land, and maritime routes. In recent years, a prime avenue for drug trafficking has occurred in the Southwest United States, along the border with Mexico. The primary agencies involved in drug interdiction include the DEA, U.S. Immigration and Customs Enforcement (ICE), U.S. Customs and Border Protection (CBP), the U.S. Coast Guard, and the U.S. military. The DEA is the only federal agency that has drug-law enforcement as its only responsibility.

- Over the years, drug-law enforcement agents have developed "drug-courier profiles" to help in the identification of potential drug smugglers. Law enforcement authorities have been criticized for developing profiles based solely on race, a practice known as racial profiling.

Street-Level Drug-Law Enforcement

- There are four basic types of undercover drug-law enforcement operations: (1) the reverse sting, (2) the controlled buy, (3) the buy-bust, and (4) the buy-walk. An important legal issue with respect to undercover operations is the possibility of entrapment. Law enforcement officers design their undercover operations in order to avoid this possibility.

- Examples of non-undercover strategies to address street-level drug crime include (1) the knock and talk, (2) the raid, (3) the crackdown, and (4) the drug diversion program. The first three interventions show just short-term effects on crime reduction; drug diversion programs, particularly those that involve a multiagency response, have demonstrated a longer term positive impact for participants.

Asset Forfeiture and the RICO Statute

- Asset forfeiture is the process by which the government seizes cash, cars, homes, and other property that it claims has been involved in or associated with criminal activity.

- Criminal forfeitures result after a conviction for a crime to which the forfeited property is related. Civil forfeitures are based upon the unlawful use of property, irrespective of its owner's culpability. With civil forfeiture, the offender does not need to be convicted or even charged with a crime, since the contention is that the property "itself" is guilty. This make civil forfeiture a more controversial practice.

- Authority for asset forfeiture in law enforcement was created as part of the Organized Crime Control Act of 1970. A section of this legislation, known as the Racketeer Influenced and Corrupt Organization (RICO) statute, pertained to the prevention of criminal infiltration of legitimate businesses.

- Equitable Sharing is a federal program that allows state and local law enforcement to adopt seized property, so that civil asset forfeitures fall under federal rather than state laws and regulations. This is a controversial program as law enforcement agencies often use Equitable Sharing to circumvent state laws in order to maximize proceeds from the seizures.

- A number of U.S. Supreme Court decisions in the 1990s confirmed the legitimacy of asset forfeiture as a tool in drug-law enforcement and established guidelines to avoid abuses of the practice.

Key Terms

asset forfeiture, p. 112	controlled buy, p. 107	Equitable Sharing, p. 113	raid, p. 110
buy-bust, p. 108	crackdown, p. 111	knock and talk, p. 109	relation-back doctrine
buy-walk, p. 109	crop eradication, p. 101	precursor chemicals, p. 102	reverse sting, p. 107
certification, p. 102	drug diversion program, p. 111	racial profiling, p. 106	search warrant, p. 110
Civil Asset Forfeiture Reform Act, p. 114	drug interdiction, p. 103	Racketeer Influenced and Corrupt Organization (RICO) statute, p. 112	source control, p. 101
consent search, p. 110	drug majors, p. 102		Weed and Seed, p. 111
	entrapment, p. 109		

Review Questions

1. Describe the four programs in drug-law enforcement that relate to source control. For each of these programs, discuss a specific difficulty that limits their effectiveness as a means for illicit drug control.

2. Discuss the recent trend toward overland drug trafficking routes along the border of the United States and Mexico. What are the challenges in securing borders from drug trafficking operations?

3. Discuss the need for drug trafficking profiles in effective drug-law enforcement. In what ways can racial profiling be avoided?

4. Compare and contrast the four undercover operations in the street-level drug-law enforcement. What would be the common procedures to avoid accusations of entrapment?

5. Discuss why non-undercover diversion programs show longer-term effects on crime prevention than the other non-undercover police strategies discussed.

6. Contrast criminal forfeitures and civil forfeitures under the RICO statute. What are the general powers that law-enforcement authorities have with respect to asset forfeiture? Why is civil asset forfeiture such a controversial practice?

Critical Thinking: What Would You Do?

Suppose you were in charge of undercover drug-law enforcement operations at the street level in a major metropolitan police department. What undercover procedures would put you and your police officers in jeopardy with respect to accusations of entrapment? What specific procedures would you put into place that would effectively avoid such accusations?

Chapter 6   Drugs and Law Enforcement   ■   115

Endnotes

1. Adapted from an interview conducted by the first author of a Police Sergeant in the New York Police Department.
2. Lyman, M. D. (2007). *Practical drug enforcement*. Boca Raton, FL: CRC Press, pp. 193–209. Marshall, E. (1971, July 27). Cold turkey: Heroin: The source supply. *New Republic*, 165(4), 23–25. Office of National Drug Control Policy (2011, August). *National drug threat assessment 2011*. Washington, D.C.: U.S. Department of Justice.
3. Vargas, R. (2002). The anti-drug policy, aerial spraying of illicit crops and their social, environmental and political impacts on Colombia. *Journal of Drug Issues, 32*, 11–61. Wyler, L. S. (2013, August 13). *International drug control policy: Background and U.S. responses*. Washington, D.C.: Report for Congress, Congressional Research Service, pp. 26–28.
4. Editorial: Afghanistan's unending addiction (2014, October 27). *The New York Times*, p. A26. Farrell, G. (1998). A global empirical review of drug crop eradication and United Nations crop substitution and alternative development strategies. *Journal of Drug Issues, 28*, 395–437. Lama-Tierramrica, A. (2002, November 18). Peru: Cash for farmers who destroy their coca crops. *Global Information Network*, p. 1. Matheson, M. (1996, August 12). Colombian leader tries to please U.S. on drugs but ignites peasant revolt. *Christian Science Monitor*, 88, 7–8.
5. Wyler, International drug control policy, p. 27.
6. Bureau for International Narcotics and Law Enforcement Affairs (2012, March). *2013 International Narcotics control strategy report, Vol. 1: Drug and chemical control*. Washington, D.C.: U.S. Department of State
7. Ibid. Lyman, *Practical drug enforcement*, pp. 206–209.
8. Presidential Memorandum for the Secretary of State — Presidential determination on Major Drug Transit or Major Illicit Drug Producing Countries for Fiscal Year 2018. The White House, Washington, D.C., September 13, 2017. U.S. Department of State (2003, January 31).
9. *The certification process: Fact sheet released by the Bureau of International Narcotics and Law Enforcement Affaires*. Washington, D.C.: U.S. Department of State. Wyler, International drug control policy, pp. 36–40.
10. U.S. Customs and Border Protection, *Snapshot: A summary of CBP Facts and Figures (based on FY 2016 data)*. U.S. Department of Homeland Security, Washington, D.C.
11. Miller, D. W. (1994, December 19). Canine carrier. *U.S. News and World Report, 117*, 14.
12. Ibid.
13. McCleland, S. (2003, July 28). Drug mules. *Maclean's, 116*, 25–31. Philbert, James (2009, November 9). Don't be drug mules ... Top cop advises women. *The Trinidad Guardian*. http://guardian.co.tt.
14. Drug Enforcement Administration (2003). *Drug intelligence brief: Common vehicle concealment methods*. Washington, D.C.: Drug Enforcement Administration.
15. U.S. Customs and Border Protection, Department of Homeland Security, Washington, D.C. U.S. Immigration and Customs Enforcement, Department of Homeland Security, Washington, D.C.
16. Office of National Drug Control Policy (2003, March). *Drug data summary fact sheet*. Washington, D.C.: Office of National Drug Control Policy. Office of National Drug Control Policy (2002, September 5). *ONDCP fact sheet: Interdiction -operations*. Washington, D.C.: Office of National Drug Control Policy. Information Courtesy of U.S. Coast Guard.
17. http://www.news.navy.mil, The official Web site for the U.S. Navy.
18. Peters, K. M. (2003, April). Troops on the beat. *Government Executive, 35*, 56. Shanker, Thom (2008, December 23). Obstacle seen in bid to curb Afghan trade in narcotics. *The New York Times*, p. A6. Zirnite, P. (1998, April). The militarization of the drug war. *Current History, 97*, 166–186.
19. Archibold, R. C. (2010, May 26). National Guard will be deployed to aid at border. *The New York Times*, pp. A1, A3. Baker, A. (2011, December 4). When the police go military. *The New York Times, Sunday Review*, p. 6. Sen. Rand Paul fights against martial law legislation. http://www.louisville.com. November 30, 2011. Vaughn, E. (1992, December). National Guard involvement in the drug war. *Justicia, the Newsletter of the Judicial Process Commission*, p. 1.
20. Ekins, E. (2014, Oct 14). *Poll: 70% of Americans Oppose Racial Profiling by the Police*. Reason: Free Minds and Free Markets. Retrieved from: http://reason.com/poll/2014/10/14/poll-70-of-americans-oppose-racial-profi
21. Hosenball, M. (1999, May 17). It is not the act of a few bad apples: Lawsuit shines the spotlight on allegations of racial profiling by New Jersey state troopers. *Newsweek*, pp. 34–35.
22. Verniero, P.; and Zoubek, P. (1999, April 20). *New Jersey Attorney General's interim report of the state police review team regarding allegations of racial profiling*. Trenton, NJ: Office of the New Jersey Attorney General.
23. Bureau of Justice Statistics (2013, September). *Special Report: Police behavior during traffic and street stops, 2011*. Washington, D.C.: Bureau of Justice Statistics, U.S. Department of Justice. International Association of Chiefs of Police (2006, September). Addressing racial profiling: Creating a comprehensive commitment to bias-free policing. *Protecting civil rights: A leadership guide for state, local, and tribal law enforcement*. Washington, D.C.: International Association of Chiefs of Police, pp. 153–191. U.S. Customs Service (1998). *Personal searches of air passengers results: Positive and negative*. Washington, D.C.: U.S. Customs Service.
24. Pierson, E.; Simoiu, C.; Overgoor, J.; Corbett-Davies, S.; Ramachandran, V.; Phillips, C.; and Goel, S. (2017). *A large-scale analysis of racial disparities in police stops across the United States*. Stanford Open Policing Project, working paper. Retrieved from https://5harad.com/papers/traffic-stops.pdf
25. Mazerolle, L.; Soole, D.; and Rombouts, S. (2007). *Crime Prevention Research Reviews No.1: Disrupting Street-Level Drug Markets*. Washington, D.C.: U.S. Department of Justice Office of Community Oriented Policing Services.
26. *Sorrells v. United States*, 287, U.S 435 (1932).
27. *Sherman v. United States*, 356, U.S. 369 (1958).
28. *Jacobson v. United States*, 503, U.S.540 (1992).
29. Lyman, *Practical Drug Enforcement*, pp. 12–46, 255–278. Council of the Inspectors General on Integrity and Efficiency (2010, June). *Guidelines on undercover operations*. Washington, D.C.: Council of the Inspectors General on Integrity and Efficiency (CIGIE).

30. Paterline, B. (2003). *Drug identification and investigation for law enforcement.* Temecula, CA: Staggs Publishing.

31. Mazerolle, Soole, and Rombouts, *Crime Prevention Research Reviews No.1.*

32. Ibid, p. 12.

33. Collins, S.; Lonczak, H.; and Clifasefi, S. (2015). *Lead Program Evaluation: Recidivism Report.* University of Washington LEAD Evaluation Team. Seattle, WA: University of Washington.

34. New York Civil Liberties Union. (April 2, 2018). Stop-and-Frisk Data. Retrieved from: https://www.nyclu.org/en/stop-and-frisk-data

35. Editorial: "Stop-and-Frisk's Legacy in Marijuana Arrests" (2018, May 15). *The New York Times*, p. A24.

36. Office of the Inspector General. (2017, March). *Review of the Department's Oversight of Cash Seizure and Forfeiture Activities.* Washington, D.C.: U.S. Department of Justice.

37. Drug Enforcement Administration (2013). *DOJ computerized asset program.* Washington, D.C.: Drug Enforcement Administration, U.S. Department of Justice. Information courtesy of the United States Marshals Service, U.S Department of Justice.

38. Bates, A. (2016, March 29). *Department of Justice Resurrects the Equitable Sharing Program.* Cato Institute. Retrieved in https://www.cato.org/blog/department-justice-restarts-equitable-sharing-program.

39. Holcomb, J.; Kovandzic, T.; and Williams, M. (2011). Civil asset forfeiture, equitable sharing, and policy for profit in the United States. *Journal of Criminal Justice*, 39, 273–285.

40. Maguire, K.; and Pastore, A. L. (Eds.) (1995). *Sourcebook of criminal justice statistics 1994.* Washington, D.C.: Bureau of Justice Statistics, U.S. Department of Justice.

41. Hawkins, C. W., Jr.; and Payne, T. E. (1999). Civil forfeiture in law enforcement: An effective tool or cash register justice? In J. D. Sewall (Ed.), *Controversial issues in policing.* Boston: Allyn and Bacon, pp. 23–34.

42. *Bennis v. Michigan*, 417, *U.S. 1163 (1996). United States v. Ursery, 518, U.S. 267 (1996). United States v. 92 Buena Vista Avenue, 507, U.S. 111 (1993).*

43. Schmalleger, F. (2009). *Criminal justice today: An -introductory text for the 21st century.* Upper Saddle River, NJ: Pearson Prentice Hall, pp. 604–605.

chapter **7**

Drugs and Correctional Interventions

After you have completed this chapter, you should have an understanding of the following:

- The four key philosophies of corrections

- The principles that guide effective practices in corrections

- Drug-abuse treatment programs in correctional facilities

- Community-based treatment programs for drug offenders

- The role of drug and other specialty courts in the criminal justice system

- Supervision of drug offenders in the community

"Hell, I saw it a whole lot different a year ago," Charlie told me.

"First off, I couldn't believe the D.A. when she told me that I had a chance not to go to jail. But then, I thought, maybe this drug court thing was just going to get in the way of getting back to using. I really felt that it wasn't a good idea."

"Yeah, I was pretty stupid then. Now, I know that if drug court didn't happen, I would never have went to Stevan House, never got me a program, never got me in line for getting sober. 'Course, like all the other guys and ladies going through it like me, I didn't want to be here. For weeks, I couldn't help thinking about getting back on the street and doin' my thing. But at the same time now that it's almost over, I'm kind of thankful for it, 'cause I probably wouldn't have no way stopped or even wanted to."

"So I'm grateful for drug court. They gave me my recovery coach to help me get straight. It was a lot of pressure to find a job and sober housing and go to treatment and meetins' all the time—my recovery coach broke them big goals down to little ones, and every time I got one done, I felt like maybe I could do this thing. I wish some of my buddies had the chance I had. 'Course most of them are in jail now. A couple of them are dead."[1]

What do we do with drug offenders once they have been arrested and processed, and they officially enter the criminal justice system? Chapter 4 reviewed the relationship between drugs and crime, while Chapter 5 focused on the penalties that drug-law violators face. The last chapter examined the role of law enforcement in detecting and apprehending drug-law violators, both locally and across the U.S. borders. This chapter will focus on the processing of drug-law violators within the criminal justice system after they have been apprehended by law enforcement and convicted of their crime. This is analogous to a relay race where once convicted or adjudicated for a crime, law enforcement passes the baton to corrections professionals to manage drug-law violators. As with law enforcement, the correctional system is charged with increasing public safety. Law enforcement does so by detecting and arresting law violators. The correctional system must monitor those under correctional supervision and attempt to dissuade offenders from engaging in future criminal behavior.

This chapter will begin with a discussion of the various philosophies of the correctional system. These philosophies drive the strategies that are employed by the correctional system to increase public safety. Next, the principles of effective practices in corrections are described. These are empirically driven strategies for managing and treating offenders aimed at stopping the cycle of offending behaviors. The correctional system itself includes both institutions for managing offenders, commonly known as jails and prisons, as well as a myriad of community-based strategies, such as community supervision and drug courts. The range of strategies that corrections uses to manage and treat drug offenders will be discussed to answer the question of what happens once a drug offender is apprehended for a drug crime, and how we best prevent those apprehended from offending again.

The Philosophies of the Correctional System

The correctional system can be divided into two categories: (1) **institutional corrections** and (2) **community-based corrections**. Institutional corrections refer to jails and prisons, while community-based corrections refer to a spectrum of interventions that occur while under community supervision (probation or parole). At the end of 2015, nearly 6.8 million individuals in the United States were under some form of adult correctional supervision, representing about 3 percent of the adult population. Since 2008, the overall correctional population has been on a slow but steady decline, falling 1.7 percent in 2015. The institutional population declined by 2.3 percent (the lowest since 2004), and those under community supervision declined by 1.3 percent (the lowest since 2000). In 2016, the institutional corrections system was at its lowest level since 2004 and community-based corrections was at its lowest since 2000.[2]

The goals of the correctional system in the United States are derived from a number of often-competing philosophies with regard to individuals who have been arrested or convicted of a crime. The four primary philosophies are (1) retribution, (2) incapacitation, (3) deterrence, and (4) rehabilitation.

- **Retribution** requires proportional punishment for a crime for the sake of justice. It can be thought of as "an eye for an eye" or the "just desserts" philosophy. Under this philosophy, the system punishes individuals who have broken the law because they morally deserve to be punished. Punishment is not for the sake of revenge, rather for the sake of justice, so it must be proportional to the crime they committed. Unlike the other philosophies, retribution focuses only on the current crime, without considering the possibility of preventing future crimes. According to the retribution philosophy, an individual convicted of a third Driving While Intoxicated (DWI) offense might undergo a three- to five-year prison term as a just action for his or her crime against society.

- Under the philosophy of **incapacitation**, the goal of punishment is to inhibit the person from engaging in contin-

institutional corrections: The correctional system that includes those confined to in jails and prisons.

community-based corrections: The correctional system that includes those persons living in the community while being supervised on probation or parole.

retribution: A correctional philosophy that believes in proportional punishment for the sake of justice.

incapacitation: A correctional philosophy that aims to prevent crime by removing a law violator from society.

Numbers Talk. . .

11	Average number of years an individual convicted of a drug offense spends in federal prison.
35	Percentage of individuals in federal prison for a drug offense with no or a minimal criminal history.
24	Percentage of individuals in federal prison who used a weapon during their most recent drug offense.

Source: Taxy, S.; Samuels, J.; and Adams, W. (2015, October). *Special Report: Drug offenders in federal prison, estimates of characteristics based on linked data.* Washington D.C.: Bureau of Justice Statistics, U. S Department of Justice.

ued criminal behavior. The individual is incapacitated from committing a future crime by being removed from the community and confined in a jail or prison. Under the incapacitation philosophy, an individual with a third DWI conviction must be sent to prison to disable him or her from continuing to drink and drive.

- Under the philosophy of **deterrence**, the goal of punishment is to dissuade the individual from continuing criminal behavior through the threat of future apprehension and punishment. There are two types of deterrence. *Specific deterrence* focuses on preventing an individual from considering future criminal behavior by the threat of punishment for a specific crime. *General deterrence* focuses on society at large—reminding the public of the consequences for breaking the law in order to deter criminal behavior. An example that combines general deterrence and specific deterrence would be Ohio's issuance of specialized license plates to individuals convicted of multiple DWI offenses. General deterrence can be achieved by alerting other drivers to the possibility that if *they* engaged in drinking and driving, they might bear the humiliation of brandishing a DWI license plate themselves. At the same time, *specific deterrence* can be achieved since the individual who is issued a DWI license plate might be persuaded to forego drinking and driving again for fear of the same or worse punishment in the future.

- Under the philosophy of **rehabilitation**, the goal of corrections is simple—to help individuals change the behavior that led to criminal justice involvement in the first place. Rehabilitation takes a more humanistic approach toward

the individual, on the belief in the capacity to change one's behavior and the responsibility of the criminal justice system to offer education and treatment interventions to facilitate that change. For an individual convicted of his or her third DWI offense, a rehabilitation strategy would be to provide residential substance abuse treatment aimed at teaching the individual decision-making skills and addressing the substance abuse problem.

Principles of Effective Intervention in Corrections

Across the field of institutional and community-based corrections, a set of principles are used to guide effective practices. The overarching goal is to reduce **recidivism**, which is a reduction of future criminal behavior or **reoffending**, among participants. A wide array of intervention programs can be employed in corrections, ranging from prison-based treatment programs to placement in a diversion program, but not all of them are effective in achieving this goal. Therefore, it is important to examine the basic principles that are considered most useful in this regard, in cases of drug-related crime as well as nondrug-related crime.

The body of research dealing with effective intervention practices can be summarized into three principles: (1) the risk principle, (2) the need principle, and (3) the responsivity principle. Collectively, these principles are referred to as the RNR principles, referring to the components of Risk, Need, and Responsivity (Figure 7.1).[3]

The Risk Principle

The **risk principle** focuses on *the risk potential of an individual who is targeted for a particular correctional intervention*. This principle argues that the intensity of the intervention should be commensurate with an offender's risk for criminal recidivism. Hence, high-risk offenders, or those with a high probability of engaging in crime again, should receive the most intensive supervision and treatment options, and low-risk individuals, or those with minimal risk of breaking the law again, should receive minimal intervention.

Quick Concept Check 7.1

Understanding the Philosophies of Corrections

Check your understanding of the primary philosophies/goals of corrections by identifying which philosophy best matches the correctional intervention. Choose from the following philosophies: (a) retribution, (b) incapacitation, (c) specific deterrence, (d) general deterrence, and (e) rehabilitation.

1. Sentencing someone arrested for cocaine possession to nine months in jail as punishment for violating a drug law.
2. Requiring a probationer to submit more frequent urinalysis tests after he fails a drug test.
3. Requiring a probationer to attend an outpatient substance abuse treatment program after he fails a second drug test.
4. Sentencing an individual to prison for drug trafficking in a school zone to prevent him from continuing to sell drugs to children.
5. Increasing advertisements about the legal consequences of DWI offenses around the holidays.

Answers: 1. a 2. c 3. e 4. b 5. d

---

deterrence: A correctional philosophy that uses the threat of apprehension and punishment to dissuade individuals and the general public from engaging in crime.

rehabilitation: A correctional philosophy that focuses on changing the behavior of the individual convicted of a criminal offense so as to reduce the likelihood of future criminal behavior.

recidivism/reoffending: The repetition of criminal behavior by one convicted of a crime.

risk principle: Assess likelihood of recidivism using a validated risk tool and ensure that supervision and treatment matches risk level.

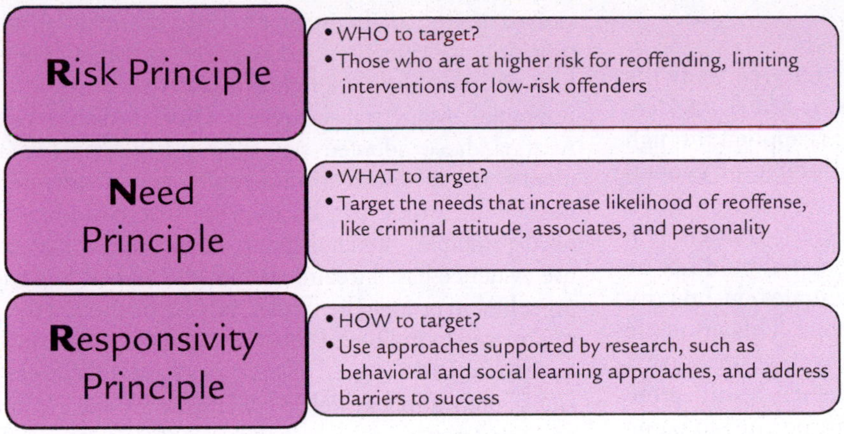

FIGURE 7.1

Summary of the RNR principles of Effective Correctional Intervention.

Sources: Based on Latessa, E., and Smith, P. (2015). *Corrections in the Community.* Routledge: New York, NY.

An important component of the risk principle is use of validated risk assessment measures. A validated risk assessment examines a range of risk factors that help to predict the individual who is most likely to reoffend. Offenders who are administered a risk assessment are classified based on their probability of reoffense. For example, an offender may be classified as low, moderate, or high risk for reoffending. Thus, according to the risk principle, effective practices would dictate that (1) offenders are assessed, using a validated risk assessment to determine their likelihood of reoffense, and (2) offenders are matched to interventions based on their risk to recidivate.

Research has found that when low-risk individuals are exposed to intensive supervision and treatment services, it can actually increase rather than decrease their likelihood of reoffending.[4] Why might this occur? Think about an adolescent, who is generally a prosocial kid (does well in school, has friends that stay out of trouble, has a supportive family, and has never been in trouble with the law before). He decides one night to go to a party and gets caught drinking and using marijuana, so is brought before the court. If a judge decides to teach the youth a lesson and refer him to a six-month residential drug treatment program, this means the youth is taken out of school, taken away from his family, and is severing ties with the friends he has that do not get into trouble. On top of this, this youth is being integrated into a program with higher-risk youth who are modeling criminal thinking and behavior. Hence, effective correctional programs are selective about what offenders go into what programs, and risk or probability of reoffending is at the forefront of those decisions.

The Need Principle

The second principle of effective intervention is the **need principle**. It focuses on *what needs* a program is targeting. The need principle suggests that offenders have a range of problems or needs. Some are **criminogenic needs**, meaning they are linked to criminal behavior, others are noncriminogenic needs. For example, if a person has a substance abuse problem, this need makes him more likely to offend in the future, so substance abuse is a criminogenic need. If a person has a mental illness, this need does not increase his likelihood of reoffending, so mental illness is a noncriminogenic need. Another term for criminogenic needs is *dynamic risk factors*. These synonymous terms describe needs that put an individual at risk for reoffending *and* can be targeted for change. *Static risk factors*, such as age, gender, and criminal history, also increase likelihood of reoffending, but cannot be changed.

The need principle argues that the goal of reduced recidivism by a correctional program is best attained through interventions that focus on dynamic risk factors/criminogenic needs. The key criminogenic needs include criminal attitudes, criminal associates, criminal personality traits, substance abuse, employment and education deficits, unstructured leisure time, and weak family support/bonding relationships. These are all needs that correctional programming and services should target for change. The risk and need principles go hand in hand. High-risk individuals have a greater number of criminogenic needs relative to low-risk individuals.

In working with high-risk drug offenders, it is important to target a range of criminogenic needs that will be most helpful in reducing not only substance abuse but also behaviors related to criminality. Thus, evidence-based interventions for high-risk drug offenders will target who the person spends time with (peers); personality traits such as impulsivity, aggression, or poor decision-making skills (criminal personality traits); family dysfunction; risky leisure activities (like going to clubs or parties); and lack of employment or education, to name a few. Programs that fail to target a range of criminogenic needs will be less effective in reducing participants' recidivism.

need principle: Target criminogenic needs in order to reduce likelihood of recidivism.

criminogenic needs: Characteristics that lead to engagement in criminal behavior.

The Responsivity Principle

The **responsivity principle**, sometimes referred to as the treatment principle, concerns *the ways in which interventions should be delivered*. This principle is applied through two approaches of responsivity. The principle of **general responsivity** focuses on programs that use research-based behavioral and social learning approaches. Models that lack evidence supporting their effectiveness should not be employed. **Specific responsivity** concentrates on how individual offenders respond to interventions. This principle argues that services must address barriers to success, such as transportation or childcare issues, mental health problems, trauma symptoms, or language barriers, just to name a few. Specific responsivity also requires programs to tailor the interventions to match the learning style and motivation of those being treated. Hence, specific responsivity calls for correctional programs to identify a spectrum of offender needs, and addresses those obstacles that may get in the way of individuals being successful in treatment or under supervision. For example, if an individual were on community supervision for a drug offense but also had an intellectual disability, the specific responsivity principle would require that the supervision officer make certain accommodations, such as additional appointment reminders or bringing in a family member to help promote the success of the probationer.

According to the responsivity principle, a probationer with a drug abuse problem should be referred to a provider that uses a behavioral/social learning approach as the primary framework for treatment, as other models fail to provide adequate support for changing an offending behavior (see Chapter 8). Likewise, if this offender is referred to a community-based group, the officer must help the individual to address possible barriers, such as transportation issues or mental health symptoms that could reduce the chances for successfully completing treatment.

Application of RNR Principles

In summary, when correctional interventions adhere to these three principles—risk, need, and responsivity—there is a greater likelihood of reducing criminal behavior, including those behaviors that are associated with drug crimes and drug-related crimes (see Chapter 4). Jurisdictions working to improve their effectiveness at reducing the rate of recidivism often use the RNR principles to guide their decision-making.

> **responsivity principle:** The principle concerned with *how* interventions are delivered—that effective approaches are used. Also called the treatment principle.
>
> **general responsivity:** The principle of using behavioral and social learning approaches to change criminal behavior.
>
> **specific responsivity:** The principle of addressing learning styles and barriers to successful completion of interventions.

For example, in the state of Texas, residential treatment programs for offenders are required to target moderate- to high-risk offenders, excluding those that are low risk (risk principle). Many states, such as Ohio, Indiana, Texas, and Arizona, have adopted statewide risk assessments used to identify risk level and criminogenic needs of offenders across the system, which can be used for case planning (risk and need principle). Federal grants often require that programs use evidence-based treatment models, such as behavioral approaches, in order to be funded (an application of the general responsivity principle). Probation agencies across the country have had officers trained in strategies to address resistance and lack of motivation, as well as specific needs like mental health and gender-responsive practices (an application of the specific responsivity). These are examples of how jurisdictions across the country have incorporated the RNR principles to improve their effectiveness.

Correctional Strategies for Drug Offenders in Confinement

A natural response to an individual whose behavior poses a significant threat to society is to remove that individual from the community and provide some form of incarceration in a jail or prison. Incarceration can be used with any of the four correctional goals described earlier in mind: retribution—to punish the drug offender for his crime; incapacitation—to prevent the sale, purchase, manufacture, or use of drugs by removing the offender from society; deterrence—to prevent crime by showing both the offender and others that the benefits of drug crimes do not outweigh the costs; and rehabilitation—by offering drug treatment while incarcerated to help prevent the offender from relapsing and recidivating once released.

How effective are U.S. penal institutions in meeting these goals? Retribution focuses on what the offender must give up for the offense that was committed, and according to retributive justice, the punishment must fit the crime. Some would argue that the mandatory minimum sentencing laws for drug offenses impose too great a cost on offenders who have committed many of the drug crimes, particularly possession and low-level drug selling. However, for high-level drug manufacturers and traffickers, many argue that the punishment of long prison sentences is justified.

With regard to incapacitation, there is an immediate impact of incarcerating a drug user or seller, prohibiting these individuals from engaging in drug crimes. Of course, drugs are contraband items available in many facilities, and prison gangs often facilitate the continuation of drug crimes in the community from prison (see Chapter 4). Nonetheless, incapacitation does limit drug access for the typical drug offender. Furthermore, many would argue that individuals such as pregnant drug users should be incapacitated so that they are prevented from harming their unborn child. Others would prefer treatment opportunities for these individuals, rather than focusing only on the use of incarceration.

Drug-control policy makers in the United States are just beginning to move away from incapacitation (particularly incarceration) as a primary tool for drug abusers. Increasingly, there is recognition that periods of confinement or the threat of confinement in absence of treatment have limited impact on the problem of addiction or public safety. A national study that examined the recidivism rates of released prisoners in 30 U.S. states between 2005 and 2010 found that among drug offenders 77 percent were arrested for a new crime within five years of their release, with most arrests occurring within the first year.[5] This suggests that incarcerating drug offenders has limited impact on deterring them from breaking the law in the future.

In Chapter 6, it was noted that the 2017 federal drug-control budget allocated a slightly higher percentage of the budget (51 percent) to "demand reduction" strategies, which includes prevention and treatment. This is the first time in the history of the Office of Drug Control Policy that resources for demand reduction strategies exceeded supply reduction strategies. This shift was largely a result of $1.1 billion budgeted for new programs/interventions in the area of opioid abuse, such as increased access to treatment, programs designed to prevent overdoses, medication assisted programs, prevention efforts, and prescription monitoring programs.[6] Policy makers are recognizing the need for additional prevention and treatment strategies, in addition to law enforcement efforts, to address America's drug problems (see Drug Enforcement . . . in Focus). This section will explore efforts to address drug crimes inside the prison setting via rehabilitative or treatment strategies.

Prison-Based Treatment Programs

For those drug-law violators who are sentenced to prison, a previous history of substance abuse continues to present difficulties that do not go away just because they are now behind bars. Substance abuse issues affect not only these drug-law offenders, but also prisoners sentenced for offenses that have no direct relationship to a history of substance abuse.[7] It is estimated that 65 percent of inmates in federal prisons, state prisons, and local jails (1.5 million individuals out of the total inmate population of 2.3 million) meet the criteria for substance use disorder according to criteria in the DSM-5 classification of mental disorders (see Chapter 8). Another 20 percent (approximately 500,000 inmates) do not meet these criteria but, nevertheless, are substance involved in that they were under the influence of alcohol or other drugs when arrested, committed some form of theft to buy drugs, or else

> **diversion programs:** Interventions designed as an alternative to incarceration or criminal justice involvement for low-level, often first-time offenders.

Drug Enforcement . . . in Focus

Diversion Programs for Low-Level, First-Time Offenders

An alternative for individuals that commit low-level, often first-time, offenses are **diversion programs**. While the objective of all community-based supervision options is diversion from prison, post-booking diversion programs allow for diversion from a criminal conviction so that successful treatment of a short-term intervention often results in a dropping of charges. Pre-booking diversion programs even allow for diversion from arrest, examples of which were described in the last chapter. While diversion programs have been around since the 1970s, of late, more low-level drug offenses have been the target of diversion programs.

One example is an initiative in Harris County Texas (Houston), where in 2017 the District Attorney's Office initiated a new program for misdemeanor possession of marijuana cases. The goal of the program was to limit expenditures on criminal justice resources (prosecutors, law enforcement, jail) and assist nonviolent offenders to avoid the stigma associated with a drug conviction. So long as program participants complete a four-hour effective decision-making course, they avoid a criminal record. This program was recently expanded so that the District Attorney could authorize officers, after a brief screening, to make a referral to the drug diversion program in lieu of arrest, thereby avoiding further prosecution and possible and jail sentences. In the decade prior to the establishment of the drug diversion program, the county had prosecuted more than 100,000 of these low-level marijuana cases, at a cost of $200 million taxpayer dollars. Other jurisdictions have initiated similar programs as both a cost saving and social justice measure. These programs allow the criminal justice system to focus on offenders who have committed more serious drug-law violations. Studies have shown evidence to support their effectiveness in recidivism beyond traditional judicial approaches.

Sources: Office of District Attorney, Harris County Texas, Misdemeanor Marijuana Diversion Program. Retrieved from: https://app.dao.hctx.net/MMDP; Center for Prison Reform (August 2015). *Diversion Programs in America's Criminal Justice System: A report by the Center for Prison Reform.* Retrieved from https://centerforprisonreform.org/wp-content/uploads/2015/09/Jail-Diversion-Programs-in-America.pdf; Wilson, H.; and Hoge, R. (2013). The effect of youth diversion programs on recidivism: A meta-analytic review. *Criminal Justice and Behavior, 40,* 497–518.

violated a specific drug or alcohol law. If incarceration is to achieve any degree of rehabilitation for these individuals, it is necessary to provide drug treatment programs of some kind. Yet, according to a major 2010 study of American prisoners, only about 11 percent of these prisoners receive any formal drug treatment at all.[8]

While prisoners with substance abuse issues are similar to non-offender populations with addiction issues, justice-involved individuals are in many ways unique. It is common for those sentenced to prison to have a lengthy history of criminal behavior and a range of criminogenic needs that tend to drive that criminality. As noted earlier, in addition to substance abuse issues, higher-risk individuals tend to have criminal thinking patterns, antisocial friends, employment and education difficulties, family issues, and lack of structured leisure. Hence, in addition to treating substance abuse, there are a host of other issues that need to be addressed if programs expect to reduce likelihood of future criminal behavior.

Jails, as opposed to prisons, house inmates on pretrial confinement (arrested but not convicted for a crime), as well as those sentenced to less than one year of incarceration. The need for substance abuse treatment for jail inmates is clear. However, the short interval of their incarceration and transient nature of this population presents a challenge in providing an effective drug treatment program while in jail.

An additional problem with establishing jail-based drug treatment programs involves the issue of **net-widening**. Net-widening occurs when an intervention casts too wide a net, bringing in individuals who would otherwise be subjected to less restrictive settings or intrusive sanctions. For example, a judge may sentence a defendant to jail confinement *in order* for him or her to have access to a jail-based substance abuse program. If the program had not existed, the defendant would have instead been mandated to participate in a community-based intervention. From a criminal justice system standpoint, net-widening is costly, since individuals who would benefit from a less intrusive and less expensive intervention are mandated to a more expensive one. Furthermore, studies suggest that putting lower-risk individuals in intensive or highly restrictive interventions can actually make them worse (see the risk principle).[9] Nonetheless, short-term programs designed for jail inmates with addiction issues do exist, such as an intensive 30-day drug treatment program,[10] but the effectiveness of such interventions varies widely based on the design of the program.

For inmates in state or federal prisons, an extended structured treatment approach can be made. The best

The Con-Quest therapeutic community program operated by the Utah State Prison for select inmates with substance abuse problems.
Credit: https://corrections.utah.gov/index.php?option=com_content &view=article&id=1060&Itemid=185

known in-prison treatment program of this type that targets inmates with a substance-abuse problem is the **therapeutic community (TC)**. Components of this program include:

- A separate residential unit isolated from the general prison population (except, at times, for meals and other standard activities) to provide a sense of safety and belonging as the TC participants begin the process of change.

- A demanding program, including active participation in several hours of structured intervention per day, that requires emotional, physical, and intellectual work on their part.

- Increased responsibilities and incentives to encourage the residents to progress through the phases of the program, as an indication of "right-living."

- Close collaboration between treatment and corrections staff, and involvement of residents in the management, operation, and treatment for the TC community.

- "Community as method" is the therapeutic strategy, whereby residents must actively participate in the community activities and take on responsibility for their peers' (as well as their own) recovery.

- Generally, a period of 6–12 months of treatment, typically available toward the end of the inmate's prison sentence.[11]

Many in-prison TC programs have been effective in reducing the rate of recidivism among participants. Examples of such programs include the Stay'n Out program in New York, KEY-CREST program in Delaware, Kyle New Vision program in Texas, and the Amity Prison TC program in California. The likelihood of positive outcomes, however, for prison-based TC programs is linked to the availability of postrelease community aftercare programs.[12] Inmates completing the prison-based programs may be required to participate in continued substance abuse services after leaving the prison. These aftercare services are important for reinforcing the skills and commitments residents have made while in

---

net-widening: A situation in which an offender becomes subject to more intrusive sanctions than are necessary.

therapeutic community (TC): A structured residential treatment program that targets the overall lifestyle of substance abusers, using mutual support and accountability to and from the community for change.

the prison-based program. Some aftercare programs involve short-term residential stays at halfway houses or residential treatment programs, while others require attendance to outpatient treatment groups.

Not all prisons utilize therapeutic communities as a treatment approach for targeting substance abuse needs. Many facilities offer specific substance abuse group programs that inmates in general population can also attend. For example, the North Dakota Department of Corrections and Rehabilitation (DOCR) assesses and classifies all inmates upon entry, and based on their risk and needs, develops a case plan for each inmate. Once placed at the appropriate facility, offenders in need of substance abuse programming attend between 8 and 14 weeks of a cognitive-behavioral substance abuse group, delivered by substance abuse counselors in the prisons.[13] These "prison outpatient models" are less intensive than therapeutic communities or other residential/unit-based interventions, and they also fail to separate the inmates who are seeking substance abuse treatment from those in general population who may not be interested in programming. However, they do equip departments with an expanded range of programming to inmates in need of substance abuse services. Many state and federal prison facilities offer unit-based programs as well as programming for those in the general population. While it is challenging to incorporate drug treatment programs in prisons, the benefits are substantial, both on a personal and monetary basis. The benefits of even a single inmate becoming substance abuse-free, crime-free, and employed following release from prison have been calculated as amounting to a savings of approximately $91,000, when compared to the substantially greater costs to society that would be expected if the individual returned to a life of substance abuse and criminal behavior. Another way of looking at the potential benefits is to imagine that if all 1.3 million inmates with untreated substance use disorders were treated in prison and approximately $12–$13 billion were spent in doing so, the "break-even" point would be reached within one year after the prisoner was released.[14]

Reentry Programs for Drug Offenders

While many citizens feel safer knowing that a convicted offender is locked up behind bars, the fact is that at least 95 percent of all state prisoners will be released from prison at some point in time.[15] Furthermore, most recidivists from prison have failed to stay out of prison for even one year after their release.[16] In 2004, in his State of the Union address, President George W. Bush announced his Prison Reentry Initiative, the goal of which was to link nonviolent returning citizens with faith-based community organizations who would help with vocational needs as well as provide services to improve community reintegration and decrease reoffending. Early studies showed a positive impact in job placement efforts as well as decreased recidivism for ex-offenders in these programs, but research in this area has been limited.[17]

Recognizing the challenges returning citizens face, support for reentry services has continued. For drug offenders, efforts have been aimed at a successful transition to the community by providing assistance with job placement, drug-free housing, treatment services, mentoring, and other supports. The National Reentry Resource Center, funded and administered by the U.S. Department of Justice, has provided information and guidance related to reentry. Since its enactment in 2009, the Second Chance Act (SCA) has provided awards of more than 800 federal grants to help state and local government, and nonprofit organizations assist returning citizens' transition from prison, jail, and juvenile facilities to the community.[18]

Community-Based Correctional Strategies for Drug Offenders

For the first time in decades, the United States has seen a drop in the use of incarceration. By the end of 2016, there were approximately 1.5 million state and federal prisoners, a drop of 7 percent since the prison population in the United States peaked in 2009.[19] One could argue that the reduction in use of prison is attributable to a reduction in crime in the United States. While overall both violent and property crime in the United States have been on a steady decline, this decline began in the early 1990s.[20] Hence, the reduction in prison population does not correspond with when the reduction in violent and property crime began. However, in just the five years between 2009 and 2013, 40 states took legislative actions to decrease penalties for drug crimes, such as shortening mandatory minimum terms of sentencing, creating alternatives to incarceration for possession charges, decriminalization and legalization of recreational marijuana, and expanding drug courts for nonviolent drug offenders. These changes at the state level have corresponded with changes at the federal level that have backed away from more punitive "War on Drugs" strategies, such as mandatory minimum sentencing.[21] Hence, decrease in the U.S. prison population since 2009 can be attributed, at least in part, to recent changes in policy and practices for drug offenders.

An important community-based correctional strategy is the adoption of **intermediate sanctions**. Positioned as an approach that fits somewhere between probation and prison, intermediate sanctions provide a range of options for a judge to tailor sentencing to the individual needs of the defendant, while also providing increased accountability for their crime. An additional benefit is that intermediate sanctions become a more justifiable sentencing option for judges who view straight probation as "a slap on the wrist." Examples of *deterrence-based* intermediate sanctions include fines, drug testing, electronic monitoring, house arrest, and boot camps. These strategies often use surveillance with the threat of punishment for criminal behaviors, including drug use. Examples of more

intermediate sanctions: A sentence positioned between probation and prison, offering a range of alternative penalties for crimes.

The Orange Street Women's Center is located in Salt Lake City, Utah, and houses 60 parolees for 4–6 months to assist with reentry from prison to the community. The program assists participants to secure a living-wage job and increases successful re-entry by providing clinical treatment, cognitive behavioral groups, education and community support. This structured facility is one example of a residential intervention. Many smaller halfway houses and sober living facilities are situated in residential communities, blending in with other residences in the area.

Credit: Utah Department of Corrections

rehabilitative intermediate sanctions include drug and alcohol treatment (residential or outpatient), mental health interventions, and drug courts. The goal with these strategies is to teach skills that defendants can use to change their behavior. Some intermediate sanctions have restorative-justice features, such as victim restitution and community service, where defendants must work to restore the damage done to the community. This section will explore some of these alternatives to incarceration for drug offenders, which have become increasingly popular over the last decade, as the pendulum has slowly begun to swing toward rehabilitation-oriented strategies.

Community Residential Drug Treatment Programs

Community residential centers represent the bridge between incarceration and community. Community residential centers serve individuals who are leaving prison with housing, job support, and treatment to assist in reentry. They also serve as an alternative to incarceration for probationers in need of intensive supervision or treatment. Historically called halfway houses, they serve people both *halfway out* and *halfway in* to prison. Some of these facilities are secure, meaning residents are not free to come and go. "Escape charges" can be filed against participants for any unauthorized leave. Other facilities operate as a more typical halfway house, in that individuals are required to seek out jobs, work, and attend self-help meetings and appointments in the community. While many community residential centers are funded and operated through state and/or county social service agencies, private and nonprofit facilities are prevalent as well.

Given the high proportion of substance abuse problems among those involved in the justice system, most of the residential treatment centers serve as drug treatment programs. However, some serve specialized nondrug populations, such as offenders with mental illness, sex offenders, or females, but nearly all offer some services to address substance abuse issues. The intensity of such services varies with the program. In more traditional halfway houses, residents work full-time, and attend groups and self-help meetings during nonwork hours. In secure treatment facilities, time is typically structured around treatment programming, so that residents attend several hours of substance abuse programming per week. These facilities also tend to offer programming or services in other need areas, such as education, vocational skills, anger management, and criminal thinking. Length of stay in such programs typically range from three to six months, depending on the program type and target population and are offered to both juveniles and adults.

Effectiveness of community residential correctional programs is as varied as the programs themselves. Effectiveness tends to be gauged along three dimensions: humaneness, recidivism, and cost.[22] There is little doubt that even in the case of the most secure facilities, community residential programs are more humanitarian than prison. They do not face the same issues with overcrowding, violence, sexual assault, and substandard health care. Residents also have greater opportunities to engage with family and supports in the community. With regard to cost effectiveness, the average cost of a residential correctional bed for adults is $50, which is about half the cost of confining someone in a jail or prison.[23] The effectiveness of these programs in decreasing recidivism can be difficult to measure and varies widely based on the individual who is admitted, what needs are targeted, and how these needs are targeted. In general, community residential programs that adhere to the principles of effective interventions (RNR) tend to show better outcomes.[24]

In addition to residential correctional treatment centers, less structured facilities include **sober living houses**. These are transitional living facilities that provide a substance-free supportive living environment. Unlike halfway houses, residents are often not limited to an offender population, and

community residential center: A facility that serves parolees and probationers as an alternative to incarceration.

sober living houses: A transitional living facility that serves as a step-down for those needing sober housing and support in the community.

these facilities can serve as a "step-down" from a more structured residential center to the community at large, where housing and aftercare services can be provided.

The Advent of Drug Courts

At the time when courts and correctional systems were inclined to pursue a punitive strategy in dealing with drug-law offenders, research in drug treatment strategies had begun to demonstrate their effectiveness in dealing with drug-taking behavior. The two opposing orientations of criminal justice professionals and public health professionals had produced a "tug-of-war" in deciding how drug-law offenders should be handled. The introduction of drug courts in prosecuting nonviolent drug offenders was essentially a compromise, combining the potential effectiveness of drug treatment programs with the structured features of proceedings within the criminal justice system.[25] As one researcher expressed it,

> Proponents of "tough on crime" approaches to drug problems were able to support drug courts and maintain face, as drug courts closely supervise and hold offenders accountable. Supports of rehabilitation and pragmatists were able to support drug courts, as they use treatment programs demonstrated to be effective outside of the drug court context.[26]

Drug courts are specialized courts designed to handle nonviolent offenders with substance abuse problems, incorporating an intensely supervised drug treatment program as an alternative to standard sentencing. The goals are to reduce drug-use relapse and criminal recidivism (repeated offenses in the future) through a risk and needs assessment, judicial proceedings, monitoring and supervision, a combination of incentives and sanctions, and, most importantly, treatment and rehabilitation services. The popularity of adult drug courts over the years has encouraged the development of comparable drug courts for juveniles, DWI offenders, veterans, and families, as well as to target populations having substance abuse problems along with difficulties with the law (Drug Enforcement . . . in Focus).[27]

Several of the characteristics of drug courts include early identification and placement of eligible participants, drug treatment with clearly defined rules and goals, a non-adversarial approach, a monitoring of abstinence, judicial involvement and extensive interaction with participants, and a team approach comprised of a judge, coordinator, public defender/defense attorney, prosecutor, evaluator, treatment provider, law enforcement officer, and probation officer. Those offenders who complete the program successfully may have their charges dropped, to avoid the long-term consequences of a drug conviction, whereas unsuccessful participants are returned to the regular court system and face possible

drug courts: Specialized court systems that handle nonviolent offenders of drug laws, incorporating a supervised drug treatment program as an alternative to standard criminal sentencing.

PORTRAIT

Jeffrey Tauber, National Association of Drug Court Professionals, President Emeritus for Life

Jeffrey Tauber was the first president of the National Association of Drug Court Professionals (NADCP). This organization was established in Alexandria, Virginia, in 1994, five years after the first drug court opened. NADCP, led by Judge Tauber, helped to fund, professionalize, and expand the role of drug courts across the country. Drug courts experienced rapid expansion in the late 1990s due to the growing number of justice involved individuals with serious substance abuse issues. NADCP was responsible for developing standards for drug courts that were sorely needed for jurisdictions interested in opening their own courts.

Judge Tauber was part of a coalition of drug court judges who lobbied Washington in the early 1990s on behalf of drug courts. This mission began when he started the Oakland Drug court in 1990 as a new judge. After spending two years witnessing one success story after another, Judge Tauber became a true believer and strong advocate for drug courts. His efforts, and that of others in the drug court coalition, led to the inclusion of drug courts in the *Violent Crime Control and Law Enforcement Act of 1994*, under President Bill Clinton. This bill was the start of the extraordinary expansion of drug courts for the next two decades.

It was in 1997 that under Judge Tauber's leadership, NADCP wrote "Defining Drug Courts: The Key Components." These 10 components became the guidelines used for the planning and implementation of drug courts across the country. In 1998, the organization developed the National Drug Court Institute to provide training and technical support to emerging drug courts, assisting them to implement best practices. This organization also began to accumulate research on effective drug court approaches. Under Judge Tauber's leadership, a national conference was established for drug court researchers and practitioners, as well as a scholarly journal to publish related research findings.

Judge Tauber resigned from his position of president of the NADCP in 2001. He went on to help create other problem-solving courts, including the San Francisco Parole Reentry Court, as he saw value in the drug court model helping other nondrug populations. He served on the board of NADCP as the "President Emeritus of NADCP for Life" until the organization's twentieth anniversary in 2013, when he officially retired. His leadership helped to drive the drug court movement, which continues to this day.

Sources: Reentry Court Solutions: A resource for community-based reentry systems. Retrieved from: http://www.reentrycourtsolutions.com/2015/07/27/excerpt-10-where-do-drug-courts-go-from-here/

Drug Enforcement . . . in Focus

Specialty Courts in Today's Criminal Justice System

Since the establishment of the first drug court in Miami-Dade County, Florida, in 1989, a number of specialty (or problem-solving) courts have appeared throughout the United States and its territories that focus on specific problem-solving strategies for one type of offender or offense. The most common specialized court is still the Drug Court. However, this model has bred a number of other specialized courts, all based upon the drug court philosophy of reducing reoffending by using therapeutic approaches and accountability, which is overseen by a multidisciplinary team led by the specialty court judge. The following list demonstrates the broad range of specialty courts that have emerged in the United States.

Drug Court: A specialized court system handling nonviolent offenders of drug laws, incorporating a supervised drug treatment program as an alternative to standard criminal sentencing. Drug courts currently exist in all 50 states and U.S. territories.

DWI Court: A specialized court for repeat Driving While Impaired (DWI) offenders, aimed at changing the behavior of individuals with alcohol or other drug-abuse problems. Like drug courts, DWI courts involve extensive interactions between offenders and the judge so as to ensure their compliance with court, supervision, and treatment conditions. There are also "hybrid" DWI/drug courts that serve those with either a DWI or drug offense.

Mental Health Court: Modeled after a drug court in response to the overrepresentation of people with mental illnesses in the criminal justice system. Individuals with (or without) substance abuse issues (depending on the program) are invited to participate following screening and assessment, but they may choose to decline participation.

Family Drug/Dependency Court: A juvenile or family court for families affected by parental drug use, where child welfare is involved with the family. These courts promote establishment of long-term recovery and increase the possibility of family reunification.

Veterans Treatment Court: A hybrid integration of adult drug court and mental health court principles, specifically serving military veterans and sometimes active-duty personnel who have legal issues tied to substance abuse and/or emotional difficulties.

Truancy Court: Addresses underlying causes of truancy by reinforcing education, using a multisystem approach with the court, school, family, mental health providers, and community. These courts are often held on school grounds.

Domestic Violence Court: Targets felony or misdemeanor offenders and addresses the legal, treatment, and social needs of both the offenders and victims, monitoring adherence to protective orders as well as substance abuse and domestic violence treatment.

Tribal Healing to Wellness Court: A component of the tribal justice system for the Native American community, aimed at addressing the impact of alcohol and other drug abuse on their lives. These courts distinguish themselves from formal drug courts as being less focused on the court-related structure and procedures and more focused on healing the individual, his/her family, and the community.

Child Support Court: Targets individuals in arrears on child support payments, so that strategies and oversight at meeting child support responsibilities can be used as an alternative to incarceration.

Community Court: A court that focuses on addressing participant needs as well as restoring, or giving back to the community where a lower-level crime occurred, using partnerships with community boards and the local police.

Federal Reentry Court: A post-incarceration cooperative effort of U.S. district attorneys, probation officers, and federal public defenders, providing a combination of treatment and sanctions to facilitate reintegration into the community for nonviolent, substance abusing offenders who have been released from federal prison.

Reentry Court: A specialty court modeled after the Federal Reentry Court for parolees who have been released from state facilities that are reintegrating with the community. The court assists them in finding jobs, housing, remaining substance free, and meeting family and personal responsibilities. There are also specialized reentry drug courts that serve returning citizens with addiction issues.

Prostitution Court: A Court designed for individuals with multiple prostitution charges, which include assessment, monitoring, and an array of social service and treatment interventions, such as substance abuse, mental health and trauma-informed services.

Homelessness Court: A court designed for homeless individuals charged with nuisance offenses, assisting them to obtain social services and permanent housing, as well as substance abuse, mental health, physical health, and other treatment services.

Sex Offender Court: A court designed to enhance community and victim safety by meeting the specialized needs of sex offenders that are maintained in the community, including treatment needs, accountability to conditions of supervision, and assistance with adhering to registration and notification requirements. These courts serve both adult and juvenile offender populations.

Sources: National Association of Drug Court Professionals, Retrieved from: http://www.nadcp.org/learn/what-are-drug-courts/types-drug-courts/problem-solving-courts; National Institute of Justice, Office of Justice Programs, Retrieved from: https://www.nij.gov/topics/courts/pages/specialized-courts. aspx; Bureau of Justice Assistance (2003, April). *Tribal healing to wellness courts: The key components.* Washington, D.C.: Bureau of Justice Assistance, U.S. Department of Justice. Information courtesy of the National Drug Court Resource Center, Alexandria, Virginia. http://www.ndcrc.org.

The court system in the United States is greatly burdened with the large number of cases that involve drug-law violations. The establishment of drug courts for nonviolent drug-law offenders is an effort to ease the judicial burden and maximize effective drug-abuse treatment.

Credit: Mark Humphrey/AP/Shutterstock

imprisonment. Since the first drug court began operation in Florida in 1989, more than 2,700 drug courts have been established in the United States and its territories as well as in other nations.[28]

The first step in the drug court program begins with defense attorneys, probation officers, or prosecutors referring a potential candidate to the drug court itself. A probation officer then screens candidates for eligibility. Candidates must be judged (using a screening instrument) to be serious drug abusers, cannot be on parole, and often cannot have a prior serious or violent felony conviction. When he or she agrees to enter the program, the candidate waives his or her right to a jury and agrees to enter a treatment program, during which he or she is subject to random drug tests. Participants are supervised by a probation officer to ensure that they adhere to program rules. Best practice standards for adult drug courts were established by the National Association of Drug Court Professionals (NADCP) in 2013 (see Table 7.1). These standards represent 25 years of studies examining what drug court practices are associated with positive outcomes.[29] It should be noted that Standards I, IV, V, and VI in particular reflect the RNR principles.

How effective are drug courts in reducing the rate of recidivism (repetition of offense) among participants? The evaluations of drug courts unfortunately do not lend themselves to a rigorous methodology in which individuals are randomly assigned to a drug court proceeding or to a traditional judicial proceeding. In most studies, drug court participants are compared to drug offenders who were eligible for participation in a drug court but declined participation ("refusers") or to drug offenders who were referred to drug court but deemed ineligible by drug court administrators ("rejects"). Making comparisons in these ways leaves open the question of whether differences could be attributed more to factors such as the motivation to take advantage of the drug court program (in the case of refusers) or the court's perception of the seriousness of the drug problem (in the case of rejects) than the actual effect of drug courts. Some efforts are made to match drug court participants with those in a comparison group on key demographic variables in order to make the two groups relatively equivalent at the start. Despite the methodological

TABLE 7.1

Adult drug court best practice standards

STANDARD	DESCRIPTION
I: Target Population	High risk (likely to recidivate) and high need (significant drug or alcohol problem) identified using a validated risk/need tool.
II: Equity and Inclusion	Must ensure equal opportunity to succeed, despite gender, race, or ethnicity, and ensure court is responsive to cultural differences among participants.
III: Roles and Responsibilities of the Judge	Judge should be "informed, approachable, fair, respectful, attentive, open, and caring" and should rely on input from clinical specialists to make treatment-related decisions.
IV: Incentives, Sanctions, and Therapeutic Adjustments	Use behavioral strategies that are consistent and fair to help change behavior, including incentives and sanctions. Use therapeutic strategies to respond to continued substance abuse rather than overuse of jail.
V: Substance Use Disorder Treatment	Provide a range of evidence-based treatment strategies, including medication assisted treatment with counseling, when recommended. Ensure participants have an adequate amount of treatment and recovery support to reach their goals.
VI: Complementary Treatment and Social Services	Assess for barriers to successful completion of drug court, such as mental health, education, or housing issues, and incorporate additional services, as needed to address additional non-substance abuse needs.
VII: Drug and Alcohol Testing	Implement comprehensive drug and alcohol tests on a random and frequent basis to ensure substance use is responded to in a timely manner.
VIII: Multidisciplinary Team	Drug court team should consist of a judge, program coordinator, prosecutor, defense attorney, probation officer, treatment provider, and law enforcement officer who attend team meetings consistently.
IX: Census and Caseloads	Caseloads should be considerably lower than traditional probation, which should be maintained if the program census rises.
X: Monitoring and Evaluation	Monitor/evaluate practices, to include an annual assessment of admission rates, services, participant outcomes, and adherence to best practices, and every five years an independent outcome evaluation on the program's quality and effectiveness.

Sources: National Association of Drug Court Professionals, Adult Drug Court Best Practice Standards. Based on information from: https://www.ndci.org/wp-content/uploads/2013/08/Best-Practice-Standards-Vol.-I.pdf and https://www.ndci.org/wp-content/uploads/2013/08/Best-Practice-Standards-Vol.-II.pdf

shortcomings, however, a major review of 92 evaluations of adult drug courts, 34 juvenile drug courts, and 28 DWI courts indicated that the vast majority of adult drug courts were effective in reducing recidivism by an average of 12 percentage points. This means if the typical drug offender recidivates within three years at a rate of 50 percent, the group that participated in drug court recidivated just 38 percent of the time. In DWI court evaluations, significant reductions in recidivism were also observed.[30] These findings average the effect size across all drug courts included in the analysis, despite adherence to best practice standards. This suggests that the drug courts with the greatest impact are those that meet the 10 standards outlined in Table 7.1 (including the standards that incorporate RNR principles).

On the other hand, drug courts that target juvenile offenders have not fared as well. Consistent with other studies in this area, the aforementioned meta-analysis found substantially smaller effects on recidivism for juvenile participants.[31] Another nationwide study of nine juvenile drug court programs found that with two exceptions, youths given traditional probation options fared better than those in juvenile drug court. Most youth in these programs were referred for alcohol- and marijuana-related offenses, and many of the failures were for technical violations, rather than new criminal behavior. This leads many to argue that drug court may be too intensive for these youths since the drug court was originally conceived for the adjudication of higher-risk adults with more serious drug addiction issues. Adults who are referred to a drug court program tend to be much further entrenched in their substance abuse and have likely experienced a range of negative consequences (legal, family, employment, and social problems) in their lives.[32] Program models designed around a youth's developmental and family needs appear to be more effective in addressing substance abuse issues that a juvenile justice population would have.

On the basis of other criteria, drug court programs have substantial benefits. They are certainly cost effective. Approximately $250 million in incarceration costs are saved each year in New York State alone by diverting 18,000 nonviolent drug offenders into treatment. Nationwide, it has been calculated that the $515 million in the annual budgets for drug courts produces $2.12 for every $1 spent.[33]

Drug courts also increase the length of time an individual remains in treatment. The coercive power of the criminal justice system with respect to getting into treatment and staying in treatment is dramatic. Ordinarily, between 40 and 80 percent of drug abusers drop out of treatment within 90 days, and between 80 and 90 percent drop out within 12 months. In sharp contrast, more than two-thirds of drug court participants complete a treatment program lasting a year or more. Interestingly, according to experts in the field of drug-abuse treatment, the mandated treatment approach in drug court programs is more likely to result in a successful outcome than in circumstances in which the decision to go for treatment is made voluntarily.[34] Furthermore, best practice standards require that drug courts use incentives for treatment

compliance and progress, which helps to reinforce and support the recovery process.

Unfortunately, it has been acknowledged that the number of drug courts around the country is far from adequate in the handling of the large numbers of nonviolent drug offenders arrested each year. One estimate is that judges and courtrooms are presently available to serve approximately 70,000 drug court clients, when there are 30 times as many actual drug offenders who could be served through a drug court system.[35]

Since the early 1990s, alternative problem-solving court programs have been created to foster treatment for other psychosocial difficulties (e.g., mental health court) or specific criminal behaviors (e.g., prostitution or child support court violations). These courts are modeled after the drug court, typically using a similar structure and philosophical focus on rehabilitation. Mental health courts, for example, provide mentally ill defendants who have committed nonviolent criminal offenses with psychiatric evaluations and treatment, as well as support with stable housing, meeting other treatment/medical needs, and adhering to the conditions of supervision (see Drug Enforcement . . . In Focus on page 128).[36]

Supervision of Drug Offenders in the Community

In 2015, more than 4.6 million individuals (1 in 53 U.S. adults) were on community supervision. Most of those on community supervision are on **probation** (nearly 3.8 million),

> **probation:** A sentence to a community supervision term, whereby individuals are monitored according to conditions set by the judge.

Quick Concept Check 7.2

Understanding Problem-Solving Courts

Check your understanding of problem-solving courts and the correctional system by answering True or False to the following statements.

1. A DWI court is an example of a problem-solving court.
2. A "refuser" refers to an individual who is eligible for a drug court but declines to participate.
3. Juvenile drug courts have yet to be established.
4. Drug courts have tremendous social value but little or no cost effectiveness.
5. Drug courts have not been found to be effective with adults, but do show promise for juveniles.
6. Judges play an important role in the rehabilitation process within problem-solving courts.

Answers: 1. True 2. True 3. False 4. False 5. False 6. True

in which a sentence of community service is given to an individual as an alternative to incarceration. The number of probationers from 2014 to 2015 decreased by about 62,000. **Parole** is another community supervision option whereby inmates are released from prison prior to the completion of their sentence and are supervised in the community. Unlike probation, the parole population in 2015 increased by nearly 13,000 offenders, to a total of about 870,000 U.S. parolees.[37]

Individuals on community supervision must abide by conditions of supervision that are imposed by the court. Some conditions are **standard conditions**. These are conditions imposed on all or nearly all individuals on community supervision. Examples include things like obeying all laws, reporting to the probation or parole officer, notifying officer of changes in residence or work status, submitting to requested searchers, no unauthorized travel outside the court's jurisdiction, no associating with known criminals, and no firearm possession. **Special Conditions** are typically driven by the needs of the individual on supervision, or the desire of the court. Special conditions might include drug testing, electronic monitoring, submitting to a substance abuse or psychiatric assessment, and then following the recommendations, attending Alcoholics Anonymous (AA) or Narcotics Anonymous (NA) meetings, or participating in a more intensive intervention, such as a residential treatment program. If the conditions that are stipulated by the court are not followed, the individual's opportunity to remain in the community can be revoked by the court for a **technical violation**, leading to a term of incarceration. Table 7.2 describes examples of special conditions that may be imposed by the court, many of which also serve as intermediate sanctions, described earlier.

As Table 7.2 suggests, interventions for individuals on community supervision include both deterrence-based strategies, such as drug testing, house arrest, and electronic monitoring, and rehabilitative strategies, such as outpatient treatment and mental health services. Some interventions combine both deterrence and rehabilitation, such as specialty courts and day reporting centers. Decisions about who receives what form of intervention should be driven by an assessment of the probationer or parolee's needs. Having a continuum of interventions is important so that strategies for managing the offender in the community can be individualized, based on his or her needs.

For individuals that do end up on community supervision, larger jurisdictions tend to have a continuum of interventions

parole: A conditional release from prison prior to serving the full term of one's sentence.

standard conditions: Conditions of community supervision that are applied to all probationers/parolees.

special conditions: Conditions of community supervision that are applied based on the needs of the probationer/parolee.

technical violation: A violation of the terms of community supervision, which may lead to a period of incarceration.

TABLE 7.2

Special conditions of community supervision

SPECIAL CONDITIONS	DESCRIPTION
Fines	Monetary penalties imposed by the court, which is often associated with specific crimes
Restitution	Payment to the victim of the offense, typically to offset any loss/expense suffered
Community service	Requirement that the offender volunteer a designated number of hours to a program or service in the community
Curfew	Requiring the offender return to his or her residence by a particular time
Drug testing	Random urinalysis screening for a range of illegal substances—might also include testing of blood or hair samples
House arrest	Requiring the offender remain at his or her residence, except for work and other approved leaves
Electronic monitoring	Use of a device that uses an electric signal to monitor whether the offender stays within range of a designated area
Global Positioning Systems (GPS) monitoring	Advanced electronic monitoring that tracks the whereabouts of an offender to identify if they go to areas prohibited by the court—often reserved for sex offenders or domestic violence offenders
Intensive supervision probation	A specialized caseload that provides increased monitoring of offender behaviors—may also include additional treatment requirements, as needed
Outpatient treatment	Referral to a community-based treatment program for substance abuse, aggression, sex offending, criminal thinking, or other need areas
Mental health services	Referral for psychiatric, case management, or counseling services for those with mental health concerns
Education or vocational training	Interventions to assist the offender to obtain and/or maintain employment or improve education status
Day Reporting Center	A requirement that the individual report regularly to a nonresidential facility for treatment or other services
Specialty court	Participation in a specialty (problem-solving) court to address a specific need area
Community residential center	A facility that serves parolees and probationers as an alternative to incarceration, providing drug (and other) treatment programs

Source: Based on Latessa, E. and Smith, P. (2015). *Corrections in the Community.* New York, NY: Routledge.

for those with a drug or alcohol problem. Those with a significant addiction issue may need to attend detox followed by a residential treatment program, so that opportunity for use is limited until that person completes treatment. Individuals with a substance abuse need who are not at high risk often attend a community drug treatment option, such as an **Intensive Outpatient Program (IOP)**. IOP is delivered in the community, typically in group format. At times, probation or parole officers are trained to conduct these drug treatment groups, or probation departments hire their own licensed substance abuse counselors to provide drug treatment services. However, more often, services are delivered by community agencies with providers that specialize in counseling or drug treatment. IOP is typically a phased intervention, so that treatment is more intensive in the beginning, and the intensity wanes as the individual successfully progresses through the program.

Intensive Outpatient Program (IOP): Substance abuse treatment delivered in the community, typically in group format.

In addition to treatment, supervision conditions typically mandate that individuals with drug crimes or substance abuse needs regularly submit random drug tests to monitor usage. Some courts also mandate attendance to self-help groups, such as AA and NA. This may be imposed based on the philosophy of the court or because the individual lives in a rural area, with limited treatment options. Figure 7.2 shows the community-based options that many moderate- or large-sized jurisdictions have in addressing offender substance abuse needs. This diagram categorizes these options from least to most intensive/restrictive. Recall that the decision about which intervention to apply should be driven by the risk and need principles, so that higher risk/need offenders receive the most intensive interventions. Note that the intervention options in Figure 7.2 are not exclusive, meaning multiple options can be used with a single offender based on his or her needs. For example, individuals in drug court also attend treatment programming, such as an intensive outpatient program, or individuals sentenced to a community residential center may be assigned an intensive supervision caseload upon discharge, as a step-down to the community.

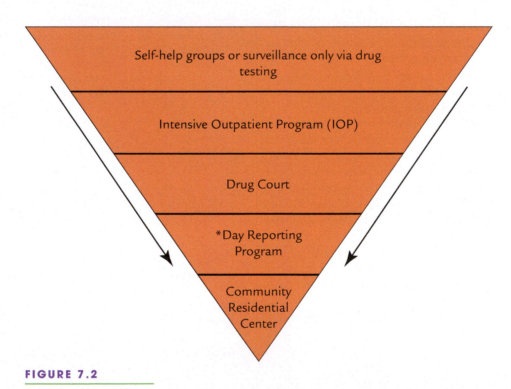

FIGURE 7.2

Least restrictive to most restrictive community-based treatment options.

*Day Reporting Programs intensity varies based on the program requirements, which may render it less intensive than drug court or IOP.

Source: Adapted from Texas Department of Criminal Justice, Community Justice Assistance Division, *Continuum of Care for Substance Abuse Treatment: https://www.tdcj.state.tx.us/documents/cjad/CJAD_SA_Continuum.pdf.*

Summary

Philosophies of the Correctional System

- The correctional system is comprised of institutional corrections (jails and prisons) and community-based corrections (probation and parole).

- Drivers for correctional interventions are based on four primary philosophies of corrections—retribution (just deserts), incapacitation (confinement), deterrence (threat of detection and apprehension), and rehabilitation (treatment).

- According to 2014 statistics, federal drug offenders spend an average of 11 years in prison.

Principles of Effective Intervention in Corrections

- Recidivism is defined as the repetition of criminal behavior by a person convicted of a crime.

- Correctional programs that adhere to the risk, need, and responsivity principles show better outcomes in terms of recidivism reduction.

- The risk principle assesses likelihood of recidivism using a validated risk tool, and ensures that supervision and treatment match risk level.

- The need principle argues that criminogenic needs, or those needs associated with risk for recidivism, must be targeted.

- The responsivity principle focuses on how correctional interventions are delivered, arguing that behavioral and social learning approaches are most effective in reducing recidivism, and that individual offender learning styles and barriers should be addressed.

Correctional Strategies for Drug Offenders in Confinement

- In a study of drug offenders release from state prison between 2005 and 2010, 77 percent were arrested for a new crime within five years.

  - The 2017 federal drug-control budget for the first time allocated more resources toward demand-reduction strategies, including drug treatment and prevention efforts, largely driven by the opioid crisis.

  - Prison-based treatment programs occur in jail and in prison, but jail programs can contribute to the problem of net-widening and can be challenging to implement due to the transient population of jails.

  - Therapeutic communities are structured residential treatment programs available in many prisons across the country that target the overall lifestyle of substance abusers using mutual support and accountability to and from the treatment community.

  - More than 95 percent of state prisoners will be released back to the community; reentry programs are designed to assist returning citizens to reintegrate.

Community-Based Correction Strategies for Drug Offenders

- Since 2009, the rate of incarceration has seen a slow but steady decline. Meanwhile, intermediate sanctions, such as intensive probation supervision, electronic monitoring, and boot camps have served as a gap between incarceration and straight probation.

- Community residential drug treatment programs bridge the gap between prison and probation, by providing an alternative to incarceration as an intensive, live-in substance abuse treatment option that focuses on the goal of rehabilitation.

- Sober living houses often serve as step-downs, or transitional living facilities for drug offenders in need of supportive housing.

- Drug courts are specialized courts designed to handle nonviolent offenders with substance abuse problems. They involve a court-supervised drug treatment program that involves a team of criminal justice and treatment professionals, as an alternative to standard sentencing.

- Other "problem-solving" courts, modeled after the drug court concept, include DWI courts, juvenile drug courts, mental health courts, veteran treatment courts, prostitution courts, reentry courts, and others.

- Evaluations of adult drug courts in terms of reduced recidivism and other measures have been generally positive, and the cost benefits have been substantial.

- Probationers and parolees must adhere to standard and specialized conditions, which often involve drug testing, and when indicated, outpatient drug treatment or other services.

Key Terms

Review Questions

1. Describe the four philosophies of corrections and how they apply to drug crimes.
2. Describe the varying treatment options an inmate with a substance abuse problem may receive in prison.
3. Describe the four standards for drug courts, as established by the National Association of Drug Court Professionals and provide one example for each.
4. Describe the purposes and operations of three problem-solving courts, modeled after the drug court concept.
5. Describe three possible intermediate sanctions that could be applied to a drug offender on probation who tests positive for an illicit substance.
6. Discuss what type of offender would be appropriate to refer to a residential drug treatment center, considering the principles of effective intervention (RNR).

Critical Thinking: What Would You Do?

If an individual received a fourth conviction for possession of a controlled substance (heroin), would you support a sentence to a community supervision option, such as drug court, knowing that these program types have demonstrated effectiveness in reducing recidivism, or would you support a prison term, due to the repeat nature of his offending? Would your opinion change if the defendant were a woman with dependent children? Would your opinion change if the individual was motivated to change his or her drug-using behavior, but did not have the resources to do so? Justify your response.

Endnotes

1. A fictional interview based on accounts of individuals who have been processed through present-day drug court systems.
2. Kaeble, D.; and Glaze, L. (2016, December). *Correctional Populations in the United States, 2015* (NCJ 250374). Washington, D.C.: Bureau of Justice Statistics, U.S. Department of Justice. Carson, A. (2018) *Prisoners in 2016* (NCJ 251149). Washington, D.C.: Bureau of Justice Statistics, U.S. Department of Justice,.
3. Bonta, J.; and Andrews, D. (2017). *The Psychology of Criminal Conduct* (6th ed.). New York, NY: Routledge.
4. Lowenkamp, C.T.; Latessa, E.; and Holsinger, A. (2006). The risk principle in action: What we have learned from 13,676 offenders and 97 correctional programs. *Crime and Delinquency, 52*(1), 1–17.
5. Durose, M.; Cooper, A.; and Snyder, H. (2014, April). *Recidivism of prisoners released in 30 states in 2005: Patterns from 2005–2010 (Special Report: NCJ 244205)*. Washington, D.C.: U.S. Department of Justice, Bureau of Justice Statistics.
6. Office of National Drug Control Policy (2017, May). *National Drug Control Budget; FY 2018 Funding Highlights*. Washington, D.C.: Executive Office of the President of the United States.
7. Chandler, R. K.; Fletcher, B. W.; and Volkow, N. D. (2009). Treating drug abuse and addiction in the criminal justice system: Improving public health and safety. *Journal of the American Medical Association, 301*, 183–190. Larney, S.; Toson, B.; Burns, L.; and Dolan, K. (2012). Effect of prison-based opioid substitution treatment and postrelease retention in treatment on risk of reincarceration. *Addiction, 107*, 372–380. Mears, D. P.; Winterfield, L.; Hunsaker, J.; Moore, G. E.; and White, R. M. (2003, January). *Drug treatment in the criminal justice system: The current state of knowledge*. Washington, D.C.: Urban Institute Justice Policy Center.
8. The National Center on Addiction and Substance Abuse at Columbia University (2010, February). *Behind bars II: Substance abuse and America's prison population*. New York: The National Center on Addiction and Substance Abuse, pp. i, 4.
9. Lowenkamp, C. T.; Latessa, E.; and Holsinger, A. (2006). The risk principle in action: What we have learned from 13,676 offenders and 97 correctional programs. *Crime and Delinquency, 52*(1), 1–17.
10. Bahr, S. J.; Harris, P. E.; Hobson, J.; and Taylor, B. M. (2011). Can drug treatment for jail inmates be effective? An evaluation of the OUT program. *Offender Programs Report, 15*, 17–22.
11. De Leon, G. (2000). *The Therapeutic Community: Theory, Model, and Method*. New York, NY: Springer Publishing Company.
12. Welsh, W. N.; and Zajac, G. (2013). A multisite evaluation of prison-based drug treatment: Four-year follow-up results. *The Prison Journal, 93*, 251–271.
13. North Dakota Department of Corrections and Rehabilitation (2014). *A guide to Evidence base treatment programming offered at the North Dakota Department of Corrections and Rehabilitation—Division of Adult Services*. Retrieved from: http://www.nd.gov/docr/adult/docs/DOCR%20Programs%20 Reference%20Guide%20(Rev.%204-14).pdf.
14. The National Center, *Behind Bars II*, pp. 95–96.
15. Hughes, T.; Wilson, D. J.; and Beck, A. (2001, October). *Trends in State Parole, 1990-2000 (NCJ 184735)*. Washington, D.C.: U.S. Department of Justice, Bureau of Justice Statistics.
16. Durose, M.; Cooper, A.; and Snyder, H. (2014, April). *Recidivism of prisoners released in 30 states in 2005: Patterns from 2005–2010 (Special Report: NCJ 244205)*. Washington, D.C.: U.S. Department of Justice, Bureau of Justice Statistics.
17. White House Fact Sheet: Prisoner Reentry. Retrieved from: https://georgewbush-whitehouse.archives.gov/government/ fbci/pdf/prisoner_reentry_factsheet.pdf.
18. Second Chance Act Grant Program. The National Reentry Resource Center. Bureau of Justice Statistics. Retrieved from: https://csgjusticecenter.org/nrrc/projects/second-chance-act/.
19. Carson, A. (2018, January). *Prisoners in 2016 (NCJ 251149)*. Washington, D.C.: U.S. Department of Justice; Bureau of Justice Statistics.
20. Gramlich, J. (2018, January). *5 facts about crime in the U.S.* Washington, D.C.: Pew Research Center.
21. Desilver, D. (2014, April). *Feds may be rethinking the drug war, but states have been leading the way*. Washington, D.C.: Pew Research Center.

22. Latessa, E.; and Allen, H. (1982). Halfway houses and parole: A national assessment. *Journal of Criminal Justice, 10,* 153–163.

23. Pratt, T.; and Winston, M. (1999). The search for the frugal grail. *Criminal Justice Policy Review, 10*(3), 447–471.

24. Lowenkamp, C.; and Latessa, E. (2002). *Evaluation of Ohio's community based correctional facilities and halfway house programs.* Technical Report. University of Cincinnati.

25. Mitchell, O. (2011). Drug and other specialty courts. In M. Tonry (Ed.), *The Oxford Handbook of crime and criminal justice.* New York: Oxford University Press, pp. 843–871.

26. Ibid., p. 849.

27. National Criminal Justice Reference Service. *In the spotlight: Drug courts.* Washington, D.C.: Office of Justice Programs, U.S. Department of Justice. http://wwwncjrs,.gov/spotlight/drug_courts/summary/html [accessed November 26, 2013].

28. Ferdinand, J.; Edwards, C.; and Madonia, J. (2012). *Addiction, treatment, and criminal justice: An inside view of the Brooklyn Treatment Court.* New York: Center for Court Innovation. Who is on an adult drug court team? National Drug Court Resource Center Web site. http://www.ndcrc.org [accessed November 26, 2013].

29. National Association of Drug Court Professionals (2013). *Adult drug court best practice standards, Vol. 1.* Alexandria, VA: National Association of Drug Court Professionals.

30. Mitchell, O.; Wilson, D.; Eggers, A.; and Mackenzie, D. (2012). Assessing the effectiveness of drug courts on recidivism: A meta-analytic review of traditional and non-traditional drug courts. *Journal of Criminal Justice, 40*(1), 60–71.

31. Ibid., p. 1.

32. Latessa, E.; Sullivan, C.; Blair, L.; Sullivan, C.; and Smith, P. (2013). *Final report outcome and process evaluation of juvenile drug courts.* Cincinnati, OH: University of Cincinnati, unpublished report.

33. Bhati, A. S.; Roman, J. K.; and Chalfin, A. (2008, April). *To treat or not to treat: Evidence on the prospects of expanding treatment to drug-involved offenders.* Washington, D.C.: Urban Institute, Justice Policy Center. Finigan, Michael W.; Carey, Shannon M.; and Cox, Anton (2007, April). *The impact of a mature drug court over 10 years of operation: Recidivism and costs.* Portland, OR: NPC Research.

34. Gottfredson, D. C.; Najaka, S. S.; and Kearley, B. (2003). Effectiveness of drug treatment courts: Evidence from a randomized trial. *Criminology and Public Policy, 2,* 401–426. Mitchell, Drug and other specialty courts. Rossman, S. B.; Roman, J. K.; Zweig, J. M.; Rempel, M.; and Lindquist, C. H. (2011, November). *The multistate adult drug court evaluation: Executive summary.* Washington, D.C.: Urban Institute, Justice Policy Center.

35. Boyum, D. A.; Caulkins, J. P.; and Kleiman, M. A. (2011). Drugs, crime, and public policy. In J. Q.; Wilson; and J. Petersilla (Eds.), *Crime and public policy.* New York: Oxford University Press, pp. 368–410. Roman, J. K.; Chalfin, A.; Reid, J.; and Reid, S. (2008). *Impact and cost-benefit analysis of the Anchorage Wellness Court.* Rockville, MD: National Criminal Justice Reference Service.

36. Huddleston, C. W.; Marlowe, D. B.; and Casebolt, R. (2008, May). *Painting the current picture: A national report card on drug courts and other problem-solving court programs in the United States.* Washington, D.C.: U.S. Department of Justice, Bureau of Justice Assistance.

37. Kaebel, D.; and Bonczar, P. (2016, December). *Probation and Parole in the United States, 2015 (NCJ 250230).* Washington, D.C.: U.S. Department of Justice, Bureau of Justice Statistics.

chapter **8**

Drug-Taking Behavior: Fundamentals and Theoretical Perspectives

After you have completed this chapter, you should have an understanding of the following:

- The ways drugs enter the body
- The ways drugs exit the body
- Critical factors in drug-taking behavior
- Drug dependence, substance use disorder, and the DSM-5
- Biological perspectives on drug use and abuse
- Psychological perspectives on drug use and abuse
- Sociological perspectives on drug use and abuse
- Risk factors and protective factors for drug use and abuse

The sorrowful look on Carrie's face said it all. The drug rehab counselor knew she was dealing with the fact that Carrie had relapsed from a previously successful treatment for cocaine abuse.

It had taken more than a year, but Carrie eventually managed to stay clean. Her life began to improve. She married a man with no drug history, and three months ago, she gave birth to a beautiful little boy. Carrie had made a complete break from her past. She saw nothing of her "cocaine buddies" in the old neighborhood. She knew all about the associations that might draw her back to cocaine. The cravings eventually subsided, and all was going well until a week ago, Carrie was changing her son's diaper when she happened to glance at some baby powder that had spilled on the changing table. Suddenly, something clicked. An intense craving for cocaine had returned. "I felt like Pavlov's dog," she said sadly.[1]

Up until now, issues surrounding drug-taking behavior have been addressed principally from a societal point of view. In this chapter, we will examine aspects of drug-taking behavior from the perspective of the drug user. Two sets of questions will be addressed:

- What are the basic facts about drug-taking behavior in general? How are drugs introduced into the body and eventually into the brain? How are they eliminated? What factors determine the effect of two drugs taken in combination, or the effect of a single drug when administered repeatedly over time? Why might two persons have different experiences even when using the same drug at the same dosage? What is the nature of drug dependence and how does it occur? How is it determined that an individual has a substance use disorder?

- Why do people use drugs in the first place? What theoretical perspectives can help to explain the inclination to engage in drug-taking behavior? How does an understanding of brain chemistry help to account for the process of drug abuse? What psychological and sociological factors underlie drug-taking behavior? What are the specific risk factors in a person's life that increase the chances of becoming a drug abuser?

Ultimately, all psychoactive drugs affect our behavior and experience through their effects on the functioning of the brain. Before they affect the brain, however, drugs need to enter the body in some way. This is where we need to begin: How do drugs get into the body in the first place?

How Drugs Enter the Body

There are four principal routes through which drugs can be delivered into the body: *oral administration, injection, inhalation,* and *absorption through the skin or membranes.* In all of the four delivery methods, the goal is to get the drug absorbed into the bloodstream. In the case of psychoactive drugs, a drug effect depends not only on reaching the bloodstream but also on reaching the brain.

Oral Administration

Ingesting a drug by mouth (later digesting it and absorbing it into the bloodstream through the gastrointestinal tract) is the oldest and easiest way of taking a drug. On the one hand, oral administration and reliance upon the digestive process for delivering a drug into the bloodstream provide a degree of safety. Many naturally growing poisons taste so vile that we normally spit them out before swallowing; others will cause us to be nauseous, causing the drug to be expelled through vomiting.

In the case of hazardous substances that are not spontaneously rejected, we can benefit from a relatively long absorption time for orally administered drugs. Most of the absorption process is accomplished between 5 and 30 minutes after ingestion, but absorption may not be complete for as long as six–eight hours. Therefore, there is at least a little time after accidental overdoses or suicide attempts to induce vomiting or pump the stomach.

On the other hand, the gastrointestinal tract contains a number of natural barriers that may prevent certain drugs that we *want* absorbed into the bloodstream from doing so. One determining factor is the degree of *alkalinity* or *acidity* in the drug, as measured by its pH value. The interior of the stomach is highly acidic, and the fate of a particular drug depends upon how it reacts with that environment. Weakly acidic drugs such as aspirin are absorbed better in the stomach than highly alkaline drugs such as morphine, heroin, or cocaine. Insulin is destroyed by stomach acid, so it cannot be administered orally, whereas a neutral substance such as alcohol is readily absorbed at all points in the gastrointestinal tract.

Numbers Talk. . .

1–7 days	Due to its fat-solubility and relatively long elimination half-life, the length of time over which metabolites from a single smoked marijuana cigarette are detectable in the urine.
5–8	Number of seconds for nicotine in an inhaled cigarette to travel from the lungs to the brain.
100 billion	Estimated number of neurons in the human brain.
2–10 times	The increased amount of dopamine released to the brain with some drugs, relative to the dopamine released with natural rewards, like eating or sex.

Sources: Brookman, R. R. (2008). Unintended consequences of drug and alcohol testing in student athletes. *AAP (American Academy of Pediatrics) Grand Rounds, 19,* 15–16. Drachman, D. (2005). Do we have brain to spare? *Neurology, 64,* 2004–2005. Di Chiara G.; and Imperato, A. (1989). Drugs abused by humans preferentially increase synaptic dopamine concentrations in the mesolimbic system of freely moving rats. *Proceedings of the National Academy of Sciences, 85,* 5274–5278. Yamaguchi, R.; Johnston, L. D.; and O'Malley, P. M. (2003). Relationship between student illicit drug use and school drug-testing policies. *Journal of School Health, 73,* 159–164.

If it survives the stomach, the drug needs to proceed from the small intestine into the bloodstream. The membrane separating the intestinal wall from blood capillaries is made up of two layers of fat molecules, making it necessary for substances to be *lipid-soluble*, or soluble in fats, to pass through. Even after successful absorption into blood capillaries, however, substances still must pass through the liver for another "screening" before being released into the general circulation. There are enzymes in the liver that destroy a drug by metabolizing (breaking down) its molecular structure prior to its excretion from the body. There is a further barrier separating the bloodstream (circulatory system) from brain tissue, called the *blood–brain barrier*, which determines a drug's psychoactive effects. Any drug that cannot pass the blood–brain barrier will not have psychoactive effects.

Injection

A solution to the problems of oral administration is to bypass the digestive process entirely and deliver the drug directly into the bloodstream. One option is to inject the drug through a hypodermic syringe and needle.

- The fastest means of injection is an **intravenous (i.v.)** injection, since the drug is delivered into a vein without any intermediary tissue. An intravenous injection of heroin in the forearm, for example, arrives at the brain in less than 15 seconds. The effects of abused drugs delivered in this way, often called *mainlining*, are not only rapid but also extremely intense. In a medical setting, intravenous injections provide an extreme amount of control over dosage and the opportunity to administer multiple drugs at the same time. The principal disadvantage, however, is that the effects of an intravenous administration drug are irreversible. In the event of a mistake or unexpected reaction, there is no turning back unless some other drug is available that can counteract the first one. In addition, repeated injections through a particular vein may cause the vein to collapse or develop a blood clot.
- With **intramuscular (i.m.)** injections, the drug is delivered into a large muscle (usually in the upper arm, thigh, or buttock) and is absorbed into the bloodstream through the capillaries serving the muscle. Intramuscular injections have slower absorption times than intravenous injections, but they can be administered more rapidly in emergency situations. Our exposure to intramuscular injections comes early in our lives when we receive the standard schedule of inoculations or get a flu shot.

- A third injection technique is the **subcutaneous (s.c. or sub-Q)** delivery, in which a needle is inserted into the tissue just underneath the skin. Because the skin has a less abundant blood supply relative to a muscle, a subcutaneous injection has the slowest absorption time of all the injection techniques. It is best suited for situations in which it is desirable to have a precise control over the dosage and a steady absorption into the bloodstream. The skin, however, may be easily irritated by this procedure. As a result, only relatively small amounts of a drug can be injected under the skin compared with the quantity that can be injected into a muscle or vein. When involved in drug abuse, subcutaneous injections are often referred to as *skin-popping*.

All injections require a needle to pierce the skin, so there is a risk of infection if the needle is not sterile. The practice of injecting heroin or cocaine with shared needles, for example, promotes the spread of infectious hepatitis and HIV. On the other hand, if administered orally, drugs do not have to be any more sterile than the foods we eat or the water we drink.

Inhalation

Next to ingesting a drug by mouth, the simplest way of receiving its effects is to inhale it in some form of gaseous or vaporous state. The alveoli within the lungs can be imagined as a huge surface area with blood vessels lying immediately behind it. Our bodies are so dependent upon the oxygen in the air we breathe that we have evolved an extremely efficient system for getting oxygen to its destinations. As a consequence of this highly developed system, the psychoactive effect of an inhaled drug is even faster than a drug delivered through intravenous injection. Traveling from the lungs to the brain takes only five to eight seconds.

- One way of delivering a drug through inhalation is to burn it and breathe in the smoke-borne particles in the air. Drugs administered through smoking include nicotine from cigarettes, opium, tetrahydrocannabinol (THC) from marijuana, free-base cocaine, crack cocaine, and crystallized forms of methamphetamine.
- Drugs such as paint thinners, gasoline, and glues also can be inhaled because they evaporate easily and the vapors travel freely through the air. In medical settings, drugs that produce general anesthesia are administered through inhalation, since the concentration of the drug can be precisely controlled.

The principal disadvantage of inhaling smoked drugs, as you probably expect, arises from the long-term hazards of breathing particles in the air that contain not only the active drug but also tar and other substances produced by the burning process. Emphysema, asthma, and lung cancer can result from smoking in general (see Chapter 15). There is also the possibility in any form of drug inhalation that the linings leading from the throat to the lungs will be severely irritated over time.

---

intravenous (i.v.): Into a vein.

intramuscular (i.m.): Into a muscle.

subcutaneous (s.c. or sub-Q): Underneath the skin.

Drugs consumed by inhalation are absorbed extremely quickly, aided by a very efficient delivery system from lungs to brain.

Absorption through the Skin or Membranes

A drug can enter the body through its transport across layers of the skin or through absorption into highly vascularized membranes of the nose, tongue, cheek, or rectum.

- Sniffing or snorting a drug in dust or its powder form into the nose is referred to as **intranasal** administration. Once inside the nose, the drug adheres to thin mucous membranes and dissolves through the membranes into the bloodstream. The intranasal technique is commonly used in taking snuff tobacco or cocaine.

- Snuff tobacco, chewing tobacco, and cocaine-containing coca leaves can be chewed without swallowing or simply placed in the inner surface of the cheek and slowly absorbed through the membranes of the mouth. Nicotine chewing gums, available for those individuals who wish to quit tobacco smoking, work in a similar way. Nitroglycerin tablets for heart disease patients are typically administered **sublingually**, with the drug placed underneath the tongue and absorbed into the bloodstream. Medicines can also be placed as a suppository into the rectum, where the suppository gradually melts, and the medicine is absorbed through thin rectal membranes. This method is less reliable than an oral administration, but it may be necessary if the individual is vomiting or unconscious.

- Another absorption technique involves a **transdermal patch**, which allows a drug to slowly diffuse through the skin without breaking the skin surface. Transdermal patches have been used for long-term administration of nitroglycerin, estrogen, motion-sickness medication, and more recently, nicotine. Newly developed procedures to enhance the process of skin penetration include the promising technique of administering low-frequency ultrasound, which allows large molecules such as insulin to pass through the skin. Alternative methods include small silicon chip patches containing a grid of microscopic needles that painlessly pierce the skin and allow the passage of large molecules into the bloodstream. Future techniques include transmitting ultrasound waves to increase skin permeability or combining medications with special compounds that help the medication slip through skin pores.[2]

How Drugs Exit the Body

How does the body eliminate drugs? The most common means of elimination is through excretion in the urine following a series of actions in the liver and kidneys. Additionally, elimination occurs through exhaled breath, feces, sweat, saliva, or (in the case of nursing mothers) breast milk. In rare cases, a drug is excreted in its intact form (i.e., in the way it was administered in the first place). In almost all other cases, however, elimination requires the drug to undergo a physical change, a process referred to as **biotransformation**. Typically, biotransformation is either accomplished literally by a breakup of the drug's molecular structure into pieces or by some modification of it. In either case, the end products of the biotransformation process, referred to as **metabolites**, are then passed along to the kidneys and eventually excreted in the urine. The customary method of drug testing is the screening for the presence or absence of metabolites in a urine sample, while other methods involve samples of saliva. It should be emphasized,

intranasal: Applied to the mucous membranes of the nose.

sublingual: Applied under the tongue.

transdermal patch: A device attached to the skin that slowly delivers the drug through skin absorption.

biotransformation: The process of changing the molecular structure of a drug into forms that make it easier to be excreted from the body.

metabolite (me-TAB-oh-lite): A by-product resulting from the biotransformation process.

however, that it is the detection of metabolites in the sample, not the detection of the drug itself, that determines the outcome of the test. The forensics of drug testing will be discussed in Chapter 16.

Each drug has a characteristic **elimination half-life**, defined as the amount of time required for the level of the drug to decline by 50 percent from its original level in the bloodstream. The elimination half-life reflects the process of biotransformation that can vary from drug to drug. In general, if a drug is fat-soluble, the rate will be slower than if a drug is water-soluble and the elimination half-life will be longer. Many drugs such as cocaine and nicotine have half-lives of only a few hours, while marijuana and some medications are examples of drugs with much longer half-lives.[3] Understanding the half-life of a specific illicit drug is important in drug-testing programs when the intention is to determine not only *whether* an illicit drug was used but also *how recently* the drug was used prior to the time of testing.

Factors Determining the Behavioral Impact of Drugs

Each type of drug administration presents specific constraints upon the effect a drug may produce. Some drug effects are optimized, for example, by an oral administration, whereas others require more direct access to the bloodstream.

Other factors must be considered as well. If a drug is administered repeatedly, the timing of the administration plays an important role in determining the final result. If two drugs are administered close together in time, we also must consider how these drugs might interact with each other in terms of their acute effects. Repeated administrations of the same drug may produce a diminished physiological or psychological effect. Finally, two identical drugs taken by two individuals in equivalent dosages may produce different effects by virtue of the characteristics of the drug users at the time of administration.

Timing

All drugs, no matter how they are delivered, share some common features when we consider their effects over time. There is initially an interval (the **latency period**) during which the concentration of the drug is increasing in the blood but is not yet high enough for a drug effect to be detected. As the concentration of the drug continues to rise, the effect will become stronger. A stage will be reached eventually when the effect attains a maximum strength, even though the concentration in the blood continues to rise. This point is unfortunately the point at which the drug may produce undesirable side effects. One solution to this problem is to administer the drug in a time-release form. In this approach, a large dose is given initially to enable the drug effect to be felt; then smaller doses are programmed

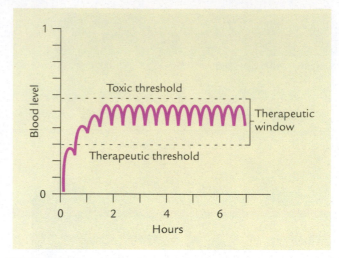

FIGURE 8.1

The therapeutic window. Time-release drugs are formulated to administer the drug in small amounts over time to stay between the therapeutic level and the toxic level.

to be released at specific intervals afterward to postpone, up to 12 hours or so, the decline in the drug's concentration in the blood. The intention is to keep the concentration of the drug in the blood within a "therapeutic window," high enough for the drug to be effective while low enough to avoid any toxic effects. When drugs are administered repeatedly, there is a risk that the second dose will boost the concentration of the drug in the blood too high before the effect of the first dose has a chance to decline (Figure 8.1).

Drug Interactions

Two basic types of interactions may occur when two drugs are mixed together.

■ In the first type, two drugs in combination can produce an acute effect that is greater than the effect of either drug administered separately. In some cases, the combination effect is purely *additive*. For example, if the effect of one drug alone is equivalent to a 4 and the effect of another drug is a 6, then the combined additive effect is equivalent to a value of 10. In other cases, however, the acute combination effect is *hyperadditive*, with the combined effect exceeding the sum of the individual drugs administered alone, as in the two drugs in the first example combining to a value of more than 10. Any hyperadditive effect produced by a combination of two or more drugs is referred to

elimination half-life: The length of time it takes for a drug to be reduced to 50 percent of its equilibrium level in the bloodstream.

latency period: An interval of time during which the effect of a drug is not observed in the blood though the drug has been administered.

as **synergism**. In some synergistic combinations, one drug may even double or triple the effect of the other. It is also possible that one drug might have no effect at all unless it is taken simultaneously with another. This special form of synergism is called **potentiation**; it is as though a drug has no effect at all by itself, but when combined with a drug having an effect of 6, produces a result equivalent to a 10. The danger of such interactions is that the combined effect of the drugs is so powerful that it can become toxic. In extreme cases, the toxicity can be lethal.

■ In the second type of interaction, two drugs can be antagonistic if the acute effect of one drug is diminished to some degree when administered with another, a situation comparable to a drug with the effect of 6 and a drug with the effect of 4 combining to produce an effect of 3. It is possible that two drugs may be totally antagonistic to each other, in that the second exactly cancels out, or neutralizes, the effect of the first.

Tolerance Effects

The concept of **tolerance** refers to the capacity of a drug dose to have a gradually diminished effect on the user as a result of repeated administrations of the drug. Another way of viewing tolerance is to say that, over repeated administrations, a drug dose needs to be *increased* to maintain an equivalent effect. A common illustration is the effect of caffeine in coffee. When you are first introduced to caffeine, the stimulant effect is usually quite pronounced; you might feel noticeably "wired" after a 5-ounce cup of coffee, containing approximately 100 mg of caffeine. After several days or perhaps a few weeks of coffee drinking, the effect is greatly diminished; you may need to be on the second or third cup by that time, consuming 200–300 mg of caffeine, to duplicate the earlier ingestions of caffeine end up remaining awake through the night after a single cup.

In general, the number of previous times the drug has been used, the greater the chance of a diminished effect, due to the diminished pharmacological effects of the drug in the body. However, there is an interaction between the pharmacological effects and the *setting* within which the drug-taking behavior occurs. Evidently, environmental cues that are present during initial

occasions of drug use have the capability of producing physiological changes that are *opposite* to the changes elicited by the drug and will become stronger as drug use is repeated *in that environment*. In other words, there will be an increasingly significant compensatory effect over time and a diminished experience on the part of the drug user. The phenomenon is referred to as **behavioral tolerance**, because it is a result of behavioral circumstances rather than any pharmacological feature of the drug itself.[4]

To have a clear idea of the role of environmental settings during drug-taking behavior in the potential for adverse consequences, we need to understand the basic principles of Pavlovian conditioning. Suppose that you consistently heard a bell ring every time you had a headache. Previously, bells had never had any negative effect on you. The association between the ringing bell and the pain of the headache over time, however, would be established so that, on some future date, the mere ringing of a bell alone would give you a headache, perhaps less severe than the one you had originally but a headache nonetheless. This effect is Pavlovian conditioning at work. Repetitions of the two events would produce a conditioned effect.

Research conducted by psychologist Shepard Siegel illustrates the application of behavioral tolerance in cases of drug overdose. In one experiment, two groups of rats were injected with doses of morphine over a series of days in a particular room. One group was then tested for tolerance effects in the same room as before. Predictably, they displayed a lessened analgesic effect. A second group was tested in a room other than the one in which the injections had been given. No tolerance developed at all. They reacted as if they had never been given morphine before, even though they had received the same number of repeated injections as the first group. If the dosage of morphine had been increased over time, the first group would have probably survived, but the second group would probably have died.

Similarly, if an individual used heroin repeatedly in the same environment over time, tolerance would develop. Typically, the dosage would be deliberately increased in order to experience the same effect as before. If the environment was changed in some way, however, the individual would now be administering the drug at a higher dosage level without the benefit of a conditioned compensatory response that had been built up from the previous environment.

Consequently, there is a greater chance of a drug overdose when the drug has been taken in a *different* environment from the one more frequently encountered or in a manner different from his or her ordinary routine.[5] Since the range of tolerated doses of heroin can be enormous, a dosage level of 200–500 mg may be lethal for a first-time heroin user, whereas amounts as high as 1,800 mg may not even be sufficient to make a long-term heroin user sick.[6] You can imagine how dangerous it would be if the conditioned compensatory response a heroin abuser had built up over time was suddenly absent.

Behavioral tolerance also helps to explain why a formerly drug-dependent individual is strongly advised to avoid the surroundings associated with his or her past drug-taking behavior. If these surroundings provoked a physiological effect opposite to the effect of the drug through their association with prior drug-taking behavior, then a return to this environment

---

synergism (SIN-er-jih-zum): The property of a drug interaction in which the combination effect of two drugs exceeds the effect of either drug administered alone.

potentiation: The property of a synergistic drug interaction in which one drug combined with another drug produces an enhanced effect when one of the drugs alone would have had no effect.

tolerance: The capacity of a drug to produce a gradually diminished physiological or psychological effect upon repeated administrations at the same dose level.

behavioral tolerance: The process of drug tolerance that is linked to drug-taking behavior occurring consistently in the same surroundings or under the same circumstances. Also known as *conditioned tolerance*.

Quick Concept Check 8.1

Understanding Drug Interactions

Check your understanding of drug interactions by assuming the following values to represent the effects of Drugs A, B, and C, when taken individually:

- Drug A   0
- Drug B   20
- Drug C   35

Identify the type of drug interaction when the following values represent the effect of two drugs in combination.

1. Drug A combined with Drug B	30
2. Drug B combined with Drug C	55
3. Drug A combined with Drug C	15
4. Drug B combined with Drug C	85
5. Drug B combined with Drug C	0
6. Drug A combined with Drug B	20

Answers: 1. potentiation   2. additive   3. antagonistic
4. synergistic (hyperadditive)   5. antagonistic   6. additive

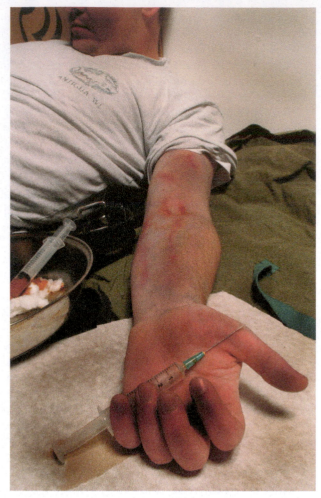

A heroin abuser suffering from a possibly lethal heroin overdose immediately after the injection. The heroin abuser may have experienced a severe allergic reaction to a massive release of histamine (see Chapter 9).

might create internal changes that only drugs could reverse. In effect, environmentally induced withdrawal symptoms would increase the chances of a relapse. The fact that conditioning effects have been demonstrated not only with respect to heroin but with alcohol, cocaine, nicotine, and other dependence-producing drugs as well makes it imperative that the phenomenon of behavioral tolerance be considered during the course of drug-abuse treatment and rehabilitation.

Cross-Tolerance

If you were taking a barbiturate (a sedation-producing drug that acts to depress bodily functioning) for an extended length of time and you developed a tolerance for its effect, you also might have developed a tolerance for another depressant drug even though you have never taken the second one. In other words, it is possible that a tolerance effect for one drug might automatically induce a tolerance for another. This phenomenon, referred to as **cross-tolerance**, is commonly observed in the physiological and psychological effects of alcohol, barbiturates, and other depressants. As a result of cross-tolerance, an alcoholic will have already developed a tolerance for a barbiturate, or a barbiturate abuser will need a greater amount of an anesthetic when undergoing surgery.

Individual Differences

Some variations in drug effects may be related to an interaction between the drug itself and specific characteristics of the person taking the drug. One characteristic is an individual's weight. In general, a heavier person will require a greater amount of a drug than a lighter person to receive an equivalent drug effect, all other things being equal. It is for this reason that drug dosages are expressed as a ratio of drug amount to body weight. This ratio is expressed in metric terms, as milligrams per kilogram (mg/kg).

Another characteristic is gender. Even if a man and a woman are exactly the same weight, differences in drug effects still can result on the basis of gender differences in body

> **cross-tolerance:** A phenomenon in which the tolerance that results from the chronic use of one drug induces a tolerance effect with regard to a second drug that has not been used before.

composition and sex hormones. Women have, on average, a higher proportion of fat, due to a greater fat-to-muscle ratio, and a lower proportion of water than men. When we look at the effects of alcohol consumption in terms of gender, we find that the lower water content (a factor that tends to dilute the alcohol in the body) in women makes them feel more intoxicated than men, even if the same amount of alcohol is consumed.

Relative to men, women also have reduced levels of enzymes that break down alcohol in the liver, resulting in higher alcohol levels in the blood and a higher level of intoxication.[7] We suspect that the lower level of alcohol biotransformation may be related to an increased level of estrogen and progesterone in women. Whether gender differences exist with regard to drugs other than alcohol is presently unknown.

Another individual characteristic that influences the ways certain drugs affect the body is ethnic background. About 50 percent of all people of Asian descent, for example, have lower than average levels of one of the enzymes that normally breaks down alcohol in the liver shortly before it is excreted. With this particular deficiency, alcohol metabolites tend to build up in the blood, producing a faster heart rate, facial flushing, and nausea.[8] As a result, many Asians find drinking to be quite unpleasant.

The Expectation Effect

It is clear that specific physiological factors must be taken into account to predict a particular drug effect. Yet, even if we controlled these factors completely, we would still frequently find a drug effect in an individual person to be different from time to time, place to place, and situation to situation. Predictions about how a person might react would be far from perfect.

In general, a good way of thinking about an individual's response to a particular drug is to view the drug effect as the product of three factors: (1) the drug's pharmacological properties (the biochemical nature of the substance), (2) the individual taking the drug (set), and (3) the immediate environment within which drug-taking behavior is occurring (setting). It is the three-way interaction of these factors that determines the final outcome.

Whether one or more of these factors dominate in the final analysis seems to depend upon the dosage level. Generally speaking, the higher the drug dose, the greater the contribution made by the pharmacology of the drug itself; the lower the dose, the greater the contribution of individual characteristics of the drug-taker or environmental conditions.

Yet probably the most uncontrollable factor in drug-taking behavior is the set of expectations a person may have about what the drug will do. If you believe that a drug will make you drunk or feel sexy, the chances are increased that it will do so; if you believe that a marijuana cigarette will make you high, the chances are increased that it will. You can consider the impact of negative expectations in the same way; when the feelings are strong that a drug will have no effect on you, the chances are lessened that you will react

to it. In the most extreme case, you might experience a drug effect even when the substance you ingested was completely inert—that is, pharmacologically ineffective. Any inert (inactive) substance is referred to as a **placebo** (from the Latin, "I will please"), and the physical reaction to it is referred to as the *placebo effect*.

The concept of a placebo goes back to the earliest days of pharmacology. The bizarre ingredients prescribed in ancient times to treat various diseases were effective to the extent that people *believed* that they were effective, not from any known therapeutic property of these ingredients. No doubt, the placebo effect was strong enough for physical symptoms to diminish. During the Middle Ages, in one of the more bizarre cases of the placebo effect, Pope Boniface VIII reportedly was cured of kidney pains when his personal physician hung a gold seal bearing the image of a lion around the pope's thigh.[9]

It would be a mistake to think of the placebo effect as involving totally imaginary symptoms or totally imaginary reactions. Physical symptoms, involving specific bodily changes, can occur on the basis of placebo effects alone. How likely is it that a person will react to a placebo? The probability will vary from drug to drug, but in the case of morphine, the data are very clear. In 1959, a review of studies in which morphine or a placebo was administered in clinical studies of pain concluded that a placebo-induced reduction in pain occurred 35 percent of the time. Considering that morphine itself had a positive result in only 75 percent of the cases, the placebo effect is a very strong one.[10]

Given the power of the placebo effect in drug-taking behavior, it is necessary to be very careful when carrying out drug research. For a drug to be deemed truly effective, it must be proved to be better not only in comparison to a no-treatment condition (a difference that could conceivably be attributed to a placebo effect) but also in comparison to an identical-looking drug that lacks the active ingredients of the drug being evaluated. For example, if the drug under study is in the shape of a round red pill, another round red pill without the active ingredients of the drug (called the *active placebo*) must also be administered for comparison.

The procedures of these studies also have to be carefully executed. Neither the individual administering the drug or placebo nor the individual receiving the drug or placebo should know which substance is actually being ingested. Such precautions, referred to as a **double-blind** procedure, represent the minimal standards for separating the pharmacological effects of a drug from the effects that arise from one's expectations and beliefs.

---

placebo (pla-SEE-bo): Latin term translated "I will please." Any inert substance that produces a psychological or physiological reaction.

double-blind: A procedure in drug research in which neither the individual administering nor the individual receiving a chemical substance knows whether the substance is the drug being evaluated or an active placebo.

Physical and Psychological Dependence

When we refer to the idea of dependence in drug abuse, we are dealing with the fact that a person has a strong compulsion to continue taking a particular drug. Two possible models or explanations for why drug dependence occurs can be considered. The first is referred to as physical dependence, and the second is referred to as psychological dependence. The two models are not mutually exclusive; the abuse of some drugs can be a result of both physical and psychological dependence, whereas the abuse of others can be a result of psychological dependence alone.

Physical Dependence

The concept of **physical dependence** originates from observations of heroin abusers, as well as of those who abuse other opioid drugs, who developed strong physical symptoms following heroin withdrawal: a runny nose, chills and fever, inability to sleep, and hypersensitivity to pain. For barbiturate abusers in a comparable situation, symptoms include anxiety, inability to sleep, and sometimes lethal convulsions. For chronic alcohol abusers, abstention can produce tremors, nausea, weakness, and tachycardia (a fast heart rate). If severe, symptoms may include delirium, seizures, and hallucinations.[11]

Although the actual symptoms vary with the drug being withdrawn, the fact that we observe physical symptoms at all suggests strongly that some kind of physical need, perhaps as far down as the cellular level, has developed over the course of drug abuse. It is as though the drug, previously a foreign substance, has become a normal part of the nervous system, and its removal and absence become abnormal.

From this point of view, it is predictable that the withdrawal symptoms would involve symptoms that are *opposite* to the effects the drug originally had on the body. For example, heroin can be extremely constipating, but eventually the body compensates for heroin's intestinal effects. Abrupt abstinence from heroin leaves the processes that have been counteracting the constipation with nothing to counteract, so the result of withdrawal is diarrhea. You may notice a strong resemblance between the action–counteraction phenomena of withdrawal and the processes Siegel has hypothesized as the basis for behavioral tolerance.

Psychological Dependence

The most important implication of the model of physical dependence, as distinct from psychological dependence, is that individuals involved in drug abuse continue the drug-taking behavior, at least in part, *to avoid the feared consequences of withdrawal.* This idea can form the basis for a general model of drug dependence only if physical withdrawal symptoms appear consistently for every drug considered as a drug of abuse. It turns out, however, that a number of abused drugs (cocaine, hallucinogens, and marijuana, for example) do not

produce physical withdrawal symptoms, and the effects of heroin withdrawal are more variable than we would expect if physical dependence alone were at work.

It is possible that drug abusers continue to take the drug not because they want to avoid the symptoms of withdrawal but because they crave the pleasurable effects of the drug itself. They may even feel that they need the drug to function at all.[12]

Many heroin abusers (between 56 and 77 percent in one major study) who complete the withdrawal process after abstaining from the drug have a relapse.[13] If physical dependence were the whole story, these phenomena would not exist. The withdrawal symptoms would have been gone by that time, and any physical need that might have been evident before would no longer be present.

When we speak of **psychological dependence**, we are offering an explanation of drug abuse based not upon the attempt of abusers to avoid unpleasant withdrawal symptoms but upon their continued desire to obtain pleasurable effects from the drug. Evidence of psychological dependence, that is, dependence *without* the presence of withdrawal symptoms, can be found in the research literature concerning animals that have been administered a number of illicit drugs.

Experiments of this type consistently show that animals would self-administer psychoactive drugs such as cocaine and other stimulants despite the fact that these drugs would not ordinarily produce physical symptoms during withdrawal. In one study, rats pressed the lever as many as 6,400 times for one administration of cocaine; others were nearly as eager for administrations of amphetamines.[14] Interestingly, researchers found that a number of other psychoactive drugs were aversive, judging from the reluctance of animals to work for them. Hallucinogens such as LSD, antipsychotic drugs, and antidepressant drugs were examples of drugs that animals clearly did not like.[15]

By connecting the concept of psychological dependence to general principles of reinforcement, it is possible for us to appreciate the powerful effects of abused drugs and differentiate among them. When an animal is presented with a choice of pressing a lever for food or pressing a lever for cocaine, cocaine wins hands down—even to the point of the animal starving to death.[16] When the effects of heroin are compared with those of cocaine, rats self-administering heroin eventually establish a stable pattern of use. They maintain their body weight and continue to groom themselves as before. For a while, they appear to be in good health, although about a third of them die in a month's time. Rats self-administering cocaine, however, show a more erratic pattern of use. Binge-like episodes of heavy use would occur, alternating with brief periods of no use

physical dependence: A model of drug dependence based on the idea that the drug abuser continues the drug-taking behavior to avoid the consequences of physical withdrawal symptoms.

psychological dependence: A model of drug dependence based on the idea that the drug abuser is motivated by a craving for the pleasurable effects of the drug.

at all. Body weight drops by 47 percent, their normal grooming behavior ends, and there is a steady deterioration in their physical health. Typically, as many as 90 percent of the rats die after 30 days of cocaine self-administration.[17]

In the final analysis, from the standpoint of drug-abuse treatment, the distinction between the concepts of physical dependence and psychological dependence may not be significant. In fact, according to many experts in the field, the patterns of compulsive drug-taking behavior among users seeking treatment are remarkably similar regardless of the drug involved. If the patterns of behavior are similar, then it can be argued that there can be common strategies for effective treatment (see Chapter 14).

The DSM-5: Defining Substance Use Disorders

For any treatment program to be effective, whether the problems are drug-related or not, a system of guidelines must be in place to establish an appropriate diagnosis. In the case of drug-related problems, health professionals in the United States use a set of *specific behavioral circumstances* that serve as criteria for a diagnosis, just as symptoms serve as criteria for a physical disease.

From the perspective of a health professional, the goal is to reduce the incidence of drug-related problems in an individual's life through a therapeutic intervention (see Chapter 14). The emphasis in making a diagnosis is on the adverse impact of drug-taking behavior on his or her life, independent of any possible illegality that may be involved in the behavior itself (see Chapter 1).

The Diagnostic and Statistical Manual of Mental Disorders (referred to as the "DSM"), issued under the auspices of the American Psychiatric Association, has been the official standard for defining and diagnosing a wide range of psychological disorders, including those related to drug-taking behavior. The fifth edition of the manual (referred to as DSM-5), issued in 2013, establishes a diagnosis of **substance use disorder** on the basis of 11 possible behavioral circumstances (or criteria). As we will see, a minimum number of criteria must be met for this diagnosis.

The 11 possible criteria for substance use disorder can be viewed in terms of four groupings of dysfunctional behavior:

- **Impaired control:** A substance may be taken in larger amounts or over a longer period of time than the individual originally intended (Criterion 1). There may be a persistent desire to cut down or regulate substance use or there may be multiple unsuccessful attempts to cut down or discontinue substance use (Criterion 2). A great deal of time may be spent obtaining the substance, using it, or recovering its effects (Criterion 3). There may be intense urges or cravings to engage in substance use or times in which the individual cannot think of anything else (Criterion 4).
- **Social impairment:** There may be a failure in fulfilling a major role obligation at work, at school, or at home

as a consequence of substance use (Criterion 5). Substance use may be continued despite the persistence or recurrence of social or interpersonal problems associated with use (Criterion 6). An individual may withdraw from, reduce, or give up on important social, occupational, or recreational activities because of substance use (Criterion 7).

- **Risky use:** There may be multiple times when substance use has occurred in a physically hazardous situation (Criterion 8). Substance use may continue despite the knowledge that it is likely to cause or exacerbate a physical or psychological problem. In other words, there is a failure to abstain from using the substance even though the individual recognizes the problems substance use is causing (Criterion 9).
- **Pharmacological effects:** Over time, there may be a development of tolerance to the effects of the substance being used (Criterion 10). For those substances for which significant withdrawal symptoms have been documented in humans (e.g., alcohol, opioids, sedative-hypnotics, and antianxiety medications), withdrawal symptoms may be observed (Criterion 11). However, in cases in which withdrawal symptoms are *not* documented to occur in humans, such as with hallucinogen use or inhalant use, Criterion 11 is not considered in arriving at a diagnosis.

According to the DSM-5, the severity of substance use disorder is defined in terms of the number of criteria that apply for a given individual. The presence of two or three criteria indicates a mild level of substance use disorder; the presence of four to five criteria indicates a moderate level; and the presence of six or more criteria indicates a severe condition.

Three major points should be made with respect to the terminology used in the DSM-5 system.

- First, the phrase "substance use" is used throughout rather than "drug use" since it is acknowledged that confusion often exists in the public mind about the consumption of alcohol or tobacco products as representing a form of drug-taking behavior.
- Second, separate diagnoses for **substance abuse** and **substance dependence** previously established in an earlier edition of the DSM (specifically DSM-IV-TR), with the latter

substance use disorder: A diagnostic term in DSM-5 (issued in 2013) identifying an individual with varying degrees of behavioral difficulties that are related to some form of drug-taking behavior.

substance abuse: A diagnostic term in an earlier edition of the DSM (DSM-IV-TR) identifying an individual who continues to take a psychoactive drug despite a pattern of drug-taking behavior that has created specific problems for that individual.

substance dependence: A diagnostic term in an earlier edition of the DSM (DSM-IV-TR) identifying an individual with significant signs of a dependent relationship upon a psychoactive drug.

indicating a greater severity of dysfunction, have been eliminated in DSM-5. It has been felt that the clinical treatment of drug-related problems can be more easily carried out with a singular diagnosis and the use of a scale of severity-of-symptoms as a rough approximation of the degree of dysfunctionality. The general guideline of fulfilling six or more criteria for substance use disorder (establishing a diagnosis of *severe substance use disorder*) can be considered equivalent to the older diagnosis of substance dependence.

- Three, when a *single* drug is involved, the diagnosis of substance use disorder is identified in the context of that drug. As examples, the DSM-5 establishes separate diagnoses of opioid use disorder (when opioids are involved), stimulant use disorder, hallucinogen use disorder, cannabis use disorder, or alcohol use disorder. With the exception of those cases in which Criterion 11 is not considered (such as hallucinogen use or inhalant use), the same behavioral criteria in the DSM-5 are used, no matter what drug is involved.[18]

Theoretical Perspectives on Drug Use and Abuse

Why do people take drugs? We all take drugs, of course, for genuine therapeutic reasons, to relieve ourselves of pain or symptoms that arise from a range of physical or psychological disorders. Yet why do people take drugs on a purely recreational basis? Is it for sheer pleasure, to escape from a life of boredom, to suppress feelings of sorrow and depression, to fit in with a group of friends, to relieve stress, or is there some propensity toward drug-taking behavior that is rooted in the neurochemistry of the brain? This section of the chapter will explore theoretical perspectives around why individuals use and abuse drugs.

The oldest theory of drug abuse, and arguably the oldest theory to explain disapproved behavior in general, has its origin in demonology. Why would you do something bad? Answer: "Because the devil made me do it." We have certainly moved away from believing that an evil spirit (or anything outside our experience) invokes bad behavior, but, strangely enough, a modern version of this belief continues to influence the way people might think about drug abuse. To some, a drug abuser is an individual who is morally deficient, who, because of personal inadequacies, overindulgence, a weakness of will, or other character flaw, has succumbed to a pattern of drug-taking behavior that has taken over his or her life and those around him or her. A nonreligious version of this point of view is the **moral model** of drug abuse. According to the moral model, drug-taking behavior is simply a matter of personal choice that we have made in our lives, and not a consequence of a biological defect, a psychological dysfunction, or sociological circumstances.

In direct contradiction to the moral model, the American Medical Association in 1956 classified addiction and alcoholism as a "disease." The **disease model** argues that addiction, like any other chronic medical condition, has a chemical/biological component, and left untreated, can be fatal. This model attributes addiction to a combination of genetic predisposition and the influence of an array of environmental factors. Due to the chronic nature of addiction, those subscribing to this model, including the founders of Alcoholics Anonymous, argue that total abstinence is the only path to recovery.

The implication for models explaining substance abuse can be profound with respect to the ways in which drug abusers are held responsible for their actions and the way the criminal justice system views drug-taking behavior. Critics of the disease model argue that classifying addiction as a disease removes the element of choice, allowing addicts to absolve themselves of responsibility for their "illness" and the consequences of their addiction. In 1988, the U.S. Supreme Court ruled that crimes committed by an alcoholic were willful misconduct, and not a consequence of a disease. Essentially, excessive alcohol use (no matter whether the individual has a pattern of chronic alcohol abuse) is the result of personal choice, and the violator of drunk driving and other alcohol-related crimes should be punished.[19]

The **biopsychosocial model** is another way of understanding substance abuse via the interplay of biological, psychological, and sociological factors. In this model, genetics, brain disease and other biological factors are recognized, as is the important role that the environment and psychological development play in the process of developing and maintaining an addiction. In this section, the three perspectives on drug-taking behavior (biological, psychological, and sociological) will form the basis for an examination of a variety of explanatory theories.[20]

Biological Perspectives on Drug Abuse

When we theorize about the origins of drug abuse from a biological perspective, we are referring to specific physical mechanisms in specific individuals that influence the initial experience with drugs or an engagement in drug abuse over

moral model: An explanation for drug abuse in which drug-taking behavior is attributed to personal inadequacies, overindulgence, a weakness of will, or other serious character flaws.

disease model: An explanation for drug abuse arguing there is a chemical/biological component to addiction, and left untreated, it can be fatal, rendering it, like any other chronic medical condition, a disease.

biopsychosocial model: A theoretical perspective on drug abuse that recognizes the biological, psychological, and sociological factors underlying drug-taking behavior and encourages an integrated approach toward drug-abuse treatment.

a period of time. Biological theories have focused primarily on genetic factors, physiological factors, and neurochemical systems in the brain.

Genetic Factors

As genetic research has advanced over the years, particularly since the completion of the mapping of the human genome in 2000, a great deal of attention has focused on the contribution that certain genetic traits make toward the abuse of a range of drugs. While environmental factors are also undoubtedly important, recent studies have shown that genetic factors play an equal or even greater role. Studies of different strains of mice and rats, for example, have found that some have a genetic propensity to become dependent upon cocaine, whereas other strains are more susceptible to the dependence-producing effects of opiates.[21]

Most studies concerning genetic factors in humans have focused on alcoholic individuals, and a growing research literature indicates that alcoholism has a genetic component (see Chapter 13). Family studies have shown that children of alcoholics are four times more likely than other children to become alcoholics (Figure 8.2). Identical twins (those who have identical genetic compositions) are more likely to have a similar risk for alcoholism than fraternal twins, who share only half their genetic traits with

each other. In addition, children who have at least one alcoholic biological parent and were adopted by nonalcoholic parents are three times more likely to have a problem with alcohol, even when they have been raised in a low-risk environment.[22]

We have yet to identify the single gene or complete set of genes responsible for the emergence of alcoholism, much less the interaction of gene expression that increases the likelihood of alcoholic behavior. Like cancer and heart disease, alcoholism is considered to be genetically complex, distinguishing it from diseases such as cystic fibrosis, which results from the mutation of a single gene. In the case of alcoholism, genes are likely to be associated with liver enzymes that metabolize (break down) alcohol as well as specific patterns of brain chemistry.[23] Even so, we are not speaking of genetic factors producing these effects in a *deterministic* manner. We are speaking of a predisposition toward alcohol misuse, which can increase the *probability* of alcoholism.[24]

Physiological Factors

One physiological factor hypothesized to be involved in drug abuse has to do with metabolic processes in the body. In other words, people might differ in the extent to which chemicals in the body are broken down or changed in some way to allow us to function normally. For example, it has

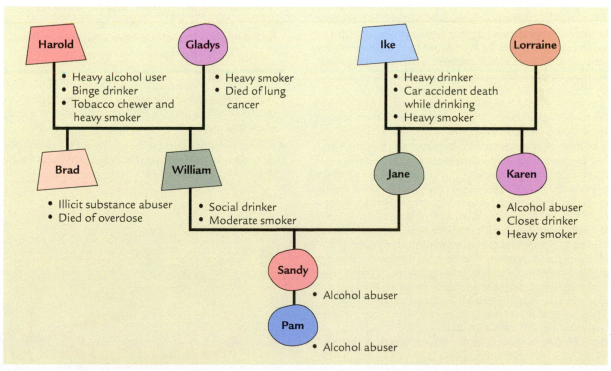

FIGURE 8.2

The genogram of two alcohol abusers, Pam and Sandy, reveals that alcohol and other substances have been abused for four generations, causing family problems and death throughout the family's history.

Source: Based on data from Stevens, P.; and Smith, R. L. (2005). *Substance abuse counseling: Theory and practice* (3rd ed.). Boston: Allyn and Bacon, p. 94.

been proposed that chronic heroin abuse might be due to a metabolic defect in the bodies of heroin abusers. Just as Type 1 diabetics have an insufficient level of insulin that prevents them from processing glucose in a normal fashion, heroin abusers may have an inborn deficiency with respect to natural opiate-like chemicals produced by the brain itself, and, as a result, they feel compelled to seek out substances from the environment to make up for that deficiency. From this perspective, heroin abusers are "normalizing" their body by indulging in heroin abuse. A specific dysfunctional system in the body of a heroin abuser, however, is yet to be discovered. At present, the evidence of a metabolic defect is only circumstantial. In other words, heroin-dependent individuals appear to behave *as if* they have a metabolic imbalance with respect to opioids (opiate-related drugs) in general.[25]

Neurochemical Systems in the Brain

Amphetamines, cocaine, heroin, alcohol, and nicotine may be very different from a pharmacological standpoint, but the way people and animals react to them are remarkably similar. Use of these substances results in a pattern of compulsive behavior that is based on an intense drive to repeat the experience. We cannot determine whether animals are "craving" these substances, but we certainly recognize feelings of craving in humans. In general, the similarities among all of these drugs and across species are numerous enough to entertain the idea that there exists a common neurochemical system in the brain that links them all together (Drugs . . . in Focus).

There are two elements in understanding the intensely rewarding effect of certain psychoactive drugs. The first of

Drugs . . . in Focus

Understanding the Biochemistry of Psychoactive Drugs

There are an estimated 100 billion neurons in the brain, specialized cells designed to receive and transmit information. The sheer number of neurons makes the brain arguably the most complex organ of the body. Communication among these neurons, through their interconnections, provides the basis for the processing of complex information and ultimately the execution of behavioral responses.

In order to understand how neurons communicate with each other, it is important first to describe the anatomy of the neuron itself (see illustration). All neurons consist of a cell body and extensions from the cell body, some of them short in length (dendrites) and one rather long (the axon).

The transfer of information from neuron to neuron is controlled by the activity of neurotransmitters. Specifically, neuron A communicates with neuron B at thousands of juncture points referred to as *synapses*. Essentially, information travels from the cell body of the neuron A to synaptic knobs, at the end of the axon. Neurotransmitters are released from these synaptic knobs and "delivered" across the synapse to the dendrites of neuron B. Special receptor sites embedded in neuron B receive the neurotransmitters that have been released. When the neurotransmitter molecules have successfully locked into the receptor sites (an event called *receptor binding*), the communication between neurons A and B has been accomplished.

Here is a partial list of neurotransmitters that play a role in the effects of alcohol and other drugs:

- *Acetylcholine* influences heart rate, learning, and memory.
- *Dopamine* affects motor control, mood, and feelings of euphoria. Dopamine plays a major role in producing feelings of craving that encourage a continuing pattern of compulsive drug-taking behavior.
- *Serotonin* affects sensory perception, sleep, mood, and body temperature. Alterations in serotonin have been related to

hallucinatory effects of such drugs as LSD and psilocybin. Abnormal levels of serotonin have been associated with depression and other mood disorders.

- *Endorphins* are natural pain killers produced by the brain and bear a remarkable resemblance to morphine.
- *Norepinephrine* influences sleep, blood pressure, heart rate, and memory. Along with serotonin, norepinephrine has been associated with the regulation of mood.
- *Gamma-aminobutyric acid (GABA)* influences levels of anxiety and general excitation in the brain. Antianxiety medications, often referred to as tranquilizers, stimulate GABA-releasing neurons, providing a reduction in feelings of stress and fear.
- *Glutamate* is the basis for the effects of PCP (angel dust) and ketamine. It is also involved in drug craving and the likelihood of drug-abuse relapse.

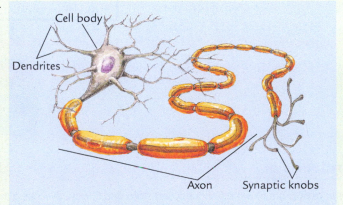

these is the existence of brain chemicals called **neurotransmitters**, which allow neurons in the brain to communicate with each other. A specific neurotransmitter of interest with respect to drug abuse is **dopamine**. The second is the existence of an area in the brain called the **nucleus accumbens**.

The significance of the nucleus accumbens is that animals will work hard to produce an increase in its activity. As with animal experiments involving self-administration of drugs, researchers have been able to conduct studies in which the pressing of a lever causes electrical brain stimulation in a localized fashion. We cannot say how animals are

> **neurotransmitter:** A chemical that makes it possible for neurons to communicate with each other in normal brain functioning. Some examples of neurotransmitters are dopamine, serotonin, GABA, and endorphins.
>
> **dopamine (DOPE-ah-meen):** A neurotransmitter in the brain whose chemical activity is related to emotionality and motor control.
>
> **nucleus accumbens (NEW-clee-us ac-CUM-buns):** A region of the brain considered to be responsible for the reinforcing effects of several drugs of abuse.

feeling at the time, but their behavior indicates that they are intensely motivated toward "turning on" this region of their brains. Their compulsive efforts to receive this stimulation are unmistakable. Since self-administration behavior in animals closely parallels the pattern of human behavior that characterizes psychological dependence, studies of this kind can be used to understand the neural changes that occur as a consequence of drug abuse.

In other words, it is reasonable to assume a connection to the human experience: the craving, the intense "rush," and compulsive drug-taking behavior associated with heroin, cocaine, amphetamines, or a host of other dependence-producing drugs. When laboratory animals are administered amphetamines, heroin, cocaine, alcohol, or nicotine, for example, there is a rapid increase in the level of dopamine activity in the nucleus accumbens. Hence, most drugs target the brain's reward system by releasing a large amount of dopamine, activating feelings of euphoria, which reinforces continued drug use. Administration of any substance that interferes with dopamine activity in this region eliminates the desire of animals to work for the self-administration of these abused drugs. Considering the evidence now in hand, a persuasive argument can be made that

PORTRAIT

Dr. Nora D. Volkow—Imaging the Face of Addiction in the Brain

It is one thing to speculate about the effects of drug dependence on the brain, to assert that the transition from initially being a voluntary drug user to becoming a compulsive drug user is a matter of subtle but significant brain changes. It is quite another thing to show the effects themselves at a neurochemical level. But that is precisely what Nora D. Volkow and her associates have done. Using a brain scanning technique called positron emission tomography (PET) neural activity in the human brain can be captured in graphic detail.

As a result of Volkow's studies, the process of drug dependence is becoming understood. As expected, the critical area in the brain is the nucleus accumbens, and the critical neurotransmitter is dopamine. However, the real key is a subset of dopamine receptors (referred to as D_2 receptors) and their change over time. All dependence-producing drugs that produce a "high" cause a very rapid increase in D_2 receptor activity in the nucleus accumbens. Conventional wisdom has held that drug dependence is a result of a sensitization of D_2 receptors, but just the opposite appears to be the case. Drug-dependent

individuals show a significant decline in D_2 receptor activity over time, with a loss of about 20 percent of the receptors themselves. Volkow has estimated that a comparable decline in dopamine receptors would take at least 40 years to accomplish in a drug-free brain. In the case of chronic cocaine abusers, these changes result in a somewhat ironic situation: They no longer feel that they enjoy the cocaine, but, at the same time, the craving for it is so strong that they feel compelled to seek it out.

Why the compulsive nature of drug dependence? Volkow's research has shown that ordinarily D_2 receptor activity causes an inhibition of systems in the prefrontal cortex of the brain, which is responsible for normal inhibitory control. (Think of the prefrontal cortex as being a "no-go" mechanism in our lives). Evidently, with fewer signals from the nucleus accumbens in chronic drug abuse, the prefrontal cortex is itself inhibited—the result being compulsive behavior, essentially an "inhibition of inhibition."

In 2003, Nora D. Volkow was appointed director of the National Institute on Drug Abuse (NIDA), the lead federal agency for research into drug abuse and

dependence, where she still serves as director today. Her work has helped to demonstrate that alcohol and drug addiction are a disease of the brain, which has helped to inform treatment for substance misuse. Among other awards, she was named one of *Time* magazine's "Top 100 People Who Shape Our World."

Sources: National Institute on Drug Abuse (2003, January 23). *Press release: Dr. Nora D. Volkow named new director of NIDA.* Rockville, MD: National Institute on Drug Abuse. Volkow, N. D.; Wang, G. J.; Tomasi, D.; and Baler, R.D. (2013). Unbalanced neuronal circuits in addiction. *Current Opinion in Neurobiology, 23*, 639–648. Volkow, N. D.; Wang, G. J.; Fowler, J. S.; Logan, J.; Gatley, S. J.; Hitzemann, R.; Chen, A. D.; and Pappas, N. (1997). Decrease in striatal dopaminergic responsiveness in detoxified cocaine-dependent subjects. *Nature, 386*, 830–833. National Institute on Drug Abuse (2017, October). *Biography of Dr. Nora Volkow.* Rockville, MD: National Institute on Drug Abuse. Retrieved from: *https://www.drugabuse.gov/about-nida/directors-page/biography-dr-nora-volkow*

dopamine-related processes in the nucleus accumbens underlie the reinforcing effects of many abused drugs (Portrait). Research also shows an involvement of the nucleus accumbens in compulsive gambling and eating disorders as well.[26]

Research on the influence of dopamine in drug dependence can help us understand why some individuals may be more susceptible than others to drug-taking behavior. In one study, for example, 23 drug-free men with no history of drug abuse were given doses of methylphenidate (brand name: Ritalin), a psychoactive stimulant when ingested by adults. Twelve of the men experienced a pleasant feeling, nine felt annoyed or distrustful, and two felt nothing at all. Measurements of **dopamine receptors** in the brains of these subjects showed a consistent pattern. *The men with the least concentration of dopamine receptors were the ones experiencing pleasant effects.*[27] It is reasonable to hypothesize that those individuals with the fewest dopamine receptors might be the most vulnerable to drug abuse. The understanding we now have about the neurochemical processes underlying dependence has significant implications for drug-abuse treatment.

It is important to note that continued drug use causes the brain to adjust. The brain counteracts surges in dopamine and other neurotransmitters from drug use by producing less dopamine or decreasing the receptors that can receive signals. This makes it difficult for a drug abuser to experience feelings of pleasure naturally. This is why drug abusers often look and feel "flat" or "burned out." This is also a contributor to drug tolerance, where individuals have to take more of a substance to get the same high. You will sometimes hear drug abusers talk about catching that first high. In addition to building tolerance, long-term addiction affects how the brain processes information, making it difficult for drug abusers to make sound decisions.[28]

Psychological Perspectives on Drug Abuse

Psychological perspectives look at how factors within the individual contribute to drug abuse. The psychological perspectives to be examined include (1) behavioral theories, (2) cognitive theories, (3) motivation theories, and (4) personality theories.

Behavioral Theories

Behavioral theories emphasize the role of learning through the principle of reinforcement. According to the behavioral point of view, practically all of human behavior is learned. In other words, addiction to a drug or alcohol is a consequence of having modified one's behaviors based on how those behaviors were rewarded.

The overarching principle of behavioral theory is that any behavior that is followed by a reward (reinforcement) is more likely to be repeated in the future. Repeated rewards will result in a continuing pattern of behavior that can be weakened only when these reinforcers are removed (a process

called *extinction*) or other behaviors are now reinforced (a process called *counterconditioning*). Think about the range of reinforcers individuals get from getting high on marijuana. Rewards might include the "high" feeling, socializing with friends that are also getting high, fitting in, feeling relaxed and free of anxiety, and having a good time.

Individuals using a drug with a high reinforcement potential typically report that they care more about obtaining and using the drug than just about anything else in their life. In this case, reinforcers related to drug-taking behavior exceed or overcome competing reinforcers, such as the benefits derived from a job, financial security, or satisfying relationships with friends and family.

While behavior theorists make the distinction between positive reinforcement (gained through the attainment of a pleasurable circumstance—for example, feeling high, having fun with friends) and negative reinforcement (gained through the reduction of a painful or uncomfortable circumstance—for example, reducing anxiety or depression), the principle of reinforcement remains the same. The reinforcement of heroin abuse can focus either on the reexperiencing of the euphoric feelings associated with heroin (positive reinforcement) or on the relief from uncomfortable feelings associated with heroin withdrawal (negative reinforcement).

Which aspect of reinforcement is emphasized among drug abusers in general can determine the pattern of drug-taking behavior. Those guided by the positive reinforcement of the drug experience are often referred to as *euphoria seekers*, and those guided by the negative reinforcement of withdrawal relief are referred to as *maintainers*. Euphoria seekers typically display a compulsive pattern of drug-taking behavior.[29]

In the case of heroin abuse, maintainers tend to consume just enough heroin to avoid the withdrawal symptoms that would occur if their pattern of heroin abuse were to cease. They try to stay within the conventionality of their social community as they "nurse" their habit along. Euphoria seekers, however, are inclined to be so heavily into the pleasurable aspects of heroin that their lives spiral out of control. They descend into a lifestyle dominated by the drug. Social conventionality is no longer possible. There are case studies of heroin abusers (called "chippers"), who have successfully maintained occasional heroin use over an extended period of time, but clearly their lives are extremely precarious.[30]

Social reinforcement for substance abuse can be just as difficult to combat as the physiological reinforcement. Think about an adolescent struggling with substance misuse who decides to stop using substances. How might this youth's peers

dopamine receptors: Specialized areas of neurons that enable dopamine to change the neuron's functioning.

behavioral theories: Theoretical explanations of behavior based upon the effect of reinforcement on learned responses to one's environment.

A visual image of white powder, resembling lines of cocaine, along with a razor blade, tends to elicit powerful feelings of craving among individuals with earlier experiences of cocaine abuse.

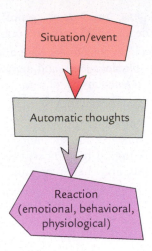

FIGURE 8.3

The cognitive model.

Source: Based on Beck, J. S. (2011). *Cognitive Behavior Therapy: Basics and Beyond* (2nd ed.). New York: Gilford Publications, p. 30.

respond when he reports that he no longer drinks, smokes, or does pills? Peers who engage in substance use are likely to reinforce use by peers and punish abstention by giving clean youth a hard time. Individuals who are justice-involved often grow up in environments where family, friends, and community members misuse substances. The ability to refrain from use, even with legal consequences, becomes a significant challenge as reinforcers for substance abuse are all around.

Behavioral theorists also assert that specific cues or situations have the capability of stimulating powerful drug cravings brought on by memories of past pleasurable (reinforcing) experiences. Through a process of Pavlovian conditioning (discussed earlier in this chapter in the context of behavioral tolerance), drug users associate drug use with certain visual cues, specific friends and situations, or even a song. Cigarette smokers, for example, commonly report that it is difficult to abstain from smoking when drinking alcohol, talking on the phone, or driving a car if these circumstances have been closely associated with smoking behavior. Some marijuana users report cravings after seeing paraphernalia used in smoking marijuana, such as a bong or pipe, while heroin injectors may crave heroin after viewing a hypodermic needle.

Conditioned cues are very difficult to break and can present major obstacles to overcome on the path to drug-abuse recovery. Drug-abuse treatment efforts are often cut short by the appearance of cues that have played an important part in previous drug-taking behavior. Counseling professionals believe that it is essential that individuals break both their pharmacological and their psychological (behavioral) dependence on drugs to return to and maintain a drug-free life. Behavioral strategies for substance abuse treatment include identifying people, places, and things that trigger the desire to use, and then practicing strategies for avoiding or managing situations that invite a person to engage in substance misuse. For example, a counselor might practice with a client what to say if a he or she runs into an old using friend who suggests they go get high, or practice how to handle the upcoming family reunion, where there is likely to be alcohol or drugs. Practicing often occurs in the form of role play, so that individuals can prepare for situations that are high risk for substance misuse.

Cognitive Theories

According to **cognitive theories**, thoughts and beliefs drive behaviors. In other words, a person's feelings (both emotions and physical sensations) and behavior are the result of that person's perception of a situation. Figure 8.3 shows how the model works. Here, Judith S. Beck, a leading cognitive therapist, identifies a situation or event, which triggers automatic thoughts (or thoughts that occur spontaneously, immediately after one encounters the situation) which then leads to a reaction or response to the situation, including a feeling and action. The feeling and action stem from how one interprets the situation.[31]

Take the example of a person just out of rehab who returns to his neighborhood and sees his old drug dealer. The following sequence may occur:

Situation: I just got out of rehab yesterday, I'm walking to the store and I see my old drug dealer.

Automatic thoughts: "Oh man, I need to stay clean"; "this guy is no good"; "I gotta get out of this situation."

Reaction: He feels nervous (*emotional*), shaky (*physiological*), and crosses the street (*behavioral response*).

Let's look at the same guy, in the same situation, and see how a change in the interpretation of the situation impacts the outcome:

Situation: I just got out of rehab yesterday, I'm walking to the store and I see my old drug dealer.

> **cognitive theories:** Theoretical explanations of behavior based upon the notion that a person's feelings and behavior is the result of that person's perception of the situation.

Automatic thoughts: "Yes! I need a score", "finally, some relief," "no big deal... no one will find out."

Reaction: He feels anxious to get high and excited (*emotional*), restless (*physiological*), and approaches the drug dealer (*behavioral reaction*).

Hence, the cognitive model assumes that it is the thoughts that drive how one ultimately responds to a situation. Cognitive strategies for substance abusers involve **cognitive restructuring**, or the process of identifying risky or irrational thoughts, and challenging and changing these thoughts, to help change behaviors. Typical risky thoughts for drug abusers are that "my drug use isn't hurting anyone," "marijuana comes from the earth," or "this will be the last time." The goal with cognitive restructuring is to identify the specific risky thoughts that accompany a person's using behavior and help them to change that pattern of thinking.

The other important component to cognitive theory is the role of beliefs. Beliefs are the ideas people have about themselves and the world. Under a cognitive model, beliefs form based on one's experiences from early childhood and beyond, and one's beliefs inform their automatic thinking, or immediate interpretation of situations.[32] Beliefs are important in a cognitive model as they are the foundation from which individuals behave. In the above situation, if it is a young man's belief that "I will never amount to anything," then whenever a high-risk situation is encountered, he is likely to revert to using drugs. Conversely, if his belief is that "drugs destroy lives," he is more likely to respond by avoiding his old drug dealer.

Albert Ellis, who developed Rational Emotive Behavior Therapy (REBT), has focused extensively on the role of thoughts and beliefs in changing problem behavior. This model was developed in the 1950s as the first **cognitive-behavior therapy (CBT)**. Cognitive-behavior therapy concentrates on developing coping strategies to target behavioral problems by helping individuals to change distorted patterns of thinking, via cognitive restructuring. Ellis simplified the process for analyzing behaviors into the ABC model (Activating event, Belief, Consequences). As in Beck's model, the activating event is the high-risk situation triggering a problem response, the belief is how that situation is interpreted, and the consequences are what follows. CBT is the most widely used cognitive strategy for treating mental health disorders and is commonly used to treat issues with addiction. This strategy has shown effectiveness in reducing patterns of unhealthy behavior, including substance misuse.[33]

Motivation Theories

Motivation theories focus on why people do what they do. In the context of substance misuse, two prominent psychologists, Carlo DiClemente and James O. Prochaska, developed the **Transtheoretical model (TTM)**, which depicts six *stages of change* that individuals experience through the course of changing a behavior. As we will see in Chapter 14, the TTM model is an important element in substance abuse treatment. Based on their experience working with alcoholics, DiClemente and Prochaska identified the following stages:

- *Precontemplation*: in denial of a problem with no intention to change—does not view behavior as problematic
- *Contemplation*: recognizes that behavior may be problematic, *but not ready to commit to change*
- *Preparation*: ready to take action to address the problem behavior, may begin to take small steps to modify behavior *or make plans to do so*
- *Action*: actively engaging in treatment or other strategies to address problem behavior and making overt changes *in behavior*
- *Maintenance*: behavior changes have been sustained and person is working toward continuing to make positive progress toward behavior change
- *Termination*: no desire to return to unhealthy behavior (not always reached with substance abuse).[34]

This model is used regularly to gauge how motivated an individual is to stop misusing substances, but the model has also been applied to other behaviors, such as health problems like diabetes, that also require changes in daily behaviors. The model recognizes that relapse can occur at any of the stages, and that individuals may weave in and out of the various stages of change.

According to the theory, those in the early stages of change require a different type of intervention than those in the later stages, who are ready to learn new skills. **Motivational Interviewing (MI)** is a popular therapeutic technique developed in the early 1990s by William R. Miller to help move individuals with a substance use disorder up the stages of change. The goal of the technique is to elicit motivational statements from the client so that the client begins to see the benefit of changing a problem behavior.[35] Table 8.1 reviews the five core principles (or strategies) of motivational interviewing.

---

cognitive restructuring: The process of identifying risky or irrational thoughts, and challenging and changing these thoughts, to help change behaviors.

cognitive-behavior therapy (CBT): Cognitive-behavior therapy concentrates on developing coping strategies to target behavioral problems by helping individuals to change distorted patterns of thinking.

Transtheoretical model (TTM): A model depicting six **stages of change** that individuals experience through the course of changing a behavior.

Motivational Interviewing (MI): A therapeutic technique designed to help move individuals up the stages of change by eliciting motivational statements from the client so that the client begins to see the benefit of changing a problem behavior.

TABLE 8.1

Motivational interviewing strategies

STRATEGY	GOAL	CLIENT STATEMENT	COUNSELOR RESPONSE
Expressing empathy	Actively listen to client, without judgment, to gain a better understanding of the client's perspective.	"Why should I change, no one cares about me."	"It must be tough to have so few people to support you."
Develop discrepancies	Help identify discrepancies between client's current choices and personal goals.	"I did miss work one day this week, but it's not a big deal."	"When you drink too much, you are often too hung over to go to work, yet you've talked about wanting a promotion."
Avoid argumentation	When resistance by client is apparent, counselor changes direction and shows support.	"You think I'm an addict too—you're just like everyone else."	"I can see where it would be upsetting to be labeled as an addict."
Roll with Resistance	Let resistance be expressed rather than trying to fight it—reflect on the client's feelings.	"You think I need inpatient treatment? There is no way I'm going to one of those places!"	"The thought of not being at home is scary—it is a big change."
Support Self-Efficacy	Self-efficacy represents confidence in one's ability to change—reinforce positive changes.	"I made it 2 weeks without a drink, but I don't know if I can do this long term."	"Taking the first step toward sobriety can be the hardest part. Two weeks without a drink is big accomplishment."

Source: Based on Velasquez, M. M.; Maurer, G. G.; Crouch, C.; and DiClemente, C. C. (2001). *Group treatment for substance abuse: A stages of change therapy manual.* New York: The Guildford Press.

Motivational Interviewing differs substantially from more traditional approaches to substance abuse treatment, whereby individuals must admit they are an alcoholic or addict, and counselors (often former addicts themselves) are confrontational about problematic attitudes and behaviors. Motivational Interviewing can be used as a pretreatment strategy, targeting only those individuals who are resistant to change, as a stand-alone treatment, or used as an adjunctive therapy, whereby it is integrated with cognitive-behavioral or other models of intervention. Studies examining the effectiveness of this approach at changing substance misuse have been promising. One meta-analysis found that use of motivational interviewing strategies yielded a 56 percent reduction in client drinking.[36] Beyond substance abuse counseling, this model has been used by probation officers and other correctional professionals as a way of interacting with justice-involved individuals, who are often resistant to changing problem behaviors and impervious to punishment and confrontational styles.

Personality Theories

Psychological explanations of drug abuse can also emphasize a constellation of personality traits that distinguish drug abusers from non-abusers. This theory argues that some individuals have an "addictive personality," or specific factors or traits that lead to substance abuse. One of the first empirical studies to examine the concept "addictive personality" found there was no single trait that led to addiction, rather a set of personality factors associated with individuals who abused alcohol or drugs. Factors included (1) impulsivity and the need for immediate gratification, (2) sensation seeking, (3) valuing nonconformity over following social norms, (4) high experience of stress with lack of coping skills, and (5) accepting defiant behavior in others and social isolation.[37]

Today, many of these traits are associated with the diagnosis of antisocial personality disorder. Individuals with antisocial personality disorder are typically impulsive, sensation seeking, and immature, and they tend to engage in law violating behaviors. Individuals displaying these traits may be more prone to abuse drugs because of their increased need for stimulation, excitement, and immediate gratification, and their apathy toward following societal norms. Sensation-seeking people are essentially risk takers, and drug use epitomizes risk-taking behavior, particularly in adolescence.[38]

Individuals that struggle with stress, anxiety and depression, and lack the coping skills to manage it, and people with a low tolerance for frustration are also susceptible to substance abuse. Issues like depression and anxiety can be immediate precursors to drug abuse, in that drugs elevate one's mood and relieve feelings of stress. In effect, individuals suffering from anxiety and depression are engaging in a pattern of self-medication. It is well known, however, that patterns of drug abuse can actually induce anxiety and depression, making it difficult at times to determine whether the drugs caused the mental health symptoms or the mental health problems led to the drug abuse. Either way, one problem exacerbates the other.

While psychologists have studied specific personality traits that are more frequently observed in drug abusers than in the general population, they have not been able to identify a unique set of personality traits for such individuals. For

Quick Concept Check   8.2

Understanding Biological and Psychological Perspectives on Drug Use and Abuse

Check your understanding of biological and psychological perspectives on drug use and abuse by matching the statement (on the left) with appropriate factor or theoretical orientation within these perspectives (on the right).

1. Identical twins are more likely than fraternal twins to develop alcoholism later in life.

2. Animals will work hard to self-stimulate in order to release dopamine in the nucleus accumbens in their brains.

3. Drug-taking behavior is strengthened through positive outcomes (rewards).

4. Sensation-seeking individuals are more likely to experiment with drugs, particularly in adolescence.

5. Individuals in the pre-contemplation stage are in denial of having a substance abuse problem.

6. Heroin-dependent individuals may have a metabolic imbalance that heroin appears to correct.

7. Automatic thoughts triggered by a high-risk situation can lead to the behavior of substance use.

a. Behavioral factor

b. Motivation factor

c. Personality factor

d. Neurochemical factor

e. Physiological factor

f. Genetic factor

g. Cognitive factor

Answers: 1. f   2. d   3. a   4. c   5. b   6. e   7. g

example, alcohol abusers tend to be more independent, non-conformist, and impulsive, but these same traits are also found in successful athletes.[39] Of the psychological theories reviewed, behavioral, cognitive, and motivation theories are those most prominent in guiding treatment for substance use disorders.

Sociological Perspectives on Drug Abuse

For sociologists, environmental and societal factors play an especially important role in drug use and abuse. The focus of sociological theories is quite different from the focus of theories associated with either a biological or psychological perspective. The emphasis is not on the individual alone, but the individual embedded in social situations, social relationships, and social structures.[40]

During the Vietnam War, for example, a large proportion of American troops used and abused heroin, which was available in Vietnam at extraordinarily high levels of purity. It is reasonable to assume that easy access to heroin in the context of being in a strange and dangerous environment encouraged them to turn to heroin for escape and relief (see Chapter 9). However, only one in eight soldiers continued to use heroin after returning home to a "normal" life. Evidently, the social context of their drug-taking behavior was a crucial factor in allowing them to make this shift.[41]

Sociological perspectives on drug use and abuse will be represented by five major theories: (1) anomie or strain theory, (2) social control or bonding theory, (3) differential association theory, (4) subcultural recruitment and socialization theory, and (5) labeling theory.

Anomie/Strain Theory

In 1893, sociologist Emile Durkheim used the term **anomie** to describe the feelings of frustration and alienation that exist among individuals who see themselves as not being able to meet the demands of society.[42] Durkheim studied the effects of anomie as they pertained to suicide, while sociologist Robert Merton in 1968 applied the concept to other forms of deviant behavior, such as drug use. Merton believed that every society includes a set of cultural goals and means to achieve them (norms). In most cases, members of society can reach these cultural goals, or at least have some hope of reaching them, by following certain socially defined means. In the United States and other economically developed nations of the world, the primary cultural goal is economic success, and individuals aspire to reach this goal through the acceptable social norm of hard work. When someone is unable to obtain economic success, the result is a feeling of frustration and anomie. This sense of anomie or strain (hence the terms "anomie theory" or "strain theory") is highest among disadvantaged segments of the population, who experience high rates of crime and drug use in their everyday lives.[43]

Merton classified five possible adaptations or responses to anomie when someone is unable to achieve cultural goals through acceptable means. The five adaptations (conformity, innovation, ritualism, retreatism, and rebellion) will be reviewed in the context of drug use and abuse.[44]

- In the first adaptation, *conformity*, individuals accept both culturally defined goals and the prescribed means for achieving them. They may find it necessary to scale down their aspirations, work hard, and save money, while continuing to follow legitimate paths. In this sense, conformity is not deviant behavior but rather an adjustment in their lives. It is also the most common mode of response when contending with anomie. This type of adaptation would

> **anomie (AN-eh-MEE):** In sociological terms, feelings of frustration and alienation when individuals see themselves as not being able to meet the demands of society. Anomie theory is sometimes referred to as strain theory.

lead to a decision not to use or abuse drugs that are outside the mainstream of our culture. It would not, however, discourage the use of alcohol or nicotine if drinking and tobacco smoking were acceptable drug-taking behaviors.

- In the second adaptation, *innovation*, individuals retain the dominant cultural goal of monetary success but choose to reject legitimate avenues of goal attainment. Unlike conformity, innovation involves illegal behavior. Aspiring to be a drug dealer in order to achieve economic success is an example of innovation.

- In the third adaptation, *ritualism*, individuals reject the goal of economic success (considering it unattainable) but continue to accept the means of working in legitimate areas of life. An example is the burnt-out factory worker who uses illicit drugs to get through the day without "making waves" and then goes home to get drunk or "stoned."

- In the fourth adaptation, *retreatism*, individuals reject both the goal of economic success and the means of hard work. They have, in effect, given up. Members belonging to this category include individuals who have developed a dependence on alcohol or other drugs. Retreatists can be viewed as double failures. First, they have been unable to find success through conformity. Second, they have not been able to find success as an innovator through criminal activity. Ironically, drug-dependent individuals retreat in this way with the expectation that they are entering a seemingly undemanding world. The harsh reality, however, is that drug dependence itself sets off a never-ending series of brutal demands, on both physical and psychological levels. Perhaps, only in the case of a Chinese opium smoker (see Chapter 9) would a retreatist adaptation approach the fantasy of a completely undemanding existence.

- In the fifth adaptation, *rebellion*, individuals not only reject both the goal of economic success and the means of working but also seek to overturn the social system and replace it with an alternate set of values. These individuals are the radicals and revolutionaries of society, who break the law in an attempt to change it. An example is the rebellious youth of the "hippie" subculture of the 1960s. Their association with marijuana and LSD use and their involvement with a wide range of psychoactive substances were components of a political act of rebellion. The popular slogan of the time, "sex, drugs, and rock and roll," represented their rebellious response to the anomie they felt at the time.

It is conceivable that someone's personal adaptation to feelings of anomie could be a combination of any of the above possibilities.

A survey of more than 9,000 high school students in 1990 found that feelings of anomie or strain were important predictors of drug use. Students who have a negative response to questions such as, "When you are older, do you expect to own more possessions than your parents do now?" or to the statement, "My life is in my hands, and I am in control of it" were more likely to engage in drug-taking behavior.[45]

Treatment for drug-related problems is optimized when there is positive involvement from the family and the social bond of attachment is strengthened.

Anomie theory, however, does tend to oversimplify a complex problem. We know that people who have attained economic success have, at the same time, become dependent on drugs and alcohol. Rock stars and celebrities of all kinds, for example, have become dependent on drugs such as cocaine, heroin, alcohol, and prescription medication. In fact, celebrity status in our society encourages such involvement. Moreover, anomie theory fails to explain why one person chooses to be a ritualist, for instance, whereas another becomes an innovator. Finally, anomie theory disregards the potential impact of interpersonal relationships, such as peer group association, differential access to drugs, and the degree of attachment to one's community and family.

Social Control/Bond Theory

A second major sociological perspective on drug use and abuse is **social control theory**. According to social control theorists, all human beings are, by nature, rule breakers. The bonds that people have to society and its moral code are what keep them from breaking the law and remaining socially controlled (hence the terms "social control theory" or "social bond theory"). When an individual is strongly bonded to his or her family, religious affiliation, school, or community, that individual is less likely to engage in delinquent behavior. When these bonds become weakened, deviant behavior, such as drug use, results.

Social control theorists identify four social bonds that promote conformity: attachment, commitment, involvement, and belief.[46] *Attachment* refers to one's closeness to significant others, such as parents, peers, and teachers. Individuals will

social control theory: A sociological theory of drug use based on weakened social bonds between an individual and social entities such as family, religious affiliation, school, and community. Social control theory is sometimes referred to as social bond theory.

conform to social norms and refrain from drug use because they seek the approval of these significant individuals. *Commitment* refers to an individual's investment and pursuit in reaching conventional goals, such as the attainment of a good education and a satisfying job. *Involvement* refers to the extent to which one is associated with conventional activities within a school, community, or religious affiliation. *Belief* refers to how well an individual has internalized the moral values of society, such as honesty, perseverance, and respect for authority. Attention to social bonds is important in the design of effective prevention and treatment programs (see Chapter 14).

Empirical tests of predictions made by social control theory with regard to drug use are mixed. Several studies have found that variables such as parental attachment and school attachment are related to lower rates of drug use among youths, whereas other studies have found that relationships with peers act as a more important predictor of drug use than attachment to one's family or school. In fact, the primary weakness of social control theory is that it underestimates the importance of the role of delinquent friends, while overestimating the importance of involvement in conventional social activities. Studies have consistently found that patterns of adolescent alcohol and drug use are strongly related to drug abusers having friends who also engage in this behavior. Yet, there is no explanatory role for peers in social control theory.[47] The next theory, however, places great importance on the nature of peer relationships.

Differential Association Theory

The third major sociological perspective is **differential association theory**. Originally proposed by sociologist Edwin Sutherland in 1939 as a general theory of deviance, differential association theory has served in recent years as a theoretical foundation for some of the most important research on illicit drug use. The basic premise of the theory is that deviant behavior such as drug use is learned in interactions and communications with other individuals. This learning takes place within relatively intimate groups, such as family and friends. Significant others (parents and friends) often communicate prodrug or antidrug messages. When one's attitudes and beliefs favoring drug use exceed one's attitudes and beliefs against it, the likelihood of drug use increases. In other words, if an adolescent has a greater number of friends who encourage and use drugs than friends who discourage and do not use drugs, he or she is more likely to engage in that behavior.[48]

From a differential association perspective, the process of learning to use drugs also involves learning the techniques to use drugs and learning how to enjoy the experience. First-time marijuana users, for example, must learn how to roll a "joint" and how to hold the marijuana smoke in their lungs for a period of time to obtain the drug's full effects (see Chapter 11). First-time heroin users must learn how to "cook" or prepare the heroin for intravenous injections by placing the drug in a spoon with water, then heating the substance with a lighter or match to liquefy the heroin. Heroin users also must learn the correct method of injecting the drug without damaging their veins (see Chapter 9). Individuals who use LSD or MDMA (Ecstasy) for the first time may be frightened. Users may experience social withdrawal, anxiety, and paranoia (Chapter 12). Peers often play an important role in calming novice users and in teaching them to focus on the positive aspects of the drug experience rather than the negative ones. These techniques are typically demonstrated in small, intimate groups. In fact, very few, if any, adolescents begin using drugs alone or with strangers present at the time.[49]

Identifying oneself as a drug user typically emerges from being immersed in a social network of friends who share a similar outlook in life. Some drug-using youths take part in a drug subculture that plays a pivotal role in teaching them about illicit drugs. A **subculture** is a subdivision within a dominant culture that has its own norms, beliefs, and values. It exists within the larger society, not apart from it. Several important American drug subcultures include the "hippie" subculture of the 1960s that promoted the use of marijuana and LSD or the rave subculture that has promoted the use of Ecstasy. Drug subcultures not only teach young users about the skills for successfully using drugs but also point out the way to obtain drugs, how to avoid getting "ripped off," and sometimes how to manufacture the drugs themselves. A strong sense of social bonding within a drug subculture, usually with its own subculture language, provides the motivation for continued drug use (Drugs... in Focus).

Subcultural Recruitment and Socialization Theory

The fourth major sociological perspective draws on the assumptions of differential reinforcement theory but focuses more directly on the dynamic relationships that drug abusers have with respect to each other. According to proponents of **subcultural recruitment and socialization theory**, such as Erich Goode and Bruce Johnson, a selective interaction exists in which individuals are drawn to drug users because they recognize a compatibility of social values.[50]

The social bonding of individuals in the subculture increases as a direct function of drug-taking behavior becoming more and more a central focus of their social interactions. The dominant influence of peers, however, applies primarily to

differential association theory: A sociological theory of drug use based upon the premise that drug-taking behavior is learned in interactions and communications with other individuals.

subculture: A subdivision within a dominant culture that has its own norms, beliefs, and values. An example is a drug subculture that provides the social bonding for continued drug use and abuse.

subcultural recruitment and socialization theory: A theoretical perspective on drug abuse that focuses on specific relationships that drug abusers have with respect to each other within a cohesive subculture and the changes that occur in this subculture over time.

Drugs . . . in Focus

The Private Language of a Drug Subculture

A powerful bond within a subculture is a common language that makes sense only for people within it and is virtually unintelligible to people on the outside. This communication system is largely hidden from the mainstream culture of the society at large. In the case of a marijuana drug subculture in New York City, a personal language provides a socially constructed way of talking, expressing, and interacting among marijuana users and distributors.

Sociologist Bruce Johnson and his associates have examined the importance of "argot" (invented slang) on maintaining the identity of the subculture, as well as establishing boundaries with subcultures defined by other types of drugs. They can be standard words with special meanings or completely new words. Here are some examples:

- *Bambu*—marijuana rolling papers
- *One and a Dutch*—a single tobacco cigarette and a blunt (marijuana in a Dutch Master cigar shell)
- *Kind*—good-quality marijuana, shortened form for *kind bud*, shortened further to *kb*

- *Crunked*—under the influence of marijuana and alcohol
- *Beastin'*—rushing the process of smoking; not willing to wait one's turn and thus rushing everyone around them
- *Puff-puff-pass*—promoting equality among smokers in group settings, meaning each person takes two inhalations and then passes the marijuana to the next person, until everyone has smoked or the marijuana joint is finished

A private language is a characteristic feature of any deviant subculture, whether the focus is a particular illicit drug such as heroin, cocaine, or Ecstasy or a specialized illicit activity such as computer hacking.

Sources: Holt, T. (2007). Subcultural evolution? Examining the influence of on- and off-line experiences on deviant subcultures. *Deviant Behavior, 28,* 171–198. Furst, R. T.; Johnson, B. D.; Dunlap, E.; and Curtis, R. (1999). The stigmatized image of the "crack head": A sociocultural exploration of a barrier to cocaine smoking among a cohort of youth in New York City. *Deviant Behavior, 20,* 153–181. Johnson, B. D.; Bardhi, F.; Sifraneck, S. J.; and Dunlap, E. (2006). Marijuana argot as subculture threads: Social constructions by users in New York City. *British Journal of Criminology, 46,* 46–77.

---

adolescent drug abuse. In later stages of drug abuse, when the drugs of choice change from a concentration on beer, wine, cigarettes, liquor, and marijuana to drugs such as cocaine and heroin, drug abusers tend to break away from a tightly focused subcultural group and move toward a set of less intimate relationships. At this point, there is typically a close relationship with only one drug-abusing friend, an individual who shares the same social attitudes, behaviors, and problems.[51]

Labeling Theory

The fifth major sociological perspective is **labeling theory**. Labeling theorists argue that virtually everyone has experimented with drugs at some time in his or her life. This experimentation is referred to as **primary deviance**, nonconformity that is temporary, exploratory, and easily concealed. Primary deviant acts, such as drug experimentation, often go unnoticed, and individuals who commit these acts do not generally regard themselves as deviants and are not labeled as such by others. Once the drug use is discovered and made public by others, however, the situation changes. At this point, drug users are labeled as deviant, and they are often seen in a new light by others as a "stoner" or "dope head." It becomes difficult for users to shed this new status.

Eventually, users begin to internalize the newly acquired label and continue to use drugs because others expect them to do so. In other words, the individual changes his or her self-perception to fit the expectations of others. Behavior now continues as **secondary deviance**, in the form of a persistent pattern of nonconformity by the individual who has been labeled as deviant. Drug users who do not wish to be labeled as deviant may choose to keep their drug use covert or, in time, may become a member of a drug subculture.

According to labeling theorists, social class distinctions play a major role in determining whether an individual might be labeled in a negative manner. A businessman who drinks three vodka martinis at lunch, for example, is much less likely to be labeled as deviant than a factory worker who drinks three beers at lunch. As discussed in Chapter 3, policy decisions regarding which drugs to outlaw and which to legitimize have often been associated with an underlying fear of a minority group whose drug use has become labeled as socially deviant.[52]

labeling theory: A sociological theory of drug use that emphasizes the process by which a drug user internalizes a newly acquired label of deviance and continues a pattern of drug-taking behavior that is based on the expectations of others.

primary deviance: Nonconformist behavior associated with drug experimentation. It is temporary, exploratory, and easily concealed from others.

secondary deviance: Persistent nonconformist behavior by an individual who has been labeled as deviant and whose deviant behavior (e.g., drug use) is based upon expectations of others.

Integrating Theoretical Perspectives on Drug Abuse

Success in drug-abuse treatment rests upon the recognition that there are multiple pathways to drug abuse. For each individual, a specific combination of biological, psychological, and sociological factors needs to be considered in assessing the origins of drug abuse and, in doing so, developing the best treatment for that individual. This integrated, combinational approach to treatment reflects the biopsychosocial model of drug-taking behavior in general. Figure 8.4 is essentially an expansion of Figure 1.1 on page 3.[53]

Risk Factors and Protective Factors

In a direct and straightforward manner, researchers have for decades asked high school seniors to report their personal reasons for taking drugs.[54] In a survey of seniors in the Class of 1983 and 1984, the most frequently given responses were "to have a good time with my friends" (65 percent), "to experiment or see what it's like" (54 percent), "to feel good or get high" (49 percent), and "to relax or relieve tension" (41 percent). The Class of 1976 had responded in a very similar way, as had the Classes of 2001 through 2005. Interestingly, the percentages of high school seniors giving these reasons for alcohol use are similar to

that found in surveys from 1976 to 2005, despite a decline of 18 percent that took place in the annual prevalence rate of alcohol consumption over that period of time. In other words, the incidence of alcohol use has declined, but the reasons for drinking in general have remained the same. Likewise, the percentages of high school seniors giving these reasons for marijuana use are similar to that found in surveys from 1976 to 2005, despite the "roller-coaster" trends in marijuana prevalence rates over that period of time (see Chapter 1).

These studies are interesting not only for the insights they have provided but also for the way they have been carried out. There was no theoretical perspective behind the question. In other words, the research was not theory-driven.

A large literature has accumulated that deals with the statistical relationships between a given variable (pertaining to an individual's lifestyle, family makeup, environmental condition, etc.) and the likelihood that drug use will occur, without assuming a particular theoretical explanation. Through studies of this kind, we can gain an understanding of the *degree of vulnerability* each individual may have with respect to drug-taking behavior.

An individual's vulnerability toward drug-taking behavior is conceptualized as being shaped by two separate groups of factors in that individual's life. The first are **risk factors**, which make it *more likely* that a person will be involved with

> **risk factors:** Factors in an individual's life that increase the likelihood of involvement with drugs.

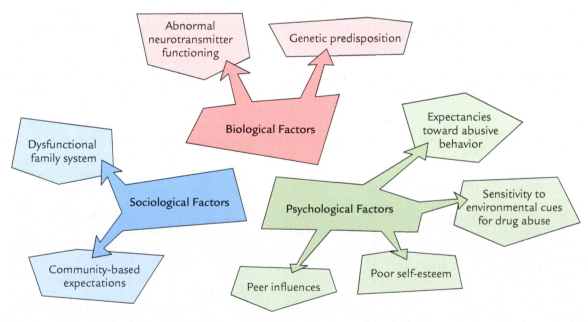

FIGURE 8.4

The biopsychosocial model with respect to effective drug-abuse treatment.

Source: Based on Margolis, R.D.; and Zweben, J. E. (1998). *Treating patients with alcohol and other drug problems: An integrated approach.* Washington, DC: American Psychological Association, pp. 76–87.

drugs; the second are **protective factors**, which make it *less likely* that a person will be involved with drugs. Together, risk factors and protective factors combine to give us some idea about the likelihood that drug-taking behavior will occur. The emphasis, however, should be on the phrase "some idea." We still cannot know for certain which individuals would use drugs and which ones would not. Any predictions about drug use would be probabilistic, not deterministic.

Nonetheless, an understanding of risk factors and protective factors in general and knowledge about which factors apply to a given individual are useful pieces of information in the development of effective drug prevention programs. Identifying the population with the highest risk toward drug use is the first step toward allocating the necessary time, effort, and money to lower the chances that drug-related problems will occur.

> **protective factors:** Factors in an individual's life that decrease the likelihood of involvement with drugs and reduce the impact that any risk factor might have.

Quick Concept Check 8.3

Understanding Sociological Perspectives on Drug Use and Abuse

Check your understanding of sociological perspectives on drug use and abuse by matching the statement (on the left) with appropriate sociological theory (on the right).

1. Virtually everyone has experimented with drugs at some time in their life. However, when this drug use is discovered, users may be stigmatized and labeled as deviant by others.
   a. Social control theory

2. People denied access to societal goals will suffer from strain and respond by conforming, rebelling, illegally innovating, or retreating. According to this theory, most drug users are retreatists.
   b. Differential association theory

3. Deviant behavior such as drug use is learned in interaction and communication with other persons.
   c. Anomie theory

4. It is the bond to society and its moral orders that keeps individuals from breaking the law.
   d. Labeling theory

5. Adolescent drug abuse is characterized by a tightly focused subcultural group based on intimate relationships among group members.
   e. Social recruitment and socialization theory

Answers: 1. d 2. c 3. b 4. a 5. e

Specific Risk Factors

Certain factors that may appear to be strong risk factors for drug-taking behavior in general (socioeconomic status, for example) turn out to have an association that is far from simple and may depend upon the particular drug under discussion. The most reliable set of risk factors consists of psychosocial characteristics that reflect a tendency toward nonconformity within society. Young people who take drugs are more inclined to attend school irregularly, have poor relationships with their parents, or get into trouble in general.[55] As discussed earlier, this may be a reflection of a deviant subculture, or youth associating with peers that have similar beliefs about nonconformity to social norms, including drug use.

Risk factors for substance abuse can stem from biological, psychological, or sociological factors. Table 8.2 displays a number of risk factors for substance use among youth aged 12–17, based on a national survey of drug use and health. These risk factors are broken down by the areas of community, family, peer/individual, and school. The drug use examined focused on alcohol and marijuana, but also surveyed use of inhalants, hallucinogens, and nonmedical use of prescription drugs. A study of the survey findings found that factors predicting use in each of these drug categories include regular conflict with parents, antisocial behavior, proclivity for risk-taking, and poor grades in school.

Many of the risk factors shown in Table 8.2 correspond with the theories we have discussed. For example, risk factors for marijuana and alcohol use include a youth *not disapproving of regular use of marijuana or alcohol by friends*. This finding lends support to cognitive theory, which suggests an excess of beliefs supportive of drug use results in drug use. The risk factor, *high risk-taking proclivity*, finds that youth not afraid to take risks are more likely to abuse any number of substances. This finding supports personality theory, which lists risk-seeking as a personality trait that puts individuals at risk for antisocial behaviors. Some of the risk factors presented also support sociological theories. For example, multiple factors point to the importance of friends (i.e., *having friends that do not strongly disagree with regular drug or alcohol use* is a risk factor for marijuana and alcohol abuse). This item lends support to differential association and the subcultural theories. *Having 10 or more parental conflicts*, another clear risk factor, supports social control theory, which argues that weak parental bonds lead to behaviors like drug use.

Of interest are the presumed risk factors in Table 8.2 that were significantly correlated to substance use, but in the wrong direction. For example, one would presume that homes with *low levels of parental monitoring* increase likelihood of substance use; however, findings from this study indicated that homes with low parental monitoring had significantly less alcohol and marijuana use. This is a finding that defies theory and is difficult to explain.

While Table 8.2 only shows *which* factors predict likelihood of use, we also know that some risk factors have a stronger relationship to drug use than others. The single strongest predictor of alcohol use among youth 12–17 was whether

TABLE 8.2

Major risk factors for substance use over the past year among youths aged 12–17

RISK FACTOR	ALC	MJ	INH	HALL	RX	1ST MJ
Community Domain						
Fairly easy or very easy to obtain marijuana	–	√	–	–	–	√
Family Domain (in past 12 months)						
Low level of parental monitoring	U	U				U
Parents would not strongly disapprove of youth monthly marijuana use	–	√	–	–	–	–
Parents would not strongly disapprove of youth daily alcohol use	√	–	–	–	–	–
10 or more conflicts with parents	√	√	√	√	√	√
Peer/Individual Domain						
High level of antisocial behavior	√	√	√	√	√	√
Youth would not strongly disapprove of peer monthly marijuana use	–	√	–	–	–	–
Youth would not strongly disapprove of peers' daily alcohol use	√	–	–	–	–	–
Friends would not strongly disapprove of youth monthly marijuana use	–	√	–	–	–	√
Friends would not strongly disapprove of youth daily alcohol use	√	–	–	–	–	–
Marijuana use not perceived as a great risk	–	√	–	–	–	√
Daily or weekly alcohol use not perceived as a great risk	√	–	–	–	–	–
High level of risk taking proclivity	√	√	√	√	√	√
Moved 2 or more times in past 5 years	√	√		√	√	
School Domain						
Perceive that most or all students in the same grade use marijuana	–	√	–	–	–	√
Perceive that most or all students in the same grade use alcohol	√	–	–	–	–	–
GPA (D or below in last grading period)		√	√	√	√	√

ALC = alcohol; MJ = marijuana; INH = inhalant; HALL = hallucinogen; Rx = illicit prescription drug; 1st MJ = initiation of marijuana use

√ = risk factor; "–" = not measured; U = significant relationship, but in the unexpected direction; blank = examined, but not a risk factor

Source: Pemberton, M.; Porter, J. D.; Hawkins, S. R.; Muhuri, P. K.; and Gfroerer, J. C. (2014). *The Prevalence and Influence of Risk and Protective Factors on Substance Use among Youths: National Findings from the 2002 to 2008 National Surveys on Drug Use and Health.* Rockville, MD: Substance Abuse and Mental Health Services Administration, CBHSQ Data Review.

they *perceived that all or most youth in the same grade engaged in regular alcohol use*. For marijuana use, the strongest risk factor was whether the *youth perceived that marijuana was easy to obtain*. For inhalant, hallucinogen, and nonmedical use of prescription drug use, the strongest risk factor was the existence of other *antisocial behavior*, like fighting at school. Hence, when youth drug use moves beyond alcohol and marijuana, the use appears accompanied by other antisocial actions.[56]

A useful tool for measuring risk factors is a **risk assessment**. Risk assessments are used to systematically identify empirically based risk factors for substance use (or other behaviors). These tools can help clinicians identify whether an individual meets the minimum criteria in the DSM-5 for a diagnosis of substance use disorder. Such tools are also used as screeners to quickly identify whether a person may be at risk for a drug or alcohol problem. One example is the Drug Abuse Screen Test (DAST-10), which helps to identify what risk factors a person possesses related to substance use, and helps to determine the level of care needed for treatment, if indicated.[57] In the criminal justice system, risk assessments are used to predict the likelihood of re-offense. These risk prediction tools typically include a substance abuse domain with items that examine past and current problems with drugs and alcohol. Risk assessments help practitioners develop case plans, determining what risk factors need to be targeted in order to help that person develop a healthier lifestyle.[58]

Specific Protective Factors

Protective factors provide the basis for someone to have stronger resistance against the temptations of drugs, to have a degree of resilience against engaging in a drug-taking lifestyle, despite the presence of risk factors in that person's life.[59] It is important that we not see these protective factors, however, as

Risk assessment: A tool used to systematically identify empirically based risk factors for substance use (or other behaviors).

TABLE 8.3

Protective factors against substance use over the past year among youths aged 12–17

PROTECTIVE FACTOR	ALC	MJ	INH	HALL	RX	1ST MJ
Community Domain						
Exposure to prevention messages in the media	U	√				
Family Domain (in past 12 months)						
High level of parental encouragement	√		√	√	√	
Parents are a source of social support	√	√	√	√	√	√
Parents communicated the dangers of substance use	U	U		U	U	U
Peer/Individual Domain (in past 12 months)						
Participate in two or more extracurricular activities		√		√	√	
Participate in substance use prevention program outside of school	√	U		U	U	
High level of religiosity	√	√	√	√	√	√
School Domain						
High level of commitment to school	√	U	√	√	√	U
Exposed to prevention messages in school during past 12 months		√		√		

ALC = alcohol; MJ = marijuana; INH = inhalant; HALL = hallucinogen; Rx = illicit prescription drug; 1st MJ = initiation of marijuana use

√ = risk factor; "–" = not measured; U = significant relationship, but in the unexpected direction; blank = examined, but not a risk factor

Source: Pemberton, M.; Porter, J. D.; Hawkins, S. R.; Muhuri, P. K.; and Gfroerer, J. C. (2014). *The Prevalence and Influence of Risk and Protective Factors on Substance Use among Youths: National Findings from the 2002 to 2008 National Surveys on Drug Use and Health.* Rockville, MD: Substance Abuse and Mental Health Services Administration, CBHSQ Data Review.

simply the inverted image, or the negation, of opposing risk factors. Rather, each group of factors operates independently of the other. One way of thinking about protective factors is to view them as a kind of "insurance policy" against the occurrence of some future event that you hope to avoid.

Protective factors can serve as a buffering element among even high-risk adolescents, allowing them to have a greater degree of resilience against drug-taking behavior and a higher resistance to drug use than they would have had otherwise. In the same national survey on drug use and health, protective factors were identified that shield against the temptation for youth to use drugs and alcohol. Table 8.3 shows that a *high level of parental support, religiosity,* and *commitment to school* helps protect youth from engagement in alcohol and drug use. This finding aligns with social control theory, which purports that attachment to parents and commitment to school promote prosocial choices. In this study however, commitment to school did show a positive correlation with marijuana use, meaning higher commitment predicted greater likelihood of marijuana use. It may be that marijuana is being viewed, even by conforming youth, as less an antisocial, or deviant, action, as time goes by.

Findings from the national data do not lend much support for direct messages aimed at drug prevention. Table 8.3 shows that when *parents communicate the dangers of drugs to youth,* in every drug type except inhalant abuse, this behavior was associated with an increased, rather than decreased, likelihood of drug and alcohol use. *Exposure to prevention messages in the media and school* had some positive impact for marijuana and hallucinogens, but not for the other drugs. It seems that lecturing youth about the many risks of drug abuse is not the best way to keep them from using, rather supportive relationships at home, at school, and in the community seem to be the stronger weapons against adolescent drug abuse.

Peer influence is a major factor in predicting the extent of drug-taking behavior during adolescence. It can represent either a risk factor or a protective factor for drug abuse.

Drug Enforcement . . . in Focus

Harm Reduction: A Strategy for Controlling Undesirable Behavior

If we were to use a metaphor of warfare in looking at the drug control policy in America and the structure of present-day drug enforcement, we would recognize that there is an acknowledged enemy (drug misuse and abuse), that there are victims or casualties (us), that there are resources at our disposal to fight the necessary battles (federal and state governments, communities, parents, etc.), and, finally, that there is a high price to pay (billions of dollars of federal funds each year, and uncounted numbers of lives lost or diminished).

Continuing the metaphor, we can ask about what our strategy should be. Do we want total victory and complete annihilation of the enemy? Or do we want some kind of negotiated settlement, some type of "truce" that gives us some semblance of peace and tranquility? If it is the former, then we have set a standard of "zero tolerance." In other words, we would not be satisfied until there is a total elimination of abusive drug-taking behavior in America (a tall order, to say the least). If it is the latter, then we have set a much lower standard for ourselves. In that case, we aim for only a reduction in the harmful consequences of abusive drug-taking behavior. The approach is referred to as the strategy of harm reduction.

Whichever strategy we adopt has profound implications for drug enforcement. It is evident that drug-taking behavior does indeed harm other people. The question, according to those advocating a harm-reduction strategy, is to look for law enforcement efforts that reduce the harm that drugs do, both directly to the drug user and indirectly to others.

A number of harm reduction tactics are controversial. They include needle-exchange programs to lower the incidence of HIV infection among intravenous drug abusers (discussed earlier), methadone maintenance programs for the treatment of heroin abusers (Chapter 9), efforts to reduce the incidence of driving while under the influence of alcohol (Chapter 13), and the use of nicotine patches or e-cigarettes to avoid the effects of cigarette smoking such as emphysema and lung cancer (Chapter 15). Probably the most controversial tactic would be to reduce the level of illicit drug use down from a heavy level of consumption to a level of occasional use. However, it is acknowledged that any level of use involving some types of illicit drugs would present a significant amount of harm to the user.

With regard to cigarette smoking and marijuana use, there is an indication that some teenagers may already be "harm reducing." Specifically, high school seniors who engaged in occasional marijuana smoking and occasional cigarette smoking reported a higher perceived risk of "regular substance use" than did high school seniors engaging in heavy use, even though there was no difference in the perceived risk of "occasional substance use." In other words, occasional users may have been moderating their behavior to minimize the harmful effects they associated with heavy drug-taking behavior. A question that advocates of the harm reduction approach will be investigating in the future with great interest is whether a prevention program that emphasizes the risks of heavy drug use, as opposed to emphasizing the risks of any level of use, is the more successful strategy in reducing significant levels of drug-taking behavior.

Sources: Denning, P. (2003). *Over the influence: The harm reduction guide for managing drugs and alcohol.* New York: Guilford Press. Levinthal, C. F. (2003). Question: Should harm reduction be our overall goal in fighting drug abuse? *Point/Counterpoint: Opposing perspectives on issues of drug policy.* Boston: Allyn and Bacon, pp. 70–73. Marlatt, G. A. (Ed.) (2002). *Harm reduction: Pragmatic strategies for managing high-risk behaviors.* New York: Guilford Press. Resnicow, K.; Smith, M.; Harrison, L.; and Drucker, E. (1999). Correlates of occasional cigarette and marijuana use: Are teens harm reducing? *Addictive behavior, 24,* 251-256.

In research by the Search Institute in Minneapolis, as many as 40 protective factors have been identified, referred to collectively as *developmental assets.*[60] These developmental assets have been found to increase resistance not only to drug-taking behavior (such as problem alcohol use and illicit drug use) but to other high-risk behaviors (such as sexual activity and violence) as well (Drug Enforcement ... in Focus).

Ultimately, the enhancement of protective factors in an individual's life can prove beneficial in reducing the likelihood of drug-related problems, even if there are significant risk factors that are present. In doing so, there will be a degree of resilience with regard to the development of a pattern of drug abuse. Chapter 14 will examine the importance of resilience in light of drug-abuse prevention programs.

Summary

How Drugs Enter and Exit the Body

- There are four basic ways to administer drugs into the body: *oral administration, injection, inhalation,* and *absorption through the skin or membranes.* Each of these presents constraints on which kinds of drugs will be effectively delivered into the bloodstream.

- Most drugs are eliminated from the body with urinary excretion. Drugs are broken down for elimination by the action of enzymes in the liver. An index of how long this process takes is called the elimination half-life.

Factors Determining the Behavioral Impact of Drugs

- The physiological effect of a drug can vary as a factor of the time elapsed since its administration, the possible combination of its administration with other drugs, and finally the personal characteristics of the individual consuming the drug, such as weight, gender, and racial or ethnic background.

- The most prominent psychological factor is the influence of personal expectations on the part of the individual consuming the drug. The impact of expectations on one's reaction to a drug is referred to as the placebo effect. Because of expectation effects, it is necessary to conduct a double-blind procedure in drug research in which neither the subject nor the experimenter knows whether an active drug or a placebo is being administered.

Physical and Psychological Dependence

- Drug dependence can be viewed in terms of a physical dependence model, in which the compulsive drug-taking behavior is tied to an avoidance of withdrawal symptoms, or a psychological dependence model, in which the drug-taking behavior is tied to a genuine craving for the drug and highly reinforcing effects of the drug on the user's body and mind.

- For health professionals, the *Diagnostic and Statistical Manual of Mental Disorders, Fifth Edition* (referred to as DSM-5) is currently the standard for defining and diagnosing a wide range of psychological problems. Specific conditions related to drug abuse are referred to as substance use disorders, based upon a set of behavioral circumstances (diagnostic criteria). A severity-of-symptoms scale identifies a mild, moderate, or severe level of substance use disorder, based upon the number of criteria met.

Theoretical Perspectives on Drug Abuse

- Explanations of drug use have shifted from the moral model (drug abusers are bad), to the disease model (drug abusers are sick), to the biopsychosocial model (there are a number of factors that contribute to drug abuse).

Biological Perspectives on Drug Abuse

- Biological perspectives on drug abuse refer to specific physical mechanisms in individuals that influence the initial experience with drugs or an engagement with drug abuse over a period of time. Theories from this perspective have focused on genetic factors, physiological factors, and neurochemical systems in the brain.

- Research on genetic factors has concentrated primarily on explanations for alcohol abuse and alcoholism. The consensus in this literature is that there is a genetic predisposition toward alcoholism.

- Physiological factors include metabolic deficiencies that set the stage for individuals to seek out drugs to "normalize" their bodies. A metabolic-defect concept has been applied to the study of heroin abuse.

- Research on the role of neurochemical systems in drug abuse has concentrated on the functioning of dopamine in the nucleus accumbens. Drug-taking behavior has been hypothesized to be a compensation for an inadequate number of dopamine receptors necessary to experience pleasurable feelings without drugs.

Psychological Perspectives on Drug Abuse

- Psychological perspectives on drug abuse draw on behavioral, cognitive, motivation, and personality theories.

- Behavioral theories emphasize the pivotal role of reinforcement in the learning of drug-taking behaviors. Behavioral theorists have studied the influence of positively reinforcing experiences inherent in the drug experience itself as opposed to negatively reinforcing experience of gaining relief from uncomfortable withdrawal symptoms.

- Cognitive theories focus on the thoughts and beliefs that lead to drug-using behaviors. According to this theory, individuals encounter high-risk situations, which trigger automatic thoughts, leading to feelings, physical sensations, and, ultimately, actions. Problems with drug abuse are attributable to what and how a person thinks, which stems from that person's belief system (or how they see themselves and the world around them).

- Motivation theories include the Transtheoretical model (or stages of change model) which depicts six stages a person experiences through the course of changing a behavior, including substance use. From this model, a therapeutic technique called motivational interviewing was developed. This approach in treatment is designed to move individuals up the stages of change, so that they are motivated to address problems with drugs or alcohol.

- Personality theories consider the personality traits that distinguish drug abusers from non-abusers. A central theme in these theories is the role of sensation-seeking among individuals as a predisposing characteristic for drug experimentation and abuse.

Sociological Perspectives on Drug Abuse

- Sociological perspectives emphasize the important role of environmental and social factors in drug use and abuse. Theories generated from a sociological perspective include anomie/strain theory, social control/bond theory, differential association theory, subcultural recruitment and socialization theory, and labeling theory.

- Anomie/strain theorists assert that drug use and abuse result from feelings of frustration and alienation existing in individuals who see themselves as not being able to meet the demands of society. Adaptations to feelings of anomie include conformity, innovation, ritualism, retreatism, and rebellion.

- Social control/bonding theory identifies attachment, commitment, involvement, and belief as four social bonds that promote conformity and the disinclination to be a drug user.

- The basic premise of differential association theory is that drug use is learned in interactions and communications with significant others such as parents and friends.

- In subcultural recruitment and socialization theory, the focus is on the dynamic relationships among drug abusers as a cohesive group. In adolescent patterns of drug abuse, peer influence is the dominant factor in maintaining the subculture; in later stages, drug abusers tend to break away from a tightly focused subcultural group and move toward a set of less intimate relationships.

- Labeling theory emphasizes the process through which individuals continue to use drugs because others expect them to do so. Drug users who are labeled as deviant may "find comfort" in being a member of a drug subculture.

Integrated Theoretical Perspectives on Drug Abuse

- The perspective that there are multiple pathways to drug abuse and for each individual, a specific combination of biological, psychological, and sociological factors needs to be considered in assessing the origins of drug abuse

and, in doing so, developing the best treatment for that individual.

Risk Factors and Protective Factors

- Risk factors and protective factors in drug-taking behavior are not theory driven. A relationship is sought between a given variable (an individual's lifestyle, family makeup, environmental condition, etc.) and the likelihood that drug use will occur.

- Risk factors for drug-taking behavior in adolescence from a national survey on drug use and health include conflict with parents, antisocial behavior, proclivity toward risk-taking, and poor grades. Identified risk factors lend support to the various theories of drug-using behavior.

- Use of validated risk assessments is the best way to identify specific risk factors an individual may have for a substance abuse problem.

- Protective factors buffering drug-taking behavior include a supportive relationship with parents, religiosity, and commitment to school.

Key Terms

anomie, p. 154
behavioral theories, p. 150
behavioral tolerance, p. 141
biopsychosocial model, p. 146
biotransformation, p. 139
cognitive-behavior therapy, p. 152
cognitive restructuring, p. 152
cognitive theories, p. 151
cross-tolerance, p. 142
differential association theory, p. 156
disease model, p. 146

dopamine, p. 149
dopamine receptors, p. 150
double-blind, p. 143
elimination half-life, p. 140
intramuscular, p. 138
intravenous, p. 138
labeling theory, p. 157
latency period, p. 140
metabolite, p. 139
moral model, p. 146
Motivational Interviewing (MI), p. 152
neurotransmitter, p. 149

nucleus accumbens, p. 149
physical dependence, p. 144
placebo, p. 143
potentiation, p. 141
primary deviance, p. 157
protective factors, p. 159
psychological dependence, p. 144
risk assessment, p. 160
risk factors, p. 158
secondary deviance, p. 157
social control theory, p. 155

subcultural recruitment and socialization theory, p. 156
subculture, p. 156
subcutaneous, p. 138
sublingual, p. 139
substance abuse, p. 145
substance dependence, p. 145
substance use disorder, p. 145
synergism, p. 141
tolerance, p. 141
transdermal patch, p. 139
Transtheoretical model (TTM), p. 152

Review Questions

1. Discuss the oral, injection, inhalation, and absorption routes of drug administration. Rank the four administrations roughly in terms of the speed by which a drug enters the bloodstream.
2. Compare and contrast the major forms of drug interactions.
3. Define drug tolerance and describe the circumstances under which environmental and contextual cues play a role in the development of behavioral (conditioned) tolerance.
4. Contrast the concepts of physical dependence and psychological dependence.
5. Describe the major behavioral criteria in the DSM-5 that are used in the diagnosis of substance use disorder.
6. Briefly discuss some evidence in favor of viewing drug-taking behavior in terms of genetic, physiological, and neurochemical factors.
7. Compare and contrast the behavioral perspective and the cognitive perspective in terms of the inclination to engage in a pattern of drug-taking behavior.

8. Describe in a few words the main tenets of strain theory, social control/bonding theory, differential association theory, subcultural recruitment and socialization theory, and labeling theory with regard to drug-taking behavior.
9. In what way is a study of risk factors and protective factors an "atheoretical" approach to examining drug-taking behavior?
10. Describe the three risk factors that pertain to all drug-taking behaviors in the Pemberton et al. (2014) study. Why do you think these risk factors would be so important for so many drug-taking behaviors? Choose a risk factor that either predicted drug-taking behavior in the opposite direction as predicted or a risk factor that pertained to only a specific drug-taking behavior. Why do you think these patterns would be observed?

Critical Thinking: What Would You Do?

Suppose you are a drug rehabilitation counselor at a local high school and you are acquainted with two students, named Tara and Debbie.

Tara, 17 years old, is an active substance abuser. Previous interviews with Tara indicate that there have been many instances in which she has gotten into a serious fight at school, and she knows several students her age who use marijuana and other drugs. What strategies could be encouraged during counseling with Tara that would provide a greater number of protective factors in her life?

Debbie, 17 years old, is not an active substance abuser. Previous interviews with Debbie indicate that she also has gotten into serious fights at school and knows several students her age who use marijuana and other drugs. What factors might be present in Debbie's life that could be responsible for her resistance to drug-related problem? Could your experience with the case of Debbie be useful in counseling Tara? Explain.

Endnotes

1. Adapted from a case history reported in Whitten, L. (2005, August). Cocaine-related environmental cues elicit physiological stress responses. *NIDA Notes, 20*(1), pp. 1, 6–7.

2. Sharma, N.; Agarwal, G.; Zulfiqar, R.; Bhat, A.; and Kumar D. (2011). A review: Transdermal drug delivery system: A tool for novel drug delivery system. *International Journal of Drug Development and Research, 3,* 70–84.

3. Advokat, C. D.; Comaty, J. E.; and Julien, R. M. (2015). A *primer of drug action* (13th ed.). New York: Worth. McKim, W. A.; and Hancock, S. D. (2013). *Drugs and behavior: An introduction to behavioral pharmacology* (7th ed.). Upper Saddle River, NJ: Pearson, pp. 1–24.

4. Siegel, S. (1990). Drug anticipation and the treatment of dependence. In B. A. Ray (Ed.), *Learning factors in substance abuse* (NIDA Research Monograph 84). Rockville, MD: National Institute on Drug Abuse, pp. 1–24.

5. Gerevich, J.; Bácskai, E.; Farkas, L.; and Danics, Z. (2005, July 25). A case report: Pavlovian conditioning as a risk factor of heroin "overdose" death. *Harm Reduction Journal, 2*(11) (online publication). Siegel, S. (1975). Evidence from rats that morphine tolerance is a learned response. *Journal of Comparative and Physiological Psychology, 89,* 489–506. Siegel, S.; Hinson, R. E.; Krank, M. D.; and McCully, .J. (1982). Heroin "overdose" death: Contribution of drug-associated environmental cues. *Science, 216,* 436–437.

6. Brecher, E. M., and the editors of *Consumer Reports*. (1972). *Licit and illicit drugs*. Mount Vernon, NY: Consumers Union.

7. Frezza, M.; DiPadova, C.; Pozzato, G.; Terpin, M.; Baraona, E.; and Lieber, C. S. (1990). High blood alcohol levels in women: The role of decreased gastric alcohol dehydrogenase activity and first-pass metabolism. *New England Journal of Medicine, 322,* 95–99.

8. Nakawatase, T. V.; Yamamoto, J.; and Sasao, T. (1993). The association between fast-flushing response and alcohol use among Japanese Americans. *Journal of Studies on Alcohol, 54,* 48–53.

9. Kornetsky, C. (1976). *Pharmacology: Drugs affecting behavior.* New York: Wiley, p. 23. Morris, D. B. (1999). Placebo, pain, and belief: A biocultural model. In A. Harrington (Ed.), *The placebo effect: An interdisciplinary exploration.* Cambridge, MA: Harvard University Press, pp. 187–207. Shapiro, A. K.; and Shapiro, E. (1997). *The powerful placebo: From ancient priest to modern physician.* Baltimore: Johns Hopkins University Press.

10. Beecher, H. K. (1959). *Measurement of subjective responses: Quantitative effects of drugs.* New York: Oxford University Press. Waber, R. L.; Shiv, B.; Cannon, Z.; and Ariely, D. (2008). Commercial features of placebo and therapeutic efficacy. *Journal of the American Medical Association, 299*(10), 1016–1017.

11. Advokat, Comaty, and Julien. A *primer of drug action.*

12. Pinel, J. P. (2003). *Biopsychology* (5th ed.). Boston: Allyn and Bacon, p. 398.

13. Simpson, D. D.; and Marsh, K. L. (1986). Relapse and recovery among opioid addicts 12 years after treatment. In F. M. Tims; and C. G. Leukefeld (Eds.), *Relapse and recovery in drug abuse* (NIDA Research Monograph 72). Rockville, MD: National Institute on Drug Abuse, pp. 86–103.

14. Halikas, J. A. (1997). Craving. In J. H. Lowinson; P. Ruiz; R. B. Millman; and J. G. Langrod (Eds.), *Substance abuse: A comprehensive textbook* (3rd ed.). Baltimore: Williams and Wilkins, pp. 85–90.

15. Yokel, R. A. (1987). Intravenous self-administration: Response rates, the effect of pharmacological challenges and drug preferences. In M. A. Bozarth (Ed.), *Methods of assessing the reinforcing properties of abused drugs.* New York: Springer-Verlag, pp. 1–34.

16. Johanson, C. E. (1984). Assessment of the abuse potential of cocaine in animals. In John Grabowski (Ed.), *Cocaine: Pharmacology, effects, and treatment of abuse.* Rockville, MD: National Institute on Drug Abuse, pp. 54–71.

17. Bozarth, M. A.; and Wise, R. A. (1985). Toxicity associated with long-term intravenous heroin and cocaine self-administration in the rat. *Journal of the American Medical Association, 254,* 81–83.

18. American Psychiatric Association (2013). *Diagnostic and statistical manual of mental disorders* (5th ed.). Washington, D.C.: American Psychiatric Publishing, pp. 483–490.

19. Fisher, G. L.; and Harrison, T. C. (2000). *Substance abuse: Information for school counselors, social workers, therapists, and counselors.* Boston: Allyn and Bacon. Miller, W. R.; and Hester, R. K. (1995). Treatment for alcohol problems: Toward an informed eclecticism. In W. R. Miller; and R. K. Hester (Eds.), *Handbook of alcoholism treatment approaches* (2nd ed.). Boston: Allyn and Bacon, pp. 1–11.

20. Goode, E. (2013). *Drugs in American society* (8th ed.). New York: McGraw-Hill Higher Education, pp. 142–172.

21. George, F. R.; and Goldberg, S. R. (1989). Genetic approaches to the analysis of addictive processes. *Trends in Pharmacological Science, 10,* 78–83. LeGrand, L. N.; Iacono, W. G.; and McGue, M. (2005, March–April). Predicting addiction. *American Scientist,* pp. 140–147.

22. Sher, K. J. (1991). *Children of alcoholics: A critical appraisal of theory and research.* Chicago: University of Chicago Press.

23. Herman, A. I.; Philbeck, J. W.; Vasilopoulos, N. L.; and DePetrillo, P. B. (2003). Serotonin transport promoter polymorphism and differences in alcohol consumption behavior in a college study population. *Alcohol and Alcoholism, 38,* 446–449. National Institute on Alcohol Abuse and Alcoholism (2003). *Is there a genetic relationship between alcoholism and depression?* Bethesda, MD: National Institute on Alcohol Abuse and Alcoholism. Nurnberger, J. I.; and Bierut, L. J. (2007, April). Seeking the connections: Alcoholism and our genes. *Scientific American,* pp. 46–53.

24. Goode, *Drugs in American society,* p. 145.

25. Goode, *Drugs in American society,* pp. 145–146. Myerson, D. J. (1969). Methadone treatment of addicts. *New England Journal of Medicine, 281,* 380. Prendergast, M. L.; and Podus, D. (1999, May 10). Methadone debate reflects deep-rooted conflicts in field. *Alcoholism and Drug Abuse Weekly,* p. 5.

26. Heidbreder, C. A.; and Hagan, J. J. (2005). Novel pharmacotherapeutic approaches to the treatment of drug addiction and craving. *Current Opinion in Pharmacology, 5,* 107–108. Nestler, E. J.; and Malenka, R. C. (2004, March). The addicted brain. *Scientific American,* pp. 78–85. Phillips, P. E.; Stuber, G. D.; Heien, M. L.; Wightman, R. M.; and Carelli, R. M. (2003). Subsecond dopamine release promotes cocaine seeking. *Nature, 422,* 614–618. Weiss, F. (2005). Neurobiology of craving, conditioned reward, and relapse. *Current Opinion in Pharmacology, 5,* 9–19.

27. Volkow, N. D.; Wang, G. J.; Fowler, J. S.; Logan, J.; Gatley, S. J.; Gifford, A.; Hitzemann, R.; Ding, Y.; and Pappas, N. (1999). Prediction of reinforcing responses to psychostimulants in humans by brain dopamine D_2 receptor levels. *American Journal of Psychiatry, 156,* 1440–1443.

28. National Institute on Drug Abuse. Drugs, Brains and Behavior: The Science of Addiction. Retrieved from: *https://www.drugabuse.gov/publications/drugs-brains-behavior-science-addiction/drugs-brain*

29. Goode, *Drugs in American society,* pp. 146–149.

30. Hser, Y.; Hoffman, V.; Grella, C.; and Anglin, M. D. (2001). A 33-year follow-up of narcotics addicts. *Archives of General Psychiatry, 58,* 503–508. Zinberg, N. E. (1984). *Drugs, set, and setting: The basis for controlled intoxicant use.* New Haven, CT: Yale University Press, pp. 46–81.

31. Beck, J. S. (2011). *Cognitive behavior therapy: Basics and beyond* (2nd ed.). New York, NY; Guilford Publications.

32. Beck, p. 32.

33. Gonzalez, J. E.; Nelson, J. R.; Gutkin, T. B.; Saunders, A.; Galloway, A.; and Shwery, C. S. (2004). Rational emotive therapy with children and adolescents: A meta-analysis. *Journal of Emotional and Behavioral Disorders, 12,* 222–235.

34. Prochaska, J. O.; and DiClemente, C. C. (1984). *The transtheoretical approach: Crossing traditional boundaries of treatment.* Homewood, IL: Dow Jones-Irwin.

35. Miller, W. R.; and Rollnick, S. (1991). *Motivational interviewing: Preparing people to change addictive behavior.* New York, NY: Guilford Publications.

36. Burke, B. L.; Arkowitz, H.; and Menchola, M. (2003). The efficacy of motivational interviewing: A meta-analysis of controlled clinical trials. *Journal of Counseling and Clinical Psychology, 71*(5), 843–861.

37. Lang, A. R. (1983). Addictive personality: A viable construct? In P. K. Levinson,; D. R. Gerstein; and D. R. Maloff (Eds.), *Commonalities in substance abuse and habitual behavior.* Lanham, MD: Lexington Books, pp. 157–336.

38. Cristie, K. A.; Burke, J.; Regier, D. A.; Rae, D. S.; Boyd, J. H.; and Locke, B. Z. (1988). Epidemiological evidence for early onset of mental disorders and higher risk of drug abuse in young adults. *American Journal of Psychiatry, 145,* 971–975. Fields, *Drugs in perspective,* p. 8. Lewis, C. E. (1984). Alcoholism, antisocial personality, narcotic addiction: An integrative approach. *Psychiatric Developments, 3,* 22–35. Shedler, J.; and Block, J. (1990). Adolescent drug users and psychological health: A longitudinal inquiry. *American Psychologist, 45,* 612–630.

39. Kerr, J. S. (1996). Two myths of addiction: The addictive personality and the issues of free choice. *Human Psychopharmacology, 11,* 39–45. Ross, H. E.; Glaser, F. B.; and Germanson, T. (1988). The prevalence of psychiatric disorders in patients with alcohol and other drug problems. *Archives of General Psychiatry, 45,* 1023–1031.

40. Goode, *Drugs in American society,* pp. 151–152.

41. Robins, L. N. (1974). *The Vietnam drug user returns.* Special Action Office for Drug Abuse Prevention Monograph Series A, No. 2, Contract HSM-42-72-75.

42. Durkheim, E. (1951). *Suicide* (translated by John Spaulding and George Simpson). New York: Free Press.

43. Agnew, R. (1992). Foundation for a general strain theory of crime and delinquency. *Criminology, 30,* 47–87. Merton, R. K. (1968). *Social theory and social structure.* New York: Free Press.

44. Merton, *Social theory and social structure.*

45. Lorch, B. D. (1990). Social class and its relationship to youth substance use and other delinquent behaviors. *Social Work Research Abstracts, 26,* 25–34.

46. Akers, R. L. (1992). *Drugs, alcohol, and society: Social structure, process, and policy.* Belmont, CA: Wadsworth, pp. 8–9. Hirschi, T. (1969). *Causes of delinquency.* Los Angeles: University of California Press.

47. Burkett, S. R.; and Warren, B. O. (1987). Religiosity, peer associations, and adolescent marijuana use: A panel study of underlying causal structures. *Criminology, 25,* 109–131. Durkin, K. F.; Wolf, T, W.; and Clark, G. (1999). Social bond theory and binge drinking among college students: A multivariate analysis. *College Student Journal, 33,* 450–462. Durkin, K. F.; Wolfe, T.; and Clark, G. A. (2005). College students and binge drinking: An evaluation of social learning theory. *Sociological Spectrum, 25,* 255–272. Guo, J.; Hill, K. J.; Hawkins, D.; Catalano, R.F.; and Abbott, R. D. (2002). A developmental analysis of sociodemographic, family, and peer effects on adolescent illicit drug initiation. *Journal of the American Academy of Child and Adolescent Psychiatry, 41,* 838–846.

48. Sutherland, E. H. (1939). *Principles of criminology* (3rd ed.). Philadelphia: Lippincott.

49. Becker, H. S. (1953). Becoming a marijuana user. *American Journal of Sociology, 59,* 235–242. Faupel, C. E. (1991). *Shooting dope: Career contingencies of hard-core heroin users.* Gainesville, FL: University of Florida Press. Hirsch, M. L.; Conforti, R. W.; and Graney, C. J. (2001). The use of marijuana for pleasure: A replication of H. S. Becker's study of marijuana use. *Journal of Social Behavior and Personality, 5,* 497–510.

50. Goode, *Drugs in American society,* pp. 159–163. Johnson, B. (1973). *Marijuana users and drug subcultures.* New York:

Wiley-Interscience. Johnson, B. (1980). Toward a theory of drug subcultures. In D. J. Lettieri; et al. (Eds.), *Theories on drug abuse*, pp. 110–119.

51. Kandel, D. B. (1973). Adolescent marijuana use: Role of parents and peers. *Science, 181,* 1067–1070. Kandel, D. B. (1980). Developmental stages in adolescent drug involvement. In D. J. Lettieri; M. Sayers; and H. W. Pearson (Eds.), *Theories on drug abuse*. Rockville, MD: National Institute on Drug Abuse, pp. 120–127. Kandel, D. B.; and M. Davies (1991). Friendship networks, intimacy, and drug use in young adulthood: A comparison of two competing theories. *Criminology, 29,* 441–467.

52. Becker, H. S. (1963). *Outsiders: Studies in the sociology of deviance*. New York: Free Press. Erickson, K. (1962). Notes on the sociology of deviance. *Social Problems, 9,* 397–414. Lemert, E. M. (1951). *Social pathology*. New York: McGraw-Hill.

53. Margolin, R. D. and Zweben, J. E. (1998). *Treating patients with alcohol and other drug problems: An integrated approach*. Washington, D.C.: American Psychological Association, pp. 76–87.

54. Johnston, L. D.; and O'Malley, P. M. (1986). Why do the nation's students use drugs and alcohol? Self-reported reasons from nine national surveys. *The Journal of Drug Issues, 16,* 29–66. T-McElrath, Y. M.; O'Malley, P. M.; and Johnston, L. D. (2009, Summer). Reasons for drug use among American youth by consumption level, gender, and race/ethnicity: 1976–2005. *Journal of Drug Issues*, 677–713.

55. Goode, *Drugs in American society*, pp. 159–162.

56. Pemberton, M. Porter, J. D.; Hawkins, S. R.; Muhuri, P. K.; and Gfroerer, J. C. (2014). *The prevalence and influence of risk and protective factors on substance use among youths: National findings from the 2002 to 2008 national surveys on drug use and health*. Rockville, MD: Substance Abuse and Mental Health Services Administration, CBHSQ Data Review.

57. Skinner H. A. (1982). The Drug Abuse Screening Test. *Addictive Behavior, 7*(4), 363–371. Yudko, E.; Lozhkina, O.; and Fouts, A. (2007). A comprehensive review of the psychometric properties of the Drug Abuse Screening Test. *Journal of Substance Abuse Treatment, 32,* 189–198.

58. Bonta J.; and Andrews, D. (2017). *The psychology of criminal conduct* (6th ed.). New York, NY: Routledge.

59. Scheier, L. M.; Botvin, G. J.; and Baker, E. (1997). Risk and protective factors as predictors of adolescent alcohol involvement and transitions in alcohol use: A prospective analysis. *Journal of Studies in Alcohol, 58,* 652–667. Scheier, L. M.; Newcomb, M. D.; and Skager, R. (1994). Risk, protection, and vulnerability to adolescent drug use: Latent-variable models of three age groups. *Journal of Drug Education, 24,* 49–82.

60. Scales, P. C.; and Leffert, N. (1999). *Developmental assets: A synthesis of the scientific research on adolescent development*. Minneapolis: Search Institute. Search Institute (2001, February). *Profiles of student life: Attitudes and behavior*. Minneapolis: Search Institute.

chapter **9**

Opioids

I had minor orthopedic knee surgery this morning and I just came home from the pharmacy with the prescription painkiller medication my doctor had ordered. Forty-two Percocet pills! (The original order had been for 90 pills, but the insurer wouldn't approve.) I was stiff and sore from minor knee surgery, but on a pain scale from 0 to 10, I was about a 4. I was told the pain would get worse and I would need some relief in a few hours. But 42 of them? Talk about using a shotgun to kill a mosquito.

A week later, I had a follow-up appointment. I was feeling fine. I asked my doctor about those 90 pills. He told me the electronic prescribing system automatically sets the default at 90. Evidently, the standard order can be overridden, but that's an extra step for a busy physician and takes some extra time.

Fortunately, I'm aware of the DEA's annual "National Prescription Drug Take-Back Day," when people can voluntarily turn in unused prescription medications. It's a great program, given all those unused opioid pills lying around that are getting into the wrong hands. I plan to take advantage of it.

But, maybe, it would be an even better program if it was held year-round. Let's call it "National Prescription Drug Take-Back EVERY DAY."[1]

Numbers Talk. . .

60.9	milligrams per capita consumption of morphine by Americans in 2015
5.4	milligrams per capita consumption of morphine worldwide in 2015
194.4	milligrams per capita consumption of oxycodone by Americans in 2015
11.4	milligrams per capita consumption of oxycodone worldwide in 2015

Source: Global opioid consumption, 2015. Pain and Policy Studies Group, University of Wisconsin at Madison. *http://www.painpolicy.wisc.edu/global/.*

For many centuries, there has been something of a love–hate relationship with opium. It has been recognized as a drug that can banish pain and transport you to a world of peace and calm, but at the same time, a drug with the potential to enslave the mind. In 1816, Samuel Taylor Coleridge in his poem "Kubla Khan" extolled its powers, calling opium "the milk of Paradise." His poetic imagery was inspired by his own frequent opium-induced dreams. Considering the dual nature of opium as a psychoactive drug, we might extend Coleridge's phrase today and more accurately refer to it as "the milk of Paradise/the milk of Hell."

It has been more than 200 years since morphine was first identified as the principal active ingredient in opium, and it has been more than a century since the introduction of heroin, a morphine derivative that tripled its potency. And as we know, most recently, a growing number of synthetic (entirely laboratory-based) compounds have become available that act in a similar way to that of morphine and heroin but are extraordinarily more powerful in their effects. This chapter will examine the full range of issues related to opioid use, with an emphasis on the current nationwide epidemic of opioid abuse and opioid-related deaths. As we will see, the history of opioids in American history provides an important perspective toward understanding the opioid-abuse crisis we face today.

We begin by explaining in detail what it means for a drug to be referred to as an opioid.

What Are Opioids?

The term **opioid** means "opium-like." An opioid drug is any drug that bears a similarity to opium in terms of its pharmacological effects on the body and the mind. Technically speaking, all opioids share the common feature of binding to a common set of receptors in the brain (see Chapter 8).

You can think of the range of opioid drugs as an "extended opium family" (Figure 9.1). Some opioids are actually components of opium itself. Some opioids are structurally derived from these components, while other opioids are not

opioids (OH-PEE-OIDS): Psychoactive drugs that share the pharmacological effects of opium on the body and the mind.

structurally derived but nonetheless have a *functional* similarity to the effects of opium. In Figure 9.1, the brand names of commonly available opioid medications in each opioid category are listed in parentheses.

In general, the diversity of opioid drugs can be understood in terms of four broad categories:

- The first category comprises three natural compounds that are directly extracted from opium itself: morphine (brand names: Avinza, Kadian, MS Contin), codeine (Tylenol with codeine 3 or 4), and thebaine. All opioids having their origin in these compounds are referred to as *opioid extracts*.

- The second category comprises derivative compounds that are created by making specific structural modifications in the chemical composition of *morphine*. Examples are heroin, hydromorphone (brand names: Dilaudid, Exalgo), and oxymorphone (brand names: Numorphan and Opana IR). Opana ER belongs in this category as well but is no longer commercially available.

- The third category comprises derivative compounds that are created by making specific structural modifications in the chemical composition of *codeine* or *thebaine*. Examples are oxycodone (brand names: Percodan, Percocet, Roxicodone), the extended-release form of oxycodone (brand name: OxyContin), hydrocodone (brand names: Hycodan, Vicodin, Lortac, Zohydro), and buprenorphine (brand names: Subutex, Suboxone, Sublocade).

- The fourth category comprises drugs that are created entirely in the laboratory and bear no structural similarity to any opioid in the first three categories. They are referred to as *synthetic opioids*. Examples of licit prescription medications of this type include methadone, meperidine (brand name: Demerol), propoxyphene (brand names: Darvon, Darvocet), LAAM (brand name: Orlaam), tramadol (brand names: Ultram, Ultracet), and fentanyl (brand names: Duragesic, Sublimaze, Actiq). Various fentanyl-analog compounds such as carfentanil, manufactured illegally in clandestine overseas laboratories and smuggled into the United States, are examples of illicit synthetic opioids.

Since the beginning of the twentieth century, opioid drugs have been commonly referred to as **narcotics** (from the Greek word for "stupor"), based on their ability to produce a

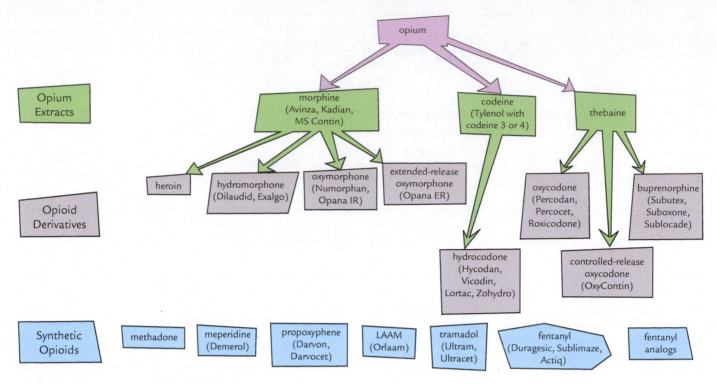

FIGURE 9.1

The "extended opium family" of opioid drugs.

Notes: Brand names are shown in parentheses. Heroin and fentanyl analogs are Schedule I controlled substances and not available for medical use. Opana ER has recently been withdrawn from the market due to the potential for abuse.

Sources: Updated from information in *Physicians' desk reference* (71st ed.) (2017). Montvale, NJ: PDR Network. Raj, P. P. (1996). *Pain medicine: A comprehensive review.* St. Louis: Mosby, pp. 126–153. Substance Abuse and Mental Health Services Administration (2018). *Key substance use and mental health indicators in the United States: Results from the 2017 National Survey on Drug Use and Health.* Rockville, MD: Substance Abuse and Mental Health Services Administration.

dreamlike experience and at higher doses induce a state of sleep. In fact, the term "narcotic" was used at one time (inappropriately) to mean *any* illicit psychoactive drug or at least any drug that caused some degree of dependence, including such unlikely drugs as cocaine and amphetamine, which are anything but sleep-inducing (see Chapter 10). Even today, it is likely that a law enforcement unit assigned to drug-law violations will be called a "narcotics unit." The name has definitely stuck, and there is little expectation that it will fade anytime soon from the lexicon of criminal justice. It is ironic that specific psychoactive drugs are available that have no relationship to opium or opioids but have far greater effectiveness in inducing sleep (see Chapter 12).

Opioids in World History

The history of heroin and the other opioid drugs can be traced back to faraway times and places. This particular story begins with a method of harvesting raw **opium** that has not

changed much in more than 3,000 years. Opium cultivation takes place today in remote areas of Myanmar (formerly Burma), Laos, Thailand, Afghanistan, Kazakhstan, Mexico, Colombia, Peru, and other countries where the weather is hot and labor is cheap (see Chapter 2). The source of opium is the opium poppy, known by its botanical name *Papaver somniferum* (literally, "the poppy that brings sleep"), an annual plant growing 3 to 4 feet high. Its large flowers are typically about 4 or 5 inches in diameter and can be white, pink, red, or purple.

The process of extracting opium out of the opium poppy is simple. When the petals of the opium poppy have fallen but the seed capsule of the plant underneath the petals is not

narcotics: A general term referring to opium, opium extracts, opioid derivatives, and related drugs. Historically, it has been used (inappropriately) to refer to non-opioid drugs as well.

opium: An analgesic and euphoriant drug acquired from the dried juice of the opium poppy.

yet completely ripe, laborers make small, shallow incisions in the capsules during the day, allowing a milky white juice to ooze out during the night. By the next morning, this substance will have oxidized and hardened by contact with cool air. Now, the laborers go from plant to plant, collecting the juice onto large poppy leaves. At this point, opium is reddish brown in color and has the consistency of heavy syrup. Later, it darkens further and forms small gumlike balls.

The first written references to opium date back to the early third century B.C., but there is evidence that opium was used at least a thousand years before that. A ceramic opium pipe has been excavated in Cyprus, dating from the Late Bronze Age, about 1200 B.C. Cypriot vases from that era depict images of incised poppy capsules.[2]

Western Europe was introduced to opium in the eleventh and twelfth centuries by returning crusaders who had learned of it from the Arabs. During the first stirrings of modern medicine in Europe, opium was regarded as a purely therapeutic drug. In 1520, a physician named Paracelsus, promoting himself as the foremost medical authority of his day, introduced a medicinal drink combining opium, wine, and an assortment of spices. He called the mixture *laudanum* (derived from the Latin phrase meaning "something to be praised"), and before long the formula of Paracelsus was being called the "stone of immortality." In 1680, the English physician Thomas Sydenham, considered the father of clinical medicine, introduced and promoted a similar version of opium drink called Sydenham's Laudanum.

Not surprisingly, Sydenham's Laudanum was enormously popular among all levels of society. For the next 200 years or so, the acceptable means of "taking opium" among Europeans and, later, Americans would be in the form of a drink, prepared according to Sydenham's recipe or a host of variations. Sydenham's enthusiasm for opium was no less than that of Paracelsus, a century earlier. "Among the remedies," Sydenham wrote, "which it has pleased Almighty God to give man to relieve his sufferings, none is so universal and so efficacious as opium." Opium was one of the very few medications that physicians had at their disposal to treat their patients in those days.[3]

Local villagers harvest opium in a poppy field in the Khogyani district of Jalalabad, east of Kabul, Afghanistan, in 2013.

Credit: Rahmat Gul/AP Images

The Geopolitics of the Opium War

Sometime in the eighteenth century, China invented a novel form of recreational opium use, opium smoking, which eventually became synonymous in the Western mind with China itself. For at least 800 years before that, the Chinese had used opium almost exclusively on a medicinal basis, consuming it orally in its raw state as a highly effective painkiller and treatment for diarrhea (see Table 9.1, page 181).

By the beginning of the nineteenth century, opium use in China was not widespread. The picture, however, was soon to change dramatically, strangely enough, when the British people discovered and fell in love with Chinese tea and Chinese silk. Sensing a business opportunity, British merchants in China sought a way to buy Chinese tea and silks, transporting it home for a handsome profit. But what could they sell to the Chinese in exchange? The problem was that there were few, if any, commodities that China really wanted from the outside. In their eyes, the rest of the world was populated by "barbarians" with an inferior culture, offering little or nothing the Chinese people needed in trade.

The answer turned out to be opium. In 1773, British forces had conquered the Bengal Province in India and suddenly had a monopoly on the cultivation of raw opium. Consequently, the British had great quantities of opium on their hands. Here was an opportunity to introduce Indian-grown opium to China as a major item of trade. Despite the understandable opposition by the Chinese government, British opium soon flooded into China, smuggled in by local British and Portuguese merchants. This tactic enabled the British government and its official trade representative, the East India Company, to maintain a public image of not being directly involved. Opium was traded for Chinese goods, a satisfactory arrangement from the perspective of Britain but certainly not from the perspective of China.

Huge quantities of opium found a ready market in southern port cities such as Canton. With the influx of opium into China, the character of opium use changed from its original medicinal purposes to a form of recreational drug-taking behavior. It did not take long for Chinese opium smoking and opium dependence to become a major social problem. Repeated edicts by the Chinese emperor to reduce the use of opium within China or cut the supply line from India failed. The situation was out of control.

In 1839, tensions had reached a peak. In a historic act of defiance against the European powers, specifically Britain, an imperial commissioner appointed by the Chinese emperor to deal with the opium problem once and for all confiscated a large shipment of opium arriving in Canton and burned it in the public squire. His courageous act was not appreciated by the British authorities. The confrontation escalated shortly thereafter, until open fighting broke out between Chinese and British soldiers. The Opium War had begun.

By 1842, British artillery and warships had overwhelmed a nation unprepared to deal with European firepower. In a humiliating treaty, China was forced to sign over to Britain the island of Hong Kong and its harbor (until the distant year of

1997), grant to British merchants exclusive trading rights in major Chinese ports, and pay a huge amount of money (equivalent to more than 600 million dollars today) to reimburse Britain for losses during the war. Despite these agreements, fighting broke out again between 1858 and 1860, with French and American forces joining the British. A second treaty signed in 1860 required China to legalize opium within its borders, causing a further growth of opium addiction in the country. In a final act of humiliation, British soldiers were ordered to burn the Summer Palace of the Emperor to the ground.

Geopolitical relations between the East and the West would never be the same. From a Western perspective, the Opium War was a major nineteenth-century victory that established European dominance over Asia for decades, a relatively minor conflict, based upon trade, that had succeeded in opening up the gates of China to the world. From a Chinese perspective, the war was viewed as a catastrophe, leaving a lasting wound to their pride and respect as a nation. To this day, contemporary Chinese scholars refer to 1842 as year one of a "Century of Humiliation" in Chinese history.[4]

Opium in Britain and the United States

To average British citizens in the mid-1800s, the Opium War in China was little more than a faraway international trade dispute, having little or no impact on their personal lives. It is ironic that, during this same period of time, opium itself was a daily fixture in their lives. The critical difference between China and Britain with respect to opium use was not in the *extent* of its consumption but in the *way* it was consumed. The acceptable form of opium use in Victorian England was opium drinking through the consumption of laudanum. The Chinese form of opium use was opium smoking, a practice that was seen by Europeans as reflecting a lifestyle of vice and degradation, a connection with the least desirable elements of society.

The social contrast was striking. Opium dens, with all the evil connotations that the phrase has carried into modern times, were the places where opium was *smoked*; the respectable parlors of middle-class British families were the places where opium was *drunk*.

Opium drinking was pervasive in British society at the time. Supplies of opium were unlimited, cheaper than gin or beer, and an entirely legal commodity. Medical opinion was at most divided on the question of any potential harm; there was no negative public opinion and seldom any trouble with the police. As long as there were no signs of opium smoking, a chronic opium abuser was considered no worse than a drunkard. Nearly all infants and young children in Britain during this period were given opium, often from the day they were born. Dozens of laudanum-based patent medicines (with appealing names such as Godfrey's Cordial, A Pennysworth of Peace, and Mrs. Winslow's Soothing Syrup) were used to dull teething pain or colic, or merely to keep the children quiet. The administration of opium to babies was particularly attractive in the new, industrial-age lifestyle of female workers, who had to leave their infants in the care of elderly women or young children when they went off to work in the factories.

Out of this climate of acceptance sprang a new cultural phenomenon: the opium-addict writer. Just as LSD and other hallucinogens were to be promoted in the 1960s as an avenue toward a greatly expanded level of creativity and imagination (see Chapter 12), a similar belief was spreading among intellectuals during this period with respect to opium. The leader of the movement was Thomas De Quincey, and his book *Confessions of an English Opium-Eater*, published in 1821, became the movement's bible. It is impossible to say how many people started to use opium recreationally as a direct result of reading De Quincey's ecstatic revelations about "opium eating" (by which he meant opium drinking in the form of laudanum), but there is no doubt that the book made the practice fashionable. Prominent English authors enamored with laudanum included Elizabeth Barrett Browning and Samuel Taylor Coleridge (whose exotic poem *Kubla Khan* was undoubtedly inspired by his numerous "opium high" experiences).

In many ways, opium consumption in the United States paralleled its widespread use in Britain. Women outnumbered men in opium use during the nineteenth century by as much as three to one, along with an opposite gender ratio in the use of alcohol. As one historian has succinctly put it, "husbands drank alcohol in the saloon; wives took opium at home."[5]

Throughout the 1800s, opium coexisted alongside alcohol, nicotine (in tobacco products), and cocaine as the dominant recreational drugs of the day. As late as 1897, the popular Sears, Roebuck and Company mail-order catalog advertised laudanum for about six cents an ounce. In a clever marketing move directed to alcoholic men, Sears's "White Star Secret Liquor Cure" was promoted as an addition to the gentleman's after-dinner coffee so that he would be less inclined to join his friends at the local saloon. In effect, he would probably fall asleep at the table or nod off shortly afterward, since the "cure" was opium. If customers became dependent on opium, perhaps as a result of taking the "liquor cure," then fortunately they could order "A Cure for the Opium Habit," being promoted on another page of the same catalog. If you guessed that the ingredients in this one included a heavy dose of alcohol, you would be right.[6]

A nineteenth-century advertising card for Mrs. Winslow's Soothing Syrup, a popular opium remedy, was directed toward young mothers and their children.

Credit: JT Vintage /Glasshouse Images/Alamy Stock Photo

Given the openness of opium drinking in the nineteenth-century United States, we can only surmise that the fanatical reaction against the practice of opium smoking was based on anti-Chinese prejudice rather than a position with respect to opium itself. It is clear that intense hostility existed toward the thousands of Chinese men and boys brought to the West in the 1850s and 1860s to build American railroads. Since most of the Chinese workers were recruited from the area around Canton (now named Guangzhou), where opium trafficking was particularly intense, the practice of opium smoking was well-known to them, and it served as a safety valve for an obviously oppressed society of men. In 1875, San Francisco outlawed opium smoking for fear, to quote local authorities of the time, that "many women and young girls, as well as young men of respectable family, were being induced to visit the dens, where they were ruined morally and otherwise."[7] No mention was ever made of any moral ruin resulting from drinking opium at home. The anti-Chinese prejudice in America with respect to opium would parallel racial prejudice with respect to cocaine (see Chapter 10).

A federal law forbidding opium smoking soon followed, whereas the regulation of opium use by any other means failed to receive legislative attention at that time. By the beginning of the twentieth century, however, the desire for social control of opium dens became overshadowed by the emergence of opium-derived drugs that presented a substantially greater threat to society than smoked opium.

Morphine and the Advent of Heroin

In 1803, a German drug clerk named Friedrich Wilhelm Adam Sertürner first isolated a yellowish-white substance in raw opium that turned out to be its primary active ingredient. He called it **morphine**, in honor of Morpheus, the Greek god of dreams. For the first time, more than three-fourths of the total weight of opium (containing inactive resins, oils, and sugars) could be separated out and discarded. Morphine represented roughly 10 percent of the total weight of opium, but it was found to be roughly 10 times stronger than raw opium. All two dozen or so compounds that were eventually isolated from opium were found to be weaker than morphine and formed a far smaller proportion of opium. Besides morphine, two other major compounds were isolated from opium: **codeine** (about 0.5 percent of raw opium) and **thebaine** (about 0.2 percent of raw opium). Both codeine and thebaine were found to have considerably weaker opioid effects.

With the invention of the hypodermic syringe in 1856, morphine could now be injected into the bloodstream rather than administered orally, thus bypassing the gastrointestinal tract and speeding the delivery of effects (see Chapter 8). The new potential for pain relief through morphine injection was welcomed by the medical profession, owing to its usefulness in dealing with the traumas of the Civil War in the United States (1861–1865) and later the Franco-Prussian War in Europe (1870–1871). It is not surprising, however, that large numbers of soldiers became dependent on morphine and maintained the condition in the years that followed.[8]

A scene of soldiers convalescing from a hospital following the Civil War. Morphine dependence was so widespread among Union and Confederate veterans that the condition was often called the "soldier's disease."

Credit: DEA Museum, Arlington, VA.

Against the backdrop of increasing worry about opiate dependence, a new painkilling morphine derivative called **heroin** was introduced into the market in 1898 by the Bayer Company in Germany, the same company that had been highly successful in developing acetylsalicylic acid as an analgesic drug and marketing it as "Bayer's Aspirin." About three times stronger than morphine, and, strangely enough, believed initially to be free of morphine's dependence-producing properties, heroin (from the German *heroisch*, meaning "powerful") was hailed as an entirely safe cough suppressant (preferable to codeine) and as a medication to relieve the chest discomfort associated with pneumonia and tuberculosis. In retrospect, it is incredible that from 1898 to 1905, no fewer than 40 medical studies concerning injections of heroin failed to recognize its potential for dependence! The abuse potential of heroin, which we now know exceeds that of morphine, was not fully recognized until as late as 1910.

Why is heroin more potent than morphine? The answer lies in its chemical composition. Heroin consists of two acetyl groups joined to a basic morphine molecule. These attachments increase fat solubility, making it more rapidly absorbed into the brain. Once inside the brain, the two acetyl groups break off,

morphine: The major active ingredient in opium.

codeine (COH-deen): One of the three active ingredients in opium, used primarily to treat coughing.

thebaine (THEE-bayn): One of the three active ingredients in opium.

heroin: A chemical derivative of morphine. It is approximately three times as potent as morphine and a major drug of abuse.

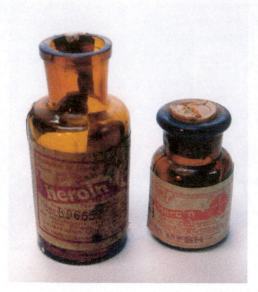

An original heroin bottle as marketed by the Bayer Company in 1898. *Credit:* DEA Museum, Drug Enforcement Administration, Arlington, VA.

leaving the chemical composition now identical to that of morphine. One way of understanding the relationship between the two drugs is to imagine morphine as the contents inside a plain cardboard box and the heroin as fancy box covered with gift wrapping. The contents inside remain the same, but the wrapping increases the chances that the box will be opened.

Opioids in American Society

The introduction of heroin at the end of the nineteenth century was the beginning of a new era in the history of opioid drugs. By 1900, there were, by one conservative estimate, 250,000 opioid-dependent people in the United States, and the actual number could have been closer to 750,000 or more. If we rely on the upper estimate and the U.S. population in 1900, then we are speaking of roughly one out of every hundred Americans, *young or old*, living at that time.

The size of the opioid-abusing population alone at that time probably would have been sufficient ground for social reformers to seek some way of controlling these drugs, but there was also the growing concern that the problems of opioid abuse were becoming intertwined with criminal elements. There was a gnawing anxiety and fear that opioid drugs, specifically heroin, were creating a significant disruption in American society. A movement began to build toward instituting some system of governmental regulation. Opioid use would soon be a focal point of attention in matters of criminal justice.

Opioid Use and Heroin Abuse after 1914

The Harrison Narcotics Tax Act of 1914 (see Chapter 3) radically changed the face of opioid use and abuse in the United States. It ushered in an era in which the abuser

(predominantly male) was no longer a victim of drugs worthy of society's sympathy. Instead, he was now viewed as weak, degenerate, and self-indulgent, a "contaminant" infecting his community's social order and, as a result, deserving society's moral outrage and whatever legal sanction it could devise.[9]

The situation, however, did not change overnight. Most importantly, the 1914 legislation did not actually ban opioids. It simply required that doctors register with the Internal Revenue Service the opioid drugs (as well as cocaine and other coca products) that they were prescribing to their patients and pay a small fee for the right to prescribe such drugs. The real impact of the new law came later, in the early 1920s, as a result of several landmark decisions sent down from the U.S. Supreme Court that interpreted the Harrison Act in broader terms. Under the Court's interpretation of the Harrison Act, no physician was permitted to prescribe opioids for "nonmedical" use. In other words, it was now illegal for addicted individuals to obtain drugs merely to maintain their habit, even from a physician. Without a legal source for their drugs, opioid abusers were forced to abandon them altogether or turn to illegal means, and the drug dealer suddenly provided the only place where opioids, particularly heroin, could be obtained.

Heroin became the perfect black-market drug. Drug traffickers found it easier and more profitable to refine heroin from raw opium overseas and then ship the heroin into the country in small bags than to transport large quantities of raw opium into the country and risk the possibility of authorities detecting its strong odor. In addition, because heroin now had to be obtained illegally and supplies were less plentiful, the price tag would skyrocket to 30–50 times what it had cost when it was available from legitimate sources, a classic example of the economic law of supply and demand.[10]

The Harrison Act also affected the sociological character of opioid drug use in general. With the emergence of restrictive legislation, the demographic profile of opioid users changed dramatically. No longer could the typical consumers of opioid drugs be characterized as female, predominantly white, middle aged, and middle class, as likely to be living on a Nebraskan farm as in a Chicago townhouse. In their place were young, predominantly white, urban adult males, whose opioid drug of choice was intravenous heroin rather than laudanum and whose drug supply was controlled by increasingly sophisticated criminal organizations.

Heroin Abuse in the 1960s and 1970s

In the minds of most Americans prior to the 1960s, heroin and heroin abusers could be comfortably relegated to the social and moral fringes of America. Three major social developments were to bring the heroin story back into the mainstream of the United States. The first began in late 1961, when a crackdown on heroin smuggling resulted in a significant shortage of heroin on the street. The price of heroin suddenly increased, and heroin dosages became more adulterated than ever before. Predictably, the high costs of maintaining heroin dependence encouraged new levels of criminal behavior and an increased response by law enforcement authorities. Heroin abuse soon imposed a cultural stranglehold on many African American and Latino communities in major U.S. cities.

A second development, beginning in the 1960s, affected the white majority more directly. Fanned by extensive media attention, a youthful countercultural movement of hippies, flower children, and the sexually liberated swept the country. The unconventionality of fashions and the antiestablishment attitudes of young people in all parts of the country led to a wave of experimentation with a variety of psychoactive drugs, including heroin. Heroin could no longer be someone else's problem. It was now making its insidious way into the homes and neighborhoods of middle America.

Finally, disturbing reports about heroin abuse began to appear, which focused not only on Americans at home but also on American armed forces personnel stationed in Vietnam. Reports beginning in the late 1960s indicated an increasingly widespread recreational abuse of heroin, along with alcohol, marijuana, and other drugs, among U.S. soldiers. With regard to heroin, in particular, the circumstances could not have been worse. Vietnamese heroin was 90–98 percent pure, compared to 2–10 percent pure in the United States at the time, and incredibly cheap to buy. A 250-milligram dose of heroin, for example, could be purchased for $10, whereas the standard intravenous dose on the streets of a major U.S. city would amount to only 10 milligrams. A comparable 250 milligram dose of highly diluted

U.S. heroin would have cost about $500. With the purity of heroin supplies so high, most U.S. soldiers smoked or sniffed heroin to get an effect; some drank it mixed with alcohol, even though most of the drug was lost as it was filtered through the liver en route to the bloodstream.[11]

In 1971, it was estimated from survey data that about 11 percent of American troops were regular users of heroin, and about 22 percent had tried it at least once. Beyond the concern for the soldiers overseas, there was the considerable worry that at least 1 in 10 Vietnam veterans would be returning home heroin dependent and continuing a pattern of heroin abuse. As a response, the military instituted a mandatory program of urinalysis testing (appropriately named Operation Golden Flow), conducted near the end of a soldier's tour of duty. In October 1971, three months of testing showed that about 5 percent of soldiers tested positive for heroin. The percentage of heroin abusers at that time could very well have been higher since there were strong indications that soldiers had voluntarily given up heroin prior to their being shipped home. Fortunately, a comprehensive investigation in 1974 showed that only 1–2 percent of Vietnam veterans were regular heroin abusers one year following their return from overseas—approximately the same percentage as those entering the military from the general population.[12]

Even if the original numbers of heroin abusers in Vietnam had been exaggerated in the first place (and evidence now suggests that the story was hyped out of proportion by the media at the time), the low number among returnees presents an interesting question. What happened to those who had been previously heroin abusers after they returned to the United States? It has been proposed that heroin use was specific to involvement in Vietnam. Once the soldiers returned home, the stressful environmental cues and motivational factors for drug abuse were no longer present.

Heroin Abuse in the 1980s and 1990s

Although the growth of crack cocaine abuse in the 1980s pushed the issue of heroin abuse temporarily off the front page, heroin abuse itself continued in new forms and variations. Two important developments occurred at this time. First, in terms of illicit drug-taking behavior, a new inexpensive form of heroin, originating in Mexico, became available under the street name of "**black tar**" (though it was actually dark orange or brown in color). While not considered by abusers to be as desirable as heroin from Southeast Asia, the greater potency and cheaper price of Mexican heroin encouraged large numbers of first-time heroin users. Second, a licit synthetic prescription opioid drug, **fentanyl**, more powerful than any form of heroin, became available on the street, after

Military involvement in Vietnam brought U.S. soldiers in contact with unusually potent doses of heroin and other psychoactive drugs.

Credit: Corbis Images

black tar: A form of heroin, generally brownish in color, originating in Mexico.

fentanyl (FEN-teh-nil): A chemical derivative of thebaine, used as a licit prescription painkiller. The street name for illicit fentanyl was, at the time, China White.

being diverted from legitimate sources. It carried the street name "China White" (not to be confused with the name given to Southeast Asian heroin in the 1970s). Twenty years later, illicit fentanyl, manufactured in clandestine overseas laboratories and smuggled into the United States, would have a major impact on opioid abuse (see next section).

Owing to existing drug laws in effect during the 1980s, it was not possible to identify a growing array of new synthetic opioids (dubbed "designer drugs") as illegal substances. Consequently, drugs of this type could not be dealt with effectively by law enforcement. Technically, since they were not chemically identical to heroin or other specific drugs covered by the Controlled Substances Act of 1970, drug-control laws did not apply to them. To remedy this problem, the Controlled Substance Analogue Act of 1986 was enacted, establishing that any drug with a chemical structure or pharmacological effect *similar to that of a controlled substance* was an illicit drug. However, as each new synthetic drug was introduced, drug-control authorities were required to designate the compound as being similar to a controlled substance before it could be covered under the law. As a consequence, there would be a continual process of "catch up" as each new formulation appeared on the scene in rapid succession.

The mid-1990s witnessed a shift in the pattern of heroin trafficking, with a greater emphasis on sources in Colombia. Street heroin from South American sources was now both cheaper and purer. The purity of Colombian heroin during this time exceeded 60 percent, at least 10 times more powerful than the typical street heroin in the 1970s. In 1994, a 90-percent-pure brand of heroin circulating in New York City took heroin abusers by surprise; several overdose deaths occurred within a period of five days. Street prices for a milligram of heroin in New York fell from $1.81 in 1988 to as little as 37 cents in 1994. As one writer put it, it was as though an automobile were suddenly redesigned to go 180 miles per hour and people could buy it at half the former price!

In the mid-1990s, there was also a shift in the social perception of heroin abuse. As the popularity of cocaine abuse declined and the incidence of crack abuse decreased, the spotlight once more turned toward the allure of heroin itself. For a brief time, popular movies (*Pulp Fiction* in 1994, *Trainspotting* in 1995), fashion photography, and the introduction of the Calvin Klein fragrance "Opium" in 1996 contributed to a glamorization of heroin abuse, soon dubbed by the media as "heroin chic." Fortunately, this phenomenon was short-lived.

As the potency of heroin increased during the 1990s, a significant change occurred in the way heroin was abused. Due to the availability of increasingly pure heroin, the drug no longer needed to be injected. Instead, it could be snorted (inhaled through the nose) or smoked. New heroin abusers were frequently smoking mixtures of heroin and crack cocaine or heating heroin and inhaling its vapors. These methods of heroin abuse avoided potential HIV infections or hepatitis that could be contracted through contaminated needles, but they did not prevent the dependence that heroin could produce or the risk of heroin overdose. Unfortunately, heroin snorting

or smoking opened the door to new populations of potential heroin abusers, who had previously stayed away from the drug because of their aversion to hypodermic needles.

The Present-Day Opioid Epidemic

The beginning of the twenty-first century marked the beginning of the latest and most deadly wave of opioid abuse in American history. Two major factors were at work during this time: (1) the rise in prescription opioid medications and (2) the introduction of illicit fentanyl and fentanyl analogs into street heroin.

Over-Prescription of Opioid Medications

Since 2000, sales of opioid pain medication have increased enormously. In terms of morphine milligram equivalent (MME) doses, the amount of opioid pain medications prescribed per person in the United States in 2015 was more than four times higher than in 1999. In some U.S. counties, the increase in opioid medication prescriptions was substantially greater than the national average. In general, six times more opioids per resident were dispensed in 2015 in the highest-prescribing counties in the United States than in the lowest-prescribing counties. Only a third of the differences in prescription rates could be explained by rural versus urban differences, income level, and demographics (Figure 9.2).[13]

Clearly, the greater numbers of opioid prescriptions set the stage for patients becoming at risk for opioid prescription abuse. In addition, as prescription opioids became more expensive and more difficult to attain, patients who had become opioid medication abusers found themselves attracted to opioid alternatives such as heroin. In response to these concerns, the Centers for Disease Control and Prevention issued in 2016 *CDC Guidelines for Prescribing Opioids for Chronic Pain*, intended for primary care clinicians (family physicians, internists, nurse practitioners, and physician assistants) who treat patients with chronic pain (defined as pain lasting more than three months or past the time of normal tissue healing). Recommendations included a close examination of a patient's prior history with opioid use, consideration of opioid therapy only if expected benefits were anticipated to outweigh risks to the patient, prescribing immediate-release opioids when starting opioid therapy instead of extended-release/long-acting medications that would increase the possibility of abuse, prescribing only the lowest effective dosage, and finally scheduling follow-up evaluations to assess any long-term abuse problems on the part of the patient. In 2017, the American College of Physicians published guidelines for the specific treatment of back pain that included drugless remedies such as yoga, acupuncture, massage, and spinal manipulation as a first-line therapy. Opioid medications were recommended only as a last resort.[14]

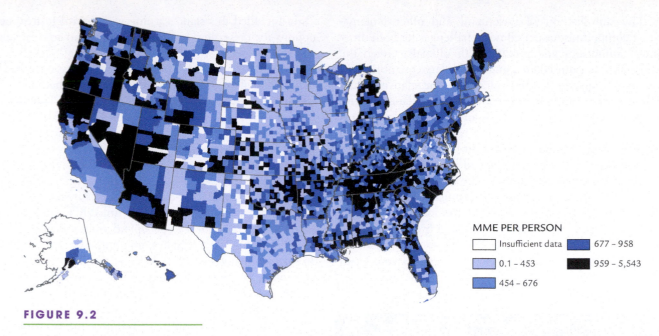

FIGURE 9.2

The quantity of opioids prescribed per person in the United States by individual counties in 2015. MME refers to *morphine milligram equivalent*. For example, a 1,000 MME dosage of an opioid drug would be equivalent to a dosage of 1,000 mg of morphine.

Source: Centers for Disease Control and Prevention (2017, July). Opioid prescribing: Where you live matters. *Vital Signs.* Atlanta, GA: Centers for Disease Control and Prevention, U.S. Department of Health and Human Services.

The Introduction of Illicit Fentanyl and Fentanyl Analogs

The second factor was the fact that heroin itself was becoming considerably more dangerous. Beginning around 2013, the synthetic opioid, fentanyl, approximately 50 times more potent than heroin, was being reported by drug-control authorities in dramatically increasing numbers of confiscations, either mixed with heroin or sold as heroin. The potency of fentanyl was so much greater than heroin that a mere two-milligram dose of fentanyl would now be potentially lethal to humans.

While fentanyl has been available since the 1960s as a valuable Schedule II opioid medication (brand names: Duragesic, Sublimaze, Aciq) for medically approved analgesic and anesthetic purposes, there began in the 1990s signs of its diversion to availability as an illicit drug of abuse. The more significant impact on opioid abuse, however, came from the influx of illicit fentanyl, manufactured in China or Mexico then smuggled into the United States. By 2015, the DEA reported estimates of confiscated opioids containing fentanyl to be more than 20 times higher than in 2012. Nearly one out of seven confiscations of fentanyl-contaminated heroin in 2015 was traced to two U.S. cities alone: Cincinnati, Ohio, and Augusta, Maine. In 2017, about three out of four individuals who died of an opioid overdose and about two out of three individuals who died of an overdose from any drug were found to have tested positive for fentanyl.

Fentanyl has also been identified in overdose cases involving cocaine and methamphetamine as well as other illicit drugs. In August, 2018, over the course of 24 hours in New Haven, Connecticut, more than 70 people required emergency treatment after an overdose of the synthetic marijuana known as K2 or Spice (see Chapter 11) that had been laced with fentanyl. There were no fatalities at that time, but some patients, upon arrival at hospitals, failed to respond initially to a single dose of Narcan, requiring higher concentrations of the opioid-antagonist before they recovered.[15]

Making matters substantially worse, new modified formulations of fentanyl (called *fentanyl analogs*) have recently entered the illicit opioid market, introducing even greater peril for the opioid abuser. One particularly powerful fentanyl analog, **carfentanil**, began to be reported in 2016 in contaminated street heroin in several U.S. cities. Carfentanil had been available as a licit synthetic opioid since the 1980s for veterinary purposes only (anesthetizing large animals, such as an elephant, musk ox, or buffalo). With a potency that is 100 times stronger than even fentanyl, an amount of carfentanil as small as 10 mg is capable of sedating or even killing an African elephant weighing 15,000 pounds (see page 178).

> **carfentanil (car-FEN-teh-nil):** An extremely potent fentanyl-analog opioid, with a potency 100 times greater than fentanyl. Originally developed as a licit opioid drug for veterinary use only, carfentanil has become available as an illicit opioid, often mixed with heroin.

The introduction of carfentanil and other fentanyl-analog compounds has raised new challenges for both drug-control authorities and public-health officials. Given the small amounts required for a single dose, large quantities can be easily smuggled into the United States in relatively small packages, often through concealments in overland vehicles and deliveries through ordinary mail services. Given its extreme potency, protective clothing is required to be worn and special safety protocol procedures must be followed by law enforcement to avoid accidental exposure, since these opioids can be absorbed through the skin. Administrations of the opioid antagonist Narcan, customarily used in emergency treatment of victims of opioid overdose and normally sufficient to revive an unconscious opioid overdose individual, are inadequate in carfentanil overdose cases. A recent public safety announcement issued by a county coroner in

A comparison of equivalent doses of heroin, carfentanil, and fentanyl. Carfentanil is 100 times stronger than fentanyl and 5,000 times stronger than heroin.

Credit: Drug Enforcement Administration.

Quick Concept Check 9.1

Understanding the History of Opium and Opioids

Check your understanding of the historical background for opium and opioids by answering the following question. Imagine yourself to be living as a male adult in the year 1900. Check yes or no to indicate whether the following psychoactive drugs would be available to you.

1. Heroin   ○ yes   ○ no
2. Opium   ○ yes   ○ no
3. Fentanyl   ○ yes   ○ no
4. Oxycodone   ○ yes   ○ no
5. Morphine   ○ yes   ○ no

Answers: 1. yes   2. yes   3. no   4. no   5. yes

Ohio included this stark warning with regard to treatment options for these new emergencies: "Narcan may not save you on this one."[16]

In 2017, the DEA instituted emergency measures to make *all* analogs of fentanyl designated as Schedule I controlled substances, rather than having to respond on a piecemeal basis to every single analog as they became introduced.

The Scope of the Opioid Overdose Crisis

The scope of the present-day opioid crisis is staggering as is the unfortunate prospect that it is unlikely to end anytime soon. In 2017, about 49,000 opioid overdose deaths were reported in the United States, amounting to approximately 134 people dying each day. As noted in Chapter 1, opioids accounted for about two-thirds of the approximately 72,000 overdose deaths occurring from all forms of drugs.

The availability of illicit fentanyl and fentanyl analogs has become the dominant factor in the rise in opioid overdose deaths and drug overdose deaths in general. It is less common in recent years for an opioid overdose fatality to be a result of heroin alone. Among the 281 overdose deaths recorded in Montgomery County, home of Dayton, Ohio, alone, in January–February 2017, toxicology analysis identified the presence of fentanyl or some type of fentanyl analog in more than 92 percent of the cases, while heroin alone was identified in only 6 percent of the cases. Figure 9.3 shows the breakdown of opioid overdose deaths from 2008 to 2016 in three categories: (1) overdose deaths involving heroin alone, (2) overdose deaths involving morphine, oxycodone (primarily Percocet and OxyContin), and hydrocodone (primarily Vicodin), and (3) overdose deaths involving fentanyl or fentanyl analogs. The rise in illicit drug involvement with fentanyl and fentanyl analogs is particularly striking.

The estimated economic costs of containing the opioid crisis in the United States has risen 600 percent since 2001 to an astounding $504 billion (equivalent to about three percent of the gross national product), according to a 2017 study by the Council of Economic Advisors. These expenditures would otherwise be allocated to research into new medication-based addiction treatments, new antidotes to overdoses and effective but nonaddictive pain medications, in addition to a vast expansion in treatment facilities for opioid-abuse individuals. The range of presently available treatment options for opioid abuse will be covered in a later section.[17]

It is uncertain how long the plague of opioid abuse and its consequences in terms of overdose deaths will continue, or how effective prevention efforts will be in stemming the tide. In the meantime, it is necessary to find ways to effectively deal with individuals who are already opioid abusers and are at risk of an accidental opioid overdose. One important response has come from the criminal justice system in the introduction of specialty drug courts, tailored for at-risk individuals who have been arrested for drug-related law violations (see Drugs . . . in Focus).

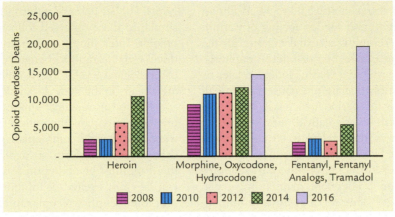

FIGURE 9.3

The number of opioid overdose deaths from 2008 to 2016 in terms of the type of opioid involved.

Note: The above numbers provide only a rough appreciation of the trends of opioid overdose deaths over these years for two reasons. First, the sum of numbers from the three categories in each year is greater than the cases since cases can involve two drugs in combination. Second, the percentage of drug overdose deaths that identified the specific drugs involved varied from 75 percent and 85 percent, depending on the year of reporting.

Source: Hedegaard, H.; Warner, M.; and Miniño, A. (2017, December). *Drug overdose deaths in the United States, 1999–2016.* NCHS Data Brief, No. 294. Atlanta, GA: Centers for Disease Control and Prevention, data from Figure 4.

Drugs . . . in Focus

Opioid Crisis Intervention Courts: A Response to the Opioid Epidemic

In a single week in 2016, three defendants in Buffalo, New York, failed to appear before the drug treatment court. Between the time of their arrest and court date, they had died of an opioid overdose. As a response to the opioid crisis in the city, a special drug court (see Chapter 7) was set up in 2017 to assure that opioid users get into treatment within hours of their arrest. The program requires defendants to check in with the judge every day for up to a month and places strict curfew restrictions on them as the judicial process proceeds. In the words of the court project director, "The idea behind it is only about how many people are still breathing each day when we 're finished." Buffalo-area health officials blamed 300 deaths in 2016 on opioid overdoses, a dramatic increase from 127 two years earlier.

As of 2018, eight other states—Alaska, Indiana, Kansas, Minnesota, North Carolina, New Jersey, Virginia, and Washington—have similar programs in the planning stage.

Source: Associated Press (2017, July 10). Opioid court's goal: Keep users alive. *Newsday,* p. A27. Quotation by Jeffrey Smith, court project director.

Opioid Effects on the Mind and the Body

While opioid abuse in the United States involves a range of opioids other than heroin itself, we have the most extensive knowledge about the effects of heroin itself. For that reason, information about heroin will be the focus here. We can assume that the behavioral and physiological effects are similar no matter what opioid is being ingested.

Even so, we need to be careful in making sweeping generalizations even about heroin. Heroin effects can be quite variable, and a number of factors should be considered. The intensity of a response to heroin is dependent upon (1) the quantity and purity of the heroin taken, (2) the route through which heroin is administered, (3) the interval since the previous dose of heroin, and (4) the degree of tolerance on the part of the user to heroin itself. In addition, there are psychological factors related to the setting and circumstances of heroin administration, as well as the expectations of the user at the time.[18]

If heroin is injected intravenously, there is an almost immediate tingling sensation and sudden feeling of warmth in the lower abdomen, resembling a sexual orgasm, for the first minute or two. There is a feeling of intense euphoria, variously described as a "rush" or a "flash," followed later by a state of tranquil drowsiness that heroin abusers often call being "on the nod." During this period, which lasts from three to four hours, any interest in sex is greatly diminished. In the case of male heroin abusers, the decline in sexual desire is due, at least in part, to the fact that opioids reduce the levels of testosterone, the male sex hormone. Withdrawal symptoms can begin in about four hours. Therefore, maintaining a relatively constant "heroin high" often requires three or four administrations in a given day.

Ironically, an individual's first-time experience with heroin may be considerably unpleasant. Opioids in general cause nausea and vomiting, as the reflex centers in the medulla are suddenly stimulated. Some first-time abusers find the vomiting so aversive that they never try the drug again; others consider the discomfort largely irrelevant because the euphoria is so powerful.

There are a number of additional physiological changes in the body. A sudden release of histamine in the bloodstream produces an intense itching over the entire body and a reddening of the eyes. Heroin also causes pupillary constriction, resulting in the characteristic "pinpoint pupils" that are used as an important diagnostic sign for narcotic abuse in general. Like sedative–hypnotic drugs (see Chapter 12), heroin reduces the sensitivity of respiratory centers in the brain to levels of carbon dioxide in the blood, resulting in a depression in breathing and potential death. Blood pressure is also depressed as a result of heroin intake. A suppression of the immune system over time as well, increasing the risk of infectious disease. Finally, a distressing, though nonlethal, effect of heroin is the slowing down of the gastrointestinal tract, causing labored defecation and intense constipation.[19]

How Opioids Work in the Brain

As a result of major discoveries in the 1970s, we now know that we are dealing with a direct effect of opioids on the activation of receptors in the brain that are specifically sensitive to morphine. During the 1960s, suspicions grew that a morphine-sensitive receptor, or a family of them, existed in the brain. One major clue came from the discovery that small chemical alterations in the morphine molecule would result in a group of new drugs with strange and intriguing properties. Not only would these drugs produce little or no *agonistic* effects—that is, they would not act like morphine—but they would instead act as *opioid antagonists*—that is, they would reverse or block the effects of morphine.

The most complete opioid antagonist to be identified, **naloxone** (brand names: Narcan and Evzio), has turned out to have enormous benefits in the emergency treatment of opioid-overdose patients. In such cases, intramuscular or intravenous injections of naloxone reverse the depressed breathing and blood pressure in a matter of a minute or so, an effect so fast that emergency department specialists view the reaction as "miraculous." The effect lasts for one to four hours. Higher doses of naloxone bring on symptoms that are similar to those observed following an abrupt withdrawal of opioids. Interestingly, in nondrugged people, naloxone produces only negligible changes, on either a physiological or a psychological level. Only if morphine or other opioid drugs are already in the body does naloxone have an effect.[20]

Beyond its practical application, the discovery of naloxone had important theoretical implications. The argument went as follows: If such small molecular changes could so dramatically transform an agonist into an antagonist, then the drug must be acting on some receptor in the brain that can be easily excited or inhibited. The concept of a special morphine-sensitive receptor fulfilled these requirements.

The actual receptors themselves were discovered in 1973, precisely where you would have expected them to be: in the spinal cord and brain, where pain signals are known to be processed, and in the limbic system of the brain, where emotional behaviors are coordinated. In other words, it was clear that the analgesic and euphoric properties of morphine were due to the stimulation of these receptors. Today, we refer to these receptors as *opioid receptors* in that all opioid drugs have the common feature of stimulating them.

Why would opioid receptors exist in the first place? No one seriously considered the possibility that receptors in the brain had been patiently waiting, during millions of years of evolutionary history, for the day that the juice of the opium poppy could finally slip inside them! The only logical answer was that we must have been producing our own opioid chemicals that had the ability to activate these receptors.

As a result of a series of important discoveries from 1975 to the early 1980s, three groups of natural morphinelike molecules have been identified: enkephalins, beta-endorphins, and dynorphins. Together, they are known as **endogenous opioid peptides**, inasmuch as they are all (1) peptide molecules (amino acids strung together like a necklace), (2) opioid in function, and (3) produced within the central nervous system. Unfortunately, this is such an unwieldy name that more frequently they are simply referred to as *endorphins*.

What can we then conclude about the effect of opioids on the brain? The answer, as we now understand it, is that the brain has the ability to produce its own "opioid" substances, called endorphins, and contains a specific set of receptors to receive them. By an amazing quirk of fate, the opium poppy yields a similarly shaped chemical that fits into these receptors, thus producing equivalent psychological and physiological effects. Naloxone acts as an opioid antagonist because its structural features enable it to fit into these receptors, replacing the opioid molecules that have gotten in. The receptors themselves, however, are *inactivated* by naloxone. This is why naloxone can "undo" the acute effects of an opioid drug such

naloxone (nah-LOX-ohn): A pure antagonist for morphine and other opioid drugs. Brand names are Narcan and Evzio.

endogenous opioid peptides (en-DODGE-eh-nus OH-pee-oid PEP-tides): Also known as *endorphins*. A class of chemicals produced inside the body that mimic the effects of opioid drugs.

as heroin. A long-acting version of naloxone, **naltrexone**, has been used as one other alternative approach in medically assisted treatments for opioid abuse. One particular formulation (brand name: ReVia, previously marketed as Trexan), taken orally three times per week, has been useful primarily for patients who are highly motivated to stop their drug-taking behavior. Such patients include doctors, nurses, and other health professionals who must terminate a pattern of opioid abuse to retain their licenses and former opioid abusers on parole who are at risk of returning to prison if they suffer a relapse. A once-per-month injectable formulation, administered by a qualified physician or health-care provider (brand name: Vivitrol), is also available, as we will see in a later section of the chapter.[21]

Patterns of Heroin Abuse

Although patterns of opioid abuse encompass, by definition, behaviors associated with the administration of a variety of opioid drugs, the focus in this section will be on heroin, for two reasons. First, heroin abuse is the most prominent and the best studied form of opioid abuse. Second, the overall patterns of heroin abuse are similar to patterns of abuse for other opioid drugs as well. Therefore, patterns of heroin abuse reviewed here can be generalized to patterns of opioid abuse. The only difference is that opioid drugs with greater potency than heroin present more intense and less reversible behavioral and physiological consequences.

The dominant route of administration in heroin abuse is intravenous injection, usually referred to as either *mainlining* or *shooting*. Heroin also can be administered through a variety of other routes. Heroin smoking is popular in Middle Eastern countries and in Asia, but until very recently it has seldom been observed in the United States. Newcomers to heroin may begin their abuse either by snorting the drug through the nose or injecting it subcutaneously (skin popping). Experienced heroin abusers may snort heroin to avoid using a needle or choose the subcutaneous route when they can no longer find veins in good enough condition to handle an intravenous injection. As mentioned earlier, an oral administration of heroin is usually worthless because absorption is extremely poor. American soldiers in Vietnam who were abusing heroin often took the drug orally, but because of the extremely high purity of the heroin being consumed, their effective dose levels equaled or slightly exceeded levels found on American streets at the time.

Tolerance and Withdrawal Symptoms

Like many other drugs, heroin and other opioids produce drug tolerance over repeated use. The tolerance symptoms themselves, however, do not occur in every bodily system. Gastrointestinal effects of constipation and spasms do not show much tolerance at all, whereas distinctive pupillary responses (the pinpoint feature

of the eyes) eventually subside with chronic use. The greatest signs of tolerance are seen in the degree of analgesia, euphoria, and respiratory depression. The intense thrill of the intravenous injection will be noticeably lessened.

The first sign of heroin withdrawal, a marked craving for another fix, generally begins about 4–6 hours after the previous dose and intensifies gradually to a peak over the next 36–72 hours, with other symptoms beginning a few hours later (Table 9.1). The abuser is essentially over the withdrawal period in five to ten days, though mild physiological disturbances, chiefly elevations in blood pressure and heart rate, are observed as long as six months later. Generally, these long-term effects are associated with a gradual withdrawal from heroin rather than an abrupt one.

The overall severity of heroin-withdrawal symptoms is a function of the dosage levels of heroin that have been sustained. When dosage levels are less than 10 percent, the withdrawal symptoms are comparable to a moderate to intense case of the flu. In more severe cases, the withdrawal process can result in a significant loss of weight and body fluids. With increases in the purities of street heroin in the 1990s, the symptoms of withdrawal are greater. Nonetheless, seldom is the process of heroin withdrawal life threatening, unlike withdrawal from barbiturate and other depressant drugs (see Chapter 12).

It should not be surprising that withdrawal symptoms are essentially the mirror image of symptoms observed when a person is under the influence of heroin. If we are dealing with a group of endorphin-sensitive receptors that are, in the case of the heroin abuser, being stimulated by the opioids

TABLE 9.1	
Symptoms of administering heroin and of withdrawing heroin	
ADMINISTERING	**WITHDRAWING**
Lowered body temperature	Elevated body temperature
Decreased blood pressure	Increased blood pressure
Skin flushed and warm	Piloerection (gooseflesh)
Pupil constriction	Pupil dilation
Constipation	Diarrhea
Respiratory depression	Yawning, panting, sneezing
Drying of secretions	Tearing, runny nose
Decreased sex drive	Spontaneous ejaculations and orgasms
Muscular relaxation	Restlessness, involuntary twitching and kicking movements*
Nodding, stupor	Insomnia
Analgesia	Pain and irritability
Euphoria and calm	Depression and anxiety

*The source of the expression "kicking the habit."

Source: Based on Grilly, D. M.; and Salamone, J. D. (2012). *Drugs, brain, and behavior* (6th ed.). Boston: Pearson Education, p. 298.

naltrexone (nal-TREX-ohn): A long-lasting form of naloxone. Formulations include the brand names ReVia (formerly known as Trexan) and Vivitrol.

coming in from the outside, then it is reasonable to assume that over time the production of endorphins would decline. Why produce something on your own when you are getting it from an external source? By that argument, withdrawal from heroin would then be a matter of cutting off those receptors from that external source, resulting in a reaction opposite to the one that would have occurred had the receptors been satisfied in the first place. Over a period of time, coinciding with the withdrawal period for a heroin abuser, we would expect that the normal production of endorphins would reestablish itself and there would be little or no need for the external supply of heroin.

The receptor explanation for heroin dependence sounds reasonable and does account for the presence of withdrawal symptoms, but unfortunately it is an oversimplification for heroin abuse in general. We would expect that once the endorphin-sensitive receptors regain their natural supply of endorphins, heroin abuse should end, but we know that it does not.

In the case of heroin abusers, their tendency to continue taking heroin is propelled by a number of factors. There is the fear and distress associated with the prospect of experiencing withdrawal symptoms that is combined with a genuine craving for the effects themselves. Long-term heroin abusers frequently develop such powerful associations with the social setting in which the drug-taking behavior occurs that, through conditioned learning, the setting itself takes on reinforcing properties of its own (see Chapter 8). Even the act of inserting a syringe into the arm can become pleasurable, since it precedes the actual delivery of heroin into the bloodstream. Some heroin abusers (so-called *needle freaks*) continue to insert needles into their skin and experience heroin-like effects even when there is no heroin in the syringe. In effect, the heroin abuser is responding to a placebo that has been created as a result of conditioned learning. Any long-term treatment for heroin abuse, as will be discussed in a later section, must address a range of physical, psychological, and social factors to be successful (Table 9.2).

The Lethality of Heroin Itself

To understand the toxicity of heroin, we first need to separate the effects of chronic heroin abuse from the drug's acute effects. Undoubtedly, the danger of acute heroin overdose is ever-present, exacerbated by the combination with much more powerful synthetic opioids such as fentanyl or fentanyl analogs. Nonetheless, from a long-term perspective with regard to one's physical health, heroin is considered relatively nontoxic, particularly when compared to several other drugs of abuse. Organ systems are not damaged or impaired by even a lifetime of heroin abuse, by virtue of ingesting the drug itself. There are no malformations, tissue damage, or physical deterioration directly tied to the use of any opioid drug, including heroin.[22] A notable exception, however, is found in the case of heroin administered by inhaling heated heroin vapors (sometimes referred to as "chasing the dragon"). This form of heroin abuse has been linked to *leukoencephalopathy*,

TABLE 9.2

Street names for opioid and opioid-combination drugs

TYPE OF OPIOID	STREET NAME
Morphine	Big M, Miss Emma, white stuff, M, dope, hocus, unkle, stuff, morpho
White heroin	Junk, smack, horse, scag, H, stuff, hard stuff, dope, boy, boot, blow, jolt, spike, slam
Mexican heroin	Black tar, tootsie roll, chapapote (Spanish for "tar"), Mexican mud, peanut butter, poison, gummy balls, black jack
Heroin combined with amphetamines	Bombitas
Heroin combined with cocaine	Dynamite, speedball, whizbang, goofball
Heroin combined with marijuana	Atom bomb, A-bomb
Heroin combined with cocaine and marijuana	Frisco special, Frisco speedball
Heroin combined with cocaine and morphine	Cotton brothers
Codeine combined with Doriden (a nonbarbiturate sedative–hypnotic)	Loads, four doors, hits

Sources: U.S. Department of Justice, Drug Enforcement Administration. (1986). *Special report: Black tar heroin in the United States*, p. 4. Bureau of Justice Statistics Clearinghouse. (1992). *Drugs, crime, and the justice system: A national report from the Bureau of Justice Statistics.* Washington, D.C.: U.S. Department of Justice, pp. 24–25.

a neurological disease in which a progressive loss of muscle coordination can lead to paralysis and death.[23]

Nonetheless, it is abundantly clear that the *practice* of heroin abuse is highly dangerous and potentially lethal. It is the *circumstances* of heroin administration that become matters of great concern.[24]

■ First of all, heroin has a relatively small ratio of LD (lethal dose) to ED (effective dose). Increase a dose that produces a high in a heroin abuser by 10 or 15 times, and you will be in the dosage range that is potentially fatal. As a result, death by overdose is an ever-present risk. If we take into account the virtually unknown potency of street heroin in any given fix, you can appreciate the hazards of a drug overdose. The "bag" sold to a heroin abuser may look like the same amount each time, but the actual heroin content may be anywhere from none at all to 90 percent. Therefore, it is easy to underestimate the amount of heroin being taken in.

■ Second, it is well known that heroin abusers are vulnerable to adverse effects from any toxic substance that has been "cut" with the heroin. The possibility of heroin being combined with synthetic opioids such as fentanyl or fentanyl analogs is an obvious hazard. Deaths from heroin overdose can also be consequences of synergistic combinations of heroin with nonopioid drugs such as stimulants like cocaine or depressants like alcohol, Valium, or barbiturates. In some cases, individuals have smoked crack as their primary drug of abuse and snorted heroin to ease the agitation associated with crack. In other cases, lines of cocaine and heroin are alternately inhaled in a single session, a practice referred to as "criss-crossing."

- Third, as mentioned earlier, it is possible that some heroin abusers develop unstable levels of tolerance that are tied to the specific environmental setting in which the heroin is administered. As a result of conditioned tolerance (see Chapter 8), a heroin dose experienced in an environment that has not been previously associated with drug taking may have a significantly greater effect on the abuser than the same dose taken in more familiar surroundings.

- Although the overriding danger of excessive amounts of heroin is the potentially lethal effect of respiratory depression, abusers can die from other physiological reactions. In some instances, death can come so quickly that the victims are found with a needle still in their veins; such deaths are usually due to a massive release of histamine or to an allergic reaction to some filler in the heroin to which the abuser was hypersensitive. Intravenous injections of heroin increase the risks of hepatitis or HIV infections, and unsterile water used in the mixing of heroin for these injections can be contaminated with bacteria. A case in

point is a situation that briefly appeared on the scene in the mid-1980s, during which "manufacturers" producing illicit heroin in clandestine laboratories failed to remove a chemical impurity called MPTP in the process. MPTP is known to destroy specific neurons in the brain that are responsible for motor control. Young people exposed to this heroin acquired severe motor control problems, including full-blown symptoms of Parkinson's disease.

Promoting the availability of naloxone for opioid overdose emergencies is an important step in reducing opioid overdose deaths.

Credit: Spencer Platt/Getty Images

Drugs . . . in Focus

Opioid Overdose Emergencies and Naloxone for First Responders

In light of the present-day opioid overdose crisis, emergency administrations of naloxone (brand names: Narcan, Evzio) have become a fixture in the battle to save lives. In 2014, the FDA approved an easy-to-use device, the size of a credit card or small cell phone, which, when turned on, provides verbal instructions for the administration of naloxone, much as defibrillators would be employed in case of cardiac arrest. Today, either Narcan or Evzio is available in auto-injectable form to a wide range of medical and nonmedical "first responders," including family members or caregivers, on a prescription basis. School districts are stocking supplies of Narcan kits onsite in school buildings for emergency use by school nurses. For heroin overdose emergencies, opioid reversal is accomplished within 2 to 3 minutes and lasts from 30 minutes to 1 hour.

A further advance is the present availability of naloxone in a nasal spray (brand name: Narcan Nasal Spray) that allows emergency administrations without any needle injections. As of 2017, nasal Narcan can be purchased as a standing order without prescription in 48 out of 50 U.S. states.

Sources: Associated Press (April 4, 2014). Overdose antidote approved. *Newsday*, p. A7. Deutsch, K. (2014, April 14). OD antidote on way. *Newsday*, p. A8. Editorial: Preventing painkiller overdoses (2014, April 15). *The New York Times*, p. A22. National Institute on Drug Abuse (2016, September). Newsletter: Opioid overdose reversal with naloxone (Narcan, Evzio). Rockville, MD: National Institute on Drug Abuse, U.S. Department of Health and Human Services. Accessed from: *http://www.narcan.com/availability*. Tyrrell, J. (2017, July 5). LI schools facing a drug test. *Newsday*, pp. A2–A3.

Quick Concept Check 9.2

Understanding the Effects of Administering and Withdrawing Heroin

Without looking at Table 9.1, check your understanding of the effects of heroin, relative to withdrawal symptoms, by noting whether the following symptoms are associated with administering heroin or withdrawing it.

Symptom	Administering	Withdrawing
1 Twitching and sneezing		
2 Skin flushed and warm		
3 Decreased sex drive		
4 Yawning and panting		
5 Pain and irritability		
6 Pupillary constriction		
7 Increased blood pressure		
8 Diarrhea		
9 Analgesia		

Answers: 1. withdrawing   2. administering   3. administering 4. withdrawing   5. withdrawing   6. administering 7. withdrawing   8. withdrawing   9. administering

Medically Assisted Treatments for Opioid Abuse

For the opioid abuser seeking treatment, the two primary difficulties are the short-term effects of opioid withdrawal and the long-term effects of opioid craving. Any successful treatment, therefore, must combine a short-term and a long-term solution. In medically assisted treatments, the primary focus is on the short-term issues, particularly with respect to the possibility of an opioid overdose, although the use of treatments of this type often extends into longer periods of treatment and recovery during which long-term drug abuse issues can be addressed.

Currently, the focus is on two medically assisted treatment approaches, through the administration of either of two prescription medication approaches. The first approach is based on the administration of the synthetic opioid, **buprenorphine**, either alone or more commonly in combination with naloxone. The second approach is based on the administration of naltrexone, the long-lasting version of naloxone (brand name: Vivitrol).

Presently, buprenorphine-based formulations are more widely used than naltrexone in medically assisted treatment programs. Buprenorphine formulations available in tablets or strips, taken sublingually by the patient on a daily basis, are marketed either as buprenorphine alone (brand name Subutex) or in combination with naloxone, (brand name **Suboxone**) or as a transdermal patch (brand name Butrans). The common naltrexone formulation is marketed under the brand name **Vivitrol** administered by injection on a monthly basis by a qualified physician or other health care provider.

There are advantages and disadvantages with either of these medically assisted approaches. Treatment with Vivitrol can only be started after detoxification has been completed (see below), while Suboxone can be started immediately, an obvious advantage when there is the possibility of a future opioid overdose. On the one hand, Suboxone is more expensive than Vivitrol. On the other hand, because Suboxone contains an opioid and Vivitrol does not, Suboxone can be potentially diverted as a street drug.

The question as to which of the two medications is more effective in opioid-abuse treatment is a matter of intense study. In a 2017 study, relapse rates with Suboxone or Vivitrol were comparable (56 percent following Suboxone versus 52 percent following Vivitrol). However, more than a quarter of study participants assigned to the Vivitrol condition dropped out of the study (upon failing to complete detoxification) and were unable to take their first dose. In 2018, extended-release buprenorphine (brand name: Sublocade) became available in an injectable formulation, to be administered on a monthly basis by a qualified physician or health care provider. Sublocade is intended to help patients attain a greater number of opioid-free weeks during their recovery period, particularly those who fail to take their daily Suboxone medication on a regular basis.[25]

In general, the medical consensus is that medically assisted treatments are a significant advance in reducing opioid overdose deaths, but unfortunately recent surveys have shown that 85 percent of U.S. counties do not have opioid treatment

buprenorphine (BYOO-preh-NOR-feen): A synthetic (laboratory-based) opioid used in the treatment of heroin abuse. Brand names are Subutex and (in combination with naloxone) Suboxone, and (as a nasal spray) Butrans.

Suboxone (soo-BOX-one, or alternatively SUB-uh-zone): The brand name for the daily sublingual medication containing buprenorphine combined with naloxone, used as a medically assisted treatment for opioid abuse.

Vivitrol (VIV-vuh-trol): The brand name for a monthly injectable medication containing naltrexone, used as a medically assisted treatment in opioid abuse.

programs that provide such options. While Suboxone or Vivitrol are most commonly employed in medically assisted treatments today, it should be noted that Vivitrol requires prior completion of opioid detoxification. Therefore, it is important to describe the detoxification procedure in those instances in which Vivitrol treatments would be employed.

Detoxification

Detoxification ("detox") is a medically supervised procedure of opioid withdrawal in which opioid levels in the bloodstream are gradually reduced over a period of three to seven days, depending on the severity of the opioid abuse. The alternative is the unsupervised process of withdrawal from opioids in an abrupt fashion (commonly referred to as "going cold turkey," a phrase supposedly inspired by the gooseflesh appearance on the skin that appears during opioid withdrawal).

To reduce the distress of detoxification, opioid drugs such as **propoxyphene** (brand name: Darvon), meperidine (brand name: Demerol), and methadone are administered orally to replace the opioids in the bloodstream, with doses decreased until complete detoxification has occurred.

Opioid Maintenance

Prior to the introduction of buprenorphine-based or naltrexone-based medications, the other medically assisted treatment for opioid abuse was the long-term administration of the synthetic opioid, **methadone**.

Since the mid-1960s, one strategy has been to have a detoxified heroin abuser participate have daily oral administrations of methadone, essentially substituted for the injected heroin or other opioids that had been central to patient's pattern of opioid abuse. This treatment approach, called **methadone maintenance**, was initiated in New York City in the 1970s through the joint efforts of Vincent Dole, a specialist in metabolic disorders, and Marie Nyswander, a psychiatrist whose interest had focused on narcotic dependence. Their idea was that if a legally and carefully controlled opioid drug was available to heroin abusers on a regular basis, the craving for heroin would be eliminated, their drug-taking lifestyle

would no longer be needed, and they could turn to more appropriate social behaviors such as steady employment and a more stable family life. The general philosophy behind this approach to heroin-abuse treatment was that heroin abuse was essentially a chronic metabolic disorder requiring a long-term maintenance drug for the body to "normalize" the drug abuser, in the same way as a diabetic patient would need a maintenance supply of insulin.

There are several advantages of the methadone maintenance approach in heroin-abuse treatment. Since it is a legal, inexpensive narcotic drug (when dispensed through authorized drug treatment centers), criminal activity involved in the purchase of heroin on the street can be avoided. Methadone is slower acting and more slowly metabolized, so that, unlike heroin, its effects last approximately 24 hours and it can be easily absorbed through an oral administration. Because it is an opioid drug, methadone binds to the same endorphin-sensitive receptors in the brain as does heroin and prevents feelings of heroin craving. The rush of a heroin high is avoided, thanks to its relatively slow rate of absorption by brain tissue.

Typically, clients in the program come to the treatment center daily for an oral dose of methadone, dispensed in orange juice, and the dose is gradually increased to a maintenance level over a period of four to six weeks. The chances of an abuser turning away from illicit drug use are increased if the higher doses of methadone are made conditional on a "clean" (drug-free) urinalysis.[26]

As a social experiment, methadone maintenance programs have met with a mixture of success and failure. On the one hand, evaluations of this program have found that 71 percent of former heroin abusers who have stayed in methadone maintenance for a year or more have stopped intravenous drug taking, thus reducing the risk of AIDS. In a major study, drug-associated problems declined from about 80 percent to between 17 and 28 percent, criminal behavior dropped from more than 20 percent to less than 10 percent, and there was a slight increase in permanent employment. Although it attracts only a fraction of the heroin-dependent community, methadone maintenance does attract those who perceive themselves as having a negligible chance of becoming abstinent on their own.[27]

Although opioid maintenance programs do help many heroin abusers, particularly those who stay in the program over an extended period of time, there are strong indications that the programs do not reduce the overall vulnerability to drug abuse in general. In other words, methadone blocks the yearning for heroin, but it is less effective in blocking the simple craving to get high. Alcohol abuse among methadone maintenance clients, for example, ranges from 10 to 40 percent, suggesting that alcohol may be substituting for opioids during the course of treatment, and one study found that as many as 43 percent of those who had successfully given up heroin had become dependent on alcohol. Furthermore, methadone is sometimes diverted away from the clinics and onto the streets for illicit use. The availability of street methadone remains a matter of great concern.[28]

detoxification: The process of drug withdrawal in which the body is allowed to rid itself of the chemical effects of the drug in the bloodstream.

propoxyphene (pro-POX-ee-feen): A synthetic (laboratory-based) opioid useful in reducing pain. Brand names are Darvon, Darvocet.

methadone: A synthetic (laboratory-based) opioid, used as an option in medically assisted treatments for opioid abuse. Long-term administration of methadone in opioid-abuse recovery is referred to as methadone maintenance.

methadone maintenance: A treatment program for heroin abusers in which heroin is replaced by the long-term intake of methadone.

The primary concern with methadone maintenance is the need to receive daily doses in designated maintenance locations, which can be logistically inconvenient. To reduce this difficulty to some extent, the opioid **LAAM** (levo-alpha-acetylmethadol), marketed under the brand name Orlaam, is available as an alternative medication for maintenance purposes. LAAM has a substantially longer duration, relative to methadone, so that treatment clients need to receive the drug only three times a week instead of every day.[29]

Behavioral and Social-Community Programs

To help deal with the tremendous social stresses that reinforce a continuation of opioid abuse as well as substance abuse in general, programs called **therapeutic communities** have been developed. Daytop Village, Samaritan Village, and Phoenix House are examples of therapeutic communities. These "mini-communities" are drug-free residential settings based on the idea that stages of treatment and recovery should reflect increased levels of personal and social responsibility on the part of the abuser. Peer influence, mediated through a variety of group processes, is used to help individuals learn

and assimilate social norms and develop more effective social skills. Typically, counselors are former heroin abusers or former abusers of other drugs.[30]

Other approaches in opioid treatment have been developed that combine detoxification, treatment with medications, psychotherapy, and vocational rehabilitation under a single comprehensive plan of action. These programs, called **multimodality programs**, are designed to focus simultaneously on the multitude of needs facing the heroin abuser, the goal being a successful reintegration into society. As a continuing effort to help the recovering heroin

> **LAAM:** The synthetic narcotic drug levo-alpha-acetylmethadol, used in the treatment of heroin abuse. Brand name is Orlaam.
>
> **therapeutic communities:** Living environments for individuals in treatment for heroin and other drug abuse, where they learn social and psychological skills needed to lead a drug-free life.
>
> **multimodality programs:** Treatment programs in which a combination of detoxification, naltrexone treatment, psychotherapy, and group support is implemented.

Drugs . . . in Focus

Buprenorphine: The Bright/Dark Side of Heroin-Abuse Treatment

When buprenorphine (brand name: Subutex) and buprenorphine combined with naloxone (brand name: Suboxone) received FDA approval in 2002, public health officials hailed it as the beginning of a new era in opioid-abuse treatment. Because buprenorphine is only a partial activator of opioid-sensitive receptors in the brain, as opposed to full activators such as heroin and methadone, clients in treatment were more likely to discontinue their heroin intake without experiencing withdrawal symptoms, and the symptoms that do occur were considerably milder. At the same time, the sustained-release formulation avoided the typical heroin effects of rapid euphoria and respiratory depression because of a slower time of release. There was also no evidence of significant impairment of cognitive or motor performance in the course of long-term buprenorphine maintenance.

In recent years, significant developments have increased the convenience of buprenorphine administration as a method of treatment, particularly as a daily administered sublingual tablet or strip (Subutex or Suboxone). The dark side of the buprenorphine story, however, has to do with an unfortunately inevitable diversion of these medications from therapeutic use to

recreational abuse purposes. It has become not only a medicine for pain but also, when crushed or dissolved, a street and prison drug. Unscrupulous physicians with prescription privileges have caused an oversupply of prescriptions that make their way into a growing black market. More than 10 percent of physicians authorized to prescribe buprenorphine have been sanctioned for offenses including excessive prescribing, insurance fraud, sexual misconduct, and practicing medicine while impaired (presumably as opioid abusers themselves). The "dissolvable filmstrip" formulation has made it easy to smuggle into prisons. Some have called it "prison heroin."

Sources: Information of buprenorphine, accessed from: *http://www.businesswire.com/news/home/20130225005607/en/Amneal-Pharmaceuticals-Receives-FDA-Approval-Generic-Suboxone%C2%AE*. Martin, K. R. (2004, September). Once-a-month medication for heroin addiction? *NIDA Notes*, p. 9. Mitka, M. (2003). Office-based primary care physicians called on to treat the "new" addict. *Journal of the American Medical Association, 290*, 735–738. Opioid detox study shows buprenorphine improves retention rate for teens (2005, October 10). *Alcoholism and Drug Abuse Weekly*, pp. 1–2. Sontag, D. (2013, November 16). Addiction treatment with a dark side. *The New York Times*, pp. A1, A20–22.

abuser over time, there are also 12-step group support programs such as Narcotics Anonymous, modeled after similar programs for those recovering from alcohol or cocaine dependence.

While a range of treatment options are available, it is important to point out that recovery from opioid dependence will be a life long endeavor. A heroin abuser successfully completing a treatment program remains a *recovering* opioid abuser, not a recovered opioid abuser. Many treatment strategies incorporate the concept of an individual continuing to be "in recovery" in cases of substance abuse in general (see Chapter 14). It is also important to recognize the devastation experienced by the families and associates of abusers over the years. The need for long-term "reconstructive surgery" with regard to a range of dysfunctional social relationships presents a continuing challenge.

Medical Uses of Opioid Drugs

While the focus in this chapter has been on opioid drugs in the context of opioid abuse, it important to look at the beneficial effects as well as the adverse side effects that these drugs can have in a medical setting (Table 9.3).

Beneficial Effects

Excluding heroin, which is a Schedule I controlled substance in the United States and therefore unavailable for medical use, opioid drugs are useful as prescription medications (Schedule II controlled substances) for three primary therapeutic purposes: the relief of pain, the treatment of acute diarrhea, and the suppression of coughing.

TABLE 9.3

Recommended dosage for adults for major opioid pain medications

GENERIC NAME	BRAND NAME*	RECOMMENDED DOSE FOR ADULTS	GENERIC NAME	BRAND NAME*	RECOMMENDED DOSE FOR ADULTS
Morphine	Avinza	30–120 mg (oral, combined immediate release, and extended release)	Hydrocodone	Hycodan	5 mg (oral)
	Duramorph	5–10 mg (i.v.)		Vicodin	5–10 mg (oral) with 300 mg acetaminophen
	Kadian	10–200 mg (oral, extended release)		Lortab	5–10 mg (oral) with 300–500 mg acetaminophen
	MS Contin	15–200 mg (oral, controlled release)		Zohydro ER	10–50 mg (oral, extended release)
	Oramorph SR	15–100 mg (oral, sustained release)		Hysingla ER	60–120 mg (oral, extended release, once daily)
	Embeda	20–100 mg morphine/ 0.8–4 mg with naltrexone (oral, sustained release)	Methadone	Dolophine	5–10 mg (oral, i.v., or s.c.)
			Meperidine	Demerol	50–100 mg (oral, i.m., i.v.)
			Propoxyphene	Darvocet-N	50 mg (oral) with acetaminophen
Codeine		30–60 mg (oral, i.m., or s.c.)		Darvon	65 mg (oral)
Hydromorphone	Dilaudid	1–8 mg (oral, i.m., i.v., or s.c.)	Fentanyl	Duragesic	12.5–100 mcg/hour (transdermal patch)
Oxymorphone	Numorphone	Suppository, injectable		Sublimaze	50 mcg/ml (IV or IM injection)
	Opana IR	5–10 mg (immediate release)		Lazanda	100–800 per nostril (nasal spray)
	Opana ER*	5–40 mg (extended release)		Actiq	200 mcg (oral transmucosal lozenge)
Oxycodone	OxyContin	10–80 mg (oral, extended release)	Tramadol	Ultracet	37.5 mg (oral) with acetaminophen
	Percocet	2.5–10 mg (oral) with acetaminophen			
	Percodan	4.5 mg (oral) with aspirin		Ultram ER	100–300 mg (oral, extended release)
	Targiniq ER	10–40 mg (oral, extended release) with 5–20 mg naloxone			

*Some opioid drugs are available only under their generic names. In 2017, Opana ER was removed from the market.

Note: i.v. = intravenous; i.m. = intramuscular; s.c. = subcutaneous.

Source: Based on information from *Physicians' desk reference* (71st ed.) (2017). Montvale, NJ: PDR Network.

- The first and foremost medical use of opioids today is for the treatment of pain. For a patient suffering severe pain following surgical procedures or from burns, the traditional drug of choice has been morphine. Recently, synthetic opioids are used.

- The second application capitalizes on the effect of opioids in slowing down peristaltic contractions in the intestines that occur as part of the digestive process. As noted earlier, one problem associated with the chronic abuse of heroin, as well as of other opioids, is constipation. However, for individuals with dysentery, a bacterial infection of the lower intestinal tract causing pain and severe diarrhea, this negative side effect becomes desirable. Therefore, the control of diarrhea by an opioid is literally lifesaving, since acute dehydration (loss of water from the body) can be fatal. Fortunately, the opioid medication loperamide (brand name: Imodium), which is available on an over-the-counter basis, effectively controls diarrhea symptoms by its action on the gastrointestinal system. Because it cannot cross the blood–brain barrier, loperamide does not produce any psychoactive effects.

- The third application focuses on the capacity of these drugs to suppress the cough reflex center in the medulla. In cases in which an **antitussive** (cough-suppressing) drug is necessary, codeine is frequently prescribed, either by itself or combined with other medications such as aspirin or acetaminophen (brand name: Tylenol, among others). As an alternative treatment for coughing, **dextromethorphan** is available in over-the-counter syrups and lozenges, as well as in combination with antihistamines. Unfortunately, the abuse of dextromethorphan among young people, who are consuming it on a recreational basis, has become a relatively new cause for concern and one of the continuing challenges of present-day substance abuse.

Prescription Opioid Medication Side Effects

Despite the overall beneficial effects of prescription opioid medications, there are serious adverse side effects. For example, respiration will be depressed for four to five hours following even a therapeutic dose of morphine, so caution is advised when the patient suffers from asthma, emphysema, or pulmonary heart disease. In addition, opioid medications decrease the secretion of hydrochloric acid in the stomach and reduce the pushing of food through the intestines, a condition that can lead to intestinal spasms. Finally, although opioids have a sleep-inducing effect in high doses, it is not recommended that they be used as a general sedative–hypnotic treatment, unless sleep is being prevented by pain or coughing.[31]

Prescription Opioid Medication Abuse

The *nonmedical* use of prescription opioid medications (in other words, the recreational use of opioid medications) has been acknowledged as a national epidemic for several years. In 2015, approximately 92 million noninstitutionalized adults in the United States (more than one-third of the population) had used prescription opioids, 11 million had misused them, and 1.9 million had a substance use disorder with regard to prescription opioids. Misuse and use disorders were most commonly reported in adults who were uninsured, were unemployed, had low income, or had behavioral health problems. In terms of public health, approximately one-half of all opioid-related overdose deaths involved a prescription opioid.[32]

Clearly, opioids are needed by millions of people who seek legitimate relief from pain. Yet, the abuse of opioids present significant personal and social problems for millions of others. This situation poses a unique challenge for law enforcement authorities and public health officials.

Patterns of OxyContin Abuse

The principal medications of concern are well known: oxycodone with acetaminophen (brand name: **Percocet**), the continuous-release form of oxycodone (brand name: **OxyContin**), hydrocodone, and hydrocodone with acetaminophen (brand name: **Vicodin**). Prior to 2013, all opioid medications were Schedule II controlled substances, with sole exception of Vicodin, which was classified as a Schedule III controlled substance. In 2013, the FDA recommended a reclassification of Vicodin from a Schedule III to a Schedule II controlled substance, a move that had been recommended by the DEA for several years. Substance abuse is common with respect to all the prescription opioid medications, but the focus here will be on patterns of OxyContin abuse, since it has received in recent years the most public attention and concern.

Introduced in 1995, OxyContin was promoted initially as being relatively safe from potential abuse and more acceptable to the general public because it lacked the social stigma associated with morphine. In its original FDA-approved continuous-release formulation, OxyContin would be taken orally and absorbed slowly over a period of 12 hours, killing pain without inducing a sudden feeling of euphoria. For several years, however, OxyContin tablets could be easily crushed and then either inhaled as a powder or injected after

antitussive: Having an effect that controls coughing.

dextromethorphan (DEX-troh-meh-THOR-fan): A popular ingredient used in over-the-counter cough remedies. The "DM" designation on these preparations refers to dextromethorphan.

Percocet: Brand name for oxycodone combined with acetaminophen, used in pain treatment.

OxyContin: Brand name for a continuous-release form of oxycodone, used in the treatment of chronic pain.

Vicodin: Brand name for hydrocodone combined with acetaminophen, used in pain treatment.

diluting the powder into a solution, producing a pharmacological effect similar to that of heroin. Even without altering the tablets in any way, some patients suffered severe withdrawal symptoms, similar to those experienced during heroin withdrawal, when they abruptly stopped taking high-dosage levels of the OxyContin.

In 2010, under intense pressure from public health authorities, Purdue Pharma, manufacturer of OxyContin, introduced a new formulation containing an added chemical called Remoxy that changed the tablet into a gummy, less easily abusable substance when crushed or dissolved. Unfortunately, some abusers have turned to microwaving the new formulation and sniffing the burned remains, a far more inconvenient but nonetheless viable option. For a time, others turned to the extended-release form of another opioid medication, oxymorphone (brand name: Opana ER), which could be crushed and dissolved like the original form of OxyContin. In 2012, a new formulation of Opana ER was launched with a modification similar to that implemented with OxyContin, though it has become apparent that even the new formulation is not immune to abuse. In 2017, the FDA requested that Endo Pharmaceuticals remove Opana ER from the market. In its news release, the FDA stated that "After careful consideration, the agency is seeking removal based on its concern that the benefits of the drug may no longer outweight its risks." It was the first time the FDA had called for a removal of a licit opioid medication for this reason.[33]

The demographic features of OxyContin abusers, unlike that of heroin abusers, cut across age, socioeconomic status, geographic location, and gender. Communities, however, that are particularly hard-hit by this form of substance abuse are in nonurban areas (Portrait) where treatment facilities are often less readily available, pharmacy security is less rigorous, and there are fewer safeguards against illegitimate access to prescription opioid medications in general.[34]

Prescription Opioid Medication Abuse and Drug Diversion

Two primary sources of drug diversion, defined as the means by which prescription medications become available for nonmedical use, have been identified (Figure 9.4). The first source includes patients who visit multiple doctors ("doctor-shoppers") and obtain multiple prescriptions by convincing doctors that there is a genuine reason for opioid treatment. Other individuals visit legal storefront stress and pain clinics (often called "pill mills") where they speak with a physician, are typically required to take a psychological test, and undergo a perfunctory physical examination, after which they leave with a prescription for a controlled substance regardless of their medical condition. Since no controlled substances are stored on the premises, no DEA license is required for these clinics to operate. Frequently, however, these clinics are raided in a "buy-bust" law enforcement operation (see Chapter 6) although it is difficult to close them down permanently. Some individuals using medications for nonmedical purposes are not patients at all, but instead the medications are obtained directly from a friend or relative.

The second source is the health-care provider, typically a private-practice physician (sometimes unlicensed) or pharmacist who has issued or dispensed prescription medications in a fraudulent manner. The DEA Drug Diversion Task Force and local law enforcement agencies are continually engaged in the prosecution of physicians and pharmacists who have abused their prescription privileges.

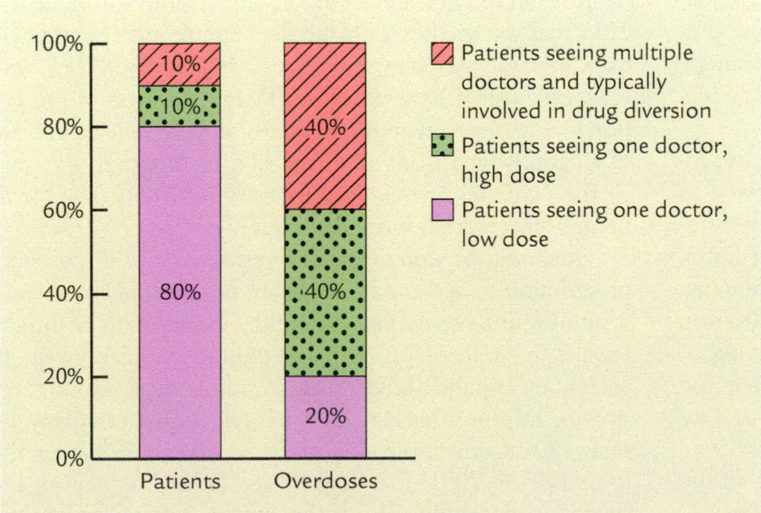

In some cases, the consequences have been deadly. In New York, for example, a 230-count indictment was issued in 2018 to a physician with a history of reckless overprescribing in opioid drugs as well as other drugs. The indictment included two charges of manslaughter, nine counts of reckless endangerment, and more than 200 counts of criminal sale of a prescription for a controlled substance. The manslaughter charges involved two men who had died from an opioid overdose in 2013 and 2014, respectively. A third overdose death in 2016 was the basis for one of the charges of reckless endangerment. Large numbers of opioid prescriptions had been issued, with some patients turning around and selling the pills as part of their own drug-trafficking operations.

In another case, reported by the DEA Drug Diversion Task Force, a physician in Tennessee received a 23-year prison sentence after being convicted of improperly writing prescriptions for opioid medications as well as other controlled substances without sufficient medical necessity. He had charged patients $80 to $100 in cash for each visit, without performing a physical examination, even after receiving information that patients were abusing their drugs or selling

FIGURE 9.4

Percentage of risk circumstances in overdose cases among pain patients and overdose cases.

Source: Based on Manchikanti, L.; Standiford, H. II; Fellows, B.; Janata, J. W.; Pampati, V.; et al. (2012). Opioid epidemic in the United States. *Pain Physician,* 15, p. ES30.

PORTRAIT

Billy Thomas and Ricky Franklin— The Two Sides of OxyContin

Billy Thomas' pain had become so excruciating that he was on the verge of suicide. A former salesman of plumbing supplies in North Plainfield, New Jersey, Thomas had endured pulsating back pain for six years. Seven surgeries, endless doctor's appointments, thousands of pills, acupuncture, and other alternative treatments had all proved unsuccessful. When Thomas began taking OxyContin, however, a relatively normal lifestyle returned. His perceived pain level (on a scale of 1 to 10, with 10 being the most horrible pain imaginable) was an acceptable 2 or 3—a dramatic improvement from his continual ratings of 8 or 9 before the advent of OxyContin. The drug had literally saved his life.

For every Billy Thomas, however, there has been a Ricky Franklin. Prescribed OxyContin following hip-replacement surgery, Franklin found that the drug was difficult to give up even after his recovery was complete. In 1999, this resident of rural Maine was convicted of selling guns to finance the purchase of a steady supply of OxyContin. In May 2001, while on parole for the firearms theft conviction, Franklin was

charged with walking into a Rite Aid pharmacy with a gun and pushing a note across the counter that read: "Give me all your OxyContin or I will shoot you." The gun turned out to be an unloaded BB gun. Franklin was sentenced in federal court in 2002 to 46 months in prison and 3 years of supervised release.

Franklin has not been alone in his descent into criminal activity as a result of compulsive OxyContin abuse. Arrests have been made in all parts of the United States (the drug has been called the "rural heroin") for crimes ranging from simple theft to murder and drug trafficking, all related to the illicit abuse of this drug. At the same time, demands to remove OxyContin from the market until a completely full-proof abuse-reducing formulation is developed would return people like Billy Thomas and millions of other Americans to a life of abject misery. The problem is that it is difficult to predict which path a patient will follow. As a neurologist and pain management specialist has expressed it, "A practicing physician has to be mindful that someone, even if they don't come with 'addict'

written all over them, may be one ... The physician has to establish a relationship with the patient they're taking care of on a long-term basis." It is unclear whether it will ever be possible to have completely positive outcomes from the development of pain medication, without the negative consequences of substance abuse.

Note: The names of the two men in this Portrait have been changed.

Sources: Adler, J. (2003, October 20). In the grip of a deeper pain. *Newsweek*, pp. 48–49. Garland, N. (2002, May 16). Teleconference used to sentence OxyContin thief. *Bangor Daily News*, p. B1. Martin, J. C. (2018, May 16). Opioid epidemic: Six states sue manufacturer of OxyContin pain pills. *USA Today Network.* Meier, B. (2003). *Pain killer: A "wonder" drug's trail of addiction and death.* New York: Rodale Press. Meier, B. (2007, May 11). Narcotic maker guilty of deceit over marketing. *The New York Times*, pp. A1, C4. Sontag, D. (2013, November 16). Addiction treatment with a dark side. *The New York Times*, p. A1. Susman, T. (2001, July 29). Good drug, bad drug: OxyContin eases pain, lures addicts. *Newsday*, pp. A6, A36. Quotations on p. A36.

them to others. Agreements had been made with patients that they would bring all or part of the drugs back to him, presumably for his personal use. He was also found guilty of willingly failing to file income tax forms for multiple years when he had a gross income exceeding $1 million.

A third case, described at the opening of Chapter 4, involved a 78-year-old physician in Alabama who received in 2018 a much lighter sentence (probation and a hefty fine) following a conviction of drug distribution, health-care fraud, and money laundering. Multiple prescriptions for fentanyl patches had been written without any medical justification. The physician was also engaging in money laundering of funds gained from illegal drug distribution. Fortunately, no deaths had resulted from his actions, and due to his age, an extended prison sentence was waived.[35]

While drug diversion continues to be challenging for the enforcement of drug laws, better communication and coordinated record-keeping systems have helped to reduce the problem, particularly with respect to opioid prescription abuse. A system of statewide prescription drug monitoring programs (PDMPs) in which electronic databases track controlled substance prescriptions has shown great promise. Implementation of a system of this kind in Florida, for example, resulted in a

decrease in the number of opioid prescriptions from 2010 to 2015 that was greater than the decrease reported nationwide over the same period of time. As of 2018, nearly all U.S. states have established statewide PDMPs for providers of prescription medications. In addition, nearly all U.S. states participate in a nationwide PDMP and data-sharing program, sponsored by the National Association of Boards of Pharmacy, for dispensers of prescription medications.

It should be noted that the providers and dispensers of prescription opioid medications are not the only ones under scrutiny as intense national attention continues to be directed toward the role of prescription opioid medications in the present-day opioid-abuse crisis. In 2007, three senior executives of Purdue Pharma, the pharmaceutical company that makes OxyContin, pleaded guilty to criminal charges that, from 1995 to 2001, they had misled federal regulators, physicians, and patients about the potential for OxyContin to be an abused drug. The company agreed to $600 million in fines and other payments; the executives themselves were convicted on misdemeanor charges and fined $34 million for their wrongdoing. In 2018, Attorney Generals of six U.S. states filed lawsuits against Purdue Pharma for misleading marketing tactics with regard to OxyContin.[36]

Abuse of Other Opioid Pain Medications

Vicodin and Percocet are based on opioids (hydrocodone and oxycodone, respectively) that have been available for a longer period of time than OxyContin and unfortunately have a longer record of abuse and dependence. An additional problem with these medications has been the addition of acetaminophen (up to 1,000 mg in the case of one form of Percocet).

This combination is particularly dangerous because excessive dosages of acetaminophen increase the risk of liver toxicity and death. In order to reduce the incidence of adverse effects, the FDA ordered in 2011 a limit of 325 milligram of acetaminophen when combined with a prescription pain medication. Two opioid medications, Zohydro ER and Hysingla ER, now contain no acetaminophen (see Table 9.3).[37]

Drug Enforcement . . . in Focus

National Prescription Drug Take-Back Day and Rogue Pharmacies

In 2010, the DEA initiated National Prescription Drug Take-Back Day in an effort to provide a more environmentally responsible and secure way to dispose of expired or unwanted medications that are highly susceptible to diversion, misuse, and abuse. At that time, individuals across the country turned in over 121 tons of medications at more than 4,000 take-back locations. In 2017, eight years later, Take-Back Day yielded a record-setting total of 456 tons of medications collected at more than 5,000 U.S. locations.

On another front, the three most-used Internet search engines in the United States adopted policies in 2010 prohibiting Internet pharmacies from advertising on the sidebars of search result pages unless they have been identified as Verified Internet Pharmacy Practice Sites by the National Association of Boards of Pharmacy and operate in compliance with U.S. pharmacy laws and practice standards. These policies are intended to reduce the number of "rogue pharmacies" that operate as unlicensed Web-based operations, often from locations in foreign countries that do not require valid prescriptions to dispense medications.

Sources: Drug Enforcement Administration (2017, November 7). Press Release: Drug Enforcement Administration collects record number of unused pills as part of its 14th Prescription Drug Take Back Day. Washington, D.C.: Diversion Control Division, Drug Enforcement Administration, U.S. Department of Justice.

Summary

Opium in History

- Opium has been used for medicinal and recreational purposes for approximately 5,000 years.
- During the nineteenth century, opium figured in global politics as the instigating factor for the Opium War fought between China and Britain. At the time, opium use was widespread in Britain and the United States at all levels of society.

Morphine and the Advent of Heroin

- The discovery of morphine in 1803 as the principal active ingredient in opium revolutionized medical treatment of pain and chronic diseases.
- At the end of the nineteenth century, heroin was introduced by the Bayer Company in Germany. Initially, it was believed that heroin lacked the dependence-producing properties of morphine.

Opioids in American Society

- The abuse potential of morphine and especially of heroin was not fully realized until the beginning of the twentieth century. Social and political developments in the United States after the passage of the Harrison Narcotics Tax Act (typically shortened to the Harrison Act) in 1914 drove heroin underground, where it soon acquired a growing association with a criminal lifestyle.
- Heroin abuse became associated with African American and other minority communities in urban ghettos after World War II, Later, the countercultural revolution and the military involvement in Vietnam during the 1960s and 1970s brought the issue of heroin abuse to a wider population in America.
- The scope of the present-day opioid crisis is staggering, as is the unfortunate prospect that it is unlikely to end anytime soon. In 2017, about 49,000 opioid overdose deaths were reported in the United States, amounting to approximately 134 people dying each day. Opioids accounted for about two-thirds of the 72,000 overdose deaths occurring from all forms of drugs. The introduction of illicit fentanyl and fentanyl analogs has been an unmistakably significant factor in the rise in opioid overdose deaths and drug overdose deaths in general.

Effects on the Mind and the Body

- The effects of opioids such as heroin include euphoria, analgesia, gastrointestinal slowing, and respiratory depression.
- Respiratory depression is the major risk factor associated with heroin intake.

How Opioids Work in the Brain

- Since the 1970s, we have known that the effects of morphine and related opioid drugs are the result of the activation of opioid-sensitive receptors in the brain.
- Three families of chemical substances produced by the brain bind to these receptors. These chemicals are collectively known as endorphins.

Patterns of Heroin Abuse

- Chronic heroin abuse is subject to tolerance effects over time. Withdrawal effects include intense craving for heroin and physical symptoms such as diarrhea and dehydration.
- One of the major problems surrounding heroin abuse is the unpredictable content of a heroin dose.

Treatment for Heroin Abuse

- Treatment for heroin abuse includes short-term detoxification and long-term interventions that address the continuing craving for the drug and physical dependence factors in the body. Medically assisted treatments currently available are based on buprenorphine (Subutex, Suboxone, Sublocade) and naltrexone (Vivitrol).
- Methadone maintenance programs focus primarily on the physiological needs of the heroin abuser, whereas therapeutic communities and support groups focus on his or her long-term reintegration into society.

Prescription Opioid Medication Use and Misuse

- In medical settings, opioid drugs have been extremely helpful in the treatment of pain, the treatment of dysentery, and the suppression of coughing.
- Side effects of opioid medications include respiratory depression, intestinal spasms, and sedation.

Prescription Opioid Medication Abuse

- There has been great concern since the late 1990s that opioid pain medications have been diverted to nonmedical purposes and are subject to abuse. Three medications of this type are OxyContin, Vicodin, and Percocet. There are numerous instances of pharmacy robberies, with the intent of securing supplies of opioid pain medication, particularly OxyContin. A continuing challenge for law enforcement has been the monitoring and prosecution of instances of prescription medication diversion, particularly with regard to opioid medications, through fraudulent actions of prescription-issuing health-care providers.

Key Terms

antitussive, p. 188
black tar, p. 175
buprenorphine, p. 184
carfentanil, p. 177
codeine, p. 173
detoxification, p. 185
dextromethorphan, p. 188

endogenous opioid peptides, p. 180
fentanyl, p. 175
heroin, p. 173
LAAM, p. 186
methadone, p. 185
methadone maintenance, p. 185
morphine, p. 173

multimodality programs, p. 186
naloxone, p. 180
naltrexone, p. 181
narcotics, p. 170
opioids, p. 169
opium, p. 170
OxyContin, p. 188

Percocet, p. 188
propoxyphene, p. 185
Suboxone, p. 184
thebaine, p. 173
therapeutic communities, p. 186
Vicodin, p. 188
Vivitrol, p. 184

Review Questions

1. Summarize the four categories of opioid drugs and give two examples in each category.
2. How did the development of morphine injections change the pattern of opioid use from a previous era of opioid ingestion through the drinking of laudanum?
3. Discuss the changes in heroin use and abuse following the Harrison Narcotics Act of 1914.
4. Discuss three significant events in the 1960s and 1970s that changed society's view of heroin abuse.
5. Discuss the basis for opioid effects in terms of brain chemistry.
6. Contrast the treatment strategies and goals of methadone maintenance and therapeutic communities.
7. How does present-day prescription opioid medication abuse take place? What is the role of drug diversion?

Critical Thinking: What Would You Do?

You are an internal medicine physician in private practice. A 50-year-old woman visits your office as a new patient. She appears extremely distraught, complaining of chronic debilitating pain. An examination of her reveals no specific physical basis for the pain. Do you prescribe an opioid medication to her? If so, what precautions do you take to reduce the likelihood of encouraging or creating a pattern of opioid medication abuse in the future? If not, are you fulfilling your professional obligations as a health-care provider?

1. Adapted from the *NPR Now* report, *90 Percocets and how easy it is to overprescribe opioids* (2017, November 17). *https://www.npr. org/.../questioning-a-doctors-prescription-for-a-sore-knee-90-percocets*.

2. Courtwright, D. T. (2001). *Forces of habit: Drugs and the making of the modern world*. Cambridge, MA: Harvard University Press, pp. 31–39. Levinthal, C. F. (1988). *Messengers of paradise: Opiates and the brain*. New York: Anchor Press/ Doubleday, p. 4.

3. Levinthal, *Messengers of Paradise*, pp. 3–25.

4. Fay, P. W. (1975). *The opium war 1840–1842*. Chapel Hill, NC: University of North Carolina Press, p. 11. Hanes, W. T. III; and Sanello, F. (2002). *The opium wars*. Napierville, IL: Sourcebooks.

5. Brecher, E. M.; and the editors of *Consumer Reports* (1972). *Licit and illicit drugs*. Boston: Little, Brown, p. 17.

6. Levinthal, *Messengers of Paradise*, pp. 16–17.

7. Brecher, *Licit and illicit drugs*, pp.42–43.

8 Courtwright, D. T. (2003). *Dark paradise: A history of opiate addiction in America*. Cambridge, MA: Harvard University Press, p. 47.

9. Smith, R. (1966). Status politics and the image of the addict. *Issues in Criminology*, 2(2), 157–175.

10. Zackon, F. (1986). *Heroin: The street narcotic*. New York: Chelsea House Publishers, p. 44.

11. Bentel, D. J.; Crim, D.; and Smith, D. E. (1972). Drug abuse in combat: The crisis of drugs and addiction among American troops in Vietnam. In D. E. Smith; and G. R. Gay (Eds.), *It's so good, don't even try it once: Heroin in perspective*. Englewood Cliffs, NJ: Prentice-Hall.

12. McCoy, A. W.; with Read, C. B.; and Adams, L. P. (1972). *The politics of heroin in Southeast Asia*. New York: Harper & Row, pp. 220–221.

13. Centers for Disease Control and Prevention (2017, July). Opioid prescribing: Where you live matters. *Vital Signs*. Atlanta, GA: Centers for Disease Control and Prevention, U.S. Department of Health and Human Services. Goodnough, A (2017, July 7). Report finds a decline in opioid prescriptions after a 2010 peak. *The New York Times*, p. A13.

14. Centers for Disease Control and Prevention (2016). *Guidelines for prescribing opioids for chronic pain*. Atlanta, GA: Centers for Disease Control and Prevention, U.S. Department of Health and Human Services. Kolodny, A. (2017, October 5). The opioid epidemic in 6 charts. *The Conversation*. *https:// www.cbsnews.com/news/opioid-epidemic-in-6-charts/*. Qaseem, A.; Wilt, T. J.; McLean, R. M.; Forciea, M. A., for the Clinical Guidelines Committee of the American College of Physicians (2017). Noninvasive treatments for acute, subacute, and chronic low back pain: A clinical practice guideline from the American College of Physicians. *Annals of Internal Medicine*, 166, 514–530.

15. Centers for Disease Control and Prevention (2017, October 27). Media Statement: Fentanyl involved in over half of opioid overdose deaths in 10 states. Atlanta, GA: Centers for Disease Control and Prevention. Courtesy of the Just Believe Recovery Center, Carbondale, PA. Public Warning: Deadly drug Carfentanil (Elephant Tranquilizer) on streets sold as heroin. https://justbelieverecoverypa.com/carfentanil-elephant-tran-quilizer.Katz, J. (2017, June 5). Katz, J. (2017, June 5). U.S.

drug deaths climbing faster than ever. *The New York Times*, pp. A1, A12. Schmidt, S. (2018, August 18). "It is taking people out": More than 70 people overdose on K2 in a single day in New Haven. *The Washington Post*. Accessed from: https:// www.washingtonpost.com/news/morning-mix/wp/2018/08/16/ it-is-taking-people-out-more-than-70-people-overdose-on-k2-in-a-single-day-in-new-haven/?utm_term=.f261af4d4c19

16. Drug Enforcement Administration (2017, November 9). News Release: Department of Justice announces significant tool in prosecuting opioid traffickers in emergency scheduling of all fentanyls. Washington, D.C.: Drug Enforcement Administration, U.S. Department of Justice. Drug Enforcement Administration (2016, December 16). DEA releases 2016 Drug Threat Assessment: Fentanyl-related overdose deaths rising at an alarming rate. Washington, D.C.: Drug Enforcement Administration, U.S. Department of Justice. Drug Enforcement Administration (2017). Carfentanil: A dangerous new factor in the U.S. opioid crisis. Officer Safety Alert. Washington, D.C.: Drug Enforcement Administration, U.S. Department of Justice. Drug Enforcement Administration (2017, March). NFLIS Brief: Fentanyl, 2001–2015. Washington, D.C.: Drug Enforcement Administration, U.S. Department of Justice. Quotation of Dr. Lakshmi Sammarco, Hamilton County coroner in Cincinnati, Ohio.

17. Daniulaityte, R.; Juliascik, M. P.; Strayer, K. E.; et al. (2017, September 1). Overdose deaths related to fentanyl and its analogs—Ohio, January–February 2017. *Morbidity and Mortality Weekly Report*, 66, 904–908. Katz, U.S drug deaths. O'Brien, E. (2017, November 27). Here's what it would cost to fix the opioid crisis, according to 5 experts. *http/time.com/ money/503244/cost-fix-opioid-crisis/*.

18. Winger, G.; Hofmann, F. G.; and Woods, J. H. (1992). *A handbook on drug and alcohol abuse: The biomedical aspects*. New York: Oxford University Press, pp. 44–46.

19. McHugh, P. F.; and Kreek, M. J. (2008). The medical consequences of opiate abuse and addiction and methadone pharmacotherapy. In J. Brick (Ed.), *Handbook of the medical consequences of alcohol and drug abuse* (2nd ed.). New York: Routledge, pp. 303–339. Winger; Hofmann; and Woods, *Handbook on drug and alcohol abuse*, pp. 46–50.

20. Advokat, C. D.; Comaty, J. E.; and Julien, R. M. (2015). *A primer of drug action* (13th ed.). New York: Worth. Yaksh, T. L.; and Wallace, M. S. (2012). Opioids, analgesia, and pain management. In L. L. Brunton; B. A. Chabner; and B. C. Knollman (Eds.), *Goodman and Gilman's the pharmacological basis of therapeutics* (12th ed.). New York: Macmillan, pp. 481–525.

21. Levinthal, *Messengers of paradise*. Mathias, R. (2003, March). New approaches seek to expand naltrexone use in heroin treatment. *NIDA Notes*, 17(6), 8. Teagle, S. (2007, April). Depot naltrexone appears safe and effective for heroin addiction. *NIDA Notes*, p. 7.

22. Goode, E. (1999). *Drugs in American society* (5th ed.). New York: McGraw-Hill, p. 328. McHugh; and Kreek, *Medical consequences*, pp. 326–327.

23. Buxton, J. A.; Sebastian, R.; Clearsky, L.; Angus, N.; Shah, L.; et al. (2011). Chasing the dragon—characterizing cases

of leukoencephalopathy associated with heroin inhalation in British Columbia. *Harm Reduction Journal, 8*, 3.

24. McHugh and Kreek, *Medical consequences*.

25. FDA approves SUBLOCADE™ (Buprenorphine Extended-Release), the first and only once-monthly injectable buprenorphine formulation to treat moderate to severe opioid use disorder. *PR Newswire*, 30 November 2017. *http://www.prnewswire.com.* Goodnough, A.; and Zernicke, K. (2017, November 15). Two opioid treatments have similar outcomes. *The New York Times*, p. A16.

26. Stitzer, M. L.; Bickel, W. K.; Bigelow, G. E.; and Liebson, I. A. (1986). Effect of methadone dose contingencies on urinalysis test results of polydrug-abusing methadone-maintenance patients. *Drug and Alcohol Dependence, 18*, 341–348.

27. Maddux, J. F.; and Desmond, D. P. (1997). Outcomes of methadone maintenance 1 year after admission. *Journal of Drug Issues, 27*, 225–238. Sees, K. L.; Delucchi, K. L.; Masson, C.; Rosen, A.; Clark, H. W.; et al. (2000). Methadone maintenance vs. 180-day psychosocially enriched detoxification for treatment of opioid dependence. *Journal of the American Medical Association, 283*, 1303–1310.

28. Wasserman, D. A.; Korcha, R.; Havassy, B. E.; and Hall, S. M. (1999). Detection of illicit opioid and cocaine use in methadone maintenance treatment. *American Journal of Drug and Alcohol Abuse, 25*, 561–571.

29. Eissenberg, T.; Bigelow, G. F.; Strain, E. C.; Walsh, S. L.; Brooner, R. K.; et al. (1997). Dose-related efficacy of levomethadyl acetate for treatment of opioid dependence: A randomized clinical trial. *Journal of the American Medical Association, 277*, 1945–1951.

30. Martin, S. S.; O'Connell, D. J.; Paternoster, R.; and Bachman, R. D. (2011). The long and winding road to desistance from crime for drug-involved offenders: The long-term influence of TC treatment on re-arrest. *Journal of Drug Issues, 11*, 179–196. National Institute on Drug Abuse (2002). Therapeutic community. *National Institute on Drug Abuse Research Report*. Rockville, MD: National Institute on Drug Abuse.

31. Advokat, Comaty, and Julien, *A primer of drug action* (13th ed.). Julien, R. M. (2005). *A primer of drug action* (10th ed.). New York: Worth.

32. Guy, G.; Zhang, K.; Bohm, M.; Losby, J.; Lewis, B.; et al (2017, July 7). Vital Signs: Changes I opioid prescribing in the United States, 2006–2015. *Mortality and Morbidity Weekly Report, 66*, 697–704. Han, B.; Compton, W. M.; Blanco, C.; Crane, E.; Lee, J.; and Jones, C. M. (2017). Prescription opioid use, misuse, and use disorders in U.S. adults: 2015 National Survey on Drug Use and Health. *Annals of Internal Medicine, 167*, 292–301.

33. Quotation in FDA requests removal of Opana ER for risks related to abuse. *FDA News Release* (2017, June 8). Washington, D.C.: U.S. Food and Drug Administration. FDA approves new formulation of OxyContin (2010, April 5). News release from the U.S. Food and Drug Administration, Washington, D.C. Goodnough, A.; and Zezima, K. (2011, June 16). Drug is harder to abuse, but users persevere. *The New York Times*, p. A21. RPT-painkiller Opana, new scourge of rural America (2012, March 12). Reuters News Service.

34. Meier, B. (2012, April 9). Tightening the lid on pain prescriptions. *The New York Times*, pp. A1, A12. Rosenberg, D. (2001, April 9). How one town got hooked. *Newsweek*, pp. 49–50. Tavernise, S. (2011, April 20). Ohio county losing its young to painkillers' grip. *The New York Times*, pp. A1, A16.

35. DeStefano, A. M. (2018, June 8). Doc faces charges over opioids, deaths. *Newsday*, p. A12. Drug Enforcement Administration, New Orleans Division News, published December 11, 2017. Accessed from: https://www.dea.gov/divisions/no/2017/no121117.shtml. Drug Diversion Task Force, Drug Enforcement Administration, U.S. Department of Justice. Accessed from: http://www.justice.gov;usao/tne/drug_diversion.html.

36. Centers for Disease Control and Prevention (2017, October 3). What states need to know about PDMPs. Atlanta, GA: Centers for Disease Control and Prevention. Meier, B. (2018, June 8). An opioid story that kept flaring up. *The New York Times*, p. A2. Schuchat, A.; Houry, D.; and Guy, G. (2017). New data on opioid use and prescribing in the United States. *Journal of the American Medical Association, 318*, 425–428. News Release: New states added to national network of Prescription Drug Monitoring Programs (2018, February 18). National Association of Boards of Pharmacy, Mount Prospect, Illinois. Accessed from https://nabp.pharmacy/category/prescription-monitoring-program.

37. FDA Drug Safety Communication: Prescription acetaminophen products to be limited to 325 mg per dosage unit: boxed warning will highlightpotential for severe liver failure (2011, January 13). Washington, D.C.: U.S. Food and Drug Administration, U.S. Department of Health and Human Services.

chapter 10

Cocaine and Methamphetamine

S.F. is a brilliant young physician attending a conference at a metropolitan hospital where he is a medical resident. He has been on call for 36 hours and can barely stay awake, much less concentrate on the presentations. S.F. is lonely, depressed, and overworked. All he can think about is his fiancée, Martha, who is several hundred miles away. He knows that Martha's father will not permit her to marry him until he is able to support her. With all his debts and meager salary, that could take years.

He excuses himself from the conference, takes a syringe from the nurses' station, and locks himself in a bathroom stall. He gets out a packet of cocaine powder, fills the syringe with a 7-percent solution, and plunges the needle into his arm. Within seconds, the young doctor feels a rush of euphoria. His fatigue is gone; his composure is regained. He is a totally rejuvenated man.

At once, S.F. rejoins the conference. He is determined to write an essay documenting the medical effects of this magical drug. If the essay is published, the entire scientific world now will know his name. Fame and fortune should likely follow.

The date is 1884, the place is Vienna, and the physician is Sigmund Freud.

After you have completed this chapter, you should have an understanding of the following:

- The history of cocaine
- Acute and chronic effects of cocaine
- Patterns of cocaine and crack cocaine abuse
- Cocaine abuse treatment options
- The history of amphetamines
- Acute and chronic effects of amphetamines
- Patterns of methamphetamine abuse
- Stimulant treatment for attention-deficit/hyperactivity disorder (ADHD)
- Stimulant abuse for cognitive enhancement

The time, place, and identity of S.F. in this fictional vignette are based on the actual life of Sigmund Freud. It may have surprised you to know that the founder of psychoanalysis, one of the most influential thinkers of the twentieth century, started out as a physician interested more in the workings of the brain and the stimulant effects of cocaine than in unlocking the mysteries of the unconscious mind. It is worth noting that the year in question could have been 1984, 1994, or any other year since then, and the individual involved could have been anyone 28 years old, as Freud was at the time, or someone either younger or older. As it turned out, Freud was extremely lucky; he never became personally dependent on cocaine, although a close friend did—and countless numbers of people have succumbed to cocaine dependence since Freud's time.

As with the story of opium, the story of cocaine is both ancient and modern. Although its origins stretch back more than 4,000 years in mountainous regions of South America, cocaine abuse continues to represent a major portion of the present-day drug scene throughout the world. Opioids may have dominated media headlines in recent years, but cocaine remains a source of significant concern in drug abuse problems today. For this reason, it is important to understand its history, the properties of the drug itself, and ways it has the potential to control and ultimately, in many cases, destroy a person's life.

This chapter will focus not only on cocaine but also on a group of stimulant drugs, referred to collectively as *amphetamines*, the most prominent example being methamphetamine (meth). Although cocaine and amphetamines are distinct in terms of their pharmacology (their characteristics as biochemical substances), there are enough similarities in their behavioral and physiological effects to warrant their being discussed together. The emphasis will be on issues surrounding abuse and dependence. We will also examine the widespread medical application of amphetamines and amphetamine-like drugs in the treatment of attention-deficit/hyperactivity disorder (ADHD), as well as recent concerns about their nonmedical use for "cognitive enhancement."

In general, cocaine and amphetamines represent the two major classes of psychoactive stimulants, drugs that energize the body and create intense feelings of euphoria.

The History of Cocaine

Cocaine is derived from small leaves of the coca shrub (*Erythroxylon coca*), grown in the high-altitude rain forests and fields that run along the slopes of the Peruvian and Bolivian Andes in South America, although coca cultivation can be found in other regions of the world with similar climate and soil conditions.

Like many other psychoactive drugs, cocaine use has a long history. We can trace the practice of chewing coca leaves, which contain about 2 percent cocaine, back to the Inca civilization, which flourished from the thirteenth century until its conquest by the Spaniards in 1532, as well as to other Andean cultures dating back 5,000 years. Coca was considered a gift from the god Inti to the Incas, allowing them to endure a harsh and physically demanding life in the Andes. [1]

To this day, coca chewing is part of cultural life in this region. It is estimated that about 2 million Peruvian men who live in the Andean highlands, representing 90 percent of the male population in that area, chew coca leaves.[2] These people, called *acullicadores*, mix their own blend of coca, chalk, lime, and ash to achieve the desired effects, whether their goal is to fight fatigue or simply relax with friends.[3]

Interestingly, this form of cocaine use among these people produces few instances of toxicity or abuse. The reason

cocaine: An extremely potent and dependence-producing stimulant drug, derived from the coca leaf.

Numbers Talk. . .

17.3	Percentage of high school seniors who had reported in 1975 that they had used cocaine sometime in their lives. Between 1979 and 1987, the lifetime prevalence rate of cocaine use among high school seniors exceeded 15 percent. The prevalence rate declined to 9.8 percent in 1999. Eight years later, in 2017, the rate dropped still further to 4.2 percent.
23,828	Number of domestic meth lab seizures by the Drug Enforcement Administration during the peak year of 2004. More than 2,900 seizures took place in the state of Missouri, the largest number in a single state in that year.
11,593	Number of domestic meth lab seizures in 2013. Missouri had dropped to third place, behind Kentucky and Indiana.
9,338	Number of domestic meth lab seizures in 2014. Missouri was now in second place, behind Indiana. Kentucky and Ohio were in third and fourth place, respectively.

Sources: Information courtesy of the Drug Enforcement Administration, U.S. Department of Justice, Washington, D.C. Miech, R. A.; Johnston, L. D.; O'Malley, P. M.; Bachman, J. G.; Schulenberg, J. E.; and Patrick, M. E. (2018). *Monitoring the future. National survey results on drug use, 1975–2017. Vol. I: Secondary school students.* Ann Arbor, MI: Institute for Social Research, The University of Michigan, Table 4-1a.

lies in the very low doses of cocaine that chewed coca leaves provide; in this form, absorption from the digestive system is slow, and relatively little cocaine enters the bloodstream and is distributed to the brain (see Chapter 8). A much more serious problem has been availability of a coca paste containing a much higher percentage of cocaine that is mixed with tobacco and smoked as a cigarette (referred to as a *bazuco*). Now delivered to the brain directly from the lungs, cocaine is more likely to produce abuse and dependence. Making matters worse, dangerously high levels of kerosene, gasoline, and ether are involved in the coca-refining process and end up as adulterants in the cigarettes themselves.[4]

Coca and Cocaine in Nineteenth-Century Life

Coca leaves were brought back to Europe from the Spanish colonies soon after the conquest of the Incas in 1533, but their potency was nearly gone after the long sea voyage. Perhaps, it was said at the time, the legendary effects of coca were merely exaggerations. Coca leaves were ignored for 300 years.

By the late 1850s, however, there was a revival of interest in coca. The active ingredient of the coca plant was chemically isolated in 1859 by the German chemist Albert Niemann, who observed its anesthetic effect on his tongue and named it "cocaine." The patent medicine industry in the United States and Europe lost no time in marketing either stimulating beverages containing coca extract or topical anesthetics (useful to relieve a toothache) containing cocaine. By the end of the nineteenth century, cocaine had gained favor among writers and intellectuals. Reportedly, cocaine inspired Robert Louis Stevenson in 1886 to write *Dr. Jekyll and Mr. Hyde*. In the stories of Sir Arthur Conan Doyle, the fictional detective Sherlock Holmes was often depicted as injecting cocaine (the "seven-percent solution") to help maintain his crime-solving powers.

The Commercialization of Coca

By far the most successful commercial use of coca in the nineteenth century was a mixture of coca and wine concocted in 1863 by a Corsican chemist and businessman, Angelo Mariani. We know now that the combination of alcohol and cocaine produces a metabolite with an elimination half-life several times longer than cocaine alone, so the mixture tends to be quite intoxicating (see Drugs ... in Focus). No wonder "Vin Mariani" became an instant sensation.

In a stroke of marketing genius, Mariani invented the concept of the "celebrity endorsement." Over the next few decades, advertisements for Vin Mariani carried testimonials from satisfied celebrities such as U.S. president William McKinley, Thomas Edison, the surgeon general of the U.S. Army, General Ulysses S. Grant, Sarah Bernhardt, Jules Verne, the Prince of Wales, the czar of Russia, and Popes Pius X and Leo XII, to name just a few of Mariani's fans. In a letter to Mariani, the sculptor Frederic Bartholdi wrote that if he had been drinking Vin Mariani while designing the Statue of Liberty, it would have ended up more than three times taller.[5] Fortunately, Bartholdi was sober at the time.

Meanwhile in the United States, Atlanta pharmacist John Pemberton promoted an imitation form of Vin Mariani that he called French Wine Cola. In 1885, however, as a concession to the American temperance movement, he removed the alcohol (see Chapter 13), added carbonated water, and reformulated the basic mixture to

Drugs . . . in Focus

Cocaine after Alcohol: The Risk of Cocaethylene Toxicity

The risk of dying from cocaine arises from the drug's powerful excitatory effects on the body, specifically abnormal heart rhythms, labored breathing, and increased blood pressure. The toxicity potential for any of these toxic reactions is, unfortunately, increased when alcohol is already in the bloodstream. The biotransformation of cocaine and alcohol (ethanol), when ingested in combination, produces a metabolite called *cocaethylene*. One effect of cocaethylene is a three- to fivefold increase in the elimination half-life of cocaine. As a result, cocaine remains in the bloodstream for a much longer time. More important, cocaethylene has a specific excitatory effect on blood pressure and heart rate that is greater than that produced by cocaine alone. In other words, there is a synergistic interaction when the two drugs are taken together (Chapter 8).

While the combination of alcohol and cocaine is associated with a prolonged and enhanced euphoria, it also brings an 18- to 25-fold increased risk of immediate death. The fact that 62–90 percent of cocaine abusers are also abusers of alcohol makes the dangers of cocaethylene toxicity a significant health concern.

Sources: Andrews, P. (1997). Cocaethylene toxicity. *Journal of Addictive Diseases, 16*, 75–84. Harris, D. S.; Everhart, E. T.; Mendelson, J.; and Jones, R. T. (2003). The pharmacology of cocaethylene in humans following cocaine and ethanol administration. *Drug and Alcohol Dependence, 72*, 169–182.

"Tired? Then drink Coca-Cola. It relieves exhaustion." In the late nineteenth century, the Coca-Cola Company advertised its beverage in medicinal terms. A company letterhead of this period spoke of Coca-Cola as containing "the tonic properties of the wonderful coca plant."

Credit: Bettmann/Getty Images

combine the coca with the syrup of the African kola nut (an ingredient containing about 2 percent caffeine). In doing so, Coca-Cola was born.

Capitalizing on the strength of a beverage containing both coca and caffeine, early advertisements for Coca-Cola emphasized the drink as a "stimulating brain tonic" that made you feel more productive and as a remedy for such assorted nervous ailments as sick headaches and melancholia (a nineteenth-century term for depression).[6] The medicinal slant to early promotions of Coca-Cola is probably the reason why soda fountains first appeared and continued for years to be located in drugstores.[7]

A number of competing brands with similar formulations soon sprang up with names such as Care-Cola, Dope Cola, Kola Ade, and Wiseola.[8] Eventually, public pressure brought about official restrictions on the patent medicine industry, which, by the beginning of the twentieth century, was marketing more than 50,000 unregulated products.[9] The Pure Food and Drug Act of 1906 specified that all active ingredients, including cocaine, had to be listed on patent medicine labels. This law led to the decline in the number of cocaine-laced patent medicines but not an outright ban. While the Proprietary and Patent Medicine Act of 1908 in Canada banned cocaine

from patent medicines entirely, no further restrictions on cocaine sales or use in the United States were imposed until the Harrison Narcotics Tax Act of 1914 (see Chapter 3).

The Coca-Cola Company, aware of the growing tide of public sentiment against cocaine, changed the formula for Coca-Cola in 1903, removing the coca leaves and substituting decocainized coca leaves. The cocaine was eliminated, while the coca leaves themselves provided the coca flavoring that remains to this day (Drugs ... in Focus). After 1903, the "pause that refreshed" America would now be due only to the presence of sugar and caffeine.

The use of cocaine served as a major advance in the practice of medicine. In the United States, William Halstead, one of the most distinguished surgeons of the time and one of the founders of the Johns Hopkins School of Medicine, studied the effect of cocaine in anesthetizing nerves and whole limbs. In the process of his experimentation, Halstead acquired a cocaine habit of his own (which was replaced several years later by dependence on morphine). It was in Europe, however, that the medical applications of cocaine were explored most extensively, largely through the promotional efforts of an obscure Viennese physician named Sigmund Freud.

Freud and Cocaine

In 1884, Freud was a struggling young physician, given to bouts of depression and self-doubt but nonetheless determined to make his mark in the medical world. Having read a report by a German army physician that supplies of pure cocaine helped soldiers endure fatigue and feel better in general, Freud secured some cocaine for himself and found the experience exhilarating. His depression lifted, and he felt a new sense of boundless energy. His friend and colleague Dr. Ernst von Fleischl-Marxow, taking morphine and enduring a painful illness, borrowed some cocaine from Freud and found favorable results as well.

Before long, Freud was distributing cocaine to his friends and his sisters and even sent a supply to his fiancée Martha Bernays. In the words of Freud's biographer Ernest Jones, "From the vantage point of our present knowledge, he was rapidly becoming a public menace."[10] We can gain some perspective on the effect cocaine was having on Freud's behavior at this time through an excerpt from a personal letter to Martha:

Woe to you, my Princess, when I come. I will kiss you quite red and feed you till you are plump. And if you are forward you shall see who is the stronger, a gentle little girl who doesn't eat enough or a big wild man who has cocaine in his body [underlined in the original]. In my last severe depression I took coca again and a small dose lifted me to the heights in a wonderful fashion. I am just now busy collecting the literature for a song of praise to this magical substance.[11]

Within four months, his "song of praise" essay, "Über Coca" (Concerning Coca), was written and published.

Unfortunately, fame that the essay brought Freud was short-lived, and the sweetness of his romance with cocaine

Drugs . . . in Focus

What Happened to the Coca in Coca-Cola?

Every day, in a drab factory building in a New Jersey suburb of Maywood, a select team of employees of the Stepan Company carries out a chemical procedure that has been one of the primary responsibilities of the company since 1903. They remove cocaine from high-grade coca leaves. The remainder, technically called "decocainized flavor essence," is then sent to the Coca-Cola Company as part of the secret recipe for the world's favorite soft drink.

Each year, the Stepan Company is legally sanctioned by the U.S. government (and carefully monitored by the DEA) to receive shipments of about 100 metric tons of raw coca leaves from Peruvian coca farms, separating the cocaine chemically, and producing about 1,750 kilograms of high-quality cocaine. Its annual output is equivalent to approximately 20 million hits of crack, worth about $200 million if it were to make it to the illicit drug market. Fortunately, the Stepan Company has an impeccable security record.

In case you are wondering what happens to the cocaine after it is removed from the coca leaves, it turns out that Stepan finds a legitimate market in the world of medicine. Since 1988, the British pharmaceutical firm, Mallinckrodt Pharmaceutical Company, with headquarters in St. Louis, is the only American company allowed by the DEA to buy the cocaine from Stepan and sell it to select medical professionals for treatment purposes. Tincture of cocaine is used regularly as a local anesthetic to numb the skin prior to minor surgical procedures such as stitching up a wound. Surgeons frequently use cocaine as a topical ointment when working on the eye, nose or throat.

As a result, the Stepan Company essentially can have it both ways. It is the exclusive U.S. supplier of cocaine for use in medical settings as well as decocainized coca for your next can of Coke. As the *Wall Street Journal* put it, "The two markets end up sending Stepan's products into virtually every bloodstream in America."

Sources: Inciardi, J. A. (2002). *The war on drugs III*. Boston: Allyn and Bacon, p. 21. Miller, M. W. (1994, October 17). Quality stuff: Firm is peddling cocaine, and deals are legit. *Wall Street Journal*, pp. A1, A14.

---

soon turned sour. Freud himself escaped becoming dependent upon cocaine, though later in his life he clearly became dependent on nicotine (see Chapter 15). His friend, Fleischl, however, was not so lucky. Within a year, Fleischl had increased his cocaine dose to 20 times the amount Freud had taken and had developed a severe cocaine-induced psychosis in which he experienced hallucinations that snakes were crawling over his skin (a phenomenon now referred to as **formication**). Fleischl suffered six years of painful agony and anguish until his death. By 1887, Freud had retracted his earlier stance on the drug.

The story of Freud's infatuation with cocaine and his later disillusionment with it can be seen as essentially a miniature version of the modern history of cocaine itself.[12] Between 1880 and 1910, the public reaction to cocaine went from wild enthusiasm to widespread disapproval. As this chapter will later describe, a similar cycle of attitudes swept the United States and the world between 1970 and 1985.

Acute Effects of Cocaine

The effects of cocaine on the user vary in degree with the route of administration, the purity of the dose, and the user's expectations about the experience, but certain features remain the same. The most prominent reaction is a powerful burst of energy. If the cocaine is injected intravenously or smoked, the extremely intense effect (often referred to as a "rush" or "high") is felt within a matter of seconds, and lasts only 5 or 10 minutes. If the drug is snorted through the nose, the effect is less intense than when injected or smoked but lasts somewhat longer, approximately 15–30 minutes.

Users also experience a general sense of well-being, although in some instances cocaine may precipitate a panic attack.[13] As levels of cocaine diminish, the mood changes dramatically. The user becomes irritable, despondent, and depressed (Figure 10.1). These aftereffects are uncomfortable enough to produce a powerful craving for another dose.

The depression induced in the aftermath of a cocaine high can lead to thoughts of suicide. In 1985, during one of the peak years of cocaine abuse in the United States, as many as one out of five suicide victims in New York City showed evidence of cocaine in their blood at autopsy. The prevalence of cocaine use was greatest among victims who were in their twenties and thirties, and for African Americans

formication: Hallucinatory behavior produced by chronic cocaine or amphetamine abuse, in which the individual feels insects or snakes crawling either over or under the skin.

Quick Concept Check   10.1

Understanding the History of Cocaine

Check your understanding of the history of cocaine by matching the names on the left with the identifications on the right. Some identifications may not match with any of the names.

1. Angelo Mariani
2. John Pemberton
3. William Halstead
4. Sigmund Freud
5. Ernst von Fleischl-Marxow

a. Friend of Sigmund Freud; first documented case of cocaine psychosis
b. Developer of Coca-Cola, originally containing cocaine
c. Early advocate of restricting cocaine use in the United States
d. Cofounder of Johns Hopkins Medical School; early developer of cocaine to anesthetize nerves and whole limbs
e. A popular figure in present-day Peru
f. Early advocate of cocaine use; originator of psychoanalysis
g. Promoter of a popular coca-laced wine

Answers: 1. g 2. b 3. d 4. f 5. a

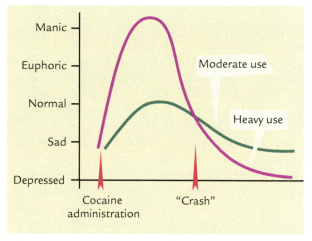

FIGURE 10.1

Ups and downs of a typical dose of cocaine.

and Latinos.[14] In a 1989 survey of teenage callers to the 1-800-COCAINE hotline, at the height of cocaine abuse, one out of seven reported a previous suicide attempt.[15]

Cocaine's effect on sexual arousal is often cited as having been the basis for its purported allure as an aphrodisiac. On the one hand, interviews of cocaine users frequently include reports of spontaneous and prolonged erections in males and multiple orgasms in females during initial doses of the drug. On the other hand, cocaine's reputation for increasing sexual performance (recall Freud's reference in his letter to Martha) may bias users toward a strong expectation that there will be a sexually stimulating reaction, when in reality the effect is a much weaker one. The fact is that chronic cocaine use results in decreased sexual performance and a loss of sexual desire, as the drug essentially takes the place of sex.[16]

Cocaine produces a sudden change in a number of systems in the body. Heart rate and respiration are increased, while appetite is diminished. Blood vessels constrict, pupils in the eyes dilate, and blood pressure rises. The cocaine user may start to sweat and appear suddenly pale. These effects can lead to a cerebral hemorrhage or congestive heart failure. Cardiac arrhythmia results from cocaine's tendency to bind to heart tissue itself.[17]

Given the extreme excitatory effects of cocaine on bodily organs, it is not surprising that behavioral skills, particularly those requiring fine motor control, would be adversely affected. In a study of drivers showing reckless behavior on the road, those found to have been under the influence of cocaine were wildly overconfident in their abilities, taking turns too fast or weaving through traffic. One highway patrol officer called this behavior "diagonal driving. They were just as involved in changing lanes as in going forward." Yet it has been determined that they are capable of passing standard sobriety tests (such as walking a straight line) that have been designed to detect alcohol intoxication.[18]

Chronic Effects of Cocaine

Repeated and continued use of cocaine produces undesirable mood changes that can be alleviated only when the person is under the acute effects of the drug. Chronic cocaine abusers are often irritable, depressed, and paranoid. As was true in Fleischl's experience with cocaine, long-term abuse can produce the disturbing hallucinatory experience of formication. The sensation of "cocaine bugs" crawling on or under the skin can become so severe that abusers may scratch the skin into open sores or even pierce themselves with a knife to cut out the imaginary creatures. These hallucinations, together with feelings of anxiety and paranoia, make up a serious mental disorder referred to as **cocaine psychosis**.

When snorted, cocaine causes bronchial muscles to relax and nasal blood vessels to constrict; the opposite effects occur when the drug wears off. As the bronchial muscles contract and nasal blood vessels relax, chronic abusers endure continuously stuffy or runny noses and bleeding of nasal membranes. In advanced cases of this problem, the septum of the nose can develop lesions or become perforated with small holes, both of which present serious problems for breathing.

cocaine psychosis: A set of symptoms, including hallucinations, paranoia, and disordered thinking, produced from chronic use of cocaine.

Medical Uses of Cocaine

When applied topically on the skin, cocaine has the ability to block the transmission of nerve impulses, deadening all sensations from the area. The use of cocaine as an anesthetic for nasal, lacrimal duct (tear duct), and throat surgery remains its only legitimate medical application.[19]

Even though cocaine is available for use in these situations, other topical anesthetics are typically preferred because they present fewer problems in their use. One disadvantage of cocaine is that it might be inadvertently absorbed into the bloodstream, leading to an acute cocaine response that is unrelated to the anesthetic effect. Another problem is that cocaine produces intense vasoconstriction (constriction of blood vessels). This can be helpful in reducing bleeding during a surgical procedure, but the intensity of the vasoconstriction may have undesirable side effects. Finally, the local anesthetic effects are brief because cocaine breaks down so rapidly and would require reapplications to be effective. Other local anesthetics, such as lidocaine (brand name: Xylocaine), have the advantage of being active over a longer period of time and not causing problems associated with cocaine.

How Cocaine Works in the Brain

Cocaine greatly enhances the activity of dopamine, and, to a lesser extent, norepinephrine in the brain (see Chapter 8). In the case of both neurotransmitters, the actual effect is to stimulate receptors longer and to a greater degree. Unlike the amphetamines (discussed later in this chapter), the structure of cocaine does not appear to resemble the structure of either dopamine or norepinephrine, so why cocaine should have this effect on receptors is not at all clear. Nonetheless, what has been determined is that the acute effect of euphoria experienced through cocaine is directly related to an increase in dopamine activity in the region of the brain that controls pleasure and reinforcement in general: the nucleus accumbens. The current scientific thinking is that this alteration in neurochemistry has a profound effect on an individual's decision-making skills and an individual's potential for developing a dependence on cocaine (or some other drug of abuse).

Chronic cocaine abuse, however, leads to the loss of about 20 percent of the dopamine receptors in this region of the brain over time. The depletion of dopamine receptors among long-term cocaine abusers has been observed up to four months after the last cocaine exposure, even though the cocaine abuser no longer has cocaine in his or her system. As a result, there is a tendency toward a decline in the experience of pleasure from any source. In fact, cocaine abusers frequently report that their craving for cocaine no longer stems from the pleasure they felt when taking it initially. Their lives may be in shambles and the acute effects of euphoria from cocaine may no longer be strong, but they still crave the drug more than ever. In other words, there is now a disconnection between "liking" and "wanting."[20]

One feature of cocaine is quite unlike that of other psychoactive drugs. Although cocaine abusers over repeated cocaine exposures develop a pattern of drug tolerance to its euphoric effect, they develop a pattern of sensitization (a heightened responsiveness) with respect to motor behavior and brain excitation. This phenomenon, referred to as the **kindling effect**, makes cocaine particularly dangerous because cocaine has the potential for setting off brain seizures. Repeated exposure to cocaine can lower the threshold for seizures, through a sensitization of neurons in the brain over time. As a result of the kindling effect, deaths from cocaine overdose may occur from relatively low dose levels.[21]

Present-Day Cocaine Abuse

The difficult problems of cocaine abuse in the United States and around the world mushroomed during the early 1970s and continue to the present day, although the incidence of abuse is down substantially from peak levels reached around 1986. In ways that resembled the brief period of enthusiasm for cocaine in 1884, attitudes during the early period of this "second epidemic" were incredibly naive. Fueled by media reports of use among the rich and famous, touted as the "champagne of drugs," cocaine became synonymous with the glamorous life. At the same time, the medical profession during this time was equally nonchalant about cocaine. The widely respected *Comprehensive Textbook of Psychiatry* (1980) stated that "if it is used no more than two or three times a week, cocaine creates no serious problem ... At present chronic cocaine use does not usually present a medical problem."[22]

These attitudes began to change as the 1980s unfolded. The death of actor-comedian John Belushi in 1982, followed by the drug-related deaths of other entertainers and sport figures (see Drugs ... in Focus, page 204), produced a reversal of opinion about the safety and desirability of cocaine. The most influential development, however, was the emergence of crack cocaine on the drug scene in the mid-1980s, which will be examined in the next sections.

From Coca to Cocaine

To understand the full picture of present-day cocaine abuse, it is necessary to examine the various forms that cocaine can take, beginning with the extraction of cocaine from the coca plant itself (Figure 10.2). During the initial extraction process, coca leaves are soaked in various chemical solvents so that cocaine can be drawn out of the plant material itself. Leaves are then crushed, and alcohol is percolated through them to remove extraneous matter. After sequential washings and a treatment with kerosene, the yield is cocaine that is approximately 60 percent pure. This is the coca paste that is,

> **kindling effect:** A phenomenon in the brain that produces a heightened sensitivity to repeated administrations of some drugs, such as cocaine. This heightened sensitivity is the opposite of the phenomenon of tolerance.

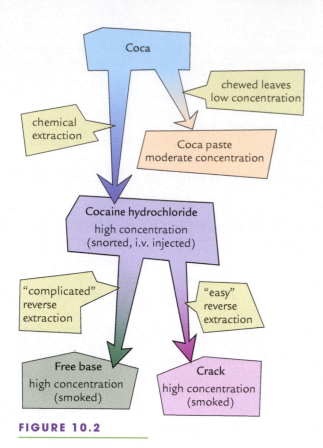

FIGURE 10.2

Steps in producing various forms of cocaine from raw coca.

as mentioned earlier, combined with tobacco and smoked in many South American countries.

Coca paste, however, is not water soluble and therefore cannot be injected into the bloodstream. An additional step of treatment with oxidizing agents and acids is required to produce a water-soluble drug. The result is a white crystalline powder called **cocaine hydrochloride**, about 99 percent pure cocaine and classified chemically as a salt. When in the form of cocaine hydrochloride, the drug can be injected intravenously or snorted. The amount injected at one time is about 16 mg. Intravenous cocaine also can be combined with heroin in a highly dangerous mixture called a *speedball*.

If cocaine is snorted, the user generally has the option of two methods. In the first method, a tiny spoonful of cocaine is carried to one nostril while the other nostril is shut, and the drug is taken with a rapid inhalation. In the second method, cocaine is spread out on a highly polished surface (often a mirror) and arranged with a razor blade in several lines, each containing from 20 to 30 mg. The cocaine is then inhaled into one nostril by means of a straw or rolled piece of paper. During the early 1980s,

a $100 bill was a fashionable choice, drawing attention to the level of income necessary to be using cocaine in the first place.[23]

From Cocaine to Crack

Options for using cocaine widened with the development of **free-base cocaine** during the 1970s and **crack cocaine (or simply crack)** during the mid-1980s. In free-base cocaine, the hydrochloride is removed from the salt form of cocaine, thus liberating it as a "free base." The aim is to obtain a smokable form of cocaine, which, by entering the brain more quickly, produces a more intense effect. The technique for producing free-base cocaine, however, is extremely hazardous, as it is necessary to treat cocaine powder with highly flammable agents such as ether. If the free base still contains some residue of ether, igniting the drug will cause it to explode into flames.

Crack cocaine is the result of a cheaper and safer chemical method, but the objective is essentially the same: a smokable form of cocaine. Treatment with baking soda yields small rocks, which can then be smoked in a small pipe.[24] When they are smoked, a cracking noise accompanies the burning, hence the origin of the name "crack."

There is no question that the effect of cocaine when smoked exceeds the effect of cocaine when snorted; for some users, it even exceeds the effect of cocaine when injected. Inhaling high-potency cocaine (the purity of cocaine in crack averages about 75 percent) into the lungs, and almost immediately into the brain, sets the stage for a pattern of psychological dependence. And at a price of $5–10 per dose, cocaine is no longer out of financial reach (Table 10.1). These factors have made crack cocaine abuse particularly problematic.

TABLE 10.1

Street names for cocaine

TYPE OF COCAINE	STREET NAME
Cocaine hydrochloride (powder)	Blow, C, coke, big C, lady, nose candy, snowbirds, snow, stardust, toot, white girl, happy dust, cola, flake, pearl, Peruvian lady, freeze, geeze, doing the line
Free-base cocaine	Freebase, base
Crack cocaine	Crack, rock, kibbles and bits, crell
Crack cocaine combined with PCP (see Chapter 12)	Beam me up Scottie, space cadet, tragic magic
Cocaine combined with heroin	Speedball, snowball
Cocaine combined with heroin and LSD	Frisco special, Frisco speedball

Source: Bureau of Justice Statistics Clearinghouse (1992). *Drugs, behavior and crime.* Washington, D.C.: U.S. Department of Justice, pp. 24–25.

cocaine hydrochloride: The powder form of cocaine that is inhaled (snorted) or injected into the bloodstream.

free-base cocaine: A smokable form of cocaine.

crack cocaine or crack: A smokable form of cocaine.

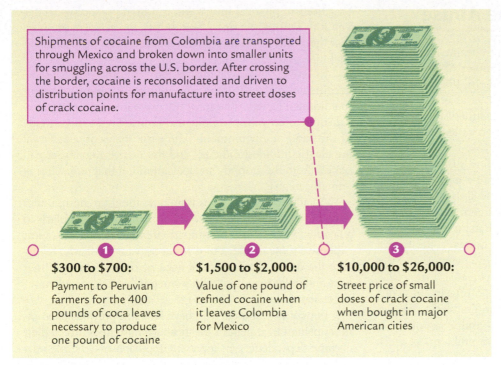

FIGURE 10.3

Shipments of cocaine from Colombia are transported through Mexico and broken down into smaller units for smuggling across the U.S. border. After crossing the border, cocaine is reconsolidated and driven to distribution points for manufacture into street doses of crack cocaine.

From the coca farm to crack cocaine on the street, values increase roughly 86 times, from $300 to as much as $26,000, for the 400 pounds of raw coca that is necessary to produce one pound of cocaine and an equivalent amount of crack cocaine.

1 **$300 to $700:** Payment to Peruvian farmers for the 400 pounds of coca leaves necessary to produce one pound of cocaine

2 **$1,500 to $2,000:** Value of one pound of refined cocaine when it leaves Colombia for Mexico

3 **$10,000 to $26,000:** Street price of small doses of crack cocaine when bought in major American cities

At its height of popularity in metropolitan regions of America, crack cocaine had major societal impact on communities where prevalence rates were high. Women who were crack abusers found that their drug cravings overwhelmed their maternal instincts, resulting in their neglecting the basic needs of their children, either in postnatal or prenatal stages of life. In New York, for example, the number of reported cases of child abuse and neglect increased from 36,000 in 1985 to 59,000 in 1989, a change largely attributed to the introduction of crack. Inner-city crime and violence skyrocketed. As the hugely profitable crack cocaine trade took root, systemic violence became a fact of life for people living in the inner cities of America. The profitability of selling crack cocaine on a domestic level was fueled by the enormous profits made by traffickers in the global illicit drug trade (Figure 10.3).[25]

Public demonstrations in urban communities in the 1980s and 1990s were one way of responding to the desolation and misery resulting from crack cocaine abuse.

Credit: Wesley Bocxe/Science Source

Although crack abuse remains a problem today, the number of new crack abusers has declined substantially, particularly in urban communities. In 1998, whereas 36 percent of all males over 36 years old who were arrested in New York in 1998 had used crack, little more than 4 percent of those 15–20 years old had done so. A principal reason for this change in prevalence rates has been the current stigmatized image of the "crack head," considered by one's peers in the community to be a social loser.[26]

Patterns of Cocaine Abuse

In 2016, the National Survey on Drug Use and Health estimated that approximately 39 million Americans aged 12 or older had used cocaine at some time in their lives, 4.8 million had used it during the past year, and 1.95 million had used it during the past month. Approximately 9 million Americans had used crack at some time in their lives, 882,000 had used it during the past year, and 432,000 had used it during the past month. The past month prevalence rate for crack in 2016 had declined by nearly 30 percent, relative to 2007, though it had increased by about the same percentage, relative to 2013. In other words, prevalence rates of crack abuse have been somewhat unstable in the last decade or so, but the incidence of crack cocaine abuse is nowhere near the levels experienced in the 1980s.

Present-day incidence of cocaine abuse in the United States is also substantially lower than it was during the 1980s. From 2006 to 2014, medical emergencies associated with cocaine use decreased by more than 50 percent, from 56,000 to 25,000. However, since 2014, there has been a surge in cocaine overdose deaths. In 2017, there were more than 14,000 cocaine overdose deaths, an increase of 114 percent over 2015, largely due to contamination with synthetic opioids such as fentanyl or fentanyl analogs (Drugs...in Focus).[27]

Treatment for Cocaine Abuse

One way of grasping the magnitude of cocaine-abuse problems in the 1980s is to look at the number of people who wanted to get help during this period. In 1983, a nationwide toll-free hotline, 1-800-COCAINE, was established as a 24-hour service for emergency and treatment information. From 1983 to 1990, more than 3 million callers responded, averaging more than 1,000 per day.[28]

The statistics gathered from the hotline during the 1980s also revealed the changing face of cocaine abuse over that span of time. In 1983, the typical cocaine abuser was college educated (50 percent), employed (83 percent), earning more than $25,000 per year (52 percent), and taking cocaine powder intranasally (61 percent). By 1988, however, the typical cocaine abuser had not gone to college (83 percent) and was earning less than $25,000 per year (80 percent). From 1983 to 1988, the percentage of individuals reporting an abuse of a free-base form of cocaine had more than doubled to 56 percent. In 1986 alone, one year after the introduction of crack, half of all calls to the hotline referred to problems of crack abuse.[29]

Treating cocaine abuse presents difficulties that are peculiar to the power of cocaine itself. Substance abuse professionals view the process of coming off cocaine as one of the most anguished and depressing of experiences. Some abusers feel like they are having a heart attack. They will do almost anything to keep from crashing.[30]

Despite its difficulties, the varieties of treatment for cocaine abuse all have certain features in common. The initial phase is detoxification and total abstinence. The cocaine abuser aims to achieve total withdrawal with the least possibility of physical injury and minimal psychological discomfort. During the first 24–48 hours, the chances are high that there will be profound depression, severe headaches, irritability, and disturbances in sleep.[31]

In severe cases involving a pattern of compulsive use, the cocaine abuser needs to be admitted for inpatient treatment in a hospital facility. The most intensive interventions, medical supervision with psychological counseling, can be made in this kind of environment. The early stages of withdrawal are clearly the most difficult, and the recovering abuser can benefit from the around-the-clock attention that only a hospital staff can give.

An alternative approach is an outpatient program, under which the individual remains at home but travels regularly to a facility for treatment. An outpatient program is clearly a less expensive route to take, but it works only for those who recognize the destructive impact of cocaine dependence on their lives and enter treatment with a sincere desire to do whatever is needed to stop.[32]

For cocaine abusers who have failed in previous attempts in outpatient treatment or for those who are in denial of their cocaine dependence, an inpatient approach may be the only answer. For most abusers, it is important to stay away from an environment where cocaine and other drugs are prevalent and peer pressure to resume drug-taking behavior is intense. The difficulty is that they have been so alienated from the mainstream and have few if any friends who are not substance abusers.[33]

A third alternative is a combined approach in which a shortened inpatient program, 7–14 days in length, is followed by an intensive outpatient program that continues for several months (Portrait).

Drugs ... in Focus

Cocaine Contamination in U.S. Paper Currency

It is a fact of life in drug enforcement that supplies of illicit drugs are very difficult to trace. As a result of a clever experiment conducted in 2001, however, the opposite appears to be true. A strange but reliable phenomenon came to light with respect to the paper currency that Americans handle every day: the contamination of this currency with detectable levels of cocaine. Analyses were made of 50 randomly sampled one-dollar bills from five cities in the United States and Puerto Rico (Baltimore, Chicago, Denver, Honolulu, and San Juan). Detectable amounts of cocaine were found in an astounding 92 percent of these bills. There is little doubt that a similar result would have been reported for bills of higher denominations, but the study focused only on one-dollar bills.

The explanation given for this finding was based on the pattern of cocaine abuse and the present-day system of currency processing and distribution. Contamination is believed to begin with the handling of currency during cocaine trafficking and with the rolling up of bills for cocaine snorting. The contaminated money is then transferred from bill to bill during automated counting in banks and other financial institutions. The extremely high incidence of cocaine-contaminated money is attributed to cross-contamination after the act of drug-taking behavior, rather than to the behavior itself. A lower incidence of contamination was found with respect to other illicit drugs such as methamphetamine or heroin, due largely to the relatively lower prevalence rates of abuse in general and the fact that currency would not as likely be directly involved in their consumption.

Source: Jenkins, A. J. (2001). Drug contamination of U.S. paper currency. *Forensic Science International, 3,* 189–193.

Whether on an inpatient or an outpatient basis, there are several approaches for treatment. One alternative is the self-help support group Cocaine Anonymous, modeled after the famous 12-step Alcoholics Anonymous program (see Chapter 13). In this program, recovering cocaine abusers meet in group sessions, learn from the life experiences of other members, and gain a sense of accomplishment from remaining drug-free in an atmosphere of fellowship and mutual support. In another drug treatment option, cocaine abusers meet with cognitive-behavioral therapists, who teach them new ways of acting and thinking in response to their environment. During the course of cognitive-behavioral therapy, cocaine abusers are urged to avoid situations that lead to drug use, recognize and change irrational thoughts, manage negative moods, and practice drug-refusal skills. While the success rates of both approaches are approximately the same for patients in cocaine-abuse treatment overall, some evidence suggests that a cocaine abuser's personal characteristics may affect the kind of treatment that will work best (Figure 10.4).

Whatever the approach taken, however, it is clear that an intensive relearning process has to go on because cocaine abusers often cannot remember a life without cocaine.[34] The potential for relapse is particularly challenging among recovering cocaine abusers, primarily as a result of powerful conditioned cues that have been associated with the drug. A specialist in cocaine abuse rehabilitation tells this story: "A woman was doing well in treatment. Then one day she was changing her baby's diaper. She used baby powder and the sight of the white powder induced a tremendous craving for cocaine."[35]

Currently, pharmacological approaches in cocaine-abuse treatment, as well as the combination of pharmacological and behavioral approaches, are being vigorously pursued. The development of any drug that reduces craving would be a great advance in the treatment of cocaine dependence and in the prevention of problems associated with cocaine dependence.[36]

Whether the strategy is behavioral or pharmacological, treatment and prevention approaches to cocaine abuse reflect a general orientation toward reducing the negative impact of drug-taking behavior on the individual and society (the "demand" side), as opposed to reducing the availability of the drugs themselves (the "supply" side). Drug Enforcement ... in Focus examines the continuing difficulties in controlling the supply line of cocaine.

Amphetamines

One of humanity's fondest dreams is to have the power of unlimited endurance, to be able to banish fatigue from our lives, to be fueled by endless energy as though we had discovered some internal perpetual motion machine. We all have wanted, at some time in our lives, to be a superhero. Cocaine, as we know, gives us that illusion. The remainder of this chapter will examine another powerful drug source for these feelings of invincibility: amphetamines. As we will see, the attractions and problems of abuse associated with cocaine and amphetamines are very similar.

The History of Amphetamines

The origin of modern amphetamines dates back almost 5,000 years to a Chinese medicinal herb called *ma huang* (*Ephedra vulgaris*) that was used to clear bronchial passageways during bouts of asthma and other forms of respiratory distress. According to Chinese legend, this herb was first identified by the Emperor Shen Nung, who also is credited with the discovery of tea and marijuana.

German chemists isolated the active ingredient of *ma huang* in 1887, naming it ephedrine. It was soon obvious that ephedrine stimulated the sympathetic nervous system in

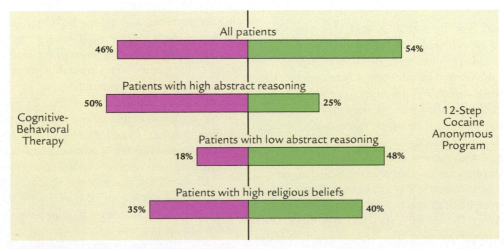

FIGURE 10.4

Percentage of patients achieving four consecutive weeks of cocaine abstinence comparing two types of treatment.

Source: Adapted from Shine, B. (2000, March). Some cocaine abusers fare better with cognitive-behavioral therapy, others with 12-step programs. *NIDA Notes, 15*(1), 9.

PORTRAIT

Robert Downey, Jr.—A Success Story Following Cocaine Abuse

The parade of celebrities who have struggled against cocaine abuse is extensive. Over the years, we have witnessed their personal triumphs and failures and have seen some lives lost (see Chapter 1), some careers lost, and occasionally careers regained. In 1986, the nation was galvanized by the untimely deaths of college basketball player Len Bias and professional football player Dan Rogers within months of each other; the death of comedian and actor John Belushi had occurred just four years earlier. The deaths of River Phoenix in 1993, Chris Farley in 1998, and Mitch Hedberg in 2005, all of them due to a lethal combination of cocaine and heroin, underscored the ever-present dangers of drug-taking behavior.

Fortunately, the story of Robert Downey, Jr., an Academy Award nominee for his performance in the title role of the movie *Chaplin* in 1992, has all the marks of a Hollywood comeback screenplay—the story of a life and career derailed for several years by the abuse of cocaine and other drugs but somehow managing to come out right in the end. For a time, his fans held their breath as events unfolded. In 2003, Downey was beginning

to recognize that he had to turn his life around. It was about one year into serving a three-year probation period, after pleading no-contest to cocaine possession and being under the influence during a November 2000 arrest in a Palm Springs hotel (see photo on left). In 1999, Downey had spent a year in prison after being convicted on charges of cocaine possession. Upon his release, he was featured on the successful *Aly McBeal* TV show, only to be fired in 2000. His drug-abuse problems had first begun making headlines in 1996 when he was found with cocaine, heroin, and a pistol in his car.

In earlier editions of *Drugs, Society, and Criminal Justice*, this Portrait feature portrayed the story of Robert Downey, Jr., in considerably less positive terms or, at best, with considerable caution. However, today there is ample reason to believe that his self-destructive lifestyle is behind him. In 2008, Downey achieved a major comeback in his starring role in the highly successful blockbuster movies *Ironman* (2008; see photo on right),

followed with *Ironman 2* (2010) and *Ironman 3* (2013), as well as *Sherlock Holmes* (2009) and its sequel (2011). His newest movie credits include *The Avengers: Infinity Wars* (2018) and *The Voyage of Doctor Doolittle* (2019).

Downey's personal life has regained a sense of stability that bodes well for the future. In 2010, Downey and his wife Susan Levin co-founded the Team Downey Production Company for the development of film and television properties. Downey has remained drug-free, frequently acknowledging his wife for her critical role in his present-day drug-free life and his continuing journey of recovery.

Sources: Carr, D. (2008, April 20). Been up, been down. Now? Super. *The New York Times*, pp. 1, 13. Downey's back, older and "mildly wiser" (2003, January 21). *Newsday*, p. A12. Lemonick, M. D. (2000, December 11). Downey's downfall. *Time*, p. 97.

Credit: Krista Kennell/Sipa Press/ironmanphotocall/ AP Images

Credit: Culver City Police department/Newsmakers/ Getty Images

Credit: Steve Vas/Featureflash/ Shutterstock

general. In 1932, the pharmaceutical company, Smith, Kline & French laboratories marketed a synthetic form of ephedrine called **amphetamine** under the brand name Benzedrine as a nonprescription CNS stimulant appetite suppressant and bronchial dilator.

During World War II, both U.S. and German troops were being given amphetamine to keep them awake and alert. Japanese kamikaze pilots were on amphetamine during their suicide missions. The advantages over cocaine, the other stimulant drug available at the time, were twofold: amphetamine was easily absorbed into the nervous system from the gastrointestinal tract, so it could be taken orally, and its effects were much longer lasting.

After the war, amphetamine use was adapted for peacetime purposes. Amphetamine, often referred to as "bennies," was a way for college students to stay awake to study for exams and for long-distance truck drivers to fight fatigue on the road. Truckers would take a "St. Louis" if they had to go from New York to Missouri and back or a "Pacific turnabout" if they needed to travel completely across country and back, without stopping to sleep.[37]

> **amphetamine (am-FEH-ta-meen):** A family of powerful stimulant drugs.

In the meantime, the word got around that amphetamine produced euphoria as well, and soon amphetamine became popular for recreational purposes. People found ways of opening up the nonprescription amphetamine inhalers, withdrawing the contents, and getting high by drinking it or injecting it intravenously. Since each inhaler contained 250 mg of amphetamine, there was enough for several powerful doses. During the early 1960s, injectable amphetamines could be bought with forged prescriptions or even by telephoning a pharmacy and posing as a physician. By 1965, amendments to federal drug laws tightened the supply of prescription amphetamines, requiring manufacturers, wholesalers, and pharmacies to keep careful records of amphetamine transactions, but amphetamines soon became available from illegal laboratories.[38]

Amphetamine abuse in the United States reached a peak about 1967, declining slowly over the 1970s as other stimulant drugs, notably cocaine, grew in popularity. By 1970, 10 percent of the U.S. population over 14 years of age had used amphetamine, and more than 8 percent of all drug prescriptions were for amphetamine in some form.[39] For about two decades afterward, amphetamine abuse steadily faded from prominence in the drug scene. Cocaine and later crack cocaine became the dominant illicit stimulant of abuse. Only since the mid-1990s has amphetamine abuse resurfaced as a significant social concern.

Drug Enforcement ... in Focus

Comparison Shopping Inside the Global Cocaine Black Market

As detailed in Chapter 2, a continuing battle rages between domestic and international drug-control authorities and illicit drug traffickers who employ increasingly sophisticated high-technology methods to distribute their drugs. A prime example is the number of Web-based marketplaces such as Silk Road 2.0 (see Drug Enforcement ... in Focus on pages 17–18) that allow anonymous purchases to be made of illicit drugs. From a criminal justice perspective, these struggles exemplify the difficulties in controlling illicit drug purchases when present-day technologies permit untraceable financial transactions.

Nonetheless, as long as Silk Road 2.0 and other Web-based marketplaces manage to exist, we can have an "inside look" at the "market conditions" for purchases of various illicit drugs. In other words, it is possible to compare the prices of various illicit drugs, as a function of the country in which the drug is being purchased. What is the going price for cocaine, for example, when purchased in a specific country?

Here is a comparison chart of prices for a gram of cocaine in eight nations of the world, as of October 7, 2013, with the virtual currency of bitcoins converted to U.S. dollars, according to the exchange rate at the time ($140 to one bitcoin). Naturally, the bitcoin currency rate, as with any other currency, fluctuates continually and often in wild gyrations. On November 3, 2014, for example, the bitcoin exchange rate was $330; on July 30, 2018 it was $8,194 after being as high as $17,680 on December 14, 2017! For a price in dollars on the day (or hour) you are reading this,

check the numerous bitcoin currency exchanges on the Internet and adjust the figures below, accordingly.

To the extent that Silk Road 2.0 accurately reflected the ongoing prices in October 2013 for illicit drugs in a particular nation, it is evident that cocaine was most expensive in Australia and relatively cheap in the United States. It was inexpensive in Peru, probably due to the fact that Peru is one of the top sources of cocaine in the world.

Source: Data accessed from: *https://money.cnn.com/2013/10/09/technology/silk-road-drug-prices/index.html*

The Different Forms of Amphetamine

To understand amphetamine abuse, both past and present, it is necessary to know something about the molecular structure of amphetamines themselves and their relationship with important neurotransmitters in the brain. As you can see at the top of Figure 10.5, amphetamine can be represented chiefly as carbon (C), hydrogen (H), and nitrogen (N) atoms, in a prescribed arrangement. What you are seeing, however, is only one version of amphetamine, the "right-handed" form, since amphetamine contains a "left-handed" version as well (imagine a mirror image of Figure 10.5). The more potent version is the right-handed form, called dextroamphetamine or **d-amphetamine** (brand name: Dexedrine). It is stronger than the left-handed form, called levoamphetamine or l-amphetamine, which is not commonly available. A modified form of d-amphetamine, formulated by substituting CH_3 (called a methyl group) instead of H at one end, is called **methamphetamine**. This slight change in the formula allows for a quicker passage across the blood–brain barrier and therefore a more powerful effect on the brain.

It is methamphetamine (*meth, speed,* or *crank*) that has been the primary form of amphetamine abuse in recent years.

Acute Effects of Amphetamines

The acute effects of amphetamine, in either d-amphetamine or methamphetamine form, closely resemble those of cocaine. However, amphetamine effects extend over a longer period of time. For intervals of 8–24 hours, there are signs of increased

> **d-amphetamine:** Shortened name for dextroamphetamine, a potent form of amphetamine, marketed under the brand name Dexedrine.
>
> **methamphetamine:** A type of amphetamine, once marketed under the brand name Methedrine. Methamphetamine abusers typically refer to the drug as meth, speed, or crank.

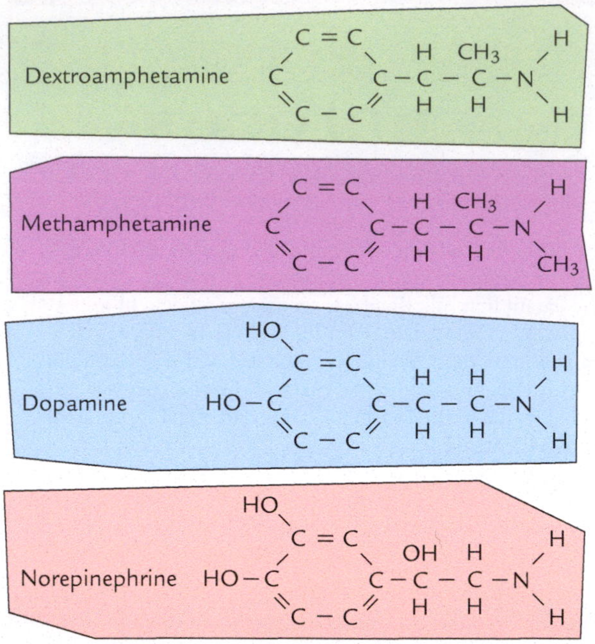

FIGURE 10.5

The molecular structures of dextroamphetamine, methamphetamine, dopamine, and norepinephrine.

sympathetic autonomic activity such as faster breathing and heart rate as well as hyperthermia (increased body temperature) and elevated blood pressure. Users experience feelings of euphoria and invincibility, decreased appetite, and an extraordinary boost in alertness and energy. Adverse and potentially lethal bodily changes include convulsions, chest pains, and stroke.[40]

Chronic Effects of Amphetamines

The chronic effects of amphetamine abuse are both bizarre and unpleasant, particularly in the case of methamphetamine. Heavy methamphetamine abusers may experience formication similar to those endured by cocaine abusers. They may become obsessed with the delusion that parasites or insects have lodged in their skin and so attempt to scratch, cut, or burn their skin in an effort to remove them. It is also likely that they will engage in compulsive or repetitive behaviors that are fixated upon ordinarily trivial aspects of life; an entire night might be spent, for example, counting the cornflakes in a cereal box. Compulsive jaw movements and teeth grinding can cause significant dental damage over time.[41]

The most serious societal consequence of methamphetamine abuse is the appearance of paranoia, wildly bizarre delusions, hallucinations, tendencies toward violence, and intense mood swings. In the words of one health professional, "It's about the ugliest drug there is."[42] Because the symptoms have been observed with the chronic abuse of amphetamines of any type, they are referred to collectively as **amphetamine psychosis**. These "psychotic" effects, often persisting for weeks or even months after the drug has been withdrawn (called "tweaking" by the drug-abuse

community), so closely resemble the symptoms of paranoid schizophrenia that it has been speculated that the two conditions have the same underlying chemical basis in the brain: an overstimulation of dopamine-releasing neurons in those regions that control emotional reactivity.[43] A study of heavy methamphetamine users has shown changes in chemical metabolites in those regions of the brain that are associated with Parkinson's disease, suggesting that this group may be predisposed to acquiring Parkinson symptoms later in life, due to their methamphetamine exposure. Fortunately, however, recent evidence indicates that chemical changes in the brain in chronic methamphetamine users can be at least partially reversed by abstaining from the drug for a year or more.[44]

How Amphetamines Work in the Brain

We can get a good idea of how amphetamines work in the brain by looking carefully at the molecular structures of dopamine and norepinephrine alongside d-amphetamine and methamphetamine in Figure 10.5. Notice how similar they all are, with only slight differences among them. Because of the close resemblance to dopamine and norepinephrine, it is not hard to imagine amphetamines increasing the activity level of these two neurotransmitters.

Methamphetamine Abuse

In the 1960s, methamphetamine abuse was intermingled with the psychedelic drug scene, most prominently during San Francisco's "Summer of Love and Peace" in 1967. Almost from the beginning, however, speed freaks—as methamphetamine abusers were called—whose behaviors were anything but loving or peaceful, became the outcasts of that society. They were more often than not wild-eyed, manic burnout cases, given to erratic and violent behavior. They were typically shunned by the rest of the drug users in the community.

As crack cocaine became increasingly associated with the urban poor and powder cocaine with upscale affluence in the 1980s, amphetamine abuse declined dramatically. In the 1990s, however, as crack cocaine and powder cocaine abuse began to diminish, methamphetamine abuse reemerged, with a totally new demographic profile. Its popularity was now concentrated among working-class people rather than among those who were associated with the drug scene of the 1960s, individuals with traditional rather than countercultural social values. Without the stigma of being a "hard drug," methamphetamine would become one of the few drugs reported as equally or more prevalent than other illicit drugs in areas outside America's inner cities.

amphetamine psychosis: A set of symptoms, including hallucinations, paranoia, and disordered thinking, resulting from high doses of amphetamines.

Methamphetamine in the Heartland of America

As methamphetamine (meth) abuse expanded into midwestern, central, and southern U.S. states, communities that had not traditionally been considered to be involved with illicit drug-taking behavior were having to deal with major problems of public safety and public health. By 2005, for example, domestic meth abuse had gotten so bad in a county in North Carolina (population 51,000) that it had nicknamed itself "the county that never sleeps." Law enforcement raids on meth laboratories in the region were a common occurrence. Because of the combustible ingredients in meth production, every fire emergency was treated as if it were a "meth-lab fire."

A survey of more than 500 county sheriffs in the United States, conducted by the National Association of Counties in 2005, documented the alarming proportions of meth abuse across the country. Fifty-eight percent of sheriffs in the survey regarded meth abuse as the biggest drug problem they faced, ahead of concerns about heroin, cocaine, or marijuana. In half of the counties surveyed, one in five current prison inmates had been incarcerated due to meth-related crimes. In 17 percent of the counties, more than half of the inmate population had been incarcerated for such crimes. A majority of sheriffs reported that methamphetamine was the major contributing factor for increases in robberies or burglaries, domestic violence, and simple assaults. At the same time, only one in six counties reported that they had the financial resources to support a rehabilitation center or program.

The impact of meth abuse on children was a particular concern. There were significant increases in cases in which children needed to be placed out of the home as a result of neglect and abuse by parents who were meth abusers or a child's proximity to the hazards of homegrown meth labs. Nearly three-fourths of county child welfare officials in California and Colorado, for example, reported an increase in such cases. More than 69 percent of counties in Minnesota reported an increase in methamphetamine-related child placements between 2004 and 2005. Meanwhile, social service networks were ill prepared to handle the increased numbers of foster children, and the chances of reunifying families torn apart by meth abuse were considerably lower than in cases involving other forms of substance abuse, due to the relatively high rate of relapse in treatment. In many respects, the crisis in social services experienced with the current opioid abuse epidemic is the same as the crisis experienced during the peak years of meth abuse a decade or so earlier. The parallel between the two crises is a clear indication of the profound negative effect drug-taking behavior can have on the social fabric of a nation.[45]

Environmental consequences included the accumulation of toxic materials remaining as waste residue from meth manufacture, seeping into the soil and contaminating rivers and streams. Families suffered from the inhalation of toxic fumes emitted during meth production and from fire and explosions resulting from flammable precursor chemicals.[46]

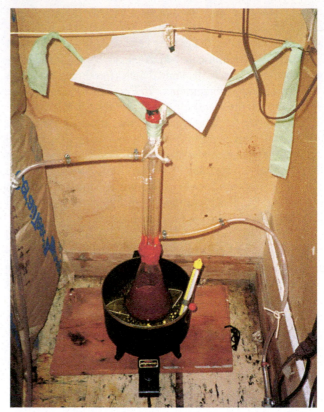

In a makeshift but sophisticated "meth factory," seized in a DEA raid in Altamont, Tennessee, a combination of ephedrine, hydrochloric acid, and red phosphorus (shown in the red liquid in the picture) was heated in a flask placed in an electric pot. Rubber tubes attached to each side of the glass condenser circulated cold water to reduce the escape of toxic fumes.

Credit: Byllwill/E+/Getty Images

Present-Day Methamphetamine Abuse

The Comprehensive Methamphetamine Control Act of 1996 increased the penalties for trafficking and manufacture of methamphetamine, but as domestic meth labs became a widespread social problem, it was apparent that more aggressive legislation was needed. In 2005, the Combat Methamphetamine Epidemic Act established nationwide sales restrictions on precursor chemicals for meth production. Since then, retail outlets have been required by federal law to limit the sales of numerous cough-and-cold remedies that contain pseudoepinephrine—an essential ingredient in the making of methamphetamine. In effect, these "over-the-counter" drugstore products have become "behind-the-counter." Under present pseudoepinephrine regulations, customers cannot make a legitimate purchase of more than the equivalent of approximately seventy 60 mg tablets per day and must provide photo identification upon purchase and sign a logbook recording the transaction. Because liquid anhydrous ammonia, commonly used as a farm fertilizer, is another ingredient in the making of methamphetamine, fertilizer dealers have resorted to the installation of security systems to protect their supplies from theft.

As described in Chapter 2, restrictions imposed under present federal law have resulted in a "downsizing" of these meth labs and a smaller role in the availability of meth. Meth cookers now rely on recipes that yield smaller quantities of methamphetamine and no longer participate in significant meth trafficking. While more than 9,000 clandestine meth laboratories in the United States were confiscated in 2014, almost 24,000 had been confiscated in 2004. Present-day methamphetamine trafficking in the United States has shifted to sources in Mexico (Drug Enforcement ... in Focus) where high-grade meth is manufactured and smuggled over the southern border.

As a result of the large quantities that are available, methamphetamine abuse continues to be a significant drug-control issue. In 2016, the National Survey on Drug Use and Health estimated that approximately 14.5 million Americans aged 12 or older had used methamphetamine at some time in their lives, 1.4 million had used it during the past year, and 667,000 had used it during the past month.

As with cocaine abuse, meth abuse has been overshadowed by the opioid abuse epidemic. Nonetheless, there is great concern that meth abuse deaths have risen quickly, particularly as a result of contamination with synthetic opioids such as fentanyl or fentanyl analogs. In 2017, there were approximately 10,700 meth overdose deaths, an increase of 87 percent over 2015.[47]

Table 10.2 includes some of the street names used by abusers of methamphetamine and other amphetamines such as dextroamphetamine.

Crystal Methamphetamine (Ice)

In the late 1980s, a smokable form of methamphetamine called **ice** (also referred to as *crystal meth*) appeared on the drug scene in Hawaii, expanding to the mainland United States a decade

ice: A smokable form of methamphetamine hydrochloride. It is often referred to as crystal meth, due to its quartz-like appearance.

TABLE 10.2

Street names for methamphetamine and other amphetamines

TYPE AMPHETAMINE	STREET NAME
Amphetamine in general	Bennies, uppers, ups, A, pep pills, white crowns, whites
Dextroamphetamine	Dexies, cadillacs, black beauties
Methamphetamine*	Meth, speed, Tina, crank, little whites, white crosstops, crystal meth, quill, yellow bam, zip, go fast, chalk, shabu, spoosh, get go
Smokable methamphetamine*	Ice, crystal, crystal meth, L.A., L.A. glass, quartz, cristy, hanyak, Christina, Tina
Methcathinone, mephedrone	Khat, cat, goob

*Slang terms often confuse smokable and nonsmokable forms of methamphetamine, so some street names may overlap the two categories.

Source: Drug Enforcement Administration and the Office of National Drug Control Policy, Washington, D.C.

later as a major club drug in New York, Los Angeles, and other cities. Its name originates from its quartz-like, chunky crystallized appearance. A combination of a purity level of 98–100 percent and a highly efficient route of administration (through the lungs), the dependence potential of this form of meth abuse is relatively high. The association with high-risk sexual behavior remains a major public health concern.[48]

Drug Enforcement . . . in Focus

North Korea and Methamphetamine Trafficking

Until recently, drug-control authorities have regarded Mexico as the primary foreign supplier of methamphetamine (meth), originating from "super lab" facilities (see Chapter 2). In 2013, there appeared signs that North Korea may have emerged as a player in meth trafficking as well. DEA officials announced the arrest and indictment of five individuals, charged with conspiring to import 100 kilograms of North Korean-produced meth into the United States. Two of the defendants, members of a Hong Kong-based criminal organization, had been responsible in 2012 for trafficking more than 30 kilograms of meth into the United States. The shipment was seized by law enforcement agents in Thailand and the Philippines; subsequent testing revealed purity levels between 96 and 99 percent. From the perspective of law enforcement, the

prospect of North Korea entering into the global illicit drug trade has become a concern in drug-trafficking control.

It is difficult to predict the extent to which North Korea will be a serious challenge to Mexico's present dominance in meth trafficking. It is safe to say that the global illicit drug trade is constantly changing, and new trafficking sources are bound to develop over time.

Sources: Five extradited, charged with North Korean drug trafficking conspiracy (2013, November 20). News release. Washington, D.C.: Drug Enforcement Administration, U.S. Department of Justice. Hays, T. (2013, November 25). New drug scourge: North Korean meth. *Newsday*, p. A31. Kwong, J. (2018, January 17). North Korea could become leading supplier of crystal meth, fake bitcoin following sanctions, expert warns. Accessed from: https://www.newsweek.com/north-korea-could-deal-crystal-meth-and-sell-counterfeit-cryptocurrency-due-783697.

Patterns of Methamphetamine Abuse

Even though methamphetamine and cocaine are similar in their stimulant effects and both trigger a major release of dopamine in the brain, the pattern of drug-taking behavior for each type of drug has its own distinctive character. Methamphetamine abusers typically use the drug throughout their waking day, at two- to four-hour intervals, in a pattern that resembles taking medication. Cocaine abusers typically use the drug in the evening and nighttime rather than during the day, taking it in a continuous (binge-like) fashion until all the cocaine on hand has been exhausted. This latter pattern of drug-taking behavior fits the typical picture of the recreational user.

The duration of response to the two drugs helps to explain the differences in usage. Methamphetamine effects generally last longer than cocaine effects. Therefore, cocaine abusers need relatively more frequent administrations to maintain their "high." On tests that evaluate different forms of cognitive functioning, methamphetamine and cocaine abusers show significant differences in the type of cognitive impairment that is produced. Methamphetamine abusers are generally impaired on tests of perceptual speed or manipulation of information, effects observed to a lesser extent among cocaine abusers. The greatest difference between the two groups is observed when tests require both speed and the manipulation of information.[49]

Quick Concept Check 10.2

Understanding Patterns of Stimulant Drug Abuse

Check your understanding of the changing patterns of stimulant drug abuse from 1975 to the present by identifying the following statements with (a) an event prior to 1986 or (b) an event subsequent to 1986.

1. Cocaine use is very expensive and restricted primarily to the wealthy.
2. Crack cocaine presents serious societal problems in the inner cities.
3. The typical cocaine abuser has not gone to college and earns less than $25,000 per year.
4. The nationwide toll-free hotline 1-800-COCAINE is established.
5. A smokable form of methamphetamine called ice becomes a major drug of abuse.
6. The number of d-amphetamine prescriptions declines by 90 percent.

Answers: 1. prior 2. subsequent 3. subsequent 4. prior
5. subsequent 6. prior

Treatment for Methamphetamine Abuse

The course of methamphetamine withdrawal—and of amphetamine withdrawal in general—is very similar to the course of events described earlier for cocaine. First, there is the "crash" when the abuser feels intense depression, hunger, agitation, and anxiety within one to four hours after the drug-taking behavior has stopped. Withdrawal from amphetamines, during total abstinence from the drug, takes between 6 and 16 weeks, during which the intense craving for amphetamine slowly subsides.

As in cocaine-abuse treatment, there are inpatient and outpatient programs for methamphetamine abuse, depending on the circumstances and motivation of the abuser. Self-help groups such as Cocaine Anonymous can be useful as well, since the symptoms of amphetamine withdrawal and cocaine withdrawal are nearly identical. Methamphetamine abusers represent approximately 1 in 12 individuals in treatment for substance abuse, but relatively few methamphetamine abusers attempt treatment, much less succeed in recovery. The reason is that they perceive themselves as remaining in control over their drug use, despite evidence to the contrary. The attitude of denial makes it difficult for methamphetamine abusers to seek treatment.[50]

Overall, methamphetamine abusers find it extremely difficult to become drug-free, and their relapse rate is one of the highest for any category of illicit or licit drug abuse.

Cathinone as a New Form of Stimulant Abuse

In the 1970s, a medicinal chemist discovered a new type of stimulant by adding an oxygen atom to a section of the amphetamine molecule, resulting in a new stimulant compound that is more powerful than amphetamine, now known as *cathinone*. Adding a methyl group to methamphetamine created a new stimulant drug called methcathinone (also referred to as mephedrone), which was still more powerful.

These discoveries were more or less scientific curiosities until 2010, when a family of white-crystal designer drugs containing cathinone or cathinone-related ingredients appeared on the drug scene, marketed to appear like legitimate bath products (specifically, common epsom salts), hence the street name "bath salts." The packaging stated that it was not intended "for human consumption" to avoid prosecution under the federal laws forbidding the sale of drugs substantially similar to already classified Schedule I controlled substances.

In 2011, dramatic increases in health emergencies involving "bath salts" were reported. Only a third of these drugs, however, were later found to contain cathinone alone; two-thirds were found to be combined with marijuana, synthetic marijuana, or other drugs. In 2012, President Obama signed into law the Synthetic Drug Abuse Prevention Act, banning synthetic drugs commonly appearing in "bath salts." The law also banned additional synthetic drugs related to marijuana that were being marketed on the street under the names "Spice" and "K2" (see Chapter 11). Fortunately, media reports of the dangers of "bath salts" have resulted in very low prevalence rates at the secondary school level. According to the University of Michigan survey in 2017, less than 1 percent of eighth, tenth, or twelfth graders reported any use in the past year.[51]

While immediate concerns about "bath salts" may have receded for now, public health and public safety concerns regarding designer synthetic drugs such as "bath salts" and similar designer synthetic drugs are likely to continue for some time. Despite the fact that these drugs are "advertised" as being synthetic forms of existing drugs such as marijuana or MDMA (Ecstasy), their chemical properties are totally unknown to the user. This serious problem will be addressed further in Chapter 11 with respect to the availability of a drug, referred to on the street as "Molly."

Amphetamines and Other Stimulants as Medications

It is well known that there are approved medical applications for amphetamines and amphetamine-like stimulant drugs in specific circumstances. Stimulants are prescribed primarily for elementary school-age children diagnosed as being unable to maintain sufficient levels of attention and impulse control in school or display hyperactive behavior in general. These symptoms are used in the determination of a diagnosis, referred to as **attention deficit/hyperactivity disorder (ADHD)**. When there is no evidence of hyperactivity, the diagnosis is referred to as *attention deficit disorder (ADD)*.

ADHD is the most common psychological disorder among children. It is estimated that 3–7 percent of all school-age children meet the criteria for ADHD. The prevalence rate is three times greater and the symptoms are generally more severe for boys than for girls. These children have average to above-average intelligence but typically underperform academically. As many as two-thirds of school-age children with ADHD have at least one other psychiatric disorder, including anxiety and depression.[52] Despite the public image of ADHD as an exclusively childhood phenomenon, longitudinal studies have shown that ADHD symptoms persist from childhood into adolescence in about 75 percent of the cases and into adulthood in about 50 percent of the cases.[53]

Stimulant Medications for ADHD

Commonly prescribed stimulant medications for the treatment of ADHD include oral administrations of an amphetamine-like drug, methylphenidate (brand name: Ritalin), a combination of dextroamphetamine and amphetamine (brand name: Adderall), and a combination of

dextroamphetamine and the amino acid lysine, lisdexamfetamine (brand name: Vyvanse).

For decades, Ritalin dominated the market as the prescription medication for ADHD. While a growing number of alternative medications are now available for this purpose, Ritalin remains the most recognizable "brand" with respect to ADHD treatment. In this drug's original formulation, the rapid onset and short duration of Ritalin require two administrations during a school day: one at breakfast and another at lunchtime as supervised by a school nurse. In the evening, blood levels of Ritalin decline to levels that permit normal sleep. Adderall has a longer duration of action, making it possible to administer a single dose and avoiding school involvement in treatment. In comparative studies, Ritalin and Adderall have been found to be equivalent in effectiveness.[54]

Newer drug treatments for ADHD have become available that are essentially variations of the traditional methylphenidate medication. They include a sustained-release formulation (brand name: Concerta), a formulation that produces an initial rapid dose of methylphenidate followed by a second sustained-release phase (brand name: Metadate), and a chemical variation of methylphenidate that allows for a longer duration of action (brand names: Attenade, Focalin). A methylphenidate patch (brand name: Daytrana), designed to release the drug through the skin slowly over a period of nine hours, was approved in 2006.

About 70 percent of the approximately 1 million children in the United States who take stimulants for ADHD each year respond successfully to the treatment. In 1999, a major study examining the effects of medication over a 14-month period found that medication was more effective in reducing ADHD symptoms than behavioral treatment and nearly as effective as a combined approach of medication and behavioral treatment.

One side effect of stimulant medications, however, is a suppression of height and weight gains during these formative years, reducing growth to about 80–90 percent normal levels. Fortunately, growth spurts during the summer, when children are typically no longer taking medication (referred to as "drug holidays"), usually compensate for this problem. Discontinuance of medication, however, has to be carefully monitored. Symptoms such as lethargy, lack of motivation, and, in some cases, depression can occur during this time.

A more serious concern is the increased risk of cardiovascular disease due to the effects of stimulant drugs. In 2006, the FDA recommended a "black box" warning on ADHD medications as a guide for patients and physicians. Recent studies indicate that stimulant treatment for ADHD in childhood does not increase the risk for substance abuse later in life. In fact, the risks for future problems with alcohol and other drugs appear to be reduced.[55]

Until recently, the phenomenon of *reducing* hyperactivity with methylphenidate and related stimulant drugs, rather than *increasing* it, had been quite puzzling to professionals in this field. It is now known that orally administered methylphenidate and related stimulant drugs produce a relatively slow but steady increase in dopamine activity in the brain (see Chapter 8).

attention deficit/hyperactivity disorder (ADHD): A behavioral disorder characterized by increased motor activity, lack of impulse control, and/or reduced attention span.

This change in brain chemistry is hypothesized to have two effects that are beneficial to an individual with ADHD. First, increased dopamine may amplify the effects of environmental stimulation, while reducing the background firing rates of neurons. Thus, there is a greater "signal-to-noise" ratio in the brain, analogous to having now a stronger radio signal received by a radio that no longer competes with high levels of background static. The behavioral result would be an improvement in attention and decreased distractibility. In other words, symptoms of ADHD may be a result of not having a sufficient "signal-to-noise" ratio in the processing of information for tasks that require concentration and focus. Second, increased dopamine may heighten one's motivation with regard to a particular task, enhancing the salience and interest in that task and improving performance. An individual might perform better on a task simply because he or she likes doing it. The slow rate of absorption achieved through oral administration (Chapter 8) and the relatively slow action of dopamine release in the brain avoids the emotional high that is experienced when stimulants are smoked, snorted, or injected.[56]

The theory that increased activity in dopamine alone accounts for the reduction in ADHD symptoms, however, may be incomplete. In 2003, a new medication, atomoxetine (brand name: Strattera), was approved by the FDA for the treatment of ADHD in both children and adults. Since Strattera produces an increase in norepinephrine activity in the brain, it is possible that lowered norepinephrine levels may play a role in ADHD as well. Strattera has been marketed as a once-a-day nonstimulant medication that reduces ADHD symptoms by increasing norepinephrine levels—not dopamine levels—in the brain. The full story may be either that both norepinephrine and dopamine are jointly involved in ADHD or that ADHD itself may be two separable disorders, one related to dopamine activity and the other related to norepinephrine activity. According to this hypothesis, the symptoms may overlap to such a degree that it is difficult to distinguish the two disorders on a strictly behavioral basis.

Other Medical Applications

Narcolepsy (an unpredictable and uncontrollable urge to fall asleep during the day) is another condition for which stimulant drugs have been applied in treatment. In 1999, modafinil (brand name: Provigil) was approved for treating narcolepsy. The advantage of Provigil over traditional stimulant treatments such as dextroamphetamine is that it does not present problems of abuse and produces fewer adverse side effects. Alternative medications for narcolepsy that do not work by stimulating the CNS are presently under development.[57]

There are also several amphetamine-like drugs available to the public, some of them on a nonprescription basis, for use as nasal decongestants. In most cases, their effectiveness stems from their primary action on the peripheral nervous system rather than on the CNS. Even so, the potential for misuse exists: Some users continue to take these drugs over a long period of time because stopping their use may result in unpleasant rebound effects such as nasal stuffiness. This reaction, by the way, is similar to the stuffy nose that is experienced in the chronic administration of cocaine.[58]

Ritalin and Adderall Abuse

In 1996, the Swiss pharmaceutical company Ciba-Geigy sent letters to hundreds of thousands of pharmacies and physicians in the United States, warning them to exert greater control over Ritalin tablets and prescriptions to obtain them. The alert came in response to reports that Ritalin was becoming a drug of abuse among young people, who were crushing the tablets and snorting the powder as a new way of getting a stimulant high. Diversion of prescription medications was beginning to be a concern.

Since then, the problem of stimulant medication abuse, primarily the nonmedical use of Adderall among young people has become a major issue, particularly among college students. In 2016, approximately one in ten college students had used Adderall and one in forty had used Ritalin for nonmedical purposes. Approximately 6 percent of high school seniors reported in 2016 using Adderall nonmedically in the past year, while 1.2 percent reported using Ritalin.[59]

Stimulant Medications as Cognitive Enhancers

In 2007, a surprising (and controversial) article entitled "Professor's Little Helper" was published in Nature, one of the world's leading scientific journals. It reported that 62 percent of respondents said that they had taken Ritalin to enhance their mental performance. More than 1,400 presumably healthy people in 60 different countries participated in the survey. Since then, the question of "cognitive enhancement" with respect to stimulant medications has become a subject of much discussion and debate. Undoubtedly, stimulants of all kinds can fight fatigue and the need for sleep as well as sharpen one's attention span and remain focused when carrying out dull, repetitive tasks. In that sense, staying up late to finish a paper or a project of some sort and the ability to focus on a routine task at hand could result in a higher level of performance (although the same could be said for caffeine), but the possible benefits for higher-level cognitive processing in areas of long-term memory, problem-solving, and creative thought are unclear.

Despite ethical concerns regarding so-called smart pills, however, the popularity of stimulant medications for these purposes has soared. Unfortunately, the ever-rising expectations of students and professionals in the workplace, as well as athletes, have made stimulant medications attractive options, despite the health risks involved. It is evident that we are dealing with the "super-motivated" rather than the "unmotivated" individual in this situation (see Chapter 16). Of course, one cannot discount the strength of a placebo effect among individuals who have reported "great benefits" from so-called smart pills.[60]

Summary

The History of Cocaine

- Cocaine, one of the two major psychoactive stimulants, is derived from coca leaves grown in the mountainous regions of South America. Coca chewing is still prevalent among certain groups of South American Indians.
- During the last half of the nineteenth century, several patent medicines and beverages were sold that contained cocaine, including the original (pre-1903) formulation for Coca-Cola.
- Sigmund Freud was an early enthusiast of cocaine as an important medicinal drug, promoting cocaine as a cure for morphine dependence and depression. Soon afterward, Freud realized the strong dependence that cocaine can bring about.

Acute and Chronic Effects of Cocaine

- Cocaine produces a powerful burst of energy and sense of well-being. In general, cocaine causes an elevation in the sympathetic autonomic nervous system.
- Long-term cocaine use can produce hallucinations and deep depression, as well as physical deterioration of the nasal membranes if cocaine is administered intranasally.

Medical Uses of Cocaine and How Cocaine Works in the Brain

- The only accepted medical application for cocaine is its use as a local anesthetic.
- Cocaine causes faster breathing and heart rate as well as elevated blood pressure and hyperthermia. Within the CNS, cocaine increases the activity of dopamine and, to a lesser extent, norepinephrine in the brain.

Present-Day Cocaine Abuse

- Compared with the permissive attitude toward cocaine use seen during the 1970s and early 1980s, attitudes toward cocaine use since the second half of the 1980s have changed dramatically.
- The emergence in the mid-1980s of relatively inexpensive, smokable crack cocaine expanded the cocaine-abuse problem to new segments of the U.S. population and made cocaine abuse one of the major social issues of our time.

Treatment Programs for Cocaine Abuse

- Cocaine abusers can receive treatment through inpatient programs, outpatient programs, or a combination of the two. Relapse is a continual concern for recovering cocaine abusers.

Amphetamines

- Amphetamines have their origin in a Chinese medicinal herb, used for thousands of years as a bronchial dilator; its active ingredient, ephedrine, was isolated in 1887.
- The drug amphetamine (brand name: Benzedrine) was developed in 1927 as a synthetic form of ephedrine. By the 1930s, various forms of amphetamines, specifically d-amphetamine and methamphetamine, became available around the world as a psychostimulant.
- Like cocaine, amphetamines cause faster breathing and heart rate as well as elevated blood pressure and hyperthermia. Unlike cocaine, however, the effects are more long-lasting. Amphetamines increase dopamine and norepinephrine activity in the brain.

Acute and Chronic Effects of Amphetamines

- Amphetamine is effective as a general arousing agent, as an antidepressant, and as an appetite suppressant, in addition to its ability to keep people awake for long periods of time.
- Although the acute effects of amphetamines resemble those of cocaine, amphetamines (when taken in large doses) have the particular feature of producing symptoms of paranoia, delusions, hallucinations, and violent behaviors, referred to as amphetamine psychosis. The bizarre behaviors of the "speed freak" illustrate the dangers of chronic amphetamine abuse.

Methamphetamine Abuse

- In the 1960s, methamphetamine (meth) abuse was intermingled with the psychedelic drug scene. At the time, meth abusers, referred to as "speed freaks," were known for erratic and often violent behavior.
- In the late 1990s and mid-2000s, meth abuse became widespread in rural and nonurban regions of the United States. The proliferation of homegrown meth labs created considerable social and public health problems in communities that were ill prepared for the consequences of illicit drug abuse.
- Federal legislation in 2005 succeeded in reducing access to precursor chemicals for domestic meth production, resulting in smaller meth labs and lesser involvement in meth trafficking. Present-day meth trafficking originates primarily in Mexico.
- Methamphetamine abusers typically use the drug throughout their waking day, while cocaine abusers typically use the drug in a binge-like fashion in the evening and nighttime rather than during the day. However, treatment for methamphetamine abuse generally follows along the same lines as treatment for cocaine abuse.

Cathinone as a New Form of Stimulant Abuse

- In 2010, a family of white-crystal designer drugs containing cathinone or cathinone-related ingredients appeared on the drug scene, marketed to resemble legitimate bath products (like epsom salts), hence the street name "bath salts."
- The designer synthetic drugs such as "bath salts" are representative of large number of recently available chemicals that are "advertised" as being synthetic forms of existing

drugs. Their chemical properties, however, are typically unknown to the user.

Amphetamines and Similar Stimulant Drugs as Medications

- Amphetamine-like stimulant drugs have been developed for a number of approved medical purposes.
- Methylphenidate (brand name: Ritalin), atomoxetine (brand name: Strattera), and dextroamphetamine (brand name: Adderall) are three examples of drugs commonly prescribed for children diagnosed with attention deficit/hyperactivity disorder (ADHD). There has been growing concern about the nonmedical use of these medications, either for recreational purposes or to stay alert for longer periods of time.

- Other medical applications for amphetamine-like drugs include their use as a treatment for narcolepsy and as a means for the temporary relief of nasal congestion.

Stimulant Medications as "Cognitive Enhancers"

- The widespread nonmedical use of stimulant medications such as Ritalin and Adderall by healthy individuals for the purpose of enhancing cognitive performance has been a subject of much discussion and debate. Beyond its effects on fighting fatigue and increasing one's focus on routine tasks, the effects they may have on higher-level processing are unclear.
- It is evident that use of stimulants for cognitive enhancement has been embraced by the "super-motivated" rather than the "unmotivated" individual in our society.

Key Terms

amphetamine, p. 206
amphetamine psychosis, p. 208
attention deficit/hyperactivity
    disorder (ADHD), p. 212

cocaine, p. 196
cocaine hydrochloride, p. 202
cocaine psychosis, p. 200
crack cocaine or crack, p. 202

d-amphetamine, p. 207
formication, p. 199
free-base cocaine, p. 202
ice, p. 210

kindling effect, p. 201
methamphetamine, p. 207

Review Questions

1. Discuss the differences in the way cocaine was treated as a form of drug-taking behavior in the nineteenth century as opposed to the twentieth and twenty-first centuries. In your answer, include some discussion of the history of Vin Mariani and Coca-Cola.
2. Describe the bodily changes involved in the acute effects of cocaine. Describe the mood changes and hallucinatory experiences in chronic cocaine abuse.
3. Describe how cocaine is extracted from the coca plant and how crack cocaine and free-base cocaine are made from cocaine.
4. Describe the current prevalence rates for cocaine, as well as the relationship between current rates and those of the past. Outline the various options for cocaine-abuse treatment.

5. Describe the various forms of amphetamines. Why is d-amphetamine more effective as a stimulant drug than l-amphetamine?
6. What are the differences in the patterns of methamphetamine abuse in the 1960s and methamphetamine abuse in the late 1990s and mid-2000s?
7. What are the benefits of stimulant medications for the treatment of attention deficit disorder? What are some of the concerns in using these drugs for treating children?
8. What are the arguments for and against the nonmedical use of stimulant medications for "cognitive enhancement" purposes, that is, as a way to increase cognitive performance?

Critical Thinking: What Would You Do?

You are a student taking a chemistry exam, and you know that a person sitting next to you (who seems as capable as you are in mastering the subject matter) used Adderall the night before and was able to study 50 percent longer than you were able to, without any stimulant medication. You later find out the exam score of that other student; it is a full letter grade higher than yours. Do you feel that you have recourse in appealing your grade to the instructor in charge? If so, how would you argue your case to the instructor?

Endnotes

1. Inciardi, J. A. (2002). *The war on drugs III*. Boston: Allyn and Bacon, p. 129. Inglis, B. (1975). *The forbidden game: A social history of drugs*. New York: Scribner's, pp. 49–50. Rivera, M. A.; Aufderheider, A. C.; Cartmell, L. W.; Torres, C. M.; and Langsjoen, O. (2005). Antiquity of coca-leaf chewing in the south central Andes: A 3,000 year archeological record of coca-leaf chewing from northern Chile. *Journal of Psychoactive Drugs*, 37(4), 455–458.

2. Jaffe, J. (1985). Drug addiction and drug abuse. In L. S. Goodman; and A. Gilman (Eds.), *The pharmacological basis of therapeutics* (7th ed.). New York: Macmillan, p. 552.

3. Nahas, G. G. (1989). *Cocaine: The great white plague*. Middlebury, VT: Paul S. Eriksson, pp. 154–162.
4. Kusinitz, M. (1988). *Drug use around the world*. New York: Chelsea House Publishers, pp. 91–95.
5. Karch, S. B. (1996). *The pathology of drug abuse* (2nd ed.). Boca Raton, FL: CRC Press, pp. 2–3. Nuckols, C. C. (1989). *Cocaine: From dependency to recovery* (2nd ed.). Blue Ridge Summit, PA: Tab Books, p. x.
6. Brecher, E. M.; and the editors of *Consumer Reports* (1972). *Licit and illicit drugs*. Boston: Little, Brown, p. 270. Weiss, R. D.; and Mirin, S. M. (1987). *Cocaine*. Washington, D.C.: American Psychiatric Press, p. 6.
7. McKim, W. A.; and Hancock, S. (2013). *Drugs and behavior: An introduction to behavioral pharmacology* (7th ed.). Boston: Pearson, p. 230.
8. Erickson, P. G.; Adlaf, E. M.; Murray, G. F.; and Smart, R. G. (1987). *The steel drug: Cocaine in perspective*. Lexington, MA: D. C. Heath, p. 9.
9. Musto, D. (1973). *The American disease: Origins of narcotic control*. New Haven, CT: Yale University Press.
10. Jones, E. (1953). *The life and work of Sigmund Freud, Vol. 1*. New York: Basic Books, p. 81.
11. Ibid. Quotation of Sigmund Freud on page 84.
12. Brecher, *Licit and illicit drugs*, pp. 272–280.
13. Aronson, T. A.; and Craig, T. J. (1986). Cocaine precipitation of panic disorder. *American Journal of Psychiatry, 143,* 643–645. National Institute on Drug Abuse (2010, March). *NIDA InfoFacts: Cocaine*. Rockville, MD: National Institute on Drug Abuse.
14. Marsuk, P. M.; Tardiff, K.; Leon, A. C.; Stajic, M.; Morgan, E. B.; and Mann, J. J. (1992). Prevalence of cocaine use among residents of New York City who committed suicide during a one-year period. *American Journal of Psychiatry, 149,* 371–375.
15. Office of Substance Abuse Prevention (1989). *What you can do about drug use in America* (DHHS publication No. ADM 88–1572). Rockville, MD: National Clearinghouse for Alcohol and Drug Information.
16. Philips, J. L.; and Wynne, R. D. (1974). *A cocaine bibliography—nonannotated*. Rockville, MD: National Institute on Drug Abuse. Cited in Abel, E. L. (1985). *Psychoactive drugs and sex*. New York: Plenum Press, p. 100.
17. Kaufman, M. J.; Levin, J. M.; Ross, M. H.; Lange, N.; Rose, et al. 1998). Cocaine-induced cerebral vasoconstriction detected in humans with magnetic resonance angiography. *Journal of the American Medical Association, 279,* 376–380.
18. Experiment in Memphis suggests many drive after using drugs (1994, August 28). *The New York Times*, p. 30.
19. Information courtesy of the American Academy of Otolaryngology-Head and Neck Surgery, Old Town Alexandria, VA.
20. National Institute on Drug Abuse (2016, May). What are some ways that cocaine changes the brain? Research Report Series on Cocaine. Rockville MD: National Institute on Drug Abuse. Accessed from: https://www.drugabuse.gov/publications/research-reports/cocaine. Volkow, N. D.; Wang, G-J.; Fowler, J. S.; Logan, J.; Gatley, S. J.; Hitzemann, R.; et al. (1997). Decrease in striatal dopaminergic responsiveness in detoxified cocaine-dependent subjects. *Nature, 386,* 830–833. Whitten, L. (2009, April). Low dopamine receptor availability may promote cocaine addiction. *NIDA Notes, 22*(3), 15, 18
21. Robinson, T. E. (1993). Persistent sensitizing effects of drugs on brain dopamine systems and behavior: Implications for addiction and relapse. In S. G. Korenman; and J. D. Barchas (Eds.), *The biological basis of substance abuse*. New York: Oxford University Press, pp. 373–402. Weiss and Mirin, *Cocaine*, pp. 48–49.
22. Kaplan, H. I.; Freedman, A. M.; and Sadock, B. J. (1980). *Comprehensive textbook of psychiatry, Vol. 3*. Baltimore, MD: Williams and Wilkins, p. 1621.
23. Flynn, J. C. (1991). *Cocaine: An in-depth look at the facts, science, history, and future of the world's most addictive drug*. New York: Birch Lane/Carol Publishing, pp. 38–46.
24. Ibid., p. 44.
25. Humphries, D. (1998). Crack mothers at 6: Prime-time news, crack/cocaine, and women. *Violence against Women, 4,* 45–61. Massing, M. (1998). *The fix*. New York: Simon and Schuster, p. 41. Singer, L. T.; Minnes, S.; Short, E.; Arendt, R.; Farkas, K.; et al. (2004). Cognitive outcomes of preschool children with prenatal cocaine exposure. *Journal of the American Medical Association, 291,* 2448–2456.
26. Egan, T. (1999, September 19). A drug ran its course, then hid with its users. *The New York Times*, pp. 1, 46. Furst, R. T.; Johnson, B. D.; Dunlap, E.; and Curtis, R. (1999). The stigmatized image of the "crack head": A sociocultural exploration of a barrier to cocaine smoking among a cohort of youth in New York City. *Deviant Behavior, 20,* 153–181.
27. Center for Behavior Health Statistics and Quality (2017). *Results from the 2016 national survey on drug use and health: Detailed tables*. Rockville, MD: Substance Abuse and Mental Health Services Administration, Table 1.1A. Data compiled from the Healthcare and Utilization Project (H-CUP) database, 2017. Agency of Healthcare Research and Quality, U.S. Department of Health and Human Services, Rockville, MD. National Institute on Drug Abuse (2018, August). Overdose death rates. Rockville, MD: National Institute on Drug Abuse. National Institute on Drug Abuse (2017, September). *Overdose death rates*. Washington, D.C.: National Institute on Drug Abuse.
28. Gold, M. S. (1990). *800–COCAINE*. New York: Bantam Books.
29. Nuckols, *Cocaine*, pp. 144–146. Lee, F. R. (1994, September 10). A drug dealer's rapid rise and ugly fall. *The New York Times*, pp. 1, 22.
30. Nuckols, *Cocaine*, p. 42.
31. Ibid., pp. 71–72.
32. Weiss and Mirin, *Cocaine*, p. 125.
33. Fox, C. L.; and Forbing, S. E. (1992). *Creating drug-free schools and communities: A comprehensive approach*. New York: HarperCollins, p. 165.
34. Shine, B. (2000, March). Some cocaine abusers fare better with cognitive-behavioral therapy, others with 12-step programs. *NIDA Notes, 15*(1), 9–11.
35. Barnes, D. M. (1988). Breaking the cycle of addiction. *Science, 241,* p. 1029. Whitten, L. (2005, August). Cocaine-related environmental cues elicit physiological stress responses. *NIDA Notes, 20*(1), 1, 6–7.
36. Brodie, J. D.; Figueroa, E.; Laska, E. M.; and Dewey, S. L. (2005). Safety and efficacy of gamma-vinyl GABA (GVG) for the treatment of methamphetamine and/or cocaine addiction. *Synapse, 55,* 122–125. Schiffer, W. K.; Marsteller, D.; and Dewey, S. L. (2003). Sub-chronic low dose gamma-vinyl GABA (vigabatrin) inhibits cocaine-induced increases in nucleus accumbens dopamine. *Psychopharmacology, 168,* 339–343. Information from ClinicalTrials.gov, a service of the U.S. National Institutes of Health, June 2009.

37. McKim, W. A.; and Hancock, S. D. (2013). *Drugs and behavior: An introduction to behavioral pharmacology* (4th ed.). Upper Saddle River, NJ: Pearson, p. 236. Ohler, N. (Translation from the German edition, 2017). *Blitzed: Drugs in the third reich.* New York: Harcourt Houghlin Mifflin.

38. Brecher, *Licit and illicit drugs*, pp. 282–283.

39. Greaves, G. B. (1980). Psychosocial aspects of amphetamine and related substance abuse. In J. Caldwell (Ed.), *Amphetamines and related stimulants: Chemical, biological, clinical, and sociological aspects.* Boca Raton, FL: CRC Press, pp. 175–192. Peluso, E.; and Peluso, L. S. (1988). *Women and drugs.* Minneapolis: CompCare Publishing.

40. McKim and Hancock, *Drugs and Behavior*, pp.,235–239.

41. Goode, E. (2005). *Drugs in American society* (6th ed.). New York: McGraw-Hill College, p. 276.

42. Bai, M. (1997, March 31). White storm warning: In Fargo and the prairie states, speed kills. *Newsweek*, pp. 66–67. Quotation by Mark A. R. Kleiman, p. 67.

43. McKim and Hancock, *Drugs and Behavior*, pp. 233–235.

44. Ernst, T.; Chang, L.; Leonido-Yee, M.; and Speck, O. (2000). Evidence for long-term neurotoxicity associated with methamphetamine abuse: A 1H MRS study. *Neurology, 54*, 1344–1349. London, E. D.; Simon, S. L.; Berman, S. M.; Mandelhern, M. A.; et al. (2004). Mood disturbances and regional cerebral metabolic abnormalities in recently abstinent methamphetamine abusers. *Archives of General Psychiatry, 61*, 73–84. Sheff, D. (2008). *Beautiful boy: A father's journey through his son's addiction.* New York: Houghton Mifflin. Sheff, N. (2008). *Tweak: Growing up with methamphetamine.* New York: Ginee See Books/Atheneum Books for Young Readers, pp. 113–115.

45. National Association of Counties (2005, July 5). The meth epidemic in America. *Two surveys of U.S. counties: The criminal effect of meth on communities and the impact of meth on children.* Washington, D.C.: National Association of Counties. Young, Stanley (1989, July). Zing! Speed: The choice of a new generation. *Spin magazine*, pp. 83, 124–125. Reprinted in Erich Goode (Ed.) (1992). *Drugs, society, and behavior 92/93.* Guilford, CT: Dushkin Publishing, p. 116. Zernike, K. (2005, July 11). A drug scourge creates its own form of orphan. *The New York Times*, pp. A1, A15.

46. Butterfield, F. (2004, January 4). Across rural America, drug casts a grim shadow. *The New York Times*, p. 10. Harris, Gardiner (2005, December 15). Fighting methamphetamine, lawmakers reach accord to curb sales of cold medicines. *The New York Times*, p. A33. Jefferson, D. J. (2005, August 5). America's most dangerous drug. *Newsweek*, pp. 41–48. Johnson, D. (2004, March 8). Policing a rural plague: Meth is ravaging the Midwest. *Newsweek*, p. 41. National Association of Counties (2006, January). *The meth epidemic in America.* Washington, D.C.: National Association of Counties. Zernicke, K. (2006, February 26). With scenes of blood and pain, ads battle methamphetamine in Montana. *The New York Times*, p. 18. National Drug Intelligence Center (2008, December). *National methamphetamine threat assessment 2009.* Washington, D.C.: National Drug Intelligence Center, U.S. Department of Justice, p. 5.

47. Center for Behavior Health Statistics and Quality (2017). *Results from the 2016 National survey on drug use and health: Detailed tables*, Table 1.1A. Methamphetamine lab incidents, 2004–2012. Washington, D.C.: Drug Enforcement Administration, U.S. Department of Justice. National Institute on Drug Abuse (2018, August). Overdose death rates. Rockville, MD: National Institute on Drug Abuse.

48. Jacobs, A. J. (2004, January 12). The beast in the bathhouse: Crystal meth use by gay men threatens to reignite an epidemic. *The New York Times*, pp. B1, B5. Shernoff, M. (2005, July–August). Crystal's sexual persuasion. *The Gay & Lesbian Review*, pp. 24–26.

49. Zickler, P. (2001). Methamphetamine, cocaine abusers have different patterns of drug use, suffer different cognitive impairments. *NIDA Notes, 16*(5), 11–12.

50. National Institute of Justice (1999, May). *Meth matters: Report on methamphetamine users in five western cities.* Washington, D.C.: National Institute of Justice, U.S. Department of Justice. Center for Behavior Health Statistics and Quality (2013). *Treatment episode data set (TEDS) 2001–2011. National admissions to substance abuse treatment services.* Rockville, MD: Substance Abuse and Mental Health Administration, Table 1.1B.

51. Chemicals used in "spice" and "K2" type products now under federal control and regulation (2011, October 21). News Release. Washington, D.C.: Office of Public Affairs, Drug Enforcement Administration. National Institute on Drug Abuse (2017). *Monitoring the future: Trends in the prevalence of various drugs.* Rockville, MD: National Institute on Drug Abuse.

52. Findling, R. L. (2008). Evolution of the treatment of attention-deficit/hyperactivity disorder in children. *Clinical Therapeutics, 30*, 942–957. Advokat, C. D.; Comaty, J. E.; and Julien, R. M. (2015). *A primer of drug action* (13th ed.). New York: Worth.

53. Advokat, Comaty, and Julien, *A primer of drug action*. Wilens, T. E. (2003). Drug therapy for adults with attention-deficit hyperactivity disorder. *Drugs, 63*, 2385–2411. Wilens, T. E.; and Fusillo, S. (2007). When ADHD and substance use disorders intersect: Relationship and treatment implications. *Current Psychiatry Reports, 9*, 408–414.

54. Advokat, Comaty, and Julien, *A primer of drug action*.

55. Nissen, S. E. (2006, April 6). ADHD drugs and cardiovascular risks. *New England Journal of Medicine*, pp. 1445–1448. The MTA Cooperative Group (1999). A 14-month randomized clinical trial of treatment strategies for attention-deficit/hyperactivity disorder. *Archives of General Psychiatry, 56*, 1073–1086. Upadhyaya, H. P. (2008). Substance use disorders in children and adolescents with attention-deficit/hyperactivity disorder: Implications for treatment and the role of the primary care physician. *Journal of Clinical Psychiatry, 10*, 211–221. Wilens, T. E.; Faraone, S. V.; Biederman, J.; and Gunawardene, S. (2003). Does stimulant therapy of attention deficit/hyperactivity disorder beget later substance abuse? A meta-analytic review of the literature. *Pediatrics, 111*, 179–185.

56. Advokat, Comaty, and Julien, *A primer of drug action*. Volkow, N. D.; Wang, G-J.; Fowler, J. S.; Logan, J.; Gerasimov, M.; et al. (2001). Therapeutic doses of oral methylphenidate significantly increase extracellular dopamine in the human being. *Journal of Neuroscience, 21* (121RC), 1–5. Volkow, N. D.; Wang, G-J., Kollins, S. H.; Wigal, T. L.; Newcorn, J. H.; et al. (2009). Evaluating dopamine reward pathway in ADHD: Clinical implications. *Journal of the American Medical Association, 302*, 1084–1091.

57. Green, P. M.; and Stillman, M. J. (1998). Narcolepsy. Signs, symptoms, differential diagnosis, and management. *Archives of*

Family Medicine, 7, 472–478. Tuller, D. (2002, January 8). A quiet revolution for those prone to nodding off. *The New York Times,* p. F7.

58. Advokat, Comaty, and Julien, *A primer of drug action.*

59. Arria, A. M.; Caldeira, K. M.; O'Grady, K. E.; Vincent, K. B.; et al. (2008). Nonmedical use of prescription stimulants among college students: Associations with attention-deficit-hyperactivity disorder and polydrug use. *Pharmacotherapy, 28,* 156–169. Miech, R. A.; Johnston, L.D.; O'Malley, P. M.; Bachman, J. G.; Schulenberg, J. E; and Patrick, M. E. (2018). *Monitoring the future. National survey results on drug use, 1975-2017. Vol. I: Secondary school students.* Ann Arbor, MI: Institute for Social Research, The University of Michigan, Table 4-1b. Thomas, K. (2000, November 27). Stealing, dealing and Ritalin: Adults and students are involved in abuse of drug. *USA Today,* p. D1. Wilens, T. E.; Adler, L A.; Adams, J.; Sgambati, S.; Rotrosen, J.; et al. (2008). Misuse and diversion of stimulants prescribed for ADHD: A systematic review of the literature. *Journal of the American Academy of Child and Adolescent Psychiatry, 47,* 21–31.

60. Carroll, B. C.; McLaughlin, T. J.; and Blake, D. R. (2006). Patterns and knowledge of nonmedical use of stimulants among college students. *Archives of Pediatric and Adolescent Medicine, 160,* 481–485. Students tapping pills for academic boost (2006, June 20). *Newsday,* p. B13. Greely, H.; Sahakian, B.; Harris, J.; Kessler, R. C.; Gazzaniga, M.; et al. (2008). Toward responsible use of cognitive-enhancing drugs by the healthy. *Nature, 456,* 702–705. Harris, J.; and Quigley, M. (2008). Commentary on "Professor's little helper": Humans have always tried to improve their condition. *Nature, 451,* 521. Stix, G. (2009, October). Turbocharging the brain. *Scientific American,* pp. 46–55.

chapter 11

Marijuana

Karen spoke about the many troubles in running a marijuana business that is legal in her state of Colorado but illegal on a federal level. "We are treated as though we are money-laundering gangsters, while we are respected business owners in our state."

Every transaction is made on a cash-only basis, she told me. The threat of robbery must be factored in every business decision. Pay schedules are staggered among her employees with a buddy system arranged to walk them to their cars to make sure they get there safely. Utility bills, taxes, and all other expenditures are paid in cash. Marijuana businesses are forced to engage private security companies with armored cars and ex-military personnel (often former members of Special Operations units) to safeguard the piles of legally acquired cash receipts. Banks refuse to offer business accounts for any deposits or credit, arguing that they would risk losing their federal charter and FDIC insurance coverage on the basis of statutes regarding money laundering. Under federal law, a 10 percent penalty is added to employee-withholding taxes because the tax isn't paid electronically.

Meanwhile, despite more than $6 billion in marijuana sales revenue in the U.S. states and the District of Columbia where recreational marijuana use has been legally sanctioned, the industry remains under a cloud of commercial illegitimacy. For marijuana company owners in these jurisdictions, the "right to use" has been won. The "right to do business" appears to be their next rallying cry.[1]

After you have completed this chapter, you should have an understanding of the following:

- Cannabis products
- The history of marijuana and hashish
- Acute effects of marijuana
- Cannabinoids and endocannabinoids
- Chronic effects of marijuana
- The gateway hypothesis
- Patterns of marijuana smoking
- Medical marijuana
- Marijuana decriminalization and legalization

It might be fair to characterize *Cannabis sativa*, the botanical source of marijuana, as a scrawny weed with an attitude. Whether the weather is hot or cold, wet or dry, cannabis plants grow abundantly from seeds that are unbelievably hardy and prolific. A handful of cannabis seeds, tossed on the ground and pressed in with one's foot, usually anchor and become plants. Its roots find whatever nutrients there are in the soil.

The pharmacological effects of marijuana show something of an independent nature as well. It is not easy to place marijuana within a classification of psychoactive drugs. When considering a category for marijuana, we are faced with an odd assortment of unconnected properties. Marijuana produces some excitatory effects, but it is not generally regarded as a stimulant. It produces some sedative effects, but a person faces no risk of slipping into a coma or dying. It produces mild analgesic effects, but it is not related chemically to opioid drugs. It produces hallucinations at high doses, but its structure does not resemble LSD or any other drug formally categorized as a hallucinogen. Marijuana is clearly a unique drug, in a league of its own.

Few other drugs have been so politicized in recent history as marijuana. It receives extravagant praise by one side or fierce condemnation by the other, often on the basis of emotionally charged issues rather than objective research data. The pro-marijuana faction tends to dismiss or downplay reports of potential dangers and emphasize the benefits; the anti-marijuana faction tends to do the opposite, pointing out that marijuana continues to be classified as a Schedule I controlled substance by the federal government, along with heroin and LSD. The present-day conflict between the position of the federal government with regard to marijuana and the position of a growing number of U.S. states that have legalized recreational use of marijuana within their jurisdictions is a major criminal-justice issue that remains to be settled. Given the well-publicized controversies surrounding marijuana in present-day American life, it is critical to examine the many aspects of marijuana as dispassionately as possible. This chapter will explore the nature of marijuana itself, the history of marijuana in American history, the acute and chronic effects of marijuana smoking, and finally the increasing trend toward the acceptance of marijuana as a fact-of-life in our contemporary society. We begin with basic facts about the plant, *Cannabis sativa*.

Cannabis Products

Marijuana (sometimes spelled *marihuana*) is frequently referred to as a synonym for cannabis, but technically the two terms need to be differentiated. Cannabis is the botanical term for the hemp plant ***Cannabis sativa***. With a potential height of about 18 feet, cannabis has sturdy stalks, four-cornered in cross-section, that have been commercially valuable for thousands of years in the manufacture of rope, twine, shoes, sailcloth, and containers of all kinds. Pots made of hemp fiber discovered at archaeological sites in China date the origins of cannabis cultivation as far back as the Stone Age. It is arguably the oldest cultivated plant not used for food.

Spaniards brought cannabis to the New World in 1545, and English settlers brought it to Jamestown, Virginia, in 1611, where it became a major commercial crop, along with tobacco. In 1619, the Virginia assembly considered hemp to be such a valuable commodity that a law was passed that *required* all farmers in the colony to plant cannabis on their plantations. Like other eighteenth-century Virginian farmers, George Washington grew cannabis in the fields of his estate at Mount Vernon. Entries in his diary indicate that he maintained a keen interest in cultivating the best possible strains of cannabis, but there is no indication that he was interested in anything more than producing a better-quality rope (Drugs ... in Focus).

Marijuana is obtained not from the stalks of the cannabis plant but from its serrated leaves. The key psychoactive factor is contained in a sticky substance, or resin, that accumulates on these leaves. Depending on the growing conditions, cannabis will produce either a greater amount of resin

Cannabis sativa (CAN-uh-bus sah-TEE-vah): A plant species, commonly called hemp, from which marijuana and hashish are obtained.

Numbers Talk. . .

122,943,000	Estimated number of Americans who reported in 2017 that they had smoked marijuana sometime in their lifetime.
25,997,000	Estimated number of Americans who reported in 2017 that they had smoked marijuana in the previous month.
33	Number of U.S. states in 2018 that have authorized marijuana use for medical purposes.
10	Number of U.S. states in 2018 that have legalized marijuana use for recreational purposes within their jurisdictions.

Sources: Center for Behavioral Health Statistics and Quality (2018). *Results from the 2017 National Survey on Drug Use and Health. Detailed tables.* Rockville, MD: Substance Abuse and Mental Health Services Administration, Table 1.1A. News media, 2018.

Drugs . . . in Focus

Growing Hemp in America: Coming Full Circle

The high-fiber stalks of the cannabis plant have been considered for centuries as one of the most sustainable, resilient and versatile crops in the world. Today, hemp fiber is used in the manufacture of a wide range of fabrics, from t-shirts, sweatshirts, pants, and hats to sailcloth, car seat upholstery, organic paper, and bioplastic products. A particularly attractive application of hemp is as a construction material. When used as a toxin-free insulation in walls and roofs, hemp mortar (so-called hempcrete) has a significantly lower carbon footprint, requiring three times less heat to create than standard limestone concrete. In many climates, a 12-foot hempcrete wall, for example, can facilitate a 60-degree indoor temperature year-round without heating or cooling systems, making it ideal for low-cost construction projects, particularly in parts of the world where building costs need to be kept to a minimum.

However, domestic cultivation and distribution of industrial hemp (even after the required sterilization to remove the psychoactive THC content) has been prohibited under the 1970 Controlled Substances Act (see Chapter 3), classifying hemp in the same category of controlled substances as marijuana. Currently, industrial hemp material for domestic use is exported from China, India, and Canada.

Beginning in 2005, faced with depressed corn and soybean prices, increasing numbers of farmers in North Dakota and other states in the region have considered high-fiber, high-protein hemp as a profitable alternative crop. Since then, the support for hemp cultivation has come from farmers and legislators elsewhere in the country, in such states as Kentucky, North Carolina, and New York. As a result, the Industrial Hemp Farming Act has been proposed in Congress with the potential for remedying this situation. The Act would define industrial hemp as a "non-narcotic agricultural commodity that is used in tens of thousands of legal and legitimate products" as long as no part of which contained a THC concentration of more than 0.3 percent on a dry weight basis. Research hemp would be defined as industrial hemp, except that a THC concentration between 0.3 percent and 0.6 percent would be permitted and the hemp would be used for scientific, medical, or industrial research. The Controlled Substances Act would be amended to allow for hemp to be grown domestically as long as these conditions are met.

For years, controversy has raged over the issue of hemp farming in America, even though it has historical roots going back to colonial times. Pro-hemp advocates have argued that the government permits manufacturers of cosmetics, clothing, paper, and foods (hemp bread being a popular example) to import hemp fiber, seed, and oil from overseas for use in their products. They consider it hypocritical to ban its domestic cultivation. Representing the opposite side of the issue, the DEA sees the proliferation of hemp fields turning into marijuana fields. According to a federal official, "The pro-dope people have been pushing hemp for 20 years because they know that if they can have hemp fields, then they can have marijuana fields. It's ... stoner logic." The retort is that industrial hemp is high in fiber, protein, vitamin E, and essential fatty acids, and because it has very low concentrations of THC, you don't get high from it.

After much debate, the Farm Act of 2018 was passed by Congress and signed into law, incorporating the important provision that hemp or any hemp derivative with less than 0.3 percent THC would now be officially recognized as a legal commodity under the supervision of the U.S. Department of Agriculture, no longer classified as a Schedule I controlled substance. Hemp would no longer be illegal in the United States. The economic ramifications for American farmers are enormous. During World War II, hemp cultivation had been permitted, even encouraged by the federal government, but only under emergency circumstances to furnish products such as rope and textiles for wartime use. As of 2019, there will be an opportunity for the United States to fully compete in a rapidly emerging global market for hemp and hemp-derived products. In effect, we will have come full circle back to an earlier time in American history, when hemp growers (notably George Washington) were dominant figures in the agricultural life of the nation.

Not incidentally, the new law legalizes all hemp derivatives with no THC-content at all. The most prominent example is cannabidiol (CBD).

Sources: Healy, J. (2013, August 6). Groundwork laid, growers turn to hemp in Colorado. *The New York Times*, p. A15. Popescu, A. (2018, January 30). Hemp for the home (construction, not smoking). *The New York Times*, pp. D1, D6. Text of H.R. 5485, U.S. House of Representatives, Hemp Farming Act of 2018, to amend the Controlled Substances Act to exclude industrial hemp. News media, 2018. https://www.congress.gov/bill/115th-congress/house-bill/5485

---

or a greater amount of fiber. In a hot, dry climate—such as in North Africa—the fiber content is weak, but so much resin is produced that the plant looks as if it is covered with dew. In a cooler, more humid climate, such as in North America, less resin is produced, but the fiber is stronger and more durable.

As many as 100 separate chemical compounds, called **cannabinoids**, have been identified from cannabis resin. The best known of these cannabinoids, **delta-9-tetrahydrocannabinol (THC)**, identified in 1964, is the "classic" compound that produces the intoxicating effects of cannabis. The

psychoactive characteristics of *Cannabis sativa* is directly related to the concentration of THC. More recently, another

> **cannabinoids (can-NAB-ih-noids):** Any of an estimated 100 compounds either synthesized in the laboratory or extracted from the cannabis plant. Cannabinoids extracted from cannabis are referred to as *phytocannabinoids*. Natural substances in the brain and elsewhere in the body that mimic phytocannabinoids are referred to as *endocannabinoids*.

A cannabis farmer carefully tends to his marijuana crop prior to final harvesting.

Credit: Eric Limon/123RF

cannabinoid, **cannabidiol (CBD)**, has been identified with properties quite different from that of THC (see pages 228–229).

In general, cannabis products are categorized in terms of two factors: (1) the resin content in the cannabis that is cultivated and (2) the relative concentration of THC that is extracted from the resin.

The best-known cannabis product, **marijuana**, consists of leaves and occasionally flowers of the cannabis plant that are first dried and then shredded. During the 1960s and 1970s, the typical THC concentration of street marijuana imported from Mexico was about 1–2 percent. Since the early 1990s, however, THC concentrations have steadily risen to 5–10 percent or higher, due primarily to advanced outdoor and indoor cultivation methods. Marijuana, smoked as a cigarette, is the form of cannabis most familiar to North Americans.

A more potent form of marijuana is obtained by cultivating only the unpollinated (or seedless) portion of the cannabis plant. Without pollination, the cannabis plant grows bushier, the resin content in the leaves is increased, and a greater THC concentration can be achieved. This form is called **sinsemilla**, from the Spanish meaning "without seed."

Another cannabis product, **hashish**, is achieved when the resin itself is scraped from cannabis leaves and then dried. Either smoked by itself or in combination with tobacco, it can have a THC concentration as high as 24 percent. The most potent forms of cannabis are **hashish oil** and **hashish oil crystals**, produced by boiling hashish in alcohol or some other solvent, filtering out the alcohol, and leaving a residue with a THC concentration ranging from 15 to 60 percent.[2]

The History of Marijuana and Hashish

The first direct reference to a cannabis product as a psychoactive drug dates from 2737 B.C., in the writings of the mythical Chinese emperor Shen Nung. The focus was on its powers as a medication for rheumatism, gout, malaria, and, strangely enough, absentmindedness. Mention was made of its intoxicating properties, but the medicinal possibilities evidently were considered more important. In India, however, its use was clearly recreational. The most popular form, in ancient times as well as in the present day, can be found in a syrupy liquid made from cannabis leaves called **bhang**, with a THC potency usually equal to that of a marijuana cigarette in the United States.[3]

The Muslim world also grow to appreciate the psychoactive potential of cannabis, encouraged by the fact that, in

delta-9-tetrahydrocannabinol (THC) (DEL-tah-9-TEH-trah-HIGH-dro-CAN-a-bih-nol): The active psychoactive compound in marijuana and other cannabis products.

cannabidiol (CBD) (can-NAB-ih-DYE-ol): A compound found in cannabis resin.

marijuana: The most commonly available psychoactive drug originating from the cannabis plant. The THC concentration ranges from approximately 1 to 6 percent. Also spelled as marihuana.

sinsemilla (SIN-sih-MEE-yah): A form of marijuana obtained from the unpollinated or seedless portion of the cannabis plant. It has a higher THC concentration than regular marijuana, as high as 15 percent.

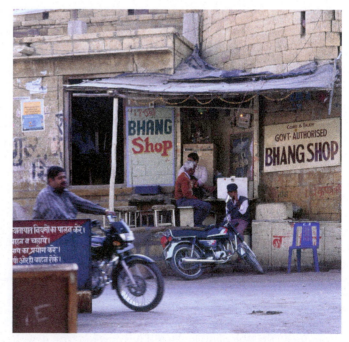

Notice the "Gov't Authorized" sign outside this bhang shop in North India. Bhang ki thandai is a popular cold drink prepared with bhang combined with almonds, spices, milk, and sugar. Bhang lassi, a mixture of bhang and iced yogurt, is another popular drink. It is traditional for many Hindus to drink bhang during Holi and Shivaratri festivals.

Credit: MI-foto/F1online digitale Bildagentur GmbH/Alamy Stock Photo

contrast to its stern prohibition of alcohol consumption, the Koran did not specifically ban cannabis use. It was here in a hot, dry climate conducive to maximizing the resin content of cannabis that hashish was born, and its popularity spread quickly during the twelfth century from Persia (Iran) in the east to North Africa in the west.

Hashish in the Nineteenth Century

In Western Europe, there was only limited knowledge about hashish or any other cannabis product until the beginning of the nineteenth century. Judging from the decree made by Pope Innocent VIII in 1484 condemning witchcraft and the use of hemp in the Black Mass, we can assume that the psychoactive properties of cannabis were known by some portions of the population. Nonetheless, there is no evidence of widespread use.

By about 1800, however, cannabis had become more widely known and the subject of a popular craze. One reason was that French soldiers who had served in Napoleon's military campaigns in Egypt brought hashish back with them to their homes in France. Another reason was a wave of romanticism that swept Europe, including an increased interest in exotic stories of the East, notably the *Arabian Nights* and the tales of Marco Polo, which contained references to hashish.

In Paris during the 1840s, a small group of prominent French artists, writers, and intellectuals formed the Club des Hachischins ("Club of the Hashish-Eaters"), where they would gather, in the words of their leader, "to talk of literature, art, and love" while consuming large quantities of hashish. The "house recipe" consisted of concentrated cannabis paste, mixed with butter, sweeteners, and flavorings such as vanilla and cinnamon. Members included Victor Hugo, Alexandre Dumas, Charles Baudelaire, Eugéne Delacroix, and Honoré de Balzac.

Marijuana and Hashish in the Twentieth Century

Chances are that anyone living in the United States at the beginning of the twentieth century would not have heard of marijuana, much less hashish. By 1890, cotton had replaced hemp as a major cash crop in southern states, although cannabis plants continued to grow wild along roadsides and in

the fields. Some patent medicines during this era contained marijuana, but it was a small percentage compared with the number of patent medicines containing opium or cocaine (see Chapter 3).[4]

It was not until the 1920s that marijuana smoking began to be a phenomenon of any social significance. Some historians have related the emergence of marijuana as a recreational drug to social changes brought on by Prohibition (see Chapter 3), when it was suddenly difficult to obtain good quality liquor at affordable prices. Recreational use was largely restricted to jazz musicians and people in show business. "Reefer songs" became the rage of the jazz world. Even the mainstream clarinetist and bandleader Benny Goodman had his popular hit "Sweet Marihuana Brown." Marijuana clubs, called *tea pads*, sprang up in the major cities; more than 500 were estimated in Harlem alone, outnumbering the speakeasies where illegal alcohol was dispensed. These marijuana establishments were largely tolerated by the authorities because at that time marijuana was not illegal and patrons showed no evidence of making a nuisance of themselves or disturbing the community at large. In the culture of the time, marijuana was not considered a societal threat at all.[5]

The Anti-Marijuana Crusade

By the 1930s, however, the picture had changed dramatically. Prior to that time, millions of Americans had never heard of marijuana, much less thought about the consequences of smoking it. Due to an intensive anti-marijuana media campaign, orchestrated by the Federal Bureau of Narcotics (FBN) under the direction of its commissioner, Harry J. Anslinger (see Portrait), the American public became introduced to marijuana in the most negative terms possible (see Chapter 3). It was not long before marijuana was viewed by the general public as a pestilence infecting the core of American life.

How did this transformation occur? To understand how marijuana smoking went from a localized and relatively innocuous form of drug-taking behavior to a national crisis, we have to look at some important changes in American society that were taking place at the time.

The practice of smoking marijuana and the cultivation of cannabis plants for that purpose had been filtering slowly into the United States since 1900 as a result of an influx of Mexican immigrants. Political turmoil in Mexico leading up to the Revolution of 1910 had encouraged large numbers of Mexicans to cross the border into towns and cities in the Southwest.

More than 1 million Mexicans are estimated to have emigrated to the United States during 1910–1930, establishing themselves as a significant minority group. By 1930, Mexicans represented one in nine residents in Texas alone. As it so often happens, they were met with an intensely hostile reception from communities unaccustomed to an introduction of a different culture and language. The fact that they were smoking an alien and foreign-sounding substance did not help. Throughout the southwestern and western United

---

hashish (hah-SHEESH): A drug containing the resin of cannabis flowers. The THC concentration ranges from approximately 8 to 14 percent.

hashish oil: A drug produced by boiling hashish, leaving a potent psychoactive residue. The THC concentration ranges from approximately 15 to 60 percent.

hashish oil crystals: A solid form of hashish oil.

bhang: A liquid form of marijuana popular in India.

States, unsubstantiated rumors began to circulate about acts of violence committed by super-strong marijuana-intoxicated Mexicans. Newspaper articles included lurid details of these stories, without any effort on the part of editors to check if there was any basis in fact.

Meanwhile, the writings of Marco Polo in which he described a twelfth-century sect of professional killers known as "hashish-eaters" (*hashashin*, from which the word, assassin, is derived) were propagated with an unfortunate modern-day twist. In the original story, the leader of the sect whose power was sustained through acts of political assassination would assemble the killers prior to their orders to carry out a particular mission. They were given hashish to allow them a drug-induced glimpse of the delights of paradise that would await them as a reward. Then, *after the effects of the drug had worn off*, the men would accomplish their assignment with great enthusiasm, despite understanding that they would most likely die in the process. The new story was that the assassins had been intoxicated as they carried out their assignment. In other words, hashish had made them killers in the first place.[6]

There were also economic issues at play. The social upheavals experienced by many Americans during the Depression made it particularly convenient to vent one's frustrations on an immigrant group viewed as competing for a

PORTRAIT

Commissioner Harry J. Anslinger: From Demon Rum to Devil Weed

Prior to his appointment in 1930 as the first commissioner of the FBN in 1930, Harry J. Anslinger had been a rising young star in the Prohibition Unit at the Treasury Department. The Harrison Act of 1914 had established the nation's drug-law enforcement policy, and Anslinger seemed like the right man for this new job. He had been quite vocal in his conviction that drug addiction was absolutely immoral and that the cure to the illicit drug problem was a matter of prosecuting people who used these drugs and preventing them from getting hold of drugs in the first place.

The end of Prohibition in 1933, however, presented a problem. Congress felt the pressure to reduce the Treasury's enforcement budget, and the Great Depression put strains on federal expenditures in general. Anslinger and the FBN faced hard times. The savior, ironically enough, was marijuana. Beginning in the early 1930s, rumors of "degenerate Spanish-speaking residents" in the Southwest going on criminal rampages while smoking marijuana were being spread in newspapers and popular magazines. Anslinger seized upon these unsubstantiated reports, legitimizing them through his frequent references to them. According to Anslinger, marijuana was the "killer weed" that had to be stopped for the sake of America.

Anslinger wasn't exactly subtle in his writings. In a 1937 article appearing in the widely read American Magazine entitled "Marijuana: Assassin of Youth," he laid out his case:

The sprawled body of a young girl lay crushed on the sidewalk the other day after a plunge from the fifth story of a Chicago apartment house. Everyone called it suicide, but actually it was murder. The killer was a narcotic known to America as marijuana, and to history as hashish. It is a narcotic used in the form of cigarettes, comparatively new to the United States and as dangerous as a coiled rattlesnake ... How many murders, suicides, robberies, criminal assaults, holdups, burglaries, and deeds of maniacal insanity it causes each year, especially among the young, can be only conjectured ... No one can predict the effect. No one knows, when he places a marijuana cigarette to his lips, whether he will become ... a joyous reveller ..., a mad insensate, a calm philosopher, or a murderer.

The answer according to Anslinger was new federal legislation outlawing marijuana, not to mention continued financial support for the agency dedicated to enforcing the law. The Marijuana Tax Act of 1937 was Anslinger's creation.

Anslinger's 32-year tenure at the FBN and his stature as defender of the purity of American youth, or at least the purity of their circulatory systems, could not have been possible without strong support from several important conservative U.S. legislators in the House and Senate. During the late 1940s and into the 1950s, Anslinger began to emphasize the link between drug addiction in the United States and the threat of international Communism from abroad.

The target was the People's Republic of China, which Anslinger repeatedly claimed was the primary source of heroin in the United States, despite the available evidence pointing to politically friendlier nations of Southeast Asia as the real culprits. According to Anslinger's testimony, China not only was the source of heroin but was also specifically selling opium and heroin to finance the expansion of Communism around the world. The concept of narcoterrorism (see Chapter 2) can be seen as having its origins at this time. On the domestic front, drug abuse was a threat to the American way of life. Only after Anslinger's resignation in 1962, following considerable pressure from President Kennedy, did the focus of attention shift to the problem of heroin trafficking in Burma, Laos, and Thailand.

Given the anti-Communist stance of the FBN, it is not surprising that one of Anslinger's staunchest supporters during the late 1940s and early 1950s was Senator Joseph R. McCarthy, whose congressional subcommittee was then engaged in a ruthless crusade against "known Communists" inside the federal government. What was not known at the time, however, was that Anslinger during this period was personally allowing McCarthy, a morphine addict as well as an alcoholic, to buy unrestricted supplies of morphine without FBN or police interference. When McCarthy died in 1957 of "acute hepatitis, cause unknown," Anslinger wrote in his memoirs, "I thanked God for relieving me of my burden."

Sources: Anslinger, H. J.; and Cooper, C. R. (1937, July). Marijuana: Assassin of youth. *American Magazine*, pp. 18–19, 150–153, excerpt on page 18.

Credit: Bettmann/Getty Images

Marijuana tax stamps were issued and valid between 1937 and 1969 when the law was overturned by the U.S. Supreme Court, though during this time stringent governmental regulations made it nearly impossible to obtain these stamps to "register" one's marijuana use. They became commercially available to stamp collectors in 2005.

Credit: Courtesy of *U.S. Customs and Border Protection*

dwindling number of American jobs and straining an already weak economy. Anti-marijuana-themed movies with provocative titles such as *Reefer Madness* and *Marihuana: Weed with Roots in Hell* were produced and distributed during the late 1930s and early 1940s with the encouragement of the FBN. By this time, these movies were reinforcing a clearly established social message: Marijuana was dangerous and single-handedly corrupting the innocent youth of America.

Considering the mounting hysteria against marijuana smoking and cannabis use in general during the 1930s, it is not surprising that the Marijuana Tax Act of 1937 had little difficulty in gaining support in Congress. As with the Harrison Act of 1914, the regulation of marijuana was accomplished indirectly. The law did not ban marijuana; it merely required everyone connected with marijuana, from growers to buyers, to pay a tax. It was a deceptively simple procedure that, in effect, made it virtually impossible to comply with the law. In the absence of compliance, a person was in violation and therefore subject to arrest. It was the state's responsibility to make possession of marijuana or any other product of *Cannabis sativa* illegal. Shortly after the 1937 legislation was enacted, all of the states adopted a uniform law that did just that.

The official stance of the federal government was that that marijuana smoking was tied to antisocial behavior, and that marijuana control was a central part of what would later evolve into a general war on drugs. For more than 20 years after passage of the Marijuana Tax Act, Harry Anslinger never let up on his anti-marijuana crusade. In 1953, he wrote:

> *Those who are accustomed to habitual use of the drug are said eventually to develop a delirious rage after its administration during which they are temporarily, at least, irresponsible and prone to commit violent crimes.... Much of the most irrational juvenile violence and killing that has written a new chapter of shame and tragedy is traceable directly to this hemp intoxication.*[7]

In the 1950s, the severity of criminal penalties for involvement with marijuana steadily increased. State judges

frequently had the option of sentencing a marijuana seller or user to life imprisonment. In Georgia, a second offense of selling marijuana to a minor could be punishable by death.

Over time, the "pharmacological violence" theory with regard to marijuana (see Chapter 4) would fade into oblivion, in the absence of any evidence to support it. In its place, a new concept regarding marijuana smoking would be introduced by the FBN: the gateway hypothesis. According to this idea, marijuana was purported to be dangerous because its abuse would lead to the abuse of heroin, cocaine, or other illicit drugs. This gateway hypothesis will be closely examined later in the chapter.

Ironically, in 1969, more than three decades after its passage, the U.S. Supreme Court ruled that the 1937 Marijuana Tax Act was unconstitutional, precisely because marijuana possession itself was illegal. The argument was made that requiring a person to pay a tax (and that was all that the 1937 law concerned) so as to possess an illegal substance amounted to a form of self-incrimination, which would be a specific violation of the Fifth Amendment to the Constitution. It turns out that the case in question here was brought to the high court by none other than Timothy Leary (see Portrait in Chapter 12), and the court's decision succeeded in overturning a marijuana conviction judged against him.[8]

This promotional poster for the 1942 film *Devil's Harvest* depicted in graphic detail the supposed evils of smoking marijuana.

Credit: Contraband Collection/Alamy Stock Photo

Challenging Old Ideas about Marijuana

Prior to 1960, arrests and seizures for possession of marijuana were relatively rare and attracted little or no public attention. The social consensus was that marijuana was a drug that could be comfortably associated with, and isolated to, ethnic and racial minorities. It was relatively easy for most Americans to avoid the drug entirely. In any event, involvement with marijuana during the 1950s was considered a deviant act and form of drug-taking behavior that could be easily ignored.

By the mid-1960s, this consensus began to dissolve. Marijuana smoking suddenly was an attraction on the campuses of U.S. colleges and universities, affecting a wide cross section of the nation. Strangely enough, the bizarre effects depicted in the anti-marijuana movies failed to occur! At the same time, the experimental use of drugs, particularly marijuana, by young people set the stage for a wholesale questioning of what it meant to respect authority, on an individual as well as a governmental level.

Acute Effects of Marijuana

In the United States, THC is usually ingested by smoking a hand-rolled marijuana cigarette referred to as a **reefer** or, more commonly, a **joint**. Exactly how much THC is administered into the body (and eventually reaches the brain) depends on the specific THC concentration level in the marijuana (often referred to as its quality), how deeply the smoke is inhaled into the lungs, and how long it is held in the lungs before being exhaled. In general, an experienced smoker will ingest more THC than a novice smoker by virtue of being able to inhale more deeply and hold the marijuana smoke in his or her lungs longer, for 25 seconds or longer, thus maximizing THC absorption into the bloodstream.

The inhalation of any drug into the lungs produces extremely rapid absorption, as noted in earlier chapters, and marijuana is no exception. In the case of THC, effects are felt within seconds. Peak levels are reached in the blood within 10 minutes and start to decline shortly afterward. Behavioral and psychological effects generally last from two to three hours. At this point, low levels of THC linger for several days because they are absorbed into fatty tissue, and excretion from fatty tissue is notoriously slow.[9]

One implication arising from a slow elimination rate is that the residual THC, left over from a previous administration, can intensify the effect of marijuana on a subsequent occasion. In this way, regular marijuana smokers often report a quicker and more easily obtained high, achieved with a smaller quantity of drug, than more intermittent smokers.[10]

reefer: A marijuana cigarette.

joint: A marijuana cigarette.

It is also important to view the fact of slow marijuana elimination in the context of drug testing. Urine tests for possible marijuana abuse typically measure levels of THC metabolites (broken-down remnants of THC); because of the slow biotransformation of marijuana, these metabolites are detectable in the urine even when the smoker no longer feels high or shows any behavioral effects. Metabolites can remain in the body for several days after smoking a single joint and for several weeks later in the case of a chronic marijuana smoker. Some drug tests are so sensitive that a positive level for marijuana can result from passive inhalation of marijuana smoke-filled air in a closed environment, even though the THC levels in these cases are substantially below levels that result from active smoking. The bottom line is that marijuana testing procedures generally are unable to indicate *when* marijuana has been smoked (if it has been smoked at all), only that exposure to marijuana has occurred (see Chapter 16).[11]

Acute Physiological Effects

Immediate physiological effects after smoking marijuana are relatively minor. It has been estimated that a human would need to ingest a dose of marijuana that was from 20,000 to 40,000 times the effective dose before death would occur.[12] Nonetheless, there is a dose-related increase in heart rate during early stages of marijuana ingestion, up to 160 beats per minute when dose levels are high. Blood pressure either increases, decreases, or remains the same, depending primarily on whether the individual is standing, sitting, or lying down.[13] A dilation of blood vessels on the cornea resulting in bloodshot eyes peaks in about an hour after smoking a joint. Frequently, there is a drying of the mouth and an urge to drink.

Other physiological reactions are inconsistent, and at least part of the inconsistency can be attributed to cultural and interpersonal influences. For example, the observation that marijuana smoking makes you feel extremely hungry and crave especially sweet things to eat (often referred to as "having the munchies") generally holds true in studies of North Americans but not for Jamaicans, who consider marijuana an appetite suppressant.

Likewise, North Americans often report enhanced sexual responses following marijuana use, whereas in India marijuana is considered a sexual depressant. These reactions, being subjective in nature, can very well be slanted in one direction or the other by the mind-set (expectations) of the marijuana smoker going into the experience. A good example is the effect on sexual responses. If you believe that marijuana turns you on sexually, the chances are that it will.

Although expectations undoubtedly play a prominent role here, we should be aware of the possibility that varying effects also may be due to differences in the THC concentration of the marijuana being smoked. In the case of sexual reactivity, studies of male marijuana smokers have shown that low-dose marijuana tends to enhance sexual desire, while high-dose marijuana tends to depress it, even to the point of impotence. It is quite possible that the enhancement is a result of a brief rise in the male sex hormone, testosterone, and the depression a result of a rebound effect that lowers testosterone below normal levels. Typically, the THC concentration in India is higher than that in North America. As a result, we would expect different effects on sexual reactivity. The same argument could be made with respect to the differences in marijuana's effect on appetite.[14]

As described in Chapter 1, hospital emergencies related to marijuana on a nationwide basis have doubled from 2006 to 2014. A consistent finding, however, has been the preponderance of emergency cases associated with the ingestion of marijuana in combination with alcohol and other drugs. Nonetheless, increased marijuana toxicity is a medical concern. It is likely that the higher THC concentrations in marijuana has contributed to greater numbers of ED visits, since these increases are greater than the increase in prevalence rates over these periods of time. It should be noted that there have been no cases on record of a death due *exclusively* to the ingestion of marijuana.[15]

Acute Psychological and Behavioral Effects

In Chapter 9, it was noted that a first-time heroin abuser frequently finds the experience more aversive than pleasurable. With marijuana, it is likely that a first-time smoker will feel no discernible effects at all. It takes some practice to be able to inhale deeply and keep the smoke in the lungs long enough for a minimal level of THC, particularly in low-quality marijuana, to take effect. Novices often have to be instructed to focus on some aspect of the intoxicated state to start to feel intoxicated, but the psychological reactions, once they do occur, are fairly predictable.

The marijuana high, as the name implies, is a feeling of euphoria and well-being. Marijuana smokers typically report an increased awareness of their surroundings, as well as a sharpened sense of sight and sound. Frequently, they feel that everything is suddenly very funny, and even the most innocent comments or events can set off uproarious laughter. Usually mundane ideas can seem filled with profound implications, and the individual may feel that creativity has been increased. As with LSD, however, no objective evidence shows that creativity is enhanced by marijuana. Commonly, time seems to pass more slowly while a person is under the influence of marijuana, and events appear to be elongated in duration. Finally, marijuana smokers frequently report that they feel sleepy and sometimes dreamy. Relatively low THC concentrations in a marijuana joint are not sufficient to be particularly sleep-inducing, though stronger cannabis preparations with higher THC can have strong sleep-inducing effects, particularly when combined with alcohol.[16]

At the same time, marijuana produces significant deficits in behavior. The major deficit is a decline in the ability to carry out tasks that involve attention and memory. Speech will be increasingly fragmented and disjointed; individuals often will forget what they, or others, have just said. The problem is that marijuana typically causes such a rush of distracting ideas to come to mind that it is difficult to concentrate on new information coming in. By virtue of a diminished focus of concentration, the performance of both short-term and long-term memory tasks is impaired. In general, these difficulties increase in magnitude as a direct function of the level of THC in the marijuana.[17]

It should not be surprising that complex motor tasks, such as driving a car, are also more poorly performed while a person is under the influence of marijuana. It is not necessarily a matter of reaction time; studies of marijuana smokers in automobile simulators indicate that they are as quick to respond as control subjects. The problem arises from a difficulty in attending to peripheral information and making an appropriate response while driving.[18] One researcher has put it this way:

> Marijuana-intoxicated drivers might be able to stop a car as fast as they normally could, but they may not be as quick to notice things that they should stop for. This is probably because they are attending to internal events rather than what is happening on the road.[19]

Given these observations in the laboratory and on the road, it should not be surprising that marijuana use would increase the risk of having an automobile accident. Surveys that

Quick Concept Check 11.1

Understanding the Effects of Marijuana

Check your understanding of the effects of marijuana by checking off the response (on the right) that you think is appropriate to the circumstances related to marijuana or other cannabis products (on the left).

CIRCUMSTANCE	INCREASES THE EFFECT	DECREASES THE EFFECT
1. The resin content in the cannabis is low.	_____	_____
2. You have decided to inhale more deeply.	_____	_____
3. You are smoking hashish instead of marijuana.	_____	_____
4. This is the first time you have ever smoked marijuana.	_____	_____
5. The THC concentration level is relatively high.	_____	_____

Answers: 1. decreases the effect 2. increases the effect 3. increases the effect 4. decreases the effect 5. increases the effect

have examined accident rates among drivers testing positive for THC in their bloodstreams have shown them to be about three to seven times more likely to be involved in an accident than drivers testing negative for THC or alcohol.[20]

An additional problem is quite serious. The decline in sensory–motor performance will persist well after the point at which the marijuana smoker no longer feels high, when there has been chronic heavy marijuana use. Significant impairments in attention and memory tasks have been demonstrated among heavy marijuana users (daily smokers) 24 hours after they had last used the drug. Therefore, we have to recognize the possibility that some important aspects of behavior can be impaired following marijuana smoking, even when an individual is not aware of it. This effect is likely due to the very slow rate with which marijuana is eliminated from the body.[21] Acute psychological effects such as mild depression, panic reactions, or mild paranoia as a result of smoking marijuana with high levels of THC are possible. With more typical THC levels, about one-half of marijuana users have reported at least one anxiety experience. Severe emotional responses such as a distortion of body image, delusions, hallucinations, and confusion can also occur, although they are associated with very high THC levels and individuals predisposed toward or recovering from a psychosis. There is little or no support for the idea that low THC doses will provoke such reactions in otherwise normal individuals. A substantially higher incidence of psychiatric problems arising from THC exposure has been reported in India and North Africa. In such cases, the THC concentrations being ingested, the frequency with which THC is ingested and the duration of THC exposure over a lifetime are all generally greater than would be encountered in the United States.[22]

Cannabinoids and Endocannabinoids

When THC was isolated in 1964 as the primary agent for the intoxicating properties of marijuana, the next step was to find out specifically how THC affects the brain to produce these effects. In 1990, the mechanism was discovered. Just as with morphine, special receptors in the brain are stimulated specifically by THC. They are concentrated in areas of the brain that are important for short-term memory and motor control. Unlike opioid receptors, however, the THC-sensitive receptors are not found in the lower portions of the brain that control breathing. As a result, no matter how high the THC concentration in the brain, there is no danger of an accidental death by asphyxiation.

Drugs . . . in Focus

The Neurochemical "Yin and Yang" of Cannabis

Considering the dozens of cannabinoids in the cannabis plant, it should not be surprising that individually they might have different neurochemical and behavioral effects. Recent studies indicate that two of the cannabinoids have diametrically opposite psychological effects. The first and best known cannabinoid, THC, is the principal psychoactive component, resulting in the marijuana high. It is also considered to be associated with acute symptoms of paranoia and increased anxiety, as well as occasional schizophrenia-like reactions, although these reactions tend to occur only when THC concentrations are extremely high. The other cannabinoid, cannabidiol (CBD), is associated with opposite effects, producing a reduction in anxiety and fewer instances of severe emotional problems. In effect, CBD can be understood as having a "neuroprotective" effect, making it less likely that adverse emotional reactions will occur. Because of the opposing properties of these cannabinoids, different strains of marijuana have been cultivated to produce varying psychological effects, depending upon the ratio of THC and CBD.

A 2008 study analyzed hair samples of individuals in three groups: nonusers of cannabis, users testing positive for both CBD and THC, and users testing positive for THC alone. There was a greater incidence of hallucinations and delusions in the THC-only group, relative to the other groups, with the THC + CBD group showing no greater incidence than nonusers.

It was not possible in this study to examine the behavior of individuals who tested positive for CBD alone, since there are no strains of natural cannabis that have this specific property. Since then, however, it has been possible to extract CBD alone from cannabis or synthesize it in the laboratory. Ironically, the ease with which synthetic cannabinoids can be made available in the illicit drug market (see Drugs ... in Focus later in the chapter) has resulted in a "new frontier" of research into potential medical benefits. The advantage of a CBD-based medical treatment, for example, is that it does not have the classic psychoactive properties of THC and it can be administered orally rather than smoked. Therefore, the potential for CBD abuse and adverse pulmonary problems due to inhaled smoke can be avoided.

Sources: Deshpande, S. R.; Taru, M.; King, K. J.; Gayathree, L; and Somashekhara, S. C. (2013). Biochemical basis for use of cannabinoids in various clinical conditions. *Journal of Drug Discovery and Therapeutics, 1,* 44–48. Gunderson, E. W. (2013). Synthetic cannabinoids: A new frontier of designer drugs. *Annals of Internal Medicine, 159,* 563–564. Morgan, C. J.; and Curran, H. V. (2008). Effects of cannabidiol on schizophrenia-like symptoms in people who use cannabis. *British Journal of Psychiatry, 192,* 306–307.

Once a specific receptor for a drug has been identified, the question inevitably becomes: Why is it there? As noted in Chapter 9, when opioid receptors were discovered, it made sense to speculate about a natural opioid-like substance that would fit into that receptor. These natural substances were subsequently identified, and we now refer to them as endorphins. The same speculation surrounded the discovery of the THC-sensitive receptor until 1992, when researchers isolated a natural substance, dubbed **anandamide** (the name derived from the Sanskrit word for "bliss"). In short, it was found that anandamide activates THC-sensitive receptors and is the basis for the effects of THC in the brain.

Anandamide is only one of dozens of natural substances collectively called *endocannabinoids* (literally "cannabinoids that exist on the inside"). These endocannabinoids activate (to varying degrees) two types of cannabinoid receptors: CB1 receptors that are located primarily in the brain and the gut and CB2 receptors that are located primarily in lymph tissue. Anandamide and THC are associated with CB1 receptors, and their increased activity level in the brain corresponds to the specific psychoactive features of marijuana.

As mentioned earlier in the chapter, another cannabinoid, cannabidiol (CBD), has been identified with psychoactive properties, though not the same as THC (see Drugs ... in Focus, page 228). It turns out that CBD has little or no association with CB1 receptors, which explains its "non-THC" effects. Instead, CBD activates CB2 receptors. It is the capability for CBD to activate CB2 receptors that has made it useful for a variety of medical applications. The medical applications for CBD will be examined in a later section.

There is an intriguing aspect to the effects of THC in the brain that connects it to other psychoactive drugs. THC stimulates neurons in the nucleus accumbens in rats, the same area that is affected by heroin, cocaine, methamphetamine, alcohol, and nicotine. The effect, however, is much weaker than with drugs that produce strong signs of dependence. Animals will self-administer marijuana in laboratory studies and, in fact, are able to discriminate high-potency from low-potency marijuana, but their behavior is not as compulsive as that observed with heroin, cocaine, alcohol, or nicotine.[23]

Chronic Effects of Marijuana

Is chronic marijuana smoking harmful over a period of time? What is the extent of tolerance and dependence? Are there long-term consequences for the health of organ systems in the body? Will marijuana lessen one's potential as a productive human being in society? Will marijuana abuse lead to the abuse of other drugs? These are questions to be considered next.

Tolerance

It is frequently reported that experienced marijuana smokers tend to become intoxicated more quickly and to a greater extent than inexperienced smokers, when exposed to marijuana joints with equivalent THC concentrations. For many years, this observation suggested that repeated administrations of marijuana produced sensitization, or reverse tolerance (a greater sensitivity), rather than tolerance (a lesser sensitivity). If this were true, then we would have been faced with the troubling conclusion that marijuana operates in a totally opposite way to any other psychoactive drug considered so far. As it turns out, when animals or humans are studied in the laboratory, marijuana smoking shows tolerance effects that are consistent and clear-cut.

Why, then, the difference with the experience of humans outside the laboratory? One important factor is the way in which we measure the quantity of THC consumed. Reaching an effective high from marijuana requires some degree of practice. For example, novice marijuana smokers may not have mastered the breathing technique necessary to allow the minimal level of THC to enter the lungs. They may have to smoke a relatively large number of marijuana joints initially before they achieve a high. Later, when they have acquired the technique, they may need fewer joints to accomplish the same effect. In these circumstances, a calculation of the number of joints consumed does not reflect the amount of THC ingested. If you were to control the THC content entering the body, as is done in laboratory studies, you would find the predictable results of tolerance over repeated administrations.

Another factor complicating tolerance studies is the slow elimination rate of marijuana. Regular marijuana smokers are likely to have a residual amount of THC still in the system. This buildup of THC would elevate the total quantity of THC consumed with every joint and induce a quicker high. Once again, the impression of sensitization is false; we are actually observing the enhanced effects of an accumulation of THC in the body. Once dosage levels are controlled, the results indicate a consistent pattern of tolerance rather than sensitization. In general, tolerance effects following repeated administrations of THC are greater as the dosage level of THC increases.[24]

Withdrawal and Dependence

On the basis of early studies conducted in the 1970s, it appeared that evidence of physical dependence (that is, the observation of withdrawal symptoms) following chronic administration of marijuana was limited to circumstances in which the level of THC ingestion was extreme. In one study, human volunteers were administered large doses of THC every 4 hours for 10–20 days. Within 12 hours after the last administration, subjects reported physical symptoms that included hot flashes, irritability, restlessness, and insomnia. In contrast, in another study in which subjects smoked one

anandamide (a-NAN-duh-mide): A naturally occurring chemical in the brain that fits into THC-sensitive receptor sites, producing many of the same effects as marijuana.

marijuana cigarette daily for 28 days, a condition closer to the typical exposure to marijuana, no withdrawal symptoms were observed.[25]

More recent studies, however, have shown that withdrawal effects can occur even with more moderate levels of THC consumed over shorter periods of time. Abstinence from smoking marijuana cigarettes with approximately 2–3 percent THC levels or equivalent oral doses of THC, administered four times a day over a four-day period, resulted in feelings of irritability, stomach pain, anxiety, and loss of appetite. These symptoms began within 48 hours and lasted at least 2 days.[26] Therefore, it is quite possible that daily marijuana use among chronic marijuana smokers is maintained, at least in part, because of its alleviation of withdrawal symptoms. Nonetheless, the symptoms involved here are substantially milder than those associated with the chronic use of heroin (Chapter 9) or alcohol (Chapter 13).

There is also evidence of significant marijuana craving, indicating a degree of psychological dependence in some marijuana smokers, but it is difficult to measure the extent of these feelings or to determine whether these effects are due to circumstances in which marijuana is used in conjunction with other drugs. As was pointed out earlier, any definitive judgment as to the possibility of psychological dependence or the extent to which psychological dependence may occur in the average marijuana smoker has to rest upon research studies involving THC concentrations that are typical of currently available marijuana.[27]

Cardiovascular Effects

THC produces significant increases in heart rate, but there is no conclusive evidence of adverse effects in the cardiovascular functioning in young, healthy people. The reason why the emphasis is on a specific age group is that most of the studies looking at possible long-term cardiovascular effects have involved marijuana smokers under the age of 35; little or no information has been compiled about older populations. For those people with preexisting disorders such as heart disease, high blood pressure, or arteriosclerosis (hardening of the arteries), it is known that the acute effects of marijuana on heart rate and blood pressure can worsen their condition.

Respiratory Effects

The technique of marijuana smoking involves the deep and maintained inhalation into the lungs of unfiltered smoke on a repetitive basis, probably the worst scenario for incurring chronic pulmonary problems. In addition, a marijuana joint (when compared with a tobacco cigarette) typically contains about the same levels of tars, 50 percent more hydrocarbons, and an unknown amount of possible contaminants (Table 11.1). Joints are often smoked more completely because the smoker tries to waste as little marijuana as possible.

Given all these factors, marijuana smoking presents several risks. One of the immediate consequences affects the

TABLE 11.1

A comparison of the components of marijuana and tobacco smoke

COMPONENT	MARIJUANA	TOBACCO
Carbon monoxide (mg)	17.6	20.2
Carbon dioxide (mg)	57.3	65.0
Ammonia (micrograms)	228.0	178.0
Acetaldehyde (micrograms)	1,200.0	980.0
Acetone (micrograms)*	443.0	578.0
Benzene (micrograms)*	76.0	67.0
Toluene (micrograms)*	112.0	108.0
Nicotine (micrograms)	—	2,850.0
Napthalene (nanograms)	3,000.0	1,200.0

Source: Based on data from Julien, R. M. (2001), A primer of drug action (9th ed.). New York: Worth, p. 317.

process of breathing. When marijuana is inhaled initially, the passageways for air entering and leaving the lungs widen, but after chronic exposure, an opposite reaction occurs. As a result, symptoms of asthma and other respiratory difficulties are increased. Molecular abnormalities in the respiratory tracts of heavy marijuana smokers have been identified that resemble the changes in the respiratory tracts of cigarette smokers. However, marijuana smoking does not increase the risk of developing emphysema, a chronic lung disease that is closely associated with tobacco smoking (see Chapter 15).

Evaluations of the effects of marijuana smoking over an extended period of time have been relatively sparse. However, one study has indicated that occasional and low-cumulative marijuana use, even over a period of more than 20 years (1985–2006), does not produce adverse effects on lung capacity as indicated by standard pulmonary breathing tests. On the other hand, most people who smoke marijuana also smoke tobacco, and the adverse effects of tobacco smoking on lung function are well known. There is a threefold increase in the risk of pulmonary disease among heavy marijuana use combined with tobacco use, suggesting that marijuana and tobacco might have a synergistic impact on lung function. It has been difficult for researchers to find a sufficient number of heavy marijuana smokers who are not also tobacco smokers to make a definitive conclusion about the pulmonary effects of heavy marijuana use alone.

Overall, while the effects of a single inhalation of marijuana smoke present greater problems than a single inhalation of tobacco smoke, we need to remember that the patterns of consumption are far from comparable. All things considered, on a statistical basis, you can think of one joint as being equivalent to five cigarettes in terms of the amount of carbon monoxide intake and four cigarettes in terms of tar intake. The use of a water pipe reduces the harm somewhat, but the risks are still present.

Risks of Lung Cancer

Does smoking marijuana produce a higher incidence of lung cancer? Once again, it has been difficult to isolate the risk of lung cancer due to marijuana use as opposed to concurrent tobacco use. An additional challenge in making a marijuana-lung cancer link is that the peak years in which lung cancer cases are typically diagnosed are decades later than the years in which marijuana smoking begins and is most frequent. It is only recently that these difficulties have been overcome. In a 40-year follow-up study of young Swedish males aged 18–20 years old identified as heavy marijuana smokers in 1969–1970, researchers have found more than a twofold increase in the incidence of lung cancer, separating out the effects of tobacco use over that period of time. The study defined heavy marijuana use as self-reports of having smoked marijuana more than 50 times over one's lifetime.

Important questions, however, remain to be answered on the issue of linking marijuana use to lung cancer. First of all, it is not known from this study to what extent marijuana smoking continued past late adolescence and early adulthood and what role that might have played in the final outcome. Were the men diagnosed with lung cancer 40 years later, the ones who smoked marijuana most of their adult life? Adolescence and early adulthood is a time of significant lung development and it is possible that marijuana smoking coincided with a "critical period" of susceptibility to the carcinogens in marijuana smoke, but we cannot determine the relationship at this time. Second, adolescents and young adults are currently smoking higher potency marijuana than was the case 40 years ago. It is possible that decades from now we might find a linkage to lung cancer at more occasional or moderate levels of marijuana use of this factor. On the other hand, the lower incidence of current tobacco smoking among adolescents and young adults, relative to the much higher incidence 40 years ago, might reduce the possibility of synergistic effects of combining marijuana and tobacco.[28]

Effects on the Immune System

When THC is administered to animals, the immune system is suppressed, resulting in a reduction in the body's defense reactions to infection and disease. In humans, the evidence is inconclusive. Some studies indicate that THC has a suppressive effect; others indicate that no immunological changes occur at all. Because marijuana smoking has not been found to be associated with a higher incidence of any major chronic disease, we can tentatively conclude that marijuana smoking does not have a major impact on the immune system. Yet, long-term epidemiological studies, in which marijuana-exposed and control populations are compared with regard to the frequency of various diseases, have not been conducted on a large-scale basis. It has been shown that cannabinoids cause a mobilization of immune-suppressor cells that may potentially have a significant effect in weakening the immune system; it is not clear whether this effect is later seen in a higher incidence of immune system-related diseases.[29]

Effects on Sexual Functioning and Reproduction

The reproductive systems of both men and women are adversely affected by marijuana smoking. In men, marijuana reduces the level of testosterone, reduces sperm count in the semen, and increases the percentage of abnormally formed sperm. In women, marijuana use results in a reduction in the level of luteinizing hormone (LH), a hormone necessary for the fertilized egg to be implanted in the uterus. As little as one marijuana joint smoked immediately following ovulation is evidently sufficient for this LH suppression to occur. Despite these hormonal changes in both males and females, however, little or no effect on fertility has been observed.[30]

The research is sparse on the question, but there does not appear to be evidence of birth defects in the offspring of women who have smoked marijuana during their pregnancy. Studies indicate, however, a lower birth weight and shorter length among newborns, as well as a reduction in the mother's milk. It may be unfair to associate these effects specifically with marijuana smoking because other drugs, including alcohol and nicotine, are often being consumed during the same period. Even so, the best advice remains that women should avoid marijuana during pregnancy.[31]

Long-Term Cognitive Effects and the Amotivational Syndrome

In the 1960s, when marijuana smoking became a mainstream concern among many in the establishment, though chronic exposure to marijuana frequently has been suspected of producing significant brain damage or long-term impairment in neural functioning, there is little or no evidence in support of this idea. It also has been suspected that marijuana may produce more subtle neurological changes that would affect one's personality, motivation to succeed, or outlook on life. In 1968, William McGlothin, a psychologist, and Louis West, a psychiatrist, proposed that chronic marijuana smoking among young people was responsible for a generalized sense of apathy in their lives and an indifference to any long-term plans or conventional goals. These changes were called the **amotivational syndrome**. In their words,

> *Regular marijuana use may contribute to the development of more passive, inward-turning personality characteristics. For numerous middle-class students, the subtly progressive change from conforming, achievement-oriented behavior to a state of relaxed and careless drifting has followed their use of sig-*

amotivational syndrome: A state of listlessness and personality change involving a generalized apathy and indifference to long-range plans.

nificant amounts of marijuana.... Such individuals exhibit greater introversion, become totally involved with the present at the expense of future goals, and demonstrate a strong tendency toward regressive, childlike magical thinking.[32]

Essentially, McGothlin and West, and probably a sizable proportion of the American public in the late 1960s, were saying, "These people don't seem to care any more about things *that we think are important*, and marijuana must be to blame for it!"

The issue of the amotivational syndrome revolves around two basic questions that need to be examined separately. The first question deals with whether such a syndrome exists in the first place, and the second deals with whether chronic abuse of marijuana is a causal factor.[33]

As to the existence of the syndrome, the evidence does suggest that students who smoke marijuana are at a disadvantage academically. Studies of high school students indicate that those who smoke marijuana on a regular basis (weekly or more frequently) earn lower grades in school (Figure 11.1), are less likely to continue on to college, are more likely to drop out, and miss more classes than those who do not smoke it.[34] In a survey of high school students graduating in the early 1980s, those who smoked marijuana on a daily basis reported several problems in their lives that are related to motivation: a loss of energy (43 percent), negative effects on relationships (39 percent), interference with work and the ability to think clearly (37 percent), less interest in other activities (37 percent), and inferior performance in school or on the job (34 percent).[35] While this survey was conducted more than 30 years ago, it is likely that these percentages would be roughly the same today.

These changes in academic performance and other aspects of cognitive activity are genuine, but we cannot easily establish a direct causal link between marijuana and such global problems, other than to acknowledge that the presence of THC in a student's system during school hours would be reflected later in a decline in overall academic performance. More broadly speaking, we cannot exclude the possibility that marijuana smoking may be, in the words of one expert in the field, "just one behavior in a constellation of related problem behaviors and personality and familial factors" that hamper an adolescent's ability to do well in school and in life.[36] We also cannot exclude the possibility that an involvement with marijuana may closely correlate with involvement in a deviant subculture, a group of friends and associates who feel alienated from traditional values such as school achievement and a promising future (see Chapter 8). Either of these factors, in combination with the regular ingestion of marijuana, can account for the motivational changes that are observed. The point is that we cannot conclude that such lifestyle changes are purely pharmacological.

Nonetheless, it is clear that acute marijuana intoxication produces significant cognitive deficits, as evidenced by reduced scores on tasks of attentiveness and memory. The question remains whether these problems are increased or perhaps may become irreversible as a result of long-term marijuana use. Large and well-controlled studies have shown that cognitive deficits in heavy marijuana smokers, relative to nonusers, are observed after 12–72 hours of abstinence. In other words, the specific signs of cognitive impairment among long-term marijuana smokers may linger for as long as three days after active marijuana smoking. In one study, however, testing after 28 days of abstinence revealed equivalent performance scores between nonusers and users of marijuana, even though the latter group had smoked a median of about 15,000 times over a period of 10–33 years. No correlation was seen between the test scores after 28 days of abstinence and the number of episodes of marijuana use over an individual's lifetime. Therefore, it appears that problems related to attention and memory among heavy marijuana smokers can be reversed by stopping marijuana use. It is a hopeful sign in the context of drug-abuse treatment (Chapter 14). On the other hand, recent studies indicate that specific brain abnormalities associated with long-term heavy marijuana use have a negative impact on successful information-processing abilities, particularly among young smokers and marijuana with high THC levels. These neuroanatomical changes may not be reversible.[37]

Examining the Gateway Hypothesis

A widely publicized theory about marijuana smoking concerns the possibility of a relationship between marijuana use and the subsequent abuse of illicit drugs such as amphetamines, cocaine, or heroin. The contention that marijuana leads to a greater incidence of drug abuse in general is referred to as the **gateway hypothesis**. As in the consideration of

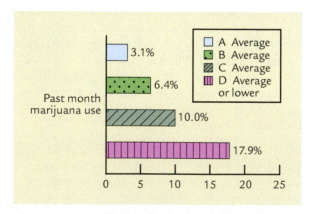

FIGURE 11.1

Percentages of past month marijuana and blunt use among students aged 12–17 and semester grade average in school.

Note: Blunts are hollowed-out cigars refilled with marijuana.

Source: Substance Abuse and Mental Health Services Administration (2007). Use of marijuana and blunts among adolescents: 2005. *The NSDUH Report,* p. 3.

gateway hypothesis: The idea that the abuse of a specific drug will inherently lead to the abuse of other, more harmful drugs.

the amotivational syndrome, the evidence for this hypothesis must be studied very carefully.

With respect to the gateway hypothesis, we should address three separate issues: (1) whether a fixed sequential relationship exists between the initiation of marijuana use and other forms of drug-taking behavior, (2) whether marijuana use represents a significant risk factor for future drug-taking behavior, specifically increasing the likelihood of using other illicit drugs, and (3) whether marijuana actually causes the use of other illicit drugs.

The Sequencing Question

One of the best-replicated findings in the long-term study of drug use is a developmental sequence of involvement (stages of progression) in drug-taking behavior. In the United States as well as other Western societies, use of alcohol and cigarettes precedes marijuana use, and marijuana use precedes use of other illicit drugs. In other words, exceedingly few people who have used cocaine or heroin have not used marijuana at a previous time. This means that *among those users of cocaine or heroin*, the use of marijuana precedes the use of cocaine or the use of heroin.[38] Yet, it is also true that an overwhelming proportion of young marijuana smokers do not go on to use other illicit drugs. As expressed in a 1999 newspaper editorial on this point, "millions of baby boomers ... once did, indeed, inhale. They later went into business, not cocaine or heroin."[39]

The Association Question

From a statistical perspective, the association between marijuana use and subsequent use of other illicit drugs is not controversial. Generally speaking, marijuana smokers are several times more likely to consume illicit drugs such as cocaine and heroin during their lifetimes than are nonmarijuana smokers. Not surprisingly, the greater the frequency of marijuana smoking and the earlier an individual first engages in marijuana smoking, the greater the likelihood of his or her becoming involved with other illicit drugs in the future.

Testing whether there is a *direct* association between marijuana use and later illicit drugs, a recent study examined marijuana use among 711 males and female participants, the reported use among their friends at ages 17, 17–22, and 22–27, and the participants' later use of illicit drugs (i.e., cocaine, methamphetamine, and opioids) at ages 22–27. It was found that marijuana use at age 17 was positively associated with perceived friends' use at age 22, which *in turn* predicted illicit drug use between ages 22 and 27. In other words, the increased likelihood of illicit drug use from early use of marijuana was mediated through a "peer ecology of drug-taking behavior." This suggests an important opportunity for prevention purposes, specifically the development of programs that focus on abstaining peers in minimizing the progression of marijuana to illicit drugs. Programs of this kind would augment prevention programs for youths that are designed to reduce the onset of marijuana use in the first place (see Chapter 14).

A precise determination of the *magnitude* of risk, however, requires studies that take into account a range of genetic and environmental variables that might act as risk or protective factors for drug-taking behavior as well (see Chapter 8). In a further analysis, a study in 2003 investigated specific subpopulations of twins, one of whom reported marijuana use by the age of 17 and the other who reported no marijuana use at all. Examining twins permitted the researchers to calculate the increased risk of future drug-taking behavior when environmental factors (in the case of fraternal twins) and both environmental and genetic factors (in the case of identical twins) were controlled. Results showed that early marijuana users were about two and one-half times more likely to use heroin later in life, four times more likely to use cocaine or other stimulants, and five times more likely to use hallucinogens. In general, they were twice as likely to become alcoholic and twice as likely to develop any form of illicit drug abuse or dependence. A question remains unanswered whether twin studies of this kind might show the increased risk from marijuana use to be *higher than the increased risk from alcohol or tobacco use.*[40]

In the final analysis, the statistical relationship between marijuana smoking and other forms of drug-taking behavior simply reflects the sequential pattern of drug use among multiple-drug (polydrug) users. Essentially, the use of high-prevalence drugs (such as alcohol, tobacco, and/or marijuana) begins earlier than the use of low-prevalence drugs (such as cocaine and/or heroin). An explanation may be due not to the types of drugs themselves but, rather, to the relative differences in prevalence rates. There are numerous examples of a statistical relationship that can be drawn when considering a common behavior and an uncommon one. Take the case of riding a motorcycle and riding a bicycle:

> For example, most people who ride a motorcycle (a fairly rare activity) have ridden a bicycle (a fairly common activity). Indeed, the prevalence of motorcycle riding among people who have never ridden a bicycle is probably extremely low. Bicycle riding, however, does not cause motorcycle riding, and increases in the former will not lead automatically to increases in the latter.[41]

The Causation Question

The strongest form of the gateway hypothesis relates to the possibility of a causal link between marijuana smoking and the use of other illicit drugs. With respect to the causation issue, Erich Goode, a sociologist and drug-abuse researcher, has distinguished between two schools of thought, which he calls the intrinsic argument and the sociocultural argument. The *intrinsic argument* asserts that some inherent property of marijuana exposure itself leads to physical or psychological dependence on other illicit drugs. According to this viewpoint, the pleasurable sensations of marijuana create a biological urge to consume more potent substances, through a combination of drug tolerance and drug dependence. In contrast, the *sociocultural argument* holds that the relationship

Quick Concept Check 11.2

Understanding the Adverse Effects of Chronic Marijuana Abuse

Check your understanding of the possible adverse effects of either acute or chronic exposure to marijuana by checking off true or false next to each of the assertions.

ASSERTION	TRUE	FALSE
1. The immune system will be suppressed.	_____	_____
2. The chances of getting lung cancer will be unaffected.	_____	_____
3. Driving ability will be significantly impaired.	_____	_____
4. Birth defects will be more frequent.	_____	_____
5. It is likely that academic performance will decline when a person smokes marijuana regularly.	_____	_____
6. Marijuana smoking will cause the smoker to experiment with cocaine or heroin in the future.	_____	_____
7. Marijuana smoking in adolescence will generally be preceded by experimentation with tobacco or alcohol.	_____	_____

Answers: 1. false   2. false   3. true   4. false   5. true   6. false   7. true

adolescent marijuana use among males also increases the risk in late adolescence of delinquency, having multiple sexual partners, not always using condoms during sex, perceiving drugs as not harmful, and having problems with cigarettes and alcohol. Generally speaking, marijuana smokers show a greater inclination toward risk-taking behavior and are more unconventional with regard to social norms.[42]

Patterns of Marijuana Smoking

From as early as their days in elementary school, most young Americans have had to come to terms with marijuana as a pervasive element in their lives. Just as nearly all adolescents have had to make the decision whether to drink or not to drink, and whether to smoke cigarettes or not to smoke them, they also have had to decide whether to smoke or not smoke marijuana.

Marijuana is undoubtedly the dominant illicit drug in U.S. society today. From the National Survey on Drug Use and Health conducted in 2017, it has been estimated that an astounding 123 million Americans, about 45 percent of the U.S. population over the age of 12, have smoked marijuana at least once during their lives. Approximately 25 million Americans are estimated to have smoked marijuana within the past 30 days. Since federal statutes define marijuana use as illicit drug use, it is fair to say that marijuana smoking for the vast majority of Americans represents the *sole form of illicit drug-taking behavior in their lives.*[43]

When examined in terms of three age groups (12–17 years, 18–25 years, 26 years and older), it is clear that the highest incidence of marijuana use is among young adults. One in five individuals in this age group report having smoked marijuana in the past month, while one in fourteen in age groups younger or older than them report doing so. The perceived risk in marijuana use among marijuana smokers in the age groups is also dramatically different (Figure 11.2). Not surprisingly, the age group showing the highest incidence of marijuana use is the group that reports the lowest level of perceived risk in doing so.[44] At the present time, one area of concern with regard to the risk of harm from marijuana smoking has been on the potential dangers of marijuana being contaminated with synthetic cannabinoids. A prominent example of a harmful synthetic cannabinoid is known by its street names, Spice or K2 (Drugs ... in Focus).

The Case for Medical Marijuana

Even though the medicinal benefits of marijuana have been noted for thousands of years, strong anti-marijuana sentiment in the United States made it difficult until the 1970s to conduct an objective appraisal of its clinical applications. Early research in the effectiveness of marijuana to reduce intraocular (within the eye) pressure and dilate bronchioles in the

exists not because of the pharmacological effects of marijuana but because of the activities, friends, and acquaintances that are associated with marijuana smoking. In other words, the sociocultural explanation asserts that those who smoke marijuana tend to have friends who not only smoke marijuana themselves but also abuse other drugs. These friends are likely to have positive attitudes toward substance abuse in general and to provide opportunities for drug experimentation.

Professionals in the drug-abuse field have concluded that if any such causal link exists, the result would be socioculturally based rather than related to the pharmacological properties of marijuana itself. The consensus is that any early exposure to psychoactive substances in general, and illicit drugs such as marijuana in particular, represents a "deviance-prone pattern of behavior" that will be reflected in a higher incidence of exposure to psychoactive drugs of many types later in life. It is interesting to note that early

Drugs . . . in Focus

Spice and Other Designer Synthetic Cannabinoids

In 2010, the Drug Enforcement Administration was alerted to a new leafy herb product, marketed under the name Spice (alternate "brand names" include K2, Fire, Blaze among others), that began to be available through smoke shops and other small retail outlets. At the time, Spice was sold officially as a "herbal incense" and therefore as a legal commodity, retailers were able to get around laws prohibiting sale of marijuana itself. In actuality, the chemical composition of Spice is highly variable, though its primary ingredient is typically a synthetic cannabinoid called JWH-018, capable of binding to CB1 receptors four times more strongly than THC itself. A powerful marijuana-like high is produced as a result. Although standard urinalysis screening tests for THC metabolites (see Chapter 16) typically do not screen for JWH-018, specialized tests have been developed for screening up to 15 synthetic cannabinoids, including JWH-018.

JWH-018 is only one of a growing number of designer synthetic cannabinoids that have entered the illegal drug market in recent years. They have obscure chemical names such as JWH-073, JWH-200, HU-210, and CP-47,497, each with individualized "signatures" with regard to their effects on CB1 and CB2 receptors (see page 229). Drugs that are sold simply as

"synthetic marijuana" may include any of these or other cannabinoids, in any proportion. As a result, it is difficult to predict the psychological and physiological responses of these drugs. Emergency physicians have reported individuals ingesting Spice with serious side effects that include convulsions, anxiety attacks, elevated heart rate and blood pressure, vomiting, and disorientation.

It has been a continuing challenge for drug enforcement authorities to keep up with the flood of new synthetic cannabinoid compounds entering the illicit drug market. Since 2011, the DEA executes expanded scheduling authority (under the Controlled Substances Act) that includes JWH-018 and many other cannabinoids as Schedule I controlled substances.

Sources: NMS Laboratories, Willow Grove, PA. Synthetic Cannabinoid Metabolites Screen Expanded Urine (Forensic) Test. Substance Abuse and Mental Health Services Administration (2012, December 4). *Drug-related emergency department visits involving synthetic cannabinoids. The DAWN Report.* Rockville, MD: Substance Abuse and Mental Health Services Administration. U.S. Drug Enforcement Administration (2014). *Schedules of controlled substances: Temporary placement of four synthetic cannabinoids into Schedule I.* Washington, D.C.: Office of Diversion Control, Drug Enforcement Administration, U.S. Department of Justice.

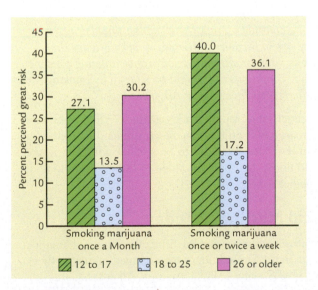

FIGURE 11.2

Perceived great risk from smoking marijuana among people aged 12–17, 18–25, and 26 and older.

Source: Lipari, R. N.; Ahmsbrak, R. D.; Pemberton, M. R.; and Porter, J. D. (2017, September). *Risk and protective factors and estimates of substance use initiations: Results from the 2016 National Survey on Drug Use and Health. NSDUH Data Review.* Rockville, MD: Substance Abuse and Mental Health Services Administration, Figure 2.

lungs suggested uses as a possible therapy for glaucoma and asthma, respectively. However, new prescription medications have been shown to be as effective as marijuana in the treatment of these disorders. Today, the focus has turned toward the treatment of chronic pain, muscle spasticity, nausea, and weight loss.

Treating Muscle Spasticity and Chronic Pain

Evidence that marijuana is useful in the treatment of muscle spasticity and lack of mobility associated with neurological diseases such as multiple sclerosis (MS) comes largely from subjective reports. In a randomized placebo-controlled study of MS patients taking oral capsules of THC or whole cannabis extract, no significant improvements were observed through objective measures of mobility but about two-thirds of the patients reported that they felt significant relief from muscle spasticity and associated chronic pain. In addition, patients frequently report relief from cancer-related pain as well as phantom limb pain (a phenomenon in which pain is experienced as coming from a limb that had been amputated). In many cases, they cite the superiority of smoked marijuana to any other form of treatment.[45]

Treating Nausea, Weight Loss, and Epilepsy

Chemotherapy in the course of cancer treatment produces an extreme and debilitating nausea, lack of appetite, and loss of body weight, symptoms that are clearly counterproductive in helping an individual contend with an ongoing fight against cancer. AIDS patients suffer from similar symptoms, as do those diagnosed with the gastrointestinal ailment Crohn's disease. Under these circumstances, standard antiemetic (antivomiting) drugs are frequently ineffective. The beneficial effect of marijuana, specifically THC, as an antiemetic drug when treatment by traditional antiemetic medications has failed, is an important therapeutic application.[46]

At the same time, the use of marijuana per se as a therapeutic agent has distinct disadvantages. First, the typical administration through smoking presents a significant health risk to the lungs. Second, because marijuana is insoluble in water, suspensions in an injectable form cannot be prepared. Since 1985, however, two legal prescription drugs containing THC or a variation of it have been made available in capsule form and classified as Schedule II controlled substances. **Dronabinol** (brand name: Marinol) is essentially THC in a sesame oil suspension; **nabilone** (brand name: Cesamet) is a synthetic variation of THC. Both drugs have been shown to be clinically effective against nausea, although the personal reactions of patients taking these drugs vary considerably.

The discovery that CBD, the cannabinoid in cannabis unrelated to THC and without intoxicating properties, has neuroprotective features has led to its use in the treatment of epileptic seizures, particularly specific seizure disorders in children and adults that have been particularly difficult to treat by available anti-seizure medications. In one study, patients treated with the medication Epidiolex (consisting of a purified, 99 percent oil-based CBD extract), had their rate of seizure activity decrease by an average of 54 percent. In 2018, the FDA approved Epidiolex for the treatment of two rare forms of epilepsy in patients two years and older. While technically limited at present for the treatment of only the most severe forms of epilepsy, the door has been opened for CBD to be investigated as a treatment for a wider range of disorders in the future.[47]

The Evolving Status of Medical Marijuana Laws

For many years, U.S. federal authorities have resisted the official reclassification of marijuana itself or of any other cannabinoid extract (including CBD) from the Schedule I category

> **dronabinol (droh-NAB-ih-nol):** A prescription drug containing delta-9-tetrahydrocannabinol (THC). Brand name is Marinol.
>
> **nabilone (NAB-ih-lone):** A prescription drug containing a synthetic variation of delta-9-tetrahydrocannabinol (THC). Brand name is Cesamet.

of controlled substances (drugs that have no medical application) to the Schedule II category (which includes morphine and cocaine). For a short period of time, a handful of "compassionate use" applications were approved by the federal government to receive marijuana as a medical treatment, but the program for reviewing new applications was curtailed in 1992.

It is interesting that a major endorsement for medical marijuana had been part of a report issued in 1999 by a federally funded institution. The Institute of Medicine, a branch of the National Academy of Sciences, was charged at that time to study the question of the potential for medical marijuana. In the preface to its final report to the president, there was a suggestion of future developments in this area:

> Although marijuana smoke delivers THC and other cannabinoids to the body, it also delivers harmful substances, including most of those found in tobacco smoke. In addition, plants contain a variable mixture of biologically active compounds and cannot be expected to provide a precisely defined drug effect. For these reasons, this report concludes that the future of cannabinoid drugs lies not in smoked marijuana, but in chemically defined drugs that act on the cannabinoid systems that are a natural component of human physiology.[48]

In response to the report, however, the federal Office of National Drug Control Strategy emphasized the potential health risks of marijuana smoking and the imprecision of its administration as a justification for the continued prohibition of marijuana for medical purposes. Largely ignored was one of the report's main conclusions within the report itself.

> Until a nonsmoked, rapid-onset cannabinoid drug delivery system becomes available, we acknowledge that there is no clear alternative for people suffering from chronic conditions that might be relieved by smoking marijuana, such as pain or AIDS wasting.[49]

In effect, the report had concluded that, although smoked marijuana could not be recommended for long-term use, short-term use appeared to be suitable for treating specific conditions when patients failed to respond well to traditional medications.

Medical Marijuana Today

In a relatively short period of time, the status of medical marijuana in the United States has changed dramatically. As of 2018, 33 U.S. states (Alaska, Arizona, Arkansas, California, Colorado, Connecticut, Delaware, Florida, Hawaii, Illinois, Louisiana, Maine, Maryland, Massachusetts, Michigan, Missouri, Minnesota, Montana, Nevada, New Hampshire, New Jersey, New Mexico, New York, North Dakota, Ohio, Oklahoma, Oregon, Pennsylvania, Rhode Island, Utah, Vermont, Washington, and West Virginia) and the District of Columbia have approved marijuana use for medical treatment, when prescribed by a physician.

There is substantial variation, however, in (1) the disorders for which marijuana treatment has been authorized, (2) the form of marijuana that is permitted for medical use, and (3) the access options for patients seeking medical treatment of this kind. In some states, the medical conditions for which marijuana treatment is permitted is quite limited. On the other hand, there are several states in which permissible medical applications for marijuana have extended to a range of conditions, including post-traumatic stress disorder. In California, there is extensive leeway in obtaining medical marijuana treatment, with applications including any "major illness where marijuana has been "deemed appropriate and has been recommended by a physician." In several states, only cannabidiol (CBD) is permitted for medical treatment; in other states, marijuana must be administered only in a nonsmokable form such as in oil extracts or capsules. There is currently a trend toward easing access to medical marijuana in those states that have authorized it, but whether there will be a greater consistency of policy across state jurisdictions in the future remains uncertain.[50]

Meanwhile, ten of these states and the District of Columbia have approved marijuana for nonmedical (recreational) use as well (see pages 237–239).

Medical Cannabinoids

In recent years, research investigations seeking new cannabis-related treatments for a variety of diseases have turned away from medications containing marijuana or THC to other cannabinoids extracted from cannabis. The most prominent cannabinoid with potential for medical applications is CBD. As mentioned earlier, in several U.S. states the only marijuana treatment permitted is treatment with CBD, specifically for treating epileptic seizures among children and a wide range of pain conditions, including spasticity-related pain in multiple sclerosis, peripheral pain, intractable cancer pain, and rheumatoid arthritis pain. A prescription drug called Sativex, containing a combination of THC and CBD extracts, holds promise as a useful treatment for spasticity and pain conditions of various kinds. Since it contains both THC and CBD, Sativex stimulates both CB1 and CB2 receptors (see pages 229 and 235). Importantly, Sativex is administered as a mouth spray rather than a cigarette, avoiding the pulmonary problems that are associated with marijuana smoking. Sativex has been approved as a medication in 24 countries (including Canada, the United Kingdom, Germany, Austria, Sweden, Denmark, and Spain). Sativex has not yet been FDA approved for treatment in the United States.[51]

Decriminalization and Legalization

What lies ahead with respect to the public stance toward marijuana smoking in the United States? Should there be a **decriminalization** of marijuana smoking, which would mean that purchase, possession, and use of marijuana would be considered a civil (noncriminal) offense, punishable by a fine rather than imprisonment? Should there be a *legalization* of marijuana smoking, which would mean that purchase, possession, or use of marijuana would no longer be an illegal act (assuming certain restrictions such as a minimum age requirement, limitations to personal use only, and prohibiting drug use while driving)?

In examining these questions, it is important to review how public policy with respect to marijuana regulation began to change in the 1970s. As described earlier in the chapter, the dramatic emergence during the 1960s of marijuana as a major psychoactive drug initiated a slow but steady reassessment of myths that had been attached to it for decades. By 1972, the American Medical Association and the American Bar Association had proposed a liberalization of laws regarding the possession of marijuana. In 1972, the National Commission on Marijuana and Drug Abuse, authorized by the Controlled Substances Act of 1970, encouraged state legislators around the country to consider changes in their particular regulatory statutes that related to marijuana.[52]

Decriminalization on a State Level

As of 2018, 12 U.S. states (Connecticut, Delaware, Illinois, Maryland, Minnesota, Mississippi, Nebraska, New Hampshire, New York, North Carolina, Ohio, and Rhode Island) have decriminalized (but not legalized) the possession of marijuana in small amounts (usually less than an ounce or so). In most decriminalized states, marijuana offenses are treated like a minor traffic violation. In a few decriminalized states, marijuana possession offenses are still considered criminal misdemeanors but do not carry any threat of jail time.

Legalization on a State Level

As of 2018, ten U.S. states (Alaska, California, Colorado, Maine, Massachusetts, Michigan, Nevada, Oregon, Vermont, and Washington) as well as the District of Columbia have approved the legalization of recreational marijuana use for individuals 21 years or older. Legal possession of marijuana for personal use is limited to 1 ounce (28 g) or less in seven of these states, with the exception of Maine where the limit has been set at 2.5 ounces (71 g). In all states, marijuana smoking in public spaces is prohibited, and commercial marijuana growers and commercial dispensaries (retail stores selling marijuana) must receive state-issued licenses to operate on a legal basis. In some states, communities in states where marijuana has been legalized can ban, if they choose, marijuana dispensaries or marijuana use in general within their local jurisdictions (see Drug Enforcement ... in Focus).

> **decriminalization:** The policy of making the possession of small amounts of a drug subject to a small fine but not criminal prosecution.

Special cannabis tours are part of growing tourism industries in those U.S. states where recreational marijuana has been legalized.

Limits on legal marijuana cultivation by individuals vary somewhat from state to state. In California, Colorado, Maine, and Massachusetts, adults over 21 are permitted to grow up to six marijuana plants in a private secure area, while the limit is lower (4 plants) in Oregon or higher (12 plants) in Alaska. In Washington State, no personal cultivation is permitted except for marijuana intended to be used for medical purposes. In Nevada, no personal cultivation of marijuana is permitted within 25 miles of a licensed marijuana dispensary, essentially eliminating circumstances under which personal cultivation can take place.

Marijuana use in those states in which legalization exists generates considerable tax revenue, as well as secondary revenue from marijuana-related tourism. Now that California has legalized marijuana in 2018, it is estimated that the $9 billion in sales revenue from legal marijuana in 2017 will grow to $11 to $21 billion by 2021. State taxes from marijuana sales amounted to $1 billion in 2016 an $11.4 billion in 2017. Generally, the sales tax paid by the consumer for retail marijuana purchases is determined either as a percentage of the total purchase price at time of sale or a flat tax based on the quantity of marijuana being sold. In most states, calculation of the total tax rate is based upon state excise tax, state sales tax, local excise tax, or local sales tax rate, the specific combination being dependent on the specific state and community in which the transaction has occurred. In Alaska, a flat tax levy of $50 per ounce of marijuana is imposed. While marijuana sales taxes are higher than the regular sales taxes on other types of retail purchases, it has been important that marijuana tax rates not be so high so as to encourage the continuation of a black market for marijuana. Recently, Colorado, Washington, and Oregon have taken steps to reduce their marijuana tax rates from initial levels when it was determined that marijuana users found black market prices to be cheaper than those found in legitimate retail outlets. There has been a general consensus that a maximal tax rate between 10 and 25 percent is sufficient in reducing black market sales. The distribution of revenue received from state taxes of marijuana varies considerably, from the support of

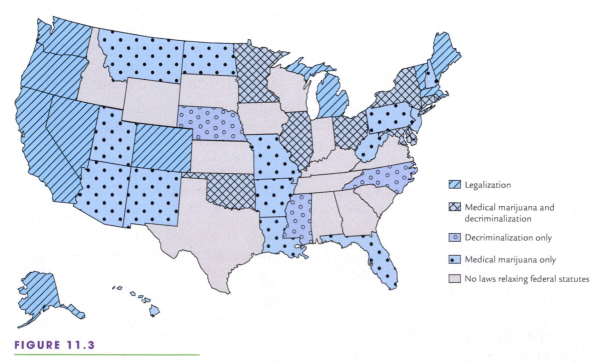

Legalization

Medical marijuana and decriminalization

Decriminalization only

Medical marijuana only

No laws relaxing federal statutes

FIGURE 11.3

A map showing U.S. states that have approved, as of 2018, medical marijuana, medical marijuana and decriminalization, decriminalization alone, or legalization. Marijuana use remains illegal in 14 states, in accordance with federal law.

Source: Used with permission from Marijuana Policy Project, Grace Donnelly/Fortune, New York, NY.

Drug Enforcement . . . in Focus

Some Communities Just Say No and Some Just Say Yes

After the repeal of Prohibition in 1933 on a nationwide basis and U.S. states eventually repealed prohibition laws of their own, there were localities that retained alcohol prohibition statutes and were entitled to do so. Therefore, there were "dry towns" in "wet states" for a number of years.

In the case of marijuana legalization, local communities have the option of banning recreational marijuana even if the state in which the community is located has legalized it. A community stands to lose the tax revenue from marijuana sales within its jurisdiction but local anti-marijuana sentiment might be a stronger factor. Prohibition of marijuana use in a state where it is officially legalized has strongest support in rural and conservative communities but surprisingly bipartisan political backing in some cases. Residents of Yakima, Washington (population 93,000), for example, have voted overwhelmingly to prohibit marijuana businesses to be licensed in their city. The Washington State Attorney General issued in 2014 a nonbinding legal opinion that local government could ban recreational marijuana, even though the intent of the state law passed in 2012, according to its supporters, was to make marijuana available to all state residents. Marijuana business owners have brought legal challenges to the localized marijuana bans. In answer to these challenges, local communities have argued that they have the legal right to act as long as marijuana remains illegal under federal law.

On the other hand, there are instances in which communities have decided to go in the opposite direction. In Atlanta, Oklahoma City, and Pittsburgh, for example, possession of small amounts of marijuana is a decriminalized offense even though in their respective states it is not. However, there is no guarantee that local ordinances remain in force on a permanent basis. In 2016, the state of Tennessee prohibited any municipal decisions to decriminalize marijuana, repealing previous ordinances instituted in Nashville and Memphis.

Sources: Donnelly, G. (2017, October 3). Atlanta is the latest U.S. city to decriminalize marijuana. Here's what that means. http://fortune.com/2017/10/03/list-of-cities-that-decriminalize-marijuana/. Johnson, K. (2014, January 27). Cannabis legal, localities begin to just say no. *The New York Times*, pp. A1, A13.

social services, public health programs and education to support of law enforcement agencies such as the state highway patrol.[53]

Marijuana in America: Federal versus State Drug Enforcement

Considering the conflict between the position of the U.S. federal government that marijuana is a Schedule I controlled substance and therefore its use in any form is prohibited and the positions of 29 U.S. states that have legalized medical marijuana and nine states that have legalized recreational marijuana, the question of drug enforcement has become a controversial issue that has yet to be resolved.

In 2009, the U.S. Attorney General Eric H. Holder, Jr. under President Obama issued the following statement on behalf of the U.S. Department of Justice with regard to medical marijuana:

It will not be a priority to use federal resources to prosecute patients with serious illnesses or their caregivers who are complying with state laws on medical marijuana, but we will not tolerate drug traffickers who hide behind claims of compliance with state law to mask activities that are clearly illegal.[54]

This statement did not change federal policy, only that the government would no longer spend time and money to carry out prosecutions in states in which medical marijuana was legally sanctioned. In effect, the Department of Justice returned the question of medical marijuana to the jurisdiction of the states without altering its official stance on a federal level that marijuana is a controlled substance without medical use.

In a memorandum issued in 2013, the Department of Justice established detailed and carefully worded guidelines for federal prosecutors, expanding its earlier position with regard to enforcement of medical marijuana to the enforcement of recreational marijuana as well. The federal government would continue its commitment to the Controlled Substances Act, but it would rely upon state and local law enforcement agencies in those states that have legalized marijuana in some form to implement "strong and effective regulatory and enforcement systems to control the cultivation, distribution, sale, and possession of marijuana." Such regulations would include preventing the distribution of marijuana to minors, preventing the diversion of marijuana from states where it is legal in some form to other states where it is illegal, and preventing state-authorized marijuana activity or revenue from such activity to support any criminal enterprise. If these conditions are met, "enforcement of state law by state and local law enforcement and regulatory bodies should remain the primary means of addressing marijuana-related activity."

In early 2018, however, the Department of Justice under the Trump administration issued another memorandum to federal prosecutors, rescinding its position that had been stated earlier in 2013. As a consequence, the question of federal and state enforcement responsibilities with regard to marijuana has returned as an unresolved issue for the time being. Recently, proposals in Congress have been made to "reschedule" marijuana as a Schedule II controlled substance, a category that identifies drugs as having some medical use. This change would remove the present conflict that exists with respect to medical marijuana, but it would not remove the conflict with respect to nonmedical (recreational) marijuana in those states that have approved such use. To resolve the conflict with respect to marijuana for any purpose, further congressional action would be needed. The proposed Marijuana Justice Act of 2018, as introduced in both the U.S. Senate and House of Representatives, amends the Controlled Substances Act to remove marijuana and tetrahydrocannabinols (THC) from Schedule I, and eliminates criminal penalties for an individual who imports, exports, manufactures, distributes, or possesses with intent to distribute marijuana. The congressional bill would also prohibit and reduce certain federal funds for a state without a statute legalizing marijuana, if the Bureau of Justice Assistance determines that such a state has a disproportionate arrest rate or disproportionate incarceration rate for marijuana offenses. This clause would allow the federal government a certain degree of control, should the legalization of marijuana exacerbate the prosecution of other drug-related offenses. On the other hand, in an effort to reverse the long-standing history of disproportionate arrest rates for marijuana possession offenses among African American and Hispanic individuals, the bill directs federal courts to expunge convictions for marijuana use or possession (see Chapter 6).[55]

Public Sentiment and Public Reality

As of 2018, 62 percent of Americans favor the legalization of marijuana. In contrast, acceptance of marijuana legalization from the late 1970s to the mid-1990s had never exceeded 25 percent. In surveys conducted in 2017, 88 percent of Americans were in favor of medical marijuana, more than one-half (53 percent) considered alcohol to be more harmful *than marijuana, and only one-fourth (23 percent) believed that marijuana use increased violent crime.*[55] The percentage of Americans favoring marijuana legalization had risen 16 percentage points in 5 years, from 52 percent in 2013 (the first time that a majority of the nation indicated holding this position) to 62 percent in 2018.

Beyond the question of public sentiment, however, is the reality of having access to legally available marijuana in present-day America. As of 2018, approximately 75 million Americans (more than 20 percent of the U.S. population) reside in a state where adults are legally permitted to use marijuana recreationally. More than 200 million

A display of cannabis-based cosmetic products on display in a state where recreational marijuana has been legalized. One product is marketed to relieve sore feet, or as one fashion stylist put it, "It's perfect for long nights in high heels."

Americans (about 62 percent of the U.S. population) live in a state where marijuana is legal to some degree. Following legalization in the state of California in 2018, recreational marijuana has become legal throughout the entire U.S. West Coast. In the meantime, Canada in 2018 became the first major industrial nation to have taken this action. It has now been possible for an adult to travel over a contiguous portion of North America, starting from eastern Nova Scotia across Canada to British Columbia then southward from Washington State to California and Nevada and find legal access to recreational marijuana (within the limits of state and local laws). With additional U.S. states currently having either proposed or pending legislation sanctioning legal access to marijuana, the number of U.S. states legalizing marijuana is certain to increase in the future. Now that Canada as a nation has approved recreational marijuana use, it is an open question whether the United States will follow suit.[56]

Clear indications of the growing sense of normalization with regard to the concept of recreational marijuana are evident throughout the United States. A sign of the times can be seen in the increasing numbers of cannabis-related products marketed in those U.S. states in which recreational marijuana use has been legalized. A case in point is the recent introduction in California of a line of cannabis-based skin care products (see Drugs...in Focus).

The Criminal-Justice Ramifications

The available evidence indicates that marijuana decriminalization laws have not affected prevalence rates of marijuana use. Statistics drawn from states in 1980 that either have or have not decriminalized show little or no difference in the prevalence rate of marijuana smoking. In addition, attitude surveys

Drugs . . . in Focus

Cannabis Skin Care Products Without the High

With nine U.S. states and the District of Columbia legalizing recreational marijuana, the skin care industry has gotten the message that they don't want to be left behind. Cannabis-derived ingredients that are mostly in cogue are isolates or crystals of cannabidiol (CBD), a cannabinoid found in cannabis (see page 240) that, unlike THC, will not get you high. While the scientific data is uneven, proponents of CBD products cite the benefits for relief from pain, reduction in anxiety and depression, appetite stimulation, as well as anti-inflammatory and anti-acne properties. There are CBD-infused gummies, caramels, and drops, but also topical lotions either for pain or soreness as well.

Lord Jones, a luxury skin care company, has introduced a chic line of body lotions (see photo), some derived purely from CBD and others from a combination of CBD and THC, that have been endorsed by well-known actresses for pain relief.

Celebratory endorsements aside, whether cannabis-derived topical products hold up to scrutiny as to effectiveness remains an open question. Dermatologists are awaiting randomized double-blind clinical trials before recommending CBD-derived skin care products over traditional remedies. Then again, skin care product companies have historically been vague as to the scientific basis for their products.

Source: Shapiro, B. (2018, February 1). Sorry, but there no contact high. Cannabis-derived ingredients are trendy in skin care. *The New York Times*, p. D5.

---

conducted in California before and after the enactment of decriminalization in 2010 indicate that the acceptance of marijuana among college students actually declined. Further studies of this kind need to be undertaken in U.S. states that have taken the further step to marijuana legalization.[57]

At the present time, states that have approved legalization have had to wrestle with a number of problems related to law enforcement, given the conflict with federal statutes that define marijuana as a Schedule I controlled substance, as well as problems related to public safety:

- In states where recreational marijuana has been legalized, college students over the age of 21 have been met with a significant restriction in marijuana use. Colleges and universities in Colorado and Washington, for example, have announced a prohibition of marijuana possession by students on college property, despite the legal status of marijuana in these states. The argument is that any institution that receives federal funding (as most colleges and universities do) must follow all federal laws, including the law defining marijuana as an illicit drug. Similar policies in other states with marijuana legalization have not been announced.[58]

- The definition of "driving while impaired" has traditionally been a matter of detecting a minimum blood alcohol concentration (BAC) adopted as the nationwide standard for drunk driving (see Chapter 13). According to popular opinion, driving while high on marijuana is not considered as dangerous as while intoxicated with alcohol, but as indicated earlier in the chapter deficits in driving behavior do occur as a result of marijuana intoxication, and there is no available information on the equivalence of the two drugs on driving performance at the present time. Moreover, while a breathalyzer test for BAC levels

can be routinely administered easily by law enforcement, there is no comparable on-site system for the detection of marijuana intoxication. The overall effect of widespread marijuana activity on driving safety is only beginning to be fully ascertained. Nonetheless, in a recent analysis of crash fatality rates in Washington and Colorado comparing pre-recreational legalization years to post-recreational legalization years, changes in rates were not significantly different from those in similar states without recreational marijuana legalization.[59]

- Newly established marijuana shop owners in states where marijuana is legally sold have found it difficult to open checking accounts, apply for business loans, or carry out any other financial transaction that is related to their business. Banks have been reluctant to be associated with a marijuana business, despite its legal status within the state, because of the potential for jeopardizing their federal deposit insurance (FDIC) eligibility. Their concern is that they would be viewed as being in violation of the Controlled Substances Act and prosecuted under federal money laundering statutes. Statements by the U.S. Attorney General on this question have suggested a relaxation of restrictions, but financial institutions await an official ruling that includes reasonable conditions for the financing of marijuana transactions.[60]

- Meanwhile, the Internal Revenue Service in 2015 reaffirmed its position that cannabis companies are required to submit payroll taxes electronically or face a 10-percent penalty. The IRS decision came as a request for an exception by a Denver-based cannabis dispensary that pays its taxes promptly in cash but cannot do so electronically because it has been unable to secure a bank account for that purpose. As a result of the IRS position, the cannabis industry currently faces millions of dollars of additional costs.

In Colorado, new marijuana-infused snacks such as chocolate-peppermint Mile High Bars and peanut butter candies infused with hashish oil have appeared on the market, as legal products. While advertised for customers over the age of 21, these products would be potentially attractive to customers under the age of 21 (the minimum age for purchasing any marijuana product). It is interesting that similar concerns have been raised with respect to the availability of alcohol or tobacco products to underage consumers (see Chapters 13 and 15).[61]

Summary

A Matter of Terminology

- Marijuana is one of several products of the *Cannabis sativa*, or common hemp plant, grown abundantly throughout the world.

- Various cannabis products are distinguished in terms of the content of cannabis resin and, in turn, the concentration of THC, the active psychoactive agent.

The History of Marijuana and Hashish

- The earliest records of marijuana come from Chinese writings nearly 5,000 years ago; hashish has its origins in North Africa and Persia in the ninth or tenth centuries A.D.

- In the United States, marijuana was available in patent medicines during the late 1800s, but its popularity did not become extensive until the 1920s.

- Federal and state regulation of marijuana began in the 1930s; penalties for possessing and selling marijuana escalated during the 1940s and 1950s.

- The emergence of marijuana on American college campuses and among American youth in general during the late 1960s, however, forced a reexamination of public policy regarding this drug, leading to a more lenient approach in the 1970s.

Acute Effects of Marijuana

- Because marijuana is almost always consumed through smoking, the acute effects are rapid, but because it is absorbed into fatty tissue, its elimination is slow. It may require days or weeks in the case of extensive exposure to marijuana for THC to leave the body completely.

- Acute physiological effects include cardiac acceleration and a reddening of the eyes. Acute psychological effects, with typical dosages, include euphoria, giddiness, a perception of time elongation, and an increased hunger and sexual desire. There are impairments in attention and memory, which interfere with complex visual–motor skills such as driving an automobile.

- The acute effects of marijuana are now known to be due to the binding of THC at special receptors in the brain.

Chronic Effects of Marijuana

- Chronic marijuana use produces tolerance effects; there is no physical dependence when doses are moderate and only a mild psychological dependence.

- Carcinogenic effects are suspected because marijuana smoke contains many of the same harmful components that tobacco smoke does, and in the case of marijuana smoking inhalation is deeper and more prolonged.

The Amotivational Syndrome and the Gateway Hypothesis

- The idea that there exists an amotivational syndrome, characterized by general apathy and an indifference to long-range planning, as a result of the pharmacological effects of chronic marijuana use has been largely discredited. An alternative explanation for the behavioral changes is that chronic marijuana users are involved in a deviant subculture that is directed away from traditional values of school achievement and long-term aspirations.

- According to the gateway hypothesis, marijuana inherently sets the stage for future patterns of drug abuse. Research studies have indicated that the use of alcohol and cigarettes precedes marijuana use, that marijuana use precedes the use of other illicit drugs, and that marijuana use and subsequent use of other illicit drugs are statistically correlated. However, there is little evidence that some inherent property of marijuana exposure itself leads to physical or psychological dependence on other drugs.

Patterns of Marijuana Smoking

- According to the National Survey on Drug Use and Health conducted in 2017, it has been estimated that an astounding 123 million Americans, about 45 percent of the U.S. population over the age of 12, have smoked marijuana at least once during their lives. Nearly 26 million Americans are estimated to have smoked marijuana within the past 30 days.

- Given the prevalence rate of marijuana smoking in the United States, there are areas of concern. In this regard, focus of attention has been drawn to the considerably greater potency of marijuana that is now available and the continuing risk of marijuana adulteration.

Medical Marijuana, Decriminalization, and Legalization

- Marijuana has been found to be helpful in the treatment of medical disorders that include muscle spasticity, chronic pain, conditions of nausea and weight loss, and epilepsy. As of the beginning of 2018, 33 U.S. states and the District of Columbia have approved medical marijuana.

- As of 2018, voters in 13 U.S. states have approved decriminalization (but not legalization) of recreational marijuana use.

As of 2018, ten U.S. states and the District of Columbia have approved recreational marijuana use for individuals 21 years or older. Canada has approved recreational marijuana use as well. Six out of ten Americans now support marijuana legalization. A growing trend toward normalization in the concept of recreational marijuana is evident throughout the United States.

- While public opinion has become increasingly favorable to medical marijuana, as well as decriminalization or legalization, several difficult issues remain to be resolved, stemming primarily from the continuing conflict between state laws that have liberalized the status of marijuana and the federal position that marijuana is a Schedule I controlled substance and therefore an illegal drug.

Key Terms

amotivational syndrome, p. 231
anandamide, p. 229
bhang, p. 223
Cannabis sativa, p. 220
cannabidiol (CBD), p. 222

cannabinoids, p. 221
decriminalization, p. 237
delta-9-tetrahydrocannabinol (THC), p. 222
dronabinol (Marinol), p. 236

gateway hypothesis, p. 232
hashish, p. 223
hashish oil, p. 223
hashish oil crystals, p. 223
joint, p. 226

marijuana, p. 222
nabilone (Cesamet), p. 236
reefer, p. 226
sinsemilla, p. 222

Review Questions

1. Explain the characteristics of marijuana, sinsemilla, hashish, and hashish oil in terms of the manner in which they are obtained from the cannabis plant and their respective levels of THC.
2. Explain the social and historical factors that changed the image of marijuana from an obscure psychoactive substance to a drug that was considered dangerous and worthy of extreme prohibitory policies.
3. Describe the distinctions between the CB1 and CB2 receptors and how various cannabinoids interact with these two receptor types and produce different behavioral and physiological effects.

4. Discuss the present understanding of the chronic effects of marijuana with respect to cardiovascular and respiratory disease, lung cancer, immunological disease, and sexual functioning.
5. Discuss the basic premises of the gateway hypothesis and present an argument that argues against the inherent property of marijuana to cause a progression to the abuse of more serious drugs.
6. Describe the present-day accepted medical applications of marijuana.

Critical Thinking: What Would You Do?

You are a bank official in a state in which marijuana has been legalized. A local businessman comes to your bank to apply for a checking account and loan to expand his thriving marijuana shop. He explains that by all standard criteria his credit rating is excellent but for the last several months he has been forced to carry out with all transactions on a cash-only basis, without a checking account. Without a commercial loan, he cannot expand his business. In the last three weeks, he has been robbed at knifepoint when transporting his cash receipts, the last time being particularly dangerous to him. He nearly lost his life, and fears that next time he may not be so fortunate. Yet you worry about the FDIC requirements for your bank. If you were to lose FDIC protection for your depositors, you would have to close your doors. Do you approve the loan? What justifications do you provide if you say Yes or if you say No?

Endnotes

1. Adapted from Berke, J. (2016, April 20). This could be the No. 1 problem facing legal weed business in America. Accessed from: https://www.sfgate.com/technology/businessinsider/article/This-could-be-the-No-1-problem-facing-legal-weed-7260996.php. Berke, J. (2018, April 10). Legal marijuana could soon be a bigger market than soda. Accessed from: https://www.businessinsider.com/marijuana-bigger-than-soda-according-to-analyst-2018-4

2. Abel, E. I. *Marijuana, the first twelve thousand years*. New York: Plenum Press, pp. x–xi. Goode, E. (2008). *Drugs in American society* (7th ed.). New York: McGraw-Hill Higher Education, p. 239. Hill, A. J.; William, C. M.; Whalley, B. J.; and Stephens, G. J. (2012). Phytocannabinoids as novel therapeutic agents in CNS disorders. *Pharmacology and Therapeutics*, 133, 79–97. National Drug Intelligence Center (2009). *Domestic cannabis cultivation assessment*

2009. Washington, D.C.: U.S. Department of Justice, p. 4. National Drug Intelligence Center (2008). *National drug threat assessment: 2009.* Washington, D.C.: U.S. Department of Justice, p. 18. *Pulse check: Marijuana report.* Washington, D.C.: White House Office of Drug Control Policy.

3. Abel, *Marihuana,* p. 12.

4. Bonnie, R. J.; and Whitebread, C. H. (1974). *The marihuana conviction: A history of marihuana prohibition in the United States.* Charlottesville, VA: University Press of Virginia, p. 3. Ramos, R. (1999). Responses to Mexican immigration, 1910–1936. In M. R. Ornelas (Ed.), *Beyond 1848: Readings in the modern Chicano historical experience.* Dubuque, IA: Kendall Hunt Publishing, p. 115.

5. Abel, *Marihuana,* pp. 218–222.

6. Bonnie and Whitebread, *The marihuana conviction,* p. 33. Polo, Marco (1300/1993). *The travels of Marco Polo: The complete Yule-Cordier edition.* Mineola, NY: Dover Publications. Ramos, Responses to Mexican immigration.

7. Anslinger, H. J.; and Tompkins, W. F. (1953). *The traffic in narcotics.* New York: Funk & Wagnalls, pp. 37–38. Cited in Inciardi, J. A. (2002). *The war on drugs III.* Boston: Allyn and Bacon, p. 46.

8. Lee, M. A.; and Shlain, B. (1985). *Acid dreams: The complete social history of LSD.* New York: Grove Weidenfeld.

9. Advokat, C. E.; Comaty, J. E.; and Julien, R. M. (2015). *A primer of drug action* (13th ed.). New York: Worth.

10. Ibid., p. 566.

11. *Allen and Hanbury's athletic drug reference* (1992). Research Triangle Park, NC: Clean Data, p. 33. Wadler, G. I.; and Hainline, B. (1989). *Drugs and the athlete.* Philadelphia: F. A. Davis, pp. 208–209.

12. Grinspoon, L.; and Bakalar, J. B. (1997). Marihuana. In J. H. Lowinson; P. Ruiz; R. B. Millman; and J. G. Langrod (Eds.), *Substance abuse: A comprehensive textbook* (3rd ed.). Baltimore, MD: Williams and Wilkins, pp. 199–206.

13. Jones, R. T. (1980). Human effects: An overview. In R. C. Petersen (Ed.), *Marijuana research findings: 1980* (NIDA Research Monograph 31). Rockville, MD: National Institute on Drug Abuse, p. 65.

14. Grilly, D.; and Salamone, J. D. (2011). *Drugs, brain, and behavior* (6th ed.). Boston: Pearson, p. 337.

15. Data compiled from the Healthcare and Utilization Project (H-CUP) database, 2017. Agency of Healthcare Research and Quality, U.S. Department of Health and Human Services, Rockville, MD.

16. Winger, G.; Hofmann, F. G.; and Woods, J. H. (1992). *A handbook on drug and alcohol abuse* (3rd ed.). New York: Oxford University Press, pp. 123–125.

17. Hooker, W. D.; and Jones, R. T. (1987). Increased susceptibility to memory intrusions and the Stroop interference effect during acute marijuana intoxication. *Psychopharmacology, 91,* 20–24. Ilan, A. B.; Gevins, A.; Coleman, M.; ElSohly, M. A.; and de Wit, H. (2005). Neurophysiological and subjective profile of marijuana with varying concentrations of cannabinoids. *Behavioural Pharmacology, 16,* 487–496.

18. Delong, F. L.; and Levy, B. I. (1974). A model of attention describing the cognitive effects of marijuana. In L. L. Miller (Ed.), *Marijuana: Effects on human behavior.* New York: Academic Press, pp. 103–117. Gieringer, D. H. (1988). Marijuana, driving, and accident safety. *Journal of Psychoactive Drugs, 20,* 93–101.

19. McKim, W. A.; and Hancock, S. D. (2013). *Drugs and behavior* (7th ed.). Boston: Pearson Education, p. 323.

20. Ramaekers, J. G.; Berghaus, G.; van Laar, M.; and Drummer, O. H. (2004). Dose related risk of motor vehicle crashes after cannabis use. *Drugs and Alcohol Dependence, 73,* 109–119.

21. Block, R. I. (1997). Editorial: Does heavy marijuana use impair human cognition and brain function? *Journal of the American Medical Association, 275,* 560–561. Pope, H. G., Jr.; and Yurgelun-Todd, D. (1996). The residual cognitive effects of heavy marijuana use in college students. *Journal of the American Medical Association, 275,* 521–527.

22. Hall, W.; Degenhardt, L.; and Teesson, M. (2004). Cannabis use and psychotic disorders: An update. *Drug and Alcohol Review, 23,* 433–443. Julien, R. A. (2005). *A primer, of drug action* (10th ed.). New York: Worth, pp. 568–572. McKim and Hancock, *Drugs and behavior,* p. 328.

23. Ameri, A. (1999). The effects of cannabinoids on the brain. *Progress in Neurobiology, 58,* 315–348. Chait, L. D.; and Burke, K. A. (1994). Preference for high- versus low-potency marijuana. *Pharmacology, Biochemistry, and Behavior, 49,* 643–647. Tanda, G.; Pontieri, F. E.; and Di Chiara, G. (1997). Cannabinoid and heroin activation of mesolimbic dopamine transmission by a common $\mu1$ opioid receptor mechanism. *Science, 276,* 2048–2049. Wickelgren, I. (1997). Research news: Marijuana: Harder than thought? *Science, 276,* 1967–1968.

24. Abood, M.; and Martin, B. (1992). Neurobiology of marijuana abuse. *Trends in Pharmacological Sciences, 13,* 201–206.

25. Frank, I. M.; Lessin, P. J.; Tyrrell, E. D.; Hahn, P. M.; and Szara, S. (1976). Acute and cumulative effects of marijuana smoking on hospitalized subjects: A 36-day study. In M. C. Braude; and S. Szara (Eds.), *Pharmacology of marijuana, Vol. 2.* Orlando, FL: Academic Press, pp. 673–680. Jones, R. T.; and Benowitz, N. (1976). The 30-day trip: Clinical studies of cannabis tolerance and dependence. In M. C. Braude; and S. Szara (Eds.), *Pharmacology of marijuana, Vol. 2.* Orlando, FL: Academic Press, pp. 627–642.

26. Haney, M.; Ward, A. S.; Comer, S. D.; Foltin, R. W; and Fischman, M. W. (1999a). Abstinence symptoms following oral THC administration in humans. *Psychopharmacology, 141,* 385–394. Haney, M.; Ward, A. S.; Comer, S. D.; Foltin, R. W; and Fischman, M. W. (1999b). Abstinence symptoms following smoked marijuana in humans. *Psychopharmacology, 141,* 395–404.

27. Duffy, A.; and Milin, R. (1996). Case study: Withdrawal syndrome in adolescent chronic cannabis users. *Journal of the American Academy of Child and Adolescent Psychiatry, 35,* 1618–1621. Julien, R. M. (2001). *A primer of drug action* (9th ed.). New York: Worth, pp. 320–322.

28. Callaghan, R. C.; Allebeck, P.; and Sidorchuk, A. (2013). Marijuana use and risk of lung cancer: A 40-year cohort study. *Cancer, Causes, and Control, 24,* 1811–1820. Joshi, M.; Joshi, A.; and Bartter, T. (2014). Review: Marijuana and lung disease. *Current Opinion in Pulmonary Medicine, 20,* 1–7. Pletcher, M. J.; Vittinghoff, E.; Kalhan, R.; Richman, Jo.; et al. (2012). Association between marijuana exposure and pulmonary function over 20 years. *Journal of the American Medical Association, 307,* 173–181.

29. Committee on Substance Abuse, American Academy of Pediatrics (1999). Marijuana: A continuing concern for

pediatricians. *Pediatrics, 104*, 982–985. Hollister, L. E. (1988). Marijuana and immunity. *Journal of Psychoactive Drugs, 20*, 3–7. Petersen, R. C. (1984). Marijuana overview. In M. D. Glantz (Ed.), *Correlates and consequences of marijuana use* (Research Issues 34). Rockville, MD: National Institute on Drug Abuse, p. 10.

30. Brands, B.; Sproule, B.; and Marshman, J. (Eds.) (1998). *Drugs and drug abuse: A reference text* (3rd ed.). Toronto: Addiction Research Foundation. Committee on Substance Abuse, Marijuana. Grinspoon and Bakalar, Marihuana, pp. 203–204. Male infertility: Sperm from marijuana smokers move too fast, too early (2003, November 3). *Health and Medicine Week*, pp. 459–460.

31. Grinspoon and Bakalar, Marihuana, p. 203.

32. McGothlin, W. H.; and West, L. J. (1968). The marijuana problem: An overview. *American Journal of Psychiatry, 125*, 372.

33. Goode, E. (2005). *Drugs in American society* (6th ed.). New York: McGraw-Hill Higher Education, pp. 246–251.

34. Brook, J. S.; Adamas, R. E.; Balka, E. B.; and Johnson, E. (2002). Early adolescent marijuana use: Risks for the transition to young adulthood. *Psychological Medicine, 32*, 79–91. Goode, Erich (2012). *Drugs in American society* (8th ed.). New York: McGraw-Hill, pp. 219–220. Roebuck, M. C.; French, M. T.; and Dennis, M. L. (2004). Adolescent marijuana use and school attendance. *Economics of Education Review, 23*, 133–141.

35. Goode, E. (1999). *Drugs in American society* (5th ed.). New York: McGraw-Hill Higher Education, p. 233.

36. Fried, P. A.; Wilkinson, B.; and Gray, R. (2005). Neurocognitive consequences of marihuana—A comparison with pre-drug performance. *Neurotoxicology and Teratology, 27*, 231–239. Pope, H. (2002). Cannabis, cognition, and residual confounding. *Journal of the American Medical Association, 287*, 1172–1174. Solowij, N.; Stephens, R. S.; Roffman, R. A.; Babor, T.; Kadden, R.; et al. (2002). Cognitive functioning of long-term heavy cannabis users seeking treatment. *Journal of the American Medical Association, 287*, 1123–1131.

37. Brook, J. S.; Zhang, C.; and Brook, D. W. (2011). Developmental trajectories of marijuana use from adolescence to adulthood. *Archives of Pediatric and Adolescent Medicine, 165*, 55–60. Gruber, S. A.; Dahlgren, M. K.; Sagar, K. A.; Gonenc, A.; and Killogre, W. D. (2012). Age of onset of marijuana use impacts inhibitory processing. *Neuroscience Letters, 511*, 89–94. Moore, A. S. (2014, November 2). This is your brain on drugs. *The New York Times*, Education Life, p. 17. Yücel, M.; Solowij, N.; Respondek, C.; Whittle, S.; Fornito, A. et al. (2008, June). Regional brain abnormalities associated with long-term heavy cannabis use. *Archives of General Psychiatry, 65*, 694–701.

38. Kandel, D. B. (2003). Does marijuana use cause the use of other drugs? *Journal of the American Medical Association, 289*, 482–483. Kandel, D. B. (Ed.) (2002). *Stages and pathways of drug involvement: Examining the gateway hypothesis.* Cambridge: Cambridge University Press.

39. Excerpt in Medical marijuana: Editorials debate "gateway" effect (1999, April 12). *American Health Line*, http://www.ahl.com.

40. Hall, W. D.; and Lynskey, M. T. (2005). Is cannabis a gateway drug? Testing hypotheses about the relationship between cannabis use and the use of other illicit drugs. *Drug and Alcohol Research, 24*, 139–48. Kandel, *Does marijuana* use cause the use of other drugs? Lynskey, M. T.; Hath, A. C.; Bucholz,

K. K.; Slutske, W. S.; Madden, P. A. F.; et al. (2003). The escalation of drug use in early-onset cannabis users vs co-twin controls. *Journal of the American Medical Association, 289*, 427–433. Martin, K. R. (2001). Adolescent treatment programs reduce drug abuse, produce other improvements. *NIDA Notes, 16*(1), 11–12. Martin, K. R. (2001). Television public service announcements decrease marijuana use in targeted teens. *NIDA Notes, 16*(1), 14. Otten, R.; Chung, J. M.; and Dishion, T. J. (2016). The social exigencies of the gateway progression to the use of illicit drug from adolescence into adulthood. *Addictive Behaviors, 73*, 144–150.

41. Zimmer, L.; and Morgan, J. P. (1997). *Marijuana myths, marijuana facts: A review of the scientific evidence.* New York: Lindesmith Center, p. 37.

42. Goode (1999). *Drugs in American society*, pp. 250–251. Nkansah-Amankra, S.; and Minelli, M. (2016). "Gateway hypothesis" and early drug use: Additional findings from tracking a population-based sample of adolescents to adulthood. *Prevention Medicine Reports, 4*, 134–141.

43. Center for Behavioral Health Statistics and Quality (2018). *Results from the 2017 National Survey on Drug Use and Health: Detailed tables.* Rockville, MD: Substance Abuse and Mental Health Services Administration, Tables 1.1A and 1.1B.

44. Lipari, R. N.; Ahmsbrak, .R. D.; Pemberton, M. R.; and Porter, J. D. (2017, September). Risk and protective factors and estimates of substance use initiations: Results from the 2016 National Survey on Drug Use and Health. *NSDUH Data Review*. Rockville, MD: Substance Abuse and Mental Health Services Administration, Figure 2.

45. Consroe, P.; Musty, R.; Rein, J.; Tillery, W.; and Pertwee, R. (1997). The perceived effects of smoked cannabis on patients with multiple sclerosis. *European Neurology, 38*, 44–48. Pertwee, R. (2001). Cannabinoid receptors and pain. *Progress in Neurobiology, 63*, 165–174. Pertwee, R. (2002). Cannabinoids and multiple sclerosis. *Pharmacology and Therapeutics, 95*, 165–174. Zajicek, J.; Fox, P.; Sanders, H.; Wright, D.; Vickery, J.; et al. (2003). Cannabinoids for treatment of spasticity and other symptoms related to multiple sclerosis (CAMS study): multicentre randomized placebo-controlled trial. *Lancet, 362*, 1517–1526.

46. Vestag, B. (2003). Medical marijuana center opens its doors. *Journal of the American Medical Association, 290*, 877–879.

47. Devinsky, O.; Marsh, E.; Friedman, D.; et al (2016). Cannabidiol win patients with treatment-resistant epilepsy: An open-label interventional trial. *The Lancet Neurology, 15*, 270–278. Epilepsy Foundation (2018). Medical marijuana and epilepsy. https://www.epilepsy.com/learn/treating-seizures-and-epilepsy.other-treatment-approaches/medical-marijuana-and-epilepsy. Plasse, T. F.; Gorter, R. W.; Krasnow, S. H.; Lane, M.; Shepard, K. V.; et al. (1991). Recent clinical experience with dronabinol. International conference on cannabis and cannabinoids, Chania, Greece. *Pharmacology, Biochemistry, and Behavior, 40*, 695–700.

48. Institute of Medicine (1999). *Marijuana and medicine: Assessing the science base.* Washington, D.C.: National Academy Press, excerpt on page vii.

49. Institute of Medicine, *Marijuana and medicine*, excerpt on page 8. Porter, B. E.; and Jacobson, C. (2013). Report of a parent survey of cannabidiol-enriched cannabis use in pediatric treatment-resistant epilepsy. *Epilepsy and Behavior, 29*, 574–577.

50. Corassaniti, N. (2018, January 24). Murphy easing "road-blocks" to medical marijuana. *The New York Times*, p. A19. ProCon.org (2018, November 13). 33 legal medical marijuana states and DC: Laws. fees. and possession limits. Accessed from : *https://medicalmarijuana.procon.org/view resources.phg?resourceID=000881*. State-by-state information about medical marijuana and decriminalization, courtesy of NORML.org, Washington, D.C.

51. Fine, P. G.; and Rosenfeld, M. J. (2013). The endocannabinoid system, cannabinoids, and pain. *Rambam Maimonides Medical Journal, 4,* e0022. Fine, E. B.; Cuy, G. W.; and Robson, P. J. (2007). Cannabis, pain, and sleep: Lessons from therapeutic clinical trials of *Sativex*, a cannabis-based medicine. *Chemistry and Biodiversity, 4,* 1729–1743. Information from GW Pharmaceuticals Web site, http://www.gwpharm.com; Sativex.aspx. Hill; Williams; Whalley; and Stephens, Phytocannabinoids as novel therapeutic agents in CNS disorders. Sharkey, K. A.; Darman, D. A.; and Parker, L. A. (2014). Regulation of nausea and vomiting by cannabinoids and the endocannabinoid system. *European Journal of Pharmacology, 722,* 134–146.

52. National Commission on Marihuana and Drug Abuse (1972). *Marihuana: A signal of misunderstanding*. Washington, D.C.: Government Printing Office, pp. 151–167.

53. Smith, A. (2018, January 31). America's legal marijuana industry is booming. Accessed from: *http://money.cnn.com/2018/01/31/news/marijuana-state-of-the-union/index.html*. Tax Foundation (2017, June 1). How high are marijuana taxes in your state? Washington D.C.: Tax Foundation. Accessed from: *https://taxfoundation.org/marijuana-taxes-state/html*.

54. U.S. Attorney General Eric Holder Jr. (2009, October 19). *Attorney General announces formal medical marijuana guidelines*. Washington, D.C.: Office of Public Affairs, U.S. Department of Justice. Stout, D.; and Moore, S. (2009, October 20). U.S. won't prosecuteS in states that allow medical marijuana. *The New York Times*, pp. A1, A21. Deputy Attorney General James M. Cole (2013, April 29). Memorandum for all United States Attorneys. Subject: Guidance regarding marijuana enforcement. Washington, D.C.: Office of the Deputy Attorney General, U.S. Department of Justice.

55. DePinto, J.; Backus, F.; Khanna, K.; and Salvanto, A. (2017, April 20). Marijuana legalization support at all-time high. Accessed from: *http://cbsnews.com/news/support-for-marijuana-legalization-at-all-time-high/*.

56. Majority now supports legalizing marijuana (2013, April 4). News release, Pew Research Center for the People and the Press, Washington, D.C. NBC News/Wall Street Journal (2014, January 22–24). Poll: Majority of Americans support efforts to legalize marijuana. Nearly 60 percent of U.S. population now lives in states with marijuana legalization (2018, January 6). Pew Research Center (2018, October 8). About six-in-ten Americans support marijuana legalization. http://www.pewresearch.org/fact-tank/2018/10/08/americans-support-marijuana-legalization/. Ross, S. (2018, June 6). All eyes on Canada as first G7 nation prepares to make marijuana legal. Accessed from: *https://www.theguardian.com/world/2018/jun/06/all-eyes-on-canada-as-first-g7-nation-prepares-to-make-marijuana-lega*. Shapiro, B. (2018, February 1). Sorry, but there no contact high. Cannabis-derived ingredients are trendy in skin care. *The New York Times*, p. D5.

57. AP-CNBC marijuana poll, responses to questions 1 and 10a. Gallup Poll (2009, October 19). Johnston, L. D. (1980, January 16). Marijuana use and the effects of marijuana decriminalization. Unpublished testimony delivered at the hearings on the effects of marijuana held by the Subcommittee on Criminal Justice, Judiciary Committee, U.S. Senate, Washington, D.C., p. 5.

58. Harvey, T. (2014, January 24). Even in Colorado and Washington, pot on campus is "not OK." *Chronicle of Higher Education*, p. A18.

59. Aydelotte, J. D.; Brown, L. H.; Luftman, K. M.; et al. Crash fatality rates after recreational marijuana legalization in Washington and Colorado. *American Journal of Public Health, 107*(8), 1329–1331. Koerth-Baker, M. (2014, February 18). Marijuana and the sobriety test. *The New York Times*, pp. D1–D2.

60. Altman, A. (2018). Pot's money problem. *Marijuana: The medical movement. Special Edition of Time Magazine*, pp. 78–82. Bova, D. (2018). Special Ops guard a budding business. *Marijuana: The medical movement. Special Edition of Time Magazine*, p. 83. Healy, J.; and Apuzzo, M. (2014, January 24). Legal marijuana business should have access to banks, Holder says. *The New York Times*, p. A20.

61. Healy, J. (2014, February 1). Snacks laced with marijuana raise concerns. *The New York Times*, pp. A1, A16.

chapter 2

Hallucinogens and Depressants

Carol remembers that terrible night as though it had happened yesterday. She had been invited to the home of her boss, along with her fellow coworkers, to celebrate his birthday. As the party wound down and the guests started to go home, she noticed that he seemed determined for her to be the last to leave. She looked dehydrated, he said, here's some water. Carol took a gulp and that was the last thing she remembered at the time.

A few hours later, Carol found herself alone in a hotel room, naked and nauseated. It was obvious that she had been drugged and raped. Emergency physicians found traces of GHB, a powerful depressant in her system. The water Carol had been offered had been laced with GHB.

Carol's boss was eventually convicted on charges of rape and the use of a Schedule I controlled substance in carrying out the rape. The prosecutor had said that GHB is the "ideal rape drug because it can so easily be concealed from the victim." Maybe, Carol thought to herself, GHB should really be called an "acquaintance-and-date rape drug."

Carol now counsels GHB victims and speaks out publicly about her personal story.[1]

This chapter will focus on two major categories of psychoactive drugs with very different attributes. The first of these are drugs referred to collectively as **hallucinogens**. These drugs cause major changes in the way we experience the world around us, often distorting our own bodies or our personal concept of reality. In effect, hallucinogens take us to a different, unexpected place from the one we know in our everyday lives. The second category of drugs do not take us necessarily to a different place but rather in specific direction. While cocaine and amphetamines make us more alert and energized, in effect more attuned to the world (Chapter 10), these drugs, referred to collectively as depressants, bring us downward to a lower level of consciousness. Some depressants, referred to as **antianxiety drugs**, help us in reducing stress and anxiety, while other depressants, referred to as **sedative-hypnotics**, help us fall asleep more easily or slow down activity in the nervous system. The oldest known depressant of them all is simply alcohol, which will be the focus of the next chapter.

Access to hallucinogens and depressants is also quite different. Most hallucinogens (examples: LSD, mescaline, psilocybin, and MDMA) are classified as Schedule I controlled substances, having been identified as illicit drugs with no accepted medical use. With the exception of GHB, depressants such as sedative-hypnotics and antianxiety drugs are classified as Schedule IV controlled substances, having been identified as licit drugs with accepted medical use. Access to these depressants requires a prescription from a physician or qualified health-care provider. A maximum of five renewals within six months is permitted. In the case of alcohol, there are no restrictions to access at all, other than a minimum age requirement on the part of the purchaser.

Despite their differences, both hallucinogens and depressants can be subject to abuse and produce significant risks to one's personal safety and health. We will take up the subject of hallucinogens first, with a focus on the best-known hallucinogen, **lysergic acid diethylamide**, abbreviated **LSD**.

A Matter of Definition

The particular terminology we use in describing things can often be a reflection of one's attitude toward them. The terminology used to describe hallucinogens is no exception. For those viewing these drugs with a "positive spin," particularly for those who took LSD in the 1960s, hallucinogens have been described as *psychedelic*, meaning "mind-expanding" or "making the mind manifest." In cases where a spiritual experience has been reported, such as with the ingestion of *ayahuasca*, hallucinogens have been *entheogenic*, meaning "generating the divine within." On the other hand, for others viewing hallucinogens with more alarm and apprehension than acceptance, the popular descriptive adjectives have been *psychotomimetic* (meaning "having the appearance of a psychosis"), *psychodysleptic* (meaning "mind-disrupting"), or even worse, *psycholytic* (meaning "mind-dissolving"). You can see that the description one chooses to use conveys a strong attitude, pro and con, with regard to these particular psychoactive substances.

Considering all this emotional baggage, describing these drugs as hallucinogenic (meaning "hallucination-producing")

hallucinogens (ha-LOO-sin-oh-jens): A class of drugs producing distortions in perception and body image at moderate doses.

antianxiety drugs: Medications that make the user feel more peaceful or tranquil; also called anxiolytic medications.

sedative-hypnotics: Medications that produce a sense of calm, induce sleep, or lower central nervous system activity in general.

lysergic acid diethylamide (LSD) (lye-SER-jik ASS-id di-ETH-il-la-mide): A synthetic, serotonin-related hallucinogenic drug, producing a variety of perceptual and emotional effects, including visual hallucinations, distorted body image, and changes in mood.

Numbers Talk. . .

566,990	Approximate number of LSD doses in 1 ounce of pure LSD, based on a typical LSD dosage level of 50 micrograms
1	The number of documented cases of deaths due to LSD ingestion alone, since 1960
1 in 3	Proportion of female undergraduates, admitted to a hospital-based sexual assault treatment center in Ontario, Canada, between 2005 and 2007 who suspected that they had been drugged.

Sources: Fysh, R. R.; Oon, M. C. H.; Robinson, K. N.; Smith, R. N.; White, P. C.; and Whitehouse, M. J. (1985). A fatal poisoning with LSD. *Forensic Science International, 28,* 109–113. Lawyer, S.; Resnick, H.; Bakanic, V.; Burkett, T.; and Kilpatrick, D. (2010). Forcible, drug-facilitated, and incapacitated rape and sexual assault among undergraduate women. *Journal of American College Health, 58,* 453–460.

is probably the most evenhanded way of describing their effects, which is the way they will be referred to in this chapter. Some problems, however, still need to be considered. Technically, a hallucination is defined as a reported perception of something that does not physically exist. For example, a schizophrenic patient might hear voices that no one else hears, and therefore we must conclude (at least the non-schizophrenic world must conclude) that such voices are not real. In the case of hallucinogens, the effect is more complicated because we are dealing with an alteration in the perception of the existing physical environment. Some researchers have suggested using the term *illusionogenic* as a more accurate way of describing drugs that produce these kinds of experiences, but understandably the term has not taken hold.

We also should be aware of another qualification when we use the term "hallucinogen." Many drugs that produce distinctive effects when taken at low to moderate dose levels turn out to produce hallucinations when the dose level is extremely high or when drug use has extended over a period of time. Examples of this possibility appeared in Chapter 10 with cocaine and amphetamines. Here, the classification of drugs as hallucinogens pertains only to those drugs that produce marked changes in perceived reality *at relatively low dosages and in acute circumstances.*

Categories of Hallucinogens

It is relatively easy to define what hallucinogens are by virtue of their effects on the users, but categorizing them can be complicated because the specific hallucinogenic experiences are so variable. One solution has been to classify hallucinogens into four groups. The first three groups are identified on the basis of the resemblance between the hallucinogen in question and a specific neurotransmitter in the brain (serotonin, norepinephrine, or acetylcholine). The fourth group includes a relatively small number of hallucinogens (referred to as miscellaneous hallucinogens) that bear no resemblance to any neurotransmitter at all.

Table 12.1 shows the overall four-group classification scheme of nine hallucinogens covered in this chapter. The first three categories are (1) hallucinogens that are chemically similar to serotonin (examples: LSD, psilocybin, LAA found in morning glory seeds, DMT, and harmine), (2) hallucinogens that are chemically similar to norepinephrine (examples: mescaline, DOM, and MDMA), and (3) hallucinogens that are chemically similar to acetylcholine (example: ibotenic acid found in *Amanita muscaria* mushrooms). The fourth category comprises the hallucinogens (example: phencyclidine, commonly known as PCP) that

TABLE 12.1

Major categories of hallucinogens

CATEGORY	SOURCE
Hallucinogens related to serotonin	
Lysergic acid diethylamide (LSD)	A synthetic derivative of lysergic acid, which is, in turn, a component of ergot
Psilocybin	Various species of North American mushrooms
Lysergic acid amide (LAA)	Morning glory seeds
Dimethyltryptamine (DMT)	The bark resin of several varieties of trees and some nuts native to Central and South America
Harmine	The bark of a South American vine
Hallucinogens related to norepinephrine	
Mescaline	The peyote cactus in Mexico and the U.S. Southwest
2, 5-dimethoxy-4-methylamphetamine (DOM)	A synthetic mescaline-like hallucinogen
MDMA (Ecstasy)	A synthetic hallucinogen
Hallucinogens related to acetylcholine	
Ibotenic acid	*Amanita muscaria* mushrooms
Miscellaneous hallucinogens	
Phencyclidine (PCP)	A synthetic dissociative anesthetic hallucinogen, often referred to as angel dust

Source: Based on information from Schultes, R. E.; and Hofmann, A. (1979). *Plants of the gods: Origins of hallucinogenic use.* New York: McGraw-Hill.

FIGURE 12.1

Botanical sources for four hallucinogenic drugs: (a) *Claviceps tulasne* (ergot from which LSD is synthetically derived), (b) *Amanita muscaria* (containing ibotenic acid), (c) *Atropa belladonna* (containing atropine), (d) *Datura stramonium*, called jimsonweed (containing atropine, scopolamine, and hyoscyamine).They are shown here scaled for illustration purposes to appear to be the same size, when in actuality they are not.

are chemically unlike any known neurotransmitter; these drugs are called miscellaneous hallucinogens. Figure 12.1 shows the botanical origin of four hallucinogenic drugs (ibotenic acid as well as atropine, hyoscyamine, scopolamine, and ergot).

Lysergic Acid Diethylamide (LSD)

Like many of the drugs that have been examined in the preceding chapters, hallucinogenic drugs such as LSD and several others have a story that belongs both in our contemporary culture and in the distant past. The discoverer of LSD and the first individual to have experienced its effects, Albert Hofmann, worked as a research chemist in the modern facilities of an international pharmaceutical company during the 1930s and 1940s, but the basic material on Hofmann's laboratory bench was an extract from a fungus that has been around for millions of years. It has been estimated that as many as 6,000 plant species around the world have some psychoactive properties.

LSD does not exist in nature but is synthetically derived from **ergot**, a fungus present in moldy rye and other grains. One of the alkaloids in ergot is highly toxic, inducing a condition called **ergotism**. Historians have surmised that widespread epidemics of ergotism (called St. Anthony's fire) occurred periodically in Europe during the Middle Ages, when extreme famine forced people to bake bread from infected grain (Drugs ... in Focus). During one particularly

deadly episode in the year 944, an outbreak of ergotism claimed as many as 40,000 lives. The features of this calamity were twofold. One form of ergotism produced a reduction in blood flow toward the extremities, leading to gangrene, burning pain, and the eventual loss of limbs. The other form produced a tingling sensation on the skin, convulsions, disordered thinking, and hallucinations.

Even though the link between this strange affliction and ergot in moldy grain has been known since the 1700s, outbreaks of ergotism have continued to occur in recent times. A major outbreak took place in a small French community in 1951 with hundreds of townspeople going totally mad on a single night.[2]

Hofmann's interest in ergot alkaloids centered on the possible medical applications, specifically ways to reduce bleeding and increase contractions in smooth muscle, particularly the uterus. His objective was to find a nontoxic chemical version of ergot that would be useful in treating problems associated with childbirth. The LSD molecule was number 25 in a series of variations that Hofmann studied in 1938, and his creation was officially named LSD-25 for that reason. He thought at the time that the compound had possibilities for medical use but then went on to other pursuits.

ergot (ER-got): A fungus infecting rye and other grains.

ergotism: A physical and/or psychological disorder acquired by ingesting ergot-infected grains. One form of ergotism involves gangrene and eventual loss of limbs; the other form is associated with convulsions, disordered thinking, and hallucinations.

Drugs ... in Focus

Strange Days in Salem: Witchcraft or Hallucinogens?

In the early months of 1692, in Salem, Massachusetts, eight young girls suddenly developed a combination of bizarre symptoms: disordered speech, odd body postures, and convulsive fits. They also began to accuse various townspeople of witchcraft. Meanwhile, the townspeople began to turn the accusations back on the girls themselves. During the summer, in a series of trials, more than 150 people were convicted of being witches and 20 were executed. Accusations were also made in neighboring villages in the county and in Connecticut. Nothing approaching the magnitude of the Salem witch trials has since occurred in American history.

Over the years, a number of theories have attempted to account for these strange events: a case of adolescent pranks, general hysteria, or some kind of political scapegoating. An interesting and controversial speculation has been advanced that these girls were showing the hallucinogenic and convulsive symptoms of ergotism, acquired from fungus-infected rye grain. Arguments that support this theory include the following:

- Rye grain, once harvested, was stored in barns for months, and the unusually moist weather in the area that year could have promoted the growth of ergot fungus during storage. Of 22 Salem households with some afflicted members, 16 were located close to riverbanks or swamps.

- Children and teenagers would have been particularly vulnerable to ergotism because they ingest more food, and hence more poison, per pound of body weight than do adults.

- The Salem girls as well as the accused "witches" frequently displayed hallucinatory behavior and physical symptoms common to convulsive ergotism

The role of ergotism in instigating the Salem witch trials has been vigorously debated by both historians and pharmacologists and remains controversial. The references listed later include readings that present arguments either for or against this intriguing possibility.

Sources: In favor: Caporael, L. R. (1976). Ergotism: The Satan loosed in Salem? *Science, 192,* 21–26. Matossian, M. K. (1982). Ergot and the Salem witchcraft affair. *American Scientist, 70,* 355–357. Matossian, M. K. (1989). *Poisons of the past: Molds, epidemics, and history.* New Haven, CT: Yale University Press, pp. 113–122. Against: Spanos, N. P.; and Gottlieb, J. (1976). Ergotism and the Salem village witch trials. *Science, 194,* 1390–1394.

Hofmann returned to these investigations five years later in 1943. It was on an April afternoon of that year, that he accidently touched an extraordinarily minute trace of the compound. As he would write in his memoirs,

> I was forced to interrupt my work in the laboratory ... in proceed home, being affected by a remarkable restlessness combined with a slight dizziness. At home I lay down and sank into a not unpleasant intoxicated-like condition, characterized by an extremely stimulated imagination in a dreamlike state.... perceived an uninterrupted stream of fantastic pictures, extraordinary shapes with kaleidoscopic play of colors.[3]

Hoffman had experienced what is now known as an "acid trip."

The Beginning of the Psychedelic Era

Interest in the commercial potential of LSD was soon to follow. Sandoz pharmaceuticals applied for FDA approval in 1953, and as was a common practice at the time, sent out samples of LSD to laboratories around the world for scientific study. The idea was that LSD might be helpful in the treatment of schizophrenia by allowing psychiatrists to gain insight into subconscious processes, which this drug supposedly unlocked. One of the researchers intrigued by the potential psychotherapeutic applications of LSD was the psychiatrist Humphrey Osmond of the University of Saskatchewan in Canada, who coined the word "psychedelic" to describe its effects and whose interest also extended to other hallucinogens such as mescaline.

In 1953, Osmond introduced the British writer Aldous Huxley to mescaline, and Huxley later reported his experiences, conducted under Osmond's supervision, in his book, *The Doors of Perception.* Prior to 1960, LSD was being administered to humans under fairly limited circumstances, chiefly as part of research studies in psychiatric hospitals and psychotherapy sessions on the West Coast. As would be revealed later in court testimony in the 1970s, there were also top-secret LSD experiments conducted by the Central Intelligence Agency (CIA), as part of their interest in the possible application in espionage work. Word of its extraordinary effects, however, gradually spread to regions outside laboratories or hospitals. One of those who picked up on these events was a young clinical psychologist and lecturer at Harvard University named Timothy Leary.

Leary's first hallucinatory experience (in fact his first psychoactive drug experience of any kind, other than alcoholic intoxication) was in Mexico in 1960, when he ate some mushrooms containing the hallucinogen psilocybin. For five hours, Leary had what he would later call the "deepest religious experience" of his life.

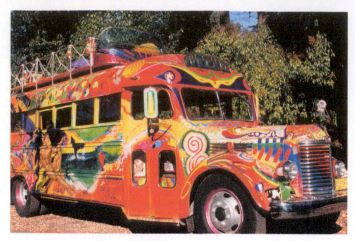

The multicolored images, inspired by the LSD experience, epitomized the psychedelic era of the 1960s.

Credit: Nancy Hoit Belcher/Alamy Stock Photo

Back at Harvard, his revelations sparked the interest of a colleague, Richard Alpert (later to be known as Baba Ram Dass). The two men were soon holding psilocybin sessions with university students and others who were interested, on and off campus. At first, these studies retained some semblance of scientific control. For example, a physician was on hand, and objective observers of behavior reported the reactions of the subjects. Later, these procedures were altered. Physicians were no longer invited to the sessions, and Leary himself began taking the drug at the same time. His argument was that he could communicate better with the subject during the drug experience, but his participation seriously undermined the scientific nature of the studies.

In 1961, Leary, Alpert, and other associates turned to LSD as the focus of their investigations, in their homes and other locations off the Harvard campus. Though these experiments were technically separate from the university itself, public relations concerns on the part of the Harvard administration were mounting. Leary further aggravated the situation through his increasingly incendiary writings. In a 1962 article published in the *Bulletin of the Atomic Scientists*, he suggested that the Soviets could conceivably dump LSD into the water supply and, to prepare for such an attack, Americans should dump LSD into their own water supply so that citizens would then know what to expect. Needless to say, the U.S. government was not amused.

In 1963, after a Harvard investigation, Leary and Alpert were dismissed from their faculty positions, making it the first time in the twentieth century that a Harvard faculty member had been fired. As you can imagine, such events brought

PORTRAIT

Timothy Leary: Mr. LSD and the Psychedelic Era

For the average college student today (or maybe for a lot of people under the age of 50), the question regarding Timothy Leary (also known as Mr. LSD) might not be "Whatever happened to him?" but rather "Who was this guy anyway?" For those of you who ask the latter question, here is a capsule rendition of Timothy Leary and his impact on the drug scene in the 1960s.

Surprisingly, until 1960, Leary's career was a world apart from what would follow. It had none of the unconventionality that would later characterize his life. As a clinical psychologist and professor at Harvard University, he had written a widely acclaimed textbook and devised a respected personality test (commonly called "the Leary"). An experience with psilocybin in Mexico in 1960, however, turned his life around. The more extensive his exposure to hallucinogenic drugs became, the more he turned away from academia and took on the self-appointed role of Pied Piper for what was then referred to as the "acid generation." Leary would be the most widely known figure of the psychedelic era.

By the middle of the 1970s, Leary had been (1) sentenced to twenty years for marijuana possession (the longest sentence ever imposed for such an offense), (2) gone to federal prison, (3) escaped and evaded recapture by the authorities for a few years by hiding out in Algeria, Afghanistan, and Switzerland, (4) recaptured, and (5) finally released after a successful appeal of his original conviction. By this time, LSD advocacy was no longer on his agenda, and in fact LSD had lost its mystique years earlier. Undeterred, Leary hit the college lecture circuit, talking about space migration and life extension. He now called himself a "stand-up philosopher."

In the late 1980s, Leary discovered computers. He formed a software company, marketed a number of successful video games, and viewed interactive computer programming and virtual reality in particular as the consciousness expansion of the 1990s, the newest route to cerebral stimulation.

Despite his newfound commercial leanings, Leary never stopped being a social activist, characterized by his own brand of opportunism. In 1994, he encouraged his detention by the local police in an Austin, Texas, airport for smoking—a cigarette, this time. After extensive media coverage of the incident, Leary said that he wanted to draw attention to people being "demonized" by no-smoking restrictions on their lives.

A year after his death in 1996, Leary's friends arranged to have his cremated remains delivered by rocket into space. It was estimated that he would orbit Earth every 90 minutes for approximately 2 years or so, before burning up during reentry. As his followers remarked at the time, the voyage was a fitting tribute to his life on earth, since it would be his "ultimate trip."

Sources: Brozan, N. (1994, May 12). Chronicle: Timothy Leary lights up. *New York Times*, p. D26. Greenfield, R. (2006). *Timothy Leary: A biography*. New York: Harcourt. Lee, M.; and Shlain, B. (1985). *Acid dreams: The complete social history of LSD*. New York: Grove Weiderfeld, pp. 71–118. Simons, M. (1997, April 22). A final turn-on lifts Timothy Leary off. *New York Times*, pp. A1, A4. Stone, J. (1991, June). Turn on, tune in, boot up. *Discover*, pp. 32–35.

Credit: Joseph Marzullo/Mediapunch/Shutterstock

enormous media exposure. Leary was now "Mr. LSD" (see Portrait), and suddenly the public became acquainted with a class of psychoactive drugs that had been previously unknown to them.[4]

For the rest of the 1960s, LSD became not only a drug but also one of the symbols for the cultural revolt of a generation of youth against the perceived inadequacies of the established, older generation. Leary himself told his followers that they were "the wisest and holiest generation that the human race has ever seen" and advised them to "turn on to the scene, tune in to what's happening; and drop out—of high school, college, graduate school ... and follow me, the hard way."[5] The era was marked with psychedelic rock festivals and light shows, psychedelic music and art, psychedelic jargon and slang—all to the considerable consternation of an older generation of Americans.[6]

To borrow the words of songwriter and singer Bob Dylan, "the times were a-changin'," but not always for the better. LSD became a battleground unto itself. In congressional hearings on LSD use by the nation's youth, scientists, health officials, and law-enforcement experts testified to a growing panic over the drug. Newspaper stories emphasized the dangers with alarmist headlines: "A monster in our midst—a drug called LSD" and "Thrill drug warps mind, kills," among them. Sandoz quietly allowed its LSD patent to lapse in 1966 and did everything it could to distance itself from the controversy. Hofmann himself called LSD his "problem child."

In 1966, LSD was made illegal, later becoming a Schedule I drug, with possession originally set as a misdemeanor and later upgraded to a felony. By the 1970s, LSD had become entrenched as a street drug, and taking LSD had become a component of the already dangerous world of illicit drugs. The story of LSD will be updated in a later section, but first it is important to understand the range of effects that LSD typically produces.

Acute Effects of LSD

LSD is considered one of the most, if not *the* most, powerful psychoactive drugs known. Its potency is so great that effective dose levels have to be expressed in terms of microgram, one-millionths of a gram, often called *mikes*. The typical street dose ranges from 50 to 150 micrograms, though sellers often claim that their product contains more. The effective dose can be as small as 10 micrograms, with only one-hundredth of a percent being absorbed into the brain. You can appreciate the enormous potency of LSD by comparing these figures to the fact that a single regular-strength aspirin tablet contains 325,000 micrograms of aspirin.

Taken orally, LSD is rapidly absorbed into the bloodstream and the brain, and its effects begin to be felt within 30 to 60 minutes. Once its concentration has peaked (in about 90 minutes), the elimination half-life, or the time it takes for 50 percent of the drug to diminish in the bloodstream (see Chapter 8), is approximately 3 hours. Within 5–12 hours, LSD effects are over.[7]

Surprisingly, given its extreme potency, the toxicity of LSD is relatively low. Generalizing from studies of animals

Perforated LSD blotters with a typical print design.

Credit: Willfried Gredler/INSADCO Photography/Alamy Stock Photo

given varying doses of LSD, we can estimate that a lethal dose of LSD for humans would have to be roughly 300 to 600 times the effective dose, a fairly comfortable margin of safety. To this day, there has been only one definitive case in which a death has been attributed solely to an LSD overdose.[8]

Street forms of LSD may contain color additives or adulterants with specific flavors, but the drug itself is odorless, tasteless, and colorless. LSD is sold on the street in single-dose "hits." It is typically swallowed in the form of powder pellets (microdots) or gelatin chips (windowpanes) or else licked off small squares of absorbent paper that have been soaked in liquid LSD (blotters). In the past, blotters soaked with LSD have been decorated with pictures of mystical symbols and signs, rocket ships, or representations of Mickey Mouse, Snoopy, Bart Simpson, or other popular characters.

LSD initially produces an excitation of the sympathetic autonomic activity: increased heart rate, elevated blood pressure, dilated pupils, and a slightly raised body temperature. There is an accompanying feeling of restlessness, euphoria, and a sensation that inner tension has been released. There may be laughing or crying, depending on one's expectations and the setting.

Between 30 minutes and 2 hours later, a "psychedelic trip" begins, characterized by a number of distinctive features.[9]

■ Images seen with the eyes closed

■ An intermingling of senses called **synesthesia**, which usually involves sounds being perceived as hallucinatory visions

■ Perception of a multilevel reality

synesthesia: A subjective sensation in a modality other than the one being stimulated. An example is a visual experience when a sound is heard.

- Strange and exaggerated configurations of common objects or experiences

During the third and final phase, approximately three to five hours after first taking LSD, the following features begin to appear:

- Great swings in emotions or feelings of panic
- A feeling of timelessness
- A feeling of ego disintegration, or a separation of one's mind from one's body

Whether any or all of these strong reactions result in a "good trip" or a "bad trip" depends heavily on the set of expectations on the part of the drug user toward possible drug effects.

Effects of LSD on the Brain

LSD closely resembles the molecular structure of serotonin. Therefore, it is not surprising that LSD should have effects on receptors in the brain that are sensitive to serotonin and LSD experiences should be related to serotonin activity. It turns out that the critical factor behind LSD's hallucinogenic effects is its ability to stimulate a special subtype of serotonin-sensitive receptors called serotonin-2A receptors. All hallucinogens, even those drugs whose structures do not necessarily resemble serotonin, are linked together by a common ability to excite these particular receptors. The ability of a particular drug to produce hallucinogenic effects is directly proportional to its ability to bind to serotonin-2A receptors. Drugs that specifically block serotonin-2A receptors, leaving all other subtypes unchanged, will block the behavioral effects of hallucinogens.[10]

Patterns of LSD Use

The enormous publicity surrounding Timothy Leary and his followers in the 1960s made LSD a household word. As many as 50 popular articles about LSD were published in major U.S. newspapers and magazines between March 1966 and February 1967 alone. By 1970, the media had lost interest. Hardly anything was appearing about LSD. Yet, while media attention was diminishing, the incidence of LSD abuse was steadily rising. The annual prevalence rate for LSD among high school seniors rose from 1 percent in 1967 to 7 percent in 1975, diminishing somewhat to 5 percent in 1985.

By the mid-1990s, prevalence rates were on the rise, reaching and later exceeding the levels of a quarter-century earlier. Since 1997, however, LSD use has declined substantially. Five percent of high school seniors in 2017 reported taking LSD at some time in their lives. A parallel trend has been observed in college students.[11]

It should be noted that today's LSD users are different from those of a previous generation in a number of ways. Typical LSD users now take the drug less frequently, and because the dosage of street LSD is presently about one-fourth the level common to the 1960s and 1970s, they remain high for a briefer period of time. Their motivation behind using LSD is also not the same. They report using LSD simply to get high, rather than to explore alternative states of consciousness or gain a greater insight into life. For current users, LSD no longer has the symbolic or countercultural significance that it had in an earlier time.

Frequently Asked Questions about LSD

Given the history of LSD use and the extensive publicity surrounding it, it is important to look carefully at the facts about LSD and to unmask the myths (of which there are many). The following four questions are frequently asked about the acute and chronic effects of this drug.

Will LSD Produce Panic Attacks or Psychotic Behavior?

One of the most notorious features of LSD is the possibility of a bad trip. Personal accounts abound of sweet, dreamlike states rapidly turning into nightmares. Perhaps the greatest risks are taken when a person is slipped a dose of LSD and begins to experience its effect without knowing that he or she has taken a drug. But panic reactions may also occur even when a person is fully aware of having taken LSD. Although the probability of having a bad trip is difficult to estimate, there are very few regular LSD abusers who have not experienced a bad trip or had a disturbing experience as part of an LSD trip. The best treatment for adverse effects is the companionship and reassurance of others throughout the period when LSD is active.

Despite the possibility of an LSD panic, there is no strong evidence that the panic will lead to a permanent psychiatric breakdown. Long-term psychiatric problems are relatively uncommon; one study conducted in 1960 showed that there was no greater probability of a person attempting suicide or developing a psychosis after taking LSD than when undergoing ordinary forms of psychotherapy.[12] The incidents that do occur typically involve people who were unaware that they were taking LSD, showed unstable personality characteristics prior to taking LSD, or were experiencing LSD under hostile or threatening circumstances.

The possible link between the character of LSD effects and certain symptoms of schizophrenia also has been examined closely. It is true that on a superficial level, the two behaviors show some similarities, but there are important differences. LSD hallucinations are primarily visual, are best seen in the dark, and, as we noted earlier, are more accurately characterized as illusions or pseudohallucinations; schizophrenic hallucinations are primarily auditory, are seen with open eyes, and qualify as true hallucinations. Individuals taking LSD are highly susceptible to suggestion and usually try to communicate the experience to others, whereas the schizophrenic individual is typically resistant to suggestion and withdrawn from his or her surroundings. Therefore, it is unlikely that LSD is mimicking the experience of schizophrenia.

Will LSD Increase Your Creativity?

The unusual visual effects of an LSD experience may lead you to assume that your creativity is enhanced, but the evidence indicates otherwise. Professional artists and musicians creating new works of art or songs while under the influence of LSD typically think that their creations are better than anything they have yet produced, but when the LSD has worn off, they are far less impressed. Controlled studies generally show that individuals under LSD *feel* that they are creative, but objective ratings do not show a significant difference from levels prior to the LSD.[13]

Will LSD Have Residual (Flashback) Effects?

One of the most disturbing aspects of taking LSD is the possibility of re-experiencing the effects of the drug long after the drug has worn off, sometimes as long as several years later. These experiences are referred to as *hallucinogen persisting perception disorder*, or simply "flashbacks." The likelihood of LSD flashbacks is not precisely known. Some studies estimate its rate of incidence as only 5 percent, whereas others estimate it as high as 33 percent. It is reasonable to assume that the range of estimates is related to differences in the dosage levels ingested.

Flashback effects sometimes can be frightening and at other times can be quite pleasant; they can occur among LSD novices or "once-only" drug takers as well as among experienced LSD abusers. They can appear without warning, but there is a higher probability that they will occur when the individual is beginning to go to sleep or has just entered a dark environment.

Because they are not common to any other psychoactive drug, the reason why LSD flashbacks might occur is not well understood. It is possible that LSD has a peculiar ability to produce some biochemical changes that remain dormant for a period of time and then suddenly reappear or that some remnant of the drug has the ability to persist over extended periods of time. It is also possible that individuals who ingest LSD are highly suggestible to social reminders about the original exposure to LSD.

Whether LSD produces major long-term deficits in the behavior of the user remains largely unknown. Memory problems and visuospatial impairments have been reported in some studies but not confirmed in others. Unfortunately, several problems persist in research studies examining long-term effects of LSD. Often, they have included either individuals with a history of psychiatric disorders prior to LSD ingestion or regular users of other illicit drugs and alcohol. As a result, it has been impossible in these studies to tease out the long-term effects of LSD alone from other factors.[14]

Will LSD Increase Criminal or Violent Behavior?

As noted in Chapter 4, it is very difficult to establish a clear cause-and-effect relationship between a drug and criminal or violent behavior. In the highly charged era of the 1960s, stories related to this question were publicized and conclusions were drawn without any careful examination of the actual facts. Take, for example, the 1964 case of a woman undergoing LSD therapy who murdered her lover three days after her last LSD session. The details of the case, overlooked by most subsequent media reports, reveal that the woman had been physically abused by the man, he had caused her to have an abortion, and the woman already had a serious mental disorder before going into treatment. The fact that the homicide took place well after the LSD had left her body indicates that the murder was not pharmacologically based (see Chapter 4). Other cases in which violent behavior appeared to be associated with an LSD experience turned out to be associated with the use of other hallucinogenic drugs instead.

It is possible, however, that an individual can "freak out" on LSD. The effects of a euphoriant drug such as LSD can lead to a feeling of invulnerability. This feeling, in turn, can lead to dangerous and possibly life-threatening behavior. We cannot reliably estimate the likelihood of these effects or pinpoint the circumstances under which they might occur; we should recognize that psychological reactions to LSD are inherently unpredictable, and caution is advised.[15]

Hallucinogens Other than LSD

There is a wide range of hallucinogens, each with an individual profile of experiences when used. Nine prominent hallucinogens other than LSD will be reviewed here. They include psilocybin, lysergic acid amide (LAA), dimethyltryptamine (DMT), harmine, mescaline, DOM, MDMA (Ecstasy), Amanita mushrooms, phencyclidine (PCP) and ketamine.

Psilocybin

The source of the drug **psilocybin** is a family of mushrooms native to southern Mexico and Central America. Spanish chroniclers in the sixteenth century wrote of "sacred mushrooms" revered by the Aztecs as *teonanacatl* (roughly translated as "God's flesh") and capable of providing extraordinary visions when eaten. Their psychoactive properties had been known for a long time, judging from stone-carved representations of these mushrooms discovered in El Salvador and dating back to as early as 500 B.C. Today, shamans in remote villages in Mexico and Central America continue the use of psilocybin mushrooms, among other hallucinogenic plants, to provide healing on both physical and spiritual levels.

In 1955, a group of Western observers documented the hallucinogenic effects of the *Psilocybe mexicana* in a native community living in a remote mountainous region of southern Mexico. Three years later, samples worked their way to Switzerland, where Albert Hofmann, already known for his work on LSD, identified

psilocybin (SIL-oh-SIGH-bin): A serotonin-related hallucinogenic drug originating from a species of mushrooms.

Psilocybe mexicana mushrooms, the source of psilocybin.

Credit: De Agostini/R. Dell'Orbo/Universal Images Group North America LLC/DeAgostini/Alamy Stock Photo

the active ingredient and named it psilocybin. As was his habit, Hofmann sampled some of the mushrooms himself and later wrote that his hallucinations took on a distinctly Mexican character. He saw Mexican designs and colors. When a doctor who was supervising the experiment bent over him to check his blood pressure, Hofmann saw him transformed into an Aztec priest![16]

An interesting question is whether the Aztec character of the hallucinations Hofmann was experiencing was simply a result of suggestion, given the environmental and social context in which drug-taking behavior was occurring, or, alternatively, Aztec designs may have been inspired over the centuries by the effects of psilocybin.

Once ingested, psilocybin loses a portion of its molecule, making it more fat soluble and therefore more easily absorbed into the brain. This new version, called **psilocin**, is the actual agent that works on the brain. Because LSD and psilocin are chemically similar, the biochemical effects are also similar.

Far less potent than LSD, psilocybin is effective at dose levels measured in the more traditional units of milligram rather than in microgram. At doses of 4 to 5 milligram, psilocybin causes a pleasant, relaxing feeling; at doses of 15 milligram and more, hallucinations, time distortions, and changes in body perception appear. A psilocybin trip generally lasts from two to five hours, considerably shorter than an LSD trip.

Individuals who have experienced both kinds of hallucinogens report that, compared to LSD, psilocybin produces effects that are more strongly visual, less emotionally intense, and more euphoric, with fewer panic reactions and less chance of paranoia. On the other hand, experimental studies of volunteers taking high doses of psilocybin have established that the drug produces drastic-enough changes in mood, sensory perception, and thought processes to qualify as a psychotic experience.

Like LSD, psilocybin (often called simply "shrooms") has become relatively easy to obtain as a drug of abuse. In 2017, about 28 percent of high school seniors reported that non-LSD hallucinogens (including "shrooms") were "fairly easy" or "very easy" to get, whereas about 26 percent felt the same way about LSD itself.[17]

Lysergic Acid Amide (LAA)

In addition to their reverence for psilocybin mushrooms, the Aztecs ingested locally grown morning glory seeds, calling them *ololuiqui*, and used their hallucinogenic effects in religious rites and healing. Like many Native American practices, the recreational use of morning glory seeds has survived in remote areas of southern Mexico. In 1961, Albert Hofmann (once again) identified the active ingredient in these seeds as **lysergic acid amide (LAA)**, after having sampled its hallucinogenic properties. As the chemical name suggests, this drug is a close relative to LSD.

The LAA experience, judging from Hofmann's report, is similar to that of LSD, though LAA is only one-tenth to one-thirtieth as potent and the hallucinations tend to be dominated by auditory rather than visual images. Commercial varieties of morning glory seeds are presently available to the public, but to minimize their abuse, suppliers have taken the precaution of coating them with an additive that causes nausea and vomiting, if they are eaten.[18]

Dimethyltryptamine (DMT)

The drug **dimethyltryptamine (DMT)** is obtained chiefly from the resin of the bark of trees and nuts native to the West Indies as well as to Central and South America, where it is generally inhaled as a snuff. An oral administration does not produce psychoactive effects. The similarity of this drug's effects to those of LSD and its very short duration gave DMT the reputation during the psychedelic years of the 1960s of being "the businessman's LSD." Presumably, someone could take a DMT trip during lunch and be back at the office in time for work in the afternoon.

An inhaled 30 milligram dose of DMT produces physiological changes within 10 seconds, with hallucinogenic effects peaking around 10 to 15 minutes later. Paranoia, anxiety, and panic also can result at this time, but most symptoms are over in about an hour.[19]

A chemical found in *Bufo* toads is similar to DMT (see Drugs ... in Focus, page 257).

Harmine

Among native tribes in the western Amazon region of South America, the bark of the *Banisteriopsis* vine yields the powerful drug **harmine**. A drink containing harmine, called *ayahuasca*,

psilocin (SIL-oh-sin): A brain chemical related to serotonin, resulting from the ingestion of psilocybin.

lysergic acid amide (LAA) (lye-SER-jik ASS-id A-mide): A hallucinogenic drug found in morning glory seeds, producing effects similar to those of LSD.

dimethyltryptamine (DMT) (dye-METH-il-TRIP-ta-meen): A short-acting hallucinogenic drug.

harmine (HAR-meen): A serotonin-related hallucinogenic drug frequently used by South American shamans in healing rituals.

is frequently used by local shamans for healing rites. It is chemically similar to serotonin, like LSD and the other hallucinogens examined so far. Its psychological effects, however, are somewhat different. Unlike LSD, harmine makes the individual withdraw into a trance, and the hallucinatory images (often visions of animals and supernatural beings) are experienced within the context of a dreamlike state. Reports among shamans refer to a sense of suspension in space or flying, falling into one's body, or experiencing one's own death.[20]

Mescaline

The hallucinogen **mescaline** is derived from the **peyote** plant, a spineless cactus with a small, greenish crown that grows above ground and has a long carrot-like root. This cactus is found over a wide area, from the southwestern United States to northern regions of South America, and many communities in these regions have discovered its psychoactive properties. Given the large distances between these groups, it is remarkable that they prepare and ingest mescaline in a highly similar manner. The crowns of the cactus are cutoff, sliced in small disks called *buttons*, dried in the sun, and then consumed. An effective dose of mescaline from peyote is 200 milligram, equivalent to about five buttons. Peak response to the drug takes place 30 minutes to 2 hours after consumption. Mescaline is still used today as part of religious worship among many American Indians in the United States and Canada (Drugs ... in Focus).

The psychological and physiological effects of mescaline are highly similar to those of LSD, though some have reported that mescaline hallucinations are more sensual, with fewer changes in mood and the sense of self. Nonetheless, double-blind studies comparing the reactions to LSD and mescaline show that subjects cannot distinguish between the two when dose levels are equivalent. Although the reactions may be the same, the mescaline trip comes at a greater price, as far as physiological reactions are concerned. Peyote buttons taste extremely bitter and can cause vomiting, headaches, and, unless the stomach is empty, distressing levels of nausea.[21] Today, mescaline can be synthesized as well as obtained from the peyote cactus. The mescaline molecule resembles the chemical structure of norepinephrine but

---

bufotenine (byoo-FOT-eh-neen): A serotonin-related drug obtained either from a bean plant in Central and South America or from the skin of a particular type of toad.

cyanosis (SIGH-ah-NOH-sis): A tendency for the skin to turn bluish purple. It can be a side effect of the drug bufotenine.

mescaline (MES-kul-leen): A norepinephrine-related hallucinogenic drug. Its source is the peyote cactus.

peyote (pay-YO-tay): A species of cactus that is the source for the hallucinogenic drug mescaline.

Drugs ... in Focus

Bufotenine and the Bufo Toad

Bufotenine is a drug with a strange past. Found in a family of beans native to Central and South America, bufotenine is better known as a chemical that can be isolated from the skin and glands of the *Bufo* toad, from which it gets its name. *Bufo* toads figured prominently in the magical potions of European witches. Evidence also exists that *Bufo* toads were incorporated into the ceremonial rituals of ancient Aztec and Mayan cultures. Largely as a result of these historical references, it has been widely assumed that bufotenine was the primary contributor to the psychoactive effects of these concoctions and that bufotenine itself is a powerful hallucinogen.

It turned out that these conclusions were wrong. The few studies in which human volunteers were administered bufotenine indicate that the substance induces strong excitatory effects on blood pressure and heart rate but no hallucinatory experiences. Some subjects report distorted images with high dosages of the drug, but this might well occur as oxygen is cutoff from parts of the body, particularly the optic nerve carrying visual information to the brain. It is likely that whatever hallucinogenic effects *Bufo* toads may produce are brought on by another

chemical also found in these toads that functions similarly to the hallucinogen DMT.

Despite the confusion as to which substance is responsible for its psychoactive properties, *Bufo* toads continue to fascinate the public. Wildly exaggerated and frequently unsubstantiated accounts of "toad licking" and "toad smoking" periodically circulate in the social media. Reportedly, a small group calling themselves Amphibians Anonymous was formed in the late 1980s; the group's motto was, "Never has it been so easy to just say no."

The bottom line, however, is that the dangers of consuming toad tissue are substantial. Besides the extreme cardiovascular reactions, toxic effects include a skin condition called **cyanosis** (literally, "turning blue"). Actually, the description may be an understatement. Skin color has been observed to be closer to an eggplant purple.

Sources: Horgan, J. (1990, August). Bufo abuse. *Scientific American*, pp. 26–27. Inciardi, J. A. (2002). *The war on drugs III.* Boston: Allyn and Bacon, pp. 4–5. Lyttle, T.; Goldstein, D.; and Gartz J. (1996). Bufo toads and bufotenine: Fact and fiction surrounding an alleged psychedelic. *Journal of Psychoactive Drugs, 28,* 267–290.

The peyote cactus, source of mescaline.

Credit: Francois Gohier/Science source

Dom

A group of synthetic hallucinogens have been developed that share mescaline's resemblance to amphetamine but do not produce the strong stimulant effects of amphetamine. One example of these synthetic drugs, **DOM** (short for 2, 5-dimethoxy-4-methylamphetamine), appeared in the 1960s and 1970s, when it was frequently combined with LSD and carried the street name of STP. To some, the nickname was a reference to the well-known engine oil additive; to others, the letters stood for "serenity, tranquility, and peace" or, alternatively, "super terrific psychedelic." It is roughly 80 times more potent than mescaline, though still far weaker than LSD. At low doses of about 3–5 milligram, DOM produces euphoria; with higher doses of 10 milligram or more, severe hallucinations result,

stimulates the same serotonin-2A receptors as LSD and other hallucinogens that resemble serotonin. As a result, mescaline and LSD share a common brain mechanism.[22]

DOM: A synthetic norepinephrine-related hallucinogenic drug, derived from amphetamine. DOM or a combination of DOM and LSD is often referred to by the street name STP.

Drugs ... in Focus

Present-Day Peyotism and the Native American Church

Among American Indians within the United States, the ritual use of peyote buttons, called *peyotism*, can be traced to the eighteenth century when the Mescalero Apaches (from whom the word *mescaline* was derived) adopted the custom from Mexican Indians, who had been using peyote for more than 3,000 years. By the late 1800s, peyotism had become widely popular among tribes from Wisconsin and Minnesota to the West Coast. It was not until the early twentieth century, however, that peyote use became incorporated into an official religious organization, the Native American Church of North America, chartered in 1918.

The beliefs of the Native American Church membership, estimated to include anywhere from 50,000 to 250,000 American Indians in the United States and Canada, combine traditional tribal customs and practices with Christian morality. To them, life is a choice between two roads that meet at a junction. The Profane Road is paved and wide, surrounded by worldly passions and temptations. The Peyote Road is a narrow and winding path, surrounded by natural, unspoiled beauty; it is also a path of sobriety (since alcohol poisons the goodness of the body), hard work, caring for one's family, and brotherly love. Only the Peyote Road leads to salvation. In their weekly ceremonies, lasting from Saturday night until Sunday afternoon, church members swallow small peyote buttons as a sacrament, similar to the ritual of taking Holy Communion, or drink peyote tea. It is considered sacrilegious to take peyote outside the ceremonies in the church.

While peyote remains classified as a Schedule I drug and therefore banned, federal law and the laws of 23 U.S. states have exempted the sacramental use of peyote from criminal penalties. The Religious Freedom Restoration Act of 1993 established an exemption from federal and state-controlled substance laws when peyote is used for religious purposes in traditional American Indian ceremonies. In 2005, a study found that peyote use among church members does not result in impairments on tests of memory, attention, and other aspects of cognitive functioning.

Today, in south Texas near Laredo, a handful of people are licensed by state and federal authorities to harvest peyote for religious purposes. This locale is the only place in the United States where peyote grows in the wild. As one of the harvesters has put it, "This is sacred ground to a lot of American Indian tribes. To some, the land here is very holy because it is the home to the sacred peyote."

Sources: Calabrese, J. D. (1997). Spiritual healing and human development in the Native American Church: Toward a cultural psychiatry of peyote. *Psychoanalytic Review, 84,* 237–255. Halpern, J. H.; Sherwood, A. R.; Hudson, J. I.; Yurgelum-Tod, D.; and Pope, H. G., Jr. (2005). Psychological and cognitive effects of long-term peyote use among Native Americans. *Biological Psychiatry, 58,* 624–631. Indian religion must say no (1990, October 6). *The Economist,* pp. 25–26. Milloy, R. E. (2002, May 7). A forbidding landscape that's Eden for peyote. *New York Times,* p. A20. Quotation on p. A20. Morgan, G. (1983). Recollections of the peyote road. In L. Grinspoon; and J. B. Bakalar (Eds.), *Psychedelic reflections.* New York: Human Sciences Press, pp. 91–99.

often lasting from 16 to 25 hours. Though similar to LSD in many respects, DOM has the reputation of producing a far greater incidence of panic attacks, psychotic episodes, and other symptoms of a very bad trip. Cases have been reported of STP being added as an adulterant to marijuana.[23]

MDMA (Ecstasy)

MDMA (generally known by its street name, Ecstasy) first appeared on the scene in the 1980s as a new designer drug. It also became known to a number of psychiatrists, who used the drug as part of their therapy, believing that MDMA had a special ability to enhance empathy among their patients. In fact, some therapists at the time suggested the name *empathogens* (meaning "generating a state of empathy") to describe MDMA and related drugs. Eventually, after several years of hesitations and reversals, the Drug Enforcement Administration put MDMA permanently on the Schedule I list of controlled substances, indicating that there is no accepted medical application for the drug. Nonetheless, MDMA remained a legally approved and regulated drug for psychiatric use in Switzerland as late as 1993. There continues to be interest in its positive role in psychiatric treatment, though its present status as a Schedule I controlled substance makes it extremely difficult to conduct research studies on this possibility. In the early 1990s, MDMA become prominent among the new club drugs, especially popular at dance clubs and all-night "rave" parties. Widely available under names such as Ecstasy, E, XTC, X, Essence, Clarity, and Adam, MDMA acquired the reputation of having the stimulant qualities of amphetamines and the hallucinogenic qualities of mescaline.[24]

Physical health concerns with respect to Ecstasy center on its short-term and long-term toxicity. The principal acute effect is severe hyperthermia (and heatstroke), which can be lethal when Ecstasy is ingested while engaged in the physical exertion of dancing in an already-overheated club environment. The dehydration associated with hyperthermia causes an elevation in blood pressure and heart rate and places a strain on kidney functioning. These problems are compounded by the highly risky practice of "Ecstasy stacking," in which multiple Ecstasy tablets are taken at once or Ecstasy is combined with LSD, alcohol, marijuana, or other drugs. Possible physical effects of Ecstasy include hyperthermia and heatstroke, dehydration and electrolyte depletion, irregular heartbeat or increased heart rate, kidney and liver failure, jaw clenching and other forms of muscle spasms, and long-term neurochemical changes. Possible psychological effects include agitation and confusion, depression and anxiety, long-term impairments in memory recall, and sleep problems. Further, the addition of elevated dosage levels of dextromethorphan (a common cough suppressant) in adulterated versions of Ecstasy produces an inhibition of sweating, increasing the risk of hyperthermia and heatstroke. In general, women show greater behavioral effects from chronic Ecstasy use than do men.

In 2003, the federal RAVE (Reducing Americans' Vulnerability to Ecstasy) Act makes it unlawful to "knowingly

MDMA (Ecstasy): A synthetic norepinephrine-related hallucinogenic drug. Once considered useful for psychotherapeutic purposes, this drug is now known to produce significant adverse side effects, including neuronal hyperthermia, dehydration, and neurochemical changes.

Drug Enforcement ... in Focus

Who (or What) Is Molly?

There are few developments in the present-day drug scene that have more greatly concerned public health and criminal justice professionals alike than the availability of designer synthetic drugs currently flooding the country. These synthetic formulations, largely created in Asian laboratories, are composed of chemical ingredients that can only be deciphered through chemical analysis in a forensic laboratory. Yet, they are often promoted as pure forms of existing drugs.

A case in point is the recent introduction of drugs referred to as "Molly." Between October 2009 and September 2013, out of more than 140 "drug exhibits" (samples of drugs obtained through DEA seizure operations in New York State) that were submitted to the Northeast Regional Laboratory for analysis, 87 percent were found to contain no amount of MDMA whatsoever. Nearly half of the samples contained methylone or 4-MEC, two substances in the cathinone family. You may recall from Chapter 10 that cathinones (particularly methylone) are

a principal ingredient in another illicit designer synthetic drug, promoted as "bath salts."

The confusion regarding the substances contained in Molly is likely to persist for some time. Health professionals are hard put to identify the exact ingredients in emergency hospitals when individuals come in with serious drug reactions. Statistics referring to an increase in hospital emergencies due to MDMA (Ecstasy) are based in large part on the assumption that patients reporting having taken Molly have been actually consuming MDMA. During Labor Day weekend in 2013, two attendees at a music festival in New York City died from drug-related causes after allegedly ingesting Molly. Given the present circumstances with respect to designer synthetic drugs, many of them promoted as Molly, it is unclear whether MDMA was involved at all.

Sources: Crowell, B. R. (2013, September). Updated "Molly" reporting. Information Bulletin issued by the Drug Enforcement Administration, New York Division. Drug Enforcement Administration (2014). *MDMA (Ecstasy) or Molly?* Washington, D.C.: Drug Enforcement Administration, U.S. Department of Justice.

open, lease, rent, use, or maintain any place, whether permanently or temporarily for the purpose of manufacturing, distributing, or using any controlled substance." Since its enactment, supporters of the law view it as helping to reduce illicit drug use in dance clubs; opponents view it more as reflection of prejudice against youth culture.[25]

About 5 percent of high school seniors and about 2 percent of eighth graders reported in 2017 having taken Ecstasy at some point in their lives. In 2001, prevalence rates had reached 12 percent and 5 percent, respectively, causing considerable alarm among public health officials. Since around 2005, however, the rates have decreased and have remained fairly steady at 5–7 percent for seniors and 2–3 percent for eighth graders.[26]

The current difficulties with Ecstasy on the drug scene go beyond the issue of MDMA toxicity per se. There is often confusion as to what is exactly being sold. Pure crystallized MDMA capsules that are promoted and sold on the street as "Molly" may not contain any MDMA at all, or else the MDMA content in the capsules has been adulterated with a number of designer stimulant drugs (see Drug Enforcement ... in Focus). Due to the proliferation of designer drugs, anything sold on the street may have a largely unknown chemical composition and, as a result, produce unpredictable pharmacological consequences.

Amanita Muscaria

The *Amanita muscaria* mushroom, also called the fly agaric mushroom because of its ability to lure and sedate flies and other insects, grows in the upper latitudes of the Northern Hemisphere, usually among the roots of birch trees. The mushroom has a bright red cap speckled with white dots; the dancing mushrooms in Walt Disney's film *Fantasia* were inspired by the appearance (if not the hallucinogenic effects) of this fungus (see Figure 12.1).

Amanita mushrooms are one of the world's oldest intoxicants. Many historians hypothesize that this mushroom was the basis for the mysterious and divine substance called soma, which is celebrated in the *Rig-Veda*, one of Hinduism's oldest holy books, dating around 1000 B.C. It is strongly suspected that amanita mushrooms were used in Greek mystery cults and were the basis for the legendary "nectar of the Gods" on Mount Olympus.[27]

The effects of amanita mushrooms can be lethal if dose levels are not watched very carefully. They produce muscular twitching and spasms, vivid hallucinations, dizziness, and heightened aggressive behavior. Viking warriors were reputed to have ingested amanita mushrooms before sailing off to battle. The drug-induced strength and savagery of these "berserk" invaders were so widely feared that a medieval prayer was written especially for protection from their attacks: "From the intolerable fury of the Norseman, O Lord, deliver us."[28]

Phencyclidine (PCP) and Ketamine

Phencyclidine (PCP) and **ketamine** are referred to as **dissociative anesthetic hallucinogens**, in that they have pain-reducing and anesthetic properties. Hallucinations also occur, but they

Quick Concept Check 12.1

Understanding the Diversity of Hallucinogenic Experiences

Check your understanding of the psychological differences among major hallucinogens by matching each hallucinatory experience (in the left column) with the hallucinogenic drug most apt to produce such effects (in the right column).

PSYCHOLOGICAL EXPERIENCE	HALLUCINOGEN
1. "The images I saw were Mexican designs as if they were created by an Aztec artist."	DMT
	LSD
2. "As I heard the bells, I also saw the vibrations of the sound move through the air."	Phencyclidine
	Psilocybin
3. "The hallucinations were gone sixty minutes after they had started."	Mescaline
	Ibotenic acid
4. "As I ate the red-topped mushrooms, I felt my muscles twitch. I could see vivid hallucinations."	
5. "As a member of the Native American Church I was feeling that I was traveling down the Peyote Road."	
6. "I look at my arms and they are three times as long as they were before!"	

Answers: 1. Psilocybin 2. LSD, principally 3. DMT
4. Ibotenic acid 5. Mescaline 6. Phencyclidine

are quite different from those experienced under the influence of LSD. There are no colorful images, no intermingling of sight and sound, no mystical sense of being "one with the world." Instead, there is a dissociative sense of being "cut off from one's body" as well as paranoia and disorientation that can lead to unpredictable aggressive behaviors. Given these properties, PCP and ketamine have the reputation of being the most notorious of all abused hallucinogens (see Table 12.2).

Amanita muscaria (a-ma-NEE-ta mus-CAR-ee-ah): A species of mushroom containing the hallucinogenic drug ibotenic acid.

Phencyclidine (fen-SIGH-klih-deen): A dissociative anesthetic hallucinogen that produces disorienting hallucinations, agitation, aggressive behavior, analgesia, and amnesia. It has various street names, including angel dust.

Dissociative anesthetic hallucinogen: A class of hallucinogens producing analgesia and disruptions of one's identity to the world, in addition to anxiety and disorienting hallucinations. Two examples are phencyclidine (PCP) and ketamine.

TABLE 12.2

Various street names for phencyclidine and ketamine

DRUG	STREET NAME
PCP	Angel dust
	Cyclones
	Jet fuel
	Killer joints
	Monkey dust
	Peep
	Sherms (derived from the reaction that it hits you like a Sherman tank)
	Supergrass
	Zombie dust
KETAMINE	Special K
	KitKat
	Ket
	Super K

Note: In the illicit drug market, PCP is frequently misrepresented and sold as mescaline, LSD, marijuana, amphetamine, or cocaine.

Source: Based on information from Milburn, H. T. (1991). Diagnosis and management of phencyclidine intoxication. *American Family Physician, 43,* 1293. Davis, K. (2017, October 12). What are the uses of ketamine? *Medical News Today.* https://www.medicalnewsto-day.com/articles/302663.php.

In the case of PCP (often called "angel dust"), behavioral effects include manic excitement, severe anxiety, sudden mood changes, disordered and confused thought, paranoid thoughts, and unpredictable aggression. Because PCP has analgesic properties as well, individuals taking the drug often feel invulnerable to threats against them and may be willing and able to withstand considerable pain. PCP abusers may imagine themselves to be so small that they feel they could walk through a keyhole or that their arm suddenly has grown to 10 times its normal length. Individuals under the influence of PCP also may stagger, speak in a slurred way, and feel depersonalized or detached from people around them. A prominent feature is a prolonged visual stare, often called "doll's eyes."

It is strange that a drug that produces so many adverse effects would have been subject to deliberate abuse, but such is the case with PCP. After its withdrawal in 1967 as a licit medication for surgical anesthesia purposes (due to a high prevalence of adverse side effects among patients), reports of illicit PCP abuse began surfacing among the hippie community in San Francisco, where it became known as the PeaCe Pill. Word quickly spread that PCP did not live up to its name. Inexperienced PCP abusers were suffering the same bizarre effects as had the clinical patients earlier in the decade. By 1969, PCP had been written off as a garbage drug, and it dropped out of sight as a drug of abuse.

In the early 1970s, PCP returned under new street names and in new forms. No longer a pill to be taken orally, PCP was now in powdered or liquid form. Powdered PCP could be added to parsley, mint, oregano, tobacco, or marijuana, rolled as a cigarette, and smoked. Liquid PCP could be used to soak leaf mixtures of all types, including manufactured cigarettes, which could then be dried and smoked. Many new users have turned to PCP as a way to boost the effects of marijuana. Making matters worse, in recent years, as many as 120 different designer-drug variations of PCP have been developed in illicit laboratories around the country and the world. The dangers of PCP abuse, therefore, are complicated by the difficulty in knowing whether a street drug has been adulterated with PCP and what version of PCP may be present. Unfortunately, the common practice of mixing PCP with alcohol or marijuana adds to its unpredictability. Today, PCP is classified as a Schedule II controlled substance in the United States and a Schedule I controlled substance in Canada.

In its medical application, ketamine (brand name: Ketalar) is administered at sub-anesthetic dosage levels in starting and maintaining surgical anesthesia, producing a trance-like state of pain relief, sedation, and memory loss. Cardiac function, breathing, and airway reflexes remain normal, and hallucinations are minimized. When properly administered by a trained medical professional, ketamine is a safe and valuable medication. It has also been used therapeutically for clinical cases of depression and posttraumatic stress disorder (PTSD) as well as a nonopioid approach to the treatment of chronic pain. Ketamine is presently classified as a Schedule III controlled substance in the United States.

Used for recreational purposes, however, ketamine abuse presents serious and dangerous physical and behavioral consequences. Like PCP, ketamine produces a dreamlike intoxication, accompanied by an inability to move or feel pain. There are also experiences of dizziness, confusion, and slurred speech. As is the case with dissociative hallucinogens, ketamine produces amnesia, in that abusers frequently cannot later remember what has happened while under its influence. A particular effect of ketamine at high doses is a profound lack of awareness of the world, a lack of control over one's body, being unable to speak or move, even though one is technically awake. Ketamine abusers have adopted the slang expression "falling into a k hole" to describe this condition.

Ketamine abuse began to be reported in the 1980s. More recently, under the names "Special K" and "Vitamin K," it has been included among current so-called club drugs on the scene. The primary hazard of acute ketamine ingestion is the depression of breathing. Little is known, however, of the chronic effects of extended ketamine abuse over time, except that experiences of "flashbacks" have been reported.[29]

Ketamine: A dissociative anesthetic hallucinogen that produces analgesia and, at high doses, dissociative hallucinations leading a lack of awareness of the world, a lack of control over one's body, being unable to speak or move, even though technically awake. Under medical supervision, ketamine is used for surgical anesthetic purposes and as a treatment for depression, posttraumatic stress disorder (PTSD), and as a nonopioid treatment for chronic pain. It has various street names, including K and Special K.

As with other drugs that produce depressive effects on the central nervous system, there is the dangerous potential for ketamine to be abused for "date-rape" purposes. Women who may unwittingly take the drug can be rendered incapacitated, without the ability to recall the experience.

Sedative-Hypnotics

Sedative-hypnotics comprised a group of non-opioid, non-alcoholic depressant drugs, so-named because they calm us down and produce sleep (from the Latin verb, *sedare*, meaning "to calm or be quiet" and the Greek noun, *hypnos*, meaning "sleep"). Sedative-hypnotic drugs range from drugs that were introduced more than 200 years ago to others that have become available only in recent years. The most prominent group of sedative-hypnotics comprises several depressants, referred to as barbiturates.

Barbiturates

In 1864, the German chemist Adolf von Baeyer combined a waste product in urine called *urea* and an apple extract called *malonic acid* to form a new chemical compound called *barbituric acid*. There are two often-told stories about how this compound got its name. One story has it that von Baeyer had gone to a local tavern to celebrate his discovery and encountered a number of artillery officers celebrating the feast day of St. Barbara, the patron saint of explosives handlers. Inspired by their celebration, the name "barbituric acid" came to mind. The other story attributes the name to a relationship with a certain barmaid (perhaps at the same tavern) whose name was Barbara.[30]

Whichever story is true (if either is), von Baeyer's discovery of barbituric acid set the stage for the development of a class of drugs called **barbiturates**. Barbituric acid itself has no behavioral effects, but if additional molecular groups combine with the acid, depressant effects are observed. In 1903, the first true barbiturate, diethylbarbituric acid, was created and marketed under the name Veronal. Over the next 30 years, several barbiturate drugs were introduced: **phenobarbital** (marketed in generic form), **amobarbital** (brand name: Amytal), **pentobarbital** (brand name: Nembutal), and **secobarbital** (brand name: Seconal). Major barbiturates currently available are listed in Table 12.3.

Categories of Barbiturates

Barbiturates all share a number of common features. They are relatively tasteless and odorless, and at sufficient dosages, they

reliably induce sleep, although the quality of sleep is a matter that will be discussed later. Because they slow down the activity of the central nervous system (CNS), the principal therapeutic application of barbiturates has been in the treatment of seizure disorders (epilepsy).

The principal difference among them lies in how long the depressant effects will last; a rough classification of barbiturates is based upon this factor. Barbiturates are categorized as *long acting* (six or more hours), *intermediate acting* (four to six hours), or *short acting* (less than four hours). Bear in mind, however, that these groups are relative only to one another. All other factors being equal, injectable forms of barbiturates are shorter acting than orally administered forms of the same drug, since it takes longer for the drug to be absorbed when taken by mouth and longer for it to be eliminated from the body (see Chapter 8).

The barbiturates used in surgical anesthesia, such as thiopental (brand name: Pentothal), take effect extremely

barbiturate (bar-BIT-chur-rit): A drug within a family of depressants derived from barbituric acid and used as a sedative-hypnotic and antiepileptic medication.

phenobarbital (Feen-oh-BAR-bih-tall): A long-acting barbiturate drug, usually marketed in generic form.

amobarbital (AY-moh-BAR-bih-tall): An intermediate-acting barbiturate drug. Brand name is Amytal.

pentobarbital (PEN-toh-BAR-bih-tall): A short-acting barbiturate drug. Brand name is Nembutal.

secobarbital (SEC-oh-BAR-bih-tall): A short-acting barbiturate drug. Brand name is Seconal.

TABLE 12.3

Major barbiturates

GENERIC NAME	BRAND NAME	DURATION OF ACTION	RELATIVE POTENTIAL FOR ABUSE
Phenobarbital	Generic*	Long	Low
Mephobarbital	Mebaral	Long	Low
Butalbarbital	Pheniline Forte**	Intermediate	Moderate
Amobarbital	Amytal	Intermediate	High
Secobarbital and amobarbital	Tuinal	Short, intermediate	High
Pentobarbital	Nembutal	Short	High
Secobarbital	Seconal	Short	High

Note: Short-acting barbiturates begin to take effect in about 15 minutes, intermediate-acting barbiturates in 30 minutes, and long-acting barbiturates in 1 hour.

*Phenobarbital is also available in combination with hyoscyamine, atropine, and scopolamine under the brand name Donnatal.

**Several brands combine butalbarbital with acetaminophen.

Sources: Henningfield, J. E.; and Ator, N. A. (1986). *Barbiturates: Sleeping potion or intoxicant?* New York: Chelsea House, p. 24. *Physicians' desk reference* (69th ed.) (2015). Montvale, NJ: PDR Network.

rapidly (within seconds) and last only a few minutes. For this reason, they are referred to as *ultra-short-acting barbiturates*. Because these features are undesirable to a person seeking a recreational drug, ultra-short-acting barbiturates are not commonly abused.

Acute Effects of Barbiturates

At very low doses, the primary result of oral administrations of a barbiturate is relaxation and, paradoxically, a sense of euphoria. These effects derive chiefly from a disinhibition of the cerebral cortex, in which normal inhibitory influences from the cortex are reduced. These symptoms are similar to the inebriating or intoxicating effects that result from low to moderate doses of alcohol (Drug Enforcement ... in Focus).

As the dose level increases, lower regions of the brain concerned with general arousal become affected. At therapeutic doses (one 100 mg capsule of secobarbital, for example), barbiturates make you feel sedated and drowsy. For this reason, patients are typically warned that barbiturates can impair the performance of driving a car or operating machinery. At higher doses, a hypnotic (sleep-inducing) effect will be achieved.

Barbiturates tend to suppress rapid eye movement (REM) sleep, a phase of everyone's sleep that represents about 20 percent of the total sleep time each night. REM sleep is associated with dreaming and general relaxation of the body. If barbiturates are consumed over many evenings and then stopped, the CNS will attempt to catch up for the lost REM sleep by producing longer REM periods on subsequent nights. This **REM-sleep rebound** effect produces vivid and upsetting nightmares, along with a barbiturate hangover the next day, during which the user feels groggy and out of sorts. In other words, barbiturates may induce sleep, but a refreshing sleep it definitely is not.[31]

The most serious acute risks of barbiturate use involve the possibility of a lethal overdose either from taking too high a dose level of the drug alone or from taking the drug in combination with alcohol, such as when a barbiturate is taken after an evening of drinking. In these instances, sleep can all too easily slip into coma and death, since an excessive dose produces an inhibition of the respiratory control centers in the brain. The mixture of barbiturates with alcohol produces a synergistic effect (see Chapter 8) in which the combined result is greater than the sum of the effects of each drug alone.

Chronic Effects of Barbiturates

Even after brief use of barbiturates, anxiety may be temporarily increased during the day, and there may be an even greater degree of insomnia than before. In addition, because

REM-sleep rebound: A phenomenon associated with the withdrawal of barbiturate drugs in which the quantity of rapid eye movement (REM) sleep increases, resulting in disturbed sleep and nightmares.

Drug Enforcement ... in Focus

Is There Any Truth Regarding "Truth Serum"?

The idea that a sedative-hypnotic drug such as amobarbital (Amytal, or "sodium amytal") may function as a "truth serum" is not at all new. It has been known for centuries that depressants can produce remarkable candor and freedom from inhibition. The oldest example is simple alcohol, whose effect on loosening the tongue has led to the Latin proverb *in vino veritas* ("in wine, there is truth").

Whether we are guaranteed truthfulness under any of these circumstances, however, is another matter entirely. Courts have ruled that expert opinion in criminal cases based solely on drug-assisted testimony cannot be admitted as evidence. Controlled laboratory studies have shown that individuals under the influence of Amytal, when pressed by questioners, are as likely to give convincing renditions of fabrications (outright lies) or fantasies as they are to tell the truth. So, perhaps, Amytal might be better described as a "tell anything serum."

Recently, the question of whether Amytal or other depressant drugs should be used to gain information has come up with regard to the interrogation of captured Al Qaeda prisoners following the September 11, 2001, attacks. The United States has determined that such individuals are unlawful combatants, a designation that excludes them from protection under the Geneva Convention guidelines prohibiting such practices for prisoners of war. Officially, U.S. officials deny that depressant drugs are being used to gain information from captives under American jurisdiction. It is possible that this practice is in effect in other countries to which captives have been transferred.

The lack of evidence that truthful information may be gained through the use of depressant drugs has not changed, however. Nonetheless, military and intelligence experts point to the potential for gaining some relevant information that might be buried in drug-induced ramblings.

Sources: CBS News (2003, April 23). Truth serum: A possible weapon. *www.cbsnews.com.* Lillienfeld, S. O.; and Landfield, K. (2008). Science and pseudoscience in law enforcement. *Criminal Justice and Behavior, 35,* 1215–1230. Michaelis, J. I. (1966). Quaere, whether "in vino veritas": An analysis of the truth serum cases. *Issues in Criminology, 2*(2), 245–267.

Barbiturates and alcohol have frequently been combined in attempts to commit suicide.

Credit: Isopix/Shutterstock

TABLE 12.4

Street names for various barbiturates

TYPE OF BARBITURATE	STREET NAME
Pentobarbital (Nembutal)	Abbotts, blockbusters, nebbies, nembies, nemmies, yellow bullets, yellow dolls, yellow jackets, yellows
Amobarbital (Amytal)	Blue angels, bluebirds, blue bullets, blue devils, blue dolls, blue heavens, blues
Secobarbital (Seconal)	F-40s, Mexican reds, R.D.s, redbirds, red bullets, red devils, red dolls, reds, seccies, seggies, pinks
Secobarbital and amobarbital (Tuinal)	Christmas trees, double trouble, gorilla pills, rainbows, tootsies, trees, tuies
Barbiturates in general	Downers, down, goofballs, G.B.s, goofers, idiot pills, King Kong pills, peanuts, pink ladies, sleepers, softballs, stumblers

Note: Like any other street drug, illicit barbiturate capsules often contain an unknown array of other substances, including strychnine, arsenic, laxatives, or milk sugars. Any yellow capsule may be "marketed" as Nembutal, any blue capsule as Amytal, or any red capsule as Seconal.

Source: Based on Henningfield, J. E.; and Ator, N. A. (1986). *Barbiturates,* Sleeping potion or intoxicant? New York: Chelsea House, p. 82.

Barbiturate Use and Abuse

Barbiturate abuse reached its peak in the 1950s and 1960s, later to be overshadowed by abuses of heroin, hallucinogens, nonbarbiturate depressants, amphetamines, and more recently, abuses of cocaine, crack, and various stimulants and hallucinogens. The principal reason was that barbiturates became less widely available as prescription drugs. Stricter controls were placed on obtaining excessive amounts of barbiturates from pharmacies, whereas physicians, concerned with the potential of barbiturates as ways of committing suicide, became reluctant to prescribe them on a routine basis. Despite their decline as major drugs of abuse, however, barbiturates are still being abused. The University of Michigan survey reported 2017 annual prevalence rates of 3 percent for high school seniors, 2 percent for college students, and 2 percent for young adults aged 19–28 years.[33]

Nonbarbiturate Sedative-Hypnotics

As the hazards of barbiturate use became increasingly evident, the search was on for sedative-hypnotic drugs that were not derivatives of barbituric acid and, it was hoped, had fewer undesirable side effects. Unfortunately, these objectives were not realized.

a barbiturate-induced sleep typically leaves a person feeling groggy the next morning, it is tempting to take a stimulant drug during the day to feel completely alert. At bedtime, the person still feels the stimulant effects and is inclined to continue taking a barbiturate to achieve any sleep at all.

Withdrawal symptoms, observed when barbiturates are discontinued, indicate a strong physical dependence on the drug. A person may experience a combination of tremors (the "shakes"), nausea and vomiting, intense perspiring, general confusion, convulsions, hallucinations, high fever, and increased heart rate. Not surprisingly, considering the parallels with alcohol, the barbiturate withdrawal syndrome closely resembles that of withdrawal after chronic alcohol abuse (Table 12.4).

Professionals in the treatment of drug dependence often view the effects of barbiturate withdrawal as the most distressing as well as the most dangerous type of drug withdrawal. From a medical perspective, the withdrawal process is life-threatening unless it is carried out in gradual fashion in a hospital setting. Without medical supervision, abrupt withdrawal from barbiturates carries approximately a 5 percent chance of death.[32]

One such drug, **chloral hydrate**, had been synthesized as early as 1832. As a depressant for the treatment of insomnia, it has the advantage of not producing the REM-sleep rebound effect or bringing on the typical barbiturate hangover. A major disadvantage, however, is that it can severely irritate the stomach. Like other depressants, it is also highly reactive when combined with alcohol. In the nineteenth century, a few drops of chloral hydrate in a glass of whiskey became the infamous "Mickey Finn," a concoction that left many an unsuspecting sailor unconscious and eventually "shanghaied" onto a boat for China. You might say that chloral hydrate was an early precursor to a modern-day "date-rape" drug.

The development of **methaqualone** (brand names: Quaalude, Sopor), first introduced in the United States in 1965, was a further attempt toward achieving the perfect sleeping pill. In 1972, methaqualone had become the sixth-best-selling drug for the treatment of insomnia. During the early 1970s, recreational use of methaqualone (popularly known as "ludes" or "sopors") was rapidly spreading across the country, aided by the unfounded reputation that it had aphrodisiac properties. The problem with methaqualone was compounded by the extensive number of prescriptions written by physicians at the time who mistakenly viewed the drug as a desirable alternative to barbiturates. On the street, quantities of methaqualone were obtained from medical prescriptions or stolen from pharmacies.

In 1984, this drug's legal status changed to that of a Schedule I controlled substance. Although methaqualone was no longer manufactured by any pharmaceutical company, it was still available as an illicit drug. It is either manufactured in domestic underground laboratories or smuggled into the country from underground laboratories abroad.

Antianxiety Drugs

If social historians consider the 1950s "the age of anxiety," then it is appropriate that this period also would be marked by the development of drugs specifically intended to combat that anxiety. These drugs were originally called *minor tranquilizers*, to distinguish them from other drugs regarded as *major tranquilizers* and developed at about the same time to relieve symptoms of schizophrenia. This terminology is no longer used today, for we now know that the pharmacological differences between the two drug categories are more than simply a matter of degree. Anxious people (or even people who are not bothered by anxiety) are not affected by drugs designed to treat schizophrenia. The current, and more logical, practice is to refer to drugs in terms of a specific action and purpose. The minor tranquilizers are now typically referred to as antianxiety medications.

The first antianxiety medication to be developed was **meprobamate** (brand name: Miltown), named in 1955 for a New Jersey town near the headquarters of the pharmaceutical company that first introduced it. It was the first psychoactive drug in history to be marketed specifically as an antianxiety medication.

Meprobamate had advantages and disadvantages. On the positive side, the toxic dose was relatively high, making the possibility of suicide more remote than with alcohol, barbiturates, and other depressants. In addition, judging from the

A person's job and other aspects of living are often sources of enormous stress and anxiety.

Credit: Eric Risberg/AP Images

reduction in autonomic responses to stressors, there were genuine signs that people on this medication were actually less anxious. On the negative side, motor reflexes were diminished, making driving more hazardous. People often complained of drowsiness, even at dose levels that should have only been calming them down. Meprobamate also produced both physical and psychological dependence.

Benzodiazepines

The introduction of a new group of drugs, called **benzodiazepines**, was a dramatic departure from all earlier attempts to treat anxiety. On the one hand, for the first time, there now were drugs that had a *selective* effect on anxiety itself, instead of producing a generalized reduction in the body's overall level of functioning. It was their "tranquilizing" effects, rather than their sedative effects, that made benzodiazepines so appealing to mental health professionals. On the other hand, it is important to distinguish between the well-publicized virtues of benzodiazepines when they were first introduced in the 1960s and the data that accumulated during the 1970s as millions of people experienced these new drugs. Although certainly very useful in the treatment of anxiety and other stress-related problems, long-acting benzodiazepines are no longer recognized as the miracle drugs they were promoted to be when they first entered the market.

chloral hydrate: A depressant drug once used for the treatment of insomnia. It is highly reactive with alcohol and can severely irritate the stomach.

methaqualone (MEH-tha-QUAY-lone): A nonbarbiturate depressant drug once used as a sedative. Brand name is Quaalude.

meprobamate (MEH-pro-BAYM-ate): A nonbarbiturate antianxiety drug and sedative. Brand name is Miltown.

benzodiazepines (BEN-zoh-dye-AZ-eh-pins): A family of antianxiety drugs. Examples are diazepam (Valium), chlordiazepoxide (Librium), and triazolam (Halcion).

TABLE 12.5

The leading benzodiazepines on the market

TRADE NAME	GENERIC NAME	ELIMINATION HALF-LIFE (IN HOURS)
Long-acting benzodiazepines		
Valium	Diazepam	20–100
Librium	Chlordiazepoxide	8–100
Limbitrol	Chlordiazepoxide and amitriptyline (an antidepressant)	8–100
Dalmane	Flurazepam	70–160
Tranxene	Clorazepate	50–100
Intermediate-acting benzodiazepines		
Ativan	Lorazepam	10–24
Klonopin	Clonazepam	18–50
Restoril	Temazepam	8–35
ProSom	Estazolam	13–35
Short-acting benzodiazepines		
Versed	Midazolam	2–5
Halcion	Triazolam	2–5
Xanax	Alprazolam	11–18

Note: Klonopin is available in orally disintegrating wafers for panic-attack patients who need the medication in an easily administered form.

Sources: Based on Physicians' desk reference (71st ed.) (2017). Montvale, NJ: PDR Network.

The first marketed benzodiazepine, **chlordiazepoxide** (brand name: Librium), was introduced in 1960, followed by **diazepam** (brand name: Valium) in 1963. Table 12.5 lists the major benzodiazepine drugs currently on the market. Although they are all chemically related, there are variations in their time course or action and, as a result, different recommendations for their medical use. Oral administrations of the relatively long-acting benzodiazepines, in general, are recommended for relief from general anxiety, with the effects beginning 30 minutes to 4 hours after ingestion. When a very quick effect is desired, an injectable form of diazepam is used either to reduce the symptoms of agitation that follow alcohol withdrawal (delirium tremens, or the DTs), as an anticonvulsant for epileptic patients, or as a pre-anesthetic drug to relax the patient just prior to surgery. In contrast, shorter-acting oral benzodiazepines are recommended for sleeping problems because their effects begin more quickly and wear off well before morning.

In general, benzodiazepines are absorbed relatively slowly into the bloodstream, so their relaxant effects last longer and are more gradual than those of barbiturates. The primary reason for these differences lies in the fact that benzodiazepines are absorbed from the small intestine rather than the stomach, as is the case with barbiturates. The relatively greater water solubility and, by implication, the relatively lower fat solubility of benzodiazepines also are factors.

The major advantage that benzodiazepines have over barbiturates and other drugs previously used to control anxiety is their higher level of safety. Respiratory centers in the brain are not affected by benzodiazepines, so it is rare that a person will die of respiratory failure from an accidental or intentional overdose. Even after taking 50 or 60 times the therapeutic dose, the person will still not stop breathing. It is almost always possible to arouse a person from the stupor that such a drug quantity would produce. In contrast, doses of barbiturates or nonbarbiturate sedatives that are 10–20 times the therapeutic dose are lethal. Yet we should understand that this higher level of safety assumes that *no alcohol or other depressant drugs are being taken at the same time.*[34]

Nonetheless, despite the relative safety of benzodiazepines, these medications pose a number of serious risks for special populations. For elderly patients, for example, the rate of elimination of these drugs is slowed down significantly, resulting in the risk of a dangerously high buildup of benzodiazepines after several doses. In the case of a long-acting benzodiazepine such as Valium or Librium, the elimination half-life is as long as 10 days. An elderly patient with this rate of elimination would not be essentially drug free until two months had passed.

The continued accumulation of benzodiazepines in the elderly can produce a form of drug-induced dementia in which the patient suffers from confusion and loss of memory. Without understanding the patient's medication history, these symptoms easily can be mistaken for the onset of Alzheimer's disease. An additional problem with benzodiazepines is the increased risk of falls and bone fractures. It is for these reasons that long-acting benzodiazepines are no longer recommended for this age group, and those who are currently taking these drugs are being encouraged to switch to shorter-acting forms or alternative antianxiety therapies.[35]

The benzodiazepines were viewed originally as having few, if any, problems relating to a tolerance effect or an acquired dependence. We now know that the *anxiety-relieving* aspects of benzodiazepines show little or no tolerance effects when the drugs are taken at prescribed dosages, but there is a tolerance to the *sedative* effects. In other words, if the drugs are taken for the purpose of relieving anxiety, there is no problem with tolerance, but if they are taken for insomnia, more of the drug may be required in later administrations to induce sleep.[36]

We also now know that physiological symptoms appear when benzodiazepines are withdrawn, an indication of benzodiazepine dependence. In the case of long-acting benzodiazepines, the slow rate of elimination delays the appearance of withdrawal symptoms until between the third and sixth day following drug withdrawal. The first signs include an anxiety level that may be worse than the level for which the drug was originally prescribed. Later, there are symptoms of insomnia, restlessness, and agitation. In general, however, withdrawal symptoms are less severe than those observed after barbiturate

chlordiazepoxide (CHLOR-dye-az-eh-POX-ide): A major benzodiazepine drug for the treatment of anxiety. Brand name is Librium.

diazepam (dye-AZ-eh-pam): A major benzodiazepine drug for the treatment of anxiety. Brand name is Valium.

withdrawal, occur only after long-term use, and are gone in one to four weeks.[37]

Benzodiazepine abuse has since declined substantially in psychiatric practice as newer approaches to anxiety disorders have been pursued. Nonetheless, benzodiazepine remains widely prescribed drugs throughout the world, particularly for people over the age of 65 years, to treat problems of insomnia and anxiety. While they are useful for short-term use, unfortunate adverse side effects can arise when benzodiazepines are taken over a long period of time. The potential for cognitive impairment among elderly people and adverse effects when combined with alcohol were discussed earlier in this chapter. These possibilities have been a particular problem in European countries where wine is consumed on a regular basis.[38]

Treating Insomnia

Just as benzodiazepines represented an advance over barbiturates, the development of new nonbenzodiazepine drugs has provided better opportunities to treat mild sleep disorders such as insomnia. Two prominent examples of this new generation of medications are zolpidem and eszopiclone.

Zolpidem (brand name: Ambien) is not a benzodiazepine drug, but it produces some of the effects usually associated with benzodiazepines. As a result, zolpidem is particularly useful in the short-term treatment of insomnia. Its strong but transient sedative effects (with a half-life of about two hours) have led to the marketing of zolpidem, since its introduction in 1993, as a sedative-hypnotic rather than an antianxiety medication. While little or no muscle relaxation is experienced with recommended dosages, there are health risks when combined with other drugs (particularly alcohol) or when exceeding the recommended dosage.

Introduced in 2004, **eszopiclone** (brand name: Lunesta, formerly known as Estorra) is also a nonbenzodiazepine drug that is prescribed for the treatment of insomnia. As a result of successful clinical trials lasting six months, the FDA has approved Lunesta for an interval of treatment that is longer than the recommended treatment with Ambien. Because its half-life of six hours is longer than that of Ambien, Lunesta has been helpful for people who have difficulty in *staying asleep* during the night as well as difficulty in *falling asleep*.[39]

In cases of both zolpidem and eszopiclone, high dosage levels have been found to produce in some patients an impairment in activities that requires full alertness, such as driving, even if they feel fully awake. As a result, the FDA required in 2014 manufacturers to include new cautionary information on the drug label and to lower the recommended starting dose. In addition, a relatively uncommon but disturbing set of side effects has been observed with these medications. Some patients have reported unusual reactions ranging from sleepwalking episodes to sensory hallucinations, binge eating during the night, and even driving while asleep. In these instances, there is no recollection of the events that occurred during the night. Although these side effects are rare from a percentage standpoint, the large number of prescriptions issued for these medications (particularly for the continuous-release form of zolpidem, marketed as Ambien CR) have resulted in a number of widely publicized cases. In 2013, Sanofi-Aventis, manufacturer of Ambien, issued the caution that "After taking Ambien, you may get up out of bed while not being fully awake and do an activity that you do not know you are doing. The next morning, you may not remember that you did anything during the night."[40]

Buspirone, Beta-Blockers, and Antidepressants

In recent years, a number of new medications have been introduced for the treatment of anxiety. They include buspirone, beta-blockers, and antidepressants.

Buspirone (brand name: BuSpar) has several remarkable features. It has been found to be equivalent to benzodiazepines in its ability to relieve anxiety, but, unlike benzodiazepines, buspirone shows no cross-tolerance effects when combined with alcohol or other depressants and no withdrawal symptoms when discontinued after chronic use. When compared with benzodiazepines, side effects are observed less frequently and are less troublesome to the patient; approximately 9 percent report dizziness, and 7 percent report headaches. Animals do not self-administer buspirone in laboratory studies, and human volunteers indicate no feelings of euphoria. Buspirone also fails to show the impairments in motor skills that are characteristic of benzodiazepines. In other words, the relief of anxiety is attainable without the accompanying feelings and behavioral consequences of sedation.

Despite its virtues, however, buspirone has a distinct disadvantage: a very long delay before anxiety relief is felt. It may take weeks for the drug to become completely effective. While this feature makes buspirone clearly inappropriate for relieving *acute* anxiety conditions, patients suffering from long-term generalized anxiety disorder find it helpful as a therapeutic drug. An extra benefit of the delay in the action of buspirone is that it becomes highly undesirable as a drug of abuse. Do not expect to see news headlines in the future warning of an epidemic of buspirone abuse.[41]

The traditional medical uses of beta-adrenergic-blocking drugs, commonly known as **beta-blockers**, include slowing the heart rate, relaxing pressure on the walls of blood vessels,

zolpidem (ZOL-pih-dem): A nonbenzodiazepine sedative-hypnotic drug, first introduced in 1993, for the treatment of insomnia. Brand name is Ambien.

eszopiclone (es-ZOP-eh-clone): A nonbenzodiazepine sedative-hypnotic, first introduced in 2005, for the treatment of insomnia. Brand name is Lunesta.

buspirone (BYOO-spir-rone): A nonbenzodiazepine anti-anxiety drug, first introduced in 1986. Brand name is BuSpar.

and decreasing the force of heart contractions. The combination of a beta-blocker drug and a diuretic is a frequent treatment for the control of high blood pressure. These drugs are also prescribed for individuals facing an anxiety-producing event, such as performing on the stage or giving a speech. Examples of beta-blockers include atenolol (brand name: Tenormin), metoprolol (brand name: Lopressor), and propanolol (brand name: Inderal).[42]

A recent development in the treatment of panic disorder, posttraumatic stress disorder, and social anxiety disorder has been the use of antidepressant medications—specifically, selective serotonin reuptake inhibitors (SSRIs) such as sertraline (brand name: Zoloft) and paroxetine (brand names: Paxil, Asima).

Depressants and Drug-Facilitated Sexual Assault

Undoubtedly, the incidence of sexual assault has become a significant social as well as personal issue, and, in many cases, occurrences of this type have been associated with the voluntary or involuntary consumption of depressant drugs. This is not to say, however, that depressants covered in this chapter are typically involved in sexual assault cases. In fact, the "classic" depressant drug in sexual assault is simple alcohol (see Chapter 13). Nonetheless, it is important to examine here the role of specific "nonalcoholic" depressant drugs, either consumed alone or in combination with alcohol (Portrait).

The Scope of the Problem

Drug-facilitated sexual assault (DFSA) is defined as an instance in which alcohol or other drugs are used to compromise an individual's ability to consent to sexual activity. In addition, drugs and alcohol are often used to minimize the resistance and memory of the victim of a sexual assault. In a national survey in 2011, about 18 percent of women in the United States reported being a victim of sexual violence at some time in their lives. In a survey of female undergraduates admitted to a hospital-based sexual assault treatment center in Ontario, Canada, between 2005 and 2007, 21 percent suspected that they were drugged. Studies vary in their reported incidences of alcohol intoxication among DFSA victims, but the numbers are very high. Between 65 and 96 percent of victims, depending on the study, report alcohol consumption on a voluntary basis prior to the assault. From police records of sexual assault cases, however, it is not often clear as to whether the perpetrator was intoxicated at the time of the crime (Figure 12.2).[43]

> **beta-blockers:** Medicinal drugs that are traditionally used to treat cardiac and blood pressure disorders. They are also prescribed for individuals who suffer from "stage fright" or anxiety regarding a specific event. Examples include atenolol (brand name: Tenormin), metoprolol (brand name: Lopressor), and propanolol (brand name: Inderal).

Quick Concept Check 12.2

Understanding the Abuse Potential in Drugs

Each of the following statements describes a particular attribute of a new drug. Based on material in this chapter, judge whether each description, when taken by itself, either increases or decreases the abuse potential of the drug.

1. Drug fails to produce euphoria at any dose levels.
2. Drug acts very quickly.
3. Drug is cross-tolerant to barbiturates and alcohol.
4. Drug is not available to the public.
5. There are tolerance effects when taking this drug.
6. The drug can be used without the need for medical supervision of dose or dosage schedule.

Answers: 1. decreases 2. increases 3. increases 4. decreases 5. increases 6. increases

Involvement of Drugs Other Than Alcohol

There are several drugs other than alcohol that have been implicated in DFSA cases. They include Ecstasy and ketamine, flunitrazepam (brand name: Rohypnol), and gamma-hydroxybutyrate (abbreviated GHB).

- Although Ecstasy is traditionally classified as hallucinogens, it has depressant-like properties. In the case of Ecstasy, DFSA victims may feel extreme relaxation and sensitivity toward others, as well as an increased sensitivity to touch. While under influence, individuals may be less likely to be aware of danger or protect themselves from attack.[44]

- **Rohypnol** is a long-acting benzodiazepine, not unlike diazepam (Valium), except that it is approximately 10 times stronger. Since it is highly synergistic with alcohol (see Chapter 8), it is particularly dangerous in DFSA situations. In one study, 9 percent of DFSA victims reported having consumed Rohypnol.[45] Street names for Rohypnol include "roofies," "rope," "wolfies," "roches," and "R2." Although it is not legally available in the United States, Rohypnol is approved for medical use in Europe and South America, where it is marketed by Hoffmann–La Roche Pharmaceuticals as a treatment for sleep disorders and as a surgical anesthetic. The U.S. supply of Rohypnol is smuggled into the country from Mexico and South America and sold for recreational use, frequently in its original bubble packaging. Since 1996, U.S. federal law provides for a 20-year sentence for the use of Rohypnol in connection with rape or other violent crime.

- **Gamma-hydroxybutyrate (GHB)** is a colorless, odorless, and virtually tasteless depressant drug, easily slipped into an alcoholic beverage without the knowledge of the drink-

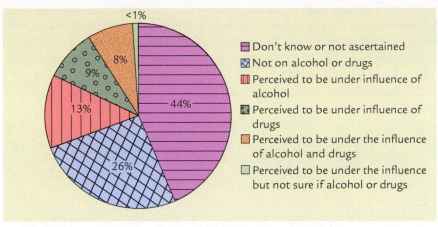

Legend:
- Don't know or not ascertained
- Not on alcohol or drugs
- Perceived to be under influence of alcohol
- Perceived to be under influence of drugs
- Perceived to be under the influence of alcohol and drugs
- Perceived to be under the influence but not sure if alcohol or drugs

Pie chart values: <1%, 8%, 9%, 13%, 44%, 26%

FIGURE 12.2

Perceptions of victims of rape, sexual assault, verbal threats of rape, or verbal threats of sexual assault with regard to alcohol and/or drug use by the perpetrator.

Source: Based on data from the Bureau of Justice Statistics (2011, May). *Criminal victimization in the United States, 2010, Statistical tables.* Washington, D.C.: Bureau of Justice Statistics, U.S. Department of Justice.

er. It produces euphoria, and an "out-of-body" high with an accompanying lowering of inhibitions. At one time, GHB was sold in health-food stores and similar establishments. It was considered to have steroid-enhancing and growth-hormone-stimulating effects, leading to interest among bodybuilders. Other promotions focused on GHB as a sedative. By 1990, however, numerous reports of GHB-related seizures and comas led to its removal from the legitimate drug market. Reports of GHB in DFSA cases are uncommon (the incidence rate varies between 1 and 4 percent). Nonetheless, the fact that it is virtually undetectable makes it potentially dangerous in these circumstances.[46]

Efforts to Reduce Drug-Facilitated Sexual Assaults

It is difficult to ascertain the relative involvement of various depressants (other than alcohol) in DFSA cases for a number of reasons. Victims of sexual assault are frequently amnesic to the circumstances prior to their attack or may be reluctant to reveal details of events leading up to the attack, particularly if voluntary drug-taking behavior had occurred. They may not acknowledge that drugs played a role.

Rohypnol (Ro-HIP-nol): The brand name for a benzodiazepine drug, illegal in the United States but available for medical use in Europe and South America. It has been implicated in instances of drug-facilitated sexual assault. The generic name is flunitrazepam.

gamma-hydroxybutyrate (GHB) (GAM-ma heye-DROX-ee-BYOO-tih-rate): A powerful depressant, often abused to induce euphoria and sedation. When slipped in an alcoholic beverage without the knowledge of the drinker, GHB has been used as a date-rape drug.

Recent developments in target screening for drugs through hair samples (see Chapter 16) have been useful in forensic studies carried out to identify specific drugs that may have been implicated in DFSA cases. In these circumstances, urine or blood samples are frequently unavailable. However, since there are only small-sample reports of hair analyses in DFSA cases, it is not possible to say which depressant drugs are most frequently involved.[47]

In some cases, the manufacturers of depressant drugs have taken steps to reduce the involvement of their product in sexual assault. Hoffmann–La Roche, the manufacturer of Rohypnol, has reformulated the drug so that it turns blue when dissolved in a clear liquid. This helps to make Rohypnol somewhat more noticeable to an unsuspecting drinker, but it is important to realize that it is difficult to notice discernible changes in beverage color under the dim illumination conditions of a typical bar. Besides, blue dye in blue tropical drinks

These bar coasters are commercially available to detect the presence of GHB in an alcoholic beverage.

Credit: Eric Risberg/AP Images

and punches produces no color change at all. A test strip developed by Drink Safe Technologies is available for the detection of GHB and ketamine (but not for Rohypnol). A straw can be used to place a few drops of one's drink on the test strip. If the liquid turns blue, there is a positive result. Unfortunately, when the drink contains dairy products, an accurate detection cannot be made. Bar coasters have been developed that incorporate this particular test strip (see Help Line).[48]

Drugs... in Focus

Protective Strategies against Drug-Facilitated Sexual Assault

There are several protective strategies to reduce the possibility of a drug-facilitated sexual assault. They include the following:

- Watch the person who pours you a drink, even if he or she is a friend or a bartender. Even better, do not drink what you cannot open or pour yourself. Avoid punch bowls and shared containers. Never accept a drink offered to you by a stranger.

- Do not leave a drink alone—not while you are dancing, using the restroom, or making a telephone call. If you have left it alone, it is better to toss the beverage.

- Appoint a designated "sober" friend to check up on you at parties, bars, clubs, and other social gatherings.

- If a friend seems extremely drunk or sick after a drink and has trouble breathing, call 911 immediately.

- If you have been slipped GHB, the drug will take effect within 10–30 minutes. Initially, you will feel dizzy or nauseous, or develop a severe headache. You can be incapacitated rapidly. This is the time when having a nondrinking friend nearby is crucial.

- If you wake up in a strange place and believe that you have been sexually assaulted while under the influence of GHB, do not urinate until you have been admitted to a hospital. There is an approximately 12-hour window of opportunity to detect GHB through urinalysis.

Where to go for assistance?

The following Web site is sponsored by the National Woman's Health Information Center, a service of the U.S. Department of Health and Human Services dedicated to women's health issues. *www.4woman.gov/faq/rohypnol.html*

Source: Information courtesy of the Rape, Abuse, and Incest National Network (RAINN), Washington, D.C.

Summary

A Matter of Definition

- Hallucinogens are, by definition, drugs that produce distortions of perception and of one's sense of reality. These drugs have also been called psychedelic ("mind-expanding") drugs. In some cases, users of hallucinogens feel that they have been transported to a new reality.

- Other classes of drugs may produce hallucinations at high-dose levels, but hallucinogens produce these effects at low- or moderate-dose levels.

Classifying Hallucinogens

- Hallucinogens can be classified under four basic groups. The first three relate to the chemical similarity between the particular drug and one of three major neurotransmitters: serotonin, norepinephrine, and acetylcholine.

- The fourth miscellaneous group includes synthetic hallucinogens, such as PCP and ketamine, which bear little resemblance to any known neurotransmitter.

Lysergic Acid Diethylamide (LSD)

- Lysergic acid diethylamide, the best-known hallucinogenic drug, belongs to the serotonin group. It is synthetically derived from ergot, a toxic rye fungus that has been

documented as being responsible for thousands of deaths over the centuries.

- Albert Hofmann synthesized LSD in 1943, and Timothy Leary led the psychedelic movement that popularized LSD use in the 1960s.

- Although the LSD experience is often unpredictable, certain features are commonly observed: colorful hallucinations, synesthesia in which sounds often appear as visions, a distortion of perceptual reality, emotional swings, a feeling of timelessness, and an illusory separation of mind from body.

- It is now known that LSD affects a subtype of brain receptors sensitive to serotonin, referred to as serotonin-2A receptors.

- In the early 1990s, there was a resurgence in LSD abuse, particularly among young individuals, a trend that began to reverse in 1997.

Frequently Asked Questions about LSD

- LSD has only a slight chance of inducing a panic or psychotic state (providing that there is a supportive setting for the taking of LSD).

- LSD does not elevate one's level of creativity. A clear relationship between LSD abuse and violent behavior has not been established. Flashback experiences, however, are potential hazards.

Hallucinogens Other Than LSD

- Other hallucinogens related to serotonin are psilocybin, lysergic acid amide (LAA), dimethyltryptamine (DMT), and harmine.

- Mescaline is chemically related to norepinephrine, even though serotonin-2A receptors are responsible for its hallucinogenic effects.

- Two synthetic hallucinogens, DOM and MDMA, are variations of the amphetamine molecule. MDMA (Ecstasy) is currently a popular club drug, presenting serious health risks to the user. Designer synthetic drugs (sold and distributed as "Molly") have purported to be a pure form of MDMA, but forensic analyses reveal that it often contains cathinones and an unknown array of other substances.

- A number of anticholinergic hallucinogens, so named because they diminish the effects of acetylcholine in the parasympathetic nervous system, have been involved in sorcery and witchcraft since the Middle Ages. One such example is ibotenic acid found in *Amanita muscaria* mushrooms.

- A dangerous form of hallucinogen abuse involves phencyclidine (PCP). Originally a psychedelic street drug in the 1960s, PCP quickly developed a reputation for producing a number of adverse reactions, including sudden mood changes, severe anxiety, as well as disordered, confused, and often paranoid thoughts. Extremely aggressive tendencies, as well as behaviors resembling acute schizophrenia, have been associated with PCP intoxication.

Barbiturates and Nonbarbiturate Sedative-Hypnotics

- Until approximately 1960, the primary sedative-hypnotics (drugs that produce sedation and sleep) belonged to the barbiturate family of drugs.

- Barbiturates are typically classified by virtue of how long their depressant effects are felt, from long acting (example: phenobarbital) to intermediate acting (examples: butalbital and amobarbital) to short acting (examples: pentobarbital and secobarbital).

- A major disadvantage of barbiturates is the potential of a lethal overdose, particularly when combined with other depressants such as alcohol. In addition, barbiturate withdrawal symptoms are very severe and require careful medical attention.

- Methaqualone (Quaalude) was introduced in the 1960s as an alternative to barbiturates for sedation and sleep. Unfortunately, this drug produced undesirable side effects and became subject to widespread abuse. It is no longer available as a licit drug.

Antianxiety Drugs

- Beginning in the 1950s, a major effort was made by the pharmaceutical industry to develop a drug that would relieve anxiety (tranquilize) rather than merely depress the CNS (sedate).

- Meprobamate (Miltown) was introduced in 1955 for this purpose, though it is now understood that the effects of this drug result more from its sedative properties than its ability to relieve anxiety.

Benzodiazepine and Nonbenzodiazepine Depressants

- The introduction of benzodiazepines, specifically diazepam (Valium) and chlordiazepoxide (Librium), in the early 1960s, was a significant breakthrough in the development of antianxiety drugs. These drugs selectively affect specific receptors in the brain instead of acting as general depressants of the nervous system.

- In general, benzodiazepines are safer drugs than barbiturates, when taken alone. When taken in combination with alcohol, however, dangerous synergistic effects are observed.

- Social problems concerning the taking of benzodiazepine drugs during the 1970s centered on the widespread misuse of the drug. Prescriptions were written too frequently and for excessive dosages.

- Recently developed nonbenzodiazepines have provided better opportunities to treat insomnia. Zolpidem (brand name: Ambien) and eszopiclone (Lunesta) have been useful as a sedative-hypnotic in the treatment of insomnia. They have strong but transient sedative effects and produce little or no muscle relaxation.

- Buspirone (brand name: BuSpar) has been useful as an antianxiety medication that does not cause sedation. Beta-blockers, traditionally used to treat cardiac and blood pressure disorders, have been prescribed for individuals who are facing an anxiety-producing event, such as performing on the stage or speaking in public.

- Certain antidepressants called selective serotonin reuptake inhibitors (SSRIs) have been successful in treating a variety of anxiety disorders.

Depressants and Drug-Facilitated Sexual Assaults

- Although alcohol is clearly the most prominent depressant drug implicated in drug-facilitated sexual assaults, other depressants have also been identified, either singly or in combination with alcohol. These depressants include Ecstasy and ketamine, Rohypnol, and gamma-hydroxybutyrate (GHB).

- Efforts have been made to reformulate Rohypnol to make it somewhat more noticeable to an unsuspecting drinker that Rohypnol and alcohol have been combined. Special bar coasters containing test strips are commercially available to aid in identifying depressant drugs that might have been slipped into an alcoholic drink.

- A number of protective strategies have been promoted to minimize the risk of drug-facilitated sexual assault.

Key Terms

Review Questions

1. Describe the characteristic features of the LSD experience. Write a sentence or two in the first-person with regard to each of these effects, as though you were taking LSD and reporting your personal reaction to the experience.
2. Discuss four frequently asked questions about LSD and provide a short answer for each.
3. Describe the effects of any four of the non-LSD hallucinogens and include the characteristics that distinguish them from those of LSD.
4. Discuss the current concerns with the designer synthetic drug called Molly. Explain how the promotion of Molly as a pure form of MDMA is likely to be inaccurate.
5. What have been the advantages of benzodiazepines as anti-anxiety medications in comparison to barbiturates and other sedative-hypnotics?
6. Describe the scope of the problem of drug-facilitated sexual assault and identify four depressant drugs (other than alcohol) that have been implicated in cases of this type.
7. Describe at least three strategies that can reduce the risk of drug-facilitated sexual assault.

Critical Thinking: What Would You Do?

You are at a music concert and a close friend of yours (someone you have known most of your life and trust implicitly) hands you a powder that he or she has obtained. He or she calls it "Molly" and assures you that it is a pure form of Ecstasy. You have used Ecstasy in the past. Your friend is willing to take this drug along with you. Given the material in this chapter, what would *you* do? How would you respond to your friend?

Endnotes

1. Adapted from Smalley, S. (2003, February 3). "The perfect crime": GHB is colorless, odorless, leaves the body within hours—and is fueling a growing number of rapes. *Newsweek*, p. 52.
2. Fuller, John C. (1967). *The day of St. Anthony's fire.* New York: Macmillan, preface.
3. Hofmann, Albert (1980). *LSD: My problem child.* New York: McGraw-Hill, p. 17.
4. Lattin, D. (2010). *The Harvard psychedelic club.* New York: HarperCollins. Leary, T. (1973). The religious experience: Its production and interpretation. In Gunther Weil; M. Ralph; and L. Timothy (Eds.), *The psychedelic reader.* Secaucus, NJ: Citadel Press. Quotation on p. 191. Lee, M. A.; and Shlain, B. (1985). *Acid dreams: The complete social history of LSD.* New York: Grove Weidenfeld, pp. 71–118.
5. Greenfield, R. (2006). *Timothy Leary: A biography.* New York: H. Silberman Book/Harcourt. Grinspoon, L.; and Bakalar, J. B. (1979). *Psychedelic drugs reconsidered.* New York: Basic Books, p. 68. Leary, T. (1968). *High priest.* New York: New American Library, p. 46. Manchester, W. R. (1974). *The glory and the dream: A narrative history of America, 1932–1972.* Boston: Little, Brown, p. 1362.
6. Grinspoon, L.; and Bakalar, J. B. (1979). *Psychedelic drugs reconsidered.* New York: Basic Books, p. 68.
7. Brown, F. C. (1972). *Hallucinogenic drugs.* Springfield, IL: Charles C. Thomas, pp. 46–49. Goode, E. (2008). *Drugs and American society* (7th ed.). New York: McGraw-Hill College, p. 260. Schuckit, M. A. (1995). *Drug and alcohol abuse: A clinical guide to diagnosis and treatment* (4th ed.). New York: Plenum, pp. 189–190.

8. Fysh, R. R.; Oon, M. C. H.; Robinson, K. N.; Smith, R. N.; White, P. C.; and Whitehouse, M. J. (1985). A fatal poisoning with LSD. *Forensic Science International, 28,* 109–113.

9. Goode, E. (2012). *Drugs in American society* (8th ed.). New York: McGraw-Hill, pp. 47–48.

10. Aghajanian, G. K.; and Marek, G. J. (1999). Serotonin and hallucinogens. *Neuropsychopharmacology, 21* (Suppl. 2), 16S–23S. Gresch, P. J.; Smith, R. L.; Barrett, R. J.; and Sanders-Bush, E. (2005). Behavioral tolerance to lysergic acid diethylamide is associated with reduced serotonin-2A receptor signaling in rat cortex. *Neuropsychopharmacology, 30,* 1693–1702. Julien, Robert M. (2005). *A primer of drug action* (10th ed.). New York: Worth, p. 602.

11. Johnston, L. D.; O'Malley, P. M.; and Bachman, J. G. (2000). *Monitoring the future. National survey results on drug use. 1975–1999. Vol. I: Secondary school students.* Ann Arbor, MI: The University of Michigan, Table D-12. Johnston, L. D.; O'Malley, P. M.; Miech, R. A.; Bachman, J. G.; Schulenberg, J. E.; and Patrick, M. E. (2018). *Monitoring the future. National survey results on drug use 1975–2017. Vol. I. Secondary school students.* Ann Arbor, MI: The University of Michigan, Table 4-1b.

12. Cohen, S. (1960). Lysergic acid diethylamide: Side effects and complications. *Journal of Nervous and Mental Diseases, 130,* 30–40. Levine, J.; and Ludwig, A. M. (1964). The LSD controversy. *Comprehensive Psychiatry, 5*(5), 314–321

13. Wells, B. (1974). *Psychedelic drugs: Psychological, medical, and social issues.* New York: Jason Aronson, pp. 170–188.

14. Abraham, H. D. (1983). Visual phenomenology of the LSD flashback. *Archives of General Psychiatry, 40,* 884–889. Halpern, J. H.; and Pope, H. G. (1999). Do hallucinogens cause residual neuropsychological toxicity? *Drugs and Alcohol Dependence, 53,* 247–256. Schlaadt, R. G.; and Shannon, P. T. (1994). *Drugs: Use, misuse, and abuse.* Englewood Cliffs, NJ: Prentice Hall, p. 273.

15. Knudsen, K. (1964). Homicide after treatment with lysergic acid diethylamide. *Acta Psychiatrica Scandinavica, 40* (Supplement 180), 389–395.

16. Hofmann, *LSD*, p. 112.

17. Johnston, O'Malley, Miech, Bachman, Schulenberg, and Patrick (2018), *Monitoring the future*, Table 9-8. Vollenweider, F. X.; Vollenweider-Scherpenhuyzen, M. F. I.; Babler, A.; Vogel, H.; and Hell, D. (1998). Psilocybin induces schizophrenia-like psychosis in humans via a serotonin-2 agonist action. *Neuroreport, 9,* 3897–3902.

18. Hofmann, *LSD*, pp. 119–127. Schultes, R. E.; and Hofmann, A. (1979). *Plants of the gods: Origins of hallucinogenic use.* New York: McGraw-Hill.

19. Brands, B.; Sproule, B.; and Marshman, J. (1998). *Drugs and drug abuse: A reference text.* Toronto, Canada: Addiction Research Foundation, pp. 512–513.

20. Frecska, E.; White, K. D.; and Luna, L. E. (2003). Effects of Amazonian psychoactive beverage *ayuhuasca* on binocular rivalry: Interhemispheric switching or interhemispheric fusion? *Journal of Psychoactive Drugs, 35,* 367–374. Grinspoon and Bakalar, *Psychedelic drugs reconsidered,* pp. 14–15. Trichter, S.; Klimo, J.; and Krippner, S. (2009). Changes in spirituality among ayahuasca ceremony novice participants. *Journal of Psychoactive Drugs, 41,* 121–134.

21. Ibid, pp. 20–21. Hollister, L. E.; and Sjoberg, B. M. (1964). Clinical syndromes and biochemical alterations following mescaline, lysergic acid diethylamide, psilocybin, and a combination of the three psychotomimetic drugs. *Comprehensive Psychiatry, 5,* 170–178.

22. Jacobs, B. I. (1987). How hallucinogenic drugs work. *American Scientist, 75,* 386–393.

23. Brecher, E.; and the editors of *Consumer Reports* (1972). *Licit and illicit drugs.* Boston: Little, Brown, pp. 376–377.

24. Cloud, J. (2000, June 5). The lure of ecstasy. *Time,* pp. 62–68. Drug Enforcement Administration (2014). *MDMA (Ecstasy) or Molly?* Washington, D.C.: Drug Enforcement Administration, U.S. Department of Justice. Feuer, A. (2000, August 6). Distilling the truth in the ecstasy buzz. *The New York Times,* pp. 25, 28. Leshner, A. I. (2002). Ecstasy abuse and control: Hearing before the Senate Subcommittee on Governmental Affairs—July 30, 2001. Statement for the record. *Journal of Psychoactive Drugs, 34,* 133–135. Martins, S. S.; Mazzotti, G.; and Chilcoat, H. D. (2005). Trends in ecstasy use in the United States from 1995 to 2001: Comparison with marijuana users and association with other drug use. *Experimental and Clinical Psychopharmacology, 13,* 244–252. Schwartz, R. H.; and Miller, N. S. (1997). MDMA (Ecstasy) and the rave: A review. *Pediatrics, 100,* 705–708. Leshner, A. I. (2002). Ecstasy abuse and control: Hearing before the Senate Subcommittee on Governmental Affairs—July 30, 2001. Statement for the record. *Journal of Psychoactive Drugs, 34,* 133–135.

25. Boils, K. I. (1999). Memory impairment in abstinent MDMA ("Ecstasy") users. *Journal of the American Medical Association, 281,* 494. Boils, K. I. (1999). Memory impairment in abstinent MDMA ("Ecstasy") users. *Journal of the American Medical Association, 281,* 494. Chonin, N. (2003, April 27). Congress acts out against club culture. *San Francisco Chronicle,* p. 35. Vollenweider, F. X.; Liechti, M. E.; Gamma, A.; Greer, G.; and Geyer, M. (2002). Acute psychological and neurophysiological effects of MDMA in humans. *Journal of Psychoactive Drugs, 34,* 171–184.

26. Johnston, O'Malley, Miech, Bachman, Schulenberg, and Patrick (2018), *Monitoring the future,* Table 4-1a.

27. Wasson, R. G. (1968). *Soma: Devine mushroom of immorality.* New York: Harcourt, Brace and World.

28. Cohen, S. (1964). *The beyond within: The LSD story.* New York: Atheneum, p. 17.

29. Cohen, S. P.; Bhatia, A.; Buvanendran, A.; Schwenk, E. S; and Wasan, A. D.; et al. (2018), Consensus guidelines on the use of intravenous ketamine infusions for chronic pain from the American Society of Regional Anesthesia and Pain Medicine, the American Academy of Pain Medicine, and the American Society of anesthesiologists. *Regional Anesthesia and Pain Medicine, 43,* 521–546. Davis, K. (2017, October 12). What are the uses of ketamine? Medical News Today. Accessed from: https://www.medicalnewstoday.com/articles/302663.php. Hartney, E. (2017, July 29). What is a k hole? Accessed from: https://www.verywell.com/what-is-a-k-hole-21861. Petersen, R. C.; and Stillman, R. C. (1978). Phencyclidine: An overview. In R. C. Petersen; and R. C. Stillman (Eds.), *Phencyclidine (PCP) abuse: An appraisal* (NIDA Research Monograph 21). Rockville, MD: National Institute on Drug Abuse, pp. 1–17.

30. Palfai, T.; and Jankiewicz, H. (1991). *Drugs and human behavior.* Dubuque, IA: W. C. Brown, p. 203.

31. Julien, R. M.; Advokat, C. D.; and Comaty, J. E. (2011). *A primer of drug action* (12th ed.). New York: Worth, p. 242.

32. Kauffman, J. F.; Shaffer, H.; and Burglass, M. E. (1985). The biological basics: Drugs and their effects. In T. E. Bratter;

and G. G. Forrest (Eds.), *Alcoholism and substance abuse: Strategies for clinical intervention.* New York: Free Press, pp. 107–136.

33. Schulenberg, J. E.; Johnston, L. D.; O'Malley, P. M.; Bachman, J. G.; Miech, R. A.; and Patrick, M. E. (2018). *Monitoring the future: National survey results on drug use, 1975–2017, Vol. II: College students and adults ages 19–55.* Ann Arbor, MI: University of Michigan, Table 2-2.

34. Tanaka, E. (2002). Toxicological interactions between alcohol and benzodiazepines. *Journal of Toxicology—Clinical Toxicology, 40,* 69–75.

35. Cumming, R. G.; and LeCouteur, D. G. (2003). Benzodiazepines and risk of hip fractures in older people: A review of the evidence. *CNS Drugs, 17,* 825–837. Salzman, C. (1999). An 87-year-old woman taking a benzodiazepine. *Journal of the American Medical Association, 281,* 1121–1125.

36. Rickels, K.; Case, W. G.; Downing, R. W.; and Winokur, A. (1983). Long-term diazepam therapy and clinical outcome. *Journal of the American Medical Association, 250,* 767–771.

37. Longo, L. P.; and Johnson, B. (2000). Addiction: Part I. Benzodiazepines—Side effects, abuse risk and alternatives. *American Family Physician, 61,* 2121–2128.

38. Lagnaouli, R.; Moore, N,; Dartigues, J. F.; Fourrier, A.; and Bégaud, B. (2001). Benzodiazepine use and wine consumption in the French elderly. *British Journal of Clinical Pharmacology, 52,* 455–456. Pimlott, N. J. G.; Hux, J. E.; Wilson, L. M.; Kahan, M.; Li, C.; and Rosser, W. W. (2003). Educating physicians to reduce benzodiazepine use by elderly patients: A randomized controlled trial. *Canadian Medical Association Journal, 168,* 835–839.

39. Gershell, L. (2006). From the analyst's couch: Insomnia market. *Nature Reviews and Drug Discovery, 5,* 15–16.

40. FDA requiring lower starting dose for sleep drug Lunesta (2014, May 15). FDA News Release, U.S. Food and Drug Administration, Washington, D.C. Medication Guide for Ambien. Sanofi-Aventis, U.S., L.L.C., Bridgewater, NJ.

41. Julien; Akvokat; and Comaty, *A primer of drug action,* pp. 261–262.

42. Naftel, K. A.; Adler, R. H.; Kappeli, L.; Rossi, M.; Dolder, M.; et al. (1982). Stage fright in musicians: A model illustrating the effect of beta blockers. *Psychosomatic Medicine, 44,* 461–469.

43. Definition courtesy of the Rape, Abuse, and Incest National Network (RAINN), Washington, D.C. Du Mont, J.; Macdonald, S.; Rotbard, N.; Asllani, E.; Bainbridge, D.; et al. (2009). Factors associated with suspected drug-facilitated sexual assault. *Canadian Medical Journal, 180,* 513–519. The National Center for Injury Prevention and Control (2011, November). *Executive summary of the national intimate partner and sexual violence survey.* Atlanta, GA: Centers for Disease Control and Prevention. Hurley, M.; Parker, H.; and Wells, D. L. (2006). The epidemiology of drug facilitated sexual assault. *Journal of Clinical Forensic Medicine, 13,* 181–185. Lawyer, S.; Resnick, H.; Bakanic, V.; Burkett, T.; and Kilpatrick, D.(2010). Forcible, drug-facilitated, and incapacitated rape and sexual assault among undergraduate women. *Journal of American College Health, 58,* 453–460.

44. Rape, Abuse, and Incest National Network (RAINN).

45. Lawyer; Resnick; Bakanic; Burkett; and Kilpatrick, Forcible, drug-facilitated, and incapacitated rape and sexual assault among undergraduate women, p. 457.

46. Dyer, J. E. (2000). Evolving abuse of GHB in California: Bodybuilding drug to date-rape drug. *Journal of Toxicology—Clinical Toxicology, 38,* 184. Lawyer; Resnic; Bakanic; Burkett; and Kilpatrick, Forcible drug-facilitated and incapacitated rape, p. 457. Németh, Z.; Kun, B.; and Demetrovics, Z. (2010). The involvement of gamma-hydrobutyrate in reported sexual assaults: A systematic review. *Journal of Psychopharmacology, 24,* 1281–1287.

47. Staikos, V.; Beyer, J.; Gerostamoulos, D.; and Drummer, O. H. (2010). Targeted screening for common drugs of abuse in hair samples. *Pathology, 42,* 528.

48. Information regarding bar coasters courtesy of Drink Safe Technologies, Wellington, Florida.

chapter **13**

Alcohol Misuse and Alcohol-Related Crime

"It's funny but at the same time, really sad," a friend and colleague said to me recently. "People don't understand that alcohol is a drug —a psychoactive drug."

"They might say something like 'Bob drinks a little too much, but at least he's not doing drugs.' It's incredible. Here we have a legal commodity in America that causes so many problems for millions of people, so many devastating effects on family life and personal health. Think of the innocent children born with fetal alcohol syndrome or the thousands of people who die from car accidents every year. And yet, we don't see it as drug abuse, when it really is. It's like talking about the drug problem in America today—over a six-pack."

"I couldn't agree with you more," I replied, "I teach a course that deals with drug abuse and its effect on society. The course is called 'Drugs and Alcohol.' Because I know that my students wouldn't expect to cover the effects of alcohol in a course that was simply called 'Drugs.'"

For the record, my friend and I were having this conversation over a cup of coffee, not beer. This is not to say we weren't engaging in drug-taking behavior. The caffeine in our coffee is a psychoactive drug, although fortunately much more benign than alcohol.

After you have completed this chapter, you should have an understanding of the following:

- How alcohol is processed in the body
- Patterns of alcohol consumption among at-risk groups
- Acute physiological and behavioral effects of alcohol
- The relationship between alcohol misuse and crime
- Strategies for responsible alcohol consumption and regulation
- Patterns of chronic alcohol abuse
- Physiological and behavioral aspects of chronic alcohol abuse
- Diagnosis, treatment, and support strategies for chronic alcohol abuse

Alcohol consumption is so tightly woven into the social fabric of our lives that it is easy to forget about the possible consequences of drinking too much too often.[1] An alcoholic drink is often regarded as simply a social beverage, when in actuality it is a social drug. This chapter deals with the psychoactive properties of alcohol and its psychological, legal, and social consequences. In the first section, we will examine the acute effects of alcohol consumption, particularly with regard to the consequences of drinking in excessive amounts. In the second section, we will examine how alcohol consumption impacts crime, and the steps that have been taken to regulate alcohol misuse. Next, the chronic effects of alcohol consumption is explored, focusing on the consequences of drinking over an extended period of time. At the end, we will review the treatment options available for chronic alcohol abuse.

We begin by asking a basic question: What happens to that alcoholic beverage after you drink it?

The Processing of Alcohol

There are three basic types of alcoholic beverages: wine, beer, and distilled spirits. Table 13.1 shows the sources of some well-known examples. The psychoactive factor in all of them is alcohol, a very small molecule that is moderately soluble in fat and highly soluble in water—all characteristics that make it easily absorbed through the gastrointestinal tract once it is ingested and easily absorbed into the brain. About 20 percent of it enters the bloodstream directly from the stomach, whereas the remaining 80 percent enters from the upper portion of the small intestine.

Because the small intestine assumes the lion's share of the responsibilities and acts extremely rapidly (more rapidly than the stomach), the rate of total alcohol absorption is based largely on the condition of the stomach when the alcohol arrives and the time required for the stomach to empty its contents into the small intestine. If the stomach is empty, the intoxicating effect ("buzz") will be felt very quickly. If the stomach is full, absorption will be delayed as the alcohol is retained by the stomach along with the food being digested, and the passage of alcohol into the small intestine slows down.

In addition to the condition of the stomach at the time, there are other factors related to the alcohol itself and the behavior of the drinker that influence the rate of alcohol absorption. The principal factor is the concentration of alcohol in the beverage being ingested. An ounce of 80-proof liquor (equivalent to an alcohol content of 40 percent) will be felt more quickly than an ounce of wine containing 12 percent alcohol, and of course the level of alcohol in the blood will be higher as well. Also, if the alcoholic beverage is carbonated, as are champagne and other sparkling wines, the stomach will empty its contents faster and effects will be felt sooner. Finally, if the alcohol enters the body at a rapid pace, such as when drinks are consumed in quick succession, the level of alcohol in the blood will be higher because the liver cannot eliminate it fast enough. All other factors being equal, a larger person requires a larger quantity of alcohol to have equivalent levels accumulating in the blood, simply because there are more body fluids to absorb the alcohol, thus diluting the overall effect.[2]

Its solubility in water helps alcohol to be distributed to all bodily tissues, with those tissues having greater water content receiving a relatively greater proportion of alcohol. The excretion of alcohol is accomplished in two basic ways. About 5 percent will be eliminated by the lungs through exhalation, causing the characteristic "alcohol breath" of heavy drinkers. Breathalyzers, designed to test for alcohol concentrations in the body and used frequently by law enforcement officials to test for drunkenness, work on this principle. The remaining 95 percent is eliminated in the urine, after the alcohol has been biotransformed into carbon dioxide and water.[3]

The body recognizes alcohol as a visitor with no real biological purpose. It contains calories but no vitamins, minerals, or other components that have any nutritional value. Therefore, the primary bodily response is to break it down for eventual removal, through a process called **oxidation**.

> **oxidation:** A chemical process in alcohol metabolism.

Numbers Talk...

24   Percentage of underage young adults in the United States, age 19–20 years, who have reported binge drinking (5+ drinks consumed on one occasion).

10   Percentage of underage young adults in the United States, age 19–20 years, who have reported high-intensity drinking (10+ drinks consumed on one occasion).

28   Percentage of all traffic-related deaths in the United States. in 2016 due to an alcohol-impaired driver.

Sources: Centers for Disease Control and Prevention (2017). Impaired driving: Get the Facts. Atlanta, GA: Centers for Disease Control and Prevention. https://www.cdc.gov/motorvehiclesafety/impaired_driving/impaired-drv_factsheet.html. Patrick, M. E.; and Terry-McElrath, Y. M. (2017). High-intensity drinking by underage young adults in the United States. *Addiction, 112,* 82–93. Data collected from the annual nationally representative Monitoring the Future study, including 1657 respondents surveyed when 19–20 years of age in 2006–2014.

TABLE 13.1

Prominent alcoholic beverages and their sources

BEVERAGE	SOURCE	BEVERAGE	SOURCE
Distilled spirits		**Wines**	
Brandy	Distilled from grape wine, cherries, or peaches	Red table wine	Fermented red grapes with skins
		White table wine	Fermented skinless grapes
Liqueur or cordial	Brandy or gin, flavored with blackberry, cherry, chocolate, peppermint, licorice, etc. Alcohol content ranges from 20% to 55%	Champagne	White wine bottled before yeast is gone so that remaining carbon dioxide produces a carbonated effect
Rum	Distilled from the syrup of sugar cane or from molasses	Sparkling wine	Red wine prepared like champagne or with carbonation added
Scotch whiskey	Distilled from fermented corn and barley malt or in the case of single malt Scotch whiskey, distilled from barley malt exclusively.	**Fortified wines**	Wines whose alcohol content is raised or fortified to 20% by the addition of brandy—for example, sherry, port, Marsala, and Madeira
Rye whiskey	Distilled from rye grain and barley malt		
Blended whiskey	A mixture of two or more types of whiskey		
Bourbon whiskey	An American whiskey distilled from fermented corn, named in honor of the French Bourbon dynasty by early settlers in Louisiana and Kentucky	**Wine-like variations**	
Gin	Distilled from barley, potato, corn, wheat, or rye, and flavored with juniper berries	Hard cider	Fermented apples
		Sake	Fermented rice
Vodka	Approximately 95% pure alcohol, distilled from grains or potatoes and diluted by mixing with water	**Beers**	Types of beer vary depending on brewing procedures.
Tequila	Distilled from the fermented juice of the maguey plant	Draft beer	Contains 3%–6% alcohol
Grain neutral spirits	Approximately 95% pure alcohol, used either for medicinal purposes or diluted and mixed in less-concentrated distilled spirits	Lager beer	Contains 3%–6% alcohol
		Ale	Contains 3%–6% alcohol
		Malt liquor	Contains up to 8% alcohol

Source: Based on Becker, C. E.; Roe, R. L.; and Scott, R. A. (1979). *Alcohol as a drug: A curriculum on pharmacology, neurology, and toxicology.* Huntington, NY: Robert Krieger Publishing, pp. 10–12.

In general, the oxidation rate for adults is approximately one-third to one-half ounce of pure alcohol per hour. If you sipped (not gulped) slightly less than the contents of one 12-ounce bottle of beer, one 5-ounce glass of wine, or any equivalent portion of alcohol (see Drugs…in Focus, page 279) very slowly over an hour's time, the enzymes in the stomach and liver would keep up, and you would not feel intoxicated. Naturally, if you consumed larger amounts of alcohol at faster rates of consumption, all bets would be off.[4]

Alcohol on the Brain

Alcohol is clearly a CNS-depressant drug, though it is often misidentified as a stimulant. The reason for this confusion is that alcohol, at low doses, first releases the cerebral cortex from inhibitory control over subcortical systems in the brain, a kind of double-negative effect. In other words, alcohol is depressing an area of the brain that normally would be an inhibitor, and the result is the illusion of stimulation. The impairment in judgment and thinking (the classic features of being drunk) stems from a loosening of social inhibitions that enable us, under nonalcoholic circumstances, to be relatively thoughtful about the consequences of our actions, as well as relatively civil and well behaved. Motor control will be reduced as well, resulting in impulsive behavior.[5]

Measuring Alcohol Levels in the Blood

The degree of alcohol intoxication is directly related to alcohol levels in the blood. Therefore, it is important to consider how these levels are measured.

The **blood alcohol concentration (BAC)** of an individual who has consumed alcohol refers to the number of grams of alcohol in the blood relative to 100 milliliters of blood, expressed as a percentage. For example, 0.1 gram (100 milligrams) of alcohol in 100 milliliters of blood is represented by a BAC of 0.10 percent.

blood alcohol concentration (BAC): The number of grams of alcohol in the blood relative to 100 milliliters of blood, expressed as a percentage. An alternate term is blood-alcohol level (BAL).

TABLE 13.2

Calculating blood concentration levels in men and women

Drinks	MEN — Approximate blood alcohol concentration (BAC) — Body weight (pounds)								
	100	120	140	160	180	200	220	240	
0	.00	.00	.00	.00	.00	.00	.00	.00	Only safe driving limit
1	.04	.03	.03	.02	.02	.02	.02	.02	Caution
2	.08	.06	.05	.05	.04	.04	.03	.03	
3	.11	.09	.08	.07	.06	.06	.05	.05	
4	.15	.12	.11	.09	.08	.08	.07	.06	Driving impaired
5	.19	.16	.13	.12	.11	.09	.09	.08	
6	.23	.19	.16	.14	.13	.11	.10	.09	
7	.26	.22	.19	.16	.15	.13	.12	.11	Legally intoxicated
8	.30	.25	.21	.19	.17	.15	.14	.13	
9	.34	.28	.24	.21	.19	.17	.15	.14	
10	.38	.31	.27	.23	.21	.19	.17	.16	

Drinks	WOMEN — Approximate blood alcohol concentration (BAC) — Body weight (pounds)									
	90	100	120	140	160	180	200	220	240	
0	.00	.00	.00	.00	.00	.00	.00	.00	.00	Only safe driving limit
1	.05	.05	.04	.03	.03	.03	.02	.02	.02	Caution
2	.10	.09	.08	.07	.06	.05	.05	.04	.04	
3	.15	.14	.11	.10	.09	.08	.07	.06	.06	
4	.20	.18	.15	.13	.11	.10	.09	.08	.08	Driving impaired
5	.25	.23	.19	.16	.14	.13	.11	.10	.09	
6	.30	.27	.23	.19	.17	.15	.14	.12	.11	
7	.35	.32	.27	.23	.20	.18	.16	.14	.13	Legally intoxicated
8	.40	.36	.30	.26	.23	.20	.18	.17	.15	
9	.45	.41	.34	.29	.26	.23	.20	.19	.17	
10	.51	.45	.38	.32	.28	.25	.23	.21	.19	

Alcohol is "burned up" by your body at .015 percent per hour, as follows:

Hours since starting first drink	1	2	3	4	5	6
Percent alcohol burned up	.015	.030	.045	.060	.075	.090

To calculate your BAC level correctly, you must consider the number of standard drinks you have consumed, your gender and body weight, and how much time has passed since the first drink. All U.S. states have now adopted the 0.08 percent standard for drunk driving.

Source: Based on information from Julien, R. M. (2001). *A primer of drug action* (9th ed.). New York: Worth, p. 317, and the Pennsylvania State Liquor Control Board, Harrisburg, PA.

As shown in Table 13.2, BAC levels are calculated in terms of four factors: (1) gender, (2) one's body weight, (3) the amount of alcohol consumed, and (4) the number of hours elapsed since starting the first drink. In order to calculate your BAC, choose the correct chart (male or female), find the column corresponding to your approximate weight in pounds and the row corresponding the number of "standard drinks" consumed (see page 279), then subtract 0.015 for every hour since drinking began.

In all U.S. states, a BAC level of 0.08 percent and higher is the standard for "legal intoxication." In some cases, the standards are more stringent. According to regulations of the U.S. Department of Transportation, truck drivers are tested and prevented from driving at a BAC level of 0.04 percent and airline pilots are prevented from flying at a BAC level of 0.02 percent (after 24 hours of abstinence).[6]

Measuring Alcohol Consumption

The estimated annual per capita consumption of pure alcohol for adults in the United States is approximately 2.3 gallons (8.7 liters). This level of consumption amounts to about three-fourths of an ounce of pure alcohol per day.[7]

How many alcoholic drinks does this estimated daily amount add up to? It is important to consider the amount of pure alcohol that is contained in each of four basic types of alcoholic beverages (Drugs…in Focus), in order to answer this question. An equivalent amount of alcohol (one-half fluid ounce) is contained in the following alcoholic beverages in the amounts indicated:

- One 5-ounce glass of wine
- One 12-ounce bottle or can of beer
- One 12-ounce bottle of wine cooler
- One shot (1.5-ounce size) of 80-proof liquor

Because all four of these drinks are approximately equal in their alcoholic content, they are referred to as "standard drinks."

Based on these equivalencies, the average alcohol consumption in the United States can be approximated as about 1.5 "standard drinks" per day. Bear in mind, however, that a "standard drink" may not be the drink you typically consume. You have to be careful in computing your own personal level of alcohol consumption. Draft beer, for example, is typically dispensed in large glasses that exceed 12 ounces in capacity. A mixed drink in a bar might contain a quantity of liquor that

Drugs . . . in Focus

Multiple Ways of Getting a Standard Drink

A standard alcoholic drink is any drink that contains about 14 grams of pure alcohol (about 0.5 fluid ounce). All of the following seven alcoholic drinks should be considered equivalently as a standard drink.

12 oz of beer or wine cooler	8–9 oz of malt liquor 8.5 oz shown in a 12-oz glass that, if full, would hold about 1.5 standard drinks of malt liquor	5 oz of table wine*	3–4 oz of fortified wine (such as sherry or port) 3.5 oz shown	2–3 oz of cordial, liqueur, or aperitif 2.5 oz shown	1.5 oz of brandy (a single jigger)	1.5 oz of spirits (a single jigger of 80-proof gin, vodka, whiskey, etc.) Shown straight and in a highball glass with ice to show level before adding mixer†
12 oz	8.5 oz	5 oz	3.5 oz	2.5 oz	1.5 oz	1.5 oz

There are so many variations in the quantity of an alcoholic beverage being served that it can be confusing to determine as to how many standard drinks are actually being consumed. Here are some examples of how the number of standard drinks can multiply when quantities increase:

- For beer or wine cooler, the approximate number of standard drinks in
  - 12 oz = 1   • 16 oz = 1.3   • 22 oz = 2   • 40 oz = 3.3
- For malt liquor, the approximate number of standard drinks in
  - 12 oz = 1.5   • 16 oz = 2   • 22 oz = 2.5   • 40 oz = 4.5
- For table wine, the approximate number of standard drinks in
  - a standard 750 mL (25 oz) bottle = 5
- For 80-proof spirits, or "hard liquor," the approximate number of standard drinks in
  - a mixed drink = 1 or more**   • a pint (16 oz) = 11   • a fifth (25 oz) = 17   • 1.75 L (59 oz) = 39

*In recent years it has been common for wines to contain an alcohol concentration of 16 percent. In these instances, 5 ounces of wine would be equivalent to 0.80 ounces of alcohol, which is 33 percent higher than when a 12 percent wine is considered. Another way of thinking about this is that for a drink of wine with 16 percent alcohol concentration to be equivalent to a 12-ounce can of beer or a typical shot of liquor, the quantity of wine consumed should be reduced to approximately 4 ounces. In this chapter, however, we will retain the concept of 5 ounces of wine as representing a standard drink, since it is traditional that alcohol equivalencies are calculated on this basis.

**It can be difficult to estimate the number of standard drinks served in a single mixed drink made with hard liquor. Depending on factors such as the type of spirits and the recipe, one mixed drink can contain from one to three or more standard drinks.

Source: National Institute on Alcohol Abuse and Alcoholism (2005). *Helping patients who drink too much: A clinician's guide.* Bethesda, MD: National Institute on Alcohol Abuse and Alcoholism, p. 12.

exceeds a standard amount, if the bartender is particularly generous. In either of these circumstances, an individual can be misled into believing that he or she is consuming an "average" amount (in terms of drinks) when, in fact, the quantity of alcohol being consumed is considerably larger.

It is useful to look at average statistics when considering alcohol consumption, but it is obvious that not everyone is "average." There is an enormous disparity in terms of how much alcohol each person actually consumes during a given year. Some people drink no alcohol at all, whereas others drink heavily. *In fact, 80 percent of the total amount of alcohol consumed in the United States each year is consumed by only the 30 percent of Americans who drink and only 20 percent of the population in general.* The following Drugs . . . in Focus provides a graphic demonstration of the lop-sided distribution in alcohol consumption in the United States today.

Drugs ... in Focus

Visualizing the Pattern of Alcohol Consumption in the United States

To appreciate the uneven pattern of alcohol consumption in the population, try the following demonstration:

Assemble 10 people and 10 bottles of beer (preferably empty).

Separate three people who hold nothing. They represent the 30 percent of the population that does not drink alcohol at all.

Separate five people; together they hold two bottles. They represent the 50 percent of the population that drinks 20 percent of the total alcohol supply.

Separate the ninth person; this person holds two bottles. This individual represents the 10 percent of the population that drinks another 20 percent of the total alcohol supply.

Separate the tenth person; this person holds a six-pack of bottles. This individual represents the 10 percent of the population that drinks 60 percent of the total alcohol supply.

The Moral of the Story

Twenty percent of the entire population (the ninth and tenth persons in this demonstration) drink 80 percent of the total alcohol consumed in the United States each year. Of those who drink some alcohol, two-sevenths (roughly 30 percent) of them drink 80 percent of the total alcohol consumed each year, while five-sevenths (roughly 70 percent) of them drink the remaining 20 percent. These figures correspond to those expressed in the text.

A Tale of 10 Beers and 10 People

3 drink none

5 share 2 beers

1 drinks 2

1 drinks 6

Source: Kinney, G. J. (2006). *Loosening the grip: A handbook of alcohol information* (8th ed.). New York: McGraw-Hill, p. 30.

Alcohol Consumption among At-Risk Groups

Unlike many of the other substances reviewed in the chapters of this book, alcohol can legally be consumed, and even abused, so long as a person is not violating a law. Easy access to alcohol, combined with a culture that looks favorably on the social aspects of alcohol consumption, makes it likely that there would be populations that are at risk for alcohol misuse, which often leads to both social and legal consequences. The pressure to engage in alcohol abuse as a college student is more pronounced than with any other group; freedom from parental supervision, alcohol availability, and the social pressure to engage in alcohol consumption create substantial risk for college students. Prior to college, middle and high school students are often pressured to engage in alcohol misuse, when they are particularly vulnerable to the need for peer acceptance. This too can lead to significant social consequences, as well as legal consequences related to underage drinking. These populations will be discussed in the section that follows.

Quick Concept Check 13.1

Understanding Alcoholic Beverages

Check your understanding of the alcohol content of various types of alcoholic beverages by rank ordering the alcohol content of the following five "bar orders," with "1" representing the largest amount and "5" the smallest. Are there any ties?

_____ A. Three 1-shot servings of liquor and one 5-oz glass of wine
_____ B. Two 1-shot servings of liquor
_____ C. One 1-shot serving of liquor, one 5-oz glass of wine, and three 12-oz beers
_____ D. Three 5-oz glasses of wine
_____ E. One 1-shot serving of liquor, one 5-oz glass of wine, and one 12-oz beer

Answers: 1 = C   2 = A   3 = D and E (tie)   5 = B

Alcohol Consumption among College Students

Not surprisingly, the prevalence of moderate alcohol consumption in college (assessed in terms of those having a drink in the last 30 days) is substantially higher than levels encountered in high school. The establishment of 21 as the mandated legal drinking age in all U.S. states has delayed the occurrence of *peak* consumption levels to the junior or senior year in college. Among young adults, *binge drinking*—defined for men as having five or more alcoholic drinks and for women as having four or more alcoholic drinks over a period of two hours—rises sharply from age 18, peaks at ages 21–22, and then steadily declines over the next 10 years. The prevalence of *daily* drinking also rises from levels encountered in high school but remains relatively stable afterward, through age 32.

An extensive series of surveys conducted from 1993 to 2015 on American college campuses have shown a fairly consistent picture of the drinking patterns of college students in the United States over this period of time. Here are the general findings:

- Overall, approximately 38 percent of college students, aged 18–22, report having engaged in binge drinking during the two weeks prior to the administration of the survey—37 percent of the women and 39 percent of the men—compared to 33 percent of 18–22-year-olds not enrolled in college. For young people reporting heavy alcohol use the past month, 13 percent were in college and 9 percent not enrolled full time in college.[8]

- College students who drank alcohol at some time over the past year frequently report alcohol-related problems while at college. One in four students report that their drinking had a negative impact on their academic performance. Problems included missing a class, failing behind on course assignments, doing poorly on exams or papers, and receiving lower grades overall.[9]

- Alcohol use among college students also has an impact on public safety. Nearly 20 percent of all 21–25-year-olds reported driving under the influence of illicit drugs or alcohol, and approximately 1,825 students, aged 18–24, die from unintended alcohol-related injuries each year, most of which involve motor vehicle accidents.[10] Additionally, nearly 700,000 students were assaulted by another student while under the influence, with about 97,000 alcohol-related sexual assaults reported.[11]

- Alcohol and drug use are common contributors to campus sexual assault. One study found that during their first year of college, 15 percent of women experience incapacitated sexual assault.[12] Incapacitation means victims are unable to give consent due to their physical state, which may be the result of voluntary or involuntary substance use (see Chapter 12 for non-alcohol circumstances). Unfortunately, only one in five college-age women who are sexually assaulted end up reporting the incident to the police.[13]

Individual, campus, and community-based interventions have been used to address the issue of college drinking, particularly targeting those in higher-risk student groups, including freshman, athletes, and Greek-involved youth. Interventions are designed to teach students the harmful effects of binge or excessive drinking, as well as address students' attitudes and behavior around drinking, by teaching skills to manage high-risk situations that involve alcohol use. Environmental, or community-based strategies are also employed, many of which are aimed at limiting alcohol access to underage drinkers. The College Alcohol Intervention Matrix (referred to as CollegeAIM) is a resource tool for schools interested in evidence-based individual and environmental strategies to combat the problem of alcohol misuse.[14]

Alcohol Consumption among Underage Drinkers

Alcohol use often begins by middle school. In fact, among young people who report some alcohol consumption between the ages of 12 and 20, *the average age when drinking began is 14 years*. In 2016, about a third of all 15-year-olds reported having had at least one drink in their lives and a fourth of them had at least one drink in the past year.[15] In the 2017 Monitoring the Future survey, 17 percent of high school seniors, 10 percent of tenth graders, and 4 percent of eighth graders reported binge drinking (5+ drinks on a single occasion). Binge drinking had declined since the 1990s by 72 percent for eighth graders, 59 percent for tenth graders, and 47 percent for seniors. However, extreme binge drinking in 2017 among underage drinkers remains a very great concern. As many as 6 percent of high school seniors surveyed in 2017 reported consuming 10 or more drinks in a row in the last two weeks, and 3 percent reported consuming 15 or more drinks in a row during that period of time.[16]

Although the downward trend in underage drinking is encouraging, the major challenge in reducing underage alcohol use still lies in the continuing access that underage drinkers have to alcoholic beverages, despite the legal restrictions on alcohol sales. Among an estimated 7.2 million underage drinkers in 2016, defined as persons aged 12–20 who drank in the past 30 days, 34 percent reported that the alcohol had

Binge drinking among young adults continues to be both a social ritual and a social concern.

Credit: FXQuadro/Shutterstock

been provided free by an adult aged 21 or older. About 19 percent of underage drinkers were given alcohol free by a parent, guardian, or another family member in the past month. About one-half (52 percent) reported drinking alcohol in someone else's home, about one-third (35 percent) drank in their own home, and about 7 percent reported drinking alcohol in a restaurant, bar, or club. When compared to comparable statistics regarding underage drinkers in 2013, the total number of underage drinkers in 2016 had decreased by roughly 16 percent, but the percentages relating to the sources of alcohol and the locations of alcohol drinking were relatively the same.[17]

Underage drinking comes with several significant risks. Youth who begin drinking prior to age 15 are four times more likely to develop an alcohol use disorder later in life, relative to those who wait to drink alcohol until age 21.[18] Among 12th graders, a higher frequency of alcohol use is significantly associated with unsafe driving, including traffic tickets, warnings, or accidents.[19] About one-third of young people have reported riding with a driver impaired on alcohol or marijuana.[20]

Fortunately, as with the drop in the prevalence of underage drinking, drunk driving fatalities have also dropped. There was an overall decrease of 51 percent in drunk driving fatalities between 1982 and 2016, and an 80 percent decrease involving drivers under 21 years of age. Twenty-two U.S. states have seen even greater decreases in drunk driving fatalities for those under 21 over this period of time.[21]

Alcohol Consumption among an Offender Population

A large number of people in the criminal justice system have problems with alcohol and other drugs. About one-third of convicted offenders on parole or probation report that they had been drinking at the time of their offense.[22] Nearly 25 percent of state inmates report having experienced problems with alcohol consistent with a diagnosis of alcohol use disorder.[23] These data suggest that alcohol misuse is an important target for correctional programs. Underscoring the importance is what we know about risk factors that predict who will become repeat offenders. Substance abuse, including the use or misuse of alcohol, is a key risk factor, meaning offenders that abuse substances are more likely to reoffend than those that do not.[24] While this certainly includes DUI and violent offenders, offender problems with alcohol and other drugs increase the risk of reoffense for a wide range of criminal behaviors.

Alcohol abuse contributes to criminal behavior in a number of ways. Those who misuse alcohol often spend time with others who consume alcohol and drugs. When offenders spend time with others who have been or are presently involved in criminal behavior, they are more likely to get in trouble again. As discussed earlier, alcohol decreases natural inhibitions, which can increase the likelihood of decisions to engage in behaviors such as breaking into a car or home, or assaulting someone at a bar. Regular alcohol misuse can interfere with getting and keeping a job, as well as developing healthy ways of coping with stress and spending time with family and friends.

In most cases, individuals on community supervision (probation or parole) are required to abstain from alcohol use and avoid establishments that sell alcohol, such as bars and clubs. Community supervision may be revoked for individuals violating this condition, requiring them to return to prison. In a study of federal probationers, substance abuse was a risk factor for violating probation or parole. Reductions in substance abuse scores for high- and moderate-risk offenders corresponded with a decreased risk of reoffending overall.[25]

Chapter 7 reviewed correctional supervision and treatment strategies specific to an offender population. If individuals in trouble with the law are to refrain from a lifetime of criminal behavior, problems with alcohol (and other drugs) must be addressed. Specific strategies for treating those with a diagnosis of alcohol use disorder will be discussed later in the chapter.

Acute Physiological Effects of Alcohol

Alcohol can produce a number of immediate physiological effects; they will be examined here. The physiological effects resulting from *chronic* alcohol consumption will be covered later in the chapter.

Toxic Reactions

First and foremost, we have to be aware that potential death by asphyxiation can occur if BAC levels are elevated, generally when levels reach 0.50 percent. In general, the therapeutic index for alcohol, as measured by the LD50/ED50 ratio (see Chapter 1), is approximately 6. This figure is not very high, and caution is strongly advised; the risks of being the "big winner" in a drinking contest should be weighed very carefully.

On the one hand, to achieve a lethal BAC level of 0.50 percent, a 160-pound man needs to have consumed approximately 23 drinks over a four-hour period.[26] On the other hand, consuming 10 drinks in one hour, a drinking schedule that achieves a BAC level of 0.23 percent, puts a person in dangerous territory (see Table 13.2). We need to remember that LD50 is a statistic referring to the dose that is likely to be lethal with 50 percent probability. There is no way to predict where a particular person might be on the normal curve!

Fortunately, two mechanisms are designed to protect us to a degree from a lethal dose of alcohol. First, alcohol acts as a gastric irritant so the drinker will feel nauseated and vomit. Second, the drinker may simply pass out, and the potential

Help Line

Emergency Signs and Procedures in Acute Alcohol Intoxication

Emergency Signs

- Stupor or unconsciousness
- Cool or damp skin
- Weak, rapid pulse (more than 100 beats per minute)
- Shallow and irregular breathing rate, averaging around one breath every three or four seconds
- Pale or bluish skin

Note: Among African Americans, color changes will be apparent in the fingernail beds, mucous membranes inside the mouth, or underneath the eyelids.

Emergency Procedures

- Seek medical help immediately.
- Drinker should lie on his or her side, with the head slightly lower than the rest of the body. This will prevent blockage of the airway and possible asphyxiation if the drinker starts to vomit.

- If drinker is put to bed, maintain some system of monitoring until he or she regains consciousness.

Note: There is no evidence that home remedies for "sobering up," such as cold showers, strong coffee, forced activity, or induction of vomiting, have any effect in reducing the level of intoxication. The only factors that help are the passage of time, rest, and perhaps an analgesic if there is a headache.

Where to go for assistance

www.postgradmed.com/issues/2002/12_02/yost1.htm.

This Web site is adapted from Yost, D. A. (2002). Acute care for alcohol intoxication: Be prepared to consider clinical dilemmas. *Postgraduate Medicine Online.*

Source: Victor, M. (1976). Treatment of alcohol intoxication and the withdrawal syndrome: A critical analysis of the use of drugs and other forms of therapy. In P. G. Bourne (Ed.), *Acute drug abuse emergencies: A treatment manual.* New York: Academic Press, pp. 197–228.

from further drinking becomes irrelevant. Nonetheless, there are residual dangers in becoming unconscious. Vomiting while in an unconscious state can prevent breathing, and death can occur from asphyxiation (Help Line).

Heat Loss and the Saint Bernard Myth

Alcohol is a peripheral dilator, which means that blood vessels near the skin surface enlarge, leading to a greater amount of blood shunted to the skin. The effect gives you the feeling that your skin is warm, which is most likely the basis for the myth that alcohol can keep you warm in freezing weather. In truth, peripheral dilation causes core body temperature to *decrease*. In other words, alcohol produces a greater loss in body heat than would occur without it. So if you are marooned in the snow and you see an approaching Saint Bernard with a cask of brandy strapped to its neck, politely refuse the offer. It will not help and could very well do you harm. (But feel free to hug the dog! That will certainly help.)

Diuretic Effects

As concentration levels rise in the blood, alcohol begins to inhibit the secretion of **antidiuretic hormone (ADH)**, a hormone that normally acts to reabsorb water in the kidneys prior to elimination in the urine. As a result, urine is more diluted and, because large amounts of liquid are typically being consumed at the time, more copious. Once blood alcohol concentrations have peaked, however, the reverse occurs. Water is now retained in a condition called **antidiuresis**, resulting in swollen fingers, hands, and feet. This effect is more

pronounced if salty foods (peanuts or pretzels, for example) were eaten along with the alcohol.

The inhibition of ADH during the drinking of alcoholic beverages can be a serious concern, particularly following vigorous exercise when the body is already suffering from a loss of water and fluid levels are low. Therefore, the advice to the marathoner, whose body may lose more than a gallon of water over the course of a warm three-hour run, is to celebrate the end of the race not with a beer but with nonintoxicating liquids such as Gatorade or similar mineral-rich drinks.[27]

Effects on Sleep

It might seem tempting to induce sleep with a relaxing "nightcap," but in fact the resulting sleep patterns are adversely affected. Alcohol reduces the duration of a phase of sleep called rapid eye movement (REM) sleep, in the same way as do barbiturates (see Chapter 12). Depending on the amount of alcohol consumed, REM sleep can be either partially or completely suppressed during the night. When alcohol is withdrawn, REM sleep rebounds and represents a higher percentage of total sleep time than before alcohol consumption began. As a result, individuals sleep poorly and experience nightmares.[28]

antidiuretic hormone (ADH): A hormone that acts to reabsorb water in the kidneys prior to excretion from the body.

antidiuresis: A condition resulting from excessive reabsorption of water in the kidneys.

Effects on Pregnancy

The consumption of alcohol during pregnancy, even in moderation, greatly increases the risk of retardation in the development of the fetus, and reducing the incidence of this behavior has been a major public health objective since the mid-1990s. National data from 2011 to 2013 estimate that 10 percent of pregnant women report consuming alcohol within the past 30 days, exposing 1 in 10 fetuses to alcohol in utero.[29]

Interactions with Other Drugs

A major concern in alcohol drinking is the complex interaction of alcohol with many drugs. There is an extremely high incidence of medical crises arising from the combination of alcohol not only with prescribed medications but also with virtually all the illicit drugs on the street. Opioids, marijuana, and many prescription medications interact with alcohol such that the resulting combination produces effects that are either the sum of the parts or greater than the sum of the parts. In other cases, the ingestion of medications with alcohol significantly lessens the medication's benefits. Anticoagulants, anticonvulsants, and MAO-inhibitors (used as antidepressant medications) fit into this second category. Table 13.3 shows a partial listing of major therapeutic drugs that interact with

alcohol and have undesirable, if not dangerous, outcomes. *The complete list is so long that it is fair to say that, whenever any medication is taken, the individual should inquire about possible interactions with alcohol.*

Hangovers

About 4–12 hours after heavy consumption of alcohol, usually the next day, unpleasant symptoms of headache, nausea, fatigue, and thirst may occur; these are collectively known as a *hangover*. At least one such experience has been undergone by 40 percent of all men and 27 percent of all women over the age of 18.[30]

The probable explanations at present focus on individual aspects of a hangover, though it is likely that several factors contribute to the total phenomenon. One factor in the development of hangover, beyond the simple fact of drinking too much, is the type of alcohol that has been consumed. Among distilled spirits, for example, vodka has a lower probability of inducing hangovers than whiskey. A possible reason is the relatively lower amount of **congeners**. These substances in alcoholic beverages, including trace amounts of nonethyl alcohol, oils, and other organic matter, are by-products of the fermentation and distillation processes and give the drinks their distinctive smell, taste, and color. A common congener is the tannin found in red wines. Although no harm is caused

---

TABLE 13.3

A partial listing of possible drug–alcohol interactions

GENERIC DRUG (BRAND NAME OR TYPE)	CONDITION BEING TREATED	EFFECT OF INTERACTION
Chloral hydrate (Noctec)	Insomnia	Excessive sedation that can be fatal; irregular heartbeat; flushing
Glutethimide (Doriden)	Insomnia	Excessive sedation; reduced driving and machine-operating skills
Antihypertensives (Apresoline, Diuril)	High blood pressure	Exaggeration of blood pressure-lowering effect; dizziness on rising
Diuretics (Aldactone)	High blood pressure	Exaggeration of blood pressure-lowering effect; dizziness on rising
Antibiotics (penicillin)	Bacterial infections	Reduced therapeutic effectiveness
Nitroglycerin (Nitro-bid)	Angina pain	Severe decrease in blood pressure; intense flushing; headache; dizziness on rising
Warfarin (Coumadin)	Blood clot	Decreased anti-blood clotting effect, easy bruising
Insulin	Diabetes	Excessive low blood sugar; nausea; flushing
Disulfiram (Antabuse)	Alcoholic drinking	Intense flushing; severe headache; vomiting; heart palpitations; could be fatal
Methotrexate	Various cancers	Increased risk of liver damage
Phenytoin (Dilantin)	Epileptic seizures	Reduced drug effectiveness in preventing seizures; drowsiness
Prednisone (Deltasone)	Inflammatory conditions (arthritis, bursitis)	Stomach irritation
Various antihistamines	Nasal congestion	Excessive sedation that could be fatal
Acetaminophen (Tylenol)	Pain	Increased risk of liver damage

Sources: National Institute on Alcohol Abuse and Alcoholism (1995, January). *Alcohol Alert: Alcohol-medication interactions.* No. 27. Bethesda, MD: National Institute on Alcohol Abuse and Alcoholism. Office of Substance Abuse Prevention (1988). *The fact is... It's dangerous to drink alcohol while taking certain medications.* Rockville, MD: National Institute on Drug Abuse. Parker, C. (1985). *Simple facts about combinations with other drugs.* Phoenix, AZ: Do It Now Foundation.

---

by congeners in minute concentrations, they are still toxic substances, and probably contribute to hangover symptoms.

Other possible factors include traces of nonoxidized acetaldehyde in the blood, residual irritation in the stomach, and a low blood sugar level rebounding from the high levels induced by the previous ingestion of alcohol. The feeling of swollenness from the antidiuresis, discussed earlier, may contribute to the headache pain. The thirst may be due to the dehydration that occurred the night before.[31]

Acute Behavioral Effects of Alcohol

The consumption of alcoholic beverages is so pervasive in the world that it seems almost unnecessary to comment on how it feels to be intoxicated by alcohol. The behavioral effects of consuming alcohol in more than very moderate quantities range from the relatively harmless effects of exhilaration and excitement, talkativeness, slurred speech, and irritability to behaviors that have the potential for causing great harm: uncoordinated movement, drowsiness, sensorimotor difficulties, and stupor. Some of the prominent behavioral problems associated with acute alcohol intoxication will be examined in this section.

Blackouts

A **blackout** is an inability to remember events that occurred during the period of intoxication, even though the individual was conscious at the time. For example, a drinker having too much to drink at a party drives home, parks the car on a nearby street, and goes to bed. The next morning, he or she has no memory of having driven home and cannot locate the car. This phenomenon is different from "passing out," which is a loss of consciousness from alcoholic intoxication. In the case of blackouts, consciousness is never lost.

Owing to the possibility of blackouts, drinkers can be misled into thinking that because they can understand some information given to them during drinking, they will remember it later. The risk of blackouts is greatest when alcohol is consumed very quickly, forcing the BAC to rise rapidly. In an e-mail survey of college students, conducted in 2002, to learn more about their experiences with blackouts, approximately half of those who had ever consumed alcohol reported having experienced a blackout at some point in their lives and 40 percent reported having had at least one experience in the 12 months prior to the survey.[32]

Sex and Sexual Desire

If they were asked, most people would say that alcohol has an enhancing or aphrodisiac effect on sexual desire and performance. The actual effect of alcohol, however, is more complex than what we commonly believe. In fact, it is because of these beliefs that people are frequently more susceptible to the expectations of what alcohol *should* do for them than they are to the actual physiological effects of alcohol.

To examine the complex relationship between alcohol and sex, we need to separate the possible pharmacological effects of alcohol and the possible expectations about what alcohol is supposed to do (see Chapter 8). It turns out that the general results of studies of this kind are quite different for men and women.

Among men, those who expected to be receiving low levels of alcohol had greater penile responses, reported greater subjective arousal, and spent more time watching erotic pictures, *regardless of whether they did indeed receive alcohol.* When alcohol concentrations rose to levels that reflected genuine intoxication, however, the pharmacological actions outweighed the expectations. The overall effect was definitely inhibitory. Drunk males had less sexual desire and a decreased capacity to perform sexually.

In contrast, expectations among women played a lesser role. They were more inclined to react to the pharmacological properties of alcohol itself, but the direction of their response depended on whether the measures being studied are subjective or physiological. For women receiving increasing alcohol concentrations, measures of subjective arousal increased but measures of vaginal arousal decreased. The pattern of their responses mirrors Shakespeare's observation in *Macbeth* that alcohol "provokes the desire, but it takes away the performance," a comment originally intended to reflect only the male point of view. Evidently, in the case of males, alcohol takes away both the desire *and* the performance.[33]

The Legal Consequences of Alcohol Misuse

Mens re is the Latin term for "guilty mind." Most crimes require mens rea, meaning that the accused must have an intention or knowledge of wrongdoing of the crime committed. The question becomes, if the accused lacked mens rea for a crime due to intoxication, is he or she culpable? The U.S Supreme Court case of *Montana v. Egelhoff* (1996) ruled that a voluntarily intoxicated person should be responsible for the consequences of the intoxication.[34] Given the number of crimes that are committed under the influence of alcohol and other drugs, this finding has had a major impact on the prosecution of criminal cases involving alcohol misuse on the part of the defendant.

The consequences of alcohol misuse can range from the mild annoyance of disorderly conduct to the heartbreaking tragedy of fatalities on the highway. We begin with the most devastating circumstance: the combination of alcohol consumption and driving.

blackout: Amnesia concerning events occurring during the period of alcoholic intoxication, even though consciousness had been maintained at that time.

congeners (KON-jen-ers): Nonethyl alcohols, oils, and other organic substances found in trace amounts in some distilled spirits.

Driving Under the Influence

There is no question that alcohol consumption significantly impairs one's ability to drive responsibly. In 2016, 10,497 people were killed in alcohol-related accidents, accounting for more than one-quarter of all motor vehicle traffic fatalities in the United States, of which 17 percent where children under age 15. To put this statistic in perspective, there were approximately 29 alcohol-related fatalities every day during that year (one instance every 50 minutes).[35]

Most of these alcohol-related fatalities resulted from conditions in which drivers had a BAC of 0.08 percent or higher, the minimum standard for legal intoxication in all U.S. states, but there were also a number of fatalities associated with the driver having a BAC less than 0.08 percent. It is important to recognize that driving can be impaired with BAC levels as low as 0.02–0.04 percent, which are well below the "driving while intoxicated" (DWI) threshold. In addition to driving a car while intoxicated, it is also illegal in many states to operate a boat under the influence. Alcohol is recognized as a major factor in more than 800 boating fatalities in the United States each year.

All these statistics could be viewed as correlational and not necessarily proof of a causal relationship between alcohol and motor vehicle accidents, were it not for laboratory-based experimental data showing a clear deterioration of sensorimotor skills following the ingestion of alcohol. Reaction times are slower, the coordination necessary to steer a car steadily is hampered, and the ability to stay awake when fatigued is impaired, but the major way that alcohol impairs driving ability is the reduction in the drinker's awareness of peripheral events and stimuli.[36]

In 2016, an estimated one million people were arrested for driving under the influence. Regionally, rates of U.S. DUI arrests were highest in west, followed by the mid-west, south, and then northeast. The most common age group for DUI arrests were 25–29 year olds, with 82 percent of those arrested being white drivers.[37]

Driving under the influence (DUI), driving while intoxicated (DWI), operating under the influence (OUI), or operating while impaired/intoxicated (OWI) are all terms used to describe drunk (or drugged) driving. Often these terms are used interchangeably, but in some states, a DWI offense is more serious, as it is used to identify drivers with a higher BAC. In other states, DWI is used for drunk driving while DUI or OUI is the term used for driving under the influence of drugs. Typically, a first- or second-time DUI is a misdemeanor level offense, which carries less serious penalties than a felony offense. However, individuals convicted of a third DUI typically face felony charges. Also, aggravating circumstances, such as having a child in the car, causing an accident or injury to someone, driving on a suspended license, or having a BAC far above the legal limit can increase DUI charges and penalties.

DUI arrests typically begin with an officer pulling over an individual who is driving erratically, but other minor driving violations can result in being pulled over, which could ultimately lead to a DUI if the driver is impaired. Once pulled over, the officer may engage in standardized field sobriety tests (SFST). There are three SFST: **Horizontal Gaze Nystagmus (HGN)**, **one-leg-stand**, and the **walk-and-turn** test. Nystagmus refers to an involuntary jerking movement in the eyes. This test is typically conducted with officers asking drivers to follow a pen moving side to side across the driver's field of vision with their eyes, while keeping their head still. The one-leg-stand requires that drivers stand with feet together and arms at their sides, then raise one leg 6 inches off the ground, while counting according to the officer's instructions. The walk-and-turn test asks that drivers walk a straight line, heal to toe for several paces, turn, and walk back several paces, with arms at their sides. The latter two tests look for balance and being able to follow the officer's instructions. Officers are supposed to demonstrate the tests and avoid making any rapid movements that could distract the driver. Of the three field tests, the HGN is generally considered the most reliable for determining intoxication.[38]

Field tests are useful for detecting impaired drivers with a high BAC, but officers are not always able to detect moderate intoxication with field tests alone. Hence, in addition to SFST, chemical tests, such as a Breathalyzer, designed to measure BAC levels can be administered at the scene. A chemical BAC test also allows for a more objective measure of driving over the limit (0.08 percent BAC), undeterminable with field tests. With the increase in drugged driving, many jurisdictions also use blood or urine tests as well to identify alcohol or drug intoxication. These are typically administered at the police station.

What if a driver simply refuses a chemical test? Under the Fourth Amendment, drivers can refuse to have their

Every community has its tragic, often heartbreaking, stories of preventable deaths due to drunk driving.

Credit: Victor Biro/Alamy Stock Photo

Horizontal Gaze Nystagmus (HGN): A field sobriety test that observes a person's eye movement while tracking a moving object.

one-leg-stand: A field sobriety test requiring a driver to stand on one leg while remaining balanced and following instructions.

walk-and-turn: A field sobriety test requiring a driver to walk a straight line while remaining balanced and following instructions.

vehicles or possessions searched without a warrant, and at one time, many drivers refused chemical testing as well. **Implied consent laws** were developed in the mid-1980s to resolve this issue. These laws are based on the premise that driving is a privilege, not a right; as such, drivers make an implicit agreement that by accepting a driver's license, they have consented to chemical tests, when requested.[39] Before these laws were put into place, drivers that refused chemical testing could still be charged with a DUI based on officer observation, but drivers had nothing to lose by refusing chemical tests, and convictions in these cases were more likely to be challenged in court. Now if individuals refuse a chemical test, they are subject to immediate license suspension, jail time, fines, and even the installation of an ignition interlock device (to be described below). If DUI charges are issued, the refusal of a chemical test can be used against the person in subsequent trial proceedings. In states like Texas, officers choose which of the three chemical tests will be used, while states like California and Florida allow drivers to decide.

Laws like implied consent were among many initiatives that sought to strengthen the penalties against drunk drivers. During the 1980s, which was the heart of the "tough on crime" era, there was strong public concern about drunk driving. Prominent victim advocacy from groups like Mothers Against Drunk Driving (MADD) helped lower the BAC limit for impaired driving and strengthen the penalties against drunk drivers (see Portrait later in the chapter). Whether a result of increasing penalties for DUIs, increasing public awareness and prevention efforts, or providing better transportation alternatives (see Drug Enforcement … in Focus), there has been a substantial drop in the number of DUIs and DUI fatalities since the 1980s.

Violent Crimes

The link between alcohol intoxication and violent behavior is well documented. Alcohol both impairs judgment and lowers inhibitions, which can increase the risk of aggression, particularly for someone with low impulse control or emotion-regulation issues. Surveys have found that among those incarcerated for a violent offense, approximately 40 percent of them report they had been drinking at the time of the offense.[40]

Drinking is particularly common with certain types of violent offenses, including intimate partner violence (IPV). Sixty percent of victims in alcohol-related incidences of violence are family members or domestic partners of the perpetrator. Moreover, alcohol-involved violence is more likely to result in injury to the victim, as opposed to violent crimes that do not involve alcohol.[41] This creates risk of serious physical harm for domestic violence victims. Even for adolescents, a study of teen dating violence found that the odds of both emotional and physical violence increase significantly when alcohol is consumed.[42]

In addition to IPV, sexual assault and homicide are also linked to alcohol misuse among perpetrators (see Chapter 12, pages 268–270). More than 60 percent of all acts of child

> **implied consent laws:** Laws requiring that drivers submit to chemical testing for alcohol or drugs when requested, or face legal penalties.

Drug Enforcement … in Focus

Does Uber Save Lives?

Ride-sharing services like Uber and Lyft help make alternative driving arrangements available with the touch of a smartphone. Many have speculated about the impact of these services on drunk driving. In 2014, Uber teamed up with MADD to explore this question. Their study concluded that DUI arrests and alcohol-related accidents fell significantly, particularly among drivers under 30, when ride-sharing was available. They also found in cities like Pittsburgh, demand for Uber increased substantially around 2 am, when most bars were closing, suggesting this service was helping prevent drunk driving.

Universities have also explored this hypothesis, offering perhaps a more independent examination of this question. A study conducted by Western Carolina University researchers found public safety benefits for communities that adopted Uber, particularly primary smartphone users, aged 25–44 (who also tend to use Uber and other ride-sharing services at a higher rate). They examined rates of crime and fatal vehicle accidents in 150 cities and counties between 2007 and 2015, where Uber (the first and largest ride-sharing service) was used. They found a decrease in fatal car crashes ranging between 17 and 40 percent when Uber was available in that county for four or more years. They also found some decline in rates of DUI, and even decreased arrests for simple assaults and disorderly conduct. However, another study published in the American Journal of Epidemiology examined alcohol-related fatalities on weekends and holidays between 2005 and 2014 in 100 metropolitan cities before and after the introduction of Uber. They found no association between traffic fatalities and the use of ride-sharing services.

Hence, the jury may still be out on this question. Nonetheless, many have taken advantage of having a convenient and cost-effective option to avoid getting behind the wheel when they have had a few drinks.

Sources: Uber and MADD report (2015, January). *More options. Shifting mindsets. Driving better choices.* Mothers Against Drunk Driving. Accessed from: https://2q72xc49mze8bkcog2f01nlh-wpengine.netdna-ssl.com/wp-content/uploads/2015/01/UberMADD-Report.pdf. Dills, A. K.; and Mulholland, S. E. (November 2017). Ride-Sharing, Fatal Crashes, and Crime. Accessed from: https://ssrn.com/abstract=2783797 or http://dx.doi.org/10.2139/ssrn.2783797. Brazil, N.; and Kirk, D. S. (2016). Uber and metropolitan traffic fatalities in the United States. *American Journal of Epidemiology, 184,* 192–198.

molestation involve drunkenness. In studies of criminal homicide, 50–60 percent of the perpetrators were found to be under the influence of alcohol when the murder took place. From the perspective of the victim, 28 percent of victims surveyed perceived that the offender had been drinking prior to the offense.[43]

The intersection between alcohol and violent crime impacts children in other important ways. A national study on child victimization found that family problems with drugs or alcohol were an important predictor of youth exposure and experience with violence.[44] This early exposure to violence can lead to an array of problems for these youth as they grow up, including the perpetuation of violence.

Yet, it is important to emphasize the well-known fact that violent behavior occurs only rarely in everyday situations in which alcohol is consumed. The major factor in an alcohol-violence association is the *quantity* of alcohol consumed. The greater the quantity of alcohol consumed, the greater is the likelihood that a person will commit some form of violence toward an individual or property.[45]

Researchers have advanced two principal ways of accounting for the linkage between alcohol intoxication and violent behavior. The *disinhibition theory* holds that ingesting alcohol on a pharmacological level impairs normal cortical mechanisms responsible for inhibiting the expression of innate or suppressed aggressive inclinations. The *cognitive-expectation theory* holds that learned beliefs or expectations about alcohol's effects can facilitate aggressive behaviors. The implication is that violence is induced by the act of drinking in combination with one's personal view of how a person is "supposed to respond" rather than by the pharmacological effects of alcohol itself (Drug Enforcement...in Focus).[46]

Other Alcohol-Related Crimes

In addition to the more serious crimes linked to alcohol consumption, there are a number of nuisance offenses associated with alcohol misuse that can lead to an individual's arrest. Examples of such offenses include public intoxication, disorderly conduct due to intoxication, underage consumption of alcohol, and contributing to the delinquency of a minor. Public intoxication (also known as being "drunk and disorderly") is a misdemeanor-level crime in states like Texas, California, and Indiana, and is subject to fines and short jail stays. In other states such as Kansas, Minnesota, and Missouri, being intoxicated in public is not a

Drug Enforcement... in Focus

Alcohol, Security, and Spectator Sports

In 2005, the National Basketball Association (NBA) issued a set of security guidelines that included "Fan Code of Conduct" specifying that "guests will enjoy the basketball experience free from disruptive behavior, including foul or abusive language or obscene gestures." In the words of NBA Commissioner David Stern, "We look at this as an opportunity to remind people that coming to an arena is an opportunity to share an experience of rooting a home team on to victory and booing the opposition, but not doing it in an antisocial way that goes against our civil society."

Acknowledging the connection between disruptive behavior and alcohol, the NBA bans alcohol sales during the fourth quarter of every game and imposes a 24-ounce limit on the size of alcoholic drinks sold in an arena, with a maximum of two alcoholic drinks per customer. Increased security measures and restrictions on alcohol sales came about after basketball players and fans brawled in the stands and on the court at the end of a game in November 2004 between the Indiana Pacers and the Detroit Pistons. Indiana's Ron Artest went into the seats after being hit by a full cup of beer that had been tossed by a spectator. As a result of the melee, considered to be one of the most violent episodes in NBA history, Artest was suspended for the rest of the 2004–2005 season, and other players were given suspensions of as many as 30 games. All told, ten players and fans were charged with fighting.

Alcohol consumption has also come under scrutiny during college and professional football games, where binge drinking at tailgating parties and after-game celebrations frequently results in property damage and sometimes leads to injuries or deaths. At the University of Virginia, a tradition that began in the 1980s has seniors individually drinking a fifth of liquor by kickoff time at the final game of the football season (the so-called Fourth-Year Fifth). This practice was associated with the deaths of 18 students between 1990 and 2002. Since 1999, a university organization, Fourth-years Acting Responsibly (FAR), has coordinated an annual pledge drive to reduce abusive drinking at the final home game, as part of a campuswide alcohol-abuse prevention program.

It should be noted that the NCAA does not permit alcohol sales at any of the 89 championship basketball games it administers. College football evidently is another matter. Beer, wine, and spirits were available for spectators at all bowl games in the 2015 inaugural playoff college football championships. The Football Bowl Subdivision in charge of the playoff games is the only NCAA-sanctioned group whose championship events are not governed by the NCAA.

Sources: Eskenazi, G. (2005, December 21). For Patriots and Jets, a sobering experience. *The New York Times*, p. D3. Football, tailgating parties, and alcohol safety (2005, October 1). *The NCADI Reporter*. Bethesda, MD: National Clearinghouse for Drug Information. NBA issuing sterner security, beer guidelines. *USA Today.com*, accessed May 8, 2005. Tracy, M. (2015, January 11). College football is powerful: The proof is in the alcohol. *The New York Times Sports Sunday*, pp. 1, 6.

criminal offense. In most of these states, cities and counties can enact ordinances against public intoxication, but it is not a state statute. If intoxication leads to belligerence, disturbing the peace or any other type of unruly behavior, then disorderly conduct can be charged. Like public intoxication, disturbing the peace under these circumstance is typically a misdemeanor offense.

In order to defray costs of low-level alcohol-related crimes, many jurisdictions have opened diversion facilities where individuals can "sleep off" a drunk, rather than be arrested and incarcerated. In Houston Texas, the Sobering Center was designed for this purpose. Such facilities offer assessment and referral to substance abuse resources, which is often not the case for individuals taken to jail. It also saves taxpayer dollars by avoiding the expense of jail stays. Chapter 6 describes the use of other police diversion options.

Twenty-one is the minimum age requirement for drinking alcohol in the United States. Underage drinking or minor-in-possession charges can be filed against juveniles who possess, attempt to purchase, purchase, or consume alcohol. Like most other crimes, penalties vary by jurisdiction. Minors are often subject to fines, community service, or license suspension, but juveniles may also be placed on probation or serve short terms of incarceration, particularly for multiple underage consumption offenses.

While in all 50 states, it is illegal for an adult to furnish alcohol to a minor, most states offer exceptions. When a parent, guardian, or spouse furnishes alcohol, states such as Arkansas, South Carolina, and Virginia allow minors to drink at home. No state, however, allows alcohol to be provided to a minor on private property by anyone other than a family member.[47] Many states also require or provide incentives to retail establishments for training on responsible alcohol beverage service. Participation in such training can decrease their liability, protect the establishment's license, or mitigate penalties for selling to a minor.[48]

Strategies for Regulating Alcohol Consumption

In light of the adverse personal and social consequences of excessive alcohol consumption, a number of regulatory controls have been adopted. Obviously, the total prohibition of alcohol, as instituted during the Prohibition Era (see Chapter 3), did not work. What other measures could be employed?

Present-Day Alcohol Regulation by Restricted Access

Regulations regarding the circumstances under which alcohol can be purchased or consumed fall under the jurisdiction of individual U.S. states or local communities. Some jurisdictions have virtually no restrictions, other than the nationwide minimum age requirement that an individual must be 21 years old or older. In these locales, alcohol can be purchased 24 hours a day, seven days a week, and alcoholic beverages can be consumed by passengers in vehicles. At the other extreme, more than half of U.S. states have cities or counties that are "dry."

Whether or not restricted access reduces alcohol consumption and alcohol-related problems is a complex question. When "dry" jurisdictions are compared to "wet" jurisdictions with respect to alcohol-related accidents, the statistics on alcohol-related accidents show a higher incidence in "dry" locales, largely due to the fact that drinkers tend to drive to nearby "wet" locales to consume alcohol and then drive home.[49]

According to the National Highway Traffic Safety Administration, more than 700 lives of persons aged 18, 19, or 20 have been saved each year as a result of laws setting 21 as the minimum drinking age. Since 1998, a nationwide minimum BAC level defining "driving while intoxicated" for drivers younger than 21 years of age has been set at 0.02 percent.[50]

Present-Day Alcohol Regulation by Taxation

One immediate benefit following the end of 13 years of Prohibition in 1933 was the return of federal revenue from taxes on alcohol. In fact, the positive impact on a struggling national economy hard hit by the Depression had been one of the arguments advanced by the Prohibition-repeal movement. In 1933 alone, excise taxes from alcohol sales brought in $500 million, a significant windfall that was put to use in financing social programs of the New Deal.

The concept of collecting taxes on the basis of alcohol consumption dates back to the very beginning of the United States as a nation. In 1794, the newly established U.S. Congress passed a law imposing an excise tax on the sale of whiskey. After a short-lived Whiskey Rebellion in which President Washington had to order federal militia to subdue Appalachian farmers who had refused to pay the new tax, the practice of taxing alcohol was accepted and has continued to the present day as a legal way of raising tax money. In 2015, more than $9 billion was collected from federal excise taxes on alcohol, with distilled spirits being taxed at a higher rate than wine and beer.[51] Total annual revenues exceed $16 billion, when additional excise taxes imposed by all U.S. states and some local communities are included.

Taxes on alcohol sales (so-called sin taxes) have been an indirect mechanism for regulating the consumption of alcohol by increasing its price, not unlike present-day taxes on tobacco products (see Chapter 15). Numerous studies have indicated that increases in the price of alcohol beverages lead to reduced alcohol consumption, both in the general population and in certain high-risk populations (heavy drinkers, adolescents, and young adults).[52] On the basis of these analyses, it has been proposed that a further step be taken, setting alcohol taxes high enough to begin to offset the total societal costs resulting from alcohol abuse. This approach would place a form of "user fee" on the consumption of alcohol. However, it has been argued that raising alcohol prices by additional taxation might lead to the development of a black market for alcohol purchases, little change in alcohol consumption, and a net decline in tax revenues.[53] One study examining two large increases in excise taxes in Illinois to determine its impact on drunk-driving fatalities found no evidence that tax increases led to a long-term reduction in alcohol-related traffic deaths.[54]

Today, alcoholic beverages are one of the most heavily taxed consumer products. Approximately 45 percent of the retail price of an average bottle of distilled spirits, for example, is earmarked for federal, state, or local taxes.

Regulations to Reduce Alcohol-Related Traffic Fatalities

Another strategy aims not at reducing alcohol consumption itself but rather reducing the incidence of adverse consequences of alcohol consumption. In that sense, it is a "harm reduction" approach in alcohol control policy. A prime example of this approach is the effort to reduce alcohol-related traffic fatalities.

With the minimum BAC level for intoxication established nationwide as 0.08 percent, there has been a significant reduction in alcohol-related traffic fatalities. According to estimates made by the National Highway Traffic Safety Administration, the reduction of the minimum BAC level to 0.08 percent has saved 500 lives each year.[55]

In addition, educational programs in schools and communities emphasizing the advantage of using "designated drivers" as well as public education and lobbying groups such as MADD and Students Against Drunk Driving (SADD) have had positive

effects. This chapter's Portrait feature highlights the origins, accomplishments, and aspirations of MADD, specifically with respect to tighter regulations on drinking and driving.

Regulations Based on Ignition Interlock Technology

A major goal in reducing alcohol-related fatalities on the road is to prevent an intoxicated individual from getting behind the wheel in the first place. We cannot prevent every intoxicated individual from driving a car, but we can at least try to prevent an individual who has had a previous DUI arrest from driving while intoxicated. The most widely used technology for preventing such a situation is an ignition interlock device (IID). IIDs are breathalyzers installed directing into a personal vehicle, typically by a private company, at the expense of the driver. When activated by the detection of a minimum BAC level in the breath of the driver, the IID will prevent the car from starting. Many states also require the placement of a video camera in the vehicle to record IID use and ensure it is the driver using the device.

In 2007, New Mexico became the first state to require ignition interlocks to be installed after a first DWI offense; alcohol-related fatalities decreased 11 percent in the first year.

PORTRAIT

Candace Lightner—Founder of MADD

In 1980, Candace Lightner's 13-year-old daughter, Cari, was killed by a hit-and-run intoxicated driver in California. The driver had been out of jail on bail for only two days, a consequence of another hit-and-run drunk-driving crash, and he had three previous drunk-driving arrests and two previous convictions. He was allowed to plea bargain to vehicular manslaughter. Although the sentence was to serve two years in prison, the judge allowed him to serve time in a work camp and later a halfway house.

It was appalling to Lightner that drunk drivers, similar to the one who had killed her daughter, were receiving such lenient sentences, with many of them never going to jail for a single day. Lightner quit her job and started an organization that has become a household name: Mothers Against Drunk Driving (MADD).

Since then, MADD has campaigned for stricter laws against drunk driving, and most of the present DWI legislation around the country is a result of its intense efforts. In addition, MADD acts as a voice for victims of drunk-driving injuries and the families of those who have been

killed. From a single act of courage, despite enormous grief, Lightner has created an organization that boasts more than 3 million members in the United States, with groups in virtually every state and more than 400 local chapters.

More recently, MADD has set for itself the goal of reducing the number of all traffic fatalities associated with alcohol drinking. These are some of the group's proposals for change:

1. More effective enforcement of the minimum-drinking-age law
2. A "0.00 percent BAC" criterion for drivers under 21, making it illegal to drive with any measurable level of blood alcohol in any state
3. Driver's license suspensions for underage persons convicted of purchasing or possessing alcoholic beverages
4. Alcohol-free zones for youth gatherings
5. Criminal sanctions against adults who provide or allow alcoholic beverages at events for underage participants
6. Mandatory alcohol and drug testing for all drivers in all traffic crashes

resulting in fatalities or serious bodily injury
7. Sobriety checkpoints to detect and apprehend alcohol-impaired drivers and to serve as a visible deterrent to drinking and driving
8. Requiring ignition interlock devices for all convicted drunk drivers
9. Support for advanced vehicle technology, such as the Driver Alcohol Detection System (DADSS) currently being tested, which determines whether a driver has a BAC above .08 percent via fingertips or an air-sampling system that tests air exhaled by the driver. Like airbags, all new vehicles could have these systems installed
10. Additional law enforcement training and support to detect drug-impaired drivers

Source: Information courtesy of Mothers Against Drunk Driving, Irving, Texas, accessed from: https://www.madd.org/the-solution/. Interview by the author with Candace Lightner.

Credit: Scott Applewhite/AP Images

TABLE 13.4

Blood alcohol concentrations at which drivers in different nations are legally drunk

BAC	0.00+	0.02	0.03	0.05	0.08
COUNTRY	Czech Republic, Slovakia, Hungary	Norway, Poland, Sweden	Japan, China	Argentina, Australia, Costa Rica, Denmark, Finland, France, Italy, Germany, Greece, The Netherlands, Peru, Russia, South Africa, Spain, Thailand	Brazil, Britain, Canada, Chile, Ecuador, Ireland, Jamaica, New Zealand, Singapore, United States

Source: Based on information from Valenti, J. (2005, July 13). U.S. lags others in DWI toughness. *Newsday*, p. A15.

When, in 2004, Maryland mandated that the system be installed after several DWI arrests, fatalities were reduced by 18 percent. As of 2014, all 50 U.S. states and the District of Columbia have enacted some form of ignition interlock law, typically during the period of license suspension and/or a specified time before fully relicensing DWI offenders. In 15 U.S. states, ignition interlock devices are mandated even after a first-time DWI offense.

In general, even though we have reason to be cautiously optimistic about reducing alcohol-related traffic fatalities, it is clear that much work remains to be done. The United States presently has one of the most lenient standards for driving while intoxicated among nations in the world (Table 13.4). The number of alcohol-related accidents, particularly among male drivers, whose involvement exceeds that of female drivers by more than 2:1, is far too high. Meanwhile, the drinking-and-driving phenomenon is widespread throughout the population. It has been estimated that nearly 28 million drivers were under the influence of alcohol at least once while driving in 2014. It should not be surprising that the peak age of drinking and driving was between 21 and 24, during which one in five reported being intoxicated on the road at least once in the past year.[56]

Ignition interlock devices are designed to prevent the starting of an automobile if the driver is intoxicated.

Credit: PA Images/Alamy Stock Photo

On the Other Hand: Alcohol and Health Benefits

The documented health benefits of moderate levels of alcohol consumption over the last 30 years of research have presented a major dilemma among medical and public health professionals. The crux of the dilemma is that moderate amounts of alcohol can possibly save your life, while immoderate amounts can possibly destroy it.

It started as an observation that did not seem to make sense. Epidemiological studies of French and other European populations who consumed large amounts of butter, cheese, liver, and other animal fats—a diet associated with elevated cholesterol and an elevated risk for coronary failure—found that these populations had a remarkably low incidence of coronary heart disease. The answer seemed to be that relatively more alcohol was consumed along with their dietary food. The "French paradox" was resolved when later research showed that alcohol increases high-density lipoprotein (HDL) cholesterol (the so-called good cholesterol) levels in the blood, with HDL acting as a protective mechanism against a possible restriction of blood flow through arteries. The greatest benefit was seen in those individuals who had high concentrations of low-density lipoprotein (LDL) cholesterol (the so-called bad cholesterol) and therefore had the greatest risk for coronary heart disease. It was estimated that consumption of approximately 8 ounces of wine (a bit less than two standard drinks) per day resulted in a 25 percent reduction in the risk of coronary heart disease.

A natural substance in red wine known as *resveratrol* has been identified as a possible factor in explaining the health benefits of drinking red wine. Mice administered resveratrol in very large quantities were higher in endurance levels, relative to controls, and were less susceptible to the elevations in glucose and insulin that normally result from eating a high-fat diet. However, these animals received a daily dosage of resveratrol far larger than a human would ingest from drinking wine, so the question of whether this substance is a key factor remains unsettled. Human intake of resveratrol at comparable dosages would have a significant potential for acute toxicity (Chapter 1).[57]

The benefits evidently extend beyond coronary heart disease. Moderate alcohol intake reduces the risk of diabetes mellitus, stroke, and dementia (possibly by reducing the incidence of mini-strokes or by boosting concentrations of vitamin B_6, which is essential for the formation of essential brain chemicals). A recent study indicates that moderate alcohol consumption can also lower the risk of rheumatoid arthritis by up to 50 percent.[58]

Of course, the key to the health benefits of alcohol consumption lies in moderation, with moderate drinking being defined as taking no more than one drink per day for women and no more than two drinks per day for men. The newest (2000) Dietary Guidelines for Americans, released by the U.S. Department of Agriculture and the U.S. Department of Health and Human Services, acknowledge that alcohol use can reduce the risk of coronary heart disease. However, they limit the recommendation of moderate drinking to men over age 45 and women over age 55, a subpopulation that carries an elevated risk for the disease.

Despite the weight of evidence tilting toward the potential health benefits of alcohol, the public health officials and medical professionals remain divided on the question of whether to encourage patients who do not drink alcohol to start at a moderate level of consumption. In some cases, moderate intake is not advisable. Even one drink per day slightly increases the risk for breast cancer in women, and in no circumstances should alcohol be consumed during pregnancy. Some public health researchers are concerned that an endorsement of moderate alcohol drinking may open up a range of possible risks, in effect, giving alcohol a kind of "halo effect" that might be confusing to the public. Even so, an argument can be made that moderate alcohol drinking is simply a behavior that coincides with a healthful lifestyle in the first place, rather than a behavior that actually makes you healthy (Help Line).[59]

Help Line
Guidelines for Responsible Drinking

The following guidelines can be useful in avoiding the numerous adverse consequences of alcohol consumption. Responsible drinking is not always an easy matter, but certain considerations can make it easier to accomplish.

- **Know how much you are drinking**. Measure your drinks. Beer is often premeasured (unless you are drinking draft beer from a keg), but wine and liquor drinks frequently are not. Learn what a 5-ounce quantity of wine or a 1½-ounce shot of liquor looks like and use these measures to guide your drinking.

- **Choose beer or wine over liquor**. Beer especially will make you feel fuller more quickly, with a smaller intake of alcohol. But be careful. A 12-ounce beer is equivalent in alcohol content to a 5-ounce glass of wine or a 1-shot drink of liquor.

- **Drink slowly**. One drink an hour stays relatively even with your body's metabolism of the alcohol you consume. Sipping your drinks is a good strategy for slowing down your consumption. If you are a man, you'll look cool; if you are a woman, you'll look refined.

- **Don't cluster your drinking**. If you are going to have seven drinks during a week, don't drink them all on the weekend.

- **Don't combine alcohol with energy drinks**. Caffeinated drinks combined with alcoholic beverages have been found to lead to increased alcohol consumption (in terms of the number of alcoholic drinks) and tend to increase the hours with an elevated BAC. Controlling for BAC levels, the combination increases the number of negative consequences.

- **Eat something substantial while you are drinking**. Protein is an excellent accompaniment to alcohol. Avoid salty foods because they will make you thirstier and more inclined to have another drink.

- **Drink only when you are already relaxed**. Chronic alcohol abuse occurs more easily when alcohol is viewed as a way to relax. If you have a problem, seek some nondrug alternative.

- **When you drink, savor the experience**. If you focus on the quality of what you drink rather than the quantity you are drinking, you will avoid drinking too much.

- **Never drink alone**. Drinking is never an appropriate answer to social isolation. Besides, when there are people around, there is someone to look out for you.

- **Beware of unfamiliar drinks**. Some drinks, such as zombies and other fruit and rum drinks, are deceptively high in types of alcohol that are not easily detected by taste.

- **Never drive a car after having had a drink**. Driving impairment begins after consumption of very low quantities of alcohol. Make plans *before* you go out as to how you are going to get home safely at the end of the night.

- **Be a good host or hostess**. If you are serving alcohol at a party, do not make drinking the focus of activity. Do not refill your guests' glasses. Discourage intoxication and do not condone drunkenness. Provide transportation options for those who drink at your party. Present nonalcoholic beverages as prominently as alcoholic ones. Prior to the end of the party, stop serving alcohol and offer coffee or other warm nonalcoholic beverages and a substantial snack, providing an interval of nondrinking time before people leave.

Where to go for assistance

www.indiana.edu/~engs/hints/holiday.html

This Web site on sensible, moderate, and responsible alcohol consumption and party hosting is adapted from Engs, R. C. (1987). Alcohol and other drugs: Self responsibility. Bloomington, IN: Tichenor Publishing.

Sources: Based on information in Gross, L. (1983). *How much is too much? The effects of social drinking.* New York: Random House, pp. 149–152. Hanson, D. J.; and Engs, R. C. (1994). Drinking behavior: Taking personal responsibility. In P. J. Venturelli (Ed.), *Drug use in America: Social, cultural, and political perspectives.* Boston: Jones and Bartlett, pp. 175–181. Steele, D. W. (1986). *Managing alcohol in your life.* Mansfield, MA: Steele Publishing and Consulting. Patrick, M. E; and Maggs, J. L. (2014). Energy drinks and alcohol: Links to alcohol behaviors and consequences across 56 days. *Journal of Adolescent Health, 54,* 454–459.

From Alcohol Misuse to Chronic Alcohol Abuse

Millions of people drink on occasion, enjoy the experience, and have never engaged in any violent or aggressive acts. They can avoid situations in which alcohol consumption would endanger their lives and the lives of others or consume quantities of alcohol that might result in problematic behavior. In other words, millions of people engage in alcohol use without engaging in alcohol misuse.

Yet, it is important to remember that alcohol remains a drug with significant potential for dependence. Unfortunately, it is easy to get hooked. As it has been said, people may plan to get drunk, but no one plans to be an alcoholic. The problems surrounding chronic alcohol abuse and alcoholism are reviewed in the next sections.

Alcoholism: Stereotypes, Definitions, and Criteria

The condition of alcoholism, through the chronic abuse of alcohol, has been called the hidden addiction. There is no need to get out on the street and find a drug dealer; for many people, it is remarkably easy to conceal their problem (at least in the beginning) from family and friends. But eventually the effects on family and friends become all too evident. In the following sections, we will review the multilayered difficulties that are encountered under these circumstances, beginning with the most prominent misconception we have about this devastating disorder.

If you were to close your eyes and try to imagine what an alcoholic looked like, some of you might be forming an image of an individual, probably male, possibly homeless and disheveled in appearance, possibly in a state of deteriorating health, possibly alone in the world with no one caring about him.

If that is so, you would be imagining less than 5 percent of all alcoholics; more than 95 percent of them look quite different. They are neatly dressed and have jobs, a home, and a family. The demographics of alcoholism include every possible category. Alcoholics can be 14 or 84 years of age, male or female, professional, or blue-collar. They can be urbanites, suburbanites, or rural residents in any community.

There is also diversity in the pattern of their drinking. Although the hallmark of alcoholism is the excessive quantity of alcohol that is consumed, there are significant differences in the way alcoholics consume their alcohol. Not all of them drink alone or begin every day with a drink. Many of them drink on a daily basis, but others are spree or binge alcoholics who might become grossly intoxicated on occasion and totally abstain from drinking the rest of the time.[60]

What aspects of their behavior tie them all together? Owing to the wide diversity of characteristics, it has been difficult to come up with one encompassing definition of alcoholism. Instead, we rely on a set of criteria—basically, a collection of signs, symptoms, and behaviors that help us make the diagnosis. A single individual may not meet all of these criteria, but if he or she fulfills enough of them, we decide that the standard has been met.

The criteria adopted here focus on four basic life problems that are tied to the consumption of alcohol: (1) problems associated with a preoccupation with drinking, (2) emotional problems, (3) vocational, social, and family problems, and (4) problems associated with physical health. Notice that these criteria make no mention of the cause or causes of alcoholism but instead reflect only its behavioral, social, and physical consequences. In short, we are recognizing that **alcoholism** is a complex phenomenon with psychological-behavioral components (criteria 1 and 2), social components (criterion 3), and a physical component (criterion 4).

All these consequences stem from a long-term pattern of alcohol consumption that we refer to as chronic alcohol abuse. For the sake of simplicity, the terms "chronic alcohol abuse" and "alcoholism" will be used interchangeably in the rest of this chapter.

Problems Associated with a Preoccupation with Drinking

The dominant characteristic of alcoholics is their preoccupation with the act of drinking and their incorporation of drinking into their everyday lives. An alcoholic may need a drink prior to a social occasion to feel "fortified." With increasing frequency, such a person sees alcohol as a way of dealing with stress and anxiety. Drinking itself becomes a routine, no longer a purely social behavior. There are two aspects to a preoccupation with drinking.

- The habit of taking a few drinks upon arriving home from work each day is an example of **symptomatic drinking**, in which alcohol is viewed specifically as a way of relieving tension. Also increasing is the incidence of unintentional states of severe intoxication and blackouts of events surrounding the time of drinking, a condition quite different from "passing out" from a high BAC level. One such occurrence may not be a particularly critical sign, but recurrences definitely are.

- Another feature often attributed to alcoholics is a loss of control over their drinking. The alcoholic typically craves a drink and frequently engages in compulsive behavior related to alcohol. There may be a stockpiling of liquor, taking a drink or two before going to a party, or feeling uncomfortable unless alcohol is present. The alcoholic may be sneaking drinks or having drinks that others do not know about, such as surreptitiously having an extra drink or two in the kitchen out of the sight of party guests. Particularly when the alcoholic is trying to totally refrain from drinking (in other words, engage in absolute **abstinence**) or to reduce the quantity of alcohol consumed, his or her thoughts become focused on the possibility of drinking in the future or on ways to rationalize it if it happens.

alcoholism: A condition in which the consumption of alcohol has produced major psychological, physical, social, and/or occupational problems.

symptomatic drinking: A pattern of alcohol consumption aimed at reducing stress and anxiety.

abstinence: The avoidance of something that is consumable or a behavior associated with its consumption.

The typical alcoholic American

Doctor, age 54

Farmer, age 35

Unemployed, age 40

College student, age 19

Counselor, age 38

Retired editor, age 86

Dancer, age 22

Police officer, age 46

Military officer, age 31

Student, age 14

Executive, age 50

Taxi driver, age 61

Homemaker, age 43

Bricklayer, age 29

Computer programmer, age 25

Lawyer, age 52

There's no such thing as typical. We have all kinds.
10 million Americans are alcoholic.
It's our number one drug problem.

Alcoholism affects such a diverse group of people that it is virtually impossible to make generalizations about the typical profile of an alcoholic. This poster shows 16 examples of individuals with whom many people might not have immediately associated the term "alcoholic." Note the example in the extreme upper right corner.

Credit: National Clearinghouse for Alcohol and Drug Information, Substance Abuse and Mental Health Services Administration.

Emotional Problems

Given that alcohol is a depressant drug on the central nervous system, it should not be surprising that chronic alcohol intake produces depressive symptoms. Serious depressions and thoughts of suicide frequently occur in the midst of heavy drinking. However, relatively few chronic alcohol abusers have experienced major depression either before the onset of their alcoholic condition or during extended periods of abstinence. Therefore, it is reasonable to conclude that the depressive symptoms are alcohol induced. Alcoholics are no more likely than others in the general population to have suffered an episode of major depression.[61]

Vocational, Social, and Family Problems

No one questions the potential problems that chronic alcohol abuse can bring to the maintenance of a job or career, social relationships, and a stable family life. These three areas frequently intertwine, and trouble in one usually exacerbates trouble in the others. A job loss puts stress on marital and family relationships, just as marital and family difficulties put stress on occupational performance.[62]

Physical Problems

There is also no question that chronic alcohol consumption has a destructive effect on the body. Not surprisingly, a principal site of damage is the brain. Neuroimaging procedures, such as CT and MRI brain scans, reveal a consistent link between heavy drinking and physical shrinkage of brain matter, particularly in the cerebral cortex, cerebellum, and regions associated with memory and other cognitive functions. These neurological changes are observed even in the absence of other alcohol-related medical conditions such as chronic liver disease and cancer.

Overall, chronic alcohol consumption accounts for 1 in 10 working-age deaths in the United States, principally among men. In other countries, the death toll to alcohol is much higher. The risk of dying before age 55 for Russian men who said they drank three or more half-liter bottles of vodka a week was 35 percent. A quarter of Russian men die before reaching 55, as compared with 7 percent of men in the United Kingdom and less than 1 percent in the United States.[63]

Interpersonal and Family Relationships

The major life problems that serve as rough criteria for determining the condition of alcoholism are often not recognized by alcoholics themselves because of their tendency to deny that their drinking has any influence on their lives or the lives of people around them. When in denial, the alcoholic can be extremely sensitive to any mention of problems associated with drinking. A hangover the next day, for example, is seldom discussed because it would draw attention to the fact that drinking has occurred.[64]

Quick Concept Check 13.2

Understanding the Psychology of Alcoholism

Check your understanding of the psychological aspects of alcoholism by matching each quotation or behavioral description (on the left) with the appropriate term (on the right).

1. Brad tries to call his estranged wife on the telephone. She hangs up on him. Now angry and frustrated, Brad takes a drink.
2. Mary stays sober during the workweek, but on the weekend she downs at least two quarts of vodka.
3. "Despite what my family says, I am convinced I am not an alcoholic."
4. "If I'm with her when she's drinking, I can make sure she doesn't overdo her drinking."
5. "I'm going to the theater later. I don't think there will be any liquor there, so I had better have a couple of drinks before I go."

a. denial
b. enabling
c. out-of-control drinking
d. spree or binge drinking
e. symptomatic drinking

Answers: 1. e 2. d 3. a 4. b 5. c

Denial can also manifest among the people around the alcoholic. Members of an alcoholic's family, for example, may try to function as if life were normal. Through their excuse making and efforts to undo or cover up the frequent physical and psychological damage the alcoholic causes, they inadvertently prevent the alcoholic from seeking treatment or delay that treatment until the alcoholism is more severe. These people are referred to as **enablers** because they enable the alcoholic to function as an alcoholic (as opposed to a sober person). Both processes of denial and enabling present major difficulties not only in establishing problem-oriented criteria for diagnosing alcoholism but also in introducing necessary interventions. Denial and enabling are clearly relevant processes in the area of alcoholism, but it is not difficult to see that they present problems with regard to *any* form of substance abuse problem.

enablers: Individuals whose behavior consciously or unconsciously encourages another person's continuation in a pattern of alcohol or other drug abuse.

The Family Dynamics of Alcoholism

Alcoholism, like any form of drug abuse, is an especially traumatizing experience for the families involved. For every one person who has a problem with alcohol, there are, on average, at least four others who are directly affected on a day-to-day basis. It is therefore important to examine some of these effects on particular family members. Since the 1950s, a **systems approach** has advocated looking at how the alcoholic and other members of the family interact. We discussed one of these aspects earlier in the chapter in connection with the adverse effects of enabling behavior on the alcoholic. Another important aspect related to an alcoholic's family is the possibility of codependency.

Since the early 1980s, the concept of **codependency** has gained widespread attention as a way of understanding people who live on a day-to-day basis with an alcoholic or any individual with a drug dependence. Definitions vary but most identify four essential features. In members of the family of an alcoholic, therapists have observed (1) an over-involvement with the alcoholic, (2) obsessive attempts to control the alcoholic's behavior, (3) a strong reliance upon external sources of self-worth, through the approval of others, and (4) an attempt to make personal sacrifices in an effort to improve the alcoholic's condition.

If people in a relationship with a codependent act badly, the codependent believes that he or she is responsible for their behavior. Because codependency is considered a learned pattern of thinking rather than an innate trait, the goal of therapy is to teach the codependent person to detach himself or herself from the alcoholic and begin to meet his or her own needs rather than being controlled by the value judgments of others.[65]

Risk Factors for Developing Alcoholism

Given the dysfunctional family dynamics that exist when one parent or both parents are chronic alcohol abusers, it is understandable that there should be negative consequences on the psychological development of the children. It is not surprising, therefore, that **children of alcoholics (COAs)** have a higher statistical risk of becoming alcoholics themselves than do children of nonalcoholics. Therefore, having an alcoholic parent or having both parents as alcoholics is a significant risk factor for the later development of alcoholism.

An equally important risk factor is related to a characteristic pattern of alcohol consumption itself. Men who, at age 20, have a relatively low response to alcohol, in that they need to drink more than other people to feel intoxicated, carry a higher risk of becoming alcoholic by the time they are 30, regardless of their pattern of drinking at an earlier age and regardless of their parents' drinking. Sons of alcoholics having a low response to alcohol have a 60 percent chance of becoming alcoholics, compared with a 42 percent chance for sons

of alcoholics in general. Sons of nonalcoholics having a low response to alcohol have a 22 percent chance of becoming alcoholics, compared with an 8 to 9 percent chance for sons of nonalcoholics in general.[66]

The combination of these two risk factors—family history and a low response to alcohol—is obviously the worst scenario for a development of alcoholism, at least in males. Nonetheless, we should remember that a large proportion of people still *do not* become alcoholics, even with both risk factors present. The question of what protective factors may account for the resilience of high-risk individuals with regard to alcoholism is a major subject of current research.[67]

Whether or not risk factor of family history is genetically based (through the transmission of genes from the parents) or environmentally based (through the living conditions in which the offspring have been brought up) is often a complex question. One way of teasing apart the influences of "nature" and "nurture" is to examine cases of adopted children and compare their behavior to behaviors of either their biological or adoptive parents. In 1981, an extensive research study in Sweden examined the adoption records of approximately 3,000 children who had alcoholic biological parents but lived with nonalcoholic adoptive parents. The results showed that, overall, a larger percentage of these children become alcoholics than would be seen in the general population. The greater incidence was present even when the children had been raised by their adoptive parents immediately after being born, indicating that a strong genetic component was operating.

There were, however, two subgroups among those children who eventually became alcoholics. One subgroup, called *Type 1 alcoholics*, developed problem drinking later in life and generally functioned well in society. In addition to a genetic predisposition toward alcoholism, there was for this subgroup a strong environmental factor as well. Whether the child was placed in a middle-class or a poor adoptive family influenced the final outcome. A second subgroup, called *Type 2 alcoholics*, developed alcoholism earlier in life and had significant antisocial patterns of behavior. A strong genetic component was operating in this subgroup, and because the socioeconomic status of the adoptive family made no difference in the outcome, we can conclude that environmental

---

systems approach: A way of understanding a phenomenon in terms of complex interacting relationships among individuals, family, friends, and community.

codependency: The concept that individuals who live with a person who has an alcohol (or other drug) dependence suffer themselves from difficulties of self-image and impaired social independence.

children of alcoholics (COAs): Individuals who grew up in a family with either one or two alcoholic parents.

TABLE 13.5

Two types of alcoholics

CHARACTERISTICS	TYPE 1	TYPE 2
Usual age at onset	(Late onset) after 25	(Early onset) before 25
Inability to abstain	Infrequent	Frequent
Fights and arrests when drinking	Infrequent	Frequent
Psychological dependence (loss of control)	Infrequent	Frequent
Guilt and fear about alcoholism	Frequent	Infrequent
Novelty-seeking personality	Low	High
Tendency to use alcohol to escape negative feelings	High	Low
Tendency to use alcohol to achieve positive feelings	Low	High
Gender	Male and female	Male only
Extent of genetic influences	Moderate	High
Extent of environmental influences	High	Low
Serotonin abnormalities in the brain	Absent	Present

Source: Based on updated information from Cloninger, C. R. (1987). Neurogenetic adaptive mechanisms in alcoholism. *Science, 236,* 410–416.

factors played a negligible role. Table 13.5 gives a more complete picture of the characteristics associated with Type 1 and Type 2 alcoholics.[68]

Patterns of Chronic Alcohol Abuse

When we consider the range of direct and indirect costs to society that result from chronic abuse of alcohol, the price we pay is enormous. These costs include the expense of treatment for alcoholism and of medical intervention for alcohol-related injuries and diseases, lost productivity from absenteeism and decreases in worker performance, legal and law enforcement costs associated with alcohol-related crimes, and losses from motor vehicle crashes. The total costs in the United States are estimated to be nearly $250 billion annually, even without taking into consideration the incalculable costs of human suffering that are associated with an estimated 88,000 alcohol-related deaths.[69]

As mentioned earlier, alcoholics can be found in every age, gender, racial, ethnic, and religious group and in all socioeconomic levels and geographic regions of the country. Nonetheless, large differences in prevalence exist within these categories. For example, the rate of alcohol abuse is higher for males than females, including binge drinking. Overall, women are more vulnerable to alcohol-related organ damage and are more likely to die of an alcohol-related accident.[70] Whether this higher risk results from differences in the pattern of drinking or from differences in the way alcohol is processed in a woman's body is at present unknown.

Figure 13.1 shows the levels of per capita consumption of alcohol in the United States on a state-by-state basis. Differences in the prevalence of alcohol-related problems are presumed to be correlated with consumption levels.

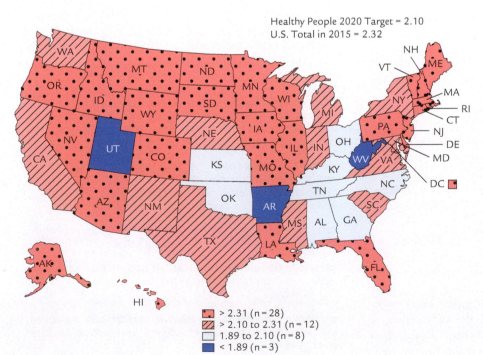

Healthy People 2020 Target = 2.10
U.S. Total in 2015 = 2.32

> 2.31 (n = 28)
> 2.10 to 2.31 (n = 12)
1.89 to 2.10 (n = 8)
< 1.89 (n = 3)

FIGURE 13.1

Total per capita alcohol consumption in gallons for the U.S. population by state in 2015.

Source: Haughwout, B. S.; and Slater, M. E. (2017, April). *Surveillance report #108: Apparent per capita alcohol consumption: National, state, and regional trends, 1977–2015.* Bethesda, MD: National Institute on Alcohol Abuse and Alcoholism, Figure 4.

Physiological Effects of Chronic Alcohol Use

Let's look at what we know about the consequences of long-term (chronic) consumption of alcohol over and above the acute effects that were discussed earlier in the chapter.

Tolerance and Withdrawal

As with other CNS depressants, alcohol consumption over a period of time will result in a tolerance effect. On a metabolic level, alcohol dehydrogenase activity during tolerance becomes higher in the stomach and liver, allowing the alcohol to leave the body somewhat faster; on a neural level, the brain is less responsive to alcohol's depressive effects.[71] Therefore, if the level of alcohol consumption remains steady, an individual feels less of an effect.

As a result of tolerance and the tendency to compensate for it in terms of drinking a greater quantity, the chronic alcohol abuser is subject to increased physical risks. There are serious behavioral risks as well; for example, an alcohol-tolerant drinker may consider driving with a BAC level that exceeds the standard for drunk driving, thinking that he or she is not intoxicated and hence not impaired. A person's driving ability, under these circumstances, will be substantially overestimated.

An alcohol-dependent person's abrupt withdrawal from alcohol can result in a range of serious physical symptoms beginning from 6 to 48 hours after the last drink, but estimates of as to how many people are typically affected vary. It is estimated that nearly 20 percent of adult patients visiting an emergency room have an alcohol use disorder, and that up to 50 percent of hospital patients with an alcohol use disorder experience some form of withdrawal symptoms.[72]. Although the exact incidence may be somewhat unclear, there is less disagreement about what takes place. Physical withdrawal effects are classified in two clusters of symptoms.

- The first cluster, called the **alcohol withdrawal syndrome**, is the more common of the two. It begins with insomnia, vivid dreaming, and a severe hangover; these discomforts are followed by tremors (the "shakes"), sweating, mild agitation, anxiety (the "jitters"), nausea, and vomiting, as well as increased heart rate and blood pressure. In some patients, there are also brief tonic-clonic (grand mal) seizures, as the nervous system rebounds from the chronic depression induced by alcohol. The alcohol withdrawal syndrome usually reaches a peak from 24 to 36 hours after the last drink and is over after 48 hours.

- The second cluster, called **delirium tremens (DTs)**, is much more dangerous and is fortunately less common. The symptoms include extreme disorientation and confusion, profuse sweating, fever, and disturbing nightmares. Typically, there are also periods of frightening hallucinations, when the individual might see snakes or insects on the walls, ceiling, or his or her skin. These effects generally reach a peak three to four days after the last drink. During this time, there is

the possibility of life-threatening events such as heart failure, dehydration, or suicide, so it is critical for the individual to be hospitalized and under medical supervision at all times. The current medical practice for treating individuals undergoing withdrawal is to administer anti-anxiety medication (see Chapter 12) to relieve the symptoms. After the withdrawal period has ended, the dose levels of the medication are gradually reduced and discontinued.[73]

Liver Disease

Chronic consumption of alcohol produces three forms of liver disease. The following conditions are presented in ascending order of severity:

- The first of these is a **fatty liver**, resulting from an abnormal concentration of fatty deposits inside liver cells. Normally, the liver breaks down fats adequately, but when alcohol is in the body, the liver breaks down the alcohol at the expense of fats. As a result, fats accumulate and ultimately interfere with the functioning of the liver. The condition is fortunately reversible, if the drinker abstains. The accumulated fats are gradually metabolized, and the liver returns to normal.

- The second condition is **alcoholic hepatitis**, an inflammation of liver tissue causing fever, jaundice (a yellowing of the skin), and abdominal pain, resulting at least in part from a lower functioning level of the immune system. It is also reversible with abstinence, though some residual scarring may remain.

- The third and most serious liver condition is **alcoholic cirrhosis**, characterized by the progressive development of scar tissue that chokes off blood vessels in the liver and destroys liver cells by interfering with the cell's utilization of oxygen. At an early stage, the liver is enlarged from the accumulation of fats, but at later stages it is shrunken as liver cells begin to degenerate (Figure 13.2). Though abstinence helps prevent further liver degeneration when cirrhosis is diagnosed, the condition is not reversible except by liver transplantation surgery.

---

alcohol withdrawal syndrome: The more common of two general reactions to the cessation of alcohol consumption in an alcoholic. It is characterized by physiological discomfort, seizures, and sleep disturbances.

delirium tremens (DTs): The less common of two general reactions to the cessation of drinking in an alcoholic. It is characterized by extreme disorientation and confusion, fever, hallucinations, and disturbing nightmares.

fatty liver: A condition in which fat deposits accumulate in the liver as a result of chronic alcohol abuse.

alcoholic hepatitis (AL-co-HAUL-ik hep-ah-TIE-tus): A disease involving inflammation of the liver as a result of chronic alcohol abuse.

alcoholic cirrhosis (AL-co-HAUL-ik seer-OH-sis): A disease involving scarring and deterioration of liver cells as a result of chronic alcohol abuse.

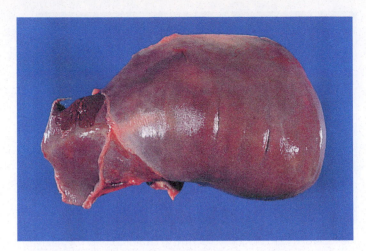

Credit: Biophoto Associates/Science Source

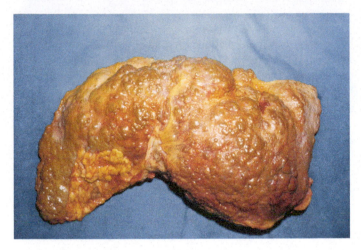

Credit: Biophoto Associates/Science Source

FIGURE 13.2

The dramatic difference between a healthy liver (top) and a cirrhotic liver (bottom).

Cirrhosis and other forms of chronic liver disease are collectively ranked as the twelfth leading cause of death in the United States, claiming more than 38,000 lives in 2014. Most deaths occur in people of ages 55–64 years. Daily drinkers are at a higher risk of developing cirrhosis than binge drinkers, though this risk may be the result of the relatively larger quantity of alcohol consumed over a long period of time. Generally, patients showing liver damage have been drinking for 10 to 20 years. Only 10–20 percent of all heavy drinkers develop cirrhosis, however, in contrast to 90–100 percent, who show evidence of either fatty liver or hepatitis. There may be a genetic predisposition to cirrhosis that puts a subgroup of alcoholics at increased risk.[74]

Cardiovascular Problems

About one in every four alcoholics develops cardiovascular problems owing to the chronic consumption of alcohol. The effects include inflammation and enlargement of the heart muscle, poor blood circulation to the heart, irregular heart contractions, fatty accumulations in the heart and arteries, high blood pressure, and stroke.[75]

Cancer

Chronic alcohol abuse is associated with the increased risk of several types of cancers—in particular, cancers of the pharynx and larynx. Nearly 50 percent of all such cancers are associated with heavy drinking. If alcohol abusers also smoke cigarettes, the increased risk is even more dramatic. An increased risk of liver cancer is also linked to chronic alcoholic abuse, whether or not cirrhosis is present as well. In addition, alcohol consumption is associated with breast cancer in women. There is either a weaker association or no association at all with cancers of the stomach, colon, pancreas, or rectum.

Alcohol is not technically considered a carcinogen (a direct producer of cancer), so why the risks are increased in certain cancer types is at present unknown. It is possible that the increased risk is a combined result of alcohol enhancing the carcinogenic effects of other chemicals and, as is true with the development of hepatitis, alcohol depressing the immune system. With a reduced immune response, the alcoholic may have a lowered resistance to the development of cancerous tumors.[76]

Dementia and Wernicke-Korsakoff Syndrome

Chronic alcohol consumption can produce longer-lasting deficits in the way an individual solves problems, remembers information, and organizes facts about his or her identity and surroundings. These cognitive deficits are commonly referred to collectively as **alcoholic dementia** and are associated with structural changes in brain tissue. Specifically, there is an enlargement of brain ventricles (the interior fluid-filled spaces within the brain), a widening of fissures separating sections of cerebral cortex, and a loss of acetylcholine-sensitive receptors. The combination of these effects results in a net decrease in brain mass, as indicated in CT and MRI brain scans, and a decline in overall intelligence, verbal learning and retention, and short-term memory, particularly for middle-aged and elderly alcoholics.

Some 50–75 percent of all detoxified alcoholics and nearly 20 percent of all individuals admitted to state mental hospitals show signs of alcohol-related dementia. Through abstinence, it is possible to reverse some of the cognitive deficits and even some of the abnormalities in the brain, depending on the age of the alcoholic when treatment begins. As you might suspect, younger alcoholics respond better than older ones.[77]

A more severe form of cognitive impairment related to chronic alcohol consumption is a two-part disease referred to

alcoholic dementia (AL-co-HAUL-ik dih-MEN-chee-ah): A condition in which chronic alcohol abuse produces cognitive deficits such as difficulties in problem-solving and memory.

as **Wernicke-Korsakoff syndrome**. In *Wernicke's encephalopathy* or simply *Wernicke's disease*, the patient shows confusion and disorientation, abnormal eye movements, and difficulties in movement, and body coordination. These neurological problems arise from a deficiency in vitamin B_1 (**thiamine**), a nutrient required for neurons in the brain to consume glucose. Extreme alcoholics may go days or weeks at a time eating practically nothing and receiving calories exclusively from drinking alcoholic beverages. As a result of thiamine deficiency, large numbers of neurons die in areas of the brain specifically concerned with thinking and movement. About 15 percent of patients with Wernicke's disease, however, respond favorably to large amounts of thiamine supplements in combination with abstinence from alcohol, restoring their previous level of orientation, eye movements, and coordination.

In some cases, Wernicke's disease patients, whether or not they recover from confusion and motor impairments, also display a severe form of chronic amnesia and general apathy called *Korsakoff's psychosis*. Such patients cannot remember information that has just been presented to them and have only a patchy memory for distant events that occurred prior to their alcoholic state. They frequently attempt, through a behavior called **confabulation**, to compensate for their gaps in memory by telling elaborate stories of imagined past events, as if trying to fool others into thinking that they remember more than they actually do. Thiamine deficiency is linked to Korsakoff's psychosis as well. After being treated with thiamine supplements, about 20 percent of patients completely recover their memory and 60 percent partially recover it. Yet, the remaining 20 percent, generally the most severely impaired patients and those with the longest history of alcohol consumption, show little or no improvement and require chronic institutionalization.[78]

Fetal Alcohol Syndrome (FAS)

The disorders just reviewed generally have been associated with consumption of large quantities of alcohol over a long period of time. In the case of the adverse effects of alcohol during pregnancy on unborn children, we are dealing with a unique situation. First of all, we need to recognize the extreme susceptibility of a developing fetus to conditions in the mother's bloodstream. In short, if the mother takes a drink, the fetus takes one, too. And to make matters worse, the fetus does not have sufficient levels of alcohol dehydrogenase to break down the alcohol properly; thus, the alcohol stays in the fetus's system longer than in the mother's. In addition, the presence of alcohol coincides with a period of time in prenatal development when critical processes are occurring that are essential for the development of a healthy, alert child.

Although it has long been suspected that alcohol abuse among pregnant women might present serious risks to the fetus, a specific syndrome was not established until 1973, when Kenneth L. Jones and David W. Smith described a cluster of characteristic features in children of alcoholic mothers that is now referred to as **fetal alcohol syndrome (FAS)**. FAS represents the most serious syndrome among the Fetal Alcohol Spectrum Disorders (FASDs).[79] Their studies, and research conducted since then,

The face of a child diagnosed as having a fetal alcohol spectrum disorder, showing the wide-set eyes and other features that are characteristic of this condition.

Credit: Rick's Photography/Shutterstock

have shown clearly that alcohol is **teratogenic**; that is, it produces specific birth defects in offspring by disrupting fetal development during pregnancy, even when differences in prenatal nutrition have been accounted for. Later in life, FAS children show deficits in short-term memory, problem-solving, and attentiveness.

Present-day diagnoses of FAS are made on the basis of three groups of observations: (1) prenatal or postnatal growth retardation in which the child's weight or length is below the tenth percentile, (2) evidence of CNS abnormalities or developmental disabilities, and (3) a characteristic skull and facial appearance that includes a smaller-than-normal head, small wide-set eyes, drooping eyelids, a flattening of the vertical groove between the mouth and nose, a thin upper lip, and a short upturned nose.

The incidence of FAS is approximately 0.2–1.5 cases per every thousand live births in the general U.S. population.[80] Risks are greatly increased when excessive drinking is taking place. Although an occasional drink may have minimal effects, no one has determined a "safe" level of drinking during pregnancy that would make this behavior risk free. The objective of prevention, therefore, is to educate women to the dangers of drinking at any level and to encourage complete abstinence from alcohol (as well as other psychoactive drugs) during pregnancy.[81] Since 1989, all containers of alcoholic beverages must

Wernicke-Korsakoff syndrome (VERN-ih-kee KOR-sa-kof SIN-drohm): A condition resulting from chronic alcohol consumption, characterized by disorientation, cognitive deficits, amnesia, and motor difficulty.

thiamine (THY-ah-meen or THY-ah-min): Vitamin B_1.

confabulation: The tendency to make up elaborate past histories to cover the fact that long-term memory has been impaired.

fetal alcohol syndrome (FAS): A serious condition involving developmental disabilities and facial-cranial malformations in the offspring of an alcoholic mother.

teratogenic (TER-ah-tuh-JEN-ik): Capable of producing specific birth defects.

contain two warning messages, one of which is that "according to the Surgeon General, women should not drink alcoholic beverages during pregnancy because of the risk of birth defects."

Fortunately, the public is aware of the problem and the number of women who consume alcohol during pregnancy has declined over the last 25 years. Nonetheless, 10 percent of pregnant women nationwide continue to consume alcohol, with 3 percent engaging in binge drinking. Among pregnant women, highest use is with those who are 35–44 years old, unmarried, and a college graduate. Unfortunately, FAS continues to be the third leading cause of intellectual disabilities, not only in the United States, but in the entire Western world, exceeded only by Down syndrome and spina bifida. The fact that the development of alcohol-related fetal defects is entirely preventable makes the incidence of these conditions all the more tragic.[82]

Diagnosis and Treatment Strategies

Since 1957, the American Medical Association has defined alcoholism as a disease, and numerous other health organizations have adopted a similar position. As reasonable as this position might sound, the disease concept has created something of a dilemma among professionals concerned with the treatment of alcohol use disorders. It places the burden on physicians to deal with the alcoholic through medical interventions, and unfortunately, the medical profession is frequently ill-equipped to help.

Diagnosis of Alcohol Use Disorder

The American Psychiatric Association, through its *Diagnostic and Statistical Manual, Fifth Edition* (known as *DSM-5*), has established a set of 11 behavioral criteria for a diagnosis of **alcohol use disorder** (see Drugs…in Focus). While the terms "alcoholism" and "chronic alcohol abuse" are not used in this diagnosis, the criteria encompass the psychological-behavioral, social, and physical components discussed earlier that accompany a pattern of problematic drinking. Essentially, an alcohol use disorder is regarded as a specific example of a substance use disorder, with the substance in question being alcohol.

On the basis of an observation of these behaviors over a 12-month period, the prevalence in the United States of alcohol use disorder is estimated to be 4.6 percent among 12–17-year-olds and 8.5 percent among adults aged 18 years or older. Peak prevalence rates are observed for individuals of ages 18–29 years.[83]

alcohol use disorder: A diagnosis in the *DSM-5* classification of mental disorders, based upon a set of behavioral criteria that reflect the psychological-behavioral, social, and physical components of chronic alcohol abuse.

Drugs . . . in Focus

Behavioral Criteria for Alcohol Use Disorder

The American Psychiatric Association considers 11 behaviors as criteria as the basis for the diagnosis of alcohol use disorder in the DSM-5 classification system (see Chapter 8). As can be seen, they parallel the criteria for a diagnosis of substance use disorder. The same scale of severity is used. Mild alcohol use disorder is indicated when two to three behaviors are observed; moderate alcohol use disorder when four to five behaviors are observed, and severe alcohol use disorder when six or more behaviors are observed.

1. Drinking alcohol in larger amounts or over a longer interval than was intended.
2. A persistent desire or unsuccessful efforts to cut down on alcohol use.
3. A great deal of time spent on activities to obtain alcohol, use it, or recover from its effects.
4. Craving or a strong urge to use alcohol.
5. Failure to fulfill major obligations at work, school, or home due to recurrent alcohol use.
6. Continuing alcohol use despite social or interpersonal problems related to the effects of alcohol.

7. Social, occupational, or recreational activities given up or reduced due to alcohol use.
8. Recurrent alcohol use when a physical hazardous situation may result.
9. Continued alcohol use despite knowing that physical or psychological problems might be caused or made worse by alcohol consumption.
10. Tolerance to the pharmacological properties of alcohol, needing increased amounts to achieve intoxication or, diminished intoxication with the same amount of alcohol.
11. Withdrawal symptoms when alcohol use is diminished or stopped.

It should be noted that none of the criteria refers to specific instances of alcohol misuse (as reviewed earlier in the chapter). Instances of alcohol misuse are assumed to occur among individuals meeting at least some other criteria for alcohol use disorder.

Source: Based upon information from the American Psychiatric Association (2013). *Diagnostic and statistical manual of mental disorders (DSM-5)* (5th ed.). Washington, D.C.: American Psychiatric Publishing, pp. 490–497.

An Abstinence versus Harm Reduction Model

A difficult issue related to the treatment for alcoholism is whether it is possible for alcoholics in the course of treatment to achieve a level of "controlled drinking" without relapsing. As we will see, well-entrenched organizations such as Alcoholics Anonymous (AA) and the National Institute on Alcohol Abuse and Alcoholism have a strong position that alcoholism is a disease, that abstinence from alcohol is the only answer, and that even the slightest level of alcohol consumption will trigger a cascade of problems that the alcoholic is constitutionally incapable of handling. Other treatment organizations, represented in greater numbers in Canada and Europe than in the United States, believe that uncontrolled drinking is a reversible behavioral disorder and that for many alcoholics the promotion of total abstinence as a treatment goal is a serious obstacle to their success in rehabilitation. The organization Moderation Management (MM) and SMART Recovery are two examples of treatment organizations holding the position that harm reduction should be the goal.

Research studies using carefully randomized assignment of alcoholic subjects to either an abstinence-oriented treatment or a controlled-drinking one have shown that long-term results are comparable for either group. This is not to say that the prospects are wonderful for either of them; the odds are still higher against long-term recovery from alcoholism than for it, no matter what the treatment, but it does appear that controlled drinking can occur.

How many alcoholics can manage to achieve a continued level of nonproblem drinking? Percentages vary from 2 to 15, though the lower figure is probably more accurate for those individuals with severe alcoholic difficulties. Perhaps a more important point is that no one knows how to predict whether an alcohol abuser will be one of that small number of successful controlled drinkers. Obviously, most alcoholics are convinced that they will be the lucky ones.[84]

Questions surrounding "controlled drinking" for individuals in treatment for chronic alcohol abuse and the appropriateness of labeling alcoholism as a physical disease have important legal ramifications in situations in which a criminal offence might be committed. The justification for using alcohol intoxication as a legal defense in these circumstances is a complex issue in present-day criminal law.[85]

Treatment and Support Options for Chronic Alcohol Abuse

The most common treatment options for alcohol use disorder are classified as either biologically-based interventions, which involve medications, or psychosocial interventions, which involve self-help programs such as AA and SMART Recovery. As we will see, programs employing a psychosocial intervention have different philosophies as to the nature of problem drinking.

Biologically Based Treatments

The use of **disulfiram** (brand name: Antabuse) as a treatment for alcohol use disorders is based on the idea that if aversive physiological reaction is induced when alcohol is consumed, then consumption will be avoided and the problems of alcoholism will be reduced. Disulfiram, taken orally as a pill once each day, inhibits alcohol dehydrogenase, allowing acetaldehyde to build up in the bloodstream. As a result, individuals who consume alcohol in combination with disulfiram experience a flushing of the face, rapid heart rate and palpitations, nausea, and vomiting. These effects are brought on not only by consuming alcoholic beverages but also by ingesting alcohol in other forms such as mouthwashes and cough mixtures, and even by the absorption of aftershave lotions and shampoos through the skin.

Studies in which disulfiram has been administered to large numbers of alcoholics indicate that it is not effective when it is the sole treatment. One major problem is that alcoholics must take the drug regularly every day, and because disulfiram does nothing to reduce the alcoholic's craving for alcohol, compliance rates are low. The consensus among professionals in this field is that disulfiram can be useful in a subgroup of higher-functioning alcoholics with exceptionally high motivation to quit drinking; for others, disulfiram can be useful as a transitional treatment until other support programs are in place.[86]

A more direct approach to treatment than aversion therapy is to reduce the actual craving for alcohol on a physiological level. As noted in Chapter 8, the craving for alcohol is related to neurochemical activity in the same dopamine-releasing receptors in the nucleus accumbens that have been implicated in craving for opioids such as heroin as well as in craving for cocaine and nicotine. Medications that interfere with dopamine activity in the nucleus accumbens, such as **naltrexone** (brand name as an alcoholism treatment: ReVia) and **nalmefene** (brand name: Revex), should be useful in treatment

An extended-release injectable form of naltrexone (brand name: Vivitrol), administered on a monthly basis, was FDA approved in 2006. The obvious advantage is that individuals do not have to remember to take their medication on a daily basis. This eliminates problems associated with individuals skipping their medication and there can be a more intensive concentration on the counseling component of recovery. The advantage of an extended-release naltrexone parallels that of an extended-release formulation of buprenorphine (brand name: Sublocade) for treating opioid abuse (see Chapter 9).

---

disulfiram (dye-SULL-fih-ram): A medication that causes severe physical reactions and discomfort when combined with alcohol. Brand name is Antabuse.

naltrexone (nal-TREX-ohn): A long-lasting opioid antagonist for the treatment of alcoholism. Brand name is ReVia. Brand name for an extended-release injectable form is Vivitrol

nalmefene (nal-MEH-feen): A long-lasting opioid antagonist for the treatment of alcoholism. Brand name is Revex.

Other neurochemical approaches have focused on other neurotransmitter systems in the brain (see Drugs…in Focus, page 148).

- FDA approved in 2004, **acamprosate** (brand name: Campral) works on the basis of regulating the neurotransmitter, GABA.

- Topiramate (brand name: Topamax) also works on the basis of regulating GABA. Other therapeutic applications include topiramate as an antiepileptic and migraine-alleviating medication.

- An anti-nausea medication that reduces serotonin levels such as **ondansetron** (brand name: Zofran) has been useful for early-onset (Type 2) alcoholics, owing to the association between this subgroup and serotonin abnormalities in the brain (see Table 13.5).

In a recent study, medications based on naltrexone (ReVia, Revex, and Vivitrol) and acamprosate (Campral) were found to be effective treatments for at least a portion of alcoholic individuals. Researchers concluded that to prevent one person from returning to drinking the number of people needed to treat for acamprosate was 12 and for naltrexone was 20. While these numbers may appear to be quite high, it is worth comparing the results to large-scale studies that have found that from 25 to more than 100 people need treatment of widely used cholesterol-lowering statin medications to prevent one cardiovascular event such as a heart attack. Yet, only a small proportion of individuals with alcohol problems receive treatment of any kind, and a still smaller proportion are prescribed medications (see Chapter 14).[87]

Alcoholics Anonymous (AA)

The best-known treatment program for alcoholism is **Alcoholics Anonymous (AA)**. Founded in 1935, this organization was conceived as a fellowship of individuals, who wished to rid themselves of their problem drinking by helping one another maintain sobriety. The philosophy of AA is expressed in the famous Twelve Steps. Members must have acknowledged that they were "powerless over alcohol" and that their lives had become unmanageable, and so must have turned their will and their lives over "to the care of God *as we understood Him.*" As the steps indicate, there is a strong spiritual component to the AA program, although the organization vigorously denies that any religious doctrine prevails.

AA functions as a type of group support with each member oriented toward a common goal: the maintenance of abstinence from alcohol despite a powerful and continuing craving for it. All meetings are completely anonymous (only first names are used in all communications), and the proceedings are dominated by members recounting their personal struggles with alcohol, their efforts to stop drinking, and their support for fellow alcoholics in their own struggles. New members are encouraged to pair up with a sponsor, typically a more experienced AA member, who has successfully completed the Twelve Steps and can serve as a personal source of support on a day-to-day basis. According to AA, no alcoholic is ever cured, but is only recovering, and the process of recovery continues throughout that person's life. In this view, alcoholism is a disease, and relapse from sobriety can occur at any moment.

AA has grown to more than 114,000 groups and more than 2 million members worldwide, although it is difficult to get a precise count because the organization is deliberately structured very loosely. Perhaps more important than its size is the powerful impact AA has had not only on the way we deal with alcoholism but also on the way we consider treatment for any compulsive behavior in general. Over the years, the Twelve-Step program has become a generic concept, as the precepts and philosophy of AA have been widely imitated. There are chapters of Gamblers Anonymous, Nicotine Anonymous, Narcotics or Cocaine Anonymous, and Overeaters Anonymous, all based on the AA model. In addition, there are two specialized fellowship organizations: Al-Anon for relatives and friends of alcoholics and Alateen for teenagers living with an alcoholic family member. These programs adopt a Twelve-Step approach to identifying and dealing with the dysfunctionality of an alcoholic family.

AA is widely regarded in the field of alcohol rehabilitation as a beneficial self-help approach, particularly when it is combined with other treatments such as individual counseling and medical interventions. It has been pointed out that AA employs four factors that have been shown to be effective in preventing relapse in alcohol use disorder: (1) the imposition of external supervision, (2) the substitution of dependence on a group activity for dependence on drug-taking behavior, (3) the development of caring relationships, and (4) a heightened sense of spirituality. Nonetheless, the inherent anonymity of AA remains a significant barrier to the precise scientific assessment of its effectiveness as an intervention program.[88]

SMART Recovery

In contrast to AA, the self-help program **SMART Recovery** holds the position that people do not need to believe that they are "powerless over alcohol" or have to submit to "a Power

---

acamprosate (A-cam-PRO-sate): A GABA-related drug for the treatment of alcoholism. Brand name is Campral.

ondansetron (on-DANS-eh-tron): A serotonin-related drug for the treatment of alcoholism. Brand name is Zofran.

Alcoholics Anonymous (AA): A worldwide organization devoted to the treatment of alcoholism through self-help groups and adherence to its principles, which include absolute abstinence from alcohol.

SMART Recovery: A treatment program for abuse of alcohol and other drugs that emphasizes a nonspiritual philosophy and a greater sense of personal control in the abuser. SMART stands for "Self-Management and Recovery Training."

greater than ourselves" (phrases taken from the Twelve Steps) to recover from alcoholism. Instead, the dominant philosophy is that individuals have the power themselves to overcome anything, including drinking. Unlike AA, Smart Recovery discourages labeling in general; a person is not required to call himself or herself an alcoholic to achieve success in recovery. The strategy is based on rational emotive behavior therapy (REBT), an approach developed by the psychologist Albert Ellis that emphasizes rooting out irrational thoughts, emotions, and beliefs that prevent the achievement of personal goals.

Another major difference is that SMART Recovery insists on professional involvement in its program, with a professional adviser (often a clinical psychologist) helping members learn the fundamentals of REBT. No reference is made to God or a higher power; the objective is "NHP (no higher power) sobriety." The goal is that within a year and a half members will be able to maintain sobriety without going to meetings. In contrast, AA members are encouraged to continue going to meetings for the rest of their lives.

Since 1990, there has been increased interest in secular (nonreligious) approaches to self-help alcoholism treatment such as that practiced by SMART Recovery. Other examples include Men for Sobriety (MFS), Women for Sobriety (WFS), Moderation Management (MM), and Secular Organization for Sobriety (SOS). Nonetheless, recent research has indicated that alcoholics benefit from participation in AA programs, regardless of their religious beliefs (Drugs…in Focus).[89]

Quick Concept Check 13.3

Understanding Alcoholics Anonymous

Check your understanding of the principles and philosophy of Alcoholics Anonymous by indicating whether each of the following statements would be subscribed to by Alcoholics Anonymous.

1. I have always had the power to control my drinking. ☐ yes ☐ no

2. I must put myself in the hands of a Higher Power if I am to be sober for the rest of my life. ☐ yes ☐ no

3. It is possible to be cured of alcoholism. ☐ yes ☐ no

4. I am capable of having a drink once in a great while without slipping back into alcoholism. ☐ yes ☐ no

5. The more meetings I attend, the better chance I have of remaining sober. ☐ yes ☐ no

Answers: 1. no 2. yes 3. no 4. no 5. yes

Summary

Processing of Alcohol in the Body

- The three basic forms of alcohol are wine, beer, and distilled spirits, all of which have different sources and concentrations.

- Absorption of alcohol into the bloodstream is extremely rapid. Several factors impact the rate of alcohol absorption.

- The effective level of alcohol in the body is measured by the blood alcohol concentration (BAC) level in the bloodstream.

- There is a great disparity in the drinking habits in the U.S. population. About a third of the population do not drink at all, and only 30 percent of those who drink account for 80 percent of total alcohol consumption.

Alcohol Consumption among At-Risk Groups

- Peak alcohol consumption occurs at ages 21–22. Alcohol problems among college students are a continuing social concern.

- Other areas of concern with respect to problematic drinking include access to alcohol beverages by underage drinkers, and the social and legal problems this creates.

- Alcohol misuse among the offender population also creates public safety concerns, particularly since problems

with alcohol and other drugs are associated with increased rates of reoffending.

Acute Physiological Effects

- Alcohol at very high levels produces a number of acute physiological effects, some of them being life-threatening. Potential death by asphyxiation can occur with BAC levels reaching 0.50 percent. At moderate levels, acute effects include a loss of body heat, increased excretion of water, an increase in heart rate and constriction of coronary arteries, disturbed patterns of sleep, and serious interactions with other drugs.

- Consumption of alcohol, even in moderate amounts, during pregnancy greatly increases the risk of retardation in the development of the fetus.

Acute Behavioral Effects

- On a behavioral level, serious adverse effects include blackouts, significant impairment in sensorimotor skills such as driving an automobile, and an increased potential for aggressive or violent acts.

- The relationship between alcohol consumption and sexual desire and performance is a complex one, with differences being observed for men and women. Expectations can play a significant role in some circumstances.

The Legal Consequences of Alcohol Misuse

- While the rate of DUI fatalities have decreased over the past decade, more than a quarter of all fatal traffic accidents are linked to alcohol.
- Law enforcement officers use a range of field and chemical tests to identify whether a person is driving while intoxicated.
- Violent crime, particularly intimate partner violence, but also murder, sexual offending, and child abuse, is associated with alcohol abuse.
- The criminalization of public intoxication varies by jurisdiction, as does the legality of parents or other family members providing alcohol to their children.

Strategies for Regulating Alcohol Consumption

- One approach to regulating alcohol consumption is to restrict access. Twenty-one years has been set nationwide as the minimum age requirement for the purchase of alcoholic beverages.
- A principal strategy for regulation has been the imposition of taxes, either at the federal or local level.
- The reduction in alcohol-related traffic fatalities has been made through a nationwide standard 0.08 percent for "driving while intoxicated" among adult drivers and 0.02 percent for drivers younger than 21 years. Anti-ignition interlock systems in automobiles have also been useful for drivers with a record of driving while intoxicated.

Chronic Alcohol Abuse and Alcoholism

- Alcoholism is a multidimensional condition that is typically defined in terms of four major criteria: (1) problems associated with a preoccupation with drinking, (2) emotional problems, (3) vocational, social, and family problems, and (4) physical problems. Dysfunctionality is a typical feature of an individual's family dynamics when one or both parents in the family are chronic alcohol abusers.
- According to health professionals, alcohol use disorder is diagnosed through a set of behavioral criteria that include uncontrolled alcohol intake, unsuccessful efforts to reduce alcohol use, life problems, and alcohol tolerance and withdrawal.

Interpersonal and Family Relationships in Alcoholism

- A systems approach to alcoholism examines the complex interacting relationships among individuals, family, friends, and community.
- The concept of codependency has helped shed light on the specific effects of alcoholism on spouses and other family members.

- The children of alcoholics (COAs) carry an increased risk of becoming alcoholic as a result of a vulnerability toward alcoholism that is genetically or environmentally based, or both.
- One risk factor is having an elevated threshold for alcohol intoxication.
- The increased risk of developing alcoholism for an alcoholic having drinking problems early in life (a Type 2 alcoholic) has been shown to be generically based, rather than environmentally based.

Patterns of Chronic Alcohol Abuse

- An estimated 88,000 alcohol-related deaths occur in the United States each year.
- Men outnumber women in the incidence of alcoholism by about six to one, although women are more vulnerable to alcohol-related organ damage.

Physiological Effects of Chronic Alcohol Abuse

- Physiological effects of chronic alcohol abuse include tolerance and withdrawal, liver disease, cardiovascular disease, cancer, and neurological disorders such as Wernicke-Korsakoff syndrome.
- A particular concern is the development of fetal alcohol syndrome (FAS) in the offspring of alcoholic mothers.

Diagnosis and Treatment Strategies

- The standard position among health care professional with respect to alcoholism is that it should be considered a disease. The American Medical Association has supported this view.
- The question of the likelihood for an alcoholic to sustain a moderate level of controlled drinking is controversial within the alcoholism treatment profession.

Treatment and Support Options for Chronic Alcohol Abuse

- Treatment options for alcohol use disorder are classified as biologically based treatments, using specific medications, or psychosocial treatments.
- Psychosocial support groups include Alcoholics Anonymous (AA) and SMART Recovery. The position of AA is that the alcoholic can never be cured and that a zero tolerance for alcohol consumption must be sustained. The position of SMART Recovery is that the alcoholic can successfully overcome problem drinking through rational-emotive behavioral therapy.

Key Terms

Review Questions

1. Describe the factors that determine the BAC level of an individual after a period of alcohol drinking.
2. Describe how alcohol consumption among at-risk groups impacts public safety.
3. Briefly describe the acute physiological effects of alcohol consumption, with reference to toxic reactions, heat and water retention, cardiovascular condition, and patterns of sleep.
4. Briefly describe the acute behavioral effects of alcohol consumption with reference to memory, driving skills, and sexual activity.
5. Identify specific crimes associated with alcohol misuse and the ways in which these crimes affect public safety.
6. In what way would taxation designed to reduce alcohol consumption have the total opposite effect?
7. What dynamics are typical of an alcoholic family?
8. Summarize the behavioral criteria for alcohol use disorder, as established by the DSM-5 classification of diagnoses.
9. Briefly describe the physiological effects of chronic alcohol abuse, with respect to tolerance and withdrawal, liver and cardiovascular disease, cancer, and certain neurological disorders.
10. Distinguish between a Type 1 and Type 2 alcoholic. What are the ramifications for treatment?
11. Contrast Alcoholics Anonymous (AA) and SMART Recovery with respect to their philosophies and general approaches toward treatment.

Critical Thinking: What Would You Do?

You are the presiding judge in a trial in which John Doe is charged with assaulting and injuring a man while outside a local fast-food establishment. The defense attorney has argued that Mr. Doe is a recovering alcoholic, having been treated in the SMART Recovery program. Mr. Doe has been engaged in controlled drinking for the past eight months, without incident. On the night of the offense, Mr. Doe returned home and fell asleep; in the morning, he had no memory of the offense for which he is charged or any aspect of the incident in question. Evidence that the offense was committed has not been contested. Would you reduce the sentence of Mr. Doe on the basis of the argument that there were mitigating circumstances?

Endnotes

1. Adapted from an observation by the first author. See also Pinel, J. P.(2003). *Biopsychology* (5th ed.). Boston: Allyn and Bacon, p. 381.
2. U.S. Department of Health and Human Services (2000). *Alcohol and health* (Tenth Special Report to the U.S. Congress). Bethesda, MD: National Institute on Alcohol Abuse and Alcoholism, p. 370.
3. Dubowski, K. M. (1991). *The technology of breath-alcohol analysis*. Bethesda, MD: National Institute on Alcohol Abuse and Alcoholism.
4. Julien, R. M. (2005). *A primer of drug action* (10th ed.). New York: Worth, pp. 96–98. National Institute on Alcohol Abuse and Alcoholism (2007, April). *Alcohol Alert: Alcohol metabolism: An update*. No. 72. Bethesda, MD: National Institute on Alcohol Abuse and Alcoholism.
5. Levinthal, C. F. (1990). *Introduction to physiological psychology* (3rd ed.). Englewood Cliffs, NJ: Prentice Hall, pp. 181–184.
6. Julien, *A primer of drug action*, p. 97.
7. LaVallee, R. A.; Kim, T.; and Yi, H. (2014, April). *Surveillance report #98: Apparent per capita alcohol consumption: National, state, and regional trends, 1977–2012*. Bethesda, MD: National Institute on Alcohol Abuse and Alcoholism, Figure 4.
8. Center for Behavioral Health Statistics and Quality (2016). Results from the *2015 National Survey on Drug Use and Health: Detailed tables*. Rockville, MD: Substance Abuse and Mental Health Services Administration, Table 6.89b.
9. Thombs, D. L.; Olds, R. S.; Bondy, S. J.; et al. (2009). Undergraduate drinking and academic performance: A

prospective investigation with objective measures. *Journal of Studies on Alcohol and Drugs, 70*(5), 776–785.

10. Hingson, R. W.; Zha, W.; and Weitzman, E. R. (2009). Magnitude of and trends in alcohol-related mortality and morbidity among U.S. college students ages 18–24, 1998–2005. *Journal of Studies on Alcohol and Drugs* (Supplement No. 16), 12–20.

11. Heeren, T.; Zakocs, R. C.; and Kopstein, A. (2002). Age of first intoxication, heavy drinking, driving after drinking and risk of unintentional injury among U.S. college students. *Journal of Studies on Alcohol, 63*, 136–144.

12. Carey, K. B.; Durney, S. E.; Shepardson, R. L.; Carey, M. P. (2015). Precollege predictors of incapacitated rape among female students in their first year of college. *Journal of Studies on Alcohol and Drugs, 76*, 829–837.

13. Bureau of Justice Statistics. (2014). Rape and Sexual Victimization Among College-Aged Females, 1995–2013. Washington, D.C.: U.S. Department of Justice.

14. National Institute on Alcohol and Alcohol Abuse (2015). *Fact sheet on college drinking*. Washington, D.C.: National Institute of Health.

15. Center for Behavioral Health Statistics and Quality (2017). *2016 National Survey on Drug Use and Health: Detailed tables*. Rockville, MD: Substance Abuse and Mental Health Services Administration, Table 2.19B.

16. Johnston, L. D.; Miech, R. A.; O'Malley, P. M.; Bachman, J. G.; Schulenberg, J. E.; and Patrick, M. E. (2017). *Monitoring the future: National survey results on drug use, 1975–2017, 2017 Overview: Key findings on adolescent drug abuse.* Washington, D.C.: National Institute on Drug Abuse and National Institutes of Health., p. 37 and Table 9.

17. Center for Behavioral Health Statistics and Quality (2017). *Results from the 2016 National Survey on Drug Use and Health: Detailed tables*, Tables 6.63B and 6.64B. Center for Behavioral Health Statistics and Quality (2014). *Results from the 2013 National Survey on Drug Use and Health: Detailed tables*. Rockville, MD: Substance Abuse and Mental Health Services Administration, Tables 6.67B and 6.69B. Substance Abuse and Mental Health Services Administration (2008, August 28). Underage alcohol use: Where do young people drink? *The NSDUH Report*. Rockville, MD: Substance Abuse and Mental Health Services Administration. Windle, M.; and Zucker, R. A. (2010). Reducing underage and young adult drinking: How to address critical drinking problems during this developmental period. *Alcohol Research and Health, 33*, 29–44.

18. National Institute on Alcohol Abuse and Alcoholism (2006, January). *Alcohol Alert*, No. 67. Bethesda, MD: National Institute on Alcohol Abuse and Alcoholism

19. Terry-McElrath, Y. M.; O'Malley, P. M.; and Johnston, L. D. (2014). Alcohol and marijuana use patterns associated with unsafe driving among U.S. high school seniors: High use frequency, concurrent use, and simultaneous use. *Journal of Studies on Alcohol and Drugs, 75*(3), 378–389.

20. Kaigang, L.; Ochoa, E.; Vaca, F. E.; and Simons-Morton, B. (2018). Emerging adults riding with marijuana, alcohol, or illicit drug-impaired peer and older drivers. *Journal of Studies on Alcohol and Drugs, 79*, 277–285.

21. Foundation for Advancing Alcohol Responsibility. *Drunk Driving Fatalities.* Accessed from: https://www.responsibility.org /get-the-facts/research/statistics/drunk-driving-fatalities/?gclid=Cj 0KCQjw5fDWBRDaARIsAA5uWTg6gFAqxo75ke5XVgEOW kYtEBqRqWW8ok9Zqo3u4ngjGBGuyFVvYukaAub XEALw_wcB

22. Bureau of Justice Statistics (2011, May). Criminal victimization in the United States, 2008. Statistical tables. Washington, D.C.: Bureau of Justice Statistics, U.S. Department of Justice, Table 32.

23. Knight, K.; Simpson, D. D.; and Hiller, M .L. (2002). Screening and referral for substance-abuse treatment in the criminal justice system. In: C. G. Leukefeld; F. Tims; and D. Farabee (Eds.),. *Treatment of drug offenders: Policies and issues.* New York: Springer, pp. 259–272.

24. Bonta, J.; and Andrews, D. (2017). *The psychology of criminal conduct* (6th ed.). New York: Routledge.

25. Cohen, T. H.; Lowenkamp, C. T.; and Van Benschoten, S. W. (2016). Does changes in risk matter? Examining whether changes in offender risk characteristics influence recidivism outcomes. *Criminology and Public Policy, 15*, 263–296.

26. Grilly, D. M.; and Salamone, J. (2012). *Drugs, brain and behavior* (6th ed.). Boston: Pearson Education, p. 238.

27. Luks, A.; and Barbato, J. (1989). *You are what you drink.* New York: Gilliard, pp. 42–43.

28. National Institute on Alcohol Abuse and Alcoholism (1998, July). *Alcohol Alert: Alcohol and sleep.* No. 41. Bethesda, MD: National Institute on Alcohol Abuse and Alcoholism.

29. Tan, C. H.; Denny, C. H.; Cheal, N. E.; Sniezek, J. E.; and Kanny, D. (2015). Alcohol use and binge drinking among women of childbearing age—United States, 2011–2013. *Morbidity and Mortality Weekly Report, 64*, 1041-1046.

30. Schuckit, M. A. (2006). *Drug and alcohol abuse: A clinical guide to diagnosis and treatment* (6th ed.). New York: Plenum, p. 88.

31. Wiese, J. G.; Shlipak, M. G.; and Browner, W. S. (2000). The alcohol hangover. *Annals of Internal Medicine, 232*, 897–902.

32. White, A. M.; Jamieson-Drake, D. W.; and Swartzwelder, H. S. (2002). Prevalence and correlates of alcohol-induced blackouts among college students: Results of an e-mail survey. *Journal of American College Health, 51*, 117–131.

33. Abel, E. L. (1985). *Psychoactive drugs and sex.* New York: Plenum Press, pp. 19–54. Cooper, M. Lynne (2006). Does drinking promote risky sexual behavior? A complex answer to a simple question. *Current Directions in Psychological Science, 15*, 19–23.

34. Morse, S. J. (2017). Addiction, Choice and Criminal Law. Faculty Scholarship, 1608. Penn Law: Legal Scholarship Repository: University of Pennsylvania Law School. Accessed from: https://scholarship.law.upenn.edu/ faculty_scholarship/1608

35. National Highway Traffic Safety Administration (2017, October). Alcohol-impaired driving. *Traffic safety facts: 2016 data.* Washington, D.C.: National Center for Statistics and Analysis, National Highway Traffic Safety Administration.

36. Hoyer, W. J.; Semenec, S. C.; and Buckler, N. E. (2007). Acute alcohol intoxication impairs controlled search across the visual field. *Journal of Studies on Alcohol and Drugs, 68*, 748–758.

37. Federal Bureau of Investigation (2016). *Uniform Crime Report 2016. Crime in the United States.* Washington, D.C.: Federal Bureau of Investigation, U. S. Department of Justice, Tables 18–21.

38. National Highway Traffic Safety Administration (NHTSA). (October, 2015). DWI Detection and Standardized Field Sobriety Testing (SFST): Instructor Guide. Accessed from:

https://www.nhtsa.gov/sites/nhtsa.dot.gov/files/documents/
sfst_ig_full_manual.pdf

39. Boas, R. B.; Kelley-Baker, T.; Romano, E.; and Vishnuvajjala, R. (2009). Implied-consent laws: A review of the literature and examination of current problems and related statutes. *Journal of Safety Research, 40, 77–83.*

40. Bureau of Justice Statistics. (revised July 2010). *Alcohol and crime: Data from 2002 to 2008.* Washington, D.C.: U.S. Department of Justice.

41. Ibid.

42. Moore T. M.; Elkins S. R.; McNulty J. K.; Kivisto A. J.; Handsel V. A. (2011). Alcohol use and intimate partner violence perpetration among college students: Assessing the temporal association using electronic diary technology. *Psychology of Violence, 4, 28.*

43. Collins, J. J.; and Messerschmidt, P. M. (1993). Epidemiology of alcohol-related violence. *Alcohol Health and Research World, 17, 93–100.* Goode, E. (2012). *Drugs in American society* (8th ed.). New York: McGraw-Hill, pp. 184–188.

44. Office of Justice Programs (2009, May). *Children exposed to violence (NCJ 251220).* Washington, D.C.:, U.S. Department of Justice.

45. Goode, *Drugs in American society,* p. 368.

46. Giancola, P. R. (2000). Executive functioning: A conceptual framework for alcohol-related aggression. *Experimental and Clinical Psychopharmacology, 8, 576–597.* Giancola, P. R. (2002). Alcohol-related aggression in men and women: The influence of dispositional aggressivity. *Journal of Studies on Alcohol, 63, 696–708.*

47. Alcohol Policy Information System. Underage Drinking: Furnishing Alcohol to Minors. National Institute on Alcohol Abuse and Alcoholism, National Institutes of Health; Washington, D.C. Accessed from: https://alcoholpolicy.niaaa.nih.gov/apis-policy-topics/furnishing-alcohol-to-minors/40

48. Alcohol Policy Information System. Beverage Service Training and Related Practices. National Institute on Alcohol Abuse and Alcoholism, National Institutes of Health; Washington, D.C. Accessed from: https://alcoholpolicy.niaaa.nih.gov/apis-policy-topics/beverage-service-training-and-related-practices/26

49. Mosher, C. J.; and Akins, S. M. (2007). *Drugs and drug policy: The control of consciousness alteration.* Los Angeles: Sage Publications, p. 370.

50. National Highway Traffic Safety Administration (2009, June). Lives saved in 2008 by restraint use and minimum drinking age laws. *Traffic Safety Facts.* Washington, D.C.: National Center for Statistics and Analysis, National Highway Traffic Safety Administration.

51. Office of Management and Budget (2017). *Budget of the United States Government, Fiscal Year 2017, Historical Tables.* Washington, D.C.: Office of Management and Budget, Table 2.4

52. Xu, X.; and Chaloupka, F. J. (2012). The effects of prices on alcohol use and its consequences. *Alcohol Research and Health, 34, 236–245.*

53. National Institute on Alcohol Abuse and Alcoholism (2001, April). *Alcohol Alert: Alcohol and transportation safety.* No. 52. Bethesda, MD: National Institute on Alcohol Abuse and Alcoholism. Wagenaar, A. C.; O'Malley, P. M.; and LaFond, C. (2001). Lowered legal blood alcohol limits for young drivers: Effects on drinking, driving, and driving-after-drinking behaviors in 30 states. *American Journal of Public Health, 91, 801–803.*

54. McClelland, R.; and Iselin, J. (2017. October). Do Alcohol Excise Taxes Reduce Motor Vehicle Fatalities? Evidence from Two Illinois Tax Increases. *Tax Policy Center.* Accessed from: http://www.taxpolicycenter.org/publications/do-alcohol-excise-taxes-reduce-motor-vehicle-fatalities-evidence-two-illinois-tax/full.

55. National Highway Traffic Safety Administration (2009, June). Lives saved in 2008 by restraint use and minimum drinking age laws. *Traffic safety facts.* Washington, D.C.: National Center for Statistics and Analysis, National Highway Traffic Safety Administration.

56. Lipari, R. N.; Hughes, M. S.; and Jonaki Bose, M. S. (2016, December). *The CBHSQ report: Driving under the influence of alcohol and illicit drugs.* Rockville, MD.: Center for Behavioral Health Statistics and Quality, Substance Abuse and Mental Health Services Administration:

57. Rimm, E. B. (2000). Moderate alcohol intake and lower risk of coronary heart disease: Meta-analysis of effects on lipids and haemostatic factors. *Journal of the American Medical Association, 283, 1269.* Zuger, A. (2002, December 31). The case for drinking (all together now: in moderation). *The New York Times,* pp. F1, F6. Quotation on p. F1.

58. Howard, A. A.; Arnsten, J. H.; and Gourevitch, M. N. (2004). Effect of alcohol consumption on diabetes mellitus: A systematic review. *Annals of Internal Medicine, 140, 211–219.* Källberg, H.; Jacobsen, S.; Bengtsson, C.; Pdersen, M.; Padyukov, L.; et al. (2009). Alcohol consumption is associated with decreased risk of rheumatoid arthritis: Results from two Scandinavian case-control studies. *Annals of the Rheumatic Diseases, 68, 222–227.* Mukamal, K. J.; Conigrave, K. M.; Mittleman, M. A.; Carmargo, C. A., Jr.; Stampfer, M. J.; et al. (2003). Roles of drinking pattern and type of alcohol consumed in coronary heart disease in men. *New England Journal of Medicine, 348, 109–118.* Mukamal, K. J.; Kuller, L. H.; Longstreth, W. T.; Mittleman, M. A.; and Siscovick, D. S. (2003). Prospective study of alcohol consumption and risk of dementia in older adults. *Journal of the American Medical Association, 289, 1405–1413.* Reynold, K.; Lewis, L. B.; Nolen, J. D.; Kinney, G. L.; Sathya, B.; et al. (2003). Alcohol consumption and risk of stroke: A meta-analysis. *Journal of the American Medical Association, 289, 579–588.*

59. Alcohol Policies Project, Center for Science in the Public Interest (2000). *Victory for public health: New U.S. guidelines on alcohol consumption drop positive spin on drinking.* Washington, D.C.: Center for Science in the Public Interest. Darby, W.; and Heinz, A. (1991, January). *The responsible use of alcohol: Defining the parameters of moderation.* New York: American Council on Science and Health, pp. 1–26. The Gallup Organization (2005, July 22). *Fewer young adults drinking to excess.* Princeton, NJ: Gallup Organization. Goldberg, I. (2003). To drink or not to drink. *New England Journal of Medicine, 348, 163–164.* Klatsky, A. (2003, February). Drink to your health? *Scientific American,* pp. 75–81. Rabin, R. C. (2009, June 19). Alcohol's good for you? Some scientists doubt it. *The New York Times,* pp. D1, D6.

60. Hofmann, F. G. (1983). *A handbook on drug and alcohol abuse* (2nd ed.). New York: Oxford University Press, p. 99.

61. Conner, K. R.; Yue, L.; Meldrum, S.; Duberstein, P. R.; and Conwell, Y. (2003). The role of drinking in suicidal ideation: Analysis of Project MATCH data. *Journal of Studies on Alcohol, 64, 402–408.* Schuckit, M. A. (2000). *Drug and*

alcohol abuse: A clinical guide to diagnostic and treatment (5th ed.). New York: Kluwer Academic/Plenum, pp. 54–97.

62. Maiden, R. P. (1997). Alcohol dependence and domestic violence: Incidence and treatment implications. *Alcohol Treatment Quarterly, 15,* 31–50. U.S. Department of Health and Human Services (1990). *Alcohol and health* (Seventh Special Report to the U.S. Congress). Bethesda, MD: National Institute on Alcohol Abuse and Alcoholism, p. 174.

63. Centers for Disease Control and Prevention (2018, January). *Fact sheets—Alcohol use and your health.* Atlanta, GA: Centers for Disease Control and Prevention. National Institute on Alcohol Abuse and Alcoholism (2000, April). *Alcohol Alert: Imaging and alcoholism: A window on the brain.* No. 47. Bethesda, MD: National Institute on Alcohol Abuse and Alcoholism. Zeridze, D.; Lewington, S.; Borode, A.; Scelo, G.; Karpov, R.; et al. (2014). Alcohol and mortality in Russia: Prospective observational study of 151,000 adults. *Lancet, 383,* 1465–1473.

64. Fishbein, D. H.; and Pease, S. E. (1996). *The dynamics of drug abuse.* Needham Heights, MA: Allyn and Bacon, pp. 122–124.

65. Beattie, M. (2009). *The new codependency.* New York: Simon and Schuster.

66. Erblich, J.; and Earleywine, M. (1999). Children of alcoholics exhibit attenuated cognitive impairment during an ethanol challenge. *Alcoholism: Clinical and Experimental Research, 23,* 476–482.

67. Hussong, A. M.; Curran, P. J.; and Chassin, L. (1998). Pathways of risk for accelerated heavy alcohol use among adolescent children of alcoholic parents. *Journal of Abnormal Child Psychology, 26,* 453–466.

68. Cloninger, C. R. (1987). Neurogenetic adaptive mechanisms in alcoholism. *Science, 236,* 410–416. Cloninger, C. R.; Gohman, M.; and Sigvardsson, S. (1981). Inheritance of alcohol abuse: Cross fostering analysis of adopted men. *Archives of General Psychiatry, 38,* 861–868. Devor, E. J.; and Cloninger, C. R. (1989). Genetics of alcoholism. *Annual Review of Genetics, 23,* 18–26. National Institute on Alcohol Abuse and Alcoholism (2008). *Genetics of alcohol use disorders.* Bethesda, MD: National Institute on Alcohol Abuse and Alcoholism.

69. Sacks, J. J.; Gonzales, K. R.; Bouchery, E. E.; Tomedi, L. E.; and Brewer, R. De. (2015). 2010 national and state costs of excessive alcohol consumption. *American Journal of Preventive Medicine, 49*(5), e73–e79.

70. Center for Behavioral Health Statistics and Quality (2014). *Results from the 2013 national survey on drug use and health: Summary of national findings.* Rockville, MD: Substance Abuse and Mental Health Services Administration.

71. Julien, *A primer of drug action,* pp. 106–109.

72. Whiteman, P. J.; Hoffman R. S.; and Goldfrank, L. R. (2000). Alcoholism in the emergency department: An epidemiologic study. *Academic Emergency Medicine, 7,* 14–20. Saitz, R. (2005). Clinical practice. Unhealthy alcohol use. *New England Journal of Medicine, 352,* 596–607.

73. Becker, H. (2008). Alcohol dependence, withdrawal, and relapse. *Alcohol Research and Health, 31,* 348–361.

74. Kochanek, K .D.; Murphy, S. L.; Xu, J.; and Tejada-Vera, B. (2016). Deaths: Final data for 2014. *National Vital Statistics Reports, 64,* 1-122, Table 10. Lieber, C. S. (2001). Alcohol and hepatitis C. *Alcohol Research and Health, 25,* 245–254.

Szabo, G.; and Mandrekar, P. (2010). Alcohol and the liver. *Alcohol Research and Health, 33,* 87–96.

75. Mukamal, K. J.; Tolstrup, J. S.; Friberg, J.; Jensen, G.; and Gronbaek, M. (2005). Alcohol consumption and risk of atrial fibrillation in men and women. *Circulation, 112,* 1736–1742.

76. Bagnardi, V.; Blangliardo, M.; and LaVecchia, C. (2001). Alcohol consumption and the risk of cancer: A meta-analysis. *Alcohol Research and Health, 25,* 263–270. Molina, P. E.; Happel, K. I.; Zhang, P.; Kolls, J. K.; and Nelson, S. (2010). Alcohol and the immune system. *Alcohol Research and Health, 33,* 97–108. Smith-Warner, S. A.; Spiegelman, D.; Shiaw-Shyuan, Y.; Van den Brandt, P. A.; Folsom, A. R.; et al. (1998). Alcohol and breast cancer in women: A pooled analysis of cohort studies. *Journal of the American Medical Association, 279,* 535–540.

77. National Institute on Alcohol Abuse and Alcoholism (2001, July). *Alcohol Alert: Cognitive impairment and recovery from alcoholism.* No. 53. Bethesda, MD: National Institute on Alcohol Abuse and Alcoholism. Department of Health and Human Services (1990). *Alcohol and health,* pp. 123–124.

78. McEvoy, J. P. (1982). The chronic neuropsychiatric disorders associated with alcoholism. In E. M. Pattison; and E. Kaufman (Eds.), *Encyclopedic handbook of alcoholism.* New York: Gardner Press, pp. 167–179.

79. Golden, J. (2005). *Message in a bottle: The making of fetal alcohol syndrome.* Cambridge, MA: Harvard University Press. Jones, K. L.; and Smith, D. W. (1973). Recognition of the fetal alcohol syndrome in early infancy. *Lancet, 2,* 999–1001. Sokol, R. J.; Delaney-Black, V.; and Nordstrom, B. (2003). Fetal alcohol spectrum disorder. *Journal of the American Medical Association, 290,* 2996–2999. Thomas, J.; Warren, K.; and Hewitt, B. G. (2010). Fetal alcohol spectrum disorders: From research to policy. *Alcohol Research and Health, 33,* 118–126.

80. Centers for Disease Control and Prevention. (March, 2018). Fetal Alcohol Spectrum Disorders (FASDs). Accessed from: https://www.cdc.gov/ncbddd/fasd/data.html.

81. Genetics of Alcohol Use Disorders. National Institute on Alcohol Abuse and Alcoholism, Bethesda, MD. Accessed from: http://niaaa.nih.gov/alcohol-health/overview-alcohol-consumption/.

82. Centers for Disease Control and Prevention (September, 2014). One in 10 pregnant women in the United States reports drinking alcohol. Accessed from: https://www.cdc.gov/media/releases/2015/p0924-pregnant-alcohol.html. Floyd, R. L.; O'Connor, M. J.; Sokol, R. J.; Bertrand, J.; and Cordero, J. F. (2005). Recognition and prevention of fetal alcohol syndrome. *Obstetrics and Gynecology, 106,* 1059–1064.

83. American Psychiatric Association (2013). *Diagnostic and statistical manual of mental disorders* (5th ed.). DSM-5. Washington, D.C.: American Psychiatric Publishing, pp. 490–497.

84. Hester, R. K.; and Miller, W. R. (1989). Self-control training. In R. K. Hester; and W. R. Miller (Eds.), *Handbook of alcoholism treatment approaches.* New York: Pergamon Press, pp. 141–149. Miller, W. R. (1989). Increasing motivation for change. In R. K. Hester; and W. R. Miller (Eds.), *Handbook of alcoholism treatment approaches.* New York: Pergamon Press, pp. 67–80. Sobell, M. B.; and Sobell, L. C. (1978). *Behavioral treatment of alcohol problems: Individualized therapy and controlled drinking.* New York: Plenum.

85. Carter-Yamauchi, C. (1998). *Drugs, alcohol, and the insanity defense: The debate over "settled" insanity.* Report No. 7, 1998. Honolulu, HI: Legislative Reference Bureau, Hawaii State Capital. Herald, J. E. (1970, Fall–Winter). Criminal law: Alcoholism as a defense. *Marquette Law Review, 53,* 445–450. Weinstock, R. (1999, January). Drug and alcohol intoxication: *mens rea* defenses. *AAPL Newsletter, American Academy of Psychiatry and the Law, 24,* 1–3.

86. Banys, P. (1988). The clinical use of disulfiram (Antabuse): A review. *Journal of Psychoactive Drugs, 20,* 243–261.

87. Jonas, D. E.; Halle, R. A.; Felmer, C.; Bobaschev, G.; Thomas, K.; et al. (2014). Pharmacotherapy for adults with alcohol use disorders in outpatient settings: A systematic review and meta-analysis. *Journal of the American Medical Association, 311,* 1889–1900.

88. Dodes, L.; and Dodes, Z. (2014). *The sober truth: Debunking the bad science behind 12-step programs and the rehab industry.* Boston: Beacon Press. Hopson, R. E.; and Beaird-Spiller, B. (1995). Why AA works: A psychological analysis of the addictive experience and the efficacy of Alcoholics Anonymous.

Alcoholism Treatment Quarterly, 12, 1–17. Morgenstern, J.; Bux, D.; LaBouvie, E.; Blanchard, K. A.; and Morgan, T. J. (2002). Examining mechanisms of action in a 12-step treatment: The role of 12-step cognitions. *Journal of Studies on Alcohol, 63,* 665–672. White, W. H. (1998). *Slaying the dragon: The history of addiction treatment and recovery in America.* Bloomington, IL: Chestnut Health Systems, pp. 127–177.

89. Ellis, A.; and Velten, E. (1992). *When AA doesn't work for you: Rational steps to quitting alcohol.* Fort Lee, NJ: Barricade Press. Kaskutas, L. A. (1996). A road less traveled: Choosing the "Women for Sobriety" program. *Journal of Drug Issues, 26,* 77–94. Schmidt, E. (1996). Rational recovery: Finding an alternative for addiction treatment. *Alcoholism Treatment Quarterly, 14,* 47–57. SMART Recovery (2004). *SMART Recovery handbook.* Mentor, OH: SMART Recovery®. Winzelberg, A.; and Humphreys, K. (1999). Should patients' religiosity influence clinicians' referral to 12-step self-help groups? Evidence from a study of 3,018 male substance abuse patients. *Journal of Consulting and Clinical Psychology, 67,* 790–794.

chapter **14**

Prevention and Strategies for Change

On his 18th birthday Alex came to a crossroads in his life. He was shooting heroin whenever and wherever he could. He was stealing money from wherever he could get it. Everything was coming apart. "Finally," he said, "it was just too much." He had to get the opioids out of his system and out of his life.

Alex could easily get through detox, but the big decision he had to make was to go for long-term treatment and recovery. He turned to a Narcotics Anonymous program at a local rehab center. He knew that he had to stay there full time if he had any chance for things to change. He knew it wouldn't be quick, but gradually he began to see that there could be a light at the end of the tunnel. "They taught me how to deal with certain triggers that made me want to use, how to deal with anger and other emotions .... Main thing, I got a Narcotics Anonymous sponsor ... I started going on passes and coming home for longer visits."

It took several months, but Alex eventually was able to leave rehab and get on with his life. He went back to school and graduated. He started college with a career in mind—a licensed drug and alcohol counselor. He still goes to NA meetings and has no intention of giving that up. As to the professionals back at the rehab center, "They showed me that recovery was possible. It gave me back my health and gave me back my life."[1]

Our national response in dealing with substance abuse can be framed in terms of two well-known concepts of economic behavior: supply and demand. In other words, we can either reduce the *supply* of drugs in our society or we can reduce the *demand* that our society has for drugs. Ideally, we can do both, but according to Economic Theory, any reduction of supply *or* reduction in demand should bring us closer to our overall goal.

The supply-reduction and demand-reduction approaches in drug-control policy have their own set of goals and associated governmental programs that have been established to achieve them. A reduction in drug supply can be accomplished through effective interdiction of drugs entering our country and effective control over international drug trafficking. The Drug Enforcement Administration (DEA) has the lead responsibility for these efforts. A reduction in drug demand can be accomplished through effective substance abuse prevention and treatment programs. The Substance Abuse and Mental Health Services Administration (SAMHSA) has the lead responsibility for these efforts. Chapters 4 through 7 focused on the supply-reduction side of the equation. This chapter will focus on the demand side, with a review of prevention and treatment programs for substance abuse in the United States.

In any given year, the relative emphasis given to supply reduction or demand reduction on a federal level is reflected in funding allocations within the annual budget of the Office of National Drug Control Strategy (ONDCS). In 2010, programs devoted to supply reduction (domestic law enforcement, interdiction, and international counterdrug support) received twice as much federal funding than did programs devoted to demand reduction (prevention and treatment). In 2016, the distribution of funding support was evenly divided. In addition, the total ONDCS budget increased from approximately $15 billion in 2010 to $30 billion in 2016. Therefore, there has been not only an increase from 2010 to 2016 in federal support for drug control efforts in general but also in a recognition of the equivalent value of supply reduction and demand reduction in dealing with the problems of substance abuse in America.[2]

We begin with interventions that are intended to promote substance abuse prevention and a particular focus on those approaches that are *effective* in doing so. As we will see, strategies that are employed by successful prevention programs can be applied to problems associated with the entire range of abusable drugs—including illicit drugs, prescription and nonprescription medications, alcohol and nicotine—and to other antisocial behaviors as well. In the second part of the chapter, we will turn to strategies for change as important components of successful treatment and recovery.

Levels of Intervention in Substance Abuse Prevention

In general, substance abuse prevention can involve three possible types of intervention. We will refer to them as primary, secondary, and tertiary levels of intervention. Each level of intervention has its own target population and specific goals. By definition, primary prevention, secondary prevention, and tertiary prevention populations vary according to the extent of prior drug use.

- In **primary prevention**, efforts are directed to those who have not had any experience with drugs or those who have been only minimally exposed. The objective is to prevent substance abuse from starting in the first place, "nipping the problem in the bud" so to speak. Targets in primary prevention programs are most frequently elementary school or middle school youths, and intervention usually occurs within a school-based curriculum or specific educational program, though community involvement is encouraged. For example, a primary prevention program would include teaching peer-refusal skills that students can use when offered marijuana, alcohol, or cigarettes ("ways to say no").

- In **secondary prevention**, the target population has already had some experience with alcohol, nicotine, and other drugs. The objective is to limit the extent of substance abuse (reducing it, if possible), prevent its spread of abuse behavior beyond the drugs already encountered, and teach strategies for the responsible use of alcohol if the legal minimum age has been met. Ordinarily, those individuals receiving secondary prevention efforts are older than those involved in primary prevention programs. High school students who are identified as alcohol or other drug users, for example, may participate in a program that emphasizes social alternatives (after-school programs, sports, etc.) to drug-taking behavior. College students may focus on the skills necessary to restrict their behavior to the moderate use of alcohol, the significant dangers of combining drinking and driving, and the signs of chronic alcohol abuse. Secondary prevention efforts are consistent with the philosophy of harm reduction rather than zero tolerance of drug-taking behavior (Drugs ... in Focus).

- In **tertiary prevention**, the objective is to ensure that an individual who has entered treatment for some form of substance abuse or substance dependence problem becomes drug free after treatment has ended, without reverting to former patterns of drug-taking behavior. Successful prevention of relapse is the ultimate indication that the treatment has taken hold. Issues related to tertiary prevention will be reviewed later in the chapter.

primary prevention: A type of intervention in which the goal is to forestall the onset of drug use by an individual who has had little or no previous exposure to drugs.

secondary prevention: A type of intervention in which the goal is to reduce the extent of drug use in individuals who have already had some exposure to drugs.

tertiary (TER-shee-eh-ree) prevention: A type of intervention in which the goal is to prevent relapse in an individual following recovery in a drug treatment program.

Numbers Talk. . .

74	Percentage of substance abuse treatment admissions aged 18 to 30 who began substance use when they were 17 years old or younger.
40	Percentage of substance abuse treatment admissions aged 18 to 30 who began substance use when they were 14 years old or younger.
89	Percentage of adults aged 18 or older in 2016 who needed substance abuse treatment but did not receive it in the past year.
$4–$7	Estimated reduction in the cost of drug-related crime, criminal justice costs, and theft alone for every $1 invested in substance abuse treatment programs. When savings related to health care are included, total savings exceed costs by a ratio of 12 to 1.

Sources: National Institute on Drug Abuse (2009, April). *Principles of drug addiction treatment: A research-based* guide (2nd ed.). Rockville, MD: National Institute on Drug Abuse, p. 13. Substance Abuse and Mental Health Services Administration (2014, July 17). Age of substance use initiation among treatment admissions aged 18 to 30. *The TEDS Report.* Rockville, MD: Substance Abuse and Mental Health Services Administration, Figure 1. Substance Abuse and Mental Health Services Administration (2017, September). Receipt of services for substance use and mental health issues among adults: Results from the 2016 National Survey on Drug Use and Health. *NSDUH Data Review.* Rockville, MD: Substance Abuse and Mental Health Services Administration, Figures 2 and 7.

In the case of primary prevention, a minimal objective is to delay the onset of drug-taking behavior in an individual's life. We are assuming that the target population for these interventions may have had some exposure to drug-taking behavior in other people but have not had significant drug-taking experiences of their own. We recognize that there are substantial temptations for young people to engage in drug use, and an effective primary prevention program can reduce the chances that these temptations will win out. It is clear that the *age of onset* for drug-taking behavior of any kind is a key factor in determining the likelihood of problems later in life, particularly with respect to licit drugs. For example, a young person who begins drinking before the age of 15 is twice as likely to develop a pattern of alcohol abuse and four times as likely to develop alcohol dependence than an individual who begins drinking at the age of 21. In general, if the age of onset can be delayed significantly or even to a moderate degree, there is the possibility of reducing the incidence of substance abuse or dependence.

In the case of secondary prevention, we are concentrating on the lifestyle of a somewhat older population, and our goal is to minimize the problems associated with drug-taking behavior, assuming that some level of that behavior already exists. Emphasis is placed on social alternatives to behaviors involving alcohol and other drugs among high school students. At the college level, the moderate use of alcohol, and particularly the avoidance of alcohol binging, as well as education about the personal risks of designer synthetic drugs and the nonmedical use of prescription medications, are all elements in a program of secondary prevention.

Goals of Substance Abuse Prevention

The U.S. federal agency specifically charged with prevention programs is the Center for Substance Abuse Prevention (CSAP), a division of the Substance Abuse and Mental Health Services Administration (SAMHSA), which is in turn a division of the U.S. Department of Health and Human Services. According to CSAP guidelines, substance abuse prevention is accomplished through two principal efforts. The first is the promotion of constructive lifestyles and norms that discourage substance abuse. The second is the development of social and physical environments that facilitate drug-free lifestyles so that they can act as buffers against the development of substance abuse behaviors.

Quick Concept Check 14.1

Understanding Levels of Intervention in Substance Abuse Prevention Programs

Check your understanding of the three basic levels of intervention in drug-abuse prevention by matching the following five scenarios with (a) primary, (b) secondary, or (c) tertiary prevention.

1. Midnight basketball sessions keep teenagers from drinking on weekends out of boredom.
2. Young children receive lessons on how to refuse the offer of drugs from a friend or acquaintance.
3. A child learns about "good drugs" and "bad drugs" in the first grade.
4. A man learns how to live without cocaine following a successful cocaine treatment program.
5. College students organize a "responsible drinking" program on campus.

Answers: 1. b   2. a   3. a   4. c   5. b

Drugs . . . in Focus

National Drug-Control Policy and the War on Drugs

From time to time in our nation's history, the metaphor of war has been invoked to carry the emotional significance of a domestic or international crisis, even when we are not waging war in the traditional sense. President Lyndon Johnson announced a "War on Poverty" in 1964 to convey the importance of creating a Great Society. President George W. Bush called on the nation in late September of 2001 to fight a "War on Terror" on an international scale. When President Richard Nixon described drug abuse as America's "Public Enemy No. 1" and declared a "War on Drugs" in 1971, it was metaphorically speaking, a call to arms.

The intense rhetoric of "waging a War on Drugs" has diminished, but we still find ourselves drawing upon metaphors that relate to war. In primary prevention, for example, we speak of engaging in the first line of defense against a powerful enemy. Critics of antidrug promotional materials that deglamorize drug-taking behavior have called them merely "magic bullets" in this fight. Protective factors in an individual's life are viewed as a kind of body armor against the onslaught of circumstances (risk factors) that increase the likelihood of substance abuse in the future. Resilience is measured by the extent to which young people emerge victorious. Essentially, primary prevention is a matter of persuading young people not to ruin the lives.

In secondary prevention, we speak of engaging in a second line of defense. We are now addressing an older population for whom some level of drug-taking behavior has already taken place. Prevention programs for high school students focus on "tactical maneuvers" such as providing social alternatives to alcohol and other drugs. Prevention programs for college students emphasize the moderate use of alcohol as opposed to no use at all. In this case, we employ a strategy of harm reduction.

Does the government have the right to issue a "War on Drugs" declaration in the first place? The nineteenth-century British philosopher, John Stuart Mill, argued that the state (meaning the government) does not have the right to intervene in order to protect individual adult citizens from harming themselves. The government does have the right, however, to intervene when there is harm done to others as a consequence. As Mill expressed it,

The only purpose for which power can be rightfully executed over any member of a civilized community, against his will, is to prevent harm to others. His own good, either physical or moral, is not a sufficient warrant. Over himself, over his own body and mind, the individual is sovereign.

By this standard, governmental intervention with respect to drug-taking behavior among adults is justified, since it is clear that drug-taking behavior causes harm to other people.

Continuing the metaphor of warfare, present-day national drug-control policy can be characterized as a series of military campaigns with specific objectives that can be assessed as to whether there has been victory or defeat. Objectives are based either on a zero-tolerance approach or harm-reduction approach toward drug-taking behavior, depending on the psychoactive substance. A campaign with respect to alcohol use places its primary focus on harm reduction rather than zero tolerance. The campaign with respect to tobacco smoking uses a hybrid approach of zero tolerance (lowering the prevalence rate of tobacco use) and harm reduction (minimizing the adverse effects of secondhand smoke). The campaigns with respect to other substances, such as heroin, cocaine, and methamphetamine, center on zero tolerance exclusively. In the case of marijuana, the nature of governmental intervention remains highly controversial. As detailed in Chapter 11, with respect to marijuana, the U.S. federal government has maintained the position of zero tolerance, while many states and communities have not. The conflict remains to be resolved.

Sources: Denning, P. (2003). *Over the influence: The harm reduction guide for managing drugs and alcohol.* New York: Guilford Press. Des Jarlais, D. C. (2000). Prospects for a public health perspective on psychoactive drug use. *American Journal of Public Health, 90,* 335–337. How did we get here? History has a habit of repeating itself (2001, July 28–August 3). *Economist,* pp. 4–5. Quotation of John Stuart Mill on p. 5. Levinthal, C. F. (2003). Question: Should harm reduction be our overall goal in fighting drug abuse? *Point/Counterpoint: Opposing perspectives on issues of drug policy.* Boston: Allyn and Bacon, pp. 70–73. Marlatt, G. A. (Ed.) (2002). *Harm reduction: Pragmatic strategies for managing high-risk behaviors.* New York: Guilford Press. Resnicow, K.; Smith, M.; Harrison, L.; and Drucker, E. (1999). Correlates of occasional cigarette and marijuana use. Are teens harm reducing? *Addictive Behaviors, 24,* 251–266.

You may recall from Chapter 8 that two groups of factors play a pivotal role in predicting the extent of drug-taking behavior in a particular individual: risk factors and protective factors. Risk factors are those circumstances in an individual's life that increase the likelihood of drug-taking behavior, while protective factors are circumstances that decrease it. You can think of the goal of substance abuse prevention in those terms. The optimal substance abuse prevention program will incorporate ways to *reduce* the impact of risk factors in an individual's life and, at the same time, *enhance* the impact of protective factors.

Creating Resilience

Successful primary prevention programs are built around the idea that an individual is less inclined to engage in substance abuse if the protective factors in his or her life are enhanced and the risk factors are diminished. Only then can a young person be resilient enough to overcome the temptations of alcohol, tobacco, and other drugs. The creation of **resilience**, defined as the inclination to resist the effect of risk factors through the action of protective factors, can be viewed as "make-or-break" element in one's social development. The promotion of positive social skills and the encouragement of a proactive rather than a passive approach to problem-solving strengthen the "buffering effect" of protective factors with respect to drug-taking behavior and other forms of deviant behavior. Since a young population is the principal target for primary prevention, programs are customarily implemented in the school. As we will see, however, for programs to be most effective, it is necessary to incorporate aspects of a young person's life outside of school. In a later section, we will turn to primary prevention programs that involve the community at large.[3]

A Matter of Public Health

It is important to recognize that a drug-free life constitutes a major element in a healthy life and, in turn, a healthy society. Figure 14.1 shows dramatically how substance abuse impacts the nation's health in general. As you can see, substance abuse of some kind accounts for almost one-half of all preventable deaths in the United States, either through the abuse of alcohol (7 percent), tobacco (38 percent), or illicit drugs (2 percent). Each year, well over a half-million deaths are attributed to these three circumstances. The concept that a reduction in the negative consequences of drug-taking behavior is part of an enhancement in the overall health of society is often referred to as the Public Health Model (see Drugs . . . in Focus).[4]

There is also an immense monetary impact on the national economy. The estimated costs of substance abuse in the United States exceed $1 trillion each year. Some of these costs arise from academic underachievement from underage drinking ($64 billion), drug-related hospital emergency visits ($4 billion), incarceration of individuals committing drug-law offenses ($30 billion), alcohol-related workplace injuries and absenteeism ($28 billion), and DWI-related collisions on highways ($230 billion). It is estimated that more than $18 could be saved for every dollar spent on effective school-based prevention programs.[5]

It should not be surprising that a national agenda for health promotion and disease prevention called Healthy People 2000 (now updated to Healthy People 2020), established by the U.S. Public Health Service in the 1990s, includes a major section devoted to behaviors related to substance abuse.[6]

The Question of Measuring Success

Given the importance of substance abuse prevention as a societal goal, it is critical that we achieve success in the prevention programs that we create. Evaluating the success or failure of a substance abuse prevention program, however, is more complicated than people often think. In the public mind, a school-based substance abuse prevention program might be considered successful, for example, if it enjoys support from parents, administrators, and teachers. There might be a long list of testimonials among participants as to their belief that they have benefitted from the program. It might be considered successful if there is evidence of a change in

> **resilience:** The inclination to resist the negative impact of risk factors in a person's life through the positive impact of protective factors. Sometimes referred to as resiliency.

FIGURE 14.1

Causes of preventable deaths annually in the United States.

Source: Center for Substance Abuse Prevention, Substance Abuse and Mental Health Services Administration, Rockville, MD.

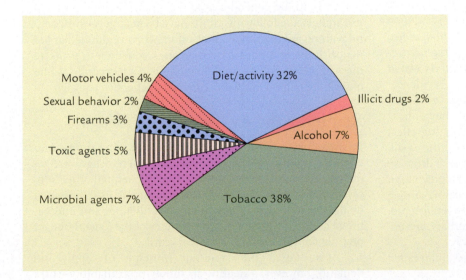

Motor vehicles 4%
Diet/activity 32%
Illicit drugs 2%
Sexual behavior 2%
Firearms 3%
Alcohol 7%
Toxic agents 5%
Microbial agents 7%
Tobacco 38%

Drugs . . . in Focus

Reducing Drug-taking Behavior and the Analogy of Infectious Disease Control

As Avram Goldstein, a prominent drug-abuse researcher and policy analyst, has pointed out, the problems of reducing drug-taking behavior have many similarities to wresting control over an infectious disease. A virus, for example, infects some people who are relatively more susceptible than others (in other words, there are risk factors), while some people will be relatively immune (in other words, there are protective factors). Public health measures can be established to reduce or eradicate the virus (just as we attempt to reduce the supply of illicit drugs from reaching the consumer); specific vaccinations can be discovered to increase a person's resistance to the virus (just as we search for effective primary prevention programs in drug abuse).

We can carry the analogy further. Medical treatment for an infectious disease is considered uncontroversial and necessary for two reasons. First, we are alleviating the suffering of the infected individual; second, we are reducing the pool of infection to limit the spread to others. Analogously, drug-abuse treatment is desirable to relieve the negative consequences of drug abuse, as well as reduce the social influence of drug abusers on non-drug abusers in our society.

Goldstein asks a provocative question:

> There are individuals who contribute to the AIDS epidemic by having promiscuous sexual contacts without taking elementary precautions. Are those behaviors, which contribute to the spread of infectious disease, really different in principle from that of pack-a-day cigarette smokers who will not try to quit, despite all the evidence of physical harm to themselves and their families?

There is certainly no consensus on how the problem of drug abuse should be conceptualized. Some have objected to the implications of the Public Health Model, arguing that it ignores the moral and ethical choices that are made in establishing a pattern of drug-taking behavior.

Sources: Goldstein, A. (1994). *Addiction: From biology to drug policy.* New York: Freeman. Quotation on p. 10. Jonas, S. (1997). Public health approaches. In J. H. Lowinson; P. Ruiz; R. B. Millman; and J. G. Langrod (Eds.), *Substance abuse: A comprehensive textbook.* Baltimore, MD: Williams & Wilkins, pp. 775–785.

---

a child's view away from drug use or a change in a child's stated inclination to engage in drug use in the future. If a child develops a nondrug lifestyle, people might automatically assume that it was due to exposure to a substance abuse prevention program.

These positive outcomes may be gratifying to the community and persuasive to the general public, but they do not impact on the core issue: Is the prevalence of substance abuse reduced as a result of the program? *The goal of any prevention program, particularly a primary prevention program aimed at young people, is to lower the numbers of new drug users or to delay the first use of alcohol and tobacco toward an age at which they are considered adults.* To be considered "evidence-based," primary prevention programs must be evaluated against a control group that did not receive the intervention; otherwise, it is impossible to determine whether the effect of the program itself was greater than doing nothing at all. Positive change per se is not enough. For example, if drug use among eighth graders has declined as a result of a prevention program but this decline is not greater than a decline among eighth graders in the control group, then the prevention program is essentially ineffective. Secondary and tertiary prevention programs must be evaluated in the same way.

The range of prevention strategies that have either failed or succeeded will be reviewed in the next section.

Prevention Approaches That Have Failed

When deciding how to solve a problem, it always helps to look at what has *not* worked in the past. That way, we can avoid wasting time, effort, and money on programs that do not work. In the general opinion of health professionals and researchers, the following efforts have been largely unsuccessful with regard to primary prevention, when positioned as the major thrust of a particular program. Nonetheless, some of these approaches have been incorporated successfully as one of several components within an overall effective package.

Reducing the Availability of Drugs

It is reasonable to expect that problems of illicit drug abuse could be prevented if the availability of these drugs were reduced or eliminated altogether. This is essentially the "supply/availability" argument in drug prevention, as represented by the domestic law enforcement, interdiction, and international counterdrug support components of the federal budget on drug control in any given fiscal year.[7]

According to the economic principle of supply and demand, however, a decline in supply or availability works to produce an increase in value and an increase in demand. If one accepts the first viewpoint, then reductions in supply or availability should help prevent drug-taking behavior; if one accepts the second viewpoint, then such reductions should exacerbate the situation. Which theoretical viewpoint is operating with respect to illicit drugs (or with respect to alcohol, tobacco, and other licit drugs) is a point of controversy among health professionals both inside and outside the government.

Given the fact that the United States has adopted the policy of reducing the supply or availability of illicit drugs as part of an overall national drug-control strategy, how successful have we been? Have we been able, for example, to reduce the production of illicit drugs around the world and their influx into the United States? Unfortunately, drug cultivation (such as the harvesting of opium, coca leaves, and marijuana) and the exportation of processed illicit drugs from their points of origin are so deeply entrenched in many regions of the world and the resourcefulness of drug producers is so great that our global efforts have been frustratingly inadequate. As was pointed out in Chapter 2, a production crackdowns in one region merely serve to create a marketing vacuum that another region quickly fills. Moreover, efforts to control international drug trafficking have been embarrassingly unsuccessful, despite well-publicized drug busts, arrests, and seizures. It is estimated that only a small fraction of illicit drugs is interdicted (intercepted) at U.S. borders.[8]

With respect to alcohol, a strategy of reduced availability has been implemented on a nationwide basis since 1984 for a specific age group, by prohibiting alcohol to young people under the age of 21 (see Chapter 13). Prior to this time, some states had adopted this policy, while neighboring states had not, allowing for comparisons in alcohol consumption rates and the incidence of alcohol-related automobile accidents. In one study, the percentage of teenage, nighttime, and single-vehicle accident fatalities in Massachusetts was found to have declined in 1979 (the year the legal drinking age in that state was raised to 21) to a significantly greater degree than in New York, which at that time still had a minimum drinking age of 18. That was the good news.

The bad news was that levels of alcohol consumption in this age range stayed the same. Therefore, although one particular consequence of immoderate alcohol use (drunk driving) was reduced as a secondary prevention intervention, the prevalence of alcohol use itself as a result of a primary prevention intervention was unaffected. As we are all aware, underage drinking still is widespread; minors still find opportunities to drink and to drink in excess. The fact that minimum-age requirements have only a limited effect on drinking among minors reinforces the complexity of dealing with primary prevention, whether we are considering licit or illicit drugs.[9]

Punitive Measures

There is a common expectation, when policies related to law enforcement and the criminal justice system are considered, that an individual would be less inclined to use and abuse illicit drugs for fear of being arrested, prosecuted, convicted, and incarcerated. The available statistics show that this deterrent factor has failed to take hold. The enticements of many psychoactive drugs are extremely powerful, and the imposition of harsh penalties has frequently been delayed or inconsistent. Mandatory minimum-sentencing laws (see Chapter 5) have resulted in a clogged judicial system and vastly overcrowded prisons, without any noticeable dent in the trafficking in or consumption of illicit drugs. Although the enforcement of these penalties may be defended in terms of an overall social policy toward illicit drugs, it has evidently failed as a means for either primary or secondary prevention.[10]

Scare Tactics

In the late 1960s, the sudden widespread use of marijuana, amphetamines, barbiturates, LSD, and other hallucinogens, first among students on college campuses and later among youth at large, spawned a number of hastily designed programs based on the arousal of fear and exaggerated or blatantly inaccurate information about the risks involved. They were the products of panic rather than careful thought.

As might be imagined, such efforts turned young people *off* precisely at the time when they were turning themselves *on* to an array of exotic and seemingly innocuous drug-taking experiences. Professionals have called it the "reefer madness approach," an allusion to the government-sponsored movie of the 1930s that attempted to scare people away from experimenting with marijuana (see Chapter 11). These programs accomplished little, except to erode even further the credibility of the adult presenters in the eyes of youths who often knew (or thought they knew) a great deal more about drugs and their effects than their elders.[11]

Objective Information Approaches

At the opposite end of the emotional spectrum are programs designed to present information about drugs and their potential dangers in a straightforward, nonjudgmental way. Unfortunately, evaluations of this "just the facts, ma'am" approach have found that youths exposed to such primary prevention programs are no less likely to use drugs later in their lives and sometimes are more likely to use them. These programs tend to increase their curiosity about drugs in general, obviously something the program planners want to avoid.[12]

Despite these failures, however, it would be a mistake to dismiss the informational aspect of any substance abuse prevention program completely out of hand, particularly when the information is presented in a low-fear atmosphere.[13] The overall value of an informational approach appears to depend on whether the target population consists of high-risk or low-risk children. When low-risk young people are presented with drug-related information, the evidence indicates that they really understand the dangers and the chances of remaining drug free are increased. High-risk youth, on the other hand, may not be so easily dissuaded, and additional intervention appears to be necessary.[14]

Magic Bullets and Promotional Campaigns

A variety of antidrug promotional materials such as T-shirts, caps, rings, buttons, bumper stickers, posters, rap songs, school assembly productions, books, and brochures are available and frequently seen as "magic bullets" that can clinch success in substance abuse prevention programs. Their appeal lies in their high visibility; these items give a clear signal to the public at large, eager for signs that the drug-abuse problem might easily go away, that something is being done. Yet, although they may be helpful in deglamorizing drug-taking behavior and providing a forum for young people to express their feelings about drugs, promotional items are inadequate by themselves to reduce substance abuse overall. They do, however, remain viable components of more comprehensive programs that have proved to be successful in primary prevention.[15]

Self-Esteem Enhancement and Affective Education

In the early 1970s, several substance abuse prevention programs were developed that emphasized the affective or emotional component of drug-taking behavior rather than specific information about drugs. In the wake of research that showed a relationship between drug abuse and psychological variables such as low self-esteem, poor decision-making skills, and poor interpersonal communication skills, programs were instituted that incorporated role-playing exercises with other assignments designed to help young people get in touch with their own emotions and feel better about themselves.

This approach, called **affective education**, was an attempt to deal with underlying emotional and attitudinal factors rather than specific behaviors related to drug use (in fact, alcohol, tobacco, and other drugs were seldom mentioned at all). Affective education was based on the observation that

Elementary school children display their handprint art projects. Designations of drug-free pledges are prominent features of many school-based drug abuse prevention programs.

Credit: Jeff Greenberg/PhotoEdit. Inc.

drug users had difficulty identifying and expressing emotions such as anger and love. In a related set of programs called **values clarification**, moral values were actively taught to children, on the assumption that they frequently had a poorly developed sense of where their life was going and lacked a "moral compass" to guide their behavior.

Difficulties arose, however, when parents, community leaders, and frequently educators themselves argued that the emphasis of affective education was inappropriate for public schools. In regard to values clarification, there was concern that a system of morality was being imposed on students without respecting their individual backgrounds and cultures. This kind of instruction, it was felt, was more suited for faith-based education settings.[16]

Beyond these social considerations, the bottom line was that neither affective education nor values clarification was effective in preventing drug-taking behavior. Some researchers have recently questioned the basic premise that self-esteem is a major factor at all. As a result, affective issues are no longer viewed as central considerations in primary or secondary prevention. Nonetheless, they can be found as components in more comprehensive prevention programs that have been more successful.[17]

Effective School-Based Prevention Programs

One of the major lessons to be learned from evaluations of previous substance abuse prevention efforts is that there is a far greater chance for success when the programs are multifaceted than when they focus on only a single aspect of drug-taking behavior. The following are elements of school-based, substance abuse prevention programs that have been shown to work.

Peer-Refusal Skills

A number of school-based programs developed during the 1980s have included the teaching of personal and social skills as well as techniques for resisting various forms of social pressure to smoke, drink, or use other drugs (often referred to as **peer-refusal skills**). The emphasis is directed toward an individual's relationships with his or her peers and an understanding of the difficult social situations that often present themselves in their developing years. Rather than simply prodding young people to "just say no" (an approach that has been

affective education: An approach in prevention programs that emphasizes the building of self-esteem and an improved self-image.

values clarification: An approach in prevention programs that teaches positive social values and attitudes.

peer-refusal skills: Techniques by which an individual can resist peer pressure to use alcohol, tobacco, or other drugs.

found to have limited success), programs that concentrate on peer-refusal skills enable them to "know how to say no."

Primary prevention programs using peer-refusal skill training have been shown to reduce the rate of tobacco smoking, as well as alcohol drinking and marijuana smoking, by 35–45 percent, considerably better than any change in control comparison groups. With respect to tobacco smoking, this approach has been even more effective for young people identified as being in a high-risk category (in that their friends or family smoked) than for other students.[18]

Anxiety and Stress Reduction

Adolescence can be an enormously stressful time, and drug-taking behavior is frequently seen as an option to reduce feelings of anxiety, particularly when an individual has inadequate coping skills to deal with that anxiety. It is therefore useful to learn techniques of self-relaxation and stress management and to practice the application of these techniques to everyday situations.

Social Skills and Personal Decision-Making

Peer-refusal skills are but one example of a range of assertiveness skills that allow young people to express their feelings, needs, preferences, and opinions directly and honestly, without fearing that they will jeopardize their friendships or lose the respect of others. Learning assertiveness skills not only helps advance the goals of primary prevention but also fosters positive interpersonal relationships throughout life. Tasks in social skills training have included the ability to initiate social interactions (introducing oneself to a stranger), offer a compliment to others, engage in conversation, and express feelings and opinions. Lessons generally involve a combination of instruction, demonstration, feedback, reinforcement, behavioral rehearsal, and extended practice through behavioral homework assignments.

A related skill is the ability to make decisions in a thoughtful and careful way. Emphasis is placed on the identification of problem situations, the formulation of goals, the generation of alternative solutions, and the consideration of the likely consequences of each. Lessons also focus on identifying persuasive advertising appeals and exploring counterarguments that can defuse them. Primary prevention programs using a social skills training approach have been shown to reduce the likelihood by 42–75 percent that a young person will try smoking and to reduce the likelihood by 56–67 percent that a nonsmoker will be a regular smoker in a one-year follow-up.[19]

An Example of an Effective School-Based Prevention Program

Substance abuse prevention professionals are in general agreement that the most effective programs should be comprehensive in nature, with special emphasis on the teaching of specific social decision-making skills such as resisting peer pressure to engage in drug-taking behavior.[20] An example of a successful school-based prevention effort is the Life Skills Training (LST) program, developed by Gilbert J. Botvin at the Cornell University Medical College in New York City. Three LST programs have been designed with developmentally appropriate content for young people in elementary school, middle school, or high school. The elementary school program can be taught either during the third grade or over the course of the fourth, fifth, and sixth grades. The middle school program is taught over the course of the seventh, eighth, and ninth grades. The high school program is taught in one year, either as a stand-alone program or as a maintenance program in conjunction with earlier sessions in middle school. The major elements include the following:

- A *cognitive component* designed to provide information concerning the short-term consequences of alcohol, tobacco, and other drugs. Unlike traditional prevention approaches, LST includes only minimal information concerning the long-term health consequences of drug-taking behavior. Evidently, it is not useful to tell young people about what might happen when they are "old." Instead, information is provided concerning immediate negative effects, the impact on social acceptability, and actual prevalence rates among adults and adolescents. This last element of the lesson is to counter the myth that drug-taking behavior is the norm in their age group—that "everyone's doing it."

- A *decision-making component* designed to facilitate critical thinking and independent decision-making. Students learn to evaluate the role of the media in behavior as well as to formulate counterarguments and other cognitive strategies to resist advertising pressures.

- A *stress reduction component* designed to help students develop ways to lessen anxiety. Students learn relaxation techniques and cognitive techniques to manage stress.

- A *social skills component* designed to teach social assertiveness and specific techniques for resisting peer pressure.

- A *self-directed behavior change component* designed to facilitate self-improvement and encourage a sense of personal control and self-esteem. Students are assigned to identify a skill or behavior that they would like to change or improve and to develop a long-term goal over an eight-week period and short-term objectives that can be met week by week.

Originally designed as a smoking prevention program, LST presently focuses on issues related to the entire spectrum of drug-taking behavior. Over a period of as long as six years following exposure to the program, participants have been found to have a 50–75 percent lower incidence of alcohol, tobacco, and marijuana use, a 66 percent lower incidence of multiple-drug use, a 25 percent lower incidence of pack-a-day cigarette smoking, and a lower incidence of inhalant, opiate, and hallucinogen use, relative to controls.[21] Reductions in drug use have been seen among inner-city minority students as well as among white middle-class youths, an encouraging sign that these primary prevention strategies can have a positive influence on adolescents from varying social backgrounds. In effect, as Botvin has expressed it, LST and similar programs work "in cities and towns and villages across the United States without having to develop separate intervention approaches for each and every different population."[22]

LST programs have also demonstrated positive influences in a number of high-risk social behaviors beyond simply drug-taking behavior. Reductions in violence and delinquency have been observed among sixth-grade LST participants, relative to controls. There has also been a reduction in risky driving behaviors among adolescent participants. Young adults who have participated in LST programs have a reduced level of HIV-risk behaviors, as indicated by multiple sex partners, frequency of intercourse while drunk or high, and recent high-risk substance use (e.g., administration by needle injection). These studies illustrate the long-term protective results of effective primary and secondary prevention programs for a range of life decisions. Similar programs emphasizing life skills and other forms of social development have been reported with equivalent success.[23]

Quick Concept Check 14.2

Understanding Substance Abuse Prevention Strategies

Check your understanding of substance abuse prevention strategies by deciding whether the following approaches would or would not be effective (in and of themselves) in reducing drug or alcohol use or delaying its onset, based on the available research.

	Would be Effective	Would not be Effective
1. Scare tactics	☐	☐
2. Life skills training	☐	☐
3. Peer-refusal skills training	☐	☐
4. Values clarification	☐	☐
5. Objective information	☐	☐
6. Anxiety reduction and stress management	☐	☐
7. Assertiveness training	☐	☐
8. Training in problem-solving and goal setting	☐	☐

Answers: 1. would not   2. would   3. would   4. would not
5. would not   6. would   7. would   8. would

Effective Community-Based Prevention Programs

Community-based prevention programs offer several obvious advantages over those restricted to schools. The first is the greater opportunity to involve parents and other family members, religious institutions, and the media as collaborative agents for change. The most important factor here is the comprehensive nature of such programs. They draw on multiple social institutions that have been demonstrated to represent protective factors in an individual's life, such as the family, religious groups, and community organizations. In addition, corporations and businesses can be contributing partners, in both a financial and nonfinancial sense. Undoubtedly, we are in a better position to tackle the complexities of drug-taking behavior through the use of multiple strategies rather than a single approach.

Community Impactors

Typically, many of the prevention components that have been incorporated in the schools are also components in community-based programs, such as the dissemination of information, stress management, and life skills training. Other approaches can be handled better in a community setting. For example, although schools can promote the possibility of alternative student activities that provide positive and constructive means for addressing feelings of boredom, frustration, and powerlessness (activities such as Midnight Basketball and Boys and Girls Clubs), the community is in a better position than the schools to actually provide these activities.

There is also a greater opportunity in the community to elicit the involvement of significant individuals to act as positive role models, referred to as **impactors**, and to enlist the help of the mass media to promote antidrug messages in the press and on television. In addition, community-based programs can be more influential in promoting changes in public policy that foster opportunities for education, employment, and self-development.[24]

Alternative-Behavior Programming

It should not be surprising that it is easier to say no to drugs when you can say yes to something else. In community-based prevention programs, a major effort is made to provide the activities and outlets that steer people away from the high-risk situations. Owing to the fact that adolescents spend a majority of their time outside school, and it is outside school that the preponderance of drug-taking behavior occurs, community programs have the best chance of providing the necessary

impactors: Individuals in the community who function as positive role models to children and adolescents in substance abuse prevention programs.

interventions. In fact, high-risk adolescents are the least likely even to be attending school on the days that prevention efforts are delivered.[25]

Alternative behaviors vary over a wide range of activities, corresponding to a particular individual's interests and needs (Table 14.1). One way of thinking about alternative-behavior programming is that a person is trading a negative dependence (on alcohol, tobacco, or other drugs) that causes harm on a physical or psychological level for a positive dependence that causes no harm and taps into pleasures from within.

In a 1986 review of its effectiveness based on well-controlled research studies, alternative-behavior programming was identified as being highly successful for at-risk adolescents such as illicit drug users, juvenile delinquents, and students having problems in school. On the basis of these evaluations, the general view is that alternative-behavior programming can work and deserves to have a place in comprehensive prevention programs.[26]

The Power of the Media

In the words of a major 2005 study analyzing the lifestyles of 8–18-year-olds, young people today live "media-saturated lives, spending an average of nearly 6½ hours a day with media." Since about one-fourth of the time they are engaged in media multitasking (reading, listening to music, and text messaging with friends, for example), they are actually crowding 8½ hours of media into each day—the equivalent of a full-time job. These individuals (dubbed "Generation M" to reflect the dominance of media in their lives) are the first generation to have grown up with easy access to computers and particularly the Internet.[27]

Because of the unprecedented media access available at home (frequently in the privacy of their bedrooms), it is important to evaluate the impact of media messages on drug-taking behavior in their lives and the potential for media exposure to promote primary prevention. It turns out that young people are exposed to more than 80 explicit references to substance use per day in the course of listening to popular music. A relationship has been identified between the amount of exposure among 10–14-year-olds to alcohol drinking in popular movies and early onset teen drinking, even after controlling for variables such as socioeconomic status, personality characteristics, school performance, and gender. In other words, exposure to movie alcohol use can be viewed as an independent risk factor for drinking behavior in this population.[28]

Traditionally, antidrug messages have been largely confined to public service announcements, brief commercials, and limited program series. Even so, the potential impact can be substantial. A prominent example is a series of memorable and persuasive antidrug advertisements on TV, on the radio, in print, and in other media sources, sponsored by the Partnership for a Drug-Free America (PDFA), a nonprofit coalition of professionals in the communications industry whose mission is to reduce demand for drugs in America. In the early 1990s, a number of PDFA spots targeted inner-city

TABLE 14.1

Alternative behaviors to drug use

LEVEL OF EXPERIENCE	NEEDS AND MOTIVES	ALTERNATIVES
Physical	Physical satisfaction, more energy	Athletics, dance/exercise, hiking, carpentry, or outdoor work
Sensory	Stimulation of sensory experience	Sensory awareness training, sky diving, "experiencing"
Emotional	Relief from anxiety, mood elevation, emotional relaxation	Individual counseling, group therapy
Interpersonal	Peer acceptance, defiance of authority figures	Confidence training, sensitivity groups, helping others in distress
Social/environmental	Promotion of social change or identification with a subculture	Social service; community action; helping the poor, aged, handicapped; environmental activism
Intellectual	Escape from boredom, curiosity, or inclination to explore one's own awareness	Reading, creative games, memory training, discussion groups
Creative/aesthetic	Increase in one's creativity or enjoyment of images and thoughts	Nongraded instruction in visual arts, music, drama, crafts, cooking, gardening, writing, singing
Philosophical	Discovery of the meaning of life, organization of a belief system	Discussions, study of ethics or other philosophical literature
Spiritual/mystical	Transcendence of organized religion, spiritual insight, or enlightenment	Study of world religions, meditation, yoga
Miscellaneous	Adventure, risk taking, "kicks"	Outward-bound survival training, meaningful employment

Source: Based on information from Cohen, A. Y. (1972). The journey beyond trips: Alternatives to drugs. In D. E. Smith; and G. R. Gay (Eds.), *It's so good, don't even try it once: Heroin in perspective.* Englewood Cliffs, NJ: Prentice Hall, pp. 191–192.

youths living in high-risk drug-use environments, and a 1994 study indicated that these messages had a significant effect in promoting increasingly antidrug attitudes, particularly among African American children attending schools in areas where many families had incomes below the poverty line.[29]

Unfortunately, Internet media has undermined these efforts. A rapidly growing number of Internet Web sites are devoted to information about marijuana cultivation, drug paraphernalia, and illicit drug use in general. These prodrug outlets have proliferated since the advent of online services. Making matters worse, the percentage of adolescents reporting that they remember seeing or hearing substance abuse prevention messages has declined.[30]

An Example of an Effective Community-Based Prevention Program

An intensive and coordinated program of preventive services and community-based law enforcement has been designed by the National Center on Addiction and Substance Abuse at Columbia University in New York, called CASASTART. (The first part of the acronym refers to the center that designed it, and the latter part stands for "Striving Together to Achieve Rewarding Tomorrows.") The target population for the program is defined as children between 8 and 13 years of age who have at least four risk factors for substance abuse problems. These risk factors may involve school (such as poor academic performance, in-school behavior problems, or truancy), family (such as poverty, violence at home, or a family member involved with gangs, drug use or sales, or a criminal conviction within five years), or the individual child (such as a history of known or suspected drug use or sales, past arrest, gang membership, or being a victim of child maltreatment).

In the CASASTART program, a case manager serving 15 children and their families coordinates a variety of services, including social support, family and educational services, after-school and summer activities, mentoring, incentives, and juvenile justice intervention. The objective is to build resilience in the child, strengthen families, and make neighborhoods safer for children and their families. Relative to controls, CASASTART children have been found to be 60 percent less likely to sell drugs, 20 percent less likely to have used drugs in the past 30 days, 20 percent less likely to commit a violent act, and more likely to be promoted to the next grade in school.[31]

Drug Abuse Resistance Education (DARE)

The Drug Abuse Resistance Education program, commonly known as DARE, is undoubtedly the best-known school-based primary prevention program in the United States and perhaps the world. It was developed in 1983 as a collaborative effort by the Los Angeles Police Department and the Los Angeles United School District to bring uniformed police officers into

kindergarten and elementary grade classrooms to teach basic drug information, peer-refusal skills, self-management techniques, and alternatives to drug use.

The DARE program has expanded quite rapidly. Today, it has been established in all 50 U.S. states, in all Native American schools administered by the Bureau of Indian Affairs, the U.S. Department of Defense schools worldwide, and school systems in many foreign countries. There are also teacher-orientation sessions, officer–student interactions at playgrounds and in cafeterias, and parent-education evenings.[32]

Responses to Project DARE from teachers, principals, students, and police officers are typically enthusiastic, and it is clear that the program has struck a responsive chord over the years for a public that has pushed for active prevention programs in the schools. Part of this enthusiasm can be seen as coming from the image of police departments shifting their emphasis from exclusively "supply reduction" to a more proactive social role in "demand reduction."

Yet, despite its success in the area of public relations, the research-based evidence supporting the effectiveness of DARE in achieving genuine reductions in drug use is weak. In general, children who participated in the DARE program have a more negative attitude toward drugs one year later than children who did not, as well as a greater capability to resist peer pressure and a lower estimate of how many of their peers smoked cigarettes. However, there are no significant differences between DARE and non-DARE control groups. There is little evidence for differences in drug use, drug attitudes, or self-esteem when young people are measured 10 years after the administration of the DARE program. Multiple studies have confirmed this conclusion.[33]

The DARE program has also been criticized for advocating that children be questioned about possible drug offenders in their families. A DARE lesson called "The Three R's: Recognize, Resist, Report" encourages them to tell friends, teachers, or police if they find drugs at home. Critics of DARE have viewed this and related elements of the program as a mechanism for turning young children into informants.[34]

Why DARE remains popular when its effectiveness and questionable practices have been consistently challenged is an interesting question. Some health professionals in this field theorize that the popularity of DARE is, in part, a result of the perception among parents and DARE supporters that it appears to work through a process of informally comparing children who go through DARE against an imagined perception of those children who do not.

The adults rightly perceive that most children who go through DARE do not engage in problematic drug use. Unfortunately, these individuals may not realize that the vast majority of children, even without any intervention, do not engage in problematic drug use ... That is, adults may believe that drug use among adolescents is much more frequent than it actually is. When the children who go through DARE are compared to this "normative" group of drug-using teens, DARE appears effective.[35]

In 2001, in response to the criticism leveled against its lack of impact on drug use, the DARE program was modified to become "enhanced DARE." In this new approach, more emphasis has been placed on student interaction, providing more opportunities for children to participate rather than being lectured by police officers.[36] In effect, DARE administrators have adopted many of the basic components of effective school-based prevention programs such as Life Skills Training.

Family Systems in Primary and Secondary Prevention

It can be argued that family influences form the cornerstone of any successful substance abuse prevention program. In effect, the family is the first line of defense against substance abuse (Figure 14.2). Reaching the parents or guardians of youths at greatest risk, however, is a difficult task. Too often, substance abuse prevention programs are attended by those parents or guardians who do not really need the information; those who need the information the most—parents who are either in denial, too embarrassed, or too out of control themselves—are notably absent. Other parents or guardians may need and genuinely want to participate, but they may have difficulty attending because of lack of child care at home, lack of transportation, scheduling conflicts with their employment, or language differences. Several of the factors that prevent their attendance are the same factors that increase the risk of substance abuse among their children.[37]

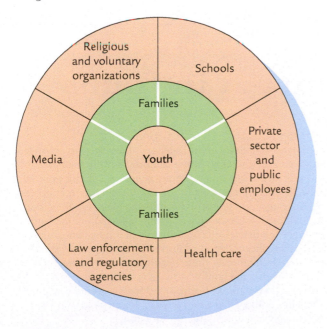

FIGURE 14.2

A schematic of various factors that impact upon young people in substance abuse prevention.

Source: Adapted from Fields, R. (1998). *Drugs in perspective* (3rd ed.). Dubuque, IA: WCB McGraw-Hill, p. 309. Reprinted with permission of the McGraw-Hill Companies. Copyright 1998.

Special Role Models in Substance Abuse Prevention

Although obstacles exist, comprehensive substance abuse prevention programs strive to incorporate parents or guardians, as well as other family members such as grandparents, into the overall effort. The reason lies in the variety of special roles they play in influencing children:

- As role models, parents or guardians may drink alcoholic beverages, smoke, or drink excessive amounts of caffeinated coffee, not thinking of these habits as drug-taking behaviors. They can avoid sending their children signals about abstinence that are inconsistent at best, hypocritical at worst.

- As educators or resources for information, they can help by conveying verbal messages about health risks that are accurate and sincere.

- As family policy-makers and rule setters, they can convey a clear understanding of the consequences of drug-taking behaviors. If a parent or guardian cannot or will not back up family rules with logical and consistent consequences, the risk increases that rules will be broken.

- As stimulators of enjoyable family activities, parents or guardians can provide alternative-behavior programming necessary to steer youth away from high-risk situations.

Communication between grandparents and grandchildren can be an important tool in substance abuse prevention.

Photo Credit: The Power of Grandparents, p. 15. © Partnership for Drug-Free Kids, New York. Accessed from: *www.drugfree.org*.

- As consultants against peer pressure, parents or guardians can help reinforce the peer-refusal skills of their children. Children and adolescents frequently report that a strongly negative reaction at home was the single most important reason for their refusing alcohol, tobacco, and other drugs from their peers.

Parental Communication in Substance Abuse Prevention

In recognition of the importance of parental communication in efforts to reduce substance abuse, the program "Parents: The Antidrug" has been a feature in public service announcements in recent years.[38] The need for better lines of communication between parents and teenagers is illustrated in a PDFA survey. When asked whether they talked to their teenagers about drugs at least once, 98 percent of parents reported that they had done so, but only 65 percent of teenagers recalled such a conversation. Barely 27 percent of teenagers reported learning a lot at home about the risks of drug use, even though virtually all of their parents said they had discussed the topic. Justifiably, antidrug media campaigns have focused on parent–child communication skills, specifically on the difficulty many parents have in talking to their children about sensitive subjects like drugs and the role of drug-taking behavior in their children's social lives.[39] Drug Enforcement ... in Focus examines an option that may be necessary, however, when family communication breaks down.

START TALKING BEFORE THEY START DRINKING

www.stopalcoholabuse.gov

Early communication between parents and children is a key factor in the prevention of underage drinking.

Photo Credit: Substance Abuse and Mental Health Services Administration. Accessed from: *www.stopalcoholabuse.gov.*

The Triple Threat: Stress, Boredom, and Spending Money

Substance abuse prevention in young people can sometimes be simpler and more straightforward than we realize. A recent survey of teenagers aged 12–17 measured the effects of three circumstances on the likelihood that a teenager might

---

Drug Enforcement . . . in Focus

Testing for Drugs in the Home: Whom Can You Trust?

Since 1995, commercial kits have been available that are capable of testing for illicit drugs in the home. Marketed for parents who wish to check for possible drug abuse among their children, these kits typically consist of a small premoistened pad that can be wiped across desktops, telephones, books, clothing, or other items. The pad is then mailed to the company, where an analysis for the presence of cocaine, crack cocaine, heroin, methamphetamine, LSD, marijuana, and PCP is performed. The testing destroys the sample, so it cannot be used later in any court proceedings. The results of the analysis are then mailed to the parents.

The fact that test kits are designed to be used by parents with or without their child's knowledge raises a number of controversial issues. On the one hand, these kits are promoted as a potent new weapon in the battle against the increased levels of drug abuse among young people. From this point of view, parents are now able to get early help for their children before drug-abuse problems become too great. On the other hand, these kits can be viewed as a new weapon in the battle of the generations. Detractors argue that it may increase an already significant degree of distrust between parents and their children. In that sense, these test kits may exacerbate dysfunctionality within the family.

What do you think? If you were a parent, would you consider using this testing kit as a step forward or a step backward in the effort to prevent drug abuse in your family?

Sources: Kit to test for drugs at home (1995, March 29). *Newsday,* p. A8. Winslow, O.; and Lam, C. (1995, March 30). Test fuels drugs debate. *Newsday,* pp. A6, A51.

engage in some form of substance abuse: (1) the degree of stress they feel they are under, (2) the frequency with which they are bored, and (3) the amount of money they have to spend in a typical week. High-stress teens (one-fourth of teens interviewed) were twice as likely as low-stress teens (a little more than one-fourth of teens interviewed) to smoke, drink, get drunk, and use illicit drugs. Teens reporting that they were frequently bored were 50 percent more likely than not-often-bored teens to engage in these behaviors. Teens with $25 or more a week in spending money were nearly twice as likely as teens with less spending money to smoke, drink, and use illicit drugs, and they were more than twice as likely to get drunk. Combining two or three of these risk factors (high stress, frequent boredom, and too much spending money) made the risk of smoking, drinking, and illicit drug use three times higher than when none of these characteristics was present.[40]

Substance Abuse Prevention and the College Student

Effective substance abuse programs among college students present an unusual challenge, in that we are hardly speaking of a homogeneous population. U.S. college students represent all racial, ethnic, and socioeconomic groups and are likely to come from all parts of the world. They include undergraduate and graduate students, full-time and part-time students, residential students and commuters, students of traditional college age, and students who are considerably older. Each of these groups has a different perspective on drug-taking behavior, different opportunities for drug-taking behavior, and different life experiences.

In particular, there are marked differences in the objectives of a prevention program between those younger than 21 years and those who are older. In the former group, the goal may be "no use of" (or abstinence from) alcohol, tobacco, and other drugs, whereas in the latter group the goal may be the low-risk (i.e., responsible) consumption of alcohol and no use of tobacco and other drugs. The term "low-risk consumption" refers to a level of use restricted by considerations of physical health, family background, pregnancy risk, the law, safety, and other personal concerns.

With respect to alcohol, secondary prevention guidelines might stipulate that pregnant women, recovering alcoholics or those with a family history of alcoholism, people driving cars or heavy machinery, people on medications, or those under the age of 21 should not drink alcohol at all. Although the distinction between "under-21" and "over-21" preventive goals is applicable in many community-oriented programs, it is an especially difficult challenge for prevention efforts on a college campus when the target population contains both subgroups so closely intermingled.[41]

Changing the Culture of Alcohol in College

A major challenge with regard to prevention programs at colleges and universities comes from the widely regarded expectation that heavy alcohol drinking, during the college years represents something of a rite of passage. College alumni (and potential benefactors) frequently impede the implementation of drug and alcohol crackdowns, arguing that "we did it when we were in school."[42] The 2017 University of Michigan survey has indicated that by the end of high school about 61 percent of all students have consumed alcoholic beverages, and 45 percent have been drunk at least once. The percentages for alcohol consumption are lower than previous years, but they are still relatively high. In other words, nearly two out of three incoming freshmen have had some experience with alcohol and almost one-half of them have drunk at some previous time.[43] Given this base of prior exposure, there is a compelling argument for secondary and tertiary prevention programs to be in place at this point.

The emphasis on most campuses is on the prevention and control of alcohol problems (Drugs ... in Focus). However, it is less common for college administrators to focus on the problems associated with drugs other than alcohol. Although alcohol-abuse programs are virtually certain to be found on college campuses, attention directed toward comparable programs related specifically to drugs other than alcohol lags behind. Frequently, the only policy in place involves a procedure of punitive action if a student athlete tests positive for an illicit drug. While no-smoking campuses exist practically everywhere, few if any programs are in place to help reduce the level of tobacco use among college students.

Prevention Programs on College Campuses

On the positive side, college campuses have the potential for being ideal environments for comprehensive substance abuse prevention programs because they combine features of school and community settings. Here are some suggested strategies for prevention on the college campus:

- Develop a multifaceted prevention program of assessment, education, policy, and enforcement. Involve students, faculty, and administrators in determining the degree of availability and demand for alcohol and other drugs on campus and in the surrounding community and initiate public information and education efforts.

- Incorporate alcohol and other drug education into the curriculum. Faculty members can use drug-related situations as teachable moments, include drug topics in their course syllabi, and develop courses or course projects on issues relating to alcohol and other drugs.

Drugs . . . in Focus

Alcohol 101 on College Campuses

A familiar experience among many students entering college for the first time is referred to by public health officials as the "college effect"—defined as an increase in drinking and negative behaviors associated with it (Chapter 13). One increasingly popular approach intended to minimize this phenomenon is a three-hour Web-based online course called AlcoholEdu, developed by Outside the Classroom, Inc. More than 500 colleges and universities nationwide are currently participating in this program.

AlcoholEdu is oriented toward responsible drinking behavior rather than abstinence. Topics include an understanding of blood alcohol concentrations, activities that increase the likelihood of blacking out, discredited remedies for hangovers, as well as an appreciation of the alcohol beverage industry's role in fostering the image of alcohol consumption as a means for advancing social and interpersonal relationships. Participants are given an exam that tests their knowledge of the information provided in the course.

Colleges and universities have varying policies regarding students taking AlcoholEdu. Some require students to complete and pass the course with a minimum score on the exam prior to the first day of classes or prior to registering for the next semester. Others convey an expectation that the AlcoholEdu should be completed and warn that severe consequences will be imposed for those students who fail to finish the course and commit an alcohol violation in the future. There are early indications that student participation in AlcoholEdu results in significantly fewer negative consequences of drinking, such as missing class, attending class with a hangover, blacking out, and abusive behavior. Intensive studies of effectiveness, both short term and long term, however, need to be carried out.

In the meantime, additional programs addressing a wider range of alcohol problems on campuses have been developed. AlcoholEdu for Sanctions is an intervention program suited for students who have violated academic policies on alcohol, aimed at reducing recidivism rates. Alcohol Innerview is a brief motivational intervention tool for students who have experienced alcohol problems or are in alcohol-abuse counseling. AlcoholEdu for Parents is designed to support parents with college-age children in fostering conversations that can help shape healthy decisions about alcohol use at college.

Recent developments in online prevention programs by Outside the Classroom, Inc. include MentalHealthEdu, raising campus community awareness of college student mental-health issues, and SexualAssaultEdu, focusing on relationships and decision-making to reduce the incidence of sexual assaults on campus.

Sources: Fact sheet on alcohol issues, University of Colorado at Boulder (2004, August 11). Boulder, CO: Office of News Services, University of Colorado. Kesmodel, D. (2005, November 1). Schools use Web to teach about booze. *Wall Street Journal Online.* Outside the Classroom (2008). *www.outsidetheclassroom.com.*

- Ensure that hypocrisy is not the rule of the day. Substance abuse prevention is not a goal for college students only but is a larger issue that affects all members of the academic community, including faculty and administration.

- Encourage environments that lessen the pressures to engage in drug-taking behavior. Foster more places where social and recreational activities can take place spontaneously and at hours when the most enticing alternative may be the consumption of alcohol and other drugs. A recent promising sign is the growing popularity of drug-free dormitories on many college campuses, where student residents specifically choose to refrain from alcohol, tobacco, and other drugs.[44]

The seriousness of the drug-taking behavior on college campuses could not be demonstrated more clearly than in the context of alcohol drinking among members of college fraternities. There is substantial risk of an alcohol-related injury, for example, from underage drinking at a university fraternity party during the first week of a new college year.[45]

Since 2000, when one in five fraternity chapters in the United States began to phase in a policy forbidding alcohol of any kind anywhere in the fraternity house, even in rooms of members who were of legal drinking age, there has been a steady upward trend in the number of alcohol-free fraternity (and sorority) houses around the country.[46]

Prevention in the Workplace

Since 1988, all U.S. federal agencies have been mandated to establish **employee assistance programs (EAPs)** in order to identify and counsel workers with personal problems associated with substance abuse or dependence and to provide referrals to community agencies where these individuals can get further help. Nongovernmental organizations have since been encouraged (but not required) by the act to establish EAPs as well. Traditionally, the emphasis on EAPs

> **employee assistance programs (EAPs):** Corporate-based services designed to identify and counsel employees with personal problems that are connected to substance abuse or dependence and to provide referrals to community agencies where these individuals can get further help.

or union-supported **member assistance programs (MAPs)** has been on problems resulting from alcohol abuse, which is understandable, given that this category represents such a large proportion of substance abuse in general (Chapter 13). In recent years, EAPs and MAPs have expanded their services to focus on psychological problems that do not necessarily concern substance abuse.

Even a modest amount of treatment that results from an EAP or MAP intervention has proven to be beneficial to both the employee and the employer. In one study, heavy drinkers who received brief intervention over a two-month period had significantly fewer accidents, hospital visits, and other events related to problem drinking during the following year. The cost of each brief intervention was $166 per employee, while the medical savings to the employee was $523.[47]

Specifically, organizations must initiate a comprehensive and continuing program of drug education and awareness. Employees must also be notified that the distribution, possession, or unauthorized use of controlled substances is prohibited in that workplace and that actions will be taken against any employee violating these rules. Supervisors are advised to be especially alert to changes in a worker that might signal early or progressive stages in the abuse of alcohol and/or other drugs. These signals include chronic absenteeism, a sudden change in physical appearance or behavior, spasmodic work pace, unexpectedly lower quantity or quality of work, partial or unexplained absences, a pattern of excuse making or lying, the avoidance of supervisors or coworkers, and on-the-job accidents or lost time from such accidents.

In effect, achieving a drug-free workplace is made possible by a combination of secondary prevention and tertiary prevention interventions.

The Economic Costs of Substance Abuse in the Workplace

High-profile instances of on-the-job accidents involving the effects of either illicit drugs or alcohol are often given as examples of the scope of substance abuse in the workplace and the need for workplace drug testing, but we have to be careful in generalizing from these reports. First of all, everyday instances of adverse effect are not covered by the news media. We cannot estimate substance abuse problems in the workplace through the news, any more than we can estimate the impact of drug toxicity on our society through stories of public figures and celebrities who have died of drug overdoses (see Chapter 1). Second, in many cases, we are limited in determining the extent to which we can connect drug use with the tragic consequences of an accident because some drugs leave metabolites in the system long after they have stopped producing behavioral effects (see Chapter 16).

Nonetheless, risk estimates have been calculated, leaving little doubt that the abuse of alcohol and other drugs has a major impact on workplace productivity. The CSAP has estimated that, relative to non-abusers, abusers of alcohol and other drugs are

- 5 times more likely to file a workers' compensation claim
- 3.6 times more likely to be involved in an accident on the job
- 5 times more likely to be personally injured on the job
- 3 times more likely to be late for work
- 2.2 times more likely to request early dismissal from work or time off
- 16 times more likely to take sick leave

Overall, the estimated costs from productivity lost as a result of such behavior amount to $60–$100 billion each year.[48]

The Impact of Drug-Free Workplace Policies

It makes sense that substance abuse prevention programs would have the greatest impact in companies within the transportation industry, owing to the close relationship between drug-induced impairments in performance and the incidence of industrial accidents. Beyond this application, however, it is widely recognized that a similar impact, if not one as dramatic in magnitude, can be demonstrated in any business setting. The reasons relate to the basic goals of prevention, as discussed earlier: deterrence and rehabilitation. The practice of testing for illicit drug use in the workplace functions as an effective deterrent among workers because the likelihood is strong that illicit drug use will be detected. Treatment options are an important component in a comprehensive plan. Substance abuse treatment programs in the workplace can function as an effective rehabilitative tool because those workers who might otherwise not receive help with drug-abuse problems will be referred to appropriate agencies for treatment services.[49]

Issues related to drug testing in the workplace as a strategy for substance abuse prevention will be examined in Chapter 16.

Multicultural Issues in Prevention

In the case of substance abuse prevention messages and administration of substance abuse treatment programs, it is important to remember that information intended to reach individuals of a specific culture passes through a series of **sociocultural filters**. Understanding this filtering process is essential to provide effective substance abuse prevention and treatment programs.

---

member assistance programs (MAPs): Corporate-based services similar to employee assistance programs (EAPs) that are sponsored and supervised by labor unions.

sociocultural filters: A set of considerations specific to a particular culture or community that can influence the reception and acceptance of public information.

Latino Communities

A good example of the need to recognize sociocultural filters is the set of special concerns associated with communicating drug-related information to Latinos, a diverse group representing more than 13 percent of the U.S. population and expected to represent more than 25 percent by 2050. The following insights concerning elements of the Latino community can enhance the chances of success in Latino-targeted prevention and treatment initiatives.

■ Because of the importance Latinos confer on the family and religious institutions, prevention and treatment efforts should be targeted to include the entire family and, if possible, its religious leaders. Prevention and treatment efforts will be most effective when counselors reinforce family units and value them as a whole.

■ Prevention programs are needed to help Latino fathers recognize how important their role or example is to their sons' and daughters' self-image regarding alcohol and other drugs. Because being a good father is part of *machismo*, it is important that the men become full partners in parenting. Mothers should be encouraged to learn strategies for including their husbands in family interactions at home.

■ Because a Latina woman with alcohol or other drug problems is strongly associated with a violation of womanly ideals of purity, discipline, and self-sacrifice, educational efforts should concentrate on reducing the shame associated with her reaching out for help. One particular Web site that addresses the needs of the Latino community is sponsored by the National Latino Council on Alcohol and Tobacco Prevention (NLCATP).[50]

African American Communities

Another set of special concerns exists with regard to communicating drug-related information in African American communities. Some basic generalizations have proven helpful in optimizing the design of prevention and treatment programs.

■ African American youths tend to use drugs other than alcohol after they form social attitudes and adopt behaviors associated with delinquency. The most common examples of delinquency include drug dealing, shoplifting, and petty theft. With regard to the designing of media campaigns, it is the deglamorization of the drug dealer that appears to be most helpful in primary prevention efforts among African American youths.

■ Drug use and social problems are likely to be interrelated in primarily African American neighborhoods. The effects of substance abuse are intensified when other factors exist, such as high unemployment, poverty, poor health care, and poor nutrition.

■ Several research studies have shown that most African American youths, even those in low-income neighborhoods, do manage to escape from the pressures to use

alcohol and other drugs. The protective factors of staying in school, solid family bonds, strong religious beliefs, high self-esteem, adequate coping strategies, social skills, and steady employment all build on one another to provide resilience on the part of high-risk children and adolescents. As noted before, prevention programs developed with protective factors in mind have the greatest chance for success.[51]

Native American Communities

Individuals in Native American communities have particular difficulties with substance abuse. In 2013, 12 percent of Native American or Alaska Natives, aged 12 or older, were current illicit drug users. Twenty-four percent reported binge alcohol drinking, and 40 percent reported current use of a tobacco product. All of these prevalence rates are higher than the average within the general U.S. population. A strong sense of ethnic identity and strong identification with a cultural group are major protective factors (see Chapter 8) with respect to substance abuse of all kinds. For this reason, the incorporation of Native American beliefs can be an effective way of promoting substance abuse prevention. For example, a program that emphasizes the values and morals passed down through the generations that define the relationship of Native Americans to their environment, society, and the universe has the best chance of success. A substance abuse prevention message that "evil spirits [referring to illicit drugs and alcohol] break the bonds between ourselves and our elders, disrupt the circle of our family, and destroys the harmony between us and all creation" reinforces these values.[52]

When Prevention Fails: Treatment Strategies

Individuals who seek help in a treatment program have typically been "jolted" by some external force in their lives. They may have no other option except imprisonment for drug offenses; they may be at risk of losing their job because their supervisor has identified an unproductive pattern of behavior; a spouse may have threatened to leave if something is not done; a friend may have died from a drug overdose or a drug-related accident. Any of these crises or others similar to them can force the question and the decision to seek treatment. You can think of successful substance abuse treatment as a tertiary level of prevention, in that the goal is to prevent an individual from relapsing back into a behavioral pattern of substance abuse.

The prospect of entering a treatment program is probably the most frightening experience the abuser has ever had in his or her life. Public health researchers have compared the early days in recovery to a climber's first step up a great mountain. Change does not happen overnight, and "road blocks" seem to appear in every step of the way. Treatment counselors frequently hear the questions, "Couldn't I just cut down?"

or "Couldn't I just give up drugs temporarily?" or "How will I be able to take the pain of withdrawal?" or "How will I be able to stand the humiliation?" Far from stalling tactics, these questions represent real fears and significant obstacles to taking the crucial first steps to recovery.[53]

In the previous chapters, substance abuse treatment options for specific abused substances have been examined. Some types of substance abuse require a specialized form of treatment. Drugs ... in Focus lists these specific treatment options and the location in previous chapters where they have been reviewed. Treatment options may vary, depending on the substance of abuse, but the *process* of treatment is the same. There is little disagreement among professionals in the substance abuse treatment field about the specific steps that must be taken for an individual to reach a level of recovery. These steps are referred to as *stages of change*.

Stages of Change

In Chapter 8, the five stages of change were discussed in terms of the transtheoretical model, as part of the discussion of the motivational aspect of drug-taking behavior. In this section, stages of change will be examined as important benchmarks along the way toward successful substance abuse recovery—bearing in mind, however, that recovery is a continuing effort without an absolute ending. In review, the stages of change (precontemplation, contemplation, preparation, action, and maintenance) are described as follows:[54]

- *Precontemplation.* Individuals who are in the **precontemplation stage** may *wish* to change but lack the serious intention to undergo change in the foreseeable future or may be unaware of how significant their problems have become. They may be entering treatment at this time only because they perceive that a crisis is at hand. They may

even demonstrate a change in behavior while the pressure is on, but once the pressure is off, they revert to their former ways. It is often difficult for a counselor to deal with a drug abuser during the precontemplation stage because the abuser still feels committed to positive aspects of drug use. A principal goal at this point is to induce inconsistencies in the abuser's perception of drugs in general.

- *Contemplation.* In the **contemplation stage**, individuals are aware that a problem exists and are thinking about overcoming it but have not yet made a commitment to take action. At this point, drug abusers may struggle with the prospect of the tremendous amount of effort and energy needed to overcome the problem. Counselors can help them by highlighting the negative aspects of drug use, making reasonable assurances about the recovery process, and building the self-confidence that is necessary to change.

- *Preparation.* Individuals in the **preparation stage** are defined as those who are seriously considering taking action in the next 30 days and have unsuccessfully taken action

precontemplation stage: A stage of change in which the individual may wish to change but either lacks the serious intention to undergo change in the foreseeable future or is unaware of how significant his or her problem has become.

contemplation stage: A stage of change in which the individual is aware that a problem exists and is thinking about overcoming it but has not yet made a commitment to take action.

preparation stage: A stage of change in which the individual seriously considers taking action to overcome a problem in the next 30 days and has unsuccessfully taken action over the past 12 months.

Drugs . . . in Focus

Reviewing Specific Treatment Strategies for Six Substances of Abuse

In the previous chapters, treatment strategies have been reviewed for specific abused substances. Here is a listing with reference to chapter and page numbers where the information can be found:

Heroin and other opioids	Chapter 9 (pages 184–187)
Cocaine	Chapter 10 (pages 204–205)
Methamphetamine	Chapter 10 (page 211)
Barbiturates	Chapter 12 (pages 263–264)
Alcohol	Chapter 13 (pages 301–304)
Tobacco (nicotine)	Chapter 15 (pages 359–361)

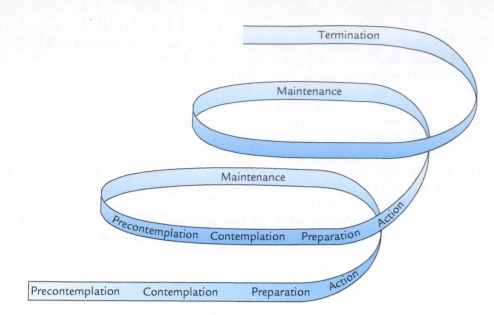

FIGURE 14.3

A spiral model of the stages of change in the recovery from drug abuse and dependence.

Source: Based on Prochaska, J. O.; DiClemente, C. C.; and Norcross, J. C. (1992). In search of how people change: Applications to addictive behaviors. *American Psychologist, 47,* 1104. Copyright © 1992 by the American Psychological Association.

over the past 12 months. Alcohol abusers or tobacco smokers may at this point set a "quit date," or a heroin abuser may make a firm date to enter a therapeutic community within the next month. Because drug abusers are fully capable of stating a clear commitment to change at the preparation stage, counselors can begin to discuss the specific steps in the recovery process, strategies for avoiding problems or postponements, and ways to involve friends and family members.

- *Action.* The **action stage** is the point at which individuals actually modify their behavior, their experiences, and their environment in an effort to overcome their problem. Drug use has now stopped. This is the most fragile stage; abusers are at a high risk of giving in to drug cravings and experiencing mixed feelings about the psychological costs of staying clean. If they successfully resist these urges to return to drug use, the counselor should strongly reinforce their restraint. If they slip back to drug use temporarily and then return to abstinence, the counselor should praise their efforts to turn their life around. An important message to be conveyed at this stage is that a fundamental change in lifestyle and a strong support system of friends and family will reduce the chances of relapse.
- *Maintenance stage.* Individuals in the **maintenance stage** have been drug free for a minimum of six months. They have developed new skills and strategies to avoid backsliding and are consolidating a lifestyle free of drugs. Here, the counselor must simultaneously acknowledge the success that has been achieved and emphasize that the struggle will never be totally over. The maintenance stage is ultimately open ended, in that it continues for the rest of the ex-user's life. Therefore, it may be necessary to have booster sessions from time to time so that the maintenance stage is itself maintained.

Rather than thinking of these stages as a linear progression, however, it is more accurate to think of them as points along a spiral (Figure 14.3); more than likely, a person will recycle through the stages multiple times before he or she is totally rehabilitated. Unfortunately, relapse is the rule rather than the exception in the process of substance abuse recovery.

Stages of Change for Other Problems in Life

If the stages of change listed earlier seem vaguely familiar to you, even without a substance abuse problem, it is no accident. Problems may take many different forms, but the difficulties that we face when we confront these problems have a great deal in common. We may wish to lose weight, get more exercise, stop smoking, end an unhappy relationship, seek out a physician to help a medical condition, or any of a number of actions that might lead toward a healthier and more productive life. We only have to witness the popularity of New Year's Eve resolutions to appreciate the fact that our desire to take steps to change is part of simply being human. And yet, we often feel frustrated when our intentions do not prevail and those New Year's Eve resolutions are left unfulfilled. You may find it helpful to look at your own personal journey toward resolving a problem in your life in terms of the five stages of change.[55]

action stage: A stage of change in which the individual actually modifies his or her behavior and environment to overcome a problem.

maintenance stage: A stage of change in which the individual has become drug free for a minimum of six months and has developed new skills and strategies that reduce the probability of relapse.

The Challenges of Recovery

Rehabilitation from substance abuse and substance dependence has three major challenging goals. First, the long decline in physical and psychological functioning that has accumulated over the years must be reversed. Drugs take a heavy toll on the user's medical condition and his or her personal relationships. Second, the use of all psychoactive substances must stop, not simply the one or two causing the immediate problem, and not merely for a limited period of time. Thus, the motivation to stop using alcohol and other drugs and to remain abstinent on a permanent basis must be strong, and it must stay strong. Third, a lifestyle free of alcohol and other drugs must be rebuilt, from scratch if necessary. This frequently means giving up the old friends and the old places where drugs were part of an abuser's life and finding new friends and places that reinforce a drug-free existence. A determination to stay clean and sober requires avoiding high-risk situations, defined as those that increase the possibility of relapse.

How successful are treatments for substance abuse? Unfortunately, relatively few treatment programs allow outside evaluators to determine whether or not there has been a genuine benefit to treatment. The need for evidence-based treatment strategies is just as important as the need for evidence-based prevention strategies, and the judgment of effectiveness must be made in the same way. All too often, treatments appear to be successful in the short term, but they end up failing in the long term. Short-term successes can be deceiving. A substance abuser may be "discharged" after 60 visits or 60 days, and everyone is crying and hugging and feeling proud. Feelings abound that the abuser has been "cured."[56]

Needing Versus Receiving Substance Abuse Treatment

According to U.S. government estimates in 2016, approximately 19.9 million people needed treatment for an illicit drug or alcohol use problem (or both), and only 11 percent received treatment at a specialty facility. Figure 14.4 shows, in visual terms, the wide gap between treatment needed and treatment received. Only 5 percent of people needing treatment in 2016 for either an illicit drug or alcohol use problem, but who did not receive it, personally felt a need to seek help.[57]

What can be done to reduce this disparity between treatment needed and treatment received? What can be done to encourage more people to seek treatment in the first place? Obviously, more work must be done to increase the number of substance abusers who recognize that they need to seek treatment and understand that treatment will have a positive impact in their lives. An encouraging new program called Screening, Brief Intervention, and Referral to Treatment

Quick Concept Check 14.3

Understanding the Stages of Change

Check your understanding of the stages of change by matching each quotation, on the left, with the appropriate stage in treatment, on the right. Quotations are assumed to be statements made by a substance abuser at a particular point in the process of treatment and recovery.

1. "Yeah, I know I drink too much but I'm not ready to do something about it yet."

2. "I may need a boost right now to help me hold on to the changes I've made. It's been nearly two years since I used drugs."

3. "I don't have any big problems. I have a right to do whatever I want."

4. "Although I like snorting coke, it might be time to quit."

5. "It's New Year's Eve and I've set two weeks from now as the day I'm quitting. I want everyone to know that."

6. "It's been six weeks since I smoked a joint, and I can tell already how different things seem to be."

a. Precontemplation stage

b. Contemplation stage

c. Preparation stage

d. Action stage

e. Maintenance stage

Answers: 1. b 2. e 3. a 4. b 5. c 6. d

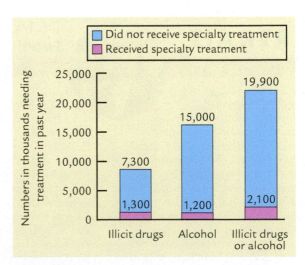

FIGURE 14.4

The gap between treatment needed and treatment received among adults aged 18 or older in the United States.

Source: Substance Abuse and Mental Health Services Administration (2017, September). Receipt of services for substance use and mental health issues among adults: Results from the 2016 National Survey on Drug Use and Health. *NSDUH Data Review.* Rockville, MD: Substance Abuse and Mental Health Services Administration, Figures 8, 10, 12, and 14.

(SBIRT) serves to help in getting individuals into treatment at an early stage and with less resistance. The program creates a system within community and/or medical settings—including physician offices, hospitals, educational institutions, and mental health centers—that screens for and identifies individuals with or at risk for substance use-related problems. The screening determines the severity of substance use and identifies the appropriate intervention. There is a brief intervention with the community setting and referral to more extensive services if needed. The intent is to make interventions in a relatively nonthreatening manner and hopefully increase the numbers of individuals who receive treatment.[58]

Additionally, more work must be done to provide accessible and affordable substance abuse treatment for those individuals who want it and are willing to seek it out. Fortunately, affordable substance abuse treatment in the United States took a major step forward to this end when the Mental Health Parity and Addiction Equity Act of 2008 was passed by the U.S. Congress. In the past, Americans seeking help for psychological problems (including problems related to substance abuse) were reimbursed differently from Americans seeking help with medical conditions. Since 2010, individuals seeking treatment for substance use or a mental health disorder do not need to face unfair and arbitrary restrictions on their benefits coverage, relative to coverage for other forms of health treatment. Since 2014, the Affordable Care Act (ACA) mandates all new small group and individual market plans to cover substance use disorder services, at parity with medical and surgical benefits. The ACA mandate builds upon the 2008 law. More than 62 million Americans have been extended "parity protection" for substance abuse treatment.[59]

For Those Who Need Help and Want to Get It

Throughout our lives, we will need to confront the reality that licit and illicit substance abuse represents a significant factor in our personal health and the public health of our communities. From everything that has been reviewed in this introduction to drug-taking behavior in today's society and its ramifications for the criminal justice system, it is clear that we need all the help we can get (Portrait).

Fortunately, information and guidance are all around us. For local referral sources for treatment programs, check out the yellow pages of your telephone book under Alcoholism Information or Drug Abuse and Addiction Information. There are also numerous Web sites on the Internet that are specifically designed to provide assistance with any problem associated with all forms of substance abuse. The most comprehensive source for substance abuse prevention and treatment information is the National Clearinghouse for Alcohol and Drug Information (NCADI). Educational materials regarding virtually any aspect of drug use, misuse, or abuse can be ordered free by calling 800-729-6686 or accessing NCADI's Web site at *www.health.org* or the Web site for the Substance Abuse and Mental Health Services Administration at *www.samhsa.gov*.

On a local level, a wide range of resources for treatment are available through recovery high schools and recovery centers, sponsored by churches and other religious organizations as well as outreach units of local police departments in the community. Many of these facilities operate on a confidential, "walk-in" basis.

PORTRAIT

Dr. Mark Willenbring: Fighting "Addiction, Inc." in the twenty-first century

Given the widespread problems of substance abuse today, the demand for treatment has never been greater. Unfortunately, the response has been the emergence of a massive and highly lucrative addiction treatment industry led by entrepreneurs who have seen this demand as an untapped market and an enormous business opportunity. Spurred on by an inadequate patchwork of regulations, little consensus among health-care experts on the most effective way to treat substance abuse, and public perception that short-fix solutions exist, addiction treatment centers thrive and prosper while, according to a recent analysis, "Only a small fraction of individuals receive interventions or treatment consistent with scientific knowledge about what works."

Dr. Mark Willenbring (see photo), former director of treatment and recovery research at the National Institute for Alcohol Abuse and Alcoholism, has pointed out, "You don't treat a chronic illness for four weeks and then send the patient to a support group. People with a chronic form of addiction need multimodal treatment that is individualized and offered continuously or intermittently for as long as they need it." Under his direction, the Alltyr Clinic in St. Paul, Minnesota was formed in 2012 as an alternative to cookie-cutter rehab programs and centers that have become so prevalent. At Alltyr, every known available evidence-based treatment is offered, with no fixed time period for treatment.

Since its founding, the Alltyr model has been adopted by other forward-looking centers around the country, all based on an evidence-based philosophy that does not presume what substance abuse treatment strategy might be best for any given patient needing services. But finding the best treatment option requires a great deal of homework. It has been said that people typically spend more research time and effort when shopping for a new car than when searching for a treatment for a problem as serious as substance abuse.

Sources: Quotation from Brody, J. E. (2013, February 5). Effective addiction treatment. *The New York Times*, p. D5. Corkery, M.; and Silver-Greenberg, J. (2017, December 28). The giant, under attack. Addiction Inc., a special report of the *New York Times*, pp. F3–F7.

Credit: Courtesy of Dr. Mark Willenbring

Summary

Levels of Intervention in Substance Abuse Prevention

● Substance abuse prevention efforts fall into three basic levels of intervention: primary, secondary, and tertiary.

● Primary prevention focuses on populations that have had only minimal or no exposure to drugs. Secondary prevention focuses on populations whose drug experience has not yet been associated with serious long-term problems. Tertiary prevention focuses on populations who have entered treatment; the goal is to prevent relapse.

The Goal of Substance Abuse Prevention

● Substance abuse prevention programs on a federal level are the responsibility of the Substance Abuse and Mental Health Services Administration.

● The overall strategy for substance abuse prevention is to minimize the risk factors in a person's life with respect to drug-taking behavior and maximize the protective factors. The inclination to resist the effects of risk factors for drug-taking behavior through the action of protective factors is referred to as resilience.

● In order to be "evidence-based," primary and secondary prevention programs must be evaluated against a control group that did not receive the intervention. Positive change per se is not enough for a judgment of success.

● The federal program, Healthy People 2020, has set specific objectives with regard to aspects of personal health, including those that pertain to substance use, recognizing that a healthy life makes for a healthy society.

Prevention Approaches That Have Failed

● Several strategies have been largely unsuccessful in meeting the goals of substance abuse prevention. They include the reliance on supply/availability reduction, punitive judicial policies, scare tactics, objective information, and self-esteem enhancement/affective education.

Effective School-Based Prevention Programs

● Effective school-based programs have incorporated a combination of peer-refusal skills training, relaxation and stress management, and training in social skills and personal decision-making.

● The Life Skills Training program is an example of a comprehensive program that incorporates several of these school-based components for effective substance abuse prevention. On the other hand, several evaluative studies have shown the popular Drug Abuse Resistance Education (DARE) program, in its original form, to be of little effectiveness in primary prevention. Later versions have incorporated many of the components that have been demonstrated to be effective.

Effective Community-Based Prevention Programs

● Community-based programs make use of a broader range of resources, including community leaders and public figures as positive role models, opportunities for alternative-behavior programming, and the media.

● Specific media sources can have a positive or negative impact on substance abuse prevention in both high-risk populations and others in the community. The Partnership for a Drug-Free America (PDFA) has been a leader in antidrug communications in the media, while numerous online Internet sources tend to promote either prodrug or misinformation about drug-taking behavior.

● CASASTART is an example of a community-based program that incorporates intensive communitywide components of substance abuse prevention.

Family Systems in Primary and Secondary Prevention

● Community-based prevention programs are increasingly mindful of the importance of the family, particularly parents, as the first line of defense in prevention efforts.

● The major emphasis in primary and secondary prevention programs has been on the special roles of parents, grandparents, guardians, and other family members. Improved lines of communication within the family are crucial elements in the promotion of substance abuse prevention.

Substance Abuse Prevention and the College Student

● On college campuses, substance abuse prevention programs are incorporating features of both school-based and community-based approaches. There is a compelling argument for the need to change the culture of alcohol and other drug use in college.

● Substance abuse prevention programs on college campuses should involve faculty and administrators, as well as students, in an overall comprehensive strategy. College fraternities have taken important strides toward an alcohol ban in fraternity houses, even when members are of legal drinking age.

Substance Abuse Prevention in the Workplace

● The 1988 Drug-free Workplace Act mandated that any company or business receiving U.S. federal contracts or grants provide a drug-free workplace. This is carried out through a comprehensive and continuing program of drug education and awareness. It is estimated that substance abuse costs as much as $60–$100 billion each year.

● One element of most drug-free workplace programs is an employee assistance program (EAP), serving to help workers with abuse problems. Where unions exist, member assistance programs (MAPs) supplement and complement the work of EAPs.

- Frequently, substance abuse prevention efforts in the workplace entail drug testing among employees, either as a prescreening procedure for new job applicants or as a continuing program for all employees.

Multicultural Issues in Prevention

- Special cultural considerations need to be made when communicating about substance abuse with specific population subgroups such as individuals in Latino, African American, and Native American communities.

Substance Abuse Treatment: Strategies for Change

- The road to recovery can be understood in terms of five distinct "stages of change." These stages are precontemplation, contemplation, preparation, action, and maintenance. It is possible to cycle through these stages multiple times in a kind of spiraling pattern before long-term recovery is attained.

- The five stages of change are applicable to the resolution of any life problems, not just those associated with substance abuse.

Needing Versus Receiving Substance Abuse Treatment

- According to U.S. government estimates, approximately 7.3 million adults 18 or older need treatment for an illicit drug problem; more than 15 million people need treatment for an alcohol problem. A small fraction, however, has received treatment at a specialized facility in the past 12 months.

- Of those individuals who have needed treatment for illicit drug or alcohol use problems but have not received it, only about 5 percent personally felt the need to seek it out. Reasons for not seeking treatment include the lack of financial means to pay for treatment services and inadequate health insurance coverage. The Mental Health Parity and Addiction Equity Act and the Affordable Care Act have allowed individuals in substance abuse treatment to receive reimbursement on a par with treatment for medical or surgical health benefits.

Final Note: For Those Who Need Help ...

- The most comprehensive sources for substance abuse treatment information in the United States are the National Clearinghouse for Alcohol and Drug Information (NCADI) and the Substance Abuse and Mental Health Administration (SAMHSA), accessible through www.health.org and www.samhsa.gov, respectively. Similar information sources exist in Canada, the United Kingdom, and most other nations.

Key Terms

action stage, p. 330
affective education, p. 318
contemplation stage, p. 329
employee assistance programs
     (EAPs), p. 326

impactors, p. 320
maintenance stage, p. 330
member assistance programs
     (MAPs), p. 327
peer-refusal skills, p. 318

precontemplation stage, p. 329
preparation stage, p. 329
primary prevention, p. 312
resilience, p. 315
secondary prevention, p. 312

sociocultural filters, p. 327
tertiary prevention, p. 312
values clarification, p. 318

Review Questions

1. Describe the primary, secondary, and tertiary levels of intervention in substance abuse prevention. Include in your answer the specific target population and goals in each level of intervention. What is the relationship between resilience and primary prevention?

2. Describe the components of effective school-based prevention programs, using the Life Skills Training program as a model for school-based interventions.

3. How is a community-based prevention program different from a school-based program? In what ways, will a community-based program be more effective in substance abuse prevention?

4. Discuss the "triple threat" concept (stress, boredom, and spending money) in drug-taking behavior among young people.

5. Why is it particular difficult to implement substance abuse prevention programs on college campuses, compared to programs in the community, in the workplace, or in earlier educational settings?

6. Discuss the particular challenges of substance abuse prevention and treatment in Latino, African American, and Native American communities?

7. Review the stages of change in substance abuse treatment.

Critical Thinking: What Would You Do?

You have a close friend who is a substance abuser, who has experienced significant problems associated with substance abuse. Your friend could be male or female; let us assume your friend is female. She is adamant in her refusal to enter into any treatment for her substance abuse. She is convinced that she does not need it; and that it is inconvenient or embarrassing to seek treatment even if she needed it. Yet, all objective evidence points to a decline in her physical, social, and psychological well-being. As a friend, what can you do to help her receive the treatment she needs?

Endnotes

1. *Adapted from* "Alex: A teen's story of overcoming addiction" (2014, August 28). Phoenix House News and Views. Accessed from: https://phoenixhouse.org/news-and-views/true-story-alex-2. Quotations slightly modified from the article.

2. Office of National Drug Control Strategy (2009, May). National Drug Control Strategy. FY 2010 Budget Summary. Washington, D.C.: Executive Office of the President. Office of National Drug Control Strategy (2015, May). *National Drug Control Strategy. FY 2016 Budget Summary.* Washington, D.C.: Executive Office of the President.

3. Brook, J. S.; and Brook, D. W. (1996). Risk and protective factors for drug use. In C. B. McCoy; L. R. Metsch; and J. A. Inciardi (Eds.), *Intervening with drug-involved youth.* Thousand Oaks, CA: Sage Publications, pp. 23–44. Clayton, Richard R.; Segress, M, J. H.; and C., Crystal A. (2008). Prevention of substance abuse. In M. Galanter; and H. D. Kleber (Eds.), *Textbook of substance abuse treatment* (4th ed.). Washington, D.C.: American Psychiatric Publishing, pp. 681–688. Glantz, M. D.; and Johnson, J. L. (Eds.) (2003). *Resilience and development: Positive life adaptations.* New York: Kluwer Academic/Plenum. Wong, M. M.; Nigg, J. T.; Zucker, R. A.; Puttler, L. I.; et al. (2006). Behavioral control and resiliency in the onset of alcohol and illicit drug use: A prospective study from preschool to adolescence. *Child Development, 77,* 1016–1033.

4. Mokdad, A. H.; Marks, J. S.; Stroup, D. F.; and Gerberding, J. L. (2004). Actual causes of death in the United States, 2000. *Journal of the American Medical Association, 291,* 1238–1245. Mokdad, A. H.; Marks, J. S.; Stroup, D. F.; and Gerberding, J. L. (2005). Correction: Actual causes of death in the United States, 2000. *Journal of the American Medical Association, 293,* 298.

5. Califano, J. A., Jr. (2007). *High society: How substance abuse ravages America and what to do about it.* New York: Public Affairs. Center for Substance Abuse Prevention (2009). *Substance abuse prevention dollars and cents: A cost-benefit analysis.* Rockville, MD: Substance Abuse and Mental Health Services Administration.

6. Public Health Service (2009, October–November). *Healthy People 2020: Public meeting. 2009 draft objectives.* Bethesda, MD: Public Health Service.

7. Office of National Drug Control Policy (2015), *National drug control strategy,* Table 1.

8. Goode, E. (2008). *Drugs in American society* (7th ed.). New York: McGraw-Hill College, pp. 400–403. National Drug Intelligence Center (2008). *National drug threat assessment 2009.* Washington, D.C.: U.S. Department of Justice, pp. 25–32.

9. Hingson, R. W.; Scotch, N.; Mangione, T.; Meyers, A.; Glantz, L.; et al. (1983). Impact of legislation raising the legal drinking age in Massachusetts from 18 to 21. *American Journal of Public Health, 73,* 163–170.

10. Goode, *Drugs in American society,* pp. 385–417. Greenhouse, L. (2007, December 11). Justices restore judges' control over sentencing. *The New York Times,* pp. A1, A28. Peters, J. W. (2009, March 11). Legislation to overhaul Rockefeller drug laws advances swiftly. *The New York Times,* p. 20. Steinberg, N. (1994, May 5). The law of unintended consequences. *Rolling Stone,* pp. 33–34.

11. Funkhouser, J. E.; and Denniston, .R. W. (1992). Historical perspective. In M. A. Jansen (Ed.), *A promising future: Alcohol and other drug problem prevention services improvement* (OSAP Prevention Monograph 10). Rockville, MD: Office of Substance Abuse Prevention, pp. 5–15.

12. Flay, B. R.; and Sobel, J. L. (1983). The role of mass media in preventing adolescent substance abuse. In T. J. Glynn; C. G. Leukenfeld; and J. P. Ludford (Eds.), *Preventive adolescent drug abuse.* Rockville, MD: National Institute on Drug Abuse, pp. 5–35.

13. Williams, R. E.; Ward, D. A.; and Gray, L. N. (1985). The persistence of experimentally induced cognitive change: A neglected dimension in the assessment of drug prevention programs. *Journal of Drug Education, 15,* 33–42.

14. Meeks, L.; Heit, P.; and Page, R. (1994). *Drugs, alcohol, and tobacco.* Blacklick, OH: Meeks Heit Publishing, p. 201.

15. Ibid., p. 202.

16. McBride, D. C.; Mutch, P. B.; and Chitwood, D. D. (1996). Religious belief and the initiation and prevention of drug use among youth. In C. B. McCoy; L. R. Metsch; and J. A. Inciardi (Eds.), *Intervening with drug-involved youth.* Thousand Oaks, CA: Sage Publications, pp. 110–130.

17. Schroeder, D. S.; Laflin, M. T.; and Weis, D. L. (1993). Is there a relationship between self-esteem and drug use? Methodological and statistical limitations of the research. *Journal of Drug Issues, 22,* 645–665. Yuen, F. K. O.; and Pardeck, J. T. (1998). Effective strategies for preventing substance abuse among children and adolescents. *Early Child Development and Care, 145,* 119–131.

18. Best, J. A.; Flay, B. R.; Towson, S. M. J.; Ryan, K. B.; et al. (1984). Smoking prevention and the concept of risk. *Journal of Applied Social Psychology, 14,* 257–273. Frakt, A.; and Humphreys, K. (2017, November 2). "Just say no"? Antidrug ads rarely work, and even risk a "yes." *The New York Times,* p. A11. Pandina, R. J.; Johnson, V. L.; and White, H. R. (2010). Peer influences on substance use during adolescence and emerging adulthood. In L. M. Scheier (Ed.), *Handbook of*

drug use etiology: Theory, methods, and empirical findings. Washington, D.C.: American Psychological Association, pp. 383–402.

19. Botvin, G. J.; and Griffin, K. W. (2010). Advances in the science and practice of prevention: Targeting individual-level etiological factors and the challenge of going to scale. In L. M. Scheier (Ed.), *Handbook of drug use etiology: Theory, methods, and empirical findings.* Washington, D.C.: American Psychological Association, pp. 631–650. Botvin, E. M. (1992). School-based and community-based prevention approaches. In J. H. Lewisohn; P. Ruiz; and R. B. Millman (Eds.), *Substance abuse: A comprehensive textbook* (2nd ed.). Baltimore, MD: Williams & Wilkins, pp. 910–927.

20. Culpers, P. (2002). Effective ingredients of school-based drug prevention programs: A systematic review. *Addictive Behaviors,* 27, 1009–1023. Faggiano, F.; Vigna-Taglianti, F.; Versino, E.; Zambon, A.; and Lemma, P. (2005). School-based prevention for illicit drugs' use. *Cochrane Database of Systematic Reviews* (2). Article No.: CD003020doi: 10.1002/14651858.CD0030. pub2.

21. Botvin, G. J.; Baker, Eli; Dusenbury, L.; Botvin, E. M.; and Diaz, T. (1995). Long-term follow-up results of a randomized drug abuse prevention trial in a white middle-class population. *Journal of the American Medical Association,* 273, 1106–1112. Botvin, G. J.; Epstein, J. A.; Baker, E.; Diaz, T.; and Ifill-Williams, M. (1997). School-based drug abuse prevention with inner-city minority youth. *Journal of Child and Adolescent Substance Abuse,* 6, 5–19. Botvin, G. J.; and Tortu, S. (1988). Preventing adolescent substance abuse through life skills training. In R. M. Price; E. L. Cowen; R. P. Lorion; and J. Ramos-McKay (Eds.), *Fourteen ounces of prevention: A casebook for practitioners.* Washington, D.C.: American Psychological Association, pp. 98–110.

22. Mathias, R. (1997, March/April). From the 'burbs to the 'hood... This program reduces student's risk of drug use. *NIDA Notes,* pp. 1, 5–6. Quotation on p. 6.

23. Beets, M. W.; Flay, B. R.; Vuchinich, S.; Snyder, F. J.; Acock, A.; et al. (2009). Use of a social and character development program to prevent substance use, violent behaviors, and sexual activity among elementary-school students in Hawaii. *American Journal of Public Health,* 99, 1438–1445. Botvin, G. J.; Griffin, K. W.; and Nichols, T. D. (2006). Preventing youth violence and delinquency through a universal school-based prevention approach. *Prevention Science,* 7, 403–408. Griffin, K. W.; Botvin, G. J.; and Nichols, T. D. (2006). Effects of a school-based drug abuse prevention program for adolescents on HIV risk behaviors in young adulthood. *Prevention Science,* 7, 103–112. Griffin, K. W.; Botvin, G. J.; and Nichols, T. D. (2004). Long-term follow-up effects of a school-based drug abuse prevention program on adolescent risky driving. *Prevention Science,* 5, 207–212.

24. Gardner, M.; Barajas, R. G.; and Brooks-Gunn, J. (2010). Neighborhood influences on substance use etiology: Is where you live important? In L. M. Scheier (Ed.), *Handbook of drug use etiology: Theory, methods, and empirical findings.* Washington, D.C.: American Psychological Association, pp. 423–442. Snyder, L. B.; and Nadorff, P. G. (2010). Youth substance use and the media. In L. M. Scheier (Ed.), *Handbook of drug use etiology: Theory, methods, and empirical findings.* Washington, D.C.: American Psychological Association, pp. 475–492. Wandersman, A.; and Florin, P. (2003). Community interventions and effective prevention. *American Psychologist,* 58, 441–448.

25. Rhodes, J. E.; and Jason, L. A. (1991). The social stress model of alcohol and other drug abuse: A basis for comprehensive, community-based prevention. In K. H. Rey; C. L. Faegre; and P. Lowery (Eds.), *Prevention research findings: 1988* (OSAP Prevention Monograph 3). Rockville, MD: Office of Substance Abuse Prevention, pp. 155–171.

26. Tobler, N. S. (1986). Meta-analysis of 143 adolescent drug prevention programs: Quantitative outcome results of program participants compared to a control group. *Journal of Drug Issues,* 16, 537–567.

27. Ridout, V.; Roberts, D. F.; and Foehr, U. G. (2005, March). *Generation M: Media in the lives of 8–18-year-olds: Executive summary.* Menlo Park, CA: Kaiser Family Foundation.

28. Masten, A. S.; Faden, V. B.; Zucker, R. A.; and Spear, L. P. (2008). Underage drinking: A developmental framework. *Pediatrics, 121,* S235–S251. Primack, B.; Dalton, M. A.; Carroll, M. V.; Agarwal, A. A.; and Fine, M. J. (2008). Content analysis of tobacco, alcohol, and other drugs in popular music. *Archives of Pediatric and Adolescent Medicine,* 162, 169–175. Sargent, J. D.; Wills, T. A.; Stoolmiller, M.; Gibson, J.; and Gibbons, F. X. (2006). Alcohol use in motion pictures and its relationship with early-onset teen drinking. *Journal of Studies in Alcohol,* 67, 54–65.

29. Partnership for a Drug-Free America (1994, July 12). Press release: New study shows children in NYC becoming more anti-drug, bucking national trends. Partnership for a Drug-Free America, New York.

30. Office of National Drug Control Policy (2006, July 21). *Media campaign fact sheets: Teens and technology fact sheet.* National Youth Anti-drug Media Campaign, Office of National Drug Control Policy, Washington, D.C. Partnership for a Drug-Free America, New York. Substance Abuse and Mental Health Services Administration (2009, April 3). *SAMHSA news release: National survey finds a decrease in the percentage of adolescents seeing substance use prevention messages in the media.* Rockville, MD: Substance Abuse and Mental Health Services Administration.

31. Information courtesy of the Substance Abuse and Mental Health Services Administration, Rockville, MD.

32. Cavazos, L. F. (1989). *What works: Schools without drugs.* Washington, D.C.: U.S. Department of Education, p. 38.

33. Clayton, R. R.; Cattarello, A. M.; and Johnstone, B. M. (1996). The effectiveness of Drug Abuse Resistance Education (Project DARE): 5-year follow-up results. *Preventive Medicine,* 25, 307–318. Lynam, D. R.; Milich, R.; Zimmerman, R.; Novak, S. P.; Logan, T. K.; et al. (1999). Project DARE: No effects at 10-year follow-up. *Journal of Consulting and Clinical Psychology,* 67, 590–593. Pan, W.; and Bai, H. (2009). A multivariate approach to a meta-analytic review of the effectiveness of the D.A.R.E. program. *International Journal of Environmental Research and Public Health,* 6, 267–277.

34. Miller, J. (2004). *Bad trip: How the war against drugs is destroying America.* New York: Nelson Thomas.

35. Lynam, D. R.; Milich, R.; Zimmerman, R.; Novak, S. P.; Logan, T. K.; et al. (1999). Project DARE: No effects at 10-year follow-up. Journal of Consulting and Clinical Psychology, 67, 590–593

36. Zernike, K. (2001, February 15). Antidrug program says it will adopt a new strategy. *The New York Times,* pp. A1, A29.

37. Kliewer, W. (2010). Family processes in drug use etiology. In L. M. Scheier (Ed.), *Handbook of drug use etiology: Theory, methods, and empirical findings.* Washington, D.C.: American

Psychological Association, pp. 365–382. National Center on Addiction and Substance Abuse at Columbia University (1999). *No safe haven: Children of substance-abusing parents.* New York: National Center on Addiction and Substance Abuse at Columbia University. Seizas, J. S.; and Youcha, G. (1999). *Drugs, alcohol, and your children: What every parent needs to know.* New York: Penguin Books.

38. The Ad Council (2008, March/April). Underage drinking prevention: Alcohol initiation rates highest during summer. *PSA Bulletin*, p. 1. Lac, A.; and Crano, W. D. (2009). Monitoring matters: Meta-analytic review reveals the reliable linkage of parental monitoring with adolescent marijuana use. *Perspectives on Psychological Science, 4,* 578–586. Wooldridge, L. Substance Abuse and Mental Health Services Administration (2007, March/April). Ads, billboards highlight younger children. *SAMHSA News*, p. 11.

39. The National Center on Addiction and Substance Abuse at Columbia University (2005, September). *The importance of family dinners II.* New York: National Center on Addiction and Substance Abuse at Columbia University. The National Center on Addiction and Substance Abuse at Columbia University (2006, August). *National survey of American attitudes on substance abuse XI: Teens and parents.* New York: National Center on Addiction and Substance Abuse at Columbia University. Partnership for a Drug-Free America (1998). Partnership attitude tracking survey: Parents say they're talking, but only 27% of teens—1 in 4—are learning a lot at home about the risk of drugs. Partnership for a Drug-Free America (1999). Partnership attitude tracking survey: More parents talking with kids about drugs more often, and appear to be having an impact. Information courtesy of Partnership for a Drug-Free America, New York.

40. The National Center on Addiction and Substance Abuse at Columbia University (2003, August). *National survey American attitudes on substance abuse VIII: Teens and parents.* New York: National Center on Addiction and Substance Abuse at Columbia University.

41. Castro, R. J.; and Foy, B. D. (2002). Harm reduction: A promising approach for college health. *Journal of American College Health, 51,* 89–91. Lewis, D. C. (2001). Urging college alcohol and drug policies that target adverse behavior, not use. *Journal of American College Health, 50,* 39–41. Weitzman, E. R.; Nelson, T. F.; Lee, H.; and Wechsler, H. (2004). Reducing drinking and related harms in college: Evaluation of the "A Matter of Degree" program. *American Journal of Preventive Medicine, 27,* 187–196.

42. Freedman, S. G. (2007, September 12). Calling the folks about campus drinking. *The New York Times*, p. B6. National Institute on Alcohol Abuse and Alcoholism (2002, October). Changing the culture of campus drinking. *Alcohol Alert*, No. 58. Bethesda, MD: National Institute on Alcohol Abuse and Alcoholism.

43. Schulenberg, J. E.; Johnston, L. D.; O'Malley, P. M.; Bachman, J. G.; Miech, R. A.; and Patrick, M. E. (2018). *Monitoring the Future national survey results on drug use, 1975–2017: Volume II, College students and adults ages 19–55.* Ann Arbor, MI: Institute for Social Research, The University of Michigan, Table 2-1.

44. Office of Educational Research and Improvement (1990). *A guide for college presidents and governing bodies: Strategies for eliminating alcohol and other drug abuse on campuses.* Washington, D.C.: U.S. Department of Education.

45. Denizet-Lewis, B. (2005, January 9). Band of brothers. *The New York Times*, pp. 32–39, 52, 73. Office of Educational Research and Improvement (1990). *A guide for college presidents and governing boards.* Washington, D.C.: U.S. Department of Education.

46. Busteed, B. (2010, March 19). Is high-risk drinking at college on the way out? *Chronicle of Higher Education*, p. A76. Crump, S. (2008, March 6). Fraternity life without keg parties safer, saner, say Phi Delta Theta guys. Accessed from: www.cleveland.com/lifestyles/2008.

47. Center for Substance Abuse Treatment (2010, April 4). Issue Brief #12 for Employers: What you need to know about substance abuse treatment. Rockville, MD: Substance Abuse and Mental Health Services Administration. Larson, S. L.; Eyerman, J.; Foster, M. S.; and Gfroerer, J. C. (2007). *Worker substance use and workplace policies and programs.* Rockville, MD: Substance Abuse and Mental Health Services Administration, p. 2. Lehman, W. E. K.; Farabee, D. J.; and Bennett, J. B. (1998). Perceptions and correlates of co-worker substance use. *Employee Assistance Quarterly, 13,* 1–22.

48. Center for Substance Abuse Prevention (1994). *Making the link: Alcohol, tobacco, and other drugs in the workplace.* Rockville, MD: Substance Abuse and Mental Health Services Administration.

49. Blum, T. C.; and Roman, P. M. (1995). *Cost-effectiveness and preventive implications of employee assistance programs.* Rockville, MD: Substance Abuse and Mental Health Services Administration.

50. Hernandez, L. P.; and Lucero, E. (1996). La Familia community drug and alcohol prevention program: Family-centered model for working with inner-city Hispanic families. *Journal of Primary Prevention, 16,* 255–272. El-Guebaly, N. (2008). Cross-cultural aspects of addiction. In M. Galanter; and H. D. Kleber (Eds.), *Textbook of substance abuse treatment* (4th ed.). Washington, D.C.: American Psychiatric Publishing, pp. 45–52. Office of Substance Abuse Prevention (1990). *The fact is ... reaching Hispanic/Latino audiences requires cultural sensitivity.* Rockville, MD: National Clearinghouse for Alcohol and Drug Information, National Institute on Drug Abuse. U.S. Census Bureau (2005). *The Hispanic population in the United States: March 2004.* Washington, D.C.: U.S. Department of Commerce.

51. Hahn, E. J.; and Rado, M. (1996). African-American Head Start parent involvement in drug prevention. *American Journal of Health Behavior, 20,* 41–51. Office of Substance Abuse Prevention (1990). *The fact is ... alcohol and other drug use is a special concern for African American families and communities.* Rockville, MD: National Clearinghouse for Drug and Alcohol Information, National Institute on Drug Abuse.

52. Kulis, S.; Napoli, M.; and Marsiglian, F. F. (2002). Ethnic pride, biculturalism, and drug use norms of urban American Indian adolescents. *Social Work Research, 26,* 101–112. Melton, A. P.; Chino, M.; May, P. A.; and Gossage, J. P. (2000). Promising practices and strategies to reduce alcohol and substance abuse among American Indians and Alaska Natives. *An OJP Issues and Practices Report.* Washington, D.C.: U.S. Department of Justice. Center for Behavioral Health Statistics and Quality (2014). *Results of the 2013 national survey on drug use and health: National summary.* Rockville, MD: Substance Abuse and Mental Health Services Administration, pp. 26, 38, and 52.

53. Connors, G. J.; Donovan, D. J.; and DiClemente, C. C. (2001). *Substance abuse treatment and the stages of change: Selecting and planning interventions.* New York: Guilford Press. DiClemente, Carlo C.; Bellino, L. E.; and Neavins, T. M. (1999). Motivation for change and alcoholism treatment. *Alcohol Research and Health, 23,* 86–92. Schuckit, M. A. (1995). *Educating yourself about alcohol and drugs: A people's primer.* New York: Plenum Press, pp. 131–153.

54. DiClemente, C. C.; Garay, M.; and Gemmell, L. (2008). Motivational enhancement. In M. Galanter; and H. D. Kleber (Eds.), *Textbook of substance abuse treatment* (4th ed.). Washington, D.C.: American Psychiatric Publishing, pp. 361–372. Dijkstra, A.; Roijackers, J.; and DeVries, H. (1998). Smokers in four stages of readiness to change. *Addictive Behaviors, 23,* 339–350. Prochaska, J. O.; DiClemente, C. C.; and Norcross, J. C. (1992). In search of how people change. *American Psychologist, 47,* 1102–1114.

55. Norman, G. J.; Velicer, W. F.; Fava, J. L.; and Prochaska, J. O. (1998). Dynamic typology clustering within the stages of change for smoking cessation. *Addictive Behaviors, 23,* 139–153. Prochaska, J. O. (1994). *Changing for good.* New York: William Morrow. Velicer, W. F.; Norman, G.y J.; Fava, J. L.; and Prochaska, J. O. (1999). Testing 40 predictions from the transtheoretical model. *Addictive Behaviors, 24,* 455–469.

56. Schuckit, *Educating yourself,* pp. 186–216.

57. Substance Abuse and Mental Health Services Administration 2017, September). Receipt of services for substance use and mental health issues among adults: Results from the 2016 National Survey on Drug Use and Health. *NSDUH Data Review.* Rockville, MD: Substance Abuse and Mental Health Services Administration, Figures 8, 10, 12, and 14.

58. McClellan, A. T. (2008). Evolution in addiction treatment concepts and methods. In M. Galanter; and H. D. Kleber (Eds.), *Textbook of substance abuse treatment* (4th ed.). Washington, D.C.: American Psychiatric Publishing, pp. 93–108. Substance Abuse and Mental Health Services Administration (2009, November/December). Screening, brief intervention, and referral to treatment. *SAMHSA News,* pp. 1–2.

59. Beronio, K.; Po, R.; Skopec, L.; and Glied, S. (2013 February). Affordable Care Act will expand mental health and substance use disorder benefits and parity protections for 62 million Americans. *ASPE Research Brief.* Washington, D.C.: U.S. Department of Health and Human Services. Parity: What does the new law mean? (2008, November/December). *SAMHSA News,* pp. 1–4. Center for Behavioral Health Statistics and Quality, *Results from 2013 national survey on drug use and health,* p. 7.

Advancing Public Health: The Regulation of Tobacco

After you have completed this chapter, you should have an understanding of the following:

- The history of tobacco and the evolution of tobacco control policy
- The three components of smoked tobacco products: carbon monoxide, tar, and nicotine
- The dependence potential of nicotine
- The health consequences of tobacco use
- Patterns of tobacco use in the United States
- Current regulatory policies for tobacco control
- Other forms of consumption: smokeless tobacco, cigars, and e-cigarettes
- Global issues in tobacco use and tobacco control
- Quitting smoking

Mark Twain used to say that quitting smoking was easy. He had done it a thousand times.

Well, I can relate to Twain on that one. It feels like I tried to quit smoking a *million times*. It's very easy. It's the other part that's hard—quitting for good.

I realize tobacco isn't good for me; I'm no fool. But diehard smokers like me think about the next one and the next one after that throughout the day. You get accustomed to the indignity and inconvenience of sneaking out of the office, standing out there in the rain and the cold, not to mention all the disapproving glances of your friends and co-workers.

Stopping a dependence on nicotine can be a living hell, but let me tell you, I won't give up. I will keep on trying and trying and trying again. Eventually I'll get there.

Anonymous

From its first introduction to the Western world in the sixteenth century, tobacco would receive mixed reviews. Many people at the time were captivated by this new indulgence. Tobacco smoking was a sign of social status. Many others, however, found it personally objectionable in the extreme. To them, tobacco smoking was personally disgusting, physically dangerous, and morally contemptible. Yet, even the critics of tobacco smoking could not deny that it was strangely alluring and hard to give up.

Until the mid-1960s, lighting up and smoking a cigarette was an unquestioned sign of maturity and sophistication. There was little or no public awareness that harm would come of it, a possibility that was concealed for decades by the tobacco industry. It was an era before the advent of surgeon general's reports, National Smoke-out Days, and smoke-free restaurants, hotels, and public buildings. Cigarette lighters were standard features on the dashboard of our cars.

The times have changed. Today, it is no longer a matter of debate that tobacco smoking is a major health hazard, both to the person involved and to other people nearby and society at large. These concerns are based on solid scientific fact. It is also no longer a matter of debate that the main psychoactive ingredient in tobacco, nicotine, is a powerful dependence-producing drug. Even tobacco companies now concede that their products are dangerous.

Yet, at the same time, the reality is that tobacco is a legally sanctioned commodity with considerable economic significance, both to the United States and to the world. There are no criminal justice issues with respect to tobacco use by adults. Tobacco companies argue that it is a matter of personal freedom for adults to engage in the consumption of a legal product, even if it may lead to premature death. Most people will agree that banning tobacco products by governmental legislation would lead to a Prohibition Era comparable to or perhaps exceeding in social upheaval to the one experienced with respect to alcohol in the last century (see Chapter 3).

Nevertheless, public outcry against tobacco has led to increasingly aggressive regulatory policies on the part of the government. For nearly a century, the major thrust of regulatory policy toward tobacco use has been through state excise taxes on cigarettes, ranging currently from 17 cents for a pack of 20 cigarettes in Missouri to $4.35 in New York. Since the 1990s, regulation of tobacco use has turned to a more direct approach, through the establishment of governmental regulatory authority over the practice of tobacco smoking, the contents of tobacco itself, and most recently tobacco use through smokeless e-cigarettes. Particular attention has been drawn to the popularity of vaping among young people. In the end, our society has adopted a "harm-reduction" position with respect to tobacco, to regulate rather than prohibit its use. What regulations are currently in place with respect to tobacco? How did we arrive at this point in our nation's history?

This chapter will explore what we know about the effects of tobacco smoking and other forms of nicotine consumption, the impact that these behaviors have had on American society and the world, and the ways in which the United States has dealt with the issue of tobacco over the years. Also, the chapter will examine current regulatory strategies as well as the law enforcement efforts that are directed toward those who violate these regulations. Finally, the chapter will examine current treatment approaches toward helping people who choose to stop smoking.

Tobacco through History

Shortly after setting foot on the small Caribbean island of San Salvador on October 12, 1492, Christopher Columbus received from the local inhabitants a welcoming gift of large, green, and sweet-smelling tobacco leaves. Never having seen tobacco before, Columbus didn't know what to make of this curious offering, except to observe in his journal that the

Numbers Talk...

>6 million	The estimated number of people worldwide who die each year from tobacco-related lung cancer, heart disease, and other illnesses as a result of direct tobacco use.
890,000	The estimated number of nonsmokers worldwide who die each year from tobacco-related lung cancer, heart disease, and other illnesses as a result of secondhand smoke.
1 billion	The projected number of people worldwide who will die prematurely of tobacco-related disease in the twenty-first century.
1921	The year Iowa became the first U.S. state to impose an excise tax on cigarettes, at 2 cents a package. Current excise tax in Iowa is $1.36 per pack. The highest cigarette tax in the nation is imposed in New York State at $4.35 per pack.
1988	The year C. Everett Koop, surgeon general of the United States, declared nicotine as addictive as either heroin or cocaine. The surgeon general's report series on smoking and health celebrated its 50-year anniversary in 2014.

Sources: National Cancer Institute (2016, December). *The economics of tobacco and tobacco control.* Monograph 21. Bethesda, MD: National Cancer Institute. Tax Foundation, Washington, D.C. Accessed from: https://taxfoundation.org/state-cigarette-taxes/. World Health Organization (2017, May). *Tobacco: Fact Sheet.* Geneva, Switzerland: World Health Organization. World Health Organization (2008). *The WHO report on the global tobacco epidemic 2008.* Geneva, Switzerland: World Health Organization.

leaves were greatly prized by the "Indians." In the first week of November, two members of the expedition ventured to the shores of Cuba, searching at Columbus's insistence for the great Khan of Cathay (China). They found no evidence of the Khan but did return with reports of natives who apparently were "drinking smoke."

Before long, some of Columbus's men were "tobacco drinking" as well. One sailor in particular, Rodrigo de Jerez, became quite fond of the practice. He was, in fact, history's first documented European smoker, though he lived to regret it. When Rodrigo returned to Spain, he volunteered to demonstrate the newfound custom to his neighbors, who instead of being impressed thought that anyone who could emit smoke from the nose and mouth without burning had to be possessed by the Devil. After being turned in to local authorities, Rodrigo was sentenced to imprisonment for witchcraft. He spent several years in jail, presumably without a supply of tobacco. Rodrigo therefore will also be remembered as the first European smoker to quit cold turkey.[1]

In 1560, the year historians mark as the year tobacco was officially introduced to Europe, a French diplomat named Jean Nicot presented tobacco seeds to the queen of France, Catherine de Medici, with a letter describing their use for curing her migraine headaches. Later, Nicot was honored by having the botanical name for modern-day tobacco, *Nicotiana tabacum*, named after him, as well as the psychoactive ingredient in tobacco, nicotine.

It was not long before news about tobacco being enjoyed among members of the French court traveled to royal courts throughout Europe. Smoking tobacco through long, elaborate pipes became a fashionable pastime among European aristocracy. This is not to say that everyone was enthusiastic about this new fad. In fact, King James I of England hated tobacco. In 1604, the king was so outraged by tobacco smoking that he wrote a lengthy treatise entitled "A Counter-blaste to Tobacco," in which he listed his reasons for condemning tobacco use. Predating modern-day surgeon general's reports by more than 350 years, he referred to tobacco as a "stinking weed," characterizing tobacco smoking as "a custom loathsome to the eye, hateful to the nose, harmful to the brain, dangerous to the lung." In the first recorded comment on its potential for causing dependence, the king observed that "he that taketh tobacco saith he cannot leave it, it doth bewitch him." King James was undoubtedly ahead of his time.

Politics and Economics

Elsewhere in the world, during the early seventeenth century, the condemnation of tobacco became extreme. In Russia, officials established penalties for smoking that included whipping, mutilation, exile to Siberia, and death. Turkey, Japan, and China tried similar tactics, but, not surprisingly, tobacco use continued to spread.[2]

By the end of the seventeenth century, however, even the fiercest opponents of tobacco had to admit that it was here to stay. A sultan of Turkey in 1648 became a smoker himself, and penalties for tobacco use vanished overnight; Czar Peter the Great in 1689 pledged to open up Russia to the West,

and tobacco suddenly became a welcome symbol of modernism. Japan and China stopped trying to enforce a prohibition that citizens obviously did not want. Even King James eventually put aside his personal disgust for tobacco in favor of the attractive prospect of sizable revenue that could come from taxing the sales of this popular new commodity.[3]

Snuffing and Chewing

One form of tobacco use observed by the early Spanish explorers was the practice of grinding a mixture of tobacco into a fine powder (**snuff**), placing or sniffing a pinch of it into the nose, and exhaling it with a sneeze. By the 1700s, this custom, called **snuffing**, overtook smoking as the dominant form of tobacco use. Among French aristocrats, both men and women, expensive snuffs, perfumed with exotic scents and carried in jeweled and enameled boxes, became part of the daily routine at the court in France and in the rest of Europe. Sneezing was considered to clear the head of "superfluous humors," invigorate the brain, and brighten the eyes. In an era when bad smells were constant features of daily living, snuffing brought some degree of relief, not to mention a highly effective way of sending nicotine to the brain (see Chapter 8).

Because of their dominance in the rapidly expanding tobacco market, the English colonies in America, particularly Virginia, enjoyed great prosperity. England benefitted from a profitable tobacco trade, but you might say that the development of colonial tobacco growing eventually backfired. In 1777, when Benjamin Franklin was sent as an envoy to France to gain support against the British in the American War for Independence, he was able to close the deal with an offer to deliver a shipment of prime Virginia tobacco. The French agreed, and the rest is history. Perhaps, had it not been for American tobacco, there might not have been a United States of America at all.[4]

In the United States, snuffing would soon be replaced by a more rough-and-ready method for using tobacco: chewing. The practice was not totally new; early Spanish explorers had found the natives chewing tobacco as well as smoking it from the earliest days of their conquest, though North American tribes preferred smoking exclusively. Chewing tobacco had the advantage of freeing the hands for work, and its low cost made it a democratic custom befitting a vigorous new nation in the nineteenth century. It also eliminated the fire hazard associated with burning tobacco. However, tobacco chewing required the spitting out of tobacco juices on a regular basis, raising the tobacco habit to unimaginable heights of gross behavior. It was enough to make the objections to smoke and possible fire fade into insignificance; now the problem was a matter of public health. Tobacco spitting became a major factor in the spread of infectious diseases such as tuberculosis. Adding to this unsavory picture was the likelihood that one's accuracy in targeting the nearest spittoon was inevitably

snuff: A quantity of finely shredded or powdered tobacco. Modern forms of snuff are available in either dry or moist forms.

snuffing: The ingestion of snuff either by inhalation or absorption through tissue in the nose.

compromised by one's level of alcohol consumption, which was setting all-time records during this period.

Cigars and Cigarettes

By the time of the American Civil War, the fashion in tobacco use began to shift once more, even as its overall popularity continued to soar. Although the plug of tobacco suitable for chewing was still a major seller and would remain so until the early twentieth century, two new trends emerged, particularly in the growing industrial cities.

The first trend was the popularity of smoking **cigars** (commonly known as "seegars"), tight rolls of dried tobacco leaves. New innovations in curing (drying) tobacco leaves had produced a milder and lighter-quality leaf that was more suitable for smoking than the older forms that had been around since the colonial period. North Carolina, with its ideal soil for cultivating this type of tobacco, began to dominate as the tobacco-growing center of the United States; it continues to do so today. With the advent of cigars, tobacco consumers could combine the feeling of chewing (since the cigar remained in the mouth for a relatively longer period of time) and the effects of ingesting tobacco smoke. Pioneers heading west could indulge in foot-long cigars called "stogies," named after the Conestoga wagons that they rode during the long and tedious journey.

The second trend was the introduction of **cigarettes**, rolls of shredded tobacco wrapped in paper. They had become popular among British soldiers returning from the Crimean War in 1856, who had adopted the practice from the Turks. Europe took to cigarettes immediately, but the United States proved a harder sell. Part of the problem was the opposition of a well-entrenched American cigar industry, which did not look kindly on an upstart competitor. Cigar makers did not discourage the circulation of rumors that the cigarette paper wrapping was actually soaked in arsenic or white lead, that cigarette factory workers were urinating on the tobacco to give it an extra "bite," or that certain Egyptian brands were mixed with crushed camel dung.[5]

An even greater marketing challenge than unsubstantiated rumors was the effeminate image of cigarette smoking itself. A cigarette was looked upon as a dainty, sissy version of the he-man cigar; cigars were fat, long, and dark, whereas cigarettes were slender, short, and light. Well into the beginning of the twentieth century, This connotation surrounding the cigarette would persist. This is what John L. Sullivan, champion boxer and self-appointed defender of American masculinity, thought of cigarettes in 1904:

> Who smokes 'em? Dudes and college stiffs—fellows who'd be wiped out by a single jab or a quick undercut. It isn't natural to smoke cigarettes. An American ought to smoke cigars.... It's the Dutchmen, Italians, Russians, Turks, and Egyptians who smoke cigarettes and they're no good anyhow.[6]

cigars: Tightly rolled quantities of dried tobacco leaves.

cigarettes: Rolls of shredded tobacco wrapped in paper, today usually fitted at the mouth end with a filter.

The public image of the cigarette eventually would change dramatically, particularly as a result of clever marketing on the part of American tobacco companies, but, until then, cigarette manufacturers had to rely on a powerful economic advantage: low cost. In 1881, James Bonsack patented a cigarette-making machine that transformed the tobacco industry. Instead of producing at most 300 cigarettes an hour by hand, three machine operators could now turn out 200 a minute, or roughly 120,000 cigarettes a day. This is a snail's pace compared to the present state-of-the-art machines capable of producing more than 10,000 cigarettes a minute, but in those days, the Bonsack machine was viewed as an industrial marvel. Cigarette prices by the end of the 1800s were as cheap as 20 for a nickel.[7]

Tobacco in the Twentieth Century

At the beginning of the twentieth century, Americans could choose from a variety of ways to satisfy their hunger for tobacco, but it was clear that cigarette smoking would be the dominant form of tobacco use. Two principal developments caused cigarette sales to soar. First, a growing number of women began to challenge the idea of masculine dominance in society, and smoking tobacco was one of the privileges of men that women now wanted to share. Not that women smoking was met with immediate acceptance; in one famous case in 1904, a New York City woman was arrested for smoking in public. Nonetheless, as smoking among women became more common, the mild-tasting, easy-to-hold cigarette was the perfect option for them. By the 1920s, advertising slogans such as "Reach for a Lucky instead of a sweet" (a clever effort to portray cigarette smoking as a weight-control aid) as well as endorsements by glamorous celebrities were being designed specifically for the women's market. A second factor was World War I, during which time cigarettes were a logical form of tobacco to take along to war. Times of tension have always been times of increased tobacco use. When the war was over, the cigarette was, in the words of one historian, "enshrined forever as the weary soldier's relief, the worried man's support, and the relaxing man's companion."[8]

Cigarettes really came into their own in the 1920s, with the introduction of heavily advertised brand names and intense competition among American tobacco companies. Cigarette sales in the United States increased from $45 billion in 1920 to $80 billion in 1925 and $180 billion by 1940.[9]

The Rise of Health Concerns and Tobacco Control Policies

A combination of promotion through mass-media advertising and the endorsement of smoking by sports celebrities and glamorous people in the entertainment industry enabled the tobacco industry, now dominated by cigarettes, to increase its volume of sales from the 1940s to the 1980s by a steady 9 billion cigarettes each year. The peak in domestic sales was reached in 1981, when approximately 640 billion were

To encourage female cigarette smokers, advertisements drew heavily on an association with popular Hollywood celebrities, including Ronald Reagan in a Christmas promotion in 1949. Other ads such as the one depicted here, highlighting prominent baseball players, were directed at male smokers. The most famous and most valuable baseball card, depicting 1909 baseball player Honus Wagner, was actually enclosed in a pack of cigarettes, long before baseball cards became associated with bubble gum.

Credit: Image courtesy of the Advertising Archives.

sold (three times more than are sold today). Owing to the increase in population, however, per capita consumption in the United States had actually peaked in 1963 at approximately 4,300 cigarettes per year (roughly 12 cigarettes per day).

Beginning in 1964, annual per capita consumption began a steady decline, from 2,076 cigarettes (roughly 6 per day) in 2000 to 1,078 cigarettes (roughly 3 per day) in 2015. With the exception of a slight increase from 2014 to 2015, annual per capita consumption levels decreased each year from 2000 to 2015 by an average of 4.6 percent each year. According to one forecast, the estimated annual per capita consumption of cigarettes in 2040 is expected to be reduced by more than 50 percent, relative to present-day consumption levels.

The year of the turnaround in cigarette smoking coincided with the U.S. surgeon general's first report on smoking and health in 1964. For the first time, the federal government asserted publicly what had been suspected for decades: that tobacco smoking was linked to cancer and other serious diseases. From the standpoint of tobacco use in America, surgeon general's reports issued from 1964 to the present day have resulted in a number of developments in smoking behavior and tobacco regulation.

- In the month or so immediately after the first report was released, there was a dramatic drop (approximately 25 percent) in per capita consumption levels. Although succeeding

months in 1964 showed a bounce upward, most likely reflecting the fact that many people who tried to quit had only temporary success, the long-term trend in U.S. tobacco consumption from that point on would never be upward again.

- As evidence of health risks accumulated, restrictions on public consumption were instituted. In 1971, all television advertising for tobacco was banned, and in 1984, a rotating series of warning labels (already on all packages of tobacco products since 1966) was required on all print advertisements and outdoor billboards.

- There was a significant change in the type of cigarette smoked by the average smoker. In the 1950s, more and more cigarette smokers began to choose *filtered* as distinct from *unfiltered* cigarettes, being persuaded by the tobacco companies that they would be ingesting less of the toxins in tobacco as a result. The surgeon general's reports accelerated this trend. By the 1990s, about 95 percent of all smokers were using filtered brands. However, after the introduction of filtered cigarettes, the industry *changed* the formulation of the tobacco to a stronger blend with an increased tar content. As a result of a stronger "filter blend" formula in the cigarette, **sidestream smoke**, the smoke directly inhaled by a nonsmoker from a burning cigarette, ended up more toxic when originating from a filtered cigarette than it was from an unfiltered one. In principle, a cigarette filter should have allowed a flow of air through small holes in the filter itself. Because a smoker typically held the cigarette with the fingers covering these holes, however, little or no filtering was accomplished. In the meantime, filtered cigarettes increased tobacco company profits. Filters were only paper and therefore cost considerably less than filling the same space with tobacco. The cork-like appearance of the filter was intended to imply that something was being filtered, when actually no filtering was taking place.

- As a consequence of the surgeon general's assertion that tar and nicotine were specifically responsible for increased health risks from smoking, new "light" and "mild" cigarette brands were introduced that were low in tar and nicotine (T/N), and the Federal Trade Commission began to issue a listing of tar and nicotine levels in major commercial brands. As later surgeon general's reports indicated, however, smokers cancelled out the benefits of switching to low T/N brands by varying the manner in which they smoked a low T/N cigarette. Smokers took more puffs, inhaled more deeply, and smoked more of the cigarette when it has a lower T/N level so as to maintain the same amount of nicotine (the same number of nicotine "hits"). Moreover, a greater number of low T/N cigarettes had to be smoked in order to satisfy the smoker's needs. In 2010, tobacco companies were required to change the branding labels to acknowledge

sidestream smoke: Tobacco smoke that is inhaled by nonsmokers from the burning cigarettes of nearby smokers. Also referred to as environmental tobacco smoke or secondhand smoke.

Drugs ... in Focus

African Americans, Smoking, and Mentholated Cigarettes

It has long been puzzling that African Americans tend to smoke fewer cigarettes than white smokers but carry a higher risk of tobacco-related diseases such as lung cancer and heart disease. One factor that has been used as an explanation is the relatively slower rate of nicotine metabolism among African Americans following cigarette smoking. African Americans may be taking in and retaining relatively more nicotine per cigarette and, as a result, may not need to smoke as many cigarettes per day to take in an equivalent dose of nicotine.

Recent studies have indicated that a major factor might be the menthol in certain brands of cigarettes. More than 75 percent of African American smokers prefer mentholated brands such as Newport and Kool over non-mentholated brands such as Marlboro and Camel, almost the complete opposite to the pattern of brand preferences among white smokers. Menthol allows smokers to take in more smoke and possibly hold it in longer, essentially canceling any benefit of choosing a "light" or "ultralight" brand to smoke. Relative to other smokers, African Americans who smoked menthol cigarettes had higher levels in their saliva of a specific nicotine by-product. The finding that smokers of mentholated cigarettes are almost twice as likely to relapse after attempts to quit smoking, compared to smokers of non-mentholated cigarettes, is consistent with the relatively higher levels of nicotine intake that are likely to occur when one is smoking mentholated brands.

The growing evidence of the effect of menthol content in cigarettes on smoking behavior and the implications with regard to smoking cessation have led to calls for the FDA to require tobacco companies to report how much menthol is contained in various cigarette brands, as they now do for levels of nicotine and tars, or even for mentholated cigarettes to be banned altogether. Such actions would be permitted under the statutes of the Tobacco Control Act of 2009. In 2013, a study published by the FDA pointed to the unique public health risks of mentholated cigarettes. The FDA concluded that mentholated cigarettes were not more or less toxic than non-mentholated cigarettes but the cooling and anesthetic properties of menthol made cigarette smoke less harsh, increasing the appeal to younger smokers starting out as tobacco users.

Sources: Celebucki, C. C.; Wayne, G. F.; Connolly, G. N.; Pankow, J. F.; and Chang, E. I. (2005). Characterization of measured menthol in 48 U.S. cigarette sub-brands. *Nicotine and Tobacco Research, 7*, 523–531. Mustonen, T. K.; Spencer, S. M.; Hoskinson, R. A.; Sachs, D. P. L.; and Garvey, A. J. (2005). The influence of gender, race, and menthol content on tobacco exposure measures. *Nicotine and Tobacco Research, 7*, 581–590. Pletcher, M. J.; Hulley, B. J.; Houston, T.; Kiefe, C.; Benowitz, N.; et al. (2006). Menthol cigarettes, smoking cessation, atherosclerosis, and pulmonary function. *Archives of Internal Medicine, 166*, 1915–1922. Substance Abuse and Mental Health Services Administration (2009, November 19). Use of menthol cigarettes. *The NSDUH Report.* Tavernise, S. (2013, July 24). FDA closer to decision about menthol cigarettes. *The New York Times,* p. A15.

---

that "light" or "mild" brands were no less harmful than regular brands. Marlboro Lights, for example, became Marlboro Gold, and Marlboro Ultra Lights became Marlboro Silver.

- In 2007, it was confirmed that cigarette manufacturers had increased the nicotine concentrations in tobacco from 1997 to 2005 by 11 percent and also had modified certain design features of the cigarettes themselves to increase the number of puffs per cigarette during smoking. In the "medium/mild" market category, nicotine levels more than doubled from 1998 to 2005 in non-mentholated cigarettes and rose by 22 percent in mentholated cigarettes (Drugs...in Focus).[10]

The Legacy of Surgeon General's Reports: 1964–2014

The first surgeon general's report on smoking and health, issued in January 1964, has been regarded as one of the most significant documents in American public health history. The reduction in the prevalence rate of tobacco use in the

50 years that have passed has been attributed to the influence of this report and others that followed. The prevalence rate for adults in the United States declined from 42 percent in 1964 to 15 percent in most recent surveys. The consequences have been significant.

- An estimated 8 million premature deaths due to tobacco use were avoided during this time.
- Tobacco control contributed 2.3 years to the 7.8-year increase in the estimated life expectancy of a male at age 40.
- Tobacco control contributed 1.6 years to the 5.4-year increase in the estimated life expectancy of a female at age 40.

Nonetheless, the consumption level of tobacco products in the United States is enormous. In 2016, Americans purchased about 258 billion cigarettes, 130 million pounds of smokeless tobacco, 12 billion large cigars, and 600 million little cigars. The tobacco industry spent $8.9 billion on cigarette advertising and promotional expenses in the United States alone, largely through price discounts on cigarettes.[11]

Changing Times: Tobacco Control since 1990

Beginning in the early 1990s, the tobacco industry in the United States began to face significant challenges from federal governmental agencies, as well as individuals and groups who brought lawsuits against tobacco companies for damages resulting from their ingestion of tobacco products.

In 1993, the U.S. Environmental Protection Agency (EPA) announced its conclusion from available research that **environmental tobacco smoke (ETS)**, the sidestream smoke in the air that is inhaled by nonsmokers as a result of tobacco smoking, causes lung cancer. This was the first time that concerns had ever been raised with respect to the *nonsmoker*. Since then, U.S. states, cities, and communities have enacted laws mandating smoke-free environments in all public and private workplaces, unless ventilated smoking rooms have been provided. It is now commonplace for restaurants, hotels, and other commercial spaces to be completely smoke free.

In 1994, congressional hearings were held on allegations that during the 1970s tobacco companies had suppressed research data obtained in their own research laboratories regarding the hazards of cigarette smoking, particularly the addictiveness of nicotine in tobacco products. At that time, tobacco company executives vehemently denied the addictiveness of nicotine.

A few years later, the Philip Morris company finally issued a statement, formally admitting that there was "overwhelming medical and scientific consensus that cigarette smoking causes cancer, heart disease, emphysema, and other serious diseases" and that "cigarette smoking is addictive, as that term is most commonly used today." Obviously, this stance was a complete reversal of the industry's 1994 congressional testimony.

The publication of undeniable data showing the dangers of tobacco smoking combined with the public reaction to testimony by tobacco industry officials during the 1994 congressional hearings made it inevitable that a more aggressive regulatory role would be taken by the federal government.

The Tobacco Settlement of 1998

In 1998, the major American tobacco corporations entered into a historic agreement with all 50 U.S. states to resolve claims that the states should be compensated for the costs of treating people with smoking-related illnesses. Under the terms of the settlement, the tobacco industry agreed to pay the states approximately $246 billion in annual installments over 24 years. The tobacco industry also agreed to refrain from marketing tobacco products to those under 18 and pay $24 million annually over 10 years for a research foundation dedicated toward finding ways to reduce smoking among youths. In contrast to earlier proposed settlements, however, tobacco corporations under this agreement would not be penalized if levels of underage smoking did not decline over that period of time. In addition, the settlement did not prevent individuals or groups of individuals from suing tobacco corporations in separate actions.

Unfortunately, compensation funds awarded to the states and intended to support tobacco use prevention programs were used instead to keep state taxes down or pay off state debt. In 2013, only six U.S. states (Alaska, Delaware, Maine, Oklahoma, North Dakota, and Wyoming) spent 50 percent or more of the funds that had been recommended by the Centers for Disease Control and Prevention for tobacco prevention programs. Twenty-three U.S. states spent less than 10 percent of the recommended amount. On the other hand, an increase in cigarette prices imposed by tobacco companies to finance the settlement, as well as higher excise taxes imposed by U.S. states, made cigarettes more expensive, especially for young people with relatively little money to spend. The decline in cigarette smoking in this age group since 1998 has been attributed, in part, to economic factors surrounding the buying of cigarettes and other tobacco products.[12]

The Tobacco Control Act of 2009

In 2009, a new era in the history of governmental relations with the tobacco industry began, with the enactment of the federal Tobacco Control Act. This legislation gave the FDA for the first time sweeping regulatory authority over tobacco products sold in the United States. The immediate results of the legislation included creation of a new FDA Center for Tobacco Products to oversee the science-based regulation of tobacco products, the banning of candy-flavored cigarettes, full disclosure of ingredients and additives in tobacco products, aggressive moves to stop youth-focused marketing, and

In 1994, tobacco industry executives testified before a congressional committee in defense of cigarette smoking. In 1999, the Philip Morris company formally reversed its earlier position that smoking was not addictive.

Credit: Terry Ashe/The LIFE Images Collection/Getty Images

environmental tobacco smoke (ETS): Tobacco smoke in the atmosphere as a result of burning cigarettes; also called sidestream or secondary smoke.

new graphic warning labels highlighting the health risks of smoking.[13]

In 2014, the FDA announced that they had authorized the introduction of two new tobacco products, both introduced as Newport cigarettes, but rejected the introduction of four others. The rejected products could not be named, according to stipulations in the 2009 law. In a ruling issued in 2011, any changes made after 2007 in the chemical components of tobacco products had to be reviewed by the FDA prior to marketing.

In 2018, an 11-year legal appeals battle between the tobacco industry and major public health advocacy organizations ended with a federal court order forcing the tobacco companies to issue a number of advertisements with statements acknowledging specific dangers of cigarette smoking (Drugs… in Focus).[14]

Tobacco Control and Global Economics

As will be discussed later in this chapter, many other nations have substantially higher prevalence rates for cigarette smoking, and their governments have taken fewer steps toward instituting policies to reduce smoking behavior. For American tobacco corporations, an expanding global marketplace for American cigarettes has given them the opportunity for an increase in profits from foreign sales that has largely compensated for their financial losses incurred from a decline in domestic sales.[15] In a larger sense, cigarette sales abroad represent a major component of overall U.S. foreign trade. In recent years, U.S. exports of tobacco products have exceeded imports by billions of dollars, creating a significant trade surplus. Therefore, the U.S. trade deficit (defined as an excess of imports over exports) would be worse than it is today were it not for the export of tobacco products to other nations.

Undoubtedly, tobacco use has presented challenges both from the standpoint of public health and from the standpoint of social and economic policies of the United States in relation to the rest of the world. At this point, it is important to examine the components of tobacco itself. What are the components of tobacco that present bodily harm to the user?

Drugs … in Focus

Court-ordered Tobacco Advertisements in 2018

In early 2018, the first of a series of full-page advertisements appeared in *The New York Times*, beginning with the words: "A Federal Court has ordered Altria, R.J. Reynolds Tobacco, Lorillard, and Philip Morris USA to make this statement about low tar and light cigarettes being as harmful as regular cigarettes." Three bullet points then followed (some words printed in bold face type).

- Many smokers switch to low tar and light cigarettes rather than quitting because they think low tar and light cigarettes are less harmful. They are **not.**
- "Low tar" and "light" cigarette smokers inhale essentially the same amount of tar and nicotine as they would from regular cigarettes.
- **All** cigarettes cause cancer, lung disease heart attacks, and premature death—lights, low tar, ultra lights and naturals. There is no safe cigarette.

Subsequent advertisements included additional bullet points such as

- Altria, R.J. Reynolds Tobacco, Lorillard, and Philip Morris SA intentionally designed cigarettes to make them more addictive.

- Cigarette companies control the impact and delivery of nicotine in many ways, including designing filters and selecting cigarette paper to maximize the ingestion of nicotine, adding ammonia to make the cigarette taste less harsh, and controlling the physical and chemical make-up of the tobacco blend.
- When you smoke, the nicotine actually changes the brain – that's why quitting is so hard.
- Secondhand smoke kills over 38,000 Americans each year.
- Secondhand smoke causes lung cancer and coronary heart disease in adults who do not smoke.
- Children exposed to secondhand smoke are at an increased risk for sudden infant death syndrome (SIDS), acute respiratory infections, ear problems, severe asthma, and reduced lung function.
- There is no safe level of exposure in secondhand smoke.

By court order, advertisements appeared in 2018 online and in the Sunday issues of more than 40 newspapers on five separate days as well as running for a year on CBS, ABC, and NBC networks in the evenings on Monday through Thursday. The TV spots featured a voice reading the statement as the text appeared on the screen. The estimated cost borne by the tobacco industry for these actions was $31 million.

Sources: Advertisement appearing in *The New York Times*, January 7, 2018, p. 9. Maheshwari, S. (2017, November 25). Honest ads for cigarettes, minus "truth." *The New York Times*, p. B1.

The Basic Components of Tobacco and Tobacco Smoke

When a smoker inhales from a lit cigarette, the temperature at the tip rises to approximately 1,700 degrees Fahrenheit (926 degrees Celsius), as oxygen is drawn through the tobacco, paper, and other additives. This accounts for the bright glow as a smoker inhales from a cigarette. At this intense heat, more than 4,000 separate compounds are oxidized and released through cigarette smoke. The smoker inhales the resultant as **mainstream smoke**, usually screened through the cigarette filter and cigarette paper. As mentioned earlier, the sidestream smoke that is released from the burning cigarette tip itself is unfiltered, and because it is a product of a slightly less intense burning process occurring between puffs, more unburned particles are contained in the smoke.

In general, we can speak of two components in tobacco smoke. The **particulate phase**, consisting of small particles (one micrometer or larger in diameter) suspended in the smoke, includes water droplets, nicotine, and a collection of compounds that will be referred to collectively as **tar**. The particles in tar constitute the primary source of carcinogenic compounds in tobacco. The second component is the **gaseous phase**, consisting of gas compounds in the smoke, including carbon dioxide, carbon monoxide, ammonia, hydrogen cyanide, acetaldehyde, and acetone. Among these gases, carbon monoxide is clearly the most toxic.

This diverse collection of physiologically active toxins is quite unique to tobacco. One way of putting it is that the 50,000–70,000 puffs per year that a one-pack-a-day cigarette smoker takes in amounts to a level of pollution far beyond even the most polluted urban environment anywhere in the world.[16] The following sections will focus on three of the most important compounds in tobacco smoke: carbon monoxide, tar, and nicotine.

Carbon Monoxide

As most people know, **carbon monoxide** is an odorless, colorless, tasteless, but extraordinarily toxic gas. It is formed when tobacco burns because the oxidation process is incomplete. In that sense, burning tobacco is similar to an inefficient engine, like a car in need of a tune-up. The danger with carbon monoxide is that it easily attaches itself to hemoglobin, the protein inside red blood cells, occupying those portions of the hemoglobin molecule normally reserved for the transport of oxygen from the lungs to the rest of the body. Carbon monoxide has about 200 times greater affinity for hemoglobin than has oxygen, so oxygen does not have much of a chance. Carbon monoxide is also more resistant to detaching itself from hemoglobin, so there is an accumulation of carbon monoxide over time.

The ultimate result of carbon monoxide is a subtle but effective asphyxiation of the body from a lack of oxygen.

Generally, people who smoke a pack a day accumulate levels of carbon monoxide in the blood of 25–35 parts per million (p.p.m.) blood components, with levels of 100 p.p.m. for short periods of time while actually smoking. Of course, greater use of tobacco produces proportionally higher levels of carbon monoxide. Carbon monoxide is the primary culprit in producing cardiovascular disease among smokers, as well as in causing deficiencies in physiological functioning and behavior.[17]

Tar

The quantity of tar in a cigarette varies from levels of 12–16 mg per cigarette to less than 6 mg. It also should be noted that the last third of each cigarette contains 50 percent of the total tar, making the final few puffs far more hazardous than the first ones.

The major problem with tar lies in its sticky quality, not unlike that of the material used in paving roads, which allows it to adhere to cells in the lungs and pulmonary airways. Normally, specialized cells with small, hair-like attachments called **cilia** are capable of removing contaminants in the air that might impede the breathing process. These cilia literally sweep the unwanted particles upward to the throat, in a process called the **ciliary escalator**, where they are typically swallowed, digested, and finally excreted from the body through the gastrointestinal system. Components in tar alter the coordination of these cilia so that they can no longer function effectively. The accumulation of sticky tar on the surface of the cells along the pulmonary system permits carcinogenic compounds that normally would have been eliminated to settle on the tissue. As will be discussed later, the resulting cellular changes produce lung cancer, and similar carcinogenic effects in other tissues of the body produce cancer in other organs.[18]

---

mainstream smoke: The smoke inhaled directly from cigarettes or other tobacco products.

particulate phase: Those components of smoke that consist of particles.

tar: A sticky material found in the particulate phase of tobacco smoke and other pollutants in the air.

gaseous phase: The portion of tobacco smoke that consists of gases.

carbon monoxide: An extremely toxic gas that prevents blood cells from carrying oxygen from the lungs to the rest of the body.

cilia: Small hair cells.

ciliary escalator: The process of pushing back foreign particles that might interfere with breathing upward from the air passages into the throat, where they can be swallowed and excreted through the gastrointestinal tract.

Nicotine

Nicotine is a toxic, dependence-producing psychoactive drug found exclusively in tobacco. It is an oily compound varying in hue from colorless to brown. A few drops of pure nicotine, about 60 mg, on the tongue would quickly kill a healthy adult, and it is commonly used as a major ingredient in all kinds of insecticides and pesticides. Cigarettes, however, contain from 0.5 to 2.0 mg of nicotine (depending on the brand), with about 20 percent being actually inhaled and reaching the bloodstream. This means that 2–8 mg of nicotine is ingested per day for a pack-a-day smoker, and 4–16 mg of nicotine for a smoker of two packs a day. Nonetheless, the toxicity of nicotine is a serious concern not only because it is ingested through cigarette smoking but also because it is ingested in a purer form in recently introduced e-cigarette products. The ramifications of nicotine ingestion with e-cigarettes will be explored in the Drugs…in Focus feature on page 357.[19]

Inhaled nicotine from smoking is absorbed extremely rapidly and easily passes through the blood–brain barrier, as well as through the blood–placental barrier in pregnant women, in a few seconds. The entire effect is over in a matter of minutes. By the time a cigarette butt is extinguished, nicotine levels in the blood have peaked, and its breakdown and excretion from the body are well underway. The elimination half-life of nicotine is approximately two to three hours.

The speed of nicotine absorption ordinarily would be much slower if it were not for the presence of ammonia as an additive in the tobacco blend. The combination of nicotine and ammonia changes the naturally acidic nicotine into an alkaline free-base form that more easily passes from body tissues into the bloodstream. As a result, ammonia increases the availability of nicotine in the blood, much as the addition of alkaline materials like baking soda converts cocaine into crack cocaine (see Chapter 10). The information that ammonia had been introduced into the manufacture of cigarette tobacco during the 1970s, in an apparent effort to increase the "kick" of nicotine, came to light in 1995 and was confirmed by tobacco industry documents released in 1998.[20]

The primary effect of nicotine is to stimulate receptors in the brain that are sensitive to acetylcholine (see Chapter 8). These receptors are called *nicotinic receptors* because they are excited by nicotine. One of the effects of activating them is the release of adrenalin, which increases blood pressure and heart rate. Another effect is to inhibit activity in the gastrointestinal system. At the same time, however, as most smokers will tell you, a cigarette is a relaxing factor in their lives. Part of this reaction may be due to an effect on the brain that promotes a greater level of clear thinking and concentration; another part may relate to the fact that nicotine, at moderate doses, serves to reduce muscle tone so that muscular tightness is decreased. Research has shown that cigarette smoking helps to sustain performance on monotonous tasks and to improve short-term memory. We can assume that it is the nicotine in cigarettes and other tobacco products that is responsible for these effects because nicotine tablets have comparable behavioral effects.[21]

The Dependence Potential of Nicotine

Historically, the dependence potential of nicotine has been demonstrated at times in which the usual availability of tobacco has suddenly been curtailed. In Germany, following the end of World War II, for example, cigarettes were rationed to two packs a month for men and one pack a month for women. This "cigarette famine" produced dramatic effects on the behavior of German civilians. Smokers bartered their food rations for cigarettes, even under the extreme circumstances of chronic hunger and poor nutrition. Cigarette butts were picked from the dirt in the streets by people who admitted that they were personally disgusted by their desperate behavior. Some women turned to prostitution to obtain cigarettes. Alcoholics of both sexes testified that it was easier to abstain from drinking alcohol than it was to abstain from smoking.[22]

It is now known that nicotine stimulates the release of dopamine in the nucleus accumbens, the same area of the brain responsible for the reinforcing properties of opioids, cocaine, and alcohol. In addition, several behavioral factors combine with this physiological effect to increase the likelihood that a strong dependence will be created. One of these factors is the speed with which smoked nicotine reaches the brain. The delivery time has been estimated as five to eight seconds. A second factor is the wide variety of circumstances and settings surrounding the act of smoking that later come to serve as learned rewards. A smoker may find, for example, that the first cigarette with a cup of coffee in the morning (a source of another psychoactive drug, caffeine) is strongly reinforcing.[23]

The Titration Hypothesis of Nicotine Dependence

There is considerable evidence that smokers adjust their smoking behavior to obtain a stable dose of nicotine from whatever cigarettes they are smoking, an idea called the **titration hypothesis**. When exposed to cigarettes of decreasing nicotine content, smokers will smoke a greater number of them to compensate and will increase the volume of each puff. When they inhale more puffs per cigarette, a greater interval of time will elapse before they light up another one. If they are given nicotine gum to chew, the intensity of their smoking behavior will decline, even though they have not been told whether the gum contains nicotine or is a placebo. All these studies indicate that experienced smokers arrive at a consistent "style" of smoking that provides their bodies with a relatively constant level of nicotine.[24]

> **nicotine:** The prime psychoactive drug in tobacco products.
>
> **titration hypothesis:** The idea that smokers will adjust their smoking of cigarettes so as to maintain a steady input of nicotine into the body.

Tolerance and Withdrawal

First-time smokers often react to a cigarette with a mixture of nausea, dizziness, or vomiting. These effects typically disappear as tolerance develops in the nicotinic receptors in the brain. Other physiological effects, such as increases in heart rate, tremors, and changes in skin temperature, show weaker tolerance effects or none at all.

The strongest dependence-related effect of nicotine consumption in cigarette smoking can be seen in the symptoms of withdrawal that follow the discontinuation of smoking. Within about six hours after the last cigarette, a smoker's heart rate and blood pressure will decrease. Over the next 24 hours, common symptoms will include headache, an inability to concentrate, irritability, drowsiness, and fatigue, as well as insomnia and other sleep disturbances. Most striking of all are the strong feelings of craving for a cigarette. Ex-smokers can attest to cravings that slowly diminish but nonetheless linger on for months and, in some cases, for years.[25]

Nicotine dependence is the central factor in the continuation of smoking behaviors. The level of dependence is significant, even when compared with dependence levels of illicit drugs available on the street. In a study of people who smoked and were also in some form of drug-abuse treatment, 74 percent judged the difficulty of quitting smoking to be at least as great as the difficulty in stopping their drug of choice. One in three considered it "much harder" to quit smoking.[26]

Health Consequences of Tobacco Use

The adverse health consequences of tobacco use can be classified in three broad categories: cardiovascular disease, respiratory disease, and cancer. In addition, there are special health difficulties that smoking can bring to women and hazards from using smokeless tobacco. An enormous literature on the adverse effects of tobacco use has grown steadily since the original surgeon general's report in 1964, though by that time more than 30,000 research studies had been conducted on the question. Smoking remains the leading cause of premature disease and death in the United States.

Beyond all the research reports are the sheer numbers of people who are affected. In the United States alone, of the more than half-million deaths each year that are attributed to substance abuse of one kind or another, approximately 480,000 are specifically tied to tobacco use or secondhand smoke from tobacco use. This figure is higher than the total number of American casualties during World War II (Drugs…in Focus). The public health community considers these deaths to be premature deaths because they are entirely preventable; these people would have been alive if their behaviors had been different.

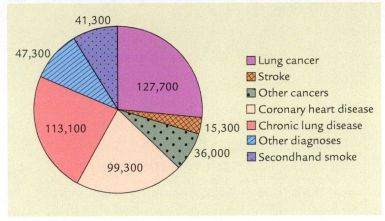

FIGURE 15.1

The distribution of approximately 480,000 annual U.S. deaths from 2005 to 2009 that have been attributed to tobacco use or secondhand smoke from tobacco use.

Source: Centers for Disease Control and Prevention (2014, February 6). *Fact Sheet: Tobacco-related mortality.* Atlanta, GA: Centers for Disease Control and Prevention.

The statistics are simple, and staggering: Smoking-related deaths account for about one out of every five deaths in the United States every year, more than 1,300 deaths each day. It has been calculated that a person's estimated life expectancy is shortened by 14 minutes every time a cigarette is smoked. Life expectancy for smokers is at least 10 years shorter than for nonsmokers. Unlike alcohol, which presents no significant health hazards when consumed in moderation, tobacco is a dangerous product *when used as intended* (Figure 15.1).[27]

Cardiovascular Disease

Cardiovascular diseases include a number of specific conditions. Some of these diseases are **coronary heart disease (CHD)**, in which damage to the heart is incurred due to the restriction of blood flow through narrowed or blocked coronary arteries; **arteriosclerosis**, in which the walls of arteries harden and lose their elasticity; **atherosclerosis**, in which fatty deposits inside arteries impede blood flow; and **ischemic stroke**, in which interruption or reduction in blood flow causes damage to the brain. In all these diseases, cigarette smoking increases the risk dramatically.

coronary heart disease (CHD): Disease that damages the heart as a result of a restriction of blood flow through coronary arteries.

arteriosclerosis (ar-TEER-ee-oh-scluh-ROH-sis): A disease in which blood flow is restricted because the walls of arteries harden and lose their elasticity.

atherosclerosis (ATH-er-oh-scluh-ROH-sis): A disease in which blood flow is restricted because of the buildup of fatty deposits inside arteries.

ischemic (iz-SKEE-mic) stroke: A disease in which there is an interruption or reduction in blood flow to the brain, causing either paralysis, sensory loss, cognitive deficits, or a combination of neuropsychological effects.

Drugs . . . in Focus

Visualizing 480,000 Annual Tobacco-Related Deaths

The estimated annual death toll in the United States due to smoking-related diseases is often difficult to visualize. In 2018, the following five U.S. cities had populations in the neighborhood of this number. Imagine the disappearance of the entire population in any one of these cities in a given year, or all of them in five years.

- Atlanta, Georgia (pop. 491,626)
- Colorado Springs, Colorado (pop. 484, 233)
- Miami, Florida (pop. 479, 909)
- Raleigh, North Carolina (pop. 476,746)
- Long Beach, California (pop. 467,512)

Source: Estimated population of major U.S. cities, 2016. United States Census Bureau, Washington, D.C.

We know now that smoking is responsible for approximately 30 percent of all CHD deaths. The risk of CHD doubles if you smoke and quadruples if you smoke heavily. On average, smoking also raises the risk of a sudden death (such as from a fatal heart attack) by two to four times, with the degree of risk increasing as a direct function of how many cigarettes are smoked per day. To put it even more boldly, it has been estimated that unless smoking patterns change dramatically in the future, about 10 percent of all Americans now alive may die prematurely from some form of heart disease as a result of their smoking behavior.[28]

These statistics are strengthened by the understanding we have of how cigarette smoking actually produces these dangerous cardiovascular conditions. The major villains are nicotine and carbon monoxide. Nicotine, as a stimulant drug, increases the contraction of heart muscle and elevates heart rate.

At the same time, nicotine causes a constriction of blood vessels, leading to a rise in blood pressure, and also increases *platelet adhesiveness* in the blood. As a result of a greater adhesiveness, platelets clump together and increase the risk of developing a blood clot. If a clot forms within coronary arteries, a heart attack can occur; a clot traveling into the blood vessels of the brain can produce a stroke. Finally, nicotine increases the body's serum cholesterol and fatty deposits, leading to the development of atherosclerosis.

While nicotine is doing its dirty work, carbon monoxide makes matters worse. A lack of oxygen puts further strain on the ability of the heart to function under already trying circumstances.

Respiratory Diseases

The general term **chronic obstructive pulmonary disease (COPD)** refers to several conditions in which breathing is impaired because of some abnormality in the air passages either leading to or within the lungs. Although only 20 percent of smokers in the United States develop COPD, 80–90 percent of all COPD cases are the result of smoking. Historically, COPD has been viewed as "a man's disease," but since 1980 the death rate in women has tripled, and since 2000, more women than men have died or been hospitalized each year as a result of COPD. With the exception of a rare genetic defect, smoking is the only established cause of clinically significant COPD.

Two examples of COPD are **chronic bronchitis**, in which excess mucus builds up in air passages, leading to an inflammation of bronchial tissue, and **emphysema**, in which air sacs in the lungs are abnormally enlarged and the air sac walls either become inelastic or rupture, leading to extreme difficulty in inhaling oxygen and exhaling carbon dioxide. In the case of advanced emphysema, more than 80 percent of a patient's energy is required merely to breathe.

Pulmonary damage, however, is not limited to adults who have been smoking for many years. Cigarette smoking is also associated with airway obstruction and slower growth of lung function in younger populations. Adolescents who smoke five or more cigarettes a day are 40 percent more likely to develop asthma and 30 percent more likely to have symptoms of wheezing but not asthma than those who do not smoke. Among smokers, girls show a greater loss of pulmonary function than boys, even though boys report that they smoke more cigarettes.[29]

Lung Cancer

At the beginning of the twentieth century, lung cancer was a rare disease. Its steady increase in the United States as well as the rest of the world since then has occurred in direct proportion to the growing prevalence of cigarette smoking and

chronic obstructive pulmonary disease (COPD): A group of diseases characterized by impaired breathing due to an abnormality in the air passages.

chronic bronchitis: A respiratory disease involving inflammation of bronchial tissue following a buildup of excess mucus in air passages.

emphysema (EM-fuh-SEE-mah): An enlargement of air sacs in the lungs and abnormalities in the air sac walls, causing great difficulty in breathing.

	Males			Females		
Prostate	180,890	21%	Breast	246,660	29%
Lung & bronchus	117,920	14%	Lung & bronchus	106,470	13%
Colon & rectum	70,820	8%	Colon & rectum	63,670	8%
Urinary bladder	58,950	7%	Uterine corpus	60,050	7%
Melanoma of the skin	46,870	6%	Thyroid	49,350	6%
Non-Hodgkin lymphoma	40,170	5%	Non-Hodgkin lymphoma	32,410	4%
Kidney & renal pelvis	39,650	5%	Melanoma of the skin	29,510	3%
Oral cavity & pharynx	34,780	4%	Leukemia	26,050	3%
Leukemia	34,090	4%	Pancreas	25,400	3%
Liver & intrahepatic bile duct	28,410	3%	Kidney & renal pelvis	23,050	3%
All Sites	**841,390**	**100%**	**All Sites**	**843,820**	**100%**

FIGURE 15.2

Leading sites of new cancer cases and death—2016 Estimates.

Source: Based on information from the American Cancer Society (2016). *Cancer facts and figures 2016.* Atlanta, GA: American Cancer Society, Inc.

other tobacco use. In 2016, approximately 86,000 men and 72,000 women died of lung cancer. It has been estimated that tobacco smoking accounts for between 80 and 90 percent of all lung cancer cases in the United States. In general, people who smoke cigarettes are 15 to 30 times more likely to get lung cancer than people who do not smoke.

Another important change has occurred over the years with respect to the incidence of lung cancer among women. Like COPD, lung cancer was once considered to be limited largely to male smokers. More recently, however, increasing numbers of women have contracted lung cancer as a result of their increased level of cigarette smoking. The age-adjusted mortality rate for women is still about one-half that for men, but the decline in mortality rates seen among men since 1990 has yet to be realized among women. Since 1988, lung cancer has exceeded breast cancer as the leading cause of cancer deaths among women (Figure 15.2).

These facts about lung cancer become even more tragic when you consider that the overall five-year survival rate after initial diagnosis of lung cancer (for all stages of cancer combined) is only 15 percent. Lung cancer patients have an approximately 50 percent chance of living five years when the disease is still localized at the time of diagnosis, but only 15 percent of lung cancers are diagnosed at this early stage.

As discussed earlier in the chapter, the exposure to tar in cigarette smoke disrupts the necessary action of ciliary cells in the bronchial tubes leading to the lungs. Without their protective function, the lungs are open to attack. Several carcinogenic compounds in the smoke can now enter the lungs and stimulate the formation of cancerous growths, **carcinomas**, in lung tissue. One of these compounds, *benzopyrene*, has been found to cause genetic mutations in cells that are identical to the mutations observed in patients who have developed carcinomas in their lungs. This finding is important because it establishes a causal link between a specific ingredient in tobacco smoke and human cases of cancer.[30]

Other Cancers

While lung cancer is the best-known and most common example of tobacco-related cancers, other organs are affected in a similar way. In the United States, approximately 30 percent of cancer deaths *of all types* have been linked to smoking. It has been estimated that smokers increase their risk by 2 to 27 times for cancer of the larynx, 13 times for mouth or lip cancer, 2 to 3 times for bladder cancer, 2 times for pancreatic cancer, and 5 times for cancers of the kidney or uterine cervix.[31]

Despite a widespread belief to the contrary, using smokeless tobacco, in the form of chewing tobacco or snuff, does not prevent the user from incurring an increased risk of cancer. Continuing contact with tobacco in the mouth has been shown to produce precancerous cell changes, as revealed by **leukoplakia** (white spots) and **erythroplakia** (red spots) inside the mouth and nasal cavity. Even though smokeless tobacco obviously avoids the problems associated with tobacco smoke, it does not prevent the user from being exposed to carcinogens, specifically a class of compounds called **nitrosamines** that are present in all tobacco products. Early signs of problems of this sort include lumps in the jaw or neck area; color changes or lumps inside the lips; white, smooth, or scaly patches in the mouth or on the neck, lips, or tongue; spots or sores on the lips or gums or inside the mouth that do not heal; repeated bleeding in the mouth; and difficulty or abnormality in speaking or swallowing.

carcinomas (CAR-sih-NOH-mas): Cancerous tumors or growths.

leukoplakia (LOO-koh-PLAY-kee-ah): Small white spots inside the mouth and nasal cavity, indicating precancerous tissue.

erythroplakia (eh-RITH-ro-PLAY-kee-ah): Small red spots inside the mouth and nasal cavity, indicating precancerous tissue.

nitrosamines (nih-TRAW-seh-meens): A group of carcinogenic compounds found in tobacco.

As a result of federal legislation enacted in 1986, all forms of smokeless tobacco must contain, on the package, a set of specific warnings that these products may cause mouth cancer as well as gum disease and tooth loss. To reinforce the idea that dangers are still present in smokeless tobacco, one of these warnings reads: "This product is not a safe alternative to cigarette smoking."

Special Health Concerns for Women

Tobacco use presents specific health risk concerns for women. Women who smoke have a more than three times greater risk of dying from stroke due to brain hemorrhaging and an almost two times greater risk of dying from a heart attack. Added to these concerns is the toxic interaction of tobacco smoke with birth control pills. If women are using birth control pills as well, the risk increases to 22 times and 20 times, respectively.

There is a higher risk of low birth weight and physical defects in the newborn due to the mother's smoking during pregnancy. In addition, it has been observed that there is a specific elevation in systolic blood pressure at about two months of age among infants whose mothers smoked during pregnancy. Even though there has been a decline in smoking in recent years among pregnant women, more than one in six pregnant women (17 percent) have smoked in the past month, with more of them smoking in their first trimester of pregnancy (22 percent) than in their second or third trimester (14 percent and 15 percent, respectively).[32]

The Hazards of Environmental Smoke

In the early days of development of methods for detecting the effects of nicotine in the bloodstream, scientists were puzzled to find traces of a nicotine metabolite in nonsmokers. They suspected at first that there was some flaw in their analysis but later had to conclude that their measurements were indeed accurate. Nonsmokers testing positive had shared car rides or workplaces with smokers shortly before their tests. Today, a large body of

evidence indicates not only the presence of tobacco smoke compounds in the bodies of nonsmokers but also the adverse consequences that such "involuntary smoking" can provoke. In other words, environmental tobacco smoke is a significant health hazard even to people who are not actively smoking.

Approximately 85 percent of the smoke in an average room where people are smoking cigarettes is generated by sidestream smoke, and about three-fourths of the nicotine originating from these cigarettes ends up in the atmosphere. In some cases, the carcinogens released in ETS are so potent that they are dangerous even in their diluted state. For example, N-nitrosamine (an example of a group of carcinogens mentioned earlier in connection with smokeless tobacco) is so much more concentrated in sidestream smoke than in mainstream smoke that nonsmokers will end up inhaling as much of it after one hour in a very smoky room as will a smoker after smoking 10–15 cigarettes.[33]

The U.S. surgeon general's report on involuntary exposure to tobacco smoke in 2006 confirmed previous data on this question and extended its conclusions to the following:

- For nonsmoking adults, exposure to environmental smoke raises the risk of heart disease by 25–30 percent in both men and women. The risk of lung cancer is increased by 20–30 percent among nonsmokers who live with a smoker.

- Environmental smoke is a cause of sudden infant death syndrome (SIDS), accounting for 430 deaths per year in the United States. The risk is higher for children whose mothers were exposed to tobacco smoke during pregnancy and for children exposed during infancy.

- Among children of parents who smoke in the home, there is an increased risk of lower respiratory illnesses such as bronchitis, middle ear disease, wheezing, and childhood asthma.

It is estimated that environmental smoke exposure accounts for 34,000 premature deaths from heart disease among nonsmokers, and 7,300 premature deaths from lung cancer among nonsmokers in the United States each year. Although the proportion of nonsmokers has declined substantially as a result of publicity about the hazards of ETS and extensive smoking bans and restrictions, more than 100 million Americans remain subject to exposure at some time in their lives.[34]

Patterns of Tobacco Use in the United States

In 1965, about 40 percent of Americans smoked cigarettes, and it is estimated that more than 50 percent did in the 1940s. In 2017, however, according to the Centers for Disease Control and Prevention, approximately 14 percent of all adults in the United States (an estimated 34 million people) were current cigarette smokers, in that they reported smoking every day or some days. As recently as 2005, the percentage had been 21 percent. Therefore, it is fair to say that cigarette use has declined significantly in American society.

Quick Concept Check 15.1

Understanding the Effects of Tobacco Smoking

Check your understanding of the effects of tobacco smoking by associating each of the following physical effects with (a) carbon monoxide, (b) tar, or (c) nicotine. It is possible to have a combination of two factors as the correct answer.

1. A decrease in oxygen in the body
2. Physical dependence
3. Cellular changes leading to cancer
4. Cardiovascular disease
5. Chronic bronchitis

Answers: 1. a 2. c 3. b 4. a and c 5. b

Nonetheless, the statistics reflect the reality that 30 million adults in the United States remain vulnerable to health hazards posed by cigarette smoking. In addition, the statistics do not include cigarette smokers younger than 18 years old.

Prevalence Rates Among Segments of the U.S. Population

Within the adult U.S. population, there are substantial variations with respect to prevalence rates. Rates are higher for males (16 percent) than for females (12 percent), substantially higher for persons living outside a metropolitan area (23 percent) than those living in a large metropolitan area (11 percent), and higher for non-Hispanic white individuals (15 percent) than Hispanic individuals (10 percent).

In 2017, 8 percent of college students reported smoking cigarettes within the previous month, a substantial decline from 20 percent reporting in 2007 and 31 percent reporting in 1999. About 10 percent of high school seniors and 5 percent of 10th graders reported cigarette smoking within the previous month. It is unlikely that many 10th and 12th graders who have *not begun smoking at this point in their lives* would ever begin smoking during their lives. The good news is that the continuing downward trend in cigarette smoking prevalence rates among young people will be seen in still lower prevalence rates among adults in future years.

Attitudes Toward Smoking Among Young People

Adolescent attitudes toward cigarette smoking have changed dramatically during the early years of the twenty-first century. In general, young people in middle and high school have become less accepting of cigarette smoking. About 88 percent of eighth graders, for example, reported in 2017 their disapproval of someone smoking a pack of cigarettes per day and 62 percent reported that such behavior would present "great risk" of harming themselves physically or otherwise.

Interestingly, adolescent attitudes toward the *social* aspects of smoking have become more negative as well. As early as 2002, about half of 10th and 12th graders agreed with the statement "I strongly dislike being near people who are smoking." Between 75 and 80 percent of them preferred to date nonsmokers. About 6 out of 10 viewed smoking as a behavior that reflects poor judgment on the part of those who smoked. The disinclination toward dating smokers was observed equally among males and females. It is unlikely that there has been a decrease in social disapproval since 2002.[35]

Regulatory Policy and Strategies for Tobacco Control

Given the reality that tobacco will remain a legal commodity in our society for the foreseeable future, we are left with a set of policies regarding the *use* of tobacco rather than tobacco itself. Since 2009, there has been a progression of governmental

authority over the availability of tobacco products to the public and the protection of the public, as much as possible, from the harm that tobacco products can do. To that end, the present-day regulatory policies can be examined in three categories: (1) regulation of tobacco purchases through taxation, (2) regulations regarding access of young people to tobacco products, and (3) regulation of tobacco use in general through educational means. In the first two categories, the prosecution of violators of regulatory statutes is the responsibility of law enforcement authorities. In all three categories, as we will see, the tobacco companies have exerted strong opposition.

Regulation by Taxation

As has been the practice throughout American history, specific commodities such as alcohol (see Chapter 3) and tobacco have been subject to taxation. The purposes are twofold. First, popular commodities provide substantial sales revenue to the government, which can be used to support governmental programs. Second, taxation provides a means of social control. Alcohol and tobacco use present substantial risk to public and private health, so it is reasonable that an extra burden be placed on the purchaser of these products. In other words, an extra cost in purchasing alcohol or tobacco can be considered to be a "sin tax."

It has been concluded, from studies on the price structure of alcohol and tobacco products, that the cost of purchase has a definite and predictable effect on the inclination to buy that product. Nonetheless, responses by U.S. states to tax cigarette sales has been uneven, to say the least. The individual state tax, for example, amounts vary from a low of 17 cents in Missouri to a high of $4.35 in New York and $5.85 in New York City. As a result of this enormous disparity, there is a substantial amount of cigarette smuggling from U.S. states that have lower tax rates (and, in particular, Native American reservations that have even lower tax rates) into U.S. states that have higher rates. It has been argued that a more equivalent rate of cigarette taxation among U.S. states would reduce this level of cigarette smuggling.[36]

Regulation by Restricted Access to Young People

Since 1997, all 50 U.S. states have established 18 as the minimum age at which tobacco products can be purchased. Vendors have been required to verify the age of purchasers up to the age of 27 as a means for reducing the access of young people to tobacco. Violators of this law face losing their vendor license. In some U.S. states, efforts are under way to raise the minimum age for tobacco purchase to 19 or 21, while other states have this higher minimum age already in effect. Any upward change from the national standard reduces the possibility of high school seniors buying cigarettes for their younger friends.

With regard to standards set in federal regulations on underage smoking, the compliance rate on the part of tobacco retail vendors nationwide reached 90 percent in 2014,

Cigarette smoking and other forms of tobacco use among minors is a continuing social and public health problem.

Credit: Paul/F1online digitale Bildagentur GmbH/Alamy Stock Photo

substantially better than the barely 60 percent compliance rate reported in 1997. Twenty-nine of the 50 U.S. states achieved a compliance rate of above 90 percent. Nonetheless, for

47 percent of 8th graders and 69 percent of 10th graders reporting in 2014, cigarettes were "fairly easy or very easy to get." While the prevalence rates for regular smoking among 8th graders and 10th graders in 2014 had fallen to only 4 percent and 7 percent, respectively, it is evident that for the relatively small numbers of smokers in these age groups, restrictions on direct retail purchases have not been entirely successful in preventing access. Problems still remain in addressing the possibility that cigarettes are obtained through older friends who can purchase them legally (see Drug Enforcement…in Focus).[37]

Regulation by Increased Awareness of Potential Harm

There are continuing efforts to educate the public about the potential harm caused by tobacco products as well as non-tobacco products containing nicotine. A powerful message was conveyed by in 2014 by a major drugstore chain in the United States to no longer sell cigarettes in their stores. The argument was made that it was inappropriate to sell products that are associated with so many health hazards in an establishment devoted to health needs.[38]

Drug Enforcement . . . in Focus

Regulating Youth Access to Tobacco—The Synar Amendment, 1992

In 1992, Congress enacted the Alcohol, Drug Abuse, and Mental Health Administration Reorganization Act with an amendment sponsored by Representative Mike Synar of Oklahoma. The amendment aimed at decreasing youth access to tobacco by mandating a number of important changes in the way young people purchase tobacco products and in the practice of commercial tobacco distribution operations. Specifically, the Synar Amendment required

- The enactment of state laws prohibiting any manufacturer, retailer, or distributor of tobacco products from selling or distributing such products to any individual younger than age 18. Law enforcement of violations was to be established "in a manner that can reasonably be expected to reduce the availability of tobacco products to youth."
- Annual, unannounced inspections in a way that provides a sampling of tobacco sales outlets that are accessible to minors.
- Each state to reduce its retail violation rate (RVR), referring to the rate at which tobacco products were sold to individuals younger than 18 years of age, to 20 percent or less by 2003. Failure to meet retail violation target rates carries a penalty of loss of up to 40 percent of federal block grant funds for substance abuse prevention and treatment.

Progress has been seen since the enactment of the Synar Amendment. In 1997, the average RVR nationwide was 40.1

percent; in 2014, it was 9.8 percent. In 2014, 44 out of the 50 states and the District of Columbia had achieved an RVR below 15 percent; 29 states had achieved an RVR below 10 percent. Ten states achieved an RVR below 5 percent. Meanwhile, prevalence rates for current cigarette smoking in 2014 among 8th graders and 10th graders were 3 percent and 5 percent, respectively. While the Synar Amendment since 1997 has succeeded in greatly reducing access to tobacco through direct retail purchases, the impact on the lower prevalence rates for cigarette smoking is less clear. The fact that cigarettes are reported to be readily available means that they are being obtained by other means, most likely from older friends who can purchase them legally.

Updated federal rules for tobacco retailers in 2018 include the following:

- Vendors are not permitted to display advertisements, sell or distribute to anyone cigarettes, cigars, hookahs, or pipe tobacco without a warning statement in the store or on the package.
- Vendors are not permitted to sell or distribute e-cigarettes, vape pens, e-hookahs, e-cigars, personal vaporizers, electronic pipe, or nicotine gels to anyone under the age of 27.

Source: Federal Drug Administration, (2018). Summary of federal rules for tobacco retailers. Washington, D.C.: Federal Drug Administration. https//www.fda.gov/TobaccoProducts/GuidanceComplianceRegulatoryInformation/Retailers/ucm205021.htm/. Substance Abuse and Mental Health Services Administration (2015). *FFY 2014 annual Synar reports: Tobacco sales to youth.* Rockville, MD: Substance Abuse and Mental Health Services Administration.

Probably the most dramatic, and controversial, strategy has been to include vivid graphic displays of packs of cigarettes, showing the health consequences of smoking. Since 1984, tobacco companies have been required to put warning labels such as "Warning: Smoking can kill you" on cigarette packs, but this move is considerably more "in the face" of the consumer. According to the Tobacco Act of 2009, large and graphic warnings showing the symptoms of cancer, strokes, and other diseases would replace the text-only warnings that have been considered unnoticed and stale, according to the Institute of Medicine. In a case brought up by the major tobacco companies in 2012, however, the U.S. Court of Appeals for the District of Columbia, in a 2-to-1 ruling, struck down this provision of the 2009 law on the grounds that it violated the First Amendment rights of the tobacco companies. The U.S. Court of Appeals for the Sixth Circuit had earlier ruled to uphold the new warnings. The U.S. Supreme Court refused to consider the case in 2013, in a decision that has been regarded as being in favor of the governmental position on the matter. Details about the implementation of new graphic displays on cigarette packs are being worked out. In the meantime, Australia and Canada have instituted graphic display warnings on cigarette packs sold in their respective countries. Since then, however, American tobacco companies have been ordered by federal courts to issue a series of print and TV advertisements attesting to the danger of cigarette smoking (see Drugs... in Focus on page 346).[39]

Other Forms of Present-Day Nicotine Consumption

Undoubtedly, concerns about the consumption of nicotine as a toxic, dependence-producing psychoactive drug have focused on the most prevalent form of tobacco use, namely specifically cigarette smoking. There are other forms of nicotine intake in other types of tobacco products, however, and, as we are all aware, new products that permit the consumption of nicotine independent of any involvement with tobacco itself.

Smokeless Tobacco

Smokeless tobacco is ingested, as the name implies, by absorption through the membranes of the mouth rather than by inhalation of smoke into the lungs (Table 15.1). The two most common forms are the traditional loose-leaf chewing tobacco (brand names include Red Man and Beech Nut) and moist, more finely shredded tobacco called **moist snuff** or simply snuff (brand names include Copenhagen and Skoal). Snuff, by the way, is no longer sniffed into the nose, as in the eighteenth century, but rather placed inside the cheek or alongside the gum under the lower lip. Some varieties of snuff are available in a small absorbent-paper sack (like a tea bag) so that the tobacco particles do not get stuck in the teeth. The practice is called "dipping."

According to the 2017 University of Michigan survey, about 2 percent of 8th graders, 4 percent of 10th graders, and 5 percent of high school seniors had used smokeless tobacco within the previous 30 days.[40]

Currently, the form of smokeless tobacco showing the most consistent gains in recent sales is moist snuff, with some brands sold in cherry or wintergreen flavors. As with cigarette tobacco, variations in the alkalinity of different brands of moist snuff allow for different percentages of the nicotine in the tobacco to be absorbed through the membranes of the mouth. Thus, snuff users typically start with brands that release relatively low levels of nicotine, then "graduate" to more potent brands. The most potent brand on the current market, Copenhagen, is also the best-selling snuff in the United States.[41]

> **moist snuff:** Damp, finely shredded tobacco, placed inside the cheek or alongside the gum under the lower lip.

TABLE 15.1

Forms of smokeless tobacco

TYPE	DESCRIPTION
Chewing tobacco	
Loose leaf	Made of cigar-leaf tobacco, sold in small packages, heavily flavored or plain
Fine cut	Similar to loose leaf but more finely cut so that it resembles snuff
Plug	Leaf tobacco pressed into flat cakes and sweetened with molasses, licorice, maple sugar, or honey
Twist	Made of stemmed leaves twisted into small rolls and then folded
(Chewing tobacco is not really chewed but rather held in the mouth between the cheek and lower jaw.)	
Snuff	
Dry, moist, sweetened, flavored, salted, scented	
(A pinch of snuff, called a *quid*, is typically tucked between the gum and the lower lip. Moist varieties are currently the most popular.)	

Source: Based on information from Popescu, C. (1992). The health hazards of smokeless tobacco. In K. Napier (Ed.), *Issues in tobacco.* New York: American Council on Science and Health, pp. 11–12.

Despite continuing warnings that smokeless tobacco presents great risk to one's health, its popularity continues. As stated earlier, while smokeless tobacco presents no immediate danger to the lungs, there are substantial adverse effects on other organs of the body. At the very least, regular use of smokeless tobacco increases the risk of gum diseases, damage to tooth enamel, and eventually the loss of teeth. More seriously, the direct contact of the tobacco with membranes of the mouth allows carcinogenic nitrosamines to cause tissue changes that can lead to oral cancer. Delay in the treatment of oral cancer increases the likelihood of the cancer spreading to the jaw, pharynx, and neck. When swallowed, saliva containing nitrosamines can produce stomach and urinary tract cancer. Moreover, all the negative consequences of ingesting nicotine during tobacco smoking are also present in the use of smokeless tobacco.[42]

Cigars: Big and Little

For a brief time in the 1990s, there was a resurgence in the popularity of cigars, spurred on by images of media stars, both male and female, who had taken up cigar smoking as the tobacco use of choice. The cigar suddenly was fashionable. By the end of the decade, however, the cigar-smoking craze had "gone up in smoke." While part of the problem related to changing market conditions for imported cigars, a major contributing factor was the increasing recognition that cigars could not be regarded as a safe alternative to cigarettes.[43] In fact, cigar smoke is more alkaline than cigarette smoke, so the nicotine content in cigars can be absorbed directly through tissues lining the mouth rather than requiring inhalation into the lungs. In addition, due to the tar content, the risk of lung cancer is 5 times higher for those who smoke cigars, 8 times higher for those smoking 3 or more cigars per day, and 11 times higher for those inhaling the smoke of cigars, relative to nonsmokers. Regular cigar smokers have a doubled risk, relative to nonsmokers, for cancers of the mouth, throat, and esophagus; they also incur a 45 percent higher risk of COPD and a 27 percent higher risk of coronary heart disease (Portrait). Major cigar manufacturers have now agreed to place warning labels on their products, alerting consumers to the risk of mouth and throat cancer, lung cancer and heart disease, and hazards to fertility and unborn children.[44] Approximately 5 percent of all adults in the United States reported cigar smoking in 2013, with African Americans and American Indian/Alaska Natives reporting a somewhat higher prevalence rate than the adult population at large.[45]

While traditional cigars have not presented a public health problem among young smokers, the recent introduction of "little cigars" with fruit or candy flavorings certainly has. Virtually indistinguishable from cigarettes in their size, filters, and outer packaging, these flavored little cigars have become popular among large numbers of middle and high school student smokers. In 2016, 9.5 percent of high school seniors and 4.9 percent of 10th graders reported smoking flavored little cigars or cigarillos within the past 30 days. Public health authorities have great concern over the significant role of flavored tobacco in the decision among adolescents to smoke, whether it is in the form of cigarettes or little cigars. More than 42 percent of students who were currently either smoking cigarettes or little cigars reported in 2016 that they favored the *flavored* varieties.[46]

E-Cigarettes, Vaping, and New Tobacco Products

The explosive rise in the popularity and availability of e-cigarettes, nontobacco products consisting of propylene glycol infused with nicotine that can be inhaled as a smokeless vapor, has raised concerns about nicotine dependence to new

PORTRAIT

Sigmund Freud—Nicotine Dependence, Cigars, and Cancer

Probably the best-known photograph of Sigmund Freud, founder of psychoanalysis and one-time proponent of cocaine use (see Chapter 10), shows him with a cigar in hand. Given that Freud typically smoked 20 cigars each day, it is not surprising that he did not set his cigar aside merely to have his picture taken. But there is a story behind this photograph, a lesson about the power of smoking over the will to stop and the tragic health consequences when the will succumbs.

In 1923, at the age of 67, Freud began to notice sores on his palate and jaw that failed to heal, a sign of oral cancer. Surgery was indicated and fortunately proved successful in removing the cancerous tissue. This would be only the first of 33 surgical operations on the jaw and oral cavity that Freud would endure for the remaining 16 years of his life. As the leukoplakia and finally carcinomas returned to his mouth, he was repeatedly warned by specialists that his practice of smoking cigars was at the root of his problems and that he must stop. Despite these warnings, Freud kept on smoking.

Freud tried very hard to stop. Sometimes he would not smoke for a few weeks at a time, but it would only be temporary. In later years, in addition to his problems with cancer, he suffered from chest pains, referred to by doctors as "tobacco angina." In 1936, the angina became acutely painful. As his biographer, Ernest Jones, noted, "It was evidently exacerbated by nicotine, since it was relieved as soon as he stopped smoking."

By this time, Freud's jaw had been entirely removed and an artificial jaw substituted in its place. He was almost constantly in pain, often could not speak and sometimes could not eat or swallow. Despite the agony, Freud still smoked a steady stream of cigars until his death at the age of 83.

Here was a man whom many consider to be one of the intellectual giants of the twentieth century. Yet the giant was a slave to tobacco.

Sources: Brecher, R.; Brecher, E. M.; Herzog, A.; Goodman, W.; Walker, G.; and the Editors of Consumer Reports (1963). *The Consumer Union's report on smoking and the public interest.* Mount Vernon, NY: Consumer Union, pp. 91–95.

Credit: GL archive/ Alamy Stock Photo

levels. While the practice of **vaping** (consuming nicotine through a container known as a vape cartridge) represents only a very small fraction of the $80 billion-a-year market for tobacco-related products in the United States, sales have shown enormous growth. In 2017, 11 percent of high school seniors, 8 percent of 10th graders, and 4 percent of 8th graders reported vaping nicotine in the past month. The prevalence rate for high school seniors and 10th graders was higher than for college students and young adults (6 percent and 7 percent, respectively). Some types of vaping devices contain a small LED light to simulate the glow of a burning ash.

Of particular concern has been the enormous popularity among young people of a particular brand of e-cigarettes called JUULs, approximately the size of a thumb drive and available in flavors from "mint" to "crème brulee." The practice of vaping through these devices has become so identified with JUULs that the practice is often referred to as "juuling." In 2018, the FDA issued the warning that teenage use of electronic cigarettes had reached "an epidemic proportion" and in letters sent to 1,100 retailers referred to substantial fines that have been imposed for selling e-cigarettes to minors. In addition, Juul Labs and four other manufacturers of similar products were put on notice that the FDA may remove their flavored products from the market completely. In late 2018, the FDA ordered strict restrictions on access to flavored e-cigarettes such as JUULs but did not impose a ban on sales.[47]

Essentially, e-cigarettes are nicotine delivery devices. While the well-known hazards of inhaling tar and carbon monoxide from traditional tobacco products are avoided in e-cigarettes, significant risks remain in two important areas. First of all, the psychoactive drug that has been the cause for tobacco-use dependence over the centuries continues to be consumed on a regular basis in e-cigarettes. Making matters worse, regular refilling of e-cigarettes with liquid nicotine (so-called e-liquids) has the potential for making available a highly toxic drug either as a new recreational drug itself or providing the basis for accidental poisoning. In an unexpected and disturbing turn of events, law enforcement authorities have begun to confiscate quantities of vape cartridges that have been emptied of nicotine and refilled with infused hashish oil and extremely high concentration levels of THC (see Chapter 11). This new development in e-cigarette technology could be opening up a new avenue for substance abusers.

Since less than a teaspoon of pure nicotine can kill an adult, significant problems exist with respect to children exposed to this toxin, either through carelessness on the part of parents or a general lack of understanding of the potential risks. In 2018, both the FDA and the Federal Trade Commission (FTC) warned tobacco companies to stop the marketing of packaging e-cigarette refill liquids that look like juice boxes and snack containers on the basis of the dangers these products pose for children.

vaping: Consuming nicotine in a nontobacco product through the inhalation of smokeless vapor. An alternate slang term is *juuling*, named for the Juul-type device that delivers flavored nicotine liquid into an inhalable vapor.

Second, recent studies have shown that vapors inhaled in e-cigarettes contain toxic organic compounds that are known to be carcinogenic (cancer producing) on the evidence that the compounds have been found to promote the development of cancer in isolated human lung cells. In one study reported in 2018, urine and saliva analyses among adolescent e-cigarette users, tested within 24 hours of e-cigarette use, showed significantly higher levels of metabolites of these compounds, relative to nonsmoking controls. Adolescents who consumed both traditional cigarettes and e-cigarettes showed higher levels than users of e-cigarettes alone.[48]

Public health authorities have noted that marketing strategies for e-cigarettes have followed along the same lines as the glamorization campaigns of tobacco products that were popular in the 1950s and 1960s. They view the present-day advertisements for e-cigarettes as having the potential for reversing more than 40 years of efforts to deglamorize smoking behavior.

Regulatory control over e-cigarettes has been focused on access to both adults and non-adults. The newest FDA regulations in 2018 regarding retail sales of e-cigarettes and associated products were detailed in an earlier section. New York State banned vaping in public places in 2018, with other U.S. states likely to do so as well in the future. Some local communities have banned all e-cigarette stores and hookah lounges within their jurisdictions. A ban on all advertising for e-cigarettes, graphic health warnings, and childproof packaging in e-cigarette products went into effect throughout the European Union in 2016.

In light of the steady decline in traditional cigarette sales in the United States and increased scrutiny of the FDA on the safety of e-cigarettes, the tobacco industry has been hard at work on developing new tobacco products that circumvent health-related concerns. One example is the application by Philip Morris International for approval of an electronic pen-like device called IQOS in which tobacco sticks are heated but not burned. When heated, the tobacco releases nicotine vapor, which the company has claimed produces fewer hazards to one's health than smoke. In recent hearings before the FDA, however, advisory committee members rejected the proposal, questioning the quality of scientific evidence that Philip Morris had presented regarding safety claims as well as their assertion that IQOS devices would not appeal to young people. Philip Morris agreed to continue research on these questions, and it is likely that they will reapply for FDA approval in the future. Meanwhile, direct sales of IQOS devices in the United States are prohibited, though they are currently being sold in as many as 30 other countries.[49]

The Global Perspective: Tobacco Use around the World

Since the seventeenth century, the practice of tobacco smoking has spread throughout the world, but until the 1980s the behavior itself outside the United States had been largely independent of American tobacco corporations. Today, the picture has changed dramatically. Between 1985 and 1994 alone, U.S. cigarette exports to Japan increased 700 percent and to South Korea increased 1200 percent. In the late 1990s, American-made cigarettes moved into significant markets in Eastern Europe and Russia, where smoking prevalence rates are substantially higher than those in the United States. Presently, U.S. tobacco exports total more than $6 billion each year.

Tobacco Use in Other Countries

The prevalence rates of smoking in most foreign countries exceed that of the United States (Figure 15.3). When broken down by gender, the differences are even more extreme. In Greece, China, South Korea, and many Eastern European countries, for example, more than 50 percent of all adult men smoke cigarettes. The public health concerns in the United States are magnified elsewhere in the world by virtue of the sheer numbers of smokers in other countries.[50]

In addition, tobacco control policies in most countries are much less stringent than in the United States. In some nations of the world, no-smoking sections in restaurants and offices are uncommon; outdoor vending machines allow minors to purchase cigarettes easily; smoking is permitted in hospitals and schools, and there is little or no governmental opposition to smoking in general. Two-thirds of the world's population have few or any programs to quit smoking, four out of five (80 percent) do not have available smoke-free environments (Figure 15.4).

Clearly, tobacco use on a global scale presents one of the most significant public health challenges we face in the twenty-first century. According to the World Health Organization (WHO), an estimated 5.4 million people worldwide die each year from tobacco-related diseases, and this figure is projected to increase to more than 8 million by 2030. In the twentieth century, tobacco smoking contributed to the deaths of 100 million people worldwide. During the twenty-first century, the death toll could rise to as high as a billion people.[51]

In recognition of the enormous health crisis that exists at present and the potential calamity that looms in the future, a Framework Convention on Tobacco Control has been signed by more than 170 members of the World Health Organization, an agency of the United Nations. Implementation of the tobacco-use reduction initiates in the agreement, however, is voluntary and progress on a global level has been slow. A major factor is the fact that governments around the world collect more than $200 billion each year in taxes imposed on tobacco sales. In some cases, governments are dependent on these tax revenues to sustain their economies. In other cases, governments receive direct profits from state-owned tobacco corporations.

On the other hand, there are success stories in the ever-changing picture of global tobacco use. In Brazil, for example, strict tobacco control efforts, begun in 1990, reduced smoking prevalence rates by 46 percent. Half of this reduction was accomplished by increasing the price of cigarettes. It is

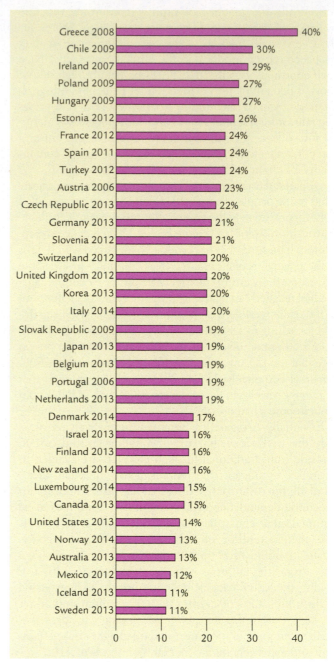

FIGURE 15.3

Smoking prevalence rates among individuals over 15 years old in 34 countries, including the United States.

Source: Based On Greenhalgh, E. M.; Bayly, M.; and Winstanley, M.H. (2015). International comparisons of prevalence of smoking. In M. M. Scollo; and M. H. Winstanley (Eds.). *Tobacco in Australia: Facts and Issues.* Melbourne: Cancer Council Victoria. Figure 1.13. Accessed from: *http://www.tobaccoinaustralia.org.au/chapter-1-prevalence/1-13-international-comparisons-of-prevalence-of-sm*; Used with permission

estimated that approximately 420,000 Brazilian deaths from smoking-related causes were averted between 1996 and 2010. It is predicted that approximately 37 million Brazilian deaths may be prevented by the year 2050 through the continuance of tobacco control programs that are presently in place.[52]

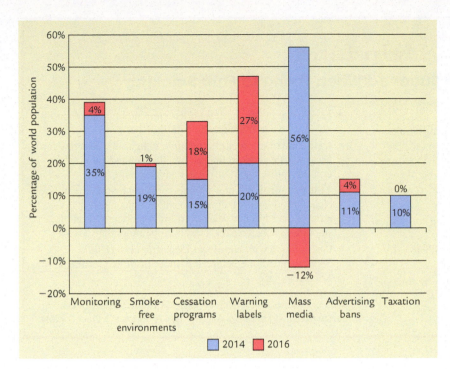

FIGURE 15.4

Growth from 2014 to 2016 in the percentage of the world population that is covered by specific tobacco control policies.

Source: Based on World Health Organization (2017). *The WHO report on the global tobacco epidemic 2017:* Geneva, Switzerland: World Health Organization.

Quick Concept Check — 15.2

Understanding Present-Day Tobacco Control Policy and Strategies

Check your understanding of present-day tobacco control policy and strategies by answering "true" or "false" to the following statements:

Statement	True	False
1. State cigarette taxes have been found to be ineffective in reducing tobacco sales by adults.		
2. The Synar Amendment of 1992 was designed to reduce retail sales of tobacco products to minors.		
3. Graphic depictions of diseases associated with tobacco use have been on packs of cigarettes in the United States since 2009.		
4. Flavored "little cigars" have a greatly reduced level of inhalable smoke.		
5. The responsibility for reducing worldwide tobacco use is assumed by the United Nations Educational, Scientific, and Cultural Organization (UNESCO).		
6. E-cigarettes contain mostly nicotine but a small amount of tar as well.		

Answers: 1. false 2. true 3. false 4. false 5. false 6. false

Quitting Smoking: The Good News and the Bad

There is no question that tobacco use of any kind is harmful to your health as well as your wallet, and it is indeed hard to quit once you have started. But, there's some good news with respect to the consequences of quitting.

The Good News: Undoing the Damage

Given the grim story of all the documented health risks associated with tobacco, it is at least reassuring to know that if a smoker does succeed in quitting, *some* of the damage can be undone. Here are the following benefits:

- Within eight hours—Carbon monoxide levels in the blood drop to normal.
- Within 24 hours—Chances of a heart attack decrease.
- Within two weeks to three months—Circulation improves. Lung function increases by up to 30 percent.
- Within one to nine months—Coughing, sinus congestion, fatigue, and shortness of breath decrease. Cilia regain normal function in the lungs, increasing the ability to handle mucus, clean the lungs, and reduce infection.
- Within one year—Excess risk of coronary heart disease is half that of a smoker.
- Within 5–10 years—Risk of stroke is reduced to that of a nonsmoker.
- Within 10 years—Lung cancer death rate is about half that of a continuing smoker.
- Within 15 years—Risk of coronary heart disease is equal to that of a nonsmoker.

Help Line

Ten Tips on How to Succeed When Trying to Quit Smoking

- Choose a quit date and stick to it.
- Remember that you are dependent, physiologically and psychologically, on nicotine and that the first few days without cigarettes will be the hardest.
- Change the habits that are associated with smoking. If you have had a cigarette with your morning coffee, drink orange juice instead.
- Tell all the people you know that you are quitting and ask for their support.
- Drink lots of water and brush your teeth frequently to rid yourself of the taste of tobacco.
- Never carry matches or a lighter with you. Put away your ashtrays or fill them with something else.
- Spend time with people who don't smoke.

- Keep a supply of sugarless gum, celery sticks, or hard candy on hand to use as a cigarette substitute.
- If you have an uncontrollable urge to light up, take 10 deep breaths instead. Hold the last breath, then exhale slowly, and tell yourself you have just had a cigarette.
- Think about all the money you are saving by not buying cigarettes. A simple calculation will convince you that the amount saved in five years from just a moderate level of smoking (say half a pack a day) can be more than $5,000.
- Get in touch with your local Department of Health Services or call the National Cancer Institute Quitline at 877-44U-QUIT.

Source: Information from the American Cancer Society (2008). *Guide to quitting smoking.* Atlanta, GA: American Cancer Society.

On the one hand, smokers who do not stop stand to lose at least one decade of life expectancy, as compared to those who have never smoked in their lifetime. On the other hand, adult smokers who had quit smoking at 25–34, 35–44, or 45–54 years of age stand to gain 10, 9, or 6 years of life, respectively, as compared to those who continue to smoke. That seems to be a powerful motivation to stop as soon as possible.[53]

The Bad News: How Hard it is to Quit

The advantages of quitting are real and most people are aware of them, but the fact remains that smoking cessation is hard to accomplish. It may be easy to quit smoking for a short while but it is very difficult to avoid a relapse, as any former or present smoker will tell you (Help Line).

About one-third of all smokers in the United States try to quit each year, the vast majority of them without any treatment, but only about 3 to 5 percent succeed with their initial attempt. Nonetheless, about half of all smokers do eventually manage to achieve long-term abstinence from the nicotine in tobacco products, but only after an average of eight attempts at quitting.

Research studies on smoking cessation indicate that there are no gender differences with regard to the likelihood that a person will quit smoking for one to four years, though men are more likely than women to have been abstinent for five years or more. Gradual reduction is as effective as abrupt cessation as a smoking cessation strategy. The fact that a higher level of smoking is consistently related to a lower level of education and family income makes it vital that smoking cessation programs be available to those who ordinarily would not be able to afford them.[54]

Part of California's antismoking campaign, this billboard focuses on the dangers of environmental tobacco smoke. Researchers have found that an approach based on the potential decline in social attractiveness reduces the desire among adolescents to start smoking. In 2005, state health officials announced that smoking rates among adolescents and adults in California had declined sharply since the inception of its antitobacco campaign in 1990.

Credit: California Department of Public Health.

The best option for quitting smoking, of course, is never to have started in the first place, which brings us back to the teenage years, when virtually all adult smokers pick up the habit. The challenge as we progress into the twenty-first century will be to maintain the communication of effective messages that prevent the initiation of cigarette smoking as well as other forms of drug-taking behavior by young people (see Chapter 14).[55]

Summary

Tobacco Use through History

- Tobacco use originated among the original inhabitants of North and South America, and its introduction to Europe and the rest of the world dates from the first voyage of Columbus. Europeans used tobacco initially in the form of pipe smoking and later in the form of snuff.

- In the nineteenth-century United States, the most popular form was tobacco chewing and later cigar smoking. It was not until the late nineteenth century and early twentieth century that cigarette smoking became popular.

Health Concerns and Smoking Behavior

- The 1964 surgeon general's report, the first official statement on the connection between smoking and adverse health consequences, produced a general reversal in the previously climbing per capita consumption rate of cigarettes.

- Since 1964, the surgeon general's reports have solidified the position that nicotine is a clearly addicting component of tobacco and that tobacco use, whether in a smoked or smokeless form, causes significant health risks.

- Since 1964, there has been increased use of filtered, low-tar, and low-nicotine cigarettes. The prevalence rate for smoking among adults has declined from 42 percent in 1964 to 15 percent in 2016. Premature deaths due to tobacco use have decreased as well.

Changing Times: Tobacco Control since 1990

- Since the early 1990s, most U.S. states, cities, and communities have enacted laws mandating smoke-free environments in all public and private workplaces.

- In 1998, the major American tobacco corporations entered into a $246 billion settlement agreement with all 50 U.S. states to resolve claims that the states should be compensated for the costs of treating people with smoking-related illnesses.

- In 2009, the Tobacco Control Act was signed into law, authorizing the FDA to regulate tobacco products sold in the United States. This legislation has been a major step toward controlling tobacco use.

- On a global level, cigarette production and sales to foreign markets have been an increasing marketing opportunity for American tobacco companies and a significant factor in the balance of U.S. foreign trade.

What's in Tobacco?

- The principal ingredients consumed during the smoking of tobacco are nicotine, tar, and carbon monoxide.

- The smoker inhales smoke in the form of mainstream smoke (through the cigarette itself) and sidestream smoke (released from the cigarette tip into the air).

The Dependence Potential of Nicotine

- Nicotine ingestion produces both tolerance effects and physical withdrawal symptoms. A prominent feature of nicotine withdrawal is the strong feeling of craving for a return to tobacco use.

- Smokers typically adjust their smoking behavior to obtain a stable dose of nicotine.

Health Consequences of Tobacco Use

- Tobacco smoking produces an increased risk of cardiovascular disease such as coronary heart disease and stroke, lung cancer and other forms of cancer, and respiratory diseases such as chronic bronchitis and emphysema.

- In addition to the hazards to the smoker through the inhalation of mainstream smoke, there are hazards to the developing fetus when the mother is smoking and hazards to nonsmokers who inhale environmental tobacco smoke.

Patterns of Smoking Behavior in the United States

- In 2017, approximately 34 million adults in the United States were current cigarette smokers.

- Between 80 and 90 percent of adult smokers are estimated to have begun to smoke by the age of 18.

- In general, young people in middle and high school have become increasingly less accepting of cigarette smoking.

Current Regulatory Policy and the Role of Law Enforcement

- The regulatory policy with regard to tobacco use has been defined by the Tobacco Control Act of 2009 under the authority of the FDA. Implementation of regulatory policy can be categorized in three general areas.

- Regulation by taxation is one area of tobacco control. As with alcohol, taxes imposed on tobacco sales vary from state to state. However, the overall intention is to reduce sales by making tobacco products more expensive to buy.

- Regulation by reduced access for young people is another area of tobacco control. Reduced access is accomplished by a minimum age requirement for tobacco sales. While retail vendor compliance with minimum age requirements is high, about half of eighth graders report that it is fairly easy or very easy to get cigarettes.

- The third area is regulation by increased awareness of potential harm. Court-ordered mandates addressed to the tobacco industry have resulted in more aggressive communications to the public regarding the dangers of tobacco use.

Other Forms of Present-Day Nicotine Consumption

- Smokeless (or chewing) tobacco is an alternative means of consuming tobacco. Its popularity continues, despite warnings that smokeless tobacco presents the same risks as tobacco smoking. In fact, smokeless tobacco is associated with increased rates of gum disease, loss of teeth, and cancers of the jaw, pharynx, and neck as well as other regions of the body.

- Cigars are another form of tobacco smoking that presents equivalent health hazards as cigarettes. Public health authorities are concerned that the recent popularity of flavored "little cigars" among young people can be an introduction to future use of tobacco products of all kinds.

- The availability of e-cigarettes, nontobacco devices containing propylene glycol infused with nicotine that is inhaled as a smokeless vapor, presents a significant public health challenge. The health hazards associated with the practice of vaping with such devices, are of particular concern, owing to their great popularity among young people.

- While tars and carbon monoxide are avoided with e-cigarettes, nicotine is consumed, often at high levels of concentration. Nicotine liquids themselves are available for refilling e-cigarettes and are highly toxic. Recent confiscations by law enforcement of vape cartridges that have been refilled with infusions of oils containing very high concentration levels of THC have raised the possibility that e-cigarette technology may have opened up a new avenue for substance abusers.

The Global Perspective: Tobacco Use around the World

- The prevalence rate of smoking in many foreign countries far exceeds that of the United States. In some countries, more than half of all adult males are tobacco smokers.

- Adding to the problem of widespread tobacco use in other countries, relative to the United States, many foreign countries promote far fewer programs that are designed to reduce tobacco use.

- The World Health Organization (WHO), an agency of the United Nations, has assumed the responsibility for the promotion of tobacco control programs in nations around the world.

Quitting Smoking: The Good News and the Bad

- Research has clearly shown that when people quit smoking, many health risks diminish rapidly. Unfortunately, nicotine dependence is very strong, and it is difficult to quit smoking. Nonetheless, a wide range of smoking cessation treatments are available, and about 50 percent of smokers eventually succeed in quitting on a permanent basis.

Key Terms

arteriosclerosis, p. 349
atherosclerosis, p. 349
carbon monoxide, p. 347
carcinomas, p. 351
chronic bronchitis, p. 350
chronic obstructive pulmonary disease (COPD), p. 350
cigarettes, p. 342

cigars, p. 342
cilia, p. 347
ciliary escalator, p. 347
coronary heart disease (CHD), p. 349
emphysema, p. 350
environmental tobacco smoke (ETS), p. 345

erythroplakia, p. 351
gaseous phase, p. 347
ischemic stroke, p. 349
leukoplakia, p. 351
mainstream smoke, p. 347
moist snuff, p. 355
nicotine, p. 348
nitrosamines, p. 351

particulate phase, p. 347
sidestream smoke, p. 343
snuff, p. 341
snuffing, p. 341
tar, p. 347
titration hypothesis, p. 348
vaping, p. 357

Review Questions

1. Explain the changes in American society that made tobacco chewing preferable over snuffing as a means of tobacco use in the 1700s.

2. Explain why it was at first difficult to introduce cigarette smoking in America. What events or circumstances helped their acceptance into American society, particularly among male smokers?

3. Discuss the changes in tobacco control policy in the United States as a result of (1) the release of a major report by the Environmental Protection Agency in 1993, (2) the Tobacco Settlement of 1998, and (3) the Tobacco Control Act of 2009.

4. Describe the composition and physiological effects of the three principal components of tobacco: (1) carbon monoxide, (2) tar, and (3) nicotine.

5. Describe and discuss two adverse health consequences of tobacco use in each of three categories of disease: (1) cardiovascular disease, (2) respiratory disease, and (3) cancer.

6. Discuss the following three categories of regulatory policy with respect to tobacco control: (1) regulation by taxation, (2) regulation by reduced access, and (3) regulation by increased awareness of potential harm. To what extent are these means for tobacco control effective?

7. Describe five health benefits that result from quitting smoking.

Critical Thinking: What Would You Do?

You are living with your parents, and your mother is a chronic tobacco smoker. You have observed a gradual increase in health issues in your mother as well as a gradual increase of health issues in your father and yourself. Your mother has failed in quitting smoking several times and has essentially given up. Obviously, you are very concerned. What would you do?

Endnotes

1. Brooks, J. E. (1952). *The mighty leaf: Tobacco through the centuries.* Boston: Little, Brown, pp. 11–14. Fairholt, F. W. (1859). *Tobacco: Its history and associations.* London: Chapman and Hill, p. 13.

2. Brooks, *The mighty leaf*, pp. 74–80. White, Jason M. (1991). *Drug dependence.* Englewood Cliffs, NJ: Prentice Hall, pp. 32–33.

3. Austin, G. A. (1978). *Perspectives on the history of psychoactive substance use.* Rockville, MD: National Institute on Drug Abuse, pp. 1–12.

4. Brooks, *The mighty leaf*, p. 181. Lehman Brothers (1955). *About tobacco.* New York: Lehman Brothers, pp. 18–20.

5. Kluger, R. (1996). *Ashes to ashes: America's hundred-year cigarette war, the public health, and the "unabashed" triumph of Philip Morris.* New York: Knopf, p. 14. Tate, C. (1989). In the 1800s, antismoking was a burning issue. *Smithsonian*, 20(4), 111.

6. Quotation originally in Bain, J.; and Werner, C. (1905). *Cigarettes in fact and fancy.* Boston: H. M. Caldwell. Cited in Brooks, *The mighty leaf*, p. 259.

7. Kluger, *Ashes to ashes*, pp. 16–20. Lehman Brothers, *About tobacco*, pp. 24–27. Slade, J. (1992). The tobacco epidemic: Lessons from history. *Journal of Psychoactive Drugs*, 24, 99–109.

8. Lehman Brothers, *About tobacco*, p. 30.

9. Lehman Brothers, *About tobacco*, p. 31.

10. Centers for Disease Control and Prevention (2017, December 9). Consumption of combustible and smokeless tobacco—United States, 2000–2015. *Morbidity and Mortality Weekly Report*, 65, 1357-1363. Connolly, G. N.; Alpert, H. R.; Wayne, G. F.; and Koh, H. (2007, January). Trends in smoke nicotine yield and relationship to design characteristics among popular U.S. cigarette brands 1997–2005. A report of the Tobacco Research Program, Harvard School of Public Health, Boston. Federal Trade Commission Report to Congress (1992). Pursuant to the Federal Cigarette Labeling and Advertising Act, p. 31. IHS Global, Inc. (2014, September 9). A forecast of U.S. cigarette consumption (2014–2040) for the Niagara Tobacco Asset Securitization Corporation. Philadelphia, PA: IHS Global Inc. Wilson, D. (2010, February 19). Coded to obey law, lights become Marlboro Gold. *The New York Times*, pp. B1, B5.

11. Brody, J. E. (2014, January 21). Changing the view on smoking. *The New York Times*, p. D5. Centers for Disease Control and Prevention (2017, November 16). Economic facts about U.S. tobacco production and use. Atlanta, GA: Centers for Disease Control and Prevention. Holford, T. R.; Mesa, R.; Warner, K. E.; Meernik, C.; Jean, J.; et al. (2014). Tobacco control and the reduction in smoking-related premature deaths in the United States, 1964–2014. *Journal of the American Medical Association*, 311, 164–171.

12. Campaign for Tobacco-Free Kids (2014, February 27). *A broken promise to our children. The 1998 state tobacco settlement 15 years later.* Washington, D.C.: Campaign for Tobacco-Free Kids. National Women's Health Information Center (2009, December 19). *States slash funding for tobacco prevention programs.* Washington, D.C.: National Women's Health Information Center, U.S. Department of Health and Human Services.

13. Office of the Press Secretary, the White House (2009, June 22). *Fact Sheet: The family smoking prevention and tobacco control act of 2009.* Washington, D.C.: Office of the President.

14. Maheshwari, S. (2017, November 25). Honest ads for cigarettes, minus "truth.". *The New York Times*, p. B1. Tavernise, S. (2013, June 26). In first, FDA rejects tobacco products. *The New York Times*, p. A18. Wilson, D. (2011, January 23). Firms told to divulge all changes to tobacco. *The New York Times*, p. B3.

15. Kell, J. (2013, April 22). Where there's smoke, there's still profit. *Wall Street Journal*, p. B2.

16. Centers for Disease Control and Prevention (2008). *Smoking and tobacco use: Frequently asked questions.* Atlanta, GA: Centers for Disease Control and Prevention.

17. Schlaadt, R. G. (1992). *Tobacco and health.* Guilford, CT: Dushkin Publishing, p. 41.

18. Gahagan, D. D. (1987). *Switch down and quit: What the cigarette companies don't want you to know about smoking.* Berkeley, CA: Ten Speed Press, p. 44.

19. Julien, R. M. (2005). *A primer of drug action* (10th ed.). New York: Worth, pp. 233–234. Richtel, M. (2014, March 24). Selling a poison by the barrel: Liquid nicotine for E-cigarettes. *The New York Times*, pp. A1, A3.

20. Meier, B. (1998, February 23). Cigarette maker manipulated nicotine, its records suggest. *The New York Times*, pp. A1, A15. Pankow, J. F.; Mader, B. T.; Isabelle, L. M.; Luo, W. T.; et al. (1997). Conversion of nicotine and tobacco smoke to its volatile and available free-base form through the action of gaseous ammonia. *Environmental Science & Technology*, 31, 2428–2433.

21. Julien, *A primer of drug action*, pp. 234–238. Phillips, S.; and Fox, P. (1998). An investigation into the effects of nicotine gum on short-term memory. *Psychopharmacology*, 140, 429–433.

22. Brecher, E. M.; and the editors of *Consumer Reports* (1972). *Licit and illicit drugs.* Boston: Little, Brown, pp. 220–228. DiFranza, J. R. (2008, May). Hooked from the first cigarette. *Scientific American*, pp. 82–87.

23. Pontieri, F. E.; Tanda, G.; Orzi, F.; and DiChiara, G. (1996). Effects of nicotine on the nucleus accumbens and similarity to those of addictive drugs. *Science*, 382, 255–257.

24. Herning, R. I.; Jones, R. T.; and Fischman, P. (1985). The titration hypothesis revisited: Nicotine gum reduces smoking intensity. In J. Grabowski; and S. M. Hall (Eds.), *Pharmacological adjuncts in smoking cessation* (NIDA Research Monograph 53). Rockville, MD: National Institute on Drug Abuse, pp. 27–41. Jarvik. M. E. (1979). Biological influences on cigarette smoking. In N. A. Krasnegor (Ed.), *The behavioral aspects of smoking* (NIDA Research Monograph 26). Rockville, MD: National Institute on Drug Abuse, pp. 7–45.

25. Schuckit, M. A. (2000). *Drugs and alcohol abuse: A clinical guide to diagnosis and treatment* (5th ed.). New York: Kluwer Academic/Plenum Publishers, pp. 262–269.

26. Koslowski, L. T.; Wilkinson, A.; Skinner, W.; Kent, C.; Franklin, T.; and Pope, M. (1989). Comparing tobacco cigarette dependence with other drug dependencies. *Journal of the American Medical Association, 261,* 898–901.

27. Centers for Disease Control and Prevention (2014, February 6). *Fact Sheet: Tobacco-related mortality*. Atlanta, GA: Centers for Disease Control and Prevention. Thun, M. J.; Carter, B. D.; Feskanich, D.; Freedman, N. D.; Prentice, R.; et al. (2014). 50-year trends in smoking-related mortality in the United States. *New England Journal of Medicine, 368,* 351–364.

28. Howard, G.; Wagenknecht, L. E.; Burke, G. L.; Diez-Roux, A.; et al. (1998). Cigarette smoking and progression of atherosclerosis. *Journal of the American Medical Association, 279,* 119–124. U.S. Department of Health and Human Services, Public Health Service, Office of Smoking and Health (1983). *The health consequences of smoking: Cardiovascular disease* (A report of the surgeon general). Rockville, MD: U.S. Public Health Service, pp. 63–156.

29. American Lung Association (2014). *Chronic obstructive pulmonary disease (COPD) Fact Sheet*. Chicago, IL: American Lung Association. Centers for Disease Control and Prevention (2017, May 31). What are the risk factors for lung cancer? Atlanta, GA: Centers for Disease Control and Prevention. Gold, D. R.; Wang, X.; Wypij, D.; Speizer, F. E.; Ware, J. H.; et al. (1996). Effects of cigarette smoking on lung function in adolescent boys and girls. *New England Journal of Medicine, 335,* 931–937. U.S. Department of Health and Human Services, Public Health Service, Office of Smoking and Health (1984). *The health consequences of smoking: Chronic obstructive lung disease* (A report of the surgeon general). Rockville, MD: U.S. Public Health Service, pp. 329–360.

30. American Cancer Society (2017). *Cancer Facts and Figures 2017*. Atlanta, GA: American Cancer Society. American Lung Association (2015). *Lung cancer Fact Sheet*. Chicago, IL: American Lung Association. Denissenko, M. F.; Pao, A.; Tang, M.; and Pfeifer, G. P. (1996). Preferential formation of benzopyrene adducts at lung cancer mutational hotspots in *P53. Science, 274,* 430–432. Landi, M. T.; Dracheva, T.; Rotunno, M., Figueroa, J. D.; et al. (2008). Gene expression signature of cigarette smoking and its role in lung adenocarcinoma development and survival. *PLoS ONE*, published online February 20, 2008, by the Public Library of Science, San Francisco, CA.

31. Freedman, N. D.; Silverman, D. T.; Hollenbeck, A. R.; Schatzkin, A.; and Abnet, C. C. (2011). Association between smoking and risk of bladder cancer among men and women. *Journal of the American Medical Association, 306,* 737–745. Huizen, J. (2017, May 30). Leukoplakia: Symptoms, causes, and prevention. *Medical News Today*. Accessed from: https://www.medicalnewstoday.com/articles/317689.php. Schuckit, *Drug and alcohol abuse*, pp. 270–272.

32. Ebrahim, S. H.; Floyd, R. L.; Merritt, R. K.; Decoufle, P.; and Holtzman, D. (2000). Trends in pregnancy-related smoking rates in the United States, 1987–1996. *Journal of the American Medical Association, 283,* 361–366. Geerts, C. C.; Grobbee, D. E.; van der Ent, C. K.; de Jong, B. M.; et al. (2007). Tobacco smoke exposure of pregnant mothers and blood pressure in their newborns. *Hypertension, 50,* 572–578. Li, Yu-Fen; Langholz, B.; Salam, M. T.; and Gilliland, F. D. (2005). Maternal and grandmaternal smoking patterns are associated with early childhood asthma. *Chest, 127,* 1232–1241.

33. Aligne, C. A.; Moss, M. E.; Auinger, P.; and Weitzman, M. (2003). Association of pediatric dental caries with passive smoking. *Journal of the American Medical Association, 289,* 1258–1264.

34. Centers for Disease Control and Prevention (2017, January). *Health effects of secondhand smoke*. Atlanta, GA: Centers for Disease Control and Prevention. U.S. Department of Health and Human Services, Public Health Service, Office of Smoking and Health (2006). *The health consequences of involuntary exposure to tobacco smoke* (A report of the surgeon general). Rockville, MD: U.S. Public Health Service.

35. Johnston, L. M.; O'Malley, P. M.; and Bachman, J. G. (2002, December 16). Centers for Disease Control and Prevention (2018, February 20). *Fast facts on tobacco*. Atlanta, GA: Centers for Disease Control and Prevention. Centers for Disease Control and Prevention (2018, January 19). Current cigarette smoking among adults—United States, 2005-2016. *Morbidity and Mortality Weekly Report, 67,* 53-59. Centers for Disease Control and Prevention (2018, November 9). Tobacco produce use among adults—United States, 2017. *Morbidity and Mortality Weekly Report, 67,* 1225-1232. Centers for Disease Control and Prevention (2018, January 19). Current cigarette smoking among adults—United States, 2005-2016. *Morbidity and Mortality Weekly Report, 67,* 53-59. Miech, R. A.; Johnston, L. M.; O'Malley, P. M.; Bachman, G. G.; Schulenberg, J. E.; and Patrick, M. E. (2018). *Monitoring the future: National survey results on drug use, 1975–2017, Vol I: Secondary school students*. Ann Arbor: Institute for Social Research, The University of Michigan, Tables 8-1 and 8-4. Schulenberg, J. E.; Johnston, L. M.; O'Malley, P. M.; Bachman, G. G.; Miech, R. A.; and Patrick, M. E. (2018). *Monitoring the future: National survey results on drug use, 1975–2017, Vol II: College students and adults ages 19–55.* Ann Arbor: Institute for Social Research, The University of Michigan, Table 2-3. National Center for Health Statistics (2018, September 18). Early release of selected estimates based on data from January-March 2018 National Health Interview Survey. Atlanta, GA: Centers for Disease Control and Prevention, Figures 8.1, 8.2, 8.4, 8.5. Teen smoking declines sharply in 2002, more than offsetting large increases in early 1990s. University of Michigan News and Information Services, Ann Arbor, pp. 4–5.

36. Federation of Tax Administrators (2017, January). State excise tax rates on cigarettes. Washington, D.C.: Federation of Tax Administrators. Accessed from: *https://www.taxadmin.org/assets/docs/Research/Rates/cigarette/.*

37. Miech, R. A.; Johnston, L. M.; O'Malley, P. M.; Bachman, G. G.; and Schulenberg, J. E. (2015). *Monitoring the future: National survey results on drug use, 1975–2014, Vol I: Secondary school students*. Ann Arbor, MI: Institute for Social Research, University of Michigan, p. 32. Substance Abuse and Mental Health Services Administration (2014, August 14).

SAMHSA News Release: State/federal effort to reduce illegal tobacco sales to minors remains effective. Substance Abuse and Mental Health Administration, Rockville, MD. Substance Abuse and Mental Health Services Administration (2015). *FFY 2014 Annual Synar Reports.* Rockville MD: Substance Abuse and Mental Health Services Administration.

38. Strom, S. (2014, February 6). CVS vows to quit selling tobacco products. *The New York Times*, p. B1.

39. Editorial: "Warning: Smoking can kill you." (2012, August 28). *The New York Times*, p. A22. Siegel, M. (2013, July 11). Labels leave a bad taste. *The New York Times*, pp. B1, B4.

40. Schulenberg, Johnston; O'Malley; Bachman; Miech; and Patrick (2018). *Monitoring the future, Vol. II*, Table 2-3.

41. Freedman, A. M. (1994, October 26). How a tobacco giant doctors snuff brands to boost their "kick." *Wall Street Journal*, pp. A1, A14.

42. Wilson, D.; and Creswell, J. (2010, January 31). Where there's no smoke, Altria hopes there's fire. *The New York Times*, pp. B1, B5.

43. Hamilton, K. (1997, July 21). Blowing smoke. *Newsweek*, pp. 54–60.

44. Ackerman, E. (1999, November 29). The cigar boom goes up in smoke. *Newsweek*, p. 55. Baker, F.; et al. (2000). Health risks associated with cigar smoking. *Journal of the American Medical Association, 284*, 735–740. Substance Abuse and Mental Health Administration (2001, December 21). *The NHSDA report: Cigar use.* Rockville, MD: Office of Applied Studies, Substance Abuse and Mental Health Administration.

45. Centers for Disease Control and Prevention (2015). Tobacco product use among middle and high school students—United States, 2011–2014. *Morbidity and Mortality Weekly Report 2015, 64*(14), 381–385. Chen, J.; Ketermann, A.; Rostron, B. L.; and Day, H. R. (2014). Biomarkers of exposure among U.S. cigar smokers: An analysis of 1999–2012 National Health and Nutrition Examination Survey (NHANES) data. *Cancer, Epidemiology, Biomarkers, and Prevention.* Published online first November 7, 2014; doi: 10.1158/1055-EPI14-0849.

46. Centers for Disease Control and Prevention (2013, November 13). Tobacco product use among middle and high school students—United States, 2011 and 2012. *Morbidity and Mortality Weekly Report, 62*, 893–897. King, B. A.; Tynan, M. A.; Dube, S. R.; and Arrazola, R. (2014). Flavored-little-cigar and flavored-cigarette use among U.S. middle and high school students. *Journal of Adolescent Health, 54*, 40–46.

47. Alderman, L. (2013, June 13). E-cigarettes at a crossroads. *The New York Times*, pp. B1, B7. Elliott, S. (2013, August 30). E-cigarette markers' ads echo tobacco's heyday. *The New York Times*, pp. B1, B5. Kaplan, S.; and Hoffman, J. (2018, September 13). F.D.A. alarmed by teenage use, targets vaping. *The New York Times*, pp. A1, A22. Kaplan, S.; and Hoffman, J. (2018, November 16). F.D.A. to limit how stores sell vaping flavors. *The New York Times*, pp. A1, A16. Meier, B. (2014, April 17). E-cigarette study data may raise concerns. *The New York Times*, pp. B1, B6. Richtel, M. (2014, July 16). E-cigarettes' fruit cocktails: Makers in an arms race for vapor flavors. *The New York Times*, pp. B1, B2. Schulenberg, Johnston; O'Malley; Bachman; Miech; and Patrick (2018). *Monitoring the future, Vol. II*, Table 2-3. Zernike, K.; and Kaplan, S. (2018, April 25). Vaping device gets attention of regulators. *The New York Times*, pp. A2. A18.

48. Brodwin, E. (2018, April 30). An e-cigarette with twice the nicotine of comparable devices is taking over high schools – and scientists are sounding the alarm. *Business Insider.* Accessed from: https://www.businessinsider.com/juul-e-cig-vaping-health-effects-2018-3. Hoffman, J. (2018, November 17). One drag on a Juul hooked a teenager for years. *The New York Times*, p. A1, A14. Meier, B. (2014, December 25). Race to deliver nicotine's punch, with less risk. *The New York Times*, p. A1. Richtel, M. (2014, March 24). Selling a poison by the barrel: Liquid nicotine for e-cigarettes. *The New York Times*, pp. A1, A3. Richtel, M. (2014, May 4). Some e-cigarettes deliver a puff of carcinogens. *The New York Times*, pp. A1, A4. Rubinstein, M. L.; Delucchi, K.; Benowitz, N. L.; and Ramo, D. E. (2018, March). Adolescent exposure to toxic volatile chemicals from e-cigarettes. *Pediatrics, 141* (4), 1–8. Yan, E. (2018, August 12). Police: THC in vape oil. *Newsday*, p. A22.

49. Cuomo adds e-cigarettes to public smoking ban (2017, October 24). *The New York Times*, p. A19. Jolly, D. (2014, February 27). Europe putting e-cigarettes under strict regulations. *The New York Times*, pp. B1, B2. Kaplan, S. (2018, January 28). F.D.A. panel rejects claim that tobacco sticks are safer than cigarettes. *The New York Times*, p. A36. Lipton, E. (2014, July 23). Officials focus on e-cigarette ads aimed at youths. *The New York Times*, p. A15.

50. Centers for Disease Control and Prevention (2018, September 28). Current tobacco smoking, quit attempts, and knowledge about smoking risks among persons aged 15 years or older—Global Adult Tobacco Survey, 28 countries, 2008–2016. *Morbidity and Mortality Weekly Report, 67*, 1072–1076. World Health Organization (2017). *The WHO report on the global tobacco epidemic 2017.* Geneva, Switzerland: World Health Organization. World Health Organization (2008). *The WHO report on the global tobacco epidemic 2008: The MPOWER package.* Geneva, Switzerland: World Health Organization.

51. Ibid.

52. Brazil slashes smoking rates (2012, December 19). *Journal of the American Medical Association, 308*, 2449. Marsh, B. (2008, February 24). A growing cloud over the planet. *The New York Times*, p. 4. Reeves, H. (2000, November 5). Blowing smoke: What's one little worldwide antismoking treaty compared to the force of 1.1 billion nicotine-craving cigarette fiends? *The New York Times Magazine*, p. 26. Shafey, O.; Eriksen, M.; Ross, H.; and MacKay, J. (2009). *The tobacco atlas* (3rd ed.). Atlanta: American Cancer Society, pp. 22–23. World Health Organization (2008). *WHO report on the global tobacco epidemic.*

53. Based on information from the American Cancer Society, Atlanta. Cited in *The world almanac and book of facts 2000* (1999). Mahwah, NJ: Primedia Reference, p. 733. Jha, P.; Ramasundarahettige, C.; Landsoman, V.; Rostron, B.; Thun, M.; et al. (2014). 21st-century hazards of smoking and benefits of cessation in the United States. *New England Journal of Medicine, 368*, 341–350.

54. American Legacy Foundation (2003). *Fact sheet: Quitting smoking.* Washington, D.C.: American Legacy Foundation. Rigotti, N. (2012). Strategies to help a smoker who is struggling to quit. *Journal of the American Medical Association, 308*, 1573–1580. Lindson-Hawley, N.; Aveyard, P.; and Hughes, J. R. (2013). Gradual reduction vs. abrupt cessation as a smoking cessation strategy in smokers who want to quit. *Journal of the American Medical Association, 310*, 91–92.

55. Fiore, M. C.; Hatsukami, D. K.; and Baker, T. B. (2002). Effective tobacco dependence treatment. *Journal of the American Medical Association, 288*, 1768–1771. Spangler, J. G.; George, G.; Foley, K. Long; and Crandall, S. J. (2002). Tobacco intervention training: Current efforts and gaps in U.S. medical schools. *Journal of the American Medical Association, 288*, 1102–1109.

chapter 6

Deterrence through Drug Testing

My friend Kenny wanted to talk about performance-enhancing drugs and baseball.

Just two years after he had been called up from the minors, Kenny was enjoying an extraordinary season on a major league baseball team that will remain nameless. A game had been cancelled due to rain that day, and Kenny had some time on his hands. The topic came up about his achievements and what they meant to him.

"I know you want me to talk about drugs," Kenny began. "When I was a little boy growing up, José Canseco and Mark McGwire were my heroes. Man, their bodies were huge, especially their arms. The power they had in their bats. Then, when I heard about all the drugs they were taking, I was mad as hell. I wanted to be another Canseco or another McGwire on the field. But I knew I couldn't be like them off the field."

"Of course, they have all those drug tests now. And I've passed them all, no reason to worry about that, I'm proud to say. From the start, I was determined that if I ever made it to the majors (and I have), it wouldn't be the way they did it. Yeah, I'm having a pretty good season this year. Don't know about the next one, but one thing I do know. I won't have to apologize to Roger Maris's widow, like McGwire did, for using drugs to break Roger's record. I will have done it on my own."

I asked Kenny if he had any regrets. "None whatsoever" was his immediate response.[1]

In the highly competitive world of sports, where running a hundredth of a second faster can make the difference between a gold medal or a silver, where hitting a baseball just a few feet farther than anyone else had done before can make you a champion, temptations abound. There has always been the allure of performance-enhancing drugs as a way of finding that winning edge. Yet, as much as we appreciate the pressures on athletes today, we continue to maintain that using performance-enhancing drugs represents a violation of the principle of fair play. We consider the use of performance-enhancing drugs as a form of cheating, and therefore unacceptable behavior. As a result, testing for the presence of performance-enhancing drugs has become an accepted fixture of modern-day sports.

Present-day drug testing, however, has been extended beyond the world of athletic competition and performance-enhancing drugs. Drug tests for a range of illicit drugs are a common feature of preemployment screening. While preemployment drug screening has been justified as part of an overall strategy for reducing substance abuse in the general population and a deterrent for engaging in substance abuse in the first place, the practice has come under considerable scrutiny, particularly when there is testing for specific drugs with questionable relevance to one's performance on the job.

This chapter will examine current issues surrounding drug testing in sports and in the workplace, as well as the physical and behavioral effects of performance-enhancing drugs in general. We begin with basic information about the forensics of drug testing. Specifically, how are drug tests conducted? What do the test results mean?

The Forensics of Drug Testing

The typical drug-testing procedure begins with a urine sample collected from the individual in question. The advantages of using urine as the basis for drug testing lie in the ease and noninvasiveness of collecting urine, the ease with which urine can be analyzed for specific factors, and the fact that drugs or their metabolites (by-products) are usually very stable in frozen urine. Therefore, it is possible to provide long-term storage of positive samples, in case the test results are disputed. The disadvantages are that many perceive urine collection to be a humiliating experience, a dehydrated athlete may find it difficult to urinate immediately after competing, and there are ways to tamper with the urine sample prior to testing.

The two major urinalysis methods are the **enzyme immunoassay (EIA)** technique and a two-stage procedure called **gas chromatography and mass spectrometry (GC/ MS)**. In both methods, the collected urine is divided into two samples prior to being sent off to the laboratory so that if the analysis of one sample yields a positive outcome, the analysis can be repeated on the other sample. A reanalysis is typically required if an individual appeals the original test result.[2]

With the EIA method, a separate test must be run on each particular drug that is being screened. First, at an earlier time, the substance to be tested for (THC or cocaine, for example) has been injected into an animal, eliciting specific immunological antibodies to that substance. The antibodies are then purified into a testing substrate. When the collected urine from the individual being tested is combined with the testing substrate, a specific reaction will occur if the urine contains the banned substance. A popular commercial testing kit for screening major controlled substances (opioids, amphetamines, cocaine, benzodiazepines, and marijuana), called **enzyme multiplied immunoassay technique (EMIT)**, has been marketed by Siemens Healthcare since the early 1970s. This kit is relatively inexpensive and can be used to screen large numbers of urine samples. Since the original patent for EMIT expired many years ago, the EIA method is available on a "generic basis" by several drug-testing companies.[2]

With the GC/MS method, the urine is first vaporized and combined with an inert gas and then passed over a number of chemically treated columns. Through the process of gas chromatography, technicians are able to identify the presence of a banned substance by the different colorations that are left on the columns. After this has been done, the gas is ionized (converted into an electrically active form) and sent through an electric current and magnetic field that separates out each of the different ions (electrically charged particles) in the gas. Through the process of mass spectrometry, a particular "fingerprint," or "signature," of each chemical substance can be detected and measured. The GC/MS technique is considered more definitive than the EIA technique, but it is considerably more expensive and time consuming. It is also the only testing procedure that adequately screens for anabolic steroids.[3]

Until the late 1990s, urinalysis was the sole means for drug testing. Since then, there has been increasing interest in oral fluid testing. In this procedure, a collection pad is placed between the lower cheek and gum for two to five minutes. The collection pad is then sealed and later analyzed by EIA. The sensitivity and specificity of the results (see next section) are comparable to those obtained through urinalysis. As with positive urinalysis tests, a confirmation of positive oral fluid test results is made by GC/MS.

Currently available FDA-approved drug-testing systems using oral fluid samples can now provide test results in approximately 15 minutes. The advantages over traditional

---

enzyme immunoassay (EIA): One of the two major drug-testing techniques for detecting banned substances or drugs.

gas chromatography/mass spectrometry (GC/MS): A drug-testing technique based on the combination of gas chromatography and mass spectrometry.

EMIT (enzyme multiplied immunoassay technique): A commercial testing kit for screening major controlled substances, based on enzyme immunoassay analysis.

urinalysis are obvious. Samples are analyzed on-site rather than having to be sent to laboratories. Specimen collection can be performed face-to-face (literally) with the donor, with little risk of sample substitution, dilution, or adulteration. Embarrassment on the part of the donor is greatly reduced, as are privacy concerns.[4]

Sensitivity and Specificity in Drug Testing

For any drug-testing procedure to be valid for the detection of any drug, two essential questions need to be asked:

- What is the *sensitivity* of the test? The sensitivity is determined by the likelihood that a specimen containing drugs (or drug metabolites) will test positive. This outcome is referred to as a "true positive." If a drug test has a high degree of sensitivity, then there will be very few "false negatives." If a test is sensitive, the subject will seldom "test negative" when drug-taking behavior has actually occurred. In other words, there will be very few "misses."

- What is the *specificity* of the test? The specificity is determined by the likelihood that a drug-free (or drug metabolite-free) specimen will test negative. This outcome is referred to as a "true negative." If a drug test has a high degree of specificity, then there will be very few "false positives." In other words, there will be very few "false alarms."

Sensitivity is an index of the ability of the test to correctly report the *presence* of drugs. Specificity is an index of the ability of the test to correctly report the *absence* of drugs. Ideally, a test for screening the presence of a drug or drug metabolite should have a high level of sensitivity and a high level of specificity. In this regard, the GC/MS test is more sensitive and specific than the EIA test for a variety of drugs. As mentioned earlier, a GC/MS analysis is typically performed as a confirmation of a positive EIA test result.

It is important to point out that no drug test can guarantee perfect sensitivity or perfect specificity, much less both in combination. It is possible that the sensitivity of a test will exceed its specificity, or vice versa. Nonetheless, efforts are made to make drug tests as sensitive and specific as possible.

Drugs ... in Focus shows the EIA and GC/MS cutoff values for a variety of drugs in a typical 9-panel or 5-panel testing procedure. Results lower than a cutoff value are reported as negative. However, it should be noted that a negative test result does not indicate that a substance was not present, only that its concentration was lower than the established cutoff concentration for a positive result.

The Possibility of False Positives and False Negatives

While less frequent than in EIA testing, false positives can occur even with GC/MS analyses. Eating a poppy seed roll prior to drug testing or taking quinolone antibiotic medications such as ofloxacin (brand name: Floxin) and ciprofloxacin (brand name: Cipro) has resulted in false-positive indications of opioid use. Therapeutic levels of ibuprofen (brand names: Advil, Motrin, and Nuprin, among others) have resulted in false-positive indications of marijuana smoking. In addition, the passive inhalation of marijuana smoke can leave sufficient levels of THC metabolites to result in false-positive indications of marijuana smoking, although the density of smoke that needs to be present for this to happen makes it unlikely that individuals would be completely unaware that they were being exposed to marijuana.

Historically, two specific tactics have been employed (unsuccessfully) by athletes attempting to create false-negative results when tested for anabolic steroids. The first tactic was to take the anti-gout drug probenecid (brand name: Benemid) prior to testing. Available since 1987, probenecid can mask the presence of anabolic steroids, but it is now on the list of banned substances for competitive athletes and is easily detected by GC/MS techniques. The second tactic was to increase the level of epitestosterone in the body. The standard procedure for determining the present or prior use of anabolic steroids is to calculate the ratio of testosterone against the level of epitestosterone, a naturally occurring hormone that is usually stable at relatively low levels in the body. Epitestosterone would essentially function as the denominator in this calculation. If epitestosterone were artificially elevated, the ratio could be manipulated downward so as to produce a false-negative result in drug testing. Using the international standard of a 4:1 ratio (formerly 6:1) or higher as indicating anabolic steroid use, an increase in the level of epitestosterone might bring the ratio down to 3:1 or lower. However, suspiciously high levels of epitestosterone can now be detected by GC/MS techniques, so this form of manipulation is no longer successful. Of course, a urine sample collected from an athlete can simply be surreptitiously substituted for a "clean" sample and then submitted for testing. As we will see in a later section, this method for creating a false-negative was the strategy used in the most brazen scandal of recent times, the infamous Russian doping incident at the Winter Olympic Games in 2014.[5]

Pinpointing the Time of Drug Use

It is important to remember that a positive result in a drug test, however genuine it may be, indicates merely that the test has detected a minimal level of a drug or its metabolite at the time of testing. It is difficult to determine *when* that drug was introduced into the body or *how long* the drug-taking behavior continued for the drug in question to be in the system. In the case of urinalysis testing, the time it takes for the body to get rid of the metabolites of a particular drug varies considerably, from a few hours to a few weeks (Table 16.1). In the case of oral fluid (saliva) drug testing, the window of detection may be different, depending on the drug of interest. Opioids and cocaine are detected within two to three days of ingestion; THC in marijuana is detected within a period ranging from 1 hour after ingestion to 14 hours later. Because THC metabolites are excreted into the urine over a period of several days

Drugs ... in Focus

EIA and GS/MS Cutoff Values in Urinalysis Drug Testing

9-Panel Testing

Drug Class	Examples	EIA Screening Cutoff	GC/MS Confirmation Cutoff
Amphetamines	Amphetamine Methamphetamine	1,000 ng/ml**	500 ng/ml
Cocaine metabolite		300 ng/ml	150 ng/ml
Marijuana metabolite		50 ng/ml	15 ng/ml
Opioids	Morphine Oxycodone	2,000 ng/ml	2,000 ng/ml
Phencyclidine (PCP)		25 ng/ml	25 ng/ml
Barbiturates	Phenobarbital Amobarbital	300 ng/ml	300 ng/ml
Benzodiazepines	Xanax Ativan	300 ng/ml	200 ng/ml
Methadone		300 ng/ml	200 ng/ml
Propoxyphene	Darvon Darvocet	300 ng/ml	200 ng/ml

5-Panel Testing*

Drug Class	Examples	EIA Screen Cutoff	GC/MS Confirmation Cutoff
Amphetamines	Amphetamine Methamphetamine	1,000 ng/ml	500 ng/ml
Cocaine metabolite		300 ng/ml	150 ng/ml
Marijuana metabolite		50 ng/ml	15 ng/ml
Opioids	Morphine Oxycodone	2,000 ng/ml	2,000 ng/ml
Phencyclidine (PCP)		25 ng/ml	25 ng/ml

*5-Panel testing is federally mandated for employees in the U.S. government. The drugs screened are sometimes referred to as the "federal-five."

**nanograms of metabolite per milliliter of urine.

Note: 10- and 12-panel tests are also available, as well as special tests for anabolic steroids, synthetic cathinones (so-called bath salts), synthetic cannabinoids (so-called Spice or K2), and a variety of new formulations that are continually being introduced.

Source: Based on data from Quest Diagnostics, Madison, NJ, and Aegis Sciences Corporation, Nashville, TN.

TABLE 16.1

Detection periods for various drugs in urinalysis testing

DRUG	DETECTION PERIOD
Alcohol	1–12 hours
Amphetamines in general	1–2 hours
Barbiturates	
Short acting	2 days
Long acting	1–3 weeks
Benzodiazepines	
Therapeutic use	3 days
Chronic use (>1 year)	4–6 weeks
Cocaine	2–4 days
Marijuana (THC)	
Single use	2–7 days
Chronic, heavy use	1–2 months
MDMA (Ecstasy)	1–2 days
Methamphetamine	1–2 hours
Opioids	
Codeine	2 days
Heroin or morphine	2 days
Darvon, Darvocet	6 hours to 2 days
Phencyclidine (PCP)	
Casual use	14 days
Chronic, heavy use	Up to 30 days

Note: The detection periods for urinalysis purposes listed here are general guidelines, which might vary according to the sensitivity of the test or the subject's physical condition, fluid balance, and state of hydration. Detection periods for hair samples are relatively longer and detection periods for blood or saliva samples are relatively shorter than for urine samples.

Sources: Based on information from Drugs of Abuse Reference Guide (2007). Occupational testing services, LabCorp, Research Triangle Park, NC. Verstraete, A. G. (2004). Detection times of drugs of abuse in blood, urine, and oral fluid. *The Drug Monitor, 26*, 200–205.

or in some cases several weeks, oral fluid testing for marijuana is better suited for determining when marijuana has been last used. In effect, the "window of detection" is narrower. If the interval between use and testing has been longer than 14 hours or so but shorter than a few days, urinalysis would pick up a positive result, but oral fluid testing would not.[6]

The question of timing has particular relevance in criminal proceedings when arrestees undergo drug testing for the presence of certain illicit drugs that may or may not be pertinent to the committing of a criminal offense. In those instances, it has been difficult to determine whether a positive test result at the time of testing is an indication of the presence of the drug at the time of the offense.

Specific Drug-Testing Programs

Drug testing for performance-enhancing drugs in sports can be carried out in conjunction with a particular athletic event such as the Olympic Games, or carried out by a sports organization on a random, unannounced schedule during the course of a season. In either case, the drugs being tested are generally limited to those that pertain to the enhancement of athletic performance, and athletes are usually well acquainted with the types of drugs under examination. When drug testing is carried out for preemployment screening purposes, the principal emphasis is on the detection of major illicit drugs rather than specific performance-enhancing drugs (see Drugs...in Focus). It can be argued that drug testing as a condition for employment represents a form of coercion and self-incrimination in situations in which illicit drugs are being screened. It can also be argued that the use of the drugs being tested may have little or no relevance to the quality of performance on the job.

Owing to the expense of randomized drug-testing programs in the workplace, not every organization can afford the costs. Large corporations may be able to budget for potentially thousands of tests for preemployment screening purposes, but smaller businesses might not. Relatively few colleges and considerably fewer high schools are able to secure the level of funding needed to test their student populations. Even if the costs were lower, it is questionable whether illicit drug-taking behavior would be reduced in the long run as a result. Interestingly, recent evidence indicates that the prospect of randomized drug testing in schools fails to act as a deterrent among students. The University of Michigan researchers in 2003 found virtually identical rates of illicit drug use in schools that had drug-testing programs and schools that did not. This general finding was replicated in a study reported in 2008. The deterrent effect of drug testing on illicit drug use in schools clearly has not been demonstrated.[7]

It should be noted that performance-enhancing drug users may not necessarily feel that they are in jeopardy of detection through drug testing. Young people who are not participants in an organized athletic program in school or individuals in general who are taking performance-enhancing drugs on their own to provide a more developed physical appearance do not need to fear a positive drug test because they will never be required to undergo *any* form of drug testing that involves performance-enhancing drugs, random or otherwise. Yet, while they may be immune to the social consequences of drug testing, they are not immune to the adverse health consequences of performance-enhancing drugs themselves, specifically the hazards of anabolic steroids. These health concerns will be examined later in the chapter. The next section will focus on the impact of performance-enhancing drugs on the world of sports, past and present.

Drug Enforcement . . . in Focus

A New Technology in Drug Testing

A new technology has been developed that does not require the use of any bodily fluid such as urine, blood, or saliva, to detect drug use. Researchers from the University of Surrey in England developed in 2018 a noninvasive way to detect drugs that simply involves a fingerprint. This new method is known as *paper spray mass spectrometry*. You may have witnessed the use of mass spectrometers in airports when a person's hand or luggage is swabbed to detect bomb residue. The drug testing technology is similar. As a person's body metabolizes drugs, it excretes molecules that can be detected via fingerprints. Pilot testing of the device show a 99-percent sensitivity rate. The test cannot be "fooled" (yielding a false-negative result) even when there has been thorough hand washing prior to testing. Results are also available within 30 seconds, so there is no longer a wait-period.

Use of such technology has major implications in criminal justice settings. Imagine if law enforcement could immediately test a driver suspected of drug intoxication or a community supervision officer could test a probationer in his or her office during a supervision meeting. In most probation settings, the individual submitting a urine sample for testing must be physically monitored to ensure that the sample in fact belongs to the person submitting it. Therefore, the new testing would be much less invasive, requiring fewer staffing resources. Large probation offices typically employ urinalysis technicians and both male and female officers who are available to monitor offenders submitting urine samples. The elimination of the need to send specimens to labs for analysis will also reduce the possibility of analysis errors, which can have significant ramifications for drug testing cases that are supervised by a court. In prisons and jails, inmates could be tested more efficiently to monitor drug use in correctional facilities, particularly in drug treatment programs within these institutions.

Devices utilizing the technology of paper spray mass spectrometry were developed initially as tests of cocaine use, but devices are now available for testing amphetamines, opioids, and THC use as well. Due to the elimination rates of various drugs (see Table 16.1), however, tests of this kind cannot identify the quantity of a substance taken nor when the substance was used. Nonetheless, this new approach to forensic drug testing appears to be the "next big thing" in law enforcement and corrections.

Sources: DrugAbuse.com (2018). New drug testing technology makes urine samples a thing of the past. Accessed from: https://drugabuse.com/new-drug-testing-technology-makes-urine-samples-a-thing-of-the-past/. McCullom. R. (April 2018). Fingerprint scanning technology leaps forward, but to what end? *Undark: Truth, Beauty, Science.* Accessed from: *https://undark.org/article/fingerprint-biometrics-drugs-law-enforcement/.* McKenna, J.; Jett, R.; Shanks, K.; and Manicke, N. E. (2018). Toxicological drug screening using pepper spray high-resolution tandem mass spectrometry (HD-MS/MS). *Journal of Analytical Toxicology, 42,* 300–310.

The History of Performance-Enhancing Drugs in Sports

The first recorded athletic competition, the Olympic Games in ancient Greece, was also the occasion for the first recorded use of drugs in sports. As early as 300 B.C.E., Greek athletes were known to eat hallucinogenic mushrooms, either to improve their performance in the competition or to achieve some kind of mystical connection to the gods. Later, Roman gladiators and charioteers used stimulants to sustain themselves longer in competition, even when injured.

By the end of the nineteenth century, world-class athletes were experimenting with a variety of stimulant and depressant drugs, including cocaine, caffeine, alcohol, nitroglycerine, opioids, strychnine, and amphetamines. In 1886, while competing in a cross-country race, a Welsh cyclist died of an overdose of a combination of morphine and cocaine (now referred to as a *speedball*), marking the first drug-related death in sports ever recorded. During the 1904 Olympics, U.S. marathoner Tom Hicks collapsed after winning the race and lost consciousness. When he was revived, doctors were told that he had taken a potentially lethal mixture of strychnine (a CNS stimulant when administered in low doses) and brandy.[8]

The Discovery of Anabolic Steroids

With the introduction in the 1930s of steroid drugs specifically patterned after the male sex hormone testosterone, a new element would enter the arena of competitive sports. Originally, these drugs had been developed by pharmaceutical companies as a treatment for anemia (low red blood cell count) and for conditions that caused muscles to waste away. In the months following the end of World War II when people in Europe were near death from starvation and weight loss, steroid drugs saved many lives. It quickly became apparent that these new drugs could find another application in otherwise healthy individuals as well. For the first time, a drug could produce **ergogenic** (performance-enhancing) effects in behavior through specific changes in the physical structure of the human body. The potential advantages to athletes and their coaches were obvious.

To understand how testosterone-based steroids produced ergogenic effects in the first place, it is necessary to recognize that physiological effects of testosterone itself. The first and

ergogenic (ER-go-JEN-ik): Performance enhancing.

most obvious effect is **androgenic** (literally, "man-producing"), in that the hormone promotes the development of male sex characteristics. As testosterone levels rise during puberty, boys acquire an enlarged larynx (resulting in a deeper voice), body hair, and an increase in body size, as well as genital changes that make them sexually mature adults. The second effect is **anabolic** (upward changing), in that it promotes the development of protein and, as a result, an increase in muscle tissue. Muscles in men are inherently larger than muscles in women because of the anabolic action of testosterone in the male body.

Steroid drugs based on alterations in the testosterone molecule are therefore referred to as **anabolic-androgenic steroids**. Obviously, the goal of pharmaceutical companies has been to develop formulations that emphasize the anabolic function while retaining as little of the androgenic function as possible. For that reason, steroid drugs of this type are most often simply called **anabolic steroids**. Unfortunately, as we will see, it has not been possible to develop a testosterone-derived drug without at least some androgenic effects. Table 16.2 shows a listing of currently available anabolic steroid drugs.

It should be pointed out that anabolic steroids not be confused with **adrenocortical steroids**, drugs that are patterned after glucocorticoid hormones secreted by the adrenal glands. The major drug of this latter type is *hydrocortisone* (brand name: Hydrocortone injection or tablets). The molecular structure of these drugs qualifies them to belong to the steroid family, but there is no relationship to testosterone or any testosterone-like effects. Adrenocortical steroids are useful in the medical treatment of tissue inflammation; in sports, they reduce the inflammation associated with muscle injuries. Their effects on muscle development can be viewed as *catabolic* (downward changing), in that they produce a weakening of the muscles, an obviously undesirable option for athletes on a long-term basis.[9]

Anabolic Steroids at the Modern Olympic Games

By the time of the 1952 Olympic Games in Helsinki, athletes were well acquainted with performance-enhancing drugs. Legally available amphetamines (see Chapter 10), in particular, were commonplace, particularly in events that emphasized speed and endurance. Among events requiring strength and size, anabolic steroids were seen to be perfectly suited for gaining a competitive advantage.

It is debatable which country first used anabolic steroids. U.S. athletic officials have claimed that Soviet weight-lifting champions were using steroids in international competitions in 1954; British officials have claimed that a U.S. hammer thrower used steroids prior to 1954. Whoever has the dubious honor of being first, steroid use became the norm by the 1956 Olympic Games in Melbourne for both men and women athletes.

Steroid use was clearly out in the open during the 1968 Olympic Games in Mexico City. An estimated one-third of the entire U.S. track and field team, not merely the strength-event and field-event competitors but sprinters and middle-distance runners as well, were using anabolic steroids. Any controversy over their use, however, did not concern the appropriateness or morality of taking steroids, only which particular steroids

TABLE 16.2		
Anabolic steroids		
TYPE OF STEROID	**GENERIC NAME**	**BRAND NAME**
Oral	Danazol	Danocrine
	Drostanolone	Masteron
	Methandrostenolone	Dianabol
	Methyltestosterone	Android, Testred, Virilon
	Oxandrolone	Oxandrin, Anavar
	Oxymetholone*	Anadrol
	Stanozolol	Winstrol
Intramuscular injection	Nandrolone decanoate	Deca-Durabolin IM
	Nandrolone phenpropionate	Durabolin IM
	Testosterone propionate*	Testex IM
	Testosterone enanthate*	Delatestryl IM
Transdermal patch	Testosterone	Androderm transdermal system, Testoderm transdermal system

Note: Anabolic steroids are Schedule III controlled substances. As such, they are considered illicit drugs under federal guidelines when not obtained with a medical prescription and restricted to medical use along with other Schedule III controlled substances. Several "brand names" marketed for performance-enhancing purposes are combinations of various steroids.

* Approved outside the United States.

Sources: Based on information from Julien, R. M. (2005). *A primer of drug action* (10th ed.). New York: Worth, p. 631. National Institute on Drug Abuse (2000, April). Anabolic steroids. *Community drug alert bulletin.* Rockville, MD: National Institute on Drug Abuse *Physicians' desk reference* (71st ed.) (2017). Montvale, NJ: PDR Network.

worked best. Strength-event athletes were taking at least two to five times the therapeutic recommendations (based on the original intent of replacing body protein). The following year,

androgenic (AN-droh-JEN-ik): Acting to promote masculinizing changes in the body.

anabolic (AN-ah-BALL-ik): Acting to promote protein growth and muscle development.

anabolic-androgenic steroids: Drugs that promote masculinizing changes in the body and increase muscle development.

anabolic steroids: Drugs patterned after the testosterone molecule that promote masculine changes in the body and increased muscle development. The full name is "anabolic-androgenic steroids."

adrenocortical steroids: A group of hormones secreted by the adrenal glands. Their anti-inflammatory action makes them useful for treating arthritis and muscle injuries.

an editor of *Track and Field News* dubbed anabolic steroids "the breakfast of champions." In 1971, one American weight lifter commented, in reference to his Soviet rival,

> Last year the only difference between me and him was I couldn't afford his drug bill. Now I can. When I hit Munich [in 1972], I'll weigh in at about 340, or maybe 350. Then we'll see which is better, his steroids or mine.[10]

In the meantime, the notable masculine features of many female athletes from eastern European countries in the 1960s and 1970s, not to mention the number of Olympic records that were suddenly broken, prompted many observers to ask whether they were either men disguised as women or genetic "mistakes." Questions about the unusually deep voices of East German women swimmers prompted their coach, at one point, to respond, "We came here to swim, not to sing."

From information that subsequently came to light, we now know that the effects were due to large doses of steroids. Until the late 1980s, the East German government was conducting a scientific program specifically to develop new steroid formulations that would benefit their national athletes and, at the same time, would be undetectable by standard drug-screening procedures. In 2000, the principal physician in the East German Swimming Federation at the time when these steroids were being administered was convicted on charges that from 1975 to 1985 the program caused bodily harm to more than four dozen young female swimmers.[11]

Russian pentathlon champion Nadezhda Tkachenko was one of several world-class female athletes in the 1970s who later tested positive for anabolic steroids.

Credit: Anonymous/AP Images

The 2000 Summer Olympic Games in Sydney, Australia, instituted the strictest drug-testing procedures to date for all competing athletes. For the first time, a specific phrase was inserted into the Olympic Oath, recited by all athletes at the beginning of the games: "... committing ourselves to a sport without doping and without drugs." Unfortunately, accusations of illegal performance-enhancing drug use and expulsions of athletes continued to plague both Summer and Winter Olympic Games, as they had in previous ones since the 1950s.

Since 2009, the World Anti-Doping Code and Standards for drug testing have been in effect for international sports events. The Code includes an agreed-upon list of prohibited performance-enhancing drugs and performance-enhancing methods in international sports competitions, testing procedures for drug screening, and specific penalties for violations. Under the auspices of the World Anti-Doping Agency (WADA), rules and regulations have been formally accepted by Olympic Committees in more than 200 nations, as well as by professional leagues (such as the National Basketball Association and the National Hockey League) representing the United States in the Olympic Games and other international competitions. The Code has been continually updated over the years as new formulations become available (see Drug Enforcement ... in Focus).[12]

Although the 2012 Summer Olympic Games in London was the first in recent history to report no specific incidences of performance-enhancing drug use among participating athletes, it did not take long before a major drug-related scandal erupted in an arena of international competition outside of the Olympic Games. In 2012, the United States Anti-Doping Agency (USADA) announced that international cycling champion Lance Armstrong would be banned for life from cycling and stripped of his seven Tour de France titles as well as his bronze medal from the 2000 Olympic Games, after finding that Armstrong had used red blood cell booster erythropoietin (EPO), testosterone, corticosteroids, and masking agents, as well as engaged in the trafficking of performance-enhancing drugs and participating in a widespread cover-up of doping activities. Armstrong never appealed the USADA decision that effectively ended his athletic career. The Lance Armstrong Foundation for cancer support that he had created was renamed the LIVESTRONG Foundation, severing all ties to the athlete. In 2013, Armstrong finally admitted his use of EPO in competitive cycling since 2000. Today, Armstrong is a *persona non grata* in the world of sports.

Perhaps the most dramatic scandal, however, took place in the 2014 Winter Olympic Games in Sochi, Russia, when it was disclosed that the entire Russian team had been subject to an elaborate state-sponsored scheme involving tainted urine samples (see Portrait). In response, the International Olympic Committee (IOC), governing the participation of all athletes in Olympic competition, ruled in 2017 that Russian medalists in the 2014 competition would be stripped of their medals and that the Russian Olympic team would be officially banned from competing in the Winter Olympic Games in 2018. Nevertheless, in January 2018, two weeks before the opening of the Winter Olympic Games, the IOC ruled that nearly 400 Russian

Drug Enforcement... in Focus

Pharmaceutical Companies and Anti-Doping Authorities in Alliance

For several years, as the World Anti-Doping Agency (WADA) engaged in a continuing and often-frustrating game of "cat and mouse" with athletes who were determined to thwart anti-doping controls, major pharmaceutical companies for the most part remained on the sidelines. Now it appears that they are getting increasingly in the game.

A case in point relates to the medication erythropoietin, marketed in its natural form as Epogen (Amgen Pharmaceuticals) or in synthetic forms as Aranesp (Amgen) and NeoRecorman (Roche Pharmaceuticals). While erythropoietin (also known as EPO) is an effective hormonal treatment for millions of anemia patients who suffer from a deficiency in production of red blood cells in bone marrow, the use of EPO for its performance-enhancing (red blood cell–boosting) effect in normal individuals, particularly trained athletes, is clearly a form of cheating, a classic example of "doping." Any prominent headline regarding EPO use as a performance-enhancing drug is a public relations nightmare of sorts for those pharmaceutical companies manufacturing EPO-related drugs for therapeutic purposes. Would the public now associate a valuable medicinal agent with the dark world of doping? Even worse, would some people accuse these companies of developing drugs that could be misused by athletes essentially as a way of enhancing sales?

In a major gesture of good "corporate citizenship," GlaxoSmithKline Pharmaceuticals sponsored the drug-testing laboratories for the 2012 London Summer Olympic Games, carrying the costs for the facilities and more than a thousand support staff involved in drug screening. It was the first time in Olympic history that an anti-doping operation had a specific corporate sponsor. But the relationship between pharmaceutical companies and international anti-doping efforts has gone beyond simply the contribution of financial support. In 2013, two major manufacturers, Glaxo and Hoffman-LaRoche, entered into an agreement with WADA to evaluate every new drug candidate in their development pipeline for potential abuse as a performance-enhancing drug. Customarily, when developing a new drug, a number of reagents are also created in company laboratories that react to the molecular structure of the drug. These reagents remain proprietary compounds, and information about them is kept secret. In the future, these reagents will be shared with WADA for use as "markers" in future drug-screening tests.

The actions of Glaxo and Roche are not entirely new. Amgen, for example, was asked by WADA officials to help develop a screening test for Aranesp, released for marketing in 2001, in anticipation of possible doping incidents in the 2002 Salt Lake City Winter Olympic Games. Not all pharmaceutical companies have been as eager to cooperate with anti-doping authorities in this regard. There remains some reluctance on the part of companies in releasing proprietary information in such a highly competitive business as pharmaceuticals. Nonetheless, there is an increasing awareness that the benefits outweigh the costs.

While there has been considerable progress in controlling performance-enhancing drugs in sports, it should be pointed out that performance-enhancing drugs can also be developed in illicit laboratories around the world and made available to athletes in nations with far weaker anti-doping controls in place. These laboratories work in the shadows of competitive athletics and have little or no incentive to cooperate with WADA or any other anti-doping agency.

Sources: Salyer, K. (2012, July 18). At London Games, a new record for doping tests. *Bloomberg Businessweek.* Accessed from: http://www.businessweek.com/articles/2012-07-18/at-london-games-a-new-record-for-doping-tests#p2. Thomas, K. (2013, February 19). An unexpected drug reaction. Manufacturers increasingly join the fight against doping. *The New York Times,* pp. B1, B4.

---

athletes who had been cleared of wrongdoing in 2014 would be permitted to participate, although they would be identified only as "Olympic Athletes from Russia (OAR)." Even so, as it turned out, two of these OAR competitors were found to be in violation of doping regulations, and their record of performance expunged.[13]

Performance-Enhancing Drugs in American Sports

The widespread use of anabolic steroids in international athletics in the 1960s quickly filtered down to sports closer to home. Trainers in the National Football League (NFL) began to administer anabolic steroids to their players. By the 1970s and 1980s, virtually all the NFL teams were familiar with these drugs. Estimates of how many NFL players were on anabolic steroids varied from 50 to 90 percent. We will never know the full extent of the practice, but it was certainly substantial.

Several professional football players remarked at the time that their steroid use had begun while they were playing on collegiate teams, and indeed, football players in several colleges and universities during the 1980s were implicated in steroid use. Football players were not alone in this regard. Use of anabolic steroids had found its way into other collegiate and even high school sports, including track and field, baseball, basketball, gymnastics, lacrosse, swimming, volleyball, wrestling, and tennis.

However, for the average American sports fan, it was not until the 1990s that the involvement of performance-enhancing drugs was fully realized, largely due to the well-publicized scandals in Major League Baseball. Record-breaking home-run performances in the late 1990s and early 2000s raised suspicions that these achievements may not have been due solely to

PORTRAIT

Dr. Grigory Rodchenkov: Whistle-Blower on the Russian Doping Scandal of 2014

"In November 2015, I escaped Russia determined to tell the world about my country's doping program for Olympic athletes… I know that I shocked many people by revealing my country's doping program (but) when senior officials in Russia direct you to do something, you do not ask questions. I had no choice."

So began a statement of Dr. Grigory Rodchenkkov, ironically the former director of Russia's antidoping center, as he referred to his detailed account of widespread breaches of drug-testing controls at the 2014 Olympic Games, a disclosure that convinced the International Olympic Committee in December 2017 to officially ban the Russian team from the 2018 Olympic Games in South Korea.

A state-sponsored program had been devised for substituting urine samples from Russian athletes who had been exposed to performance-enhancing drugs with clean samples and fraudulently altering test results that were later submitted to WADA for analysis and evaluation. Russian athletes had been given a three-drug "cocktail" of banned substances mixed with alcohol that had been developed by Russian officials for performance-enhancing purposes. Then, during the Games, agents of the Russian intelligence service broke into supposedly tamper-proof collection bottles, replacing the bottles containing drug-tainted urine with those containing clean urine. The bottle switch was accomplished at night through a concealed hole in the hole. Rodchenkov's detailed accounts of these events and the participation of officials at the highest levels of Russian sports were instrumental in revealing to the world what may never have come to light.

It would be the most comprehensive doping scandal in the history of the modern Olympic Games.

Threatened for his life in Russia, Rokchenkov escaped to the United States in 2015 and now lives at an undisclosed location under the U.S. Federal Witness Protection Program. His story is the basis for the documentary film *Icarus*, released in late 2017.

Sources: Mather, V. (2018, February 2). Heavily represented despite being ineligible. *The New York Times*, p. B9. Quotation from Rodchenkov, G. (2017, September 22). Russia's Olympic cheating, unpunished. *New York Times*, p. A27. Ruiz, R. R.; and Panja, T. (2017, December 6). Russia banned from Winter Olympics by I.O.C. *The New York Times*, p. A1.

Credit: Lifestyle pictures/Alamy Stock Photo

---

athletic prowess but rather to some pharmacological assistance as well. Matters were made worse by the fact that the sport of baseball had stood apart from other professional sports in the United States and sports organizations around the world by failing to establish regulatory policies on steroid abuse and the use of other performance-enhancing drugs.

In 2004, two executives of BALCO, a nutritional supplements laboratory in California, and the personal trainer for outfielder Barry Bonds, Greg Anderson, were indicted on charges of illegally distributing steroids and other performance-enhancing drugs to dozens of professional athletes in baseball and other sports. Anderson pled guilty in 2005 to conspiracy to distribute steroids and money laundering and was later sentenced to three months in prison and three months of home arrest. The BALCO executives served short prison sentences, as well. In another development, a New York Mets clubhouse assistant pled guilty to having supplied performance-enhancing drugs to dozens of current and former major MLB players and their associates between 1995 and 2005 and subsequently laundering the proceeds from these transactions.

Under intense pressure from public opinion and from government officials, the MLB players union agreed in early 2005 to a policy of steroid testing that was more in line with those of the National Football League and the National Basketball Association. In late 2005, MLB penalties for steroid use were stiffened. Testing procedures and penalties for the use of amphetamine and other stimulants, which had been omitted from consideration in the earlier agreement, were added and later extended to minor league players (see Drug Enforcement… in Focus).

Despite changes in policy with regard to performance-enhancing drugs in MLB baseball, it became evident that abuses had not ended. In 2011, Barry Bonds was convicted of one felony count of obstruction of justice in connection with BALCO investigations. He was sentenced to two years' probation and 30 days of house arrest, fined $4,000, and asked to complete 250 hours of community service, but he was exonerated on appeal in 2015. In 2012, pitcher Roger Clemens was found not guilty of lying to Congress in 2008, when he testified that he never administered performance-enhancing drugs during his baseball career.

Fans expressed their opinion on steroid use at Major League Baseball's All-Star Game in 2002. Between 5 and 7 percent of MLB players tested positive for anabolic steroids when randomized screening was conducted during spring training in 2003. Players involved in steroid use were dubbed "the syringe generation."

Credit: MIKE BLAKE/REUTERS/Newscom

Drug Enforcement . . . in Focus

Suspension Penalties for Performance-Enhancing Drug Use in Sports

The 2005 agreement on regulations against performance-enhancing drug use in MLB included a ban on "all substances regarded now, or in the future, by the federal government as steroids," as well as human growth hormone and steroid precursor hormones such as androstenedione. Suspension penalties for positive-test infractions under these new regulations are shown in comparison to previous MLB regulations and those of other U.S. and international athletic organizations. In 2013, MLB announced an expansion of its drug-testing program, with players required to undergo in-season (as opposed to spring-training and off-season) blood testing for human growth hormone, as well as a new test for synthetic testosterone.

	POSITIVE TEST PENALTIES				
	First	*Second*	*Third*	*Fourth*	*Fifth*
Major League Baseball					
Pre-2005	Counseling	15 days	25 days	50 days	1 year
Late 2005	50 games	100 games	Lifetime suspension, with right of reinstatement after two years		
Minor League Baseball	15 days	30 days	60 days	1 year	Lifetime
National Football League	4 games	6 games	1 year	1 year	1 year
National Basketball Association	5 games	10 games	25 games	25 games	25 games
National Hockey League			—no testing for steroids—		
World Anti-Doping Association (Olympic sports)	2 years	Lifetime			

Sources: Curry, J. (2006, November 16). Baseball lacks stiffer penalties for steroid use. *The New York Times*, pp. A1, D2. NFL will ban amphetamines as enhancers (2006, June 28). *Newsday*, p. A53. Schmidt, M. S. (2013, January 13). Baseball to expand drug-testing program. *The New York Times*, pp. B13, B17. Schmidt, M. S. (2010, February 24). Baseball plans to start testing for human growth hormone in minors. *The New York Times*, p. B11.

In 2014, Yankees third baseman Alex Rodriguez was barred for 162 games and the 2014 postseason for using performance-enhancing drugs in previous baseball seasons. It was the longest suspension for doping in baseball history. Shortly before returning to the Yankees in 2015, Rodriguez issued a handwritten letter in which he apologized for his actions. He wrote, "To Major League baseball, the Yankees, the Steinbrenner family, the Players Association and you, the fans, I can only say I'm sorry."[14]

Present-Day Federal Regulations

In 1990, as a response to increased public awareness of anabolic steroid abuse both in and outside of competitive sports, Congress passed the Anabolic Steroid Control Act, reclassifying anabolic steroids as Schedule III controlled substances. Jurisdiction was transferred from the Food and Drug Administration (FDA) to the Drug Enforcement Administration (DEA). As a result of this legislation, pharmacies are now permitted to fill anabolic steroid prescriptions only up to a maximum of five times. Penalties for violating the law can result in a five-year prison term and a $250,000 fine for illegal nonmedical sales, and a one-year term and a $1,000 fine for nonmedical possession. Penalties are doubled for repeated offenses or for selling these drugs to minors. States are permitted to draft their own laws regarding the definition of anabolic steroids and to set sentencing guidelines for steroid offenders. Although most states follow the federally mandated Schedule III classification, New York lists steroids in Schedule II, while other states have their own classification systems. In some U.S. states, possession of small quantities of steroids is regarded as a misdemeanor; others regard it as a felony. In most but not all jurisdictions, first-time offenses do not result in imprisonment, unless there are aggravating circumstances, such as possession of large quantities or evidence of intent to sell or distribute the drugs.[15]

Despite the regulations now in effect, steroid abuse today remains a major problem. Steroid distribution has become an enormous black-market enterprise. With their use commonly referred to as being "on the juice," these drugs are channeled principally through people associated with body-building gyms and through Internet Web sites that frequently change a company's name and location in an effort to stay one step ahead of the law. Some Internet-based suppliers include a warning on their Web sites, "Due to their profound effects and potencies, it is recommended to seek the guidance of a physician prior to use," to protect themselves from liability, although few if any customers would voluntarily divulge their steroid abuse, much less seek medical guidance.

Patterns of Anabolic Steroid Abuse

Some anabolic steroids can be taken orally and others through intramuscular injections, but abusers often administer a combination of both types in a practice called *stacking*. Hard-core abusers may take a combination of three to five different pills and injections simultaneously, or they may consume any steroid that is available ("shotgunning"), with the total exceeding a dozen. In addition to the complications that result from so many different types of steroids being taken at the same time, multiple injections into the buttocks or thighs, with 1.5-inch needles (called "darts" or "points"), are painful and inevitably leave scars. If these needles are shared, as they frequently are, the risk of hepatitis or HIV contamination is significant.

Steroid abusers often follow a pattern called *cycling*, in which steroids are taken for periods lasting from 4 to 18 weeks, the "on" periods being separated by "off" periods of abstinence. Unfortunately, when the drugs are withdrawn, the newly developed muscles tend to "shrink up," throwing the abuser into a panic that his or her body is losing the gains that have been achieved. In addition, abstinence from steroids can lead to signs of depression, such as problems sleeping, lack of appetite, and general moodiness. All these effects encourage a return to steroids, frequently in even larger doses, and generate a craving for the euphoria that the person felt while on them.

A variation of the cycling pattern is the practice of *pyramiding*. An individual starts with low doses of steroids, gradually increases the doses over several weeks prior to an athletic competition, and then tapers off entirely before the competition itself in an attempt to escape detection during drug testing. However, pyramiding leads to the same problems during abstinence and withdrawal as cycling, except that the symptoms occur during the competition itself.

The Potential for Steroid Dependence

A major problem associated with steroid abuse is the potential for an individual to believe that his or her physique will forever be imperfect. In a kind of "reverse anorexia" that has been called **muscle dysmorphia**, some body builders continue to see their bodies as weak and small when they look at themselves in the mirror, despite their greatly enhanced physical development. Peer pressure at the gyms and clubs is a factor in never being satisfied with the size of one's muscles, but it is becoming apparent that societal pressures play a

Whether or not aided by anabolic steroids, massive development of musculature continues to be greatly prized in competitive body building.

Credit: Nattanan726/Shutterstock

role as well. In the case of males, it is interesting to examine the evolution of the design of G.I. Joe action figures over the years, from the original toy introduced in 1964 to the most recent incarnation introduced in 1998 (Table 16.3). Just as the Barbie doll has been criticized as setting an impossible ideal for the female body among girls, male-oriented action figures can be criticized on the same basis for boys.[16]

Traditional estimates of substance dependence among steroid users range from 13 to 18 percent, but more recent studies indicate that the prevalence rate may be somewhat higher. In an Internet survey, about one in four weight lifters and body builders using steroids have reported that they were taking larger amounts of steroids over a longer period of time than originally intended, that they needed increased amounts of steroids to achieve the desired effect, or that they experienced physical or emotional problems when steroids were discontinued. One in eight admitted that they had resumed steroid use to relieve a problem that occurred when they stopped. By the present-day DSM-5 guidelines (see Chapter 8), about one-third of them would meet the criteria for moderate to severe substance use disorder.

The Hazards of Anabolic Steroid Abuse

One of the problems in evaluating the adverse effects of steroid abuse is that the dosage levels can vary over an enormous range. Since nonmedical steroid use is illegal, it is virtually impossible to know the exact dosage levels or even the exact combinations of steroids a particular individual may be taking. It is estimated that a "typical" body builder on anabolic steroids takes in a minimum of five to twenty-nine times the therapeutic doses recommended for the medical use of these drugs, but in some cases, the estimates have gone as high as a hundred to a thousand times the recommended therapeutic dose.

At these huge dosages, anabolic steroids are literally flooding into the body, upsetting the delicate balance of hormones

muscle dysmorphia (dis-MORF-ee-ah): The perception of one's own body as small and weak and of one's musculature as inadequately developed, despite evidence to the contrary. Also known as megorexia, the condition of muscle dysmorphia is a form of body dysmorphic disorder.

TABLE 16.3

Promoting muscular development in the marketing of an action figure: The evolution of G.I. Joe (1964–1998)—with a comparison to Mark McGwire in 1998

YEAR OF INTRODUCTION	GENERAL APPEARANCE	BICEP CIRCUMFERENCE (EXTRAPOLATED TO A 6-FOOT TALL MAN)
1964	Relatively normal chest and body proportions, no weapon	12.2 inches
1974	Chest and body "bulked up" with a "Kung-fu grip"	15.2 inches
1994	Named Gung-Ho, the ultimate Marine, with moustache and tattoo	16.4 inches
1998	Named G.I. Joe Extreme with grenade launcher	26.8 inches
	Mark McGwire MLB first-baseman, 70 home runs in 1998, an all-time single-season record (until Barry Bonds hit 73 home runs in 2001)	20.0 inches

Sources: Based on information in Week in Review: As G.I. Joe bulks up, concern for the 98-pound weakling (1999, May 30). *The New York Times,* p. D2.

and other chemicals that are normally controlled by testosterone. The primary effect in men is for the testes gland to react to the newly increased testosterone levels in the blood by producing *less* testosterone on its own. In other words, the gland is getting the incorrect message that its services are no longer needed. As a result, the testicles shrink, and a lower sperm count leads to sterility, reversible for most men but irreversible in a small number of cases. Paradoxically, the male breasts enlarge (a condition called *gynecomastia*) because steroids eventually break down into estradiol, the female sex hormone. Other related consequences include frequent, sustained, and often painful penile erections (a condition called *priapism*) and an enlargement of the prostate gland. Severe acne, particularly on the shoulders and back, results from an increase in the secretions of the sebaceous glands in the skin. Other testosterone-related effects include two changes in hair growth patterns: increased facial hair growth and accelerated balding on the top of the head. Among women taking anabolic steroids, the dramatically increased levels of testosterone in bodies that normally have only trace amounts produce major masculinizing changes, only some of which return to normal when steroids are withdrawn.

Given the fact that the liver is the primary mechanism for clearing drugs from the body (see Chapter 3), it is not surprising that large doses of anabolic steroids take their toll on this organ. The principal result is a greatly increased risk of developing liver tumors. The type of liver tumors that are frequently seen in these circumstances are benign (noncancerous) blood-filled cysts, with the potential for causing liver failure. In addition, a rupture in these cysts can produce abdominal bleeding, requiring life-saving emergency treatment. Fortunately, these liver abnormalities are reversible when steroids are withdrawn from use.

Chronic steroid abuse has also been associated with an increased risk of cardiovascular disease. There are documented cases of heart-related sudden death among athletes who have been steroid users, even though there was no history of illness or any family history that would predispose them to heart trouble. Cardiac abnormalities such as enlargement of the left ventricle are not reversible when steroid use is discontinued.

Stories abound of mood swings and increased aggressiveness, often referred to by athletes as "roid rage," when taking anabolic steroids. While numerous anecdotal reports force us to consider the possibility that real psychological changes are going on, more rigorous laboratory investigations into the relationship between anabolic steroid use and psychological problems are needed to provide a better understanding of the phenomenon.[17]

Counterfeit Steroids and the Placebo Effect in Sports

As with many illicit drugs, some products marketed to look like anabolic steroids are not the real thing. The problem here is that athletes are notoriously superstitious and easily leave themselves open to placebo effects. On the one hand, in the case of anabolic steroids, the effects on muscle development are usually so dramatic that it is difficult to mistake the response as simply a result of a placebo effect. On the other hand, some performance-enhancing drugs have far more subtle effects, and psychological factors can end up playing a greater role. In relating his own experience with steroids, MLB superstar Alex Rodriguez spoke of the placebo effect:

> *I'm not sure what the benefit was... I will say this: when you take any substance, especially in baseball, it's half mental and half physical. If you take this glass of water and say you're going to be a better baseball player, if you believe it, you probably will be. I certainly felt more energy, but it's hard to say.*[18]

Testing for Other Performance-Enhancing Drugs

While anabolic steroids have dominated the performance-enhancing drug scene, other drugs have been promoted as having performance-enhancing properties. They include human growth hormone, androstenedione, and creatine, all of which can be detected by present-day drug-testing procedures.

Human Growth Hormone

One illicit alternative, **human growth hormone (hGH)**, has become increasingly popular, according to experts in this field, because it is more widely available and cheaper than in previous years, in contrast to the evermore costly illicit steroids. Those who take this pituitary hormone, however, face the increased risk of developing a significant side effect called **acromegaly**, a condition resulting in a coarse and misshapen head, enlarged hands and feet, and damage to various internal organs.

Prior to 1985, hGH was obtained from the pituitary glands of human cadavers, but now genetically engineered hGH (brand names: Protropin and Humatrope) is available, having been approved by the FDA for the treatment of rare cases of stunted growth in children. Although the distribution of these drugs is controlled by their manufacturers as carefully as possible, supplies manage to get diverted for illicit use.

Testimony in 2008 that prominent MLB players had used hGH for performance-enhancing purposes revealed the abuse potential of this hormone in professional sports. It is doubtful, however, that its reputation for performance enhancement is justified, according to a major review of more than 40 studies of hGH in healthy athletes, conducted between 1966 and 2007. The conclusion is that hGH use increases lean body mass, but the increased bulk does not raise levels of strength or endurance. Indeed, hGH produces higher levels of lactate in muscle tissue, leading to fatigue; hGH users are more likely than others to develop joint pain and carpal tunnel syndrome. In the absence of scientific evidence of any performance-enhancing effects, it has been suggested that reports by athletes that hGH helped to increase their athletic performance are probably due to a placebo effect. Nonetheless, despite hGH's dubious value, hGH screening, capable of differentiating naturally produced hGH from synthetic hGH, became a fixture of drug testing at the 2008 Summer Olympic Games in Beijing. Because hGH has a relatively short half-life, athletes tested positive only if the drug had been injected in the previous 12–24 hours. No major hGH-related scandals occurred in the 2010 Winter Olympic Games in Vancouver.[19]

Dietary Supplements

As recently as 10 years ago, fitness-oriented young people might have taken only basic vitamins and minerals to help them build muscle mass or improve cardiovascular performance. Today, the fitness market is inundated with a growing number of dietary supplement products with presumed performance-enhancing properties; sales of such products exceed $2 billion each year in the United States. They are sold under short, appealing names such as Adenergy and Lean Stack, alongside impressive before-and-after photographs, or under long, pseudoscientific names like Vaso XP Xtreme Vasodilator and Xenadrine-NRG that are accompanied by complex molecular diagrams. An advertisement for Aftermath, for example, promises to help "swell your muscles to grotesque size" and eliminate the chances of "dooming yourself to girly man status."[20]

A prominent example of a dietary supplement used for performance-enhancing purposes is **androstenedione**. Technically, androstenedione is not an anabolic steroid because it is not based on the specific structure of testosterone itself. Nonetheless, it is testosterone related because it is a naturally occurring metabolic precursor to testosterone. In other words, the body converts androstenedione to testosterone via the action of specific enzymes in the liver. At the recommended daily dose of 300 milligram, androstenedione has been found to increase testosterone levels by an average of 34 percent above normal. Despite the increase in testosterone, however, no change in body composition or strength is observed when its effect is compared to that of placebo controls. There is no evidence that androstenedione promotes muscle protein synthesis at these dosage levels.[21]

Androstenedione rose to prominence in the late 1990s when it became public that St. Louis Cardinals baseball player Mark McGwire had been taking the supplement during his phenomenal 1998 hitting season (70 home runs, far eclipsing the historic record set by Babe Ruth in 1927). A storm of controversy ensued, with some commentators suggesting that McGwire's record be disallowed because of his androstenedione use. Although it had been banned by the National Football League and other professional and amateur sports organizations, androstenedione had not yet been banned in MLB at that time, so McGwire's use of it was not illegal. The publicity surrounding McGwire's use of androstenedione and its easy availability were blamed for a 30-percent increase among eighth-grade boys and a 75-percent increase among tenth-grade boys in the use of anabolic steroids from 1998 to 2000.

In 2005, the FDA banned the over-the-counter sale of androstenedione (Andro) and other testosterone precursors. By this time, the Anabolic Steroid Control Act of 2004 had expanded the Schedule III of controlled substances to include androstenedione and other testosterone precursors, along with anabolic steroids themselves. In early 2010, it was disclosed that androstenedione had not been the only performance-enhancing drug in McGwire's life. He admitted what had been suspected for some time: that during the 1990s he had used anabolic steroids, as well. McGwire has denied that his home-run record-breaking achievements could be attributed to steroid use, but it will never be known whether the performance-enhancing drugs he took did indeed enhance his performance.[22]

---

human growth hormone (hGH): A naturally occurring hormone promoting growth, particularly in the long bones of the body.

acromegaly (A-kroh-MEG-ah-lee): A condition resulting in structural abnormalities of the head, hands, and feet, as well as damage to internal organs.

androstenedione (AN-dro-steen-DYE-own): A dietary supplement, acting as a metabolic precursor to testosterone and used as an ergogenic agent.

Another dietary supplement marketed as a performance-enhancing agent is **creatine** (brand names: Creatine Fuel, Muscle Power, and many other products), a nonprotein amino acid synthesized in the kidney, liver, and pancreas from L-arginine, glycine, and L-methionine. Ingestion of creatine has been found to enhance the retention of water by muscle cells, causing them to expand in size. One hypothesis is that water retention might stimulate protein synthesis and increase muscle mass as a result, but there is no evidence from controlled studies that this is the case. Although creatine appears to enhance performance in repetitive bouts of high-intensity cycling and sprints, the weight gain experienced by creatine users makes it undesirable for runners or swimmers. Short-term use of creatine has been found to produce muscle cramping, and its long-term adverse effects have not been fully explored.[23]

Stimulant Medications

In the nineteenth century, world-class athletes experimented with stimulants of all kinds in attempts to achieve some level of performance enhancement in their sport through sheer elevation of central nervous activity. More than a century later, stimulants have continued to be an attractive option, particularly in baseball.

Amphetamines were officially banned from MLB in 2005. Before that time, amphetamine use was a likely choice for baseball players to stay focused and ward off fatigue during a grueling and lengthy competitive season. A professional baseball team psychiatrist testified in congressional hearings in 2008 that amphetamines "were the real performance-enhancing drugs that people should always have been worried about."

It is therefore not surprising that since 2005, some players have attempted to circumvent the amphetamine ban by taking Adderall (see Chapter 10), a medication for the treatment of attention-deficit/hyperactivity disorder (ADHD). In 2007, 103 therapeutic-use exemptions for ADHD were approved for MLB players—a suspiciously high number considering that only 28 players received such approval in 2006. Whether these exemptions reflected a fourfold increase in the incidence of ADHD symptoms over a single year or an effort to benefit from the performance-enhancing effects of stimulant drugs, without violating the amphetamine ban, continues to be a matter of concern to MLB management as well as baseball fans. From 2007 to 2013, the number of ADHD exemptions for Adderall use was steady at about 110 cases each year. The number of ADHD cases represented about 9 percent of the MLB player community, more than twice the national prevalence rate for ADHD (4 percent) among adults in the general population (Drugs... in Focus on this page).[24]

> **creatine (CREE-ah-teen):** A dietary supplement available for ergogenic uses.

Drugs... in Focus

ADHD/ADD Exemption Requirements for the Use of Adderall in Sports

The following requirements are necessary as of 2013 to be exempt from the ban on Adderall use in competitive sports:

- **National Football League (NFL):** A physician must fill out an exhaustive diagnostic form documenting the presence of lifelong impairments, and childhood history must be confirmed by a physician or health-care provider who treated the player as a child. An independent expert in ADHD/ADD is required to confirm the diagnosis. Exemptions must be renewed each year.
- **Major League Baseball (MLB):** A diagnosis of ADHD or ADD must be made by an MLB-certified clinician. If a diagnosis is not made, the case is referred to the MLB Expert Panel on ADHD/ADD, which can request additional information or tests before issuing the exemption.
- **National Basketball Association (NBA):** Players can apply for an exemption with the medical director of the NBA Anti-Drug Program.

- **National Hockey League (NHL):** A player must apply to the NHL Program Committee for a review of the application and approval to grant an exemption. Applications must be renewed annually.
- **National Collegiate Athletic Association (NCAA):** The student-athlete must show proof of an earlier ADHD/ADD diagnosis and course of treatment, or undergo an assessment through the university in order to receive an exemption. The athletic administration maintains the player's record in the event of a positive drug test.
- **United States Anti-Doping Agency/Olympic Sports:** The athlete's physician must submit a sport-specific application and provide supporting documentation of ADHD or ADD. Submissions are received by organizers of the event in which the athlete is preparing to compete.

Source: Swieca, C. (2013, September 10). NFL, other leagues deal with players' use of amphetamine Adderall. *Denver Post.* Accessed from: *http://denverpost.com/.*

Drug Testing in the Workplace

Drug testing in the workplace serves a number of purposes in today's world of business. For those industries with a direct impact on the public, drug testing serves as a protective measure, instilling consumer confidence that employees are working in a safe environment. For organizations in general, drug testing is viewed as a way of deterring current employees from abusing alcohol and other drugs and to prevent the hiring of new employees who use illicit drugs. Where applicable, organizations need to comply with federal, state, and local regulations, as well as receive benefits from Workers' Compensation Prevention Premium Discount programs.

Drug testing in an organization may be required under five basic circumstances:

- *Preemployment screening.* Preemployment screening is the most common circumstance for the occurrence of drug testing in organizations. Typically, drug testing can take place after a conditional offer of employment has been made. Applicants agree to be tested as a condition of employment and are not hired if they fail to produce a negative test result. Some states restrict this practice and since the Americans with Disabilities Act of 1990, organizations are prohibited from conducting preemployment testing for alcohol use.

- *Reasonable suspicion.* Drug testing can be required if there is reasonable suspicion that an employee has shown observable signs or symptoms that suggest drug use or some violation of drug-free workplace policies. Substantive documentation is needed before drug testing is authorized.

- *Post-accident.* Drug testing maybe required following accidental property damage or personal injury to help determine whether drugs and/or alcohol were a factor. Objective criteria must be used to trigger a test under these circumstances. Some employers expand the trigger for drug testing to include incidents even if an accident or injury was averted, in which case the term "post-incident" is used.

- *Return-to-duty.* Drug testing may be required as a one-time announced test when any employee who has tested positive has completed treatment for substance abuse and is ready to return to the workplace. Some employees use this category to include any employee who has been absent for an extended period of time.

- *Random.* Random testing is performed on an unannounced, unpredictable basis on employees, with selection being computer generated to ensure that each employee has an equal chance of being selected at any point in time. Because no advance notice is made, this practice is considered to serve as a deterrent. If a notice of the scheduled test is made in advance and uniformly administered (such as on annual basis), such practices are referred to as *periodic testing*. The disadvantage, however, is that employees can prepare for testing by stopping their drug use several days beforehand in order to receive a negative test result.

A typical notification of drug testing policies for employees in businesses designated as a drug free workplace.

Credit: Chuck Rausin/Shutterstock

The History of Drug Testing in the Workplace

As discussed in Chapter 14, the 1988 Drug-Free Workplace Act required that all companies and businesses receiving any U.S. federal contracts or grants provide a drug-free workplace and specifically to establish employee assistance programs (EAPs) in order to identify and counsel workers who have personal problems associated with substance abuse or dependence and to provide referrals to community agencies where these individuals can get further help. In addition, organizations must initiate a comprehensive and continuing program of drug education and awareness. Employees must also be notified that the distribution, possession, or unauthorized use of controlled substances is prohibited in that workplace and that action will be taken against any employee who violates these rules. Supervisors are advised to be especially alert to changes in a worker that might signal early or progressive stages in the abuse of alcohol and/or other drugs. These signals include chronic absenteeism, a sudden change in physical appearance or behavior, spasmodic work pace, unexpectedly lower quantity or quality of work, partial or unexplained absences, a pattern of excuse making or lying, the avoidance of supervisors or coworkers, and on-the-job accidents or lost time from such accidents. As mentioned above, accidents or incidents related to possible drug use as well as long-term worker absence are one of the five circumstances under which drug testing may be conducted.

By executive order of President Reagan in 1986, all federal employees involved in "law enforcement, national security, the protection of life and property, public health or safety, or other functions requiring a high degree of public trust" are subject to mandatory drug testing. Most state and local law enforcement officers and emergency service providers are also required to undergo drug testing. While there is no current federal requirement for non-federal "first responders," it is common for mandatory drug testing to be required in these instances as well. About three out of four U.S. companies surveyed in 2011 reported that they conducted some form of preemployment drug testing. In 84 percent of cases in which drug testing was carried out, urine tests were employed. A majority of companies with drug-testing programs reported some perceived benefits in reduced absenteeism, workers' compensation claims, and increased worker productivity or performance.[25]

Nongovernmental organizations have since been encouraged (but not required) by the Drug-Free Workplace Act of 1988 to establish EAP services as well. Thus, though they are not technically required to do so, steadily increasing numbers of American businesses have set up EAPs and are becoming committed to treatment as well as prevention. Traditionally, the emphasis in EAPs, as well as in union-supported member assistance programs (MAPs), has been on problems resulting from alcohol abuse; this is understandable, given that alcohol abuse represents such a large proportion of substance abuse in general (Chapter 13). In recent years, EAPs and MAPs have expanded their services to focus on psychological problems that do not necessarily concern substance abuse.

Drug Testing and Concerns about Individual Rights

Although it is not difficult to understand the rationale for drug testing in the workplace, the procedure has raised a number of important questions regarding individual rights. Does taking a urine sample violate a person's freedom from "unreasonable search and seizure" as guaranteed by the Fourth Amendment to the U.S. Constitution? It turns out that if the government requires it, the decision rests on the question of whether there is reasonable or unreasonable cause for the drug testing to occur. In cases in which a threat to public safety is involved, the cause has been ruled reasonable. However, if a private business requires it, the legal rights of employees are somewhat murky. An employee typically accepts his or her job offer with the assumption and agreement that periodic monitoring of drug use will take place, but whether this understanding is a form of implied coercion is an open question.

If a worker loses his or her job as a result of testing positive in a drug test, has there been a violation of that individual's right to "due process" as guaranteed by the Fifth Amendment? The courts have ruled that this right would be violated only if the method of drug screening were unreliable, if the analysis and reporting were carried out in an unreliable manner, or if it could not be shown that the presence of any one of the screened substances was related to job impairment. In general, screening methods are not perfectly reliable, the handling of drug tests is not perfectly controlled, and the relationship between drug use and a decline in job performance is not perfectly clear. Nonetheless, for the most part, drug tests have been judged to have met reasonable standards, and the practice has been allowed. The bottom line is that drug testing, despite its obvious infringements on individual privacy, has become a fact of life in corporate America.[26]

Yet, despite the increasing acceptance of drug testing as a tool for drug-abuse prevention or deterrence in the workplace, there will always be questions about the impact on workers themselves. For example, the possibility of false positives and false negatives can have unfortunate consequences, beyond the potential consequences of a competitive athlete. Consider this possible preemployment screening scenario:

> *Suppose that the EMIT test were 100 percent effective in spotting drug users (it is not) and that it has a false-positive rate of 3 percent (which is not unreasonable). In a group of 100 prospective employees, one person has recently taken an illegal drug. Since the test is 100 percent effective, that person will be caught, but three other people (the 3 percent false-positive rate) will also. Therefore, 75 percent of those who fail the test are innocent parties.*[27]

Another problem is that companies are not required to follow up a positive EIA test result with a more sensitive method, such as one using the GC/MS analysis. Some companies allow for retesting in general, but most do not.

Summary

The Forensics of Drug Testing

- The two major urinalysis methods for drug testing are the enzyme immunoassay (EIA) technique and a procedure combining gas chromatography and mass spectrometry (GC/MS). In both methods, the collected urine is divided into two samples prior to being sent off to the laboratory so that if the analysis of one sample yields a positive outcome, the analysis can be repeated on the other sample.

- The accuracy in a drug test is measured in terms of sensitivity and specificity. Sensitivity indicates the ability of the test to correctly report the *presence* of drugs. Specificity indicates the ability of the test to correctly report the *absence* of drugs. Ideally, a test for screening the presences of a drug or drug metabolite should have a high level of sensitivity and a high level of specificity.

The History of Performance-Enhancing Drugs in Sports

- In the 1960s, the introduction of performance-enhancing (ergogenic) drugs, particularly anabolic steroids, became a pervasive feature of athletic competition in the Olympic Games. Despite rigorous controls imposed by the World Anti-Doping Association, established in 2009, scandals continued to be reported, as athletes and their trainers turn to increasing sophisticated schemes to circumvent anti-doping regulations.

- In the 1990s, anabolic steroids and other performance-enhancing drugs were the basis for scandals in Major League Baseball. Suspension penalties for violations have been established in baseball and other sports.

Present-Day Federal Regulations

- Since 1990, anabolic steroids have been classified as Schedule III controlled substances, making their possession and sale without a specific medical prescription illegal. In 2004, steroid precursors were added to the category of Schedule III controlled substances. These drugs are now distributed through illicit black-market channels.

Patterns of Steroid Abuse

- In typical patterns of steroid abuse, multiple steroids are administered, usually at dosage levels that far exceed recommended levels when used for medical purposes.
- Hazards associated with steroid abuse include serious physiological changes that result from an elevation in testosterone, as well as liver tumors and cardiovascular abnormalities. Psychological changes include mood swings and increased aggressiveness among male steroid abusers, a phenomenon often referred to as "'roid rage."
- Significant signs and symptoms of dependence can occur, including a phenomenon called muscle dysmorphia, in which an individual perceives his or her body as exceedingly small despite an increase in musculature. Placebo effects are commonly observed.

Testing for other Performance-Enhancing Drugs

- Other performance-enhancing drugs used in athletic competitions include human growth hormone (hGH) and dietary supplements such as androstenedione and creatine.

Stimulant medications such as Adderall have also been used on a nonmedical basis for performance-enhancing purposes.

Drug Testing in the Workplace

- Drug testing in an organization may be required under five basic circumstances: preemployment screening, reasonable suspicion of drug use or violation of drug-free workplace policies, post-accident or post-incident occasions following a possible drug-related accident or injury, return-to-duty occasions for employees who had completed substance abuse treatment or been absent for an extended period of time, and random (unscheduled) testing.
- The 1988 Drug-Free Workplace Act requires that all companies and businesses receiving any U.S. federal contracts or grants provide a drug-free workplace and specifically to establish employee assistance programs (EAPs) in order to identify and counsel workers who have personal problems associated with substance abuse and to provide referrals to community agencies where these individuals can get further help. Member assistance programs (MAPs) are equivalent programs sponsored by labor unions.
- By executive order of President Reagan in 1986, all federal employees involved in "law enforcement, national security, the protection of life and property, public health or safety, or other functions requiring a high degree of public trust" are subject to mandatory drug testing. Most state and local law enforcement officers and emergency service providers are also required to undergo drug testing. Mandatory drug testing for non-federal "first responders" is typically required as well.
- Despite the increasing acceptance of drug testing as a tool for drug-abuse prevention or deterrence in the workplace, there are questions of the possible adverse consequences when drug tests with imperfect sensitivity and specificity are conducted.

Key Terms

acromegaly, p. 379
adrenocortical steroids, p. 372
anabolic, p. 372
anabolic-androgenic steroids, p. 372
anabolic steroids, p. 372

androgenic, p. 372
androstenedione, p. 379
creatine, p. 380
enzyme immunoassay (EIA), p. 367

enzyme multiplied immunoassay technique (EMIT), p. 367
ergogenic, p. 371
gas chromatography/mass spectrometry (GC/MS), p. 367

human growth hormone (hGH), p. 379
muscle dysmorphia, p. 377

Review Questions

1. Describe and distinguish between the techniques of enzyme immunoassay (EIA) and gas chromatography/mass spectrometry (GC/MS) in drug testing.
2. Define the terms "sensitivity" and "specificity" in drug testing. What unforeseen consequences might there be with respect to drug testing in preemployment screening?
3. Discuss the major events of the Olympic Games with respect to performance-enhancing drug use prior to the creation of the World Anti-Doping Agency (WADA). What effects has the WADA had on athletic competition in the Olympic Games?

4. Explain the terms "stacking," "shotgunning," "cycling," and "pyramiding" as practices involved in anabolic steroid abuse.
5. Explain how the phenomenon of muscle dysmorphia poses a great challenge in treating anabolic steroid abuse.
6. Discuss the five major circumstances under which drug testing in the workplace are typically conducted. Which of the circumstances raises questions regarding an employee's individual rights?

Critical Thinking: What Would You Do?

You are a voting member of the Baseball Hall of Fame, and you are about to cast your vote for the induction of an MLB player (XYZ). All the usual eligibility requirements have been met, but there is documented evidence of androstenedione use during the years in which his record is being considered. While androstenedione is currently a banned substance in the MLB, androstenedione was not a banned substance in the years in question nor was it a Schedule III controlled substance at that time. Some of your colleagues oppose his election into the Hall of Fame. What would you do?

Endnotes

1. A fictional account of an interview, based on historic events in the history of major league baseball.
2. Wadler, G. I.; and Hainline, B. (1989). *Drugs and the athlete.* Philadelphia: F. A. Davis, pp. 201–202.
3. Hatton, C. K. (2007). Beyond sports-doping headlines: The science of laboratory tests for performance-enhancing drugs. *Pediatric Clinics of North America, 54,* 713–733. Meer, *Drugs and sports,* pp. 92–95.
4. Alternate specimen testing policies may be set soon (2005, September). *Occupational Health and Safety,* p. 26. Cone, E. J.; Presley, L.; Lehrer, M.; Seiter, W.; Smith, M.; et al. (2002). Oral fluid testing for drugs of abuse: Positive prevalence rates by Intercept immunoassay screening and GC-MS-MS confirmation and suggested cutoff concentrations. *Journal of Analytical Toxicology, 26,* 540–546.
5. Catlin, D.; Wright, J.; Pope, H.; and Liggett, M. (1993). Assessing the threat of anabolic steroids: Sportsmedicine update. *The Physician and Sportsmedicine, 21,* 37–44.
6. Rosenberg, R. (2000, October 12). Citgo to use Avitar drug tests, job applicants to undergo new saliva-based exam. *Boston Globe,* p. C3.
7. Brookman, R. R. (2008). Unintended consequences of drug and alcohol testing in student athletes. *AAP (American Academy of Pediatrics) Grand Rounds, 19,* 15–16. Yamaguchi, R.; Johnston, L. D.; and O'Malley, P. M. (2003). Relationship between student illicit drug use and school drug-testing policies. *Journal of School Health, 73,* 159–164.
8. Dolan, E. F. (1986). *Drugs in sports* (rev. ed.). New York: Franklin Watts, pp. 17–18. Meer, Jeff (1987). *Drugs and sports.* New York: Chelsea House, pp. 2, 61–75. Taylor, W. N. (1991). *Macho medicine: The history of the anabolic steroid epidemic.* Jefferson, NC: McFarland and Co., pp. 3–16. Wadler, G. I.; and Hainline, B. (1989). *Drugs and the athlete.* Philadelphia: F. A. Davis, pp. 3–17.
9. Bhasin, S.; Storer, T. W.; Berman, N.; Callegari, C.; Clevenger, B.; et al. (1996). The effects of supraphysiologic doses of testosterone on muscle size and strength in normal men. *New England Journal of Medicine, 335,* 1–7. Lombardo, J. (1993). The efficacy and mechanisms of action of anabolic steroids. In C. E. Yesalis (Ed.), *Anabolic steroids in sport and exercise.* Champaign, IL: Human Kinetics Publishers, p. 100.
10. Scott, J. (1971, October 17). It's not how you play the game, but what pill you take. *New York Times Magazine,* p. 41.
11. Maimon, A. (2000, February 6). Doping's sad toll: One athlete's tale from East Germany. *The New York Times,* pp. A1, A6. Yesalis, C. E.; Courson, S. P.; and Wright, J. (1993). History of anabolic steroid use in sport and exercise. In C. E. Yesalis (Ed.), *Anabolic steroids,* pp. 1–33.
12. Longman, J. (2003, October 24). Steroid is reportedly found in top runner's urine test. *The New York Times,* p. D2. Macur J. (2008, October 9). Beijing Games blood samples to be retested for new drug. *The New York Times,* pp. B17, B20. Vecsey, G. (2002, March 1). More curious material in skiing's closet. *The New York Times,* pp. D1, D4. World Anti-Doping Agency (2013, September 11). *The 2014 Prohibited List, International Standard, effective 1 January 2014.* Montreal: World Anti-Doping Agency. World Anti-Doping Agency (2012, January). *International Standard for Testing.* Montreal: World Anti-Doping Agency.
13. Macur, J. (2012, October 11). Details of doping scheme paint Armstrong as leader. *The New York Times,* pp. A1, B15. Macur, J. (2013, January 5). In reversal, Armstrong is said to weigh admitting drug use. *The New York Times,* pp. A1, D4. Pania, T. (2018, February 25). Russian athletes won't get to march behind their flag. *The New York Times,* p. SP4. Ruiz, R. R. (2018, January 20). I.O.C. clears nearly 400 Russians to compete in Winter Games. *The New York Times,* p. D1, D3. Ruiz, R. R. and Panja, T. (2017, December 6). Russia banned from Winter Olympics by I.O.C. *The New York Times,* p. A1.
14. Curry, J. (2005, November 16). Baseball backs stiffer penalties for steroid use. *The New York Times,* pp. A1, D2. Eder, S. (2014, January 12). Rodriguez out for all of 2014, arbitrator says. *The New York Times,* pp. A1, SP7. Fainaru-Wada, M.; and Williams, L. (2006). *Game of shadows: Barry Bonds, Balco and the steroids scandal that rocked professional sports.* New York: Gotham Books. Kepner, T. (2009, July 31). A stain keeps spreading. *The New York Times,* pp. B10, B11. Schmidt, M. S.; and Macur, J. (2010, August 30). Clemens enters not guilty plea. *The New York Times,* p. B14. Vecsey, G. (2008, January 16). Spring training and the syringe generation. *The New York Times,* pp. D1, D3. Quotation of Alex Rodriguez in Waldstein, D. (2015, February 18). Exchanging sword for pen, Rodriguez apologizes to Yankees and fans. *The New York Times,* p. B11.
15. National Institute on Drug Abuse (2000, April). Anabolic steroids. *Research report series.* Rockvile, MD: National Institute on Drug Abuse. Collins, R. (2003, January 5). Federal and state steroid laws. Posted on the Web site of Collins, McDonald, and Gann, P. C., Attorneys-at-law, Nassau County and New York, NY, www.steroidlaw.com.
16. Pope, H. G.; Gruber, A. J.; Choi, P.; Olivardia, R.; and Phillips, K. A. (1997). Muscle dysmorphia: An underrecognized form of body dysmorphic disorder. *Psychosomatics, 38,* 548–557. Wroblewska, A.M. (1997). Androgenic-anabolic steroids and body dysmorphia in young men. *Journal of Psychosomatic Research, 42,* 225–234.

17. American Psychiatric Association (2013). *Diagnostic and statistical manual of mental disorders* (5th ed.). Washington, D.C.: American Psychiatric Publishing, pp. 483–490. Beel, A.; Maycock, B.; and McLean, N. (1998). Current perspectives on anabolic steroids. *Drug and Alcohol Review, 17,* 87–103. DiPaolo, M.; Agozzino, M.; Toni, C.; Luciani, A. B; et al. (2005). Sudden anabolic steroid abuse–related death in athletes. *International Journal of Cardiology, 114,* 114–117. Hartgens, F.; and Kuipers, H. (2004). Effects of androgenic-anabolic steroids in athletes. *Sports Medicine, 34,* 513–554. Monaghan, L. F. (2000). *Bodybuilding, drugs, and risk.* New York: Routledge. Neri, M.; Bello, S.; Bonsignore, A.; Cantatore, S.; Riezzo, I. et al. (2011). Anabolic androgenic steroids and liver toxicity. *Mini Reviews in Medicinal Chemistry, 11,* 430–437. Perry, P. J.; Lund, B. C.; Deninger, M. J.; Kutscher, E. C.; and Schneider, J. (2005). Anabolic-steroid use in weightlifters and bodybuilders: An Internet survey of drug utilization. *Clinical Journal of Sport Medicine, 15,* 326–330. Stocker, S. (2000). Study provides additional evidence that high steroid doses elicit psychiatric symptoms in some men. *NIDA Notes, 15*(4), 8–9. Straus, R. H.; and Yesalis, C. E. (1993). Additional effects of anabolic steroids in women. In C. E. Yesalis (ed.) *Anabolic steroids in sport and exercise.* Champaign, IL: Human Kinetics Publishers, pp. 151–160. Trenton, A. J.; and Currier, G. W. (2005). Behavioral manifestations of anabolic steroid use. *CNS Drugs, 19,* 571–595.

18. Quotation of Alex Rodriguez in Kepner, T. (2009, February 17). As team looks on, Rodriguez details his use of steroids, *The New York Times,* p. B12.

19. Interlandi, J. (2008, February 25). Myth meets science. *Newsweek,* p. 48. Juhn, M. S. (2003). Popular sports supplements and ergogenic aids. *Sports Medicine, 33,* 921–939. Liu, H.; Bravata, D. M.; Olkin, I.; Friedlander, A.; et al. (2008). Systematic review: The effects of growth hormone on athletic performance. *Annals of Internal Medicine, 148,* 747–748. Macur, J. (2008, June). Who has the horse tranquilizers? *Play,* p. 18. Macur, J. (2008, October 9). Olympic blood samples to be retested. *The New York Times,* p. B17. Macur, J. (2010, February 28). No doping scandals at Games, but time will tell. *The New York Times,* Sports p. 9.

20. Tuller, D. (2005, January 18). For sale: "muscles" in a bottle. *The New York Times,* pp. F5, F10. Quotation on p. F5.

21. Juhn, Popular sports supplements and ergogenic aids. Leder, B. Z.; Longcope, C.; Catlin, D. H.; Ahrens, B.; and Schoenfeld, J. S. (2000). Oral androstenedione administration and serum testosterone concentrations in young men. *Journal of the American Medical Association, 283,* 779–782.

22. Denham, B. E. (2006). The Anabolic Steroid Control Act of 2004: A study in the political economy of drug policy. *Journal of Health and Social Policy, 22,* 51–78. Kepner, McGwire admits steroid use in 1990s, his years of magic. Mravic, M. (2000, February 21). Ban it, bud. *Sports Illustrated,* pp. 24, 26.

23. Buford, T. W.; Kreider, R. B.; Stout, J. R.; et al. (2007). International Society of Sports Nutrition position stand: Creatine supplementation and exercise. *Journal of the International Society of Sports Nutrition, 4,* 6. Freeman, M. (2003, October 21). Scientist fears athletes are using unsafe drugs: Discovery of an undetected steroid confirms suspicions. *New York Times,* p. D2. Gregory, A. J. M.; and Fitch, R. W. (2007). Sports medicine: Performance-enhancing drugs. *Pediatric Clinics of North America, 54,* 797–806.

24. Schmidt, M. S. (2008, January 16). Baseball is challenged on rise in stimulant use. *The New York Times,* pp. A1, A16. Quotation on page A16. Schmidt, M. S. (2009, January 10). Baseball officials give report on amphetamine use among players. *The New York Times,* p. D5. Swieca, C. (2013, September 10). NFL, other leagues deal with players' use of amphetamine Adderall. *Denver Post.* Accessed from: *http://www.denverpost.com/broncos/ci_24055922/.*

25. American Management Association (2004). *AMA 2004 workplace testing survey: Medical testing.* New York: American Management Association, p. 3. Fortner, N. A.; Martin, D. M.; Esen, S. E.; and Shelton, L. (2011). Employee drug testing: Study shows improved productivity and attendance and decreased workers' compensation and turnover. *Journal of Global Drug Policy, and Practice, 5,* 6, 18. Substance Abuse and Mental Health Services Administration (2008, March 15). *Making your workplace drug-free: A kit for employers.* Rockville, MD: Substance Abuse and Mental Health Services Administration.

26. Comerford, A. W. (1999). Work dysfunction and addiction. *Journal of Substance Abuse Treatment, 16,* 247–253. Moeller, K. E.; Kissack, J. C.; Atayee, R. S.; and Lee, K. C. (2016). Clinical interpretation of urine drug tests: What clinicians need to know about urine drug screens. *Mayo Clinic Proceedings, 92,* 774–796. Normand, J.; Lempert, R.; and O'Brien, C. (Eds.) (1994). *Under the influence? Drugs and the American work force.* Washington, D.C.: National Academy Press.

27. Avis, H. (1996). *Drugs and life* (3rd ed.). Dubuque, IA: Brown and Benchmark. Quotation on, p. 256.

INDEX

Note: Boldface indicates key terms and the pages where they are defined.

AA (Alcoholics Anonymous), 205, **303,** 303–4
Absorption, 139
   through gastrointestinal tract, 137–8
   through skin or membranes, 139
Abstinence, 293
Acamprosate, 303
Acetaldehyde dehydrogenase, 302
Acetaminophen, 187, 188, 284
Acetic acid, 302
Acetic anhydride, 101
Acetylcholine, 148
Acetylsalicylic acid (ASA), 173
Acid blotters, 253
Acne, steroid use and, 378
Acquired immuno-deficiency syndrome. *See*
   AIDS (acquired immuno-deficiency
   syndrome)
Acromegaly, 379
Action stage of change, **330**
Actiq (fentanyl), 187
Active placebo, 143
Acullicadores, 196
Acute toxicity, 8, 8, 12
ADAM II (Arrestee Drug Abuse Monitoring
   Program), 68–9
Adaptations to anomie, 154
Adderall, 212, 213
Addiction, brain effects of, 149. *See also*
   Dependence
Additive effect, 140
Adenergy, 379
ADHD. *See* Attention-deficit hyperactivity
   disorder (ADHD)
ADHD/ADD, Adderall in sports, 380
Adhesiveness, platelet, 350
Adjudication, 87
Administration
   routes of, 137–9
   timing of, 140
Adolescents, drug use among
   alcohol, 281
   crime and, 71
   marijuana, 231, 234
   peers and, 72, 156
   reasons for, 158–9
   smoking, 352–3
   social bonds and, 156
   steroids, 377
Adopted children, alcoholism among, 296
Adrenocortical steroids, 372
Advertising for tobacco, 342, 344, 355
Advil (ibuprofen), 368
Affective education, 318, 318
Affordable Care Act (ACA), 332
Afghanistan, heroin from, 26, 27
African Americans
   acute alcohol intoxication, 283
   cocaine propaganda, 45
   cocaine use, 200
   drug abuse prevention approaches
     among, 316
   and ethnicity association of cocaine
     with, 45
   mentholated cigarettes smoked by, 344
   nicotine metabolism in, 344
   racial profiling and, 128
Aggression. *See* Crime; Violence

AIDS (acquired immuno-deficiency syndrome),
   185, 236
   spread through injections, 138
Air Branch, U.S. Customs, 104
Al-Anon, 303
Alateen, 303
Alcohol, 4, 6, 275–304
   acute behavioral effects of, 285–9
   acute physiological effects of, 282–5
   barbiturates mixed with, 263–4
   benzodiazepines combined with, 265
   biotransformation rate of, 139
   black-market, during Prohibition, 289
   blood levels of, 277, 285
   BluntGen subculture and use of, 72
   in brain, effects of, 277, 299–300
   cardiovascular effects, 299
   chronic physiological effects of, 298–301
   cocaine and, 197
   in college, 15, 281, 325
   cross-tolerance and, 142
   deaths from, 11, 50
   demographics of consumption, 293
   detection periods for, 370
   diuretic effects of, 283
   driving while under the influence of, 53, 285
   elimination of, 283
   emergency signs and procedures for
     intoxication, 283
   gender and, 143
   hangovers from, 284–5
   health benefits of, 291–2
   heat loss and, 283
   interactions with other drugs, 10, 284
   legality of, 6
   lethal dosage of, 282
   Life Skills Training program to combat,
     319–20
   as men's recreational drug in 1800s, 172
   methadone-maintenance clients' abuse of, 185
   minimum drinking age, 291
   neurochemical system in brain and, 148–9
   neurotransmitters and effects of, 149–50
   patterns of consumption, 278–9
   pharmacological violence and, 65
   pharmacology of, 277–80
   pregnancy and consumption of, 284, 300
   Prohibition Era in America, 48
   regulation of, 45–50
   restricted access, regulation by, 289
   security and spectator sports, 288
   sexual desire and performance, 285–6
   sleep patterns and, 283
   Temperance Movement, 48–9
   toxic reactions to, 282–3
   traffic fatalities, regulation to reduce, 290
   withdrawal from, 144, 266, 298–9
Alcohol, Drug Abuse, and Mental Health
   Administration Reorganization Act (1992), 354
Alcohol abuse
   cancer from, 299
   cardiovascular problems from, 299
   dementia, 299
   effects of chronic, 298–301
   fetal alcohol syndrome (FAS) from, 300
   liver disease from, 299
   patterns of, 297–8
   regulation of, 289–90
   tolerance to and withdrawal from, 181–2
   Wernicke-Korsakoff's syndrome from, 300

Alcohol consumption
   at risk groups, 280–2
   offender population, 282
   underage drinkers, 281–2
Alcohol misuse, consequences of, 285–9
AlcoholEdu, 326
AlcoholEdu for Sanctions, 326
Alcoholic beverages
   alcohol equivalencies of, 278
   sources of, 276
Alcoholic cirrhosis, 298, 298–304
Alcoholic dementia, 299, 299–300
Alcoholic hepatitis, 298
Alcoholics
   benzodiazepine use, 265
   children of (COAs), 296
   types of, 297
Alcoholics Anonymous (**AA**), **131,** 131–2, 205
Alcoholism, 293, 293
   biologically based treatments of, 302–3
   demographics of, 293
   emotional problems and, 295
   family dynamics, 296–7
   genetics of, 147–8
   physical problems associated with, 295
   preoccupation with drinking and, 293
   SMART Recovery for, 304
   vocational, social, family dynamics of, 295
Alcohol use disorder, 301, **301**
Alcohol withdrawal syndrome, 298
Aldactone, 284
Ale, 277
Alpert, Richard, 252
Alprazolam, 266
Al Qaeda in the Lands of the Islamic Maghreb
   (AQIM), 38
Alternative-behavior programming, 320
Alternative maintenance programs, 185
Altria, 346
Alzheimer's disease, drug-induced dementia
   versus, 266
Amado Carrillo-Fuentes Organization
   (ACFO), 34
Amanita muscaria, 249, 250, **260,** 260
Ambien (zolpidem), 267
American Bar Association, 94
American Cancer Society, 351
American Medical Association, 45, 301
American Psychiatric Association, 7, 145, 301
American Temperance Society, 48
Amitriptyline, 266
Ammonia as cigarette additive, 348
Amobarbital, 262, **262,** 263, 264
Amotivational syndrome, 231–2, **231**
Amphetamine psychosis, 208
Amphetamines, 195–6, 205–7, **208**
   acute and chronic effects of, 207–8
   brain and, 208
   detection periods for, 370
   forms of, 207
   heroin combined with, street names for, 181
   history of, 205–6
   medications and stimulants, 212
   molecular structure of, 208
   neurochemical system in brain and, 148
   patterns of abuse and treatment, 211
   in sports, 371, 376
   street names, 182
   withdrawal from, 211
Amytal (amobarbital), 262, 264

Cognitive restructuring, 152
Cognitive theories, 151, 151–2
Cold medications
　detection periods for, 370
College students
　alcohol, 76, 281–2, 325
　amphetamines, 207
　drug abuse prevention, 325–6
　drug use among, 15. (See also Youth)
Collegiate sports, steroid use in, 374
Colombia, 55, 103, 104
　cocaine production in, 203
　cocaine trafficking, 30–2
　crop eradication in, 101
　heroin from, 181
　Medellin and Cali drug cartels, 31–2
　money laundering by traffickers in, 79
　opium and heroin from, 26, 28, 176
Columbus, Christopher, 340
Combat Methamphetamine Epidemic Act
　(2005), 54, 56, 102
Commitment (social bond), 155
Communication within family, dysfunctional,
　323–4
Communism, 50
Community-based corrections, 119
Community-based prevention, 320–2
　alternative-behavior programming, 320–1
　CASASTART, 322
Community residential center, 126
Comprehensive Crime Control Act of 1984, 53, 54
Comprehensive Drug Abuse Prevention and
　Control Act of 1970, 48, 51, 54, 89–90,
　112, 237
Comprehensive Methamphetamine Control Act
　(1996), 54, 55
Comprehensive Textbook of Psychiatry, 201
Compulsive behavior
　amphetamine abuse, 208
　economically compulsive crime, 76
　neurochemical system in brain and, 148, 150
Concerta, 212
Conditioned cues, 151, 205
Conditioned-learning effects, heroin abuse
　and, 182
Conditioned tolerance, 141–2
　heroin abuse and, 182–3
Conditioning, Pavlovian, 141, 151
Confabulation, 300
Confessions of an English Opium Eater
　(DeQuincey), 172
Confiscation Act of 1862, 112
Conformity
　adaptation to anomie, 154
　social bonds promoting, 155
Congeners, 285
Consent search, 110
Constipation, heroin abuse and, 180, 188
Constitution, U.S.
　Eighteenth Amendment, 49, 54
　Fourth Amendment, 382
　Twenty-first Amendment, 50, 54
Contemplation stage of change, **329**, 329–30
Contraceptives, smoking and, 352
Controlled buy, 107
Controlled Substance Analogue Act (1986), 176
Controlled substances
　federal trafficking penalties, 90
　schedules of, 57
　violation type and, 89
Controlled Substances Act. *See* Comprehensive
　Drug Abuse Prevention and Control Act
　of 1970
**COPD (chronic obstructive pulmonary
　disease), 350**, 350

Copenhagen (chewing tobacco), 355
Cordial, 277
Coronary heart disease (CHD), 291, **349**, 356
Correctional system
　cost of building and maintaining prisons, 53
　drug use among inmates, 68–9, 91
　philosophies of, 119–20
　principles of effective intervention, 120–2
　prison-based treatment programs, 123–4
Coughing
　narcotic drugs to treat, 187–8
Coumadin (warfarin), 284
Couriers, drug, 28
　"mules," 28, 103
Courts, drug, 127, 127
Crack cocaine (crack), 53, 202, **202**, 203
　dealing organizations, 77, 78
　economically compulsive crime and, 71–2
　federal penalties for, 91, 93
　freelance sale of, 76
　heroin mixed with, 183
　pharmacological violence and, 71
　street names, 210
　systemic violence and, 66, 203
　use among American youth, 55
Crackdown, 112
CrackGen subculture, 72
"Crank," 33
Creatine, 380
Creativity
　LSD and, 255
　marijuana and, 226
Crime, 63–80
　as cause of drug use, 75
　causes, 75
　crack cocaine and, 202
　deviant life-style and, 74
　drug-defined offenses, 64
　drug-related offenses, 65
　drug trafficking (*See* Drug trafficking)
　drug use and, 67–70
　drug use as cause of, 67, 75
　drug using lifestyle, 66–7
　economically compulsive, 65, 71–4
　heroin abuse and, 174, 182, 185
　illicit drug dealing, 75–6
　incarceration rates of drug offenders, 68
　methadone maintenance and reduction of, 185
　methamphetamine-related, 208
　money laundering, 79
　OxyContin abuse and, 188–9
　during Prohibition, 49
　psychopharmacological, 70–1
　statistics, 67
　systemic, 74–5
　violence and, 72
Criminal justice, drug trade and, 25
Criminal justice system, drugs and, 99–114. *See
　also* Drug laws
　community-based correctional strategy, 125–32
　community residential centers, 126–7
　community supervision, 130–2
　correctional strategies for, 122–5
　drug courts, 127–30
　drug-law violators in, 88–9
　interdiction, 103–5
　judicial events, phases of, 86
　mandatory minimum sentencing, 92–5, 317
　source control, 101–3
　specialty courts in, 128
　street-level drug-law enforcement, 106–12
Criminal Justice System, specialty courts in, 128
Criminal model of drug use and crime, 75
Criminal organizations, Prohibition and, 49. *See also*
　Drug cartels; Organized crime

Criminogenic needs, 121
"Criss-crossing," 183
Crohn's disease, 236
Crop eradication, 101, 101
Cross-tolerance, 142
　alcohol and, 212
　from benzodiazepines, 265
　buspirone, 267
　between LSD and psilocin, 256
Crystal meth (ice), 210
CSAP (Center for Substance Abuse Prevention), 313
Cuba, cocaine trafficking and organized crime
　from, 30
Customs and Border Protection (CBP), U.S., 17,
　103, 104
　interdiction by, 105
Cyanosis, 257
Cycling pattern of steroid abuse, 377

Dalmane (flurazepam), 266
DALYs. *See* Disability-adjusted life years statistic
　(DALYs)
D-amphetamine, 207, 207
Danazol, 372
Danocrine capsules (danazol), 272
DARE, 58, 322
Dark Web, policing the, 17
Darvocet-N (propoxyphene), 187
Darvon (propoxyphene), 185, 187, 370
Date-rape drugs, 265, 269
Datura stramonium, 250
Daytrana, 212
DCE. *See* Digital Currency Exchange (DCE)
DEA, 38, 51, 104
　anabolic steroids, 376
　asset forfeitures, 112
　interdiction by, 104–5
　MDMA, 259
　meth lab seizure, 55
　precursor chemical monitoring, 102
Death(s)
　from alcohol, 11, 277
　drug-related (1962-2007), 9
　lethal dose, 8–9
　from LSD, 253
　from tobacco, 349–50, 352
de Blasio, Bill, 110
Deca-Durabolin IM (nandrolone decanoate), 372
Decision making, training in, 319–20
Decriminalization, 237
　of marijuana, 237
Delatestryl IM (testosterone enantrate), 372
Delirium tremens (DTs), 298
Delta-9-tetrahydrocannabinol (THC), 222,
　227–8
Deltasone (prednisone), 284
Dementia
　alcoholic, 299–300
　drug-induced, 266
　moderate alcohol consumption and, 291–2
Demerol (meperidine), 187
　toxicity, 9
Dendrites, 148
Denial of alcoholism, 295
"Deodand" (forfeiture), 112
Dependence, 144–5. *See also* Physical
　dependence; Psychological dependence
　alcohol, 298
　on barbiturates, 263–4
　on benzodiazepines, 265
　on heroin, 144–5
　LSD and, 253
　on marijuana, 229–30
　on meprobamate, 265
　on nicotine, 348–9

Ibotenic acid, 249, 250
Ibuprofen, 368
Ice (crystal meth), **210**, 210
ICE. *See* Immigration and Customs Enforcement (ICE)
Ignition interlock device, 290–1
Illicit Drug Anti-Proliferation Act (2003), **56**, 56
Illicit drugs, 6, 56
   drug subcultures, 156–7
   emergencies related to, 11
   global business, 22
   use among adults aged 12 and older, 13–14
   use among eighth graders and tenth graders, 15
   use among youth, 15
   worldwide prevalence rates, 23
Illicit drug trade. *See* Drug trafficking
Illusionogenic drugs. *See* Hallucinogens
Immigrants
   Mexican, 256
   Prohibition and anti-immigrant sentiment, 48–9
Immigration and Customs Enforcement (ICE), 52, 104
Immune system, marijuana effects on, 231
Imodium, 188
Impactors, 320
Implied consent laws, 287
Inca civilization, 196
Incapacitation, 119
Incarceration, 86
Inderal (propanolol), 268
India, 171, 223
Individual differences in drug effects, 142–3
Infants, opium given to, 172
Infectious disease control, analogy to drug abuse prevention, 316
Inhalation, 138, 139
Inhalers
   amphetamine, 206
Injection, 138
Inmates. *See* Prisoners
Innocent VIII, Pope, 223
Innovation, as adaptation to anomie, 154
Inpatient treatment for cocaine, 204–5
In rem civil forfeitures, 113
Insomnia
   barbiturates to treat, 263–4
   benzodiazepine to treat, 266
   non-barbiturates to treat, 267
   nonbenzodiazepine drugs to treat, 267
Institute of Medicine, 236
Institutional corrections, 119
Instrumental use, 4, 5
Insulin, 137–8, 284
Intensification model of drug use and crime, 67
Intensive Outpatient Program (IOP), 132
Interactional circumstances, 74, 74–5
Intermediate sanctions, 125
Internal Revenue Service (IRS), 47, 63, 79, 174
International Association of Chiefs of Police, 106
International drug code for sport competitions, 373
International Monetary Fund, 102
International Narcotics Control Strategy Report on Money Laundering, 79
International Narcotics Trafficking Emergency Response by Detecting Incoming Contraband with Technology (INTERDICT) Act, 29
International Olympic Committee (IOC), 373
INTERDICT. *See* International Narcotics Trafficking Emergency Response by Detecting Incoming Contraband with Technology (INTERDICT) Act
Internet
   steroid suppliers on, 376–7

Intervention, levels of, 312–13. *See also* Prevention strategies
Intestinal spasm, 188
Intimate partner violence (IPV), 287
Intramuscular (i.m.) injections, 138
Intravenous (i.v.) injection, 138
   heroin, 183
Involvement (social bond), 156
Iran, heroin from, 26
IRS. *See* Internal Revenue Service (IRS)
ischemic stroke, 349
IRS. *See* Internal Revenue Service (IRS)
Israel smoking in, 358

Jackson, Michael, 9
Jamaica, marijuana in, 226
James I of England, King, 341
Japan, smoking in, 357, 358
Japanese Yakuza, 31
Jazz world, marijuana's popularity in, 223
Jerez, Rodrigo de, 341
Jimsonweed, 250
"Jitters," 298
Johnson, Bruce, 156, 157
Joint, 226. *See also* Marijuana
Jones, Ernest, 198, 356
Jones, Kenneth L., 300
Joplin, Janis, 9
Jungle, The (Sinclair), 45
Justice, Department of, 74, 239–40
"Just Say No" campaign, 53
Juvenile Drug Court, 130

Kadian (morphine), 187
Kefauver-Harris Amendment of, 1962, 45
Kenya, 38
Ketalar. *See* Ketamine
Ketamine, 255, 260–2, **261**
   ED visits for, 11
   trafficking, 33–4
Kindling effect, 201
Klonopin (clonazepam), 266
Knock and talk, 109
Korsakoff's psychosis, 299–300

LAA (lysergic acid amide), 255, 256
LAAM (levo-alpha-acetylmethadol), 186, 186
Labeling theory, 157, 157
Labor, endorphins and, 180
Lager beer, 277
Laissez-faire, 44
L-amphetamine, 207
Language of drug subculture, private, 157
Laos, 26, 170
Latency period, 140
Latino groups
   cocaine use, 199
   drug abuse prevention approaches in, 328
   racial profiling, 106
Laudanum, 171
Laundromats, money laundering originating from, 79
Law Enforcement Assisted Diversion (LEAD), 111
LDL (low-density lipoprotein), 291
LEAD. *See* Law Enforcement Assisted Diversion (LEAD)
Leary, Timothy, 251, 252–3, 254
Ledger, Heath, 9
Legal status of drugs, 6
Leo XII, Pope, 197
Lethal dose, 8, 8–9
   alcohol, 282
   heroin, 182
Lethal emergencies. *See* Deaths

Leukoencephalopathy, 182
Leukoplakia, 351
Levoamphetamine (l-amphetamine), 207
Leyva, Arturo Bertrán, 36
Librium (chlordiazepoxide), 265, 266
Licit (legal) drugs, 6
   emergencies related to, 11
Lidocaine, 201
Life Skills Training (LST), 319–20
Lightner, Candace, 290
Limbic system, 180
Limbitrol (chlordiazepoxide and amitriptyline), 266
Lincoln, Abraham, 48
Lipid-soluble, 138
Liqueur, 277
Liquor. *See* Distilled spirits
Liver
   alcohol abuse and, 298–9
   cancer of, 299
   fatty, 298
   screening of orally-administered drugs by, 137–8
   steroid use and, 378
London Summer Olympic Games, 374
Loperamide, 188
Lopressor (metoprolol), 268
Lorazepam, 266
Lortab (hydrocodone), 187
Low-density lipoprotein (LDL), 291
LSD. *See* Lysergic acid diethylamide (LSD)
LST (Life Skills Training), 319–20
Lunesta (eszopiclone), 267
Lung cancer, 231, 350–1, 352, 356
Luteinizing hormone (LH), 231
Lysergic acid amide (LAA), 255, **256**, 256
Lysergic acid diethylamide (LSD), 33, **248,** 250–1
   acute effects of, 253–4
   bad trip on, 254
   brain and, 254
   cocaine combined with, 202
   creativity and, 255
   criminal or violent behavior and, 255
   cross tolerance between psilocin and, 256
   ED visits for, 11
   effective dose of, 253
   facts about, 254–5
   learning techniques to use and enjoy, 156
   mescaline effects compared to, 257–8
   panic or psychosis produced by, 254
   patterns of use, 254
   penalties for, 90
   personality disorder, 153
   production of, 75
   psychedelic era and, 251–3
   residual effect of, 255
   toxicity of, 253
   trafficking in, 33
   use among youth, 15

MADD, 287, 290
Mafia, money laundering by, 78, 79. *See also* Organized crime
"Magic bullets" approach to prevention, 318
Ma huang (*Ephedra vulgaris*), 205
Mainlining, 138, 181
Mainstream smoke, 347, 347
Maintainers, 150
Maintenance stage of rehabilitation, **330**
Major League Baseball, 374, 380
Malt liquor, 277, 279
Mandatory minimum sentencing, 92, 92–5, 317
MAO inhibitors, alcohol mixed with, 284
MAPs (member assistance programs), 327, **327**, 382

Reefer, 226. *See also* Marijuana
Reentry Drug Court, 128
Reefer Madness (film), 47, 225
Reefer madness approach, 317
Reefer songs, 223
Regulation, 45–50, 52–5
   of alcohol, 48
   of anabolic steroids, 379
   lack of, in 19th century, 44
   of marijuana, 47, 234–5
   minimum-age, for smoking, 353
   of narcotics, 46–7
   tobacco, economics and, 341
Rehabilitation, 120
Rehabilitation, stages of change and, 329–30
Rehnquist, William H., 106
Reinforcement
   behavioral theory of, 150
   dopamine and, 149
   negative, 150
   positive, 150
Religious Freedom Restoration Act of 1993, 258
Remoxy, 189
REM sleep
   alcohol and reduction of, 283
   barbiturates, 263
REM sleep rebound, 263
Reoffending, 120
Reproduction
   LSD effects on, 255
   marijuana effects on, 229
Resilience, 315, 315
Respiratory depression
   heroin use and, 180, 182
   opioid pain medications, 187
Respiratory disease from tobacco, 349–50
Respiratory effects of marijuana, 230
Responsivity principle, 122
Restoril (temazepam), 266
   resveratrol, 291
Retail service business, money laundering using cash-based, 79
Retail violation rate (RVR), 354
Retreatism, as adaptation to anomie, 154–5
Retribution, 119
Reverse anorexia, 377
Reverse sting, 107
Reverse sting operation, anatomy of, 107
Reverse tolerance, 229
Revex (nalmefene), 302
ReVia (naltrexone), 181, 302
Revolutionary Armed Forces of Colombia (FARC), 38
RICO. *See* Racketeer Influenced and Corrupt Organization (RICO)
RICO statute, 112, 112–13
Rig-Veda, 260
Rise of the Temperance Movement, 48
Risk assessment, 160
Risk factors, 158–9, **158**
Risk principle, 120
Ritalin (methylphenidate), 150, 212, 215
Ritualism, as adaptation to anomie, 154
Road to National Prohibition, 48
"Roaring Twenties," 49
Robbery, 65
Rockefeller Drug Laws, 92, 94
Rodchenkov, Dr. Grigory, 375
Rodriguez, Alex, 376, 378
Rogers, Don, 206
Rogue Pharmacies, 191
Rohypnol (flunitrazepam), 268, 269
"Roid rage," 378
Role models, parents and guardians as, 323–4
Roosevelt, Franklin D., 45

Roosevelt, Theodore, 45
Routes of administration, 137–8
Rum, 277
Runner (street dealing), 76
Russia, smoking in, 341, 342, 358
RxPatrol, 73
Ryan Haight Online Pharmacy Consumer Protection Act (2008), 54, **56**
Rye whiskey, 277

SADD (Students Against Drunk Driving), 290
Safe and Secure Drug Disposal Act (2010), 54, **56**
Safety, margin of, 10
Saint Bernard myth, 283
Sake, 277
Salem witch trials, role of ergotism in, 251
Salt Lake City Winter Olympic Games, 374
Sandoz Pharmaceuticals, 251
Sarin and chemical warfare, 39
Sativex, 237
Scare tactics, 317
Schedules of controlled substances, 57
Schizophrenia
   amphetamine psychosis and, 208
   LSD hallucinations compared to, 254
   tranquilizers, 265
School-based prevention, 318–20
   anxiety and stress reduction, 319
   Drug Abuse Resistance Education (DARE), 322–3
   drug testing, 53
   Life Skills Training (LST) program, 319–20
   peer-refusal skills, 318–19
   social skills and personal decision making, 318–19
Scopolamine, 250, 262
Scotch whiskey, 277
Screening, Brief Intervention, and Referral to Treatment (SBIRT), 331–2
Search Institute, 162
Search warrant, 110
Sears, Roebuck catalog, 172
Secobarbital, 262, 263
Seconal (secobarbital), 263, 264
Secondary deviance, 157
Secondary prevention, 312, 313, 317
Second Chance Act (SCA), 125
Secular Organization for Sobriety (SOS), 304
Sedative-hypnotics, 248. *See also* Barbiturates
   nonbarbiturate, 264
Seizures
   alcohol withdrawal syndrome and, 298
   cocaine and, 201
Selective serotonin reuptake inhibitors (SSRIs), 268, 271
Self-esteem enhancement, 318
Sentencing, mandatory minimum, 92, 92–5, 317
Sentencing and sanctions, 88
September 11, 2001 attacks
   drug smuggling methods since, 103
Serotonin, 148, 249, 254
   hallucinogens related to, 249, 255
Serotonin-sensitive receptors, 254
Sertraline, 268
Sertürner, Friedrich Wilhelm Adam, 173
Sex and sexual desire
   alcohol and, 71, 285–6
   cocaine's effect on, 200
   heroin's effect on, 181
   marijuana and, 226, 230
Sexual assault, 270
"Shakes," 264, 298
Shen Nung, emperor, 205, 222
Shooting, 181

"Shotgunning," 377
Shrooms. *See* Psilocybin
Sidestream smoke, 343, 352
SIDS (sudden infant death syndrome), 352
Siegel, Shepard, 141, 145
Silicon chip patches, 139
Simple possession, 89
Sinclair, Upton, 45
Sinsemilla, 222
Skin-popping, 138, 181
Skoal, 355
Sleep
   barbiturates, 263
   neurotransmitters and, 149
   opiates for medical use, 148
   patterns, alcohol and, 283
Sleep aids, 267. *See also* Barbiturates
"Smart pills," stimulants used as, 213
SMART Recovery, 303
Smith, David W., 300
Smith, Kline and French Laboratories, 206
Smoke, tobacco
   comparison of components of marijuana and, 230
   components in, 347–8
   environmental tobacco smoke (ETS), 352
   hazards of, 352
   mainstream, 347–8
   sidestream, 343, 352
Smokeless tobacco, 351–2, 355–6
Smoking. *See also* Cigarettes; Marijuana; Nicotine; Tobacco
   by American youth, 312, 352–3
   behavioral theory, 150–1
   cessation, medications for, 360–1
   of crack cocaine, 202
   drugs administered through, 138
   health concerns and, 342
   of heroin, 176, 181
   Life Skills Training program to combat, 319–20
   methamphetamine, 208
   of opium, 173
   oral contraceptives and, 352patterns of, 352–3
   patterns of marijuana, 234
   Pavlovian conditioning and associations with, 151
   physiological responses, 143
   in post-World War II U.S., 50–1
   quitting, 359–61
Smuggling, drug interdiction to prevent, 103–5
"Smurfing," 79
Snorting heroin, 176, 181
Snuff, 341, 355
Snuffing, 341
Sober living houses, 126
Social class. *See* Socioeconomic status
Social-community programs, 186
Social control theory, 155, 155–6
   subcultural recruitment and socialization theory and, 156–7
Socialization theory, subcultural recruitment and, 156–7
Social problems, alcoholism and, 295
Social skills training, 319
Sociocultural filters, 327
Socioeconomic status
   labeling of behavior and, 157
Sociological perspectives on drug abuse, 154–7
Sokolow, Andrew, 106
Sopor (methaqualone), 265
SOS, 304
Source control, 101, 101–3
   chemical controls, 101–2
   crop eradication, 101–2
   U. S. certification, 102

South America, opium and heroin from, 176. *See also* Colombia
Southeast Asia, Golden Triangle of, 26, 175–6
South Korea, cigarette smoking in, 358
Spain, smoking in, 358
Sparkling wine, 277
Speakeasies, 49
Special conditions, 131
Special K, 261
Specific responsivity, 122
Speed. *See* Methamphetamine
Speedball, 202, 371
Speed freaks, 208, 214
Spending money, teenage drug abuse and, 376
Spiral model of recovery, 330
Sports. *See also* Anabolic steroids
    alcohol and security issues in, 288
    amphetamines, 372
    drug testing in, 370
    performance-enhancing drugs, 374–6
    spectator, 288
Spousal abuse, alcohol intoxication and, 71
SSRIs, 268
Stacking, 377
Standard conditions, 131
Stanozolol, 372
St. Anthony's fire, 250
Standardized field sobriety tests (SFST), 286
States' rights, regulation of drugs and, 45
Stepan Company, 199
Stern, David, 288
Steroids, anabolic. *See* Anabolic steroids
Stimulants, 35. *See also* Amphetamines; Cocaine
    for ADHD, 212–13
    nonmedical use in baseball, 215
    as "smart pills," 213
STP, 258, 259
Strain/anomie theory, 154–5
Strattera (atomoxetine), 213
Street dealing, business model of, 76
Street gangs, 77–8
Street-level drug-law enforcement, 106–7
Street names
    amphetamines, 208
    cocaine, 202
    marijuana, 234
    opioid, 182
    PCP, 261
Stress, 265
    endorphins and, 180
    teenage drug abuse and, 319, 326
Stress reduction, 319
Stroke, moderate alcohol consumption and, 350
Strychnine, 371
Students, drug use by, 17–18. *See also* College students; High school students
Students Against Drunk Driving (SADD), 290
Subcultural recruitment and socialization theory, 156, 156–7
Subculture, 156
    deviant, 157
    "hippie," of 1960s, 50, 155, 156
    in New York City, 72
    private language of drug, 157
    rise and fall of drugs and violence, 72
Subcutaneous (s.c. or sub-Q) delivery, 138
Sublingual administration, 139
Suboxone (buprenorphine in combination with naloxone), 170, 184
Substance abuse, 145
Substance Abuse and Mental Health Services Administration (SAMHSA), 312, 313
Substance dependence, 145
Substance use disorder, 145
Subutex (buprenorphine), 184

Sudden infant death syndrome (SIDS), 352
Suicide, suicide attempts, suicidal thoughts
    alcohol abuse and, 295
    barbiturates and, 263, 265
    cocaine abuse and, 199–200
Sullivan, John L., 342
Supply/availability argument, 316
Suppository, 139
Surgeon general's report on smoking, 341
Sutherland, Edwin, 156
Sweden, smoking in, 358
Sydenham, Thomas, 171
Sydenham's Laudanum, 171
Sympathetic branch of autonomic nervous system, cocaine's effect on, 205–6
Symptomatic drinking, 293
Synaptic knob, 148
Synar, Mike, 354
Synar Amendment, 354
Synergism, 141
    between alcohol and barbiturates, 263
Synesthesia, 253
Synthetic Drug Abuse Prevention Act (2012), 56, 56
Synthetic hallucinogens, 258–9
Synthetic heroin, 182
Syringe, invention of, 173
Systemic crime, 65
Systemic violence, 65
Systems approach, 296, 296

Tactical Analysis Teams (TATs), 105
Taliban, 37
Tannin, 284
Tar and nicotine (T/N), 343
Tar in cigarettes, **347,** 347
TAT. *See* Tactical Analysis Teams (TATs)
Tauber, Jeffrey, 127
Taverns, 262
Taxes
    alcohol regulation through, 289–90
    on cigarettes, 347
    drug abuse regulation through, 47
Tea pads (marijuana clubs), 223
Technical violation, 131
Temperance movement, 48
Tenormin (atenolol), 268
Tenth graders, drug use among, 15, 16
Teonanacatl, 255. *See also* Psilocybin
Teratogenic, 300
Tertiary prevention, 312
Testing for drugs at home, 324
Testing for ergogenic drugs, 380
Testoderm transdermal system, 372
Testosterone, 372, 376
    aggression and, 378
    anabolic steroids and level of, 377–8
    effects of, 371
    marijuana's effect on level of, 226, 231
Testosterone enanthate, 372
Testred (methyltestosterone), 372
Tetrahydrocannabinol (THC), 138, 236, 237, 240
Thailand, 26
THC, 222, 226–7
    detection periods for, 370
THC-sensitive receptors, 228–9
Thebaine, 169, 173
Theoretical perspectives on drug use and abuse, 146–62
    biological perspectives, 146–50
    biopsychosocial model, **146**
    integrating, 158
    protective factors, 158–62
    psychological perspectives, 150–3

    risk factors, 158–62
    sociological perspectives, 154–9
Therapeutic communities, 124, 186, 192
Therapeutic index, 9
    for alcohol, 282
    "Therapeutic window," 140
Thiamine, 300
Thiopental, 262
Timing of drug administration, 140
Titration hypothesis, 348
Tkachenko, Nadezhda, 373
Tobacco, 339–42. *See also* Cigarettes; Nicotine; Smoking
    advertising for, 342, 343
    cancers linked to, 351–2
    cardiovascular disease from, 349, 352
    chewing, 139, 341–2
    cigars and cigarettes, 342, 356
    coca paste mixed with, 197
    components of, 347
    control since 1990, 361
    economics and, 341–2
    global marketplace for, 346
    health risks, 343, 349–52
    high school and college students, 17–18
    legality of, 6
    lung cancer from, 350–1
    minimum age for purchase of, 353–4
    politics and, 341
    regulation, 345–6
    respiratory disease from, 350
    smokeless, 138, 341, 352, 355–6
    through history, 340–2
    in twentieth century, 342
    women and, 342, 352
    worldwide use of, 358–9
Tobacco angina, 356
Tobacco control (1990), 345
Tobacco control, policy and strategy
    potential harm, awareness of, 354–5
    taxation, regulation by, 353
    young people, reduced access by, 353–4
Tobacco Control Act (2009), 54, 345
Tobacco settlement (1998), 345
Tobacco smoke. *See* Smoke, tobacco
Tolerance, 141–2, 141
    to alcohol, 298
    to barbiturates, 263–4
    behavioral, 141
    to benzodiazepines, 265–7
    chronic heroin abuse and, 181–2
    to cocaine, 201
    conditioned, 141, 183
    cross-tolerance, 142, 267
    to LSD and other hallucinogens, 270
    to marijuana, 228–9
    to nicotine, 349
    reverse, 229
Toluene, 230
"Tootsie Roll" (heroin), 27
Toxicity, 7–11, 8
    acute, 8, 12
    of alcohol, 277
    chronic, 12
    cocaethylene, 197
    of drug interactions, 140–1
    drug-related deaths, 23
    ergot, 250
    of LSD, 253–4
    of MDMA, 259
Trafficking. *See* Drug trafficking
Tramadol, 187
Tranquilizers, 265. *See also* Antianxiety drugs
Transdermal patch, 139, 184, 372
Transnational Narcoterrorism, 37